Irwin

BUSINESS: AN INTEGRATIVE APPROACH
Published by McGraw-Hill/Irwin, a business unit of The McGraw-Hill Companies, Inc.,
1221 Avenue of the Americas, New York, NY, 10020. Copyright © 2004, 2001, 1998 by
The McGraw-Hill Companies, Inc. All rights reserved. No part of this publication may be
reproduced or distributed in any form or by any means, or stored in a database or retrieval
system, without the prior written consent of The McGraw-Hill Companies, Inc.,
including, but not limited to, in any network or other electronic storage or transmission,
or broadcast for distance learning.
Some ancillaries, including electronic and print components, may not be available to
customers outside the United States.

This book is printed on acid-free paper.

Domestic   1 2 3 4 5 6 7 8 9 0 VNH/VNH 0 9 8 7 6 5 4 3
International   1 2 3 4 5 6 7 8 9 0 VNH/VNH 0 9 8 7 6 5 4 3

ISBN 0-07-253780-9

Publisher: *John E. Biernat*
Sponsoring editor: *Ryan Blankenship*
Senior developmental editor: *Christine Scheid*
Senior marketing manager: *Ellen Cleary*
Producer, media technology: *Todd Labak*
Project manager: *Natalie J. Ruffatto*
Senior production supervisor: *Michael R. McCormick*
Coordinator freelance design: *Artemio Ortiz Jr.*
Photo research coordinator: *Jeremy Cheshareck*
Photo researcher: *David Tietz*
Supplement producer: *Betty Hadala*
Senior digital content specialist: *Brian Nacik*
Cover design: *Kiera Cunningham*
Interior design: *Artemio Ortiz*
Typeface: *10/12 Times Roman*
Compositor: *Precision Graphics*
Printer: *Von Hoffmann Press, Inc.*

Library of Congress Cataloging-in-Publication Data

Fry, Fred L.
    Business : an integrative approach / Fred L. Fry, Charles R. Stoner, Richard E.
Hattwick.—3rd ed.
        p. cm.
    Includes bibliographical references and index.
    ISBN 0-07-253780-9 (alk. paper) — ISBN 0-07-121460-7 (international : alk. paper)
    1. Industrial management—Case studies. I. Stoner, Charles R. II. Hattwick, Richard E.
III. Title.
HD31 .F79 2004
658—dc21
                                                2002037986

INTERNATIONAL EDITION ISBN 0-07-121460-7
Copyright © 2004. Exclusive rights by The McGraw-Hill Companies, Inc., for manufacture and export. This
book cannot be re-exported from the country to which it is sold by McGraw-Hill.
The International Edition is not available in North America.

www.mhhe.com

The Path (or Model) to a Success

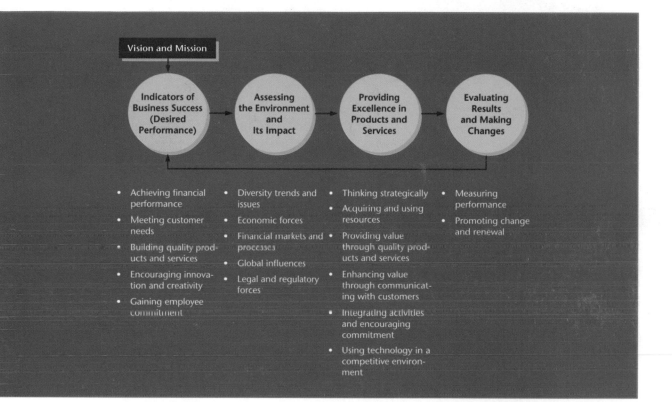

From the mission and vision to the evaluation of decisions, the model parallels the steps people/businesses must make to be competitive and successful. Chapter 2 explains more about how this model will be followed and referred to throughout the text.

Make sure to check the inside back cover for information about our new Student Interactive Study Guide on CD-ROM, and the Online Learning Center at

www.mhhe.com/fry3e

Business

AN INTEGRATIVE APPROACH

Third Edition

Fred L. Fry
Bradley University

Charles R. Stoner
Bradley University

Richard E. Hattwick
Western Illinois University

 Irwin

Boston   Burr Ridge, IL   Dubuque, IA   Madison, WI   New York   San Francisco   St. Louis
Bangkok   Bogotá   Caracas   Kuala Lumpur   Lisbon   London   Madrid   Mexico City
Milan   Montreal   New Delhi   Santiago   Seoul   Singapore   Sydney   Taipei   Toronto

Meet the Authors

Fred L. Fry is a Professor of Management in the Foster College of Business Administration at Bradley University. His Ph.D. is from Oklahoma State University. He has taught a variety of business classes, including Contemporary Business, Introduction to Business, Entrepreneurship, Small Business Management, Management of the Nonprofit Organization, Technology Entrepreneurship, and Strategic Management.

Dr. Fry's research has centered on entrepreneurship and small business management. He has published or presented over 40 articles and papers in journals such as *Business Horizons, Journal of Small Business Strategy, Journal of Small Business Management, Business Forum, Personnel,* and *Journal of Behavioral Economics,* and at national and regional professional conferences. Dr. Fry is the newsletter editor for the United States Association of Small Business and Entrepreneurship. He has written three other books—*Entrepreneurship: A Planning Approach* (1993), *Strategic Planning in New and Emerging Businesses* (1995, 1999), and *Strategic Planning in the Small Business* (1987). The last two of these were co-authored with Charles Stoner.

Charles R. Stoner is the Robert A. McCord Professor of Executive Management Development at Bradley University. His D.B.A. is from Florida State University. He has published over 40 articles and papers in journals such as the *Journal of Occupational Psychology, Journal of Business and Psychology, Journal of Applied Business Research, Business Horizons, Journal of Services Marketing, The Journal of Marketing Management,* and *International Journal of Management.* His recent research has focused on applied leadership topics. He co-authored *Strategic Planning for New and Emerging Businesses* (1995, 1999) and *Strategic Planning in the Small Business* (1987) with Dr. Fry, and he is the author of *The Adversity Challenge: How Successful Leaders Bounce Back from Setbacks* (2002). His course teaching includes Contemporary Business, Organizational Behavior, and Leadership and Interpersonal Dynamics. Dr. Stoner has done extensive consulting in the areas of team dynamics, organization culture, conflict resolution, and leadership. Much of his consulting has been with CEOs of large and midsize companies.

Richard E. Hattwick is a Professor of Economics in the College of Business and Technology at Western Illinois University. He teaches a variety of courses for majors in both business and economics. Dr. Hattwick holds a Ph.D. in Economics from Vanderbilt University. He has taught economics to business and economics students at the University of Houston, the University of Colorado, the State University of Guanabara (Brazil), and Vanderbilt University, in addition to teaching at Western Illinois University. For 23 years he served as director of the Center for Business and Economic Research at Western Illinois University.

Dr. Hattwick is the founder and current editor of the *Journal of Socio-Economics.* He is also the founder and president of the Illinois Business Hall of Fame and serves as the current president of the American National Business Hall of Fame. Dr. Hattwick is the author of numerous business leadership articles and is a frequent guest lecturer on business ethics and business history at various universities.

Brief Contents

Contents

10 The Impact of Globalization

11 The Impact of Legal and Regulatory Forces

Part 5

Assessment and Change

18 Measuring Performance

19 Promoting Change and Renewal

BECAUSE IT'S INTEGRATED LIKE A BUSINESS

The authors firmly believe that students don't want simply to learn about business; they want to know how businesses succeed. The goal of *Business: An Integrative Approach* is to show students how businesses win by integrating their resources and functions. Students learn how external forces, such as economics, diversity, globalization, and financial markets, have an impact on the world of business. The integrated approach also allows for a more focused concentration on such skills as decision making, strategic thinking, delivering quality and value, and using technology competitively.

A Model for Success

The text uses an integrative model that illustrates the elements of a successful business. The model is clearly described in the second chapter and is repeated and explained at the beginning of each Part Opener.

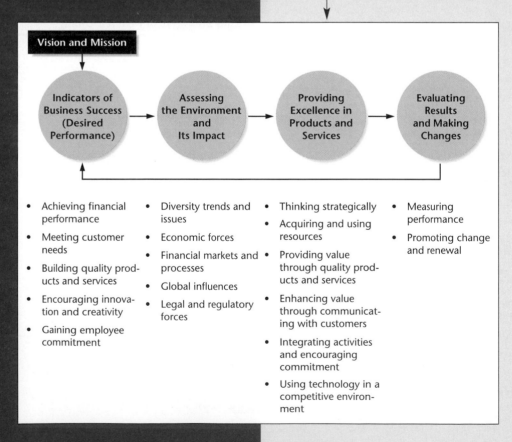

Vision and Mission

| Indicators of Business Success (Desired Performance) | → | Assessing the Environment and Its Impact | → | Providing Excellence in Products and Services | → | Evaluating Results and Making Changes |

- Achieving financial performance
- Meeting customer needs
- Building quality products and services
- Encouraging innovation and creativity
- Gaining employee commitment

- Diversity trends and issues
- Economic forces
- Financial markets and processes
- Global influences
- Legal and regulatory forces

- Thinking strategically
- Acquiring and using resources
- Providing value through quality products and services
- Enhancing value through communicating with customers
- Integrating activities and encouraging commitment
- Using technology in a competitive environment

- Measuring performance
- Promoting change and renewal

We have only skimmed the surface of information sources here. Most managers today have more information available to them than they can use effectively. The key to effective use of information resources is to identify what information is needed, what form it is needed in, and where to find it.

THE BIG PICTURE

When a large company is considering buying another company, one of the key considerations is the concept of strategic fit. In other words, does the new company fit in with the overall strategy and culture of the buying firm? Managers must consider this issue before committing to an action that could turn out to be disastrous.

Considering resources is much the same. Managers must ask: Do the resources we currently have at our disposal fit with the overall strategy of the firm? Further, if we are considering a new strategy—especially a growth strategy—do we either have or can we get the resources we need to make that new strategy work? If we have insufficient resources or the wrong mix of resources, the new strategy could end badly.

In the 1970s, McDonald's grew far faster than either Hardee's or Burger King. Why? It was because McDonald's had the financial resources to underwrite the expansion and the associated national advertising that would be needed. Its fast-food competitors did not have those resources.

As you read the next few chapters, which deal with product development, marketing, technology, and people, keep in mind that each of the four types of resources we discussed in this chapter will be involved. The role of managers is to integrate those resources so that the overall strategy can be successful.

Summary

1. This book emphasizes the importance of integrative thinking in business.
   - What are some of the issues of integration you must consider when dealing with resource acquisition and use?

   Resource acquisition demands that managers work with many people throughout the company to acquire and use resources in the most effective and least expensive manner. This strategy is important because changes in one resource can affect the use of others. It is also important because of the concept of trade-offs. Trade-offs mean that using funds for one thing precludes using them for another. Opportunity costs, the value of activities that are sacrificed, must also be considered. Resource acquisition and use involve the movement of goods, equipment, inventory, money, people, and information from outside the organization to inside and back.

2. Resource acquisition provides two major challenges to a business.
   - What are two major resource challenges?

   The two challenges are (1) acquiring an adequate amount, and (2) acquiring the proper mix.

3. CEOs of most companies are quick to tell you that their people are the key to their company's success. What they do not tell you is how they happen to have such superior employees.

The Big Picture

Reinforcing the main theme of the book, this learning feature near the end of each chapter reinforces how the topics of that chapter relate to the operation of a successful business. These features help students see businesses as a whole instead of a set of unrelated functions.

Chapter Opener and Learning Objectives

Each chapter begins with a thought-provoking story that sparks students' interest in the chapter. After each opening vignette, a preview, which provides students with the chapter objectives, acts as a framework for chapter success. The chapter summaries carefully mirror the chapter objectives, thereby serving as a check on students' learning.

2

The Path toward a Successful Business

It is an impressive list of businesses—Southwest Airlines, Wal-Mart, Microsoft, Berkshire Hathaway, Home Depot, Johnson & Johnson, FedEx, Citigroup, and Intel. These well-known businesses were recently named to *Fortune* magazine's all-star list. This designation means they were considered America's most admired businesses. But which business sits atop this lofty list? For the fifth straight year, the most admired business in America, as well as the most admired in the world, was General Electric.

GE's reputation is well deserved. First, the company made money. Year after year it has shown impressive earnings. It has huge cash reserves, and its various businesses have generated over a billion dollars of revenue every month. In business parlance, GE "made the numbers."

But that's not all there is to the GE story. The business has been known for being innovative, even entrepreneurial. That's quite an accomplishment given a business that employs over 315,000 people worldwide. And it has been known for taking risks—well-thought-out risks. For example, in the midst of a weakened international economy in 2001, GE realized it had an opportunity to expand and grow faster in China. So, the company went for it.

Although GE operates a number of different businesses, it is known, in all cases, for the quality of its products and services. Its wide range of operations has helped GE deal with fluctuations in the economy. For instance, as the economy plummeted in 2001, GE realized that some of its businesses (such as appliances and lightbulbs) would miss their targets. That meant more costs would have to be cut. It also meant

other businesses (such as turbines and CT scanners) would have to pick up the slack. And not surprisingly, GE rose to the challenge.

GE has also been known for training great managers. These were managers who stepped up and made tough decisions. And that culture starts at the top. GE's new CEO, Jeff Immelt, followed one of the most popular leaders in business history—Jack Welch. Welch's tough, hard-driving imprint is all over the company. Welch was known for comments like the one that he made to a division chief who had missed his targets: "I love you, and I know you can do better. But I'm going to take you out if you can't get it fixed." GE has a record for making the right calls and, when it has to, getting the problem fixed.[1]

Chapter 2 is titled "The Path toward a Successful Business" to show you the kind of thought process that business leaders use to make sound judgments and decisions. It will show you the complexity of decision making. More than that, however, it will show you how the pieces fit together. Indeed, that is the nature of this entire book—to study a business and discover how the business as a whole operates.

We call this approach an integrative framework because it looks at a business as an integrated and interactive process that is affected by decisions throughout the organization. We recognize that owners or managers of every business make decisions related to marketing, finance, human resources, facilities, and many other elements of the business. But each of these decisions affects other areas in the business. And each decision affects the overall success of the organization by both its individual impact and its interaction with the other parts. It is important that you keep this big picture in mind throughout this book and, indeed, throughout your business career.

After studying this chapter, you should be able to:

1. Explain the concepts of vision and mission statements.
2. Understand the significance of the indicators of business success.
3. Understand the basic nature of the influences of the environment in which a business operates.
4. Describe the types of decisions a company's leaders must make to succeed.
5. Note the relationship between performance measures and the indicators of business success and the need for change once performance has been measured.

The Path toward a Successful Business

How does a business get started, and how does it become successful? What is the path toward business success? To an extent, each business takes a unique path. Yet there are some themes that all successful businesses have in common. These themes and the way service be done right the first time. Often little can be done to correct service errors other than make some type of restitution—frequently a costly matter. For example, if an airline overbooks flights and all passengers show up, the airline then must offer some type of incentive to get volunteers to take a later flight. A restaurant whose service does not meet the expectations of a customer often simply will not charge that patron for the meal rather than risk having an unhappy customer. Both of these examples can be expensive if the problem occurs frequently. In addition, poor service often leads to lost customers. Think of the number of businesses that you refuse to patronize because you received bad service. You may or may not have complained, but you most likely told your friends about the bad service you received.

The role of the employee is critical in service businesses. Since services depend on the interaction between customers and business representatives, employees must always be well trained both in the technical aspects of the service and in interpersonal skills. Few things are more frustrating to customers than representatives who cannot answer questions or who do not care about customer satisfaction.

A key issue for managers is the trade-off between cost and customer satisfaction. We have probably all complained that a bank is irresponsible because not enough drive-up windows were open. But the bank's managers must decide how many tellers are needed to service the windows properly. Too many tellers means that the bank is paying labor costs for idle workers. Too few tellers means that unhappy customers must wait. Similarly, too many trained dental hygienists in a dentist's office can be costly, but too few means that patients must be turned away. Unfortunately, labor costs increase in large increments. For example, each hygienist can clean 20 patients' teeth per day. But hiring an additional hygienist may bring in only five new patients per day because of insufficient demand. Thus, the owner of the dental business must decide whether the additional business is worth the expense.

Changes in Service through Technology

We have emphasized that service delivery depends on customer contact and that satisfaction with that contact is critical. Yet one trend in the service industry seems to be toward less direct contact between the service providers and the customers. For example, you probably have little if any contact with your bank other than through the ATM. You probably use a self-service gasoline station, and you may even pay for the gas by swiping your credit card through a reader on the pump. You may check into and out of hotels without talking to a human being. These lower levels of contact are convenient and in some cases allow providers to offer services at lower prices.

Many improvements in service provision are the result of increasing technology. You couldn't have done banking from your computer 10 years ago. Technology even permits some medical services without going to a doctor. Now some doctors' offices allow patients to ask nonemergency questions via e-mail. This option saves travel and waiting time for the patients and allows the doctors to use their time and resources more efficiently.

We illustrate the service industries with a profile of Southwest Airlines. You have already learned a great deal about Southwest Airlines. Now observe in Profile 4.4 how Southwest does so well in providing services in a tough industry and still consistently makes a profit.

THINK ABOUT THIS

1. Service industries differ from manufacturing in a number of ways. One major way is customer contact. What employee skills are most important for service industries?

2. We mentioned that services cannot be back ordered or stored. Are there any exceptions to this rule?

3. How can technology be used effectively in services such as real estate sales? car rentals?

Think About This

At the end of each major topic within a chapter, students are asked a series of thought-provoking questions to cultivate critical thinking. These questions relate to specific business situations introduced in the chapter and often require the use of analytical skills. Effective for sparking in-class discussion, these questions are purposely expansive.

Business Profiles

These in-chapter profiles of well-known as well as entrepreneurial businesses illustrate how particular strategies and decisions have led to a company's success. To reflect the real world, these profiles depict a wide array of small, medium, and large companies, and even nonprofit organizations. Special attention has been placed on using examples from businesses that students will recognize, relate to from real-life experience, and enjoy reading.

FIGURE 5.1

Typical Top Management Positions

finance to be the chief financial officer of the business. In some companies, two or more vice presidents will report to an executive vice president, who then reports to the president. This is the case at Best Buy, as shown in Profile 5.2. Figure 5.1 presents the typical top management positions.

PROFILE 5.2   BEST BUY'S TOP MANAGEMENT

Best Buy's top management structure recognizes the different aspects of the overall company. From the list below, you will see that Richard Schulze is founder and chairman, while Bradbury Anderson is CEO. Both of them have responsibilities for the overall strategic direction of the company. Allen Lenzmeier, president and COO, has overall responsibility for the internal workings of the company. Below them are several other individuals, many of whom are listed as president of either a division or a function within the company. For example, Kevin Freeland is president of Musicland, one of the Best Buy subsidiaries. Marc Gordon is CIO, the chief information officer, in charge of ensuring that information is communicated effectively throughout the organization. John Walden, who is now the executive vice president of human capital and leadership, was previously president of BestBuy.com. It is not unusual for large companies to have several presidents of subsidiaries or functional areas among the officers of the overall company.

Richard M. Schulze
Founder and Chairman

Bradbury H. Anderson
Vice Chairman and CEO

Allen Lenzmeier
President and COO

Michael Kesky
President, Best Buy Stores

Wade R. Fenn
President, Business Development and Strategic Alliances

Philip Schoonover
Executive Vice President, Business Development

Kevin Freeland
President, Musicland

Marc Gordon
Chief Information Officer

Darren Jackson
Chief Financial Officer

Jim Tweten
President, Magnolia Hi-Fi

John Walden
Executive Vice President, Human Capital and Leadership

Source: Best Buy website, www.bestbuy.com (accessed September 13, 2002).

Middle Managers

Decision makers with positions of vice president and higher are typically considered top management. Managers who work at levels from just below vice president down to just above first-line supervisors are referred to as **middle managers.** These people have direct supervisory responsibility over other managers or employees and have significant decision-making authority.

Let's think for a moment about middle managers and what they really do. Middle managers are responsible for translating broad policies and strategies into doable tasks. They receive orders from their own superiors and then must divide those orders into parts for each of their areas to accomplish. They spend much of their time in meetings with their subordinates to explain and gain commitment to plans set forth by their own superiors.

Middle managers sometimes find themselves in difficult situations, particularly in today's world. They depend heavily on those who work for them to achieve the goals that they and their superiors have set. But sometimes those goals were dictated to the middle manager because of the situation at hand—the competitive environment, the wishes of the company's top management, or pressure from outsiders. Middle managers are often held accountable for achieving challenging goals they did not have free rein in

middle managers
Managers below vice presidents down to just above first-line supervisors; they are responsible for translating broad policies into doable tasks.

Partly offsetting the revenue drop were declines in operating expenses (from \$3,780 million to \$3,718 million), in provision for income taxes (from \$958 million to \$485 million), and in the cumulative effect of a change in accounting principles (from \$59 million to zero). But adding to the drop in net revenue was a decline in investment and other income (loss). In the year ending February 1, 2001, Dell received revenue of \$531 million from that category. The following year, Dell actually lost \$58 million on its investment and other income accounts. The 2002 report explains the details of these losses.

Table 18.4 shows Dell's balance sheet, which Dell calls a consolidated statement of financial position. A **balance sheet** lists a company's assets (what it owns), liabilities (what it owes), and net worth (owners' equity) at a specific point in time. Note that Dell's assets fell slightly from \$13,670 million in 2001 to \$13,535 million in 2002. All but one of the listed components of assets declined. The one exception was the value of investments, which increased significantly. Note also that total liabilities rose from \$8,048 million in 2001 to \$8,841 million in 2002. Finally, note that stockholders' equity declined as a result of a large drop in the value of treasury stock—the stock that Dell, itself, owns.

Large companies typically send press releases to the media when their financial reports are completed. Analysts and other interested individuals can then seek additional information from the companies, including their annual reports and other financial statements. Profile 18.2 is an abbreviated version of such a press release. It reports Southwest Airlines' first quarter earnings for 2002.

Target has been recognized for its financial performance and strength. It has been honored as one of America's most admired companies, one of the best companies for both working mothers and Latinos, one of the best corporate citizens, and as a leader in its commitment to the education and training of its people. To what extent do you think its positive work environment affects its financial success?

balance sheet
A financial statement that shows a company's assets (what it owns), liabilities (what it owes), and net worth (owners' equity) at a specific point in time.

SOUTHWEST AIRLINES REPORTS FIRST QUARTER EARNINGS FOR 2002   PROFILE 18.2

Dallas, Texas, April 18, 2002—Southwest Airlines' net income for first quarter 2002 was \$21.4 million, compared to first quarter 2001 net income of \$121.0 million, a decrease of 82.3 percent. . . .

Total operating revenues for first quarter 2002 decreased 12.0 percent to \$1.26 billion, compared to \$1.43 billion for first quarter 2001. Revenue passenger miles decreased 2.5 percent in first quarter 2002 . . .

Total first quarter 2002 operating expenses were \$1.21 billion, which declined slightly from first quarter 2001. Operating expenses . . . decreased . . . primarily due to lower jet fuel prices, agency commissions, and profit sharing. These decreases more than offset increases in airport security and aviation insurance costs . . .

Summary

1. Daily newspapers make it look easy to measure the performance of a business. They present reports on profits and sales and leave the reader with the impression that everything important has been covered. But measurement is much more complicated. To begin with, a number of important caveats must be kept in mind with any attempt to measure business performance.
   - What are some of the important cautions that should be considered in the measurement process?

   Five caveats are as follows: (1) Measurements are interrelated and not performed in a vacuum, (2) we must measure both efficiency and effectiveness, (3) we must measure processes as well as results, (4) we must measure dynamically, not just statically, and (5) measurement must foster communication.

2. Another aspect of the complexity of measurement is that it involves far more than simply looking at the financial performance of a company.
   - What are the elements of a comprehensive model of performance measurement for a business?

FROM THE PAGES OF
BusinessWeek

Steve Ballmer Turns to Metrics

There isn't another company in the world as closely identified with its leader as Microsoft Corp. has been with William H. Gates III . . . But Gates no longer runs Microsoft. He gave up the chief executive role 2 1/2 years ago to his best friend and longtime management sidekick, Steven A. Ballmer . . . The 46-year-old Ballmer is not content to tend the machine Gates designed. His goal: to create a "great, long-lasting company" that will be even more successful.

(T)he new CEO is calling on his colleagues to do nothing less than rethink every aspect of the way they do their jobs. He has put in place a set of management processes aimed at bridging the gap between the sales and product development sides of the company . . . To make it all stick, Ballmer has concocted a dizzying array of meetings, reviews, and examinations that force people to do their jobs differently. It includes everything from rank-and-file employees grading their supervisors to an accounting system for managers that helps them weigh spending trade-offs . . . Each new process is designed to hook into the next so decisions can be made quickly—and can later be measured. This is light-years away from the ad hoc way Microsoft took action before. The final touch: Ballmer is making adoption of the new corporate values a part of every employee's annual performance review. Ballmer's hope is that his code of conduct will also make Microsoft a better corporate citizen. He says the company's core values of honesty, integrity, and respect must shine through with customers, partners and the tech industry.

Ballmer's chief challenges . . . are internal. One is the danger that so much attention to management processes and the myriad metrics of evaluating performance could stifle innovation . . . "Policy is an abdication of thought," says former Microsoft chief technologist Nathan Myhrvold. "If you hire process-oriented guys, it's probable that an idea never bubbles up."

Decision Questions

1. What are the benefits of measurement suggested by this article?
2. Ballmer says he wants the company's core values to "shine through" and expects to measure each employee's performance in terms of the company's values. How might a company measure an employee's performance in this regard?
3. Some say that measurement can be overdone. What is the major danger of overdoing measurement according to this article? Can you think of other undesirable results that could come from too much measurement?
4. The article indicates that under Bill Gates, Microsoft was a company that did not closely or systematically measure employee performance. Does this indicate that Gates was not as good a manager as he could have been?

Source: Jay Greene, Steve Hamm, and Jim Kerstetter, "Ballmer's Microsoft," *Business Week*, June 17, 2002, pp. 66–75.

Key Terms

absenteeism, p. 479	income statement, p. 462
balance sheet, p. 465	integrated assessment, p. 456
current ratio, p. 466	inventory turnover ratio, p. 466
debt ratio, p. 466	net worth, p. 462
dynamic measurements, p. 457	performance appraisal, p. 478
earnings per share (EPS), p. 460	return on equity (ROE), p. 460
effectiveness, p. 456	second-level communications, p. 473
efficiency, p. 456	turnover, p. 479
gap analysis, p. 470	

Exercises and Applications

1. Most large businesses post their annual reports on their websites. These annual reports contain both balance sheets and income statements. Evaluate the balance sheet and income statement for one of the following businesses: Apple Computer, Southwest Airlines, AT&T, or Kodak. What can you tell about the business, its level of success, and the direction it's likely to move in the future?
2. As a team, identify five important measures of customer satisfaction. Then select a business with which you are familiar. How does it rate on your five measures?
3. Using the measures of service quality discussed in the chapter, evaluate the service quality of your school's food-service provider.
4. In teams, brainstorm measures of employee satisfaction. Then discuss how easy each would be to measure and how accurate the measure might be. Write a two-page summary of your conclusions.
5. As this chapter has noted, measurement must take into account a number of factors. In teams, discuss how this course should be evaluated. Prepare a one-page paper

---

Designed for Today's Visual Learner

Most students today are visual learners. The text uses an attractive design and incorporates tables and figures whenever possible to illustrate concepts visually as an aid in comprehension.

End-of-Chapter Material

The end-of-chapter material has been carefully tailored to provide students and instructors plenty of in-class exercises and applications and other tools to review and reinforce the key concepts introduced in each chapter.

Key Terms   Important terms in each chapter are set in **boldface type,** with definitions placed in the margins. Key terms are also listed at the end of each chapter and are defined in the Glossary at the end of the book.

Summary   The chapter summaries mirror the learning objectives introduced at the beginning of each chapter. Students are provided with response questions in the summaries to ensure that they are mastering the key points.

Exercises and Applications   Each chapter has a series of exercises and applications that relate to the material presented in the chapter. Some of the exercises and applications are to be carried out by teams; others require individual research or consideration. Many suggest a brief writing assignment or Internet exercise.

From the Pages of BusinessWeek   Each chapter concludes with a discussion adapted from a recent article from a well-recognized business magazine—*BusinessWeek*. These articles apply chapter concepts to what is going on in the real world. Students will appreciate the connection and trust that what they are learning is relevant. Following each article are questions that can be assigned as homework or used as discussion generators in class.

STUDENT RESOURCES

PowerWeb

This online reservoir of course-specific news articles and essays offers a great way to keep the course current, while complementing textbook concepts with real-world applications. Articles and essays from leading periodicals and niche publications in specific business disciplines are reviewed by professors to ensure fruitful search results every time. PowerWeb also offers current news, weekly updates with assessments, interactive exercises, a Web research guide, study tips, and much more.

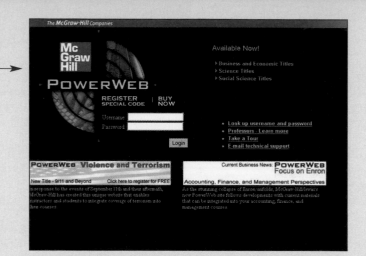

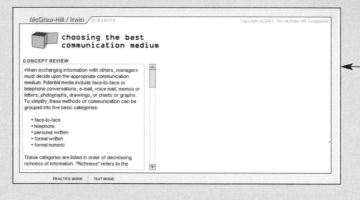

Student CD-ROM

The student CD contains exercises to help students succeed in class. For each chapter, there are quizzes, study outlines, self-assessment exercises, and video clips from the business world.

Online Learning Center

The book's website contains quizzes, Internet exercises, and media-enhanced student PowerPoint slides unique to the text. Each chapter's slides contain lecture outlines, text art and embedded video clips, and Web links.

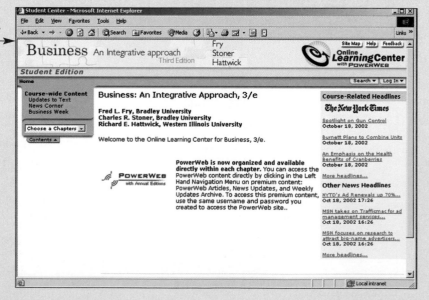

INSTRUCTOR RESOURCES

Online Learning Center with PowerWeb

Online Learning Center (OLC) with PowerWeb is a website that follows the text chapter by chapter with digital supplementary content germane to the text. As students read the book, they can go online to take self-grading quizzes, review material, and work through interactive exercises. Thanks to embedded PowerWeb content, students can get quicker access to real-world news and essays that pertain directly to their introductory business course. OLCs can be delivered multiple ways—through the textbook website, through PageOut, or within a course management system (e.g., WebCT or Blackboard).

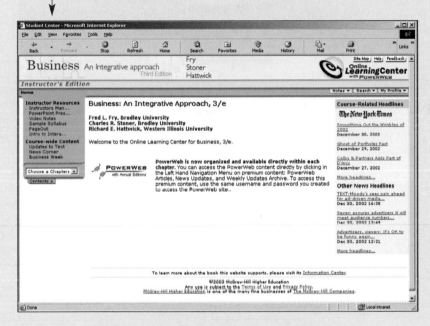

Instructor CD-ROM

With the Instructor CD-ROM, you no longer need to lug home your supplements. All the major supplements are included on this convenient CD—the Instructor's Manual and Video Guide, Test Bank, Computerized Test Bank, and PowerPoint slides. Also included are additional videos, separate from those on the Student CD-ROM.

Videos

Chapter-specific video clips are offered on VHS, with selections from PBS and NBC. Additional clips can be found on the Instructor CD-ROM under the heading "Management Hot Seat Collection." These nine situation-analysis features cover topics such as diversity, teamwork, and negotiation.

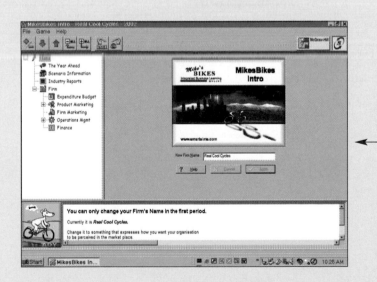

Mike's Bikes

To provide your students with a true and exciting business experience, try Mike's Bikes business simulation, specifically designed for your introductory business course. Students make decisions that will have an impact on a simulated mountain bike company in an interactive game scenario. This feature helps students understand how all the functions of a business come together to make a company successful.

Preface

The third edition of *Business: An Integrative Approach* comes during a period of intense challenges for contemporary business. Since the previous edition, the booming U.S. economy has experienced a devastating slump after years of unbridled prosperity. The dot-com darlings of the late 1990s have become a disappointing page of business history, replete with dashed fortunes and ravaged hopes. The moral and ethical integrity of businesses and their leaders, arguably the foundation of a free enterprise system, has been shaken more profoundly than at any other time in recent memory.

Against this backdrop, we write a book that explores the excitement, the energy, and the renewal of the business world. This book offers a realistic, but upbeat portrait of the nature of business. It speaks of basics that we know have worked for years in successful businesses—attention to customers, financial discipline, belief in people, and sound ethical practices. But the book does more.

Business: An Integrative Approach, Third Edition, is the most integrative introductory business textbook on the market. It is built around how business works. Look at the model of the book (Figure 2.1) to see the importance of the presentation. We start with the mission and vision, and then look at indicators of success, the assessment of environmental influences, the decisions business leaders must make, and the evaluation of those decisions. Thus, the book parallels how people think in business.

The topics covered in the text are contemporary: cross-functional teams, customer-centered thinking, the use of technology both inside the company and between the company and its customers, the role of stakeholders in business decision making, the need for quality. In this edition, we have added a discussion of crisis decision making—a compelling need in the current business and social environment. We look at the environment that business faces—many of the topics you are familiar with from traditional textbooks—but we treat it from the perspective of how it really affects businesses rather than from an isolated view that is unrelated to other chapters in the text.

Business: An Integrative Approach, Third Edition, purposely de-emphasizes an isolated discussion of functional areas. Rather than talk about finance, human resources, and production, for example, we discuss the acquisition of resources that allow the company to function efficiently and effectively. The functional topics are covered, but the focus is on how business leaders use those resources and the information around them to make decisions leading to successful strategies. Everything we do in the text is oriented around the big picture for the company. As in the previous edition, we end each chapter with a feature that is unique to *Business: An Integrative Approach*—"The Big Picture." In this feature, we ask the readers to pause, step back, and think about how the preceding information is used in a business or how it affects decision making. Not a summary, "The Big Picture" truly is an attempt to get readers to look at a business as a system of interrelated activities, a system that affects and is affected by forces and institutions around it.

Changes in the Third Edition

Since we preach the virtues of customer-centered strategies, it is only right that we listened to our own customers—faculty who teach introductory business courses and students who take those courses. We solicited critical evaluation of the second edition from professors who used that edition as well as those who used competing texts. We listened to what they liked about our book and—more important—what they did not like. We listened to what they liked and did not like about competing books. We have added a plethora of topics that reviewers requested. For example, we added more marketing-related topics and more information on the use of technology inside the organization rather than having just an external communication orientation. We moved the discussion of industry sectors from the environmental forces to the nature of business. We added a section on entrepreneurship and starting one's own business. And we shortened some chapters and lengthened others to give more appropriate coverage and to balance teaching schedules. We have kept the use of three focus companies because students overwhelmingly reported a high value in having known companies that relate to topics covered, but in this edition our three companies are Best Buy, Dell, and Southwest Airlines.

We have also done an amazing amount of updating. This text is truly the first introductory business text that covers the effects of the dot-com crash; the terrorist attacks of September 11, 2001; the recession; and the accounting ethics scandal. Virtually every one of our examples is new or significantly updated. Most citations are from 2002, and nearly all, except classic references, are from 2000 or later. We have replaced two of the three focus companies because we felt different companies would better illustrate the principles of good management. We chose three: Dell in manufacturing, Best Buy in retail, and Southwest Airlines in service—all companies that students can relate to and that have done well in their respective industry sectors. We have replaced every one of our From the Pages of *BusinessWeek* features at the end of each chapter to make sure they are current and relevant. All are from 2001 or 2002, with most from mid-2002. We replaced almost all the introductory vignettes to give students exciting and up-to-date introductions to chapters. And all the vignettes reflect well-known companies—Coca-Cola and PepsiCo, General Electric, Disney, MTV, Swatch, Nike, and others.

We think you will not only see the value in *Business: An Integrative Approach, Third Edition,* but also find it enjoyable to read. Students using the second edition have consistently said that the book was very readable and really came alive more than the books in their other classes. We think the third edition is even better than the second, and we hope you will agree.

Instructor Support Material

Instructor's Manual (Available on the Instructor CD-ROM and the Online Learning Center)

The Instructor's Manual, prepared by the authors, includes many valuable tools for teaching an integrative course, including expanded chapter outlines and teaching suggestions, a teaching strategy for each chapter, and links to other chapters and books. We have added "Attention Grabbers" and "Fun Things To Do in Class" for each chapter. Many of these come from our own teaching experiences in introductory business classes.

Test Bank (Available on the Instructor CD-ROM)

Our thanks to Sharon Niblock of Spokane Community College for revising the Test Bank for this edition. It includes at least 100 true-false, multiple-choice, and essay questions, designated with degree of difficulty, for each chapter.

Computerized Testing for Windows (Available on the Instructor CD-ROM)

A computerized version of the Test Bank allows instructors to generate random tests and to add their own questions.

PowerPoint Presentation Slides (Available on the Instructor CD-ROM and the Online Learning Center)

Our thanks also go to Bernie Yevin of the Marketing Department at Virginia Intermont College, in Bristol, Virginia, for revising the PowerPoint Presentation slides. Each chapter contains 15 to 20 slides for use in the classroom or as handouts; they are packaged ready to run with a Windows installation program and a slide viewer. No additional software is required. They can be modified, however, with Microsoft PowerPoint for Windows. One hundred of these slides were chosen for the color acetates.

Instructor CD-ROM (ISBN: 007-253784-1)

This state-of-the-art technology provides a single resource for faculty to customize in-class presentations. The Instructor CD-ROM contains:

- Instructor's Manual
- Test Bank
- Computerized Testing
- PowerPoint Classroom Presentation Software
- Additional videos

Videos (ISBN: 007-253785-X)

Featured with this edition is a video collection, one video for nearly each chapter, with footage obtained from sources such as NBC and Public Broadcasting. The collection includes programs about Carly Fiorina, Southwest Airlines following the 9/11 attacks, and a report on ethics in America in light of the Enron–Arthur Andersen debacle. Additional video selections, dealing with such topics as workplace perks, humor in the workplace, and Peapod, can be found on the Instructor CD-ROM. Student and instructor material to go with the videos can be found in the appropriate section of the textbook website.

Website: www.mhhe.com/fry3e, with Instructor Online Learning Center

A resource for faculty and students, our website contains information for lecture and learning enhancement. Along with a sample chapter, features of the text, and author biographical information, our website contains downloadable supplements for your convenience, sample syllabi, and the now fully integrated PowerWeb. This online resource provides high-quality, peer-reviewed content, including up-to-date articles from leading periodicals and journals, current news, weekly updates, interactive exercises, study tips, and much more. Ask your sales representative how to harness the power of PowerWeb with the Online Learning Center.

Student Resources

Student CD-ROM

A student CD-ROM, free with the purchase of a new textbook, contains activities, chapter outlines, chapter quizzes, video selections, and links for students to go above and beyond the boundaries of the printed textbook. Additional exercises use Flash technology along with detailed feedback to bring exercises and concepts to life in three-dimensional form. To have the text packaged with the Student CD and PowerWeb, use this ISBN: 007-284530-9.

Website: www.mhhe.com/fry3e, with Student Online Learning Center

The student section of the website houses many interactive resources, including "Introduction to Business Online," online quizzes, Internet exercises, a career corner, and the new fully-integrated PowerWeb, where students can get up-to-the-minute articles and information. Along with these assets, we introduce the new Student PowerPoint slides for the textbook website. A road map for studying, the PowerPoint slides consist of an outline of the text with interactive links to animations, video clips, and URLs to enhance the learning process for the student.

Acknowledgments

We are indebted to many people for this third edition of *Business: An Integrative Approach*. We have solicited assistance from a number of our colleagues at Bradley University, who have graciously provided information and advice. In particular, we thank Mark Brown, Jennifer Burgess, Ross Fink, Matt McGowan, and Larry Weinzimmer of the Business Management and Administration Department; Ed Bond and Mitch Griffin of the Marketing Department; Ray Wojcikewych of the Economics Department, and Joyce Shotick, who has taught BUS 100 Contemporary Business for a number of years. We owe a special thanks to Garrett Ringness, one of our former students in Contemporary Business, who assisted us with the research for the book, and Karen Olehy and Cindy McGowan, our administrative support staff. We also owe thanks to Mary Sherwood at Western Illinois University for her assistance.

Second, we would like to thank our panel of reviewers, who once again gave us a myriad of ideas and suggestions to ponder and use. The reviewers were:

Patricia Bernson
County College of Morris

Lana Carnes
Eastern Kentucky University

Ron Cereola
James Madison University

Richard Drury
George Mason University

Don Gordon
Illinois Central College

Inez Heal
Youngstown State University

Joshua Holt
Brigham Young University—Idaho

Jerry Kozlowski
Genesee Community College

Sharon Niblock
Spokane Community College

Jack Partlow
Northern Virginia Community College—Annandale

Marcie Satterwhite
Lake Land College

Janet I. Boring Seggern
Lehigh Carbon Community College

Joyce Shotick
Bradley University

Marc Titel
Long Beach City College

Glen Van Whye
Pacific Lutheran University

Mary Williams
Community College of Southern Nevada

Greg Young
North Carolina State University

Third, we are grateful to the 10 professors who formally reviewed the first edition. Some of them had used the book; others had used competing books. All gave us good advice. The reviewers were:

Linda Anglin
Mankato State University

John Antsey
University of Nebraska—Omaha

John Bowdidge
Southwest Missouri State University

Kitty Campbell
Southeastern Oklahoma State University

Ron Cereola
James Madison University

Mary Meredith
University of Southwestern Louisiana

Lizbeth Ellis
New Mexico State University

Bob Muir
Coastal Carolina Community College

Mary Gorman
University of Cincinnati

At McGraw-Hill/Irwin, we have had wonderful cooperation and encouragement from Christine Scheid, Senior Development Editor. We have been truly fortunate to have worked with Christine over two editions. We also appreciate the efforts of Natalie Ruffatto, Project Manager; Ryan Blankenship, Sponsoring Editor; and John Biernat, Publisher.

Finally, our wives—Lois Fry, Julie Stoner, and Nazareth Hattwick—have provided moral support as well as being excellent sounding boards for both content and writing issues. For their input on the book as well as their support for over 25 years, we are grateful beyond words.

Model of the Path toward a Successful Business

1

The Integrative Nature of Business

In Part One of this book, we introduce you to the world of business and the integrative nature of business activity. The four chapters in Part One are devoted to helping you better understand the landscape and scope of business in our contemporary world.

In Chapter 1, we take a broad look at the nature of business. You will gain a sense of the excitement and challenge that the study of business holds. The chapter defines *business* and introduces our focus companies, which you will encounter throughout the text.

Chapter 2 presents the big picture—our model of the path toward a successful business. You will study the key outcomes a business must achieve if it is to succeed over time. You will begin to recognize the tough, interrelated issues that business decision makers encounter as they grapple to make the right choices in an increasingly competitive international environment.

Chapter 3 helps you understand the scope of business. You will learn that businesses come in an array of sizes and forms. You will recognize the attraction of small business ownership. You will learn some of the opportunities that a business achieves only as it grows. This chapter describes some of the complexity of business ownership and provides an important foundation for further study.

Chapter 4 examines the key industry sectors of business. You will recognize some of the unique competitive features of each sector, and you will see how industries (and businesses within industries) intersect and affect one another. You will gain a deeper sense of the integrative nature of the overall business system.

Many of the topics discussed in Part One will appear throughout the text. As you read the text and study the business examples presented, recognize the excitement, challenge, and opportunity of the business world. Think and enjoy.

1

The Nature of Business: The Big Picture

As you head to the ski slopes for a weekend getaway, there's a good chance that you will participate in the fastest-growing winter sport of the past 20 years—snowboarding. There's an even better chance that the board you ride will be made by Burton, the leading snowboard maker.

Jake Burton Carpenter grew up as an avid New England skier. Yet even as a youngster, he thought it was cool to surf on the snow with his Snurfer, a single-ski sledding toy popular at the time. After high school, Jake enrolled at the University of Colorado at Boulder, hoping to join its NCAA champion ski team. But fate intervened as a car accident dashed his hopes of making the team.

After taking a year off from school, Jake earned a degree in economics from New York University. He accepted a job with an investment firm where he had interned. But it wasn't what he wanted. Leaving a good-paying job, Jake moved to Vermont in 1977 and started Burton Snowboards. The beginnings were basic. With two relatives, he converted a house and barn into a makeshift factory.

The early days were tough and even discouraging. Jake tended bar at night and taught tennis in the summers just to get by. He knew snowboarding combined fun, adventure, and athleticism. He believed that his vision of this sport, with its youthful and extreme edge, would catch on. Convinced that the only way for the business to succeed was for the sport to gain acceptance, Jake became a great promoter of the sport. He encouraged the riders. And he focused on convincing resort owners to consider the potential of snowboarding. Not surprisingly, once resorts allowed snowboards on their mountains, the sport exploded in popularity.

Today, amid competition, Burton Snowboards remains the industry leader. In addition to its boards, the company produces and sells apparel, boots, bindings, packs, and outerwear. Its products, which are in 3,000 specialty shops, are distributed to more than 30 countries. In addition to the one in Vermont, Burton Snowboards now has factories in Austria and Japan.[1]

Jake had an idea and a vision. He believed there was a demand for the sport and his product, and he built a company around that idea. He took risks, and he made some tough decisions.

Jake Carpenter's story is unique but not unusual. Businesses are complex. They always face an array of challenges. They require ideas, an understanding of customer needs, and the ability to satisfy those needs. They require dedication and commitment from people who believe in the business. They require an understanding of the competitive environment and the ability to make appropriate decisions to compete successfully in that environment.

This chapter sets the stage for the rest of the book. It discusses the excitement, the rewards, and the challenges of the world of business. It introduces the definitions of *business* and *successful business*. It also introduces you to the three focus companies that we will refer to throughout the book.

After studying this chapter, you should be able to:

1. Explain why business is exciting, rewarding, dynamic, and challenging.
2. Recognize the need for business leadership.
3. Understand the definition of *business*.
4. Understand the requirements of a successful business.
5. Identify our three focus companies and know why we chose them.
6. Discuss how business fits within society as a whole.

Business Is Exciting

Business is exciting. The process of creating a new product or service, doing all the work necessary to make it marketable, and delivering it in a way that customers value and appreciate can be exhilarating. The business landscape is constantly changing as

Burton Snowboards, introduced in the chapter opener, was featured prominently in the 2002 Winter Olympics in Salt Lake City, Utah. The excitement of the sport meets the excitement of business. How can Burton use scenes like this one to improve its profits?

new products replace old ones, and new services tap the latest interests and needs of some group of consumers. New technologies are developed that make older technologies obsolete. And every day, new companies are started that challenge existing companies.

Some of these new companies will thrive, while others will not survive. That uncertainty is part of the dynamic and risky nature of the world of business. In many ways, the standard of living we enjoy today is largely a result of entrepreneurs and other businesspeople who have taken the risks necessary to bring new products and services to the market.

Consider the following information: In the United States, there were over 100 million cell phones by 2001.[2] Cell phones are nearly a requirement for businesspeople. Fifteen years ago, however, there were virtually no cell phones. Today personal digital assistants (PDAs) have more computing power than entire computers did a decade or two ago. On another front, the fastest-growing demographic group today on a percentage basis is those over 80 years old and, more specifically, those over 100! This growth is primarily due to the advances in medicine and medical treatment that simply did not exist even 20 years ago. All these developments are made possible by businesses. Developments such as these and the prospects for even more new products and services make business an interesting and exciting subject to study.

Every year, approximately 600,000 new businesses are started. Some are small businesses that are started to give the entrepreneur a livelihood. Others are growth-oriented businesses that have high potential for financial returns. Many new businesses are built primarily around high-tech innovations. For example, have you ever heard of Foveon Inc.? Foveon was started in 1997, with a commitment to develop innovative products and technology so that photographers could capture the potential of digital photography. Now Foveon has developed a new chip technology that's more efficient and offers far better picture quality than current digital cameras. Industry experts suggest that the chip is a breakthrough that will literally change the face of digital photography. Or consider another newcomer, ArrayCom, Inc. It is revolutionizing the cell phone industry with its new wireless network that sends data 20 times faster than the competition. Often, as is the case with Foveon and ArrayCom, new companies aren't big companies. But they are poised to make big splashes in the business world.[3]

Business Is Rewarding

More to Come
Chapter 6

Although business is not risk-free, it can be quite rewarding. The most tangible form of reward is dollars—wealth. Look at the list of the wealthiest people in America, provided in Table 1.1. As you can see, almost all these people made their wealth by owning a business.

TABLE 1.1

North America's
Richest People, 2001
($ in billions)

	Net Worth	Source
William Gates	58.8	Microsoft
Warren Buffet	35.0	Investments
Paul Allen	25.2	Microsoft
Lawrence Ellison	23.5	Oracle
Five members of Sam Walton's estate	20.5 each	Wal-Mart
Steven Ballmer	14.8	Microsoft
Michael Dell	11.1	Dell
John Kluge	10.5	Metromedia
Barbara Cox Anthony and Ann Cox Chambers	10.1 each	Media
Forrest Mars, Jacqueline Badger Mars, and John Mars	9.0 each	Candy
Abigail Johnson	8.6	Fidelity
Sumner Redstone	8.1	Viacom

Source: Luisa Kroll with Lea Goldman, "The Global Billionaires," *Forbes,* March 18, 2002, pp. 119–150.

However, the financial rewards of business affect more than just a few successful entrepreneurs. The retirement income of millions of people comes from the savings accumulated while working in business. Still more comes from investments in the stock market.

Further, rewards from working in or owning businesses include psychological rewards, such as the personal accomplishments of owners or employees of businesses. These accomplishments may come from inventing a new product or developing a new idea. They may also come from writing new computer code to solve some business problem. They may come from making a significant sale to a customer. They may come from leading a team that does well in an organization. In many cases, business is also fun. Employees of well-run companies report that working for those companies is fun. You will read about some of those companies in this book. Thus, rewards of working in business come in many forms.

Business Is Dynamic

Successful businesses never stand still. They realize that they must always be willing to change or risk losing their competitive position. Sometimes, as a business becomes successful, it becomes vulnerable because it fails to adjust to new technology, shifting customer needs, and the unique approaches that other businesses take. Remember, the competition never stands still either.

Consider the way new technology drives business innovation. Today the name of the game in laptop computing is "smaller and lighter." Customers want the best lightweight laptop they can get at an affordable price. Dell has pioneered a new 2.8-pound version. But it's not the lightest. That honor goes to Toshiba's Portégé 2000. Using a very thin hard disk and battery, the Portégé is a full-width laptop with a 12.1-inch, high-resolution screen and all the amenities, and weighs a mere 2.6 pounds.[4] Of course, we know that the story will not end here. Soon there will be another version that is smaller and lighter and has even more features. Such is the nature of business innovation, and it's an example of how dynamic, change-oriented businesses drive progress. Some businesses even have change as part of their basic mission. Profile 1.1 takes a look at IDEO, a company whose business is innovation.

Business Is Challenging

Business is exciting. It is rewarding. It is dynamic. Business is also challenging. Business is often risky. Even in the midst of opportunities and success, potential problems and pitfalls are never far away. Sometimes businesses have problems that are beyond their control. The year 2001 is a good example. The economy was already cooling off after a record 10-year run of growth when the tragic events of September 11, 2001, shook the country and, indeed, the world. Although the personal costs of that period are simply immeasurable and cannot be discounted, the

PROFILE 1.1   IDEAS FROM IDEO

It is a bit of an understatement to say that IDEO is in the business of innovation. The company creates and sells new ideas. In fact, IDEO is probably the most famous design company in the world. It has designed thousands of products for hundreds of business clients. Although IDEO is not a household name, the company's accomplishments are nonetheless impressive.

For starters, consider just a few of its successes: IDEO designed the first commercial mouse for Apple, the first single-use instant camera for Polaroid (Polaroid Popshots), the Palm V, Cisco's IP phones, the Heartstream portable defibrillator, the Logitech video game controller, the virtual reality headset for Sega, and PDAs for Handspring. The company also designed the Acela train interiors for Amtrak, furniture systems for Steelcase, medical devices for Baxter and Eli Lilly, and consumer products for businesses from PepsiCo to Nike. Not everything is high-tech and high-profile either. IDEO has designed containers for Rubbermaid, bike locks for Specialized, the Oral-B gripper toothbrush, and even Crest's Neat Squeeze toothpaste dispenser.

IDEO stays relatively small. It employs about 600 people worldwide, many of whom are engineers. They practice brainstorming, in which ideas are generated and judgments, at least initially, are withheld. They regularly bring consumers in to look at products and offer suggestions and ideas for options or changes. Recently, IDEO launched Project 2010. This six-month project evaluates trends in technology and then tries to visualize the products of the future.

What will the next generation of products look like? What features will they sport? IDEO has at least some of the ideas that will frame our future. By the way, the company also has a great website. Check it out at www.ideo.com.

Source: IDEO website, www.ideo.com (accessed September 4, 2002).

economic cost to businesses in some industries was great. Businesses in the travel and hospitality industry—including airlines, hotel chains and resorts, car rental firms, and insurance carriers—were hit especially hard. Also hit hard were many small firms, such as independent travel agents and taxi services.

The economy as a whole has ups and downs, but some industries magnify those peaks and valleys. The technology industry is a good example. Throughout the late 1990s and into the early 2000s, the dot-com industry experienced years of uninterrupted growth. Thousands of new companies were launched to take advantage of the Internet and Web-based business processes. That growth was fueled by millions of dollars of capital being invested with the hopes of high returns. Many people lost much of that investment in the dot-com bust, which occurred in a relatively few months in late 2000 and in 2001.

But not all the problems that businesses face are beyond their control. Sometimes poor management decisions wipe out years of progress in the company. Misguided or even unethical decision making can affect the livelihood of workers, investors, and customers. Examples in the energy industry and even the accounting industry in 2002 showed how a few key managers making questionable decisions pushed an entire huge business into bankruptcy almost overnight.

> **More to Come**
> *CHAPTER 8*

The Need for Business Leadership

Business is not a precise science. Executives are intelligent, but they possess no special powers that assure their decisions will be correct. Most decisions require high levels of judgment. Issues are not always clear, and rarely is enough information available. However, any organization that succeeds requires leaders who can make carefully thought-out and reasoned decisions, who possess a strong sense of ethics, and who use the best information about the future that is available. Business leaders must exhibit high levels of courage, a willingness to listen to others in order to collect and analyze information, the logic to assess risks associated with courses of action, and the ability to change those decisions whenever the company's experience suggests that an incorrect strategy is being used.

Many examples of good management and good leadership will be included in this book. You have no doubt already heard of Sam Walton of Wal-Mart, Bill Gates of Microsoft, and Andy Grove of Intel. But there are other companies you likely have not encountered that also exemplify good business leadership. You will read about James Goodnight of SAS Institute, a privately held software development firm that perennially ranks in the top five among the best companies in America for employees. You will read about Mannie Jackson, who bought the Harlem Globetrotters and saved a business icon from going out of business.

Leadership is a key focus in today's organizations. The quality of a firm's leadership is a key ingredient for its success, especially in the long run. Likewise, efforts to understand business failures point to poor leadership as a dominant factor. A survey of top executives at Fortune 100 firms indicated that decisiveness and vision, along with effectiveness as a communicator and motivator, were the most important qualities that CEOs should have. They need to have a firm conviction, or vision, about where they think the company should go and strong instincts about how to get it there. Above all, they need to be flexible in everything except integrity.[5] Leaders must be visionaries, always looking ahead for new opportunities. Leaders must be promoters of change, moving their businesses to think and act in new ways consistent with shifts in the business environment. Effective leaders build people up and inspire them to want to give their best for the business.

One other dimension of leadership is also important. Leaders set the moral tone for the business. Although we will discuss business ethics and morality in more detail in

> **More to Come**
> *CHAPTERS 5, 6*

Chapter 6, a brief perspective on ethics and leadership is needed here. When leader ethics go awry, the entire organization becomes suspect. That is one of the reasons good leaders are so concerned with ethics and appropriate ethical actions. Despite the high-profile and unfortunate examples that make the headlines, the vast majority of business leaders are men and women of strong moral character who demand the highest levels of ethical behavior from their organizations.

Southwest Airlines CEO Jim Parker offers a wonderful perspective on the role of leadership in contemporary business. Parker notes that "leadership is . . . defining and communicating the mission; providing guidance as to how it might be accomplished; equipping people with the proper tools (information, training, etc.); motivating and inspiring through selfless dedication and respect for others; providing positive and negative feedback, including recognition for achievement; and, ultimately, getting out of the way and giving people the ability and authority to accomplish the mission, with the full confidence they will be supported."[6]

A Definition of *Business*

> **business**
> Any organization that strives for profits by providing goods and services that meet customer needs.

Before proceeding further, we need to define what we are talking about. Just what is a business, and what is a successful business? A **business** is any organization that strives for profits by providing goods and services that meet customer needs. Although this definition is basic, you will soon see how rich and complex it really is.

Recognize that business really deals with a fundamental exchange, an exchange of products and services for money. Now understand how fragile this exchange can be. The business must produce and offer products and services that customers need and desire. If it doesn't, customers will not exchange their dollars for these products and services. At the same time, the business must receive a fair and reasonable amount of money for its products and services. If it doesn't, it will see little value to be gained through the exchange. So a business is really an *integrated* process of exchanging value between the organization and its clients.

> **successful business**
> Any business that excels over a long period of time.

We define a **successful business,** or healthy business, as one that excels over time. A business that happens to make a lot of money for a short time but then falls far short of its objectives later is not successful. Neither is a business that makes great financial returns but only at the expense of low morale, uncommitted workers, shoddy products, or unethical behavior. To be truly successful, a business must excel, and it must excel over the long run.

As you read this book, you will enjoy the many examples we use of successful businesses throughout the world. You will read about large companies, such as Caterpillar, IBM, and Kraft. You will learn about some remarkable entrepreneurial companies that are making critical inroads in their respective industries. And you will read about many small companies, the true backbone of our economy, that few people know about outside the company's community.

Let's make one further distinction. Many organizations exist that do not have the goal of making a profit. Known as *not-for-profit* or *nonprofit organizations,* they share many of the characteristics of businesses. For example, the American Red Cross, the YWCA, the Girl Scouts, and your college are all nonprofit organizations. We will discuss these organizations in more depth in Chapter 3.

THINK ABOUT THIS

1. We discussed the fact that business is rewarding, but challenging. Is there a relationship between the two? Do more challenges lead to more rewards?
2. Is the need for strong business leadership greater now than it was 5 or 10 years ago? Or has it always been high, just with different challenges?

Our Three Focus Companies

In addition to the many examples of businesses you will see throughout the book, we have chosen three companies to illustrate specifically how successful companies operate and how business leadership abounds. We will refer to these three companies throughout the book to illustrate business concepts. All three companies were started by entrepreneurs who were willing to defy odds to create a new model of business. All represent highly ethical business practices. All are businesses that have excelled over time when their competitors were performing at a much lower level.

We have chosen one company each from the manufacturing, retail, and service industries. Our manufacturing firm is Dell, started by Michael Dell in his dorm room at the University of Texas. The retail company is Best Buy, started by Richard Schulze in Minneapolis. We note how it evolved from his earlier interest in audio electronics. The service company is Southwest Airlines, launched by Herb Kelleher in Dallas as one of the first no-frills airlines. It is the only airline to have shown 29 years of consistent profits. We introduce these focus companies in the following profiles. We will then refer to them time and again throughout the book to illustrate business leadership

---

DELL   **PROFILE 1.2**

Michael Dell was speaking to an entrepreneurship class at the University of Texas business school when a student asked Dell why he still kept going to work. "You've got so much money," the student blurted. "Why don't you just sell out, buy a boat, and sail off to the Caribbean?" Dell stared at him and said, "Sailing's boring. Do you have any idea how much fun it is to run a billion-dollar company?"

Michael Dell was like many of you reading this book. He was 19 and a freshman in college—The University of Texas at Austin. He crafted an idea—buy computer parts,

Michael Dell personifies the challenge and excitement of building a successful business. He is one of the most recognized young leaders today.

assemble the computers, and sell them to willing customers. He started with $1,000 to underwrite his venture. And, as they say, the rest is history.

Dell ended fiscal year 2002 with $31.2 billion of revenues, a slight decrease from 2001, and a net profit of $1.8 billion. Its sales just six years earlier were only $7.7 billion. Dell's market share approaches 40 percent. Dell now has domestic manufacturing plants in Austin, Texas, and Nashville, Tennessee, as well as plants in Brazil, Ireland, Malaysia, and China.

Dell's award-winning customer service, industry-leading growth, and financial performance continue to differentiate the company from competitors. At the heart of that performance is Dell's unique direct-to-customer business model. "Direct" refers to the company's relationships with its customers, from home-PC users to the world's largest corporations. Until recently, there were no retailers or other resellers adding unnecessary time and cost, or diminishing Dell's understanding of customer expectations. Dell also built little for stock or inventory, having only four or five days' worth of inventory. Every computer it produced was made to order, so there was little cost for storing perhaps thousands of finished computers as other companies did. Having little inventory also reduced the chances of having obsolete products as changes were made. In 2001, for example, Dell had only 0.05 percent obsolete inventory—virtually zero.

In the summer of 2002, Dell announced a new strategy of selling unbranded PCs to U.S. dealers. These dealers would then add their own brand and sell the PCs to small businesses. Dell did not abandon its core strategy of made-to-order Dell computers. Rather, it added an additional strategy to capture a potentially lucrative market.

Dell shares its wealth with its communities. With plants in Austin and Nashville, Dell has made a commitment to the communities in central Texas and middle Tennessee, supporting local community charitable causes both financially and through its volunteers. It also contributes to international agencies.

Source: Richard Murphy, "Michael Dell," *Success,* January 1999, pp. 50–53, reprinted in Robert Price, ed., *Annual Editions: Entrepreneurship* (Guilford, CT: McGraw-Hill/ Dushkin, 2002), pp. 29–31; J. Bonasia, "Supply Chain Issues Take on New Urgency," *Investor's Business Daily,* February 27, 2002, p. A-10; Dell website, www.dell.com (accessed September 5, 2002); *Wall Street Journal,* August 20, 2002, p. B1.

PROFILE 1.3   BEST BUY

"Aggressive entrepreneurship, willingness to change, and strong ethics." This statement captures the mode of operation for Best Buy Co., Inc., or just Best Buy.

Richard Schulze was born and raised in St. Paul, Minnesota. Although he never attended college, Schulze gained practical, secondary, and technical electronics training in the U.S. Air Force with the Minnesota Air National Guard. He began his career in consumer electronics as an independent manufacturer's representative, selling national name brand consumer electronics components throughout a four-state area. This experience, coupled with an aggressive, contagious, and enthusiastic management style, led Schulze to found Sound of Music with his wife, Sandy, in 1966. This chain of six stereo component retail stores served as the forerunner to the present Best Buy Co., Inc., formed in 1983.

Best Buy is more, however, than just the warehouse-looking store with the bright yellow tag on the front. The company also owns Sam Goody, Media Play, On Cue, Suncoast, Magnolia Hi-Fi, and the Canadian chain Future Shop. Each of these store chains also has an associated Internet business, such as BestBuy.com and Suncoast.com. The company reaches consumers throughout the United States (including its recently opened first store in Alaska), Canada, Puerto Rico, and the U.S. Virgin Islands.

Best Buy is now the nation's largest retailer of consumer electronics and appliances. In 2002, it had 1,900 stores, generating nearly $20 billion in annual revenues and more than $500 million in profits. *The Wall Street Journal* ranked shares of Best Buy first in total return to shareholders among 1,000 publicly traded companies during the five years ending December 31, 2001.

Schulze turned the operation of Best Buy over to Bradbury Anderson, who became CEO of Best Buy on June 30, 2002. Schulze still remains chairman of the board, however, focusing on strategic growth and fostering the company's culture through the development of future leadership. Even with the competitive nature of retailing that exists today, the culture and leadership that Richard Schulze created for Best Buy will serve the business well.

Richard Schulze is a classic entrepreneur. He started with a single music store business that has grown to 1,900 stores. What personal characteristics are needed to achieve this growth?

Source: Best Buy website, www.bestbuy.com (accessed September 5, 2002); communication with Best Buy staff, Summer, 2002.

SOUTHWEST AIRLINES   PROFILE 1.4

It is second on *Fortune's* list of the most admired companies. It is regularly featured among the best companies to work for. And it has consistently made a profit since it was founded. In fact, it was the only airline that did not lay off any employees as a result of both the September 11, 2001, tragedy and the faltering economy. It even added 4,000 new employees and bought additional planes in 2002.

Southwest Airlines is known for many things. It is known for its on-time performance. It is known for the quickness of its turnaround time at a gate. It is known for its discount fares and limited frills, no-meals service. It is known for its first-come, first-served seating. Because of Southwest's dedication to efficiency, it has had 29 consecutive years of profit when many of its competitors have struggled. It is now the fourth largest airline in terms of domestic customers carried, flying 2,800 flights per day to 58 cities in 30 states. It is known for many things, but among its more than 35,000 employees, it is best known as a fun place to work.

Herb Kelleher and Rollin King started Southwest Airlines as an intrastate airline in Texas. They were forced to overcome numerous challenges from other airlines that resisted an intruder in their markets. Much of the initial funding they arranged was

Now Chairman at Southwest, founder Herb Kelleher (pictured) set the tone for Southwest Airlines by promoting humor and family culture. Why do you think this is important to Southwest employees?

spent in arguing legal cases before a variety of court venues to gain the right to fly, first within Texas and later from Texas to other points.

In spite of the company's early travails, Herb Kelleher set the tone that an airline need not be a stodgy place to work. His sense of humor helped make up for the long hours that his employees worked. Even as Southwest has grown into a nationwide airline, employees still feel a family culture and are quick to say that they are convinced that there is no better airline to work for than Southwest. Flight attendants and reservationists often state that they know people who work for other airlines who do not have the advantage of Southwest's culture.

Southwest has received so many awards and recognitions and has so many interesting facts to share about the airline, its planes, and its employees, that it has a special link to that information. Go to www.southwest.com, and click on "About SWA" and then "Fact Sheet."

Herb Kelleher, like Richard Schulze of Best Buy, recently announced that he was giving up the day-to-day operations of Southwest Airlines and turning them over to Jim Parker, CEO, and Colleen Barrett, president— both long-time employees. Kelleher will stay active in the company. As chairman of Southwest, he will focus on government regulation and airline security. It is clear, however, that the culture of Southwest Airlines will still have the innovative, entrepreneurial, and customer-oriented edge that has long been associated with Kelleher.

Source: Terry Maxon, "Southwest Airlines to Create 4000 New Jobs," *Dallas Morning News,* February 19, 2002, p. 10. Southwest Airlines website, www.southwest.com (accessed September 5, 2002).

THINK ABOUT THIS

1. Visualize a small business in your hometown. Compare it with one or more of our focus companies. Obviously, it is smaller. What else is different? What is similar?

2. Recently, both Herb Kelleher and Richard Schulze have scaled back their involvement with their businesses and turned them over to capable executives. Speculate as to the changes that might occur now, if any. Why might there be changes even though the new leaders have been with the companies for many years?

The Plan for This Book

Business: An Integrative Approach, third edition, follows a very logical path. In the next chapter, we lay out a model of how a business works, starting with the company's mission and vision. We then consider indicators of a successful business, the broad goals that drive a business. We follow that discussion in Chapter 2 with a discussion in Chapters 3 and 4 of the nature of businesses in our economy.

In Part Two, we discuss decision makers and decision making, including how the decisions affect others outside the business. We also present an in-depth view of business ethics.

In Part Three, we look at the many forces that affect a company's success, including our society's diversity, the economy, financial markets, the global business environment, and government and regulatory influences.

In Part Four, we look at the kinds of decisions that business leaders make. First, they must craft a strategy for the firm. Then they must acquire the resources to implement the strategy. They must design and produce products or services that customers desire. Producing products is of little value if there is no communication with customers, so we discuss marketing-related issues. None of these outcomes are possible without an effective organization in which individuals can make their best contribution to the firm's success. Managers must also consider how to use technology to make the business more competitive in the industry in which it operates.

Finally, Part Five considers how to evaluate the company's performance in comparison with the indicators of success discussed earlier. If change is necessary, business leaders must have the boldness to adapt the company's strategy or operations to increase performance.

> **open systems approach**
> The view that any system is comprised of interrelated parts, each influencing and being influenced by the other parts.

THE BIG PICTURE

This feature appears in each chapter just before the Summary. It is designed to help you integrate the material discussed in the chapter into the overall understanding of how a business operates.

In this first chapter, we have suggested to you that business is exciting, dynamic, and challenging. At the outset of your study of business, we also want you to step back and see business as it fits in the larger society. A given business is just one of many in an industry. That industry is but one part of the overall business system. And the business system itself is only one of many that make up society. Others include government, education, religious organizations, the natural environment, other countries, and, of course, society itself—over 410 million people in North America alone and 6.2 billion in the world.[7] Visualize the world as a giant assortment of interlaced rubber bands, each of which tugs gently—or not so gently—on the others. Business is only one of those rubber bands, but it is influenced by and also influences all the others. Business leaders must react to the dynamics of the business system as well as all the pushes and pulls of the overall society. Thus, decisions that a business leader makes may be incredibly complicated and may have an impact far beyond that single business.

We call this viewpoint a holistic approach, or the **open systems approach,** to studying business. Any system—business, education, government—both influences and is influenced by all other systems. Business leaders must consider these impacts in the decision-making process.

Summary

1. Business is an exciting career choice. In addition, business is rewarding, dynamic, and challenging.
   - Why does business exhibit these characteristics?

   Business is exciting because of all the new products that enter the market. Over 600,000 new companies are formed each year. Businesses create new technology, products, and services that make our standard of living higher. Business is rewarding both from a financial standpoint and from the psychological rewards individuals get from achieving results in business. It is dynamic in that it is always changing. And it is challenging because all decisions carry a certain amount of risk.

2. There is a constant or even increasing need for business leadership today. The complexities of business decisions create a need for carefully thought-out decisions.

   • Why is business leadership so critical?

   Business decision making requires leaders who can examine the environment, analyze information, and make decisions that affect an entire business. Many times, insufficient information is available, so business leaders must make judgment calls. Leaders must be able to make bold decisions, change when necessary, and exhibit high moral character at all times.

3. There are millions of businesses around the world.

   • What is a business?

   A business is any organization that strives for profits by providing goods and services that meet customer needs.

4. Some businesses are far more successful than others.

   • What is a successful business?

   A successful business is one that excels in all aspects of its operations over time.

5. We chose Dell, Best Buy, and Southwest Airlines as focus companies that will be featured throughout the book.

   • Why were these companies chosen?

   We chose a manufacturing company—Dell, a retail company—Best Buy, and a service company—Southwest Airlines. We chose these specific companies because they exhibit several common characteristics. They are all entrepreneurial and were all founded by an individual who was willing to take the risk associated with starting a company. They have all been successful over time, usually exceeding the performance of their competitors. And they all represent companies that exhibit high levels of ethical conduct.

6. In the Big Picture feature for this chapter, we noted that business is but one part of society as a whole.

   • Why is the big picture important, and how does business really fit in society?

   It is important to always take a broad view. Regardless of whether we are discussing how a specific business sells products or how the business system operates, it is important to step back and see how everything fits together. Looking at a business as a system, we see that it interacts with other systems, such as government, education, the natural environment, and of course, society in general. Everything each part of the system does affects the other parts of the system.

Key Terms

business, p. 10   successful business, p. 10
open systems approach, p. 15

Exercises and Applications

1. In a group, discuss the following terms: *excitement, rewarding, dynamic,* and *challenging.* Discuss an example from your own work life that is an example of each. Do the examples that each of you suggest share common characteristics? Do the terms overlap?

2. Assume you have just been given $500,000 to start a business. What business would you form? Justify why this business is a good choice, given today's business environment.

3. Using one of your library's online search engines, type in the term *business leadership*. Look for articles that discuss either the concept of business leadership or companies that exemplify good business leadership. Write what you have learned in one to two pages.

4. Look up any one of our three focus companies on its company website. List in some detail the type of information that is available. Now consider the different audiences that might be looking at those sites. Which information is targeted toward each audience?

5. In teams, discuss the term *open system*. What does it mean to you? What parts of our society does business interact with most? How would your answer differ for education? for government?

6. Look up the term *holistic* in the dictionary. Compare the use of the word in medicine to our use of the word to describe the study of business.

More Torture for Tech

FROM THE PAGES OF

BusinessWeek

Ross Holman, chief information officer for Southwest Airlines, typifies Michael Dell's dilemma. Dell had predicted that Southwest, as well as thousands of other companies, would replace their laptops and other computers bought just before the year 2000 as a hedge against expected Y2K problems. He reasoned that the computers would be three years old and ready for replacement. However, Holman of Southwest has decided to keep those computers for one or two more years. This, of course, helps Southwest Airlines remain profitable, but it causes great grief to the computer industry.

The decision to keep computers longer comes from at least two sources. First, today's computers have sufficient power and accessories to meet most companies' needs. Home computers are also not being replaced as often as previously was the case. Second, the recession that began in 2001 reduced the growth—and hence the need for additional computing power—of many of the computer industry's customers. This implosion of the computer market was certainly a contributing factor to Compaq's merger with Hewlett-Packard in 2002. In addition, Gateway decided to abandon its efforts to sell abroad, and Toshiba pulled out of the U.S. desktop market.

Making matters worse, the soft market has forced computer companies into a price war which shows no sign of stopping for awhile. Although unit sales of PCs were projected to rise slightly in 2002, revenues were projected to fall by 4.3 percent.

All this bad news for computer manufacturers is good news for customers. The recession has caused customers to look carefully at how badly they need new computers. And when they do decide to buy, there will certainly be lots of bargains.

Decision Questions

1. Businesses must constantly react to changes in their external environment. Sometimes the changes represent new opportunities. At other times the changes represent threats. According to this article, what are the environmental threats faced by Southwest Airlines? Dell? other computer makers? Best Buy?

2. Does the article suggest any opportunities presented to Southwest Airlines? Dell? Best Buy?

Source: Adapted from Andrew Park, "More Torture for Tech," *BusinessWeek*, January 14, 2002, p. 98.

References

1. Hans Prosl, "Jake Burton Carpenter: Snowboard Pioneer," http://classic.mountain.snowboarding/99/interviews/burton (accessed February 19, 2002); "Burton Snowboards," www.hoovers.com (accessed February 19, 2002).

2. "Trends in Telephone Service," Federal Communications Commission, August 2001, pp. 12–13.

3. Don Clark, "Tech Innovation Thrives, Despite Stock-Market Blues," *The Wall Street Journal,* February 11, 2002, pp. B1, B4.

4. Walter S. Mossberg, "Going for the Gold, Toshiba Offers a Skinny and Very Light Portégé," *The Wall Street Journal,* February 14, 2002, p. B1.

5. Pamela Goett, "Myths and Legends," *Journal of Business Strategy,* March–April 2002, p. 2.

6. From the Southwest Airlines Officer Biography for Jim Parker. www.southwest.com (accessed March 4, 2002).

7. *The World Fact Book, 2001,* Central Intelligence Agency (CIA) website, www.cia.gov/publications/factbook (accessed March 4, 2002).

2

The Path toward
a Successful Business

It is an impressive list of businesses—Southwest Airlines, Wal-Mart, Microsoft, Berkshire Hathaway, Home Depot, Johnson & Johnson, FedEx, Citigroup, and Intel. These well-known businesses were recently named to *Fortune* magazine's all-star list. This designation means they were considered America's most admired businesses. But which business sits atop this lofty list? For the fifth straight year, the most admired business in America, as well as the most admired in the world, was General Electric.

GE's reputation is well deserved. First, the company made money. Year after year it has shown impressive earnings. It has huge cash reserves, and its various businesses have generated over a billion dollars of revenue every month. In business parlance, GE "made the numbers."

But that's not all there is to the GE story. The business has been known for being innovative, even entrepreneurial. That's quite an accomplishment given a business that employs over 315,000 people worldwide. And it has been known for taking risks—well-thought-out risks. For example, in the midst of a weakened international economy in 2001, GE realized it had an opportunity to expand and grow faster in China. So, the company went for it.

Although GE operates a number of different businesses, it is known, in all cases, for the quality of its products and services. Its wide range of operations has helped GE deal with fluctuations in the economy. For instance, as the economy plummeted in 2001, GE realized that some of its businesses (such as appliances and lightbulbs) would miss their targets. That meant more costs would have to be cut. It also meant other businesses (such as turbines and CT scanners) would have to pick up the slack. And not surprisingly, GE rose to the challenge.

GE has also been known for training great managers. These were managers who stepped up and made tough decisions. And that culture starts at the top. GE's new CEO, Jeff Immelt, followed one of the most popular leaders in business history—Jack Welch. Welch's tough, hard-driving imprint is all over the company. Welch was known for comments like the one that he made to a division chief who had missed his targets: "I love you, and I know you can do better. But I'm going to take you out if you can't get it fixed." GE has a record for making the right calls and, when it has to, getting the problem fixed.[1]

Chapter 2 is titled "The Path toward a Successful Business" to show you the kind of thought process that business leaders use to make sound judgments and decisions. It will show you the complexity of decision making. More than that, however, it will show you how the pieces fit together. Indeed, that is the nature of this entire book—to study a business and discover how the business as a whole operates.

We call this approach an integrative framework because it looks at a business as an integrated and interactive process that is affected by decisions throughout the organization. We recognize that owners or managers of every business make decisions related to marketing, finance, human resources, facilities, and many other elements of the business. But each of these decisions affects other areas in the business. And each decision affects the overall success of the organization by both its individual impact and its interaction with the other parts. It is important that you keep this big picture in mind throughout this book and, indeed, throughout your business career.

After studying this chapter, you should be able to:

1. Explain the concepts of vision and mission statements.
2. Understand the significance of the indicators of business success.
3. Understand the basic nature of the influences of the environment in which a business operates.
4. Describe the types of decisions a company's leaders must make to succeed.
5. Note the relationship between performance measures and the indicators of business success and the need for change once performance has been measured.

The Path toward a Successful Business

How does a business get started, and how does it become successful? What is the path toward business success? To an extent, each business takes a unique path. Yet there are some themes that all successful businesses have in common. These themes and the way they fit together are the focus of this book. Consider Southwest Airlines, one of our focus companies, which was detailed in Profile 1.4.

Southwest Airlines was started in the early 1970s against a backdrop of intense competition in the airline industry. The owners understood how customers think. Southwest reasoned that if fares were low enough, routes were convenient, quality of service was high, and on-time arrival was consistent, large numbers of customers would choose flying over other travel options. That is exactly what happened. Southwest's approach was innovative. It also offered employees a fun place to work and made them feel part of the team.

Today, over 30 years later, Southwest Airlines is still one of the country's most successful businesses. How did this success happen? The company understood its customers. It recognized the changing nature of its environment. It controlled costs. It assured customers of quality service. It innovated. It created a motivating culture. Most importantly, it has been consistently profitable. In short, Southwest successfully integrated its decisions and actions to build a healthy business.

Like those at Southwest Airlines, managers in every other business must make decisions based on careful consideration of what it takes to be successful and the environment the business faces. Becoming a successful business is the result of a carefully formulated process, or path. Figure 2.1 shows a model of that process. We will briefly discuss the model and then break it down into its various parts. Follow this model carefully; it forms the basis for the rest of the book.

The first step is to consider the vision and mission of the company, which set the general direction the company will take. On the basis of the vision and mission, we determine what is important to us. In other words, we determine what the indicators of success will be for us. We then consider a number of forces that have an impact on the company and the decisions it makes. This is a careful and analytical process. Next we move into the action stage, in which we make decisions for the company that lead it toward success. Then we measure how we did in terms of the indicators of success determined earlier. But measuring success is not the end. We must introduce change and renewal to bring the company even closer to the goals we have set.

Look again at the model as it is presented in Figure 2.1. Note the arrows between groups of topics, especially the arrow from "Evaluating Results and Making Changes" back to "Indicators of Business Success." These arrows suggest that the actions in each successive step build on the previous one. For example, it is important to have the vision and mission and the success indicators firmly in mind before studying the environment. It is important to know the environment well before developing strategies and actions for the business. And it is important to have a firm grasp on the actions taken to create value before trying to measure performance.

But reality is more complex than a model, and it is important to understand that these are continuing processes. We are always studying the environment. We measure performance frequently, and we regularly update our approaches and improve our products and services. It is important to see the model of the path toward a successful business as a circular flow.

We will now consider the parts of the model in depth. As we do that, we encourage you to refer often to Figure 2.1, which also appears on the inside front cover of the book for your convenience. Figure 2.1 will help you see how each piece fits into the larger picture.

THINK ABOUT THIS

1. Why is it important for business leaders to look at the total framework or model before looking at individual parts?

2. What are some of the significant events that have occurred in the environment in the past year or two that have affected business? How would knowledge of those events have affected decisions for a large manufacturer? a small, independent retailer?

FIGURE 2.1

Model of the Path toward a Successful Business

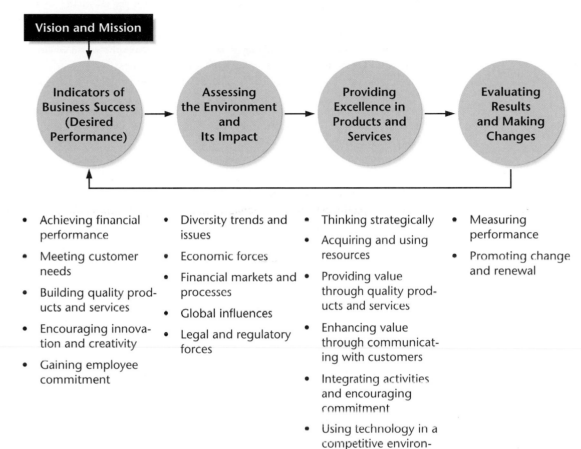

Vision and Mission

The first decision that the key people in a business must make is the direction they wish the business to take. This is shown in Figure 2.2. Here leaders present the big picture of what the business actually will do and what they hope it will become. Leaders should indicate a desirable and possible future for the business. This broad statement of what they would like the business to achieve is termed the **vision** of the business.

Armed with a broad sense of vision, leaders next spell out why the business exists and what the business will do. This more specific statement is referred to as the **mission** of the business. The mission adds substance to the broad theme of the vision. It defines more clearly the aim, scope, and direction of the business.

vision
A broad statement of what a business would like to achieve.

mission
A statement that spells out why a business exists and what the business will do.

Vision and Mission

FIGURE 2.2

Vision and Mission

FIGURE 2.3

Mission Statements

eBay

ebay's mission is to help practically anyone trade practically anything on earth.

Starbucks

Establish Starbucks as the premier purveyor of the finest coffee in the world while maintaining our uncompromising principles while we grow.

Dell

Dell's mission is to be the most successful computer company in the world at delivering the best customer experience in the markets we serve. In doing so, Dell will meet customer expectations of:

Highest quality

Leading technology

Competitive pricing

Individual and company accountability

Best-in-class service and support

Flexible customization capability

Superior corporate citizenship

Financial stability

Best Buy

We improve people's lives by making technology and entertainment products affordable and easy to use. Best Buy's core values include:

Having fun while being the best

Learn from challenge and change

Show respect, humility, and integrity

Unleash the power of our people

Southwest Airlines

The mission of Southwest Airlines is dedication to the highest quality of Customer Service delivered with a sense of warmth, friendliness, individual pride, and Company Spirit.

Source: Company websites: www.ebay.com, www.starbucks.com, www.dell.com, www.onlinepressroom.net/bestbuy, and www.southwest.com (accessed September 6, 2002).

The mission spells out what the business seeks to do and the reasons it exists. Notice that the mission statements in Figure 2.3 share certain common themes. In fact, a mission statement generally addresses three areas. First, it defines the company's basic business. In other words, it broadly specifies the activities or services the business provides. Second, it specifies the markets or constituents the business serves. These first two areas are important. In them, the business designates not only what it does and whom it serves but also, by implication, the areas it will not serve. Third, the mission statement specifies the basic philosophy of the business. This third area is growing in popularity. More and more businesses are using the mission statement to state their core values. These core values are held as standards of behavior for all to see and for all to meet.

Achieving financial performance

Meeting customer needs

Building quality products and services

Encouraging innovation and creativity

Gaining employee commitment

FIGURE 2.4

Indicators of Success

Look carefully at the Dell mission statement. Since the nature of the business is somewhat obvious, Dell uses its mission statement to express its customer-focused philosophy. It emphasizes customer service, quality, cutting-edge technology, customization, and corporate citizenship. These themes, which are so critical at Dell, are stated clearly in its mission statement.

The vision and mission statements are critical because they set the tone and direction of the business. These statements also suggest the relative emphasis that will be placed on each of the five key indicators of business success.

The Indicators of a Successful Business

Once we have an understanding of the key themes laid out by the vision and mission, we can then look at how we measure progress toward the vision of the business. Indicators of success are built around the vision of the company. Indeed, this is the integrating force within a business—that success, and how we define it, must be a function of the vision and mission of the company. These indicators become both the performance targets that businesses try to achieve and the basis for measuring actual performance to determine if corrective action is needed. Today's businesses must be sensitive to these indicators. We suggest five indicators of success that affect all businesses. Although individual businesses may have additional indicators that are unique to their particular business or industry, we see the following five as relevant to virtually all businesses and organizations. Figure 2.4 shows the five indicators. As we will see, strength in each area is important. These indicators, along with the vision and mission, are the big picture for the organization. So when someone asks you to consider the big picture, think of the following sections.

Achieving Financial Performance

Perhaps the single most dramatic measure of organizational health and business success is financial performance. This is the *bottom line* we hear mentioned so often. Regardless of what else goes on in the business, if bottom-line performance is not good enough, the business will not survive.

The most direct indicator of financial performance is captured in the concept of profit. Indeed, the managers of successful businesses constantly strive to make a profit, thereby adding value to the firm. Let's explore what profit really means.

On the way to class today, you stopped at Natural Joe's Pushcart and bought one of Joe's special concoctions, his all-natural multifruit juice, to quench your thirst. The unique blend of strawberry, banana, papaya, and cherry seems to help you concentrate better in class. You paid Joe 90 cents for the drink. That 90 cents is revenue for Joe and his business. In other words, **revenue** is the amount customers pay for the goods and services they purchase.

Of course, that 90 cents does not represent a profit for Joe's business. Joe must pay out money to make his products and provide services to his customers. These payouts include the raw materials he uses in his drinks. He must buy strawberries, bananas, papayas, and cherry extract. He must also pay for the sugar he uses in each drink, as well as the biodegradable cups. He even has to pay the university a royalty (a percentage of sales) to rent pushcart space on campus. Stated concisely, the money a business must pay out to make its products and provide its services is known as **expenses.** Each drink Joe makes includes expenses that total 65 cents.

It is only when revenues exceed expenses that the business realizes a profit, or, in other words, makes money. Thus, **profit** is the amount of money left over after the business records all its revenues and subtracts all its expenses. The difficulty in making a profit is illustrated by the case of the Fox Network in Profile 2.1.

The example of Natural Joe's Pushcart offers some important business insights. First, it lets you see how important revenue is to business. A business needs revenue to survive. Consequently, businesses are always looking for ways to increase their total revenues.

Let's explore that idea of total revenue for a moment. What is Joe's total revenue for the day? Do you have enough information to know? Not really. You know he charges 90 cents for each drink. But you don't know how many drinks he sells in a day. Today, with students streaming by and the temperature pushing 90 degrees, Joe sold 500 drinks. So his total revenue for the day was $450. The price per drink (90 cents) times the quantity sold (500) equals the total revenue ($450). Businesses are always playing the price–quantity trade-off game. If Joe lowers his price, will he sell more drinks? If he raises his price, will he sell fewer? The answers and Joe's subsequent actions are critical because they affect the total revenue that Joe's business will earn.

The 500 drinks Joe sold represent an expense of $325 for the day. Accordingly, his profit for the day is $125 ($450 − $325).

Businesses must always be concerned with expenses. They realize that if they can find ways to reduce expenses while still giving customers the desired products and services, they will make more money. This idea is fundamental, and it is a popular theme in business today. Businesses produce goods and services. Of course, it takes money and other resources to do so. A business converts its resources into goods and services that customers value enough to pay for them. The ratio of goods and services produced to resources used is known as the rate of **productivity** of the business. If a business can increase its level of goods and services offered without increasing the resources it uses, it is increasing its productivity. If a business can produce the same level of output while reducing the resources it uses, it is said to be operating more efficiently. Both actions, increased productivity and efficiency, should give the business a more favorable bottom line. Throughout the book, we will see some of the innovative ways businesses are trying to control expenses, operate more efficiently, and increase their productivity. The logic for this effort is simple: It is profitable to do so.

---

revenue
The amount customers pay for the goods and services they purchase.

expenses
The money a business must pay out to make its products and provide its services.

profit
The amount of money left over after the business records all its revenues and subtracts all its expenses.

productivity
The ratio of goods and services provided to resources used.

"Noisy, unruly, brash, unpredictable, and impossible to ignore." No, it's not a description of your roommate. It is how one critic described TV's most outrageous network—Fox.

From the beginning, over 15 years ago, Fox was unique, bold, and aggressive. The network sported huge hits, such as "The Simpsons" and "The X-Files." It expanded into popular sports entertainment through the National Football League, Major League Baseball, and NASCAR. Even Fox News had a certain edge and popularity.

Through all its years, one thing has remained. The network is an innovator. Fox always appears poised to try new things and stir up the stale mix of standard TV fare. The network has pushed the boundaries. It has taken us to the edge of what could be said and done on TV. And in the process, it has built a more youthful and culturally diverse set of programming options.

But there is one more surprise. The Fox Network has not been a moneymaker! That's right. With all those shows, all that popularity, all that advertising revenue, how is this possible? It is just the bottom line. Fox has managed to spend more money than it has taken in. Recently, that gap exceeded $1 billion.

Fox is not unique and its financial situation is affected by some tough factors beyond its control. For example, Fox was affected by the severe advertising recession that has hit the industry. As businesses worldwide pare their advertising budgets, they drained a major source of Fox revenues. Another issue is escalating costs. As production costs for network shows rose, Fox took a hit. Plus, keep in mind all the up-front money it takes to secure those popular sports contracts.

But there is hope. Many think that Fox's huge investments are about to pay off. Plus, Fox is part of the giant Fox Entertainment Group that is owned by media mogul Rupert Murdoch. Fox executives state their case boldly, "We've been in an investment mode. . . Now we're in the payback cycle."

Source: Marc Gunther, "Will Fox Ever Grow Up?" *Fortune*, March 4, 2002, pp. 137–140.

A final note on profits. Some people seem to have an impression that there is something sinister about a business seeking profits. Let's recognize right up front that there is nothing negative, manipulative, or corrupt about a firm's pursuit of profits. In fact, profit is the incentive for which individuals invest in a business. It is the reward for risking one's wealth and/or efforts in a venture. For example, Joe may have committed his life savings to getting his pushcart business started. He works hard, and he sacrifices for his business. Profit is a reasonable and fair incentive to encourage Joe's actions.

Profit may be taken out of the business for the owner's personal use, or it can be reinvested in the business. It can be shared with employees or invested in other ventures or donated to charitable causes. Profit is one of the key aspects of a capitalist society. The quest for profit drives innovation and efficiency.

Remember, profit is one of the primary measures of a firm's success. It certainly is not the only measure, but it is the most commonly accepted one. If a business fails to make a profit over time, it will ultimately go out of business.

Analyzing the overall financial performance of a business, however, is more complicated than simply looking at profits. In later chapters, you will learn that financial performance can be calculated from the financial statements and reports that the managers prepare. Even though such measures are objective and numerically based, you should exercise care in using and interpreting them. For example, a relatively new business may not make much money. In fact, it may actually lose money each month that it operates. Yet it may be poised for growth. In essence, the business may be healthy given its situation. It just has not taken off yet.

More to Come
CHAPTER 18

In contrast, a business may appear to be in good financial condition and yet be far from healthy. Other measures of success may indicate that there are problems. It may take some time for the effect of inattention to those factors to appear on the bottom line. For example, the business may be making a lot of profit for its investors, yet it may not be buying new equipment, updating its facilities, or investing in new technology. Therefore, even if the business seems financially successful, its failure to modernize may cast doubt on its longer-term success. Given this perspective, we will now look more closely at the nonfinancial indicators of success.

Meeting Customer Needs

Every business has customers, regardless of whether it produces a product or provides a service. The amount of profit a business makes is ultimately determined by how well it meets its customers' needs over the long run. There are many different kinds of customers. Some customers are other businesses. Some are individuals. Some purchase goods or services from the business only once. Others purchase often and repeatedly. Some purchase products costing a few pennies. Others spend thousands of dollars for a single product. Customers may be next door to the business or thousands of miles away. They may talk face-to-face with a sales representative or order via direct mail or the Internet. Whatever the nature of the customer, the key to business profits is satisfying customer needs over time.

Today many experts feel that customers are the key indicator of business health and success. Note that rather than thinking of profits first, these experts think of customers first. They recognize that if customers are satisfied, the base for financial profitability is in place. Without customer acceptance, the business will not survive. If a business does not meet the needs of a customer, that customer will go to a competitor.

Many businesses recognize this relationship and focus their efforts on customer satisfaction. Many say they want to not only meet but also exceed customer expectations. Some even talk about delighting the customer. Many organizations are quite creative about how they approach the customer and try to satisfy customer needs. Some organizations even "guarantee" customer satisfaction.

Consider the example of a well-known retail business, Spiegel. Spiegel has a tradition of customer service that has defined the business for over 135 years. Today, as a premier retailer of clothing and home furnishings, the Spiegel

Spiegel is noted for its customer service. Whether its sales are in retail stores, the Internet, or catalogs, sales are backed by Spiegel's culture and promise of happy customers. What is your opinion of a "happy customer" philosophy?

THINK ABOUT THIS

1. Consider a company that saw its sales increase significantly and, at the same time, incurred a loss. How could that happen?

2. How could you increase productivity in a service business such as, say, a small, independent accounting firm?

Group's businesses include not only Spiegel but also Eddie Bauer and Newport News. These businesses reach customers through catalogs, e-commerce, and more than 560 specialty and retail outlets. One theme dominates the businesses, and they say it proudly: "We want you to be happy with every Spiegel purchase. If you're not . . . give us the chance to make things right."[2]

How do businesses know if they are meeting customer needs? Ultimately, they know through the purchases and selections that customers make. However, that may be too late. A successful business keeps a watchful eye on two factors: (1) customer sensitivity and service and (2) timeliness. Let's look at each of these factors.

Customer Sensitivity and Service

Customer sensitivity is about awareness; it means being aware of customer desires and needs, and anticipating changes in customer preferences. Customer sensitivity leads to customer service, which is action-oriented. **Customer service** is the set of actions a business takes to meet customer needs and preferences.

In customer service, a successful business must be proactive. It must anticipate customer trends and respond quickly to new needs. Proactive businesses constantly look for new trends, new ways to serve customers, and new ways to operate more efficiently. They try to stay ahead of the game and anticipate what may be coming. Large businesses even have marketing research professionals and customer relations specialists to help them better understand and predict customer needs and how those needs are changing.

Customer service is an ongoing process, a goal that is never fully realized. As soon as customers' needs are met, their expectations rise. The bar on customer service is always being raised higher and higher. Clearly, a business without a proactive awareness of customers will not remain healthy for long.

Southwest Airlines has built its entire company around the concept of customer service. Customer service is part of the culture at Southwest Airlines. Employees from reservation agents to flight attendants to mechanics are encouraged to be friendly and to make decisions that similar employees at other airlines might expect to refer to a higher level. In addition, employees are encouraged to have fun on their jobs because their attitude makes flying easier for customers. As a result, the U.S. Department of Transportation has ranked Southwest number one in fewest customer complaints for the past 11 consecutive years.[3]

customer sensitivity	The awareness of customer desires and needs.

customer service	The actions a business takes to meet customer needs and preferences.

SOUTHWEST

Timeliness

In today's volatile business environment, speed and response time are extremely important. A wonderful new product idea or a vision of a novel area of service is meaningless unless it can be delivered to customers in a timely way. True, managers must analyze their decisions and carefully reflect on available information. This process of analysis is the backbone of effective decision making. Yet leaders must be action-oriented. They must avoid the tendency to overevaluate decisions. Indeed, while they wait for more information and gain assurance that the risk is acceptable, a competitor may act. That competitor will have gained initial consumer acceptance, achieving *first-comer advantages*. The slow mover is then playing catch-up. The phrase "if you snooze, you lose" has real business implications.

Consider the case of handheld computers, which are booming in popularity. You can schedule appointments, look up phone numbers, check your e-mail, and even have a mobile Internet kit right there in the palm of your hand. As in any growing industry, competition intensifies. But who do you think is the industry leader? It's not even close. The dominant company is the one that pioneered the first handheld device only a few

FedEx has always been known for its overnight delivery of packages. It has expanded into ground transportation of packages over shorter distances. Still, timeliness is a key to its success.

years ago—Palm, Inc. In fact, its first device, the Palm Pilot, is so well recognized that many people still use the phrase "palm pilot" to refer to any handheld computing machine.[4] Palm is definitely reaping the benefits of being the first comer.

Timeliness is a tough issue for many businesspeople. No one wants to rush to a decision without all the necessary information. No one wants to risk a premature entry into a new market without sufficient study. But there is never as much information available as you would like. All decisions carry some element of risk. Successful businesses are always studying, anticipating, developing, and looking for new options—but they are poised to act. Indeed, their health and even their survival demand that they act with speed and conviction.

In addition to being a major issue in larger, more strategic actions of a business, timeliness is important in specific customer situations. Lands' End, a mail-order seller of quality clothes, prides itself on getting every order out within 24 hours. It ships by an express delivery service, so the package usually reaches the customer's door within three days after the order is placed. In recent years, banks have moved to almost exclusive use of ATMs because quick service has become more of a priority for customers than seeing a bank teller face-to-face. In later chapters, you will learn about just-in-time delivery in manufacturing, yet another example of how timeliness has become a key factor in business today.

More to Come
CHAPTER 14

Building Quality Products and Services

Increasingly, today's businesses must focus on the quality and value of their products and services. Customers won't tolerate low quality unless low prices are more important to them than the quality of the product. The trend in recent years, however, has been to emphasize quality even if the cost is higher. In a competitive environment, customers will readily abandon any business that fails to meet their quality expectations. Some businesses may generate initial sales and revenues by offering low prices that lure customers to their products. But if quality is low, these customers generally do not return.

Quality is a near obsession for many companies. In fact, **quality management** is the expected way of operating for most businesses today. Quality management is nothing more than a company's unique approach for ensuring quality. The foundation of quality management is a philosophy known as **continuous improvement,** which refers to a company's efforts to provide steadily higher levels of quality throughout all phases of its operations. Each step in the production process is examined and altered to make it better. This approach often results in more efficient and less costly ways of making a product. Continuous improvement also means that the products and services provided to customers are getting better all the time.

Some businesses are known for the quality of their products and services. These businesses use their quality reputations to distinguish themselves from their competitors. For example, in the industrial equipment industry, Caterpillar is recognized for building top-quality, dependable machines. In the semiconductor industry, Intel is highly regarded for the consistent quality of its products. United Parcel Service (UPS) is known for its innovative efforts to make the shipping process easier and more convenient and for making the timely delivery of packages a virtual certainty. This reputation has led a number of business experts to single out UPS as a great example of service quality. But which company do you think is number one on *Forutne*'s more recent list of businesses with the best reputations in the world for quality? That honor goes to Toyota.[5]

Encouraging Innovation and Creativity

In today's volatile business setting, the only constant is change. Customer tastes and preferences are constantly changing. Employee demands are always shifting. Competitors are always searching for new ways to edge rivals out of the market. Organizations are always looking for methods of operation that will bring greater efficiency and productivity. New technologies are always being developed. The only way a business can stay on top and compete is to be creative and innovative. If a firm does not have the ability to change, its success will surely be short-lived.

Consider Nokia. At a time when the rest of the telecom industry is struggling, Nokia is going stronger than ever, posting dazzling operating profits year after year. How does Nokia do it? It realizes that size and strength are never enough, particularly in a business that is driven by technology innovation and rising customer expectations. Nokia's growth in the late 1990s came from the boom in the cell phone industry. But most people think that growth has leveled off today, since most people who want a cell phone probably have one. So Nokia keeps changing and innovating. It is bringing out a new line of "technophones" that will let users send and receive images and cruise the Internet as easily as they can from a PC. Nokia CEO Jorma Ollila, echoing the need for change, says it best: "This isn't a business where you can do one big strategic thing right and you're set for the next 5 years."[6]

A fundamental way to think about creativity and innovation is to look at how the two terms are related. Creativity is a process; innovation is an outcome. **Creativity** is new and different patterns of thinking and behaving. **Innovation** is the result, or what is produced through these creative activities. Innovation deals with new approaches and options. In short, creativity leads to innovation.

Innovation is quite difficult because it requires a business to think about change and improvement even when things look quite good. Indeed, one of the biggest barriers to innovation is success. The argument goes, Why should we change when the bottom line looks so good?

---

quality management
A company's unique approach to ensuring quality.

More to Come
CHAPTER 14

continuous improvement
The efforts by a business to provide steadily higher quality throughout all phases of its operation.

Nokia has become the fastest selling brand of cell phones in the U.S. Its phones are on the forefront of technology and style.

More to Come
CHAPTER 19

creativity
New and different patterns of thinking and behaving.

innovation
New approaches and options that are the result of creative activities.

Innovation is done not simply to be creative. Innovation can yield profits. It can help meet customer needs. It can add to the quality of products or processes. Check out Profile 2.2 about 3M. It is one of the best-known examples of creativity and innovation and the culture required to achieve that innovation. And the innovation pays off. 3M's net income has averaged over $1.6 billion per year for the past five years.

PROFILE 2.2   3M

You have heard about Post-it™ Notes made by 3M. You know Scotch tape. You may even recall Scotchgard protective treatments on furniture fabrics. And you may have Thinsulate gloves or jacket linings. But how about the following diverse products?

Accentrim tapes and films that give the illusion of beveled glass without the weight or cost.

Sleeping bags for snakes (endangered species of grass snakes in Germany) that use the Thinsulate material.

Inflata-Pak packaging material made of high-quality plastic that seals itself around breakable products, eliminating the need for packing peanuts or shredded newspaper.

Sandblaster high-performance abrasives that sand three times faster than traditional sandpaper and last three times as long.

3M light-management technology that applies breakthrough physics in telecommunications, photonics, lighting, medical, automotive, packaging, and horticulture.

Scotchprint Printer 2000, a large-format graphics printer that produces a colorful, durable 8- by 10-foot display in two minutes and, in less than 20 minutes, can produce graphics to cover a standard semitrailer truck.

3M has long been known for its innovations. The development of Post-it Notes, for example, is an intriguing story itself. The more important aspect of 3M, however, is the culture that encourages innovation. The following quote from 3M's website captures the spirit of innovation: "There's opportunity in the air every day at 3M. It's part of our atmosphere of innovation, the excitement and anticipation of knowing the next new product discovery or technological breakthrough is right around the corner. It's the exhilaration of being able to take risks every day, the freedom of trying your own ideas—because you're encouraged and empowered to! We do everything possible to champion your creative thinking, to streamline the process of taking your ideas from concept to implementation. We expect 30% of our sales each year to come from products that are less than 4 years old—innovative new products that begin every day with creative initiatives from you and your colleagues."

The Post-it Note is one of 3M's most famous innovations. It was made using an adhesive that had been rejected for other products because it would not stick well enough. Scientists at 3M have substantial freedom to experiment with new ideas.

Source: 3M website, www.3m.com (accessed March 7, 2002).

Businesses today are encouraged to operate as learning organizations. **Learning organizations** are those that not only adapt to change but also search creatively for new and better ways to operate and meet the needs of their employees and customers. A learning organization is highly proactive. It is ripe with creativity and is more likely to produce useful innovations. Increasingly, this focus must be present if a business is to be considered truly successful.

> **learning organizations**
> Organizations that adapt to change and search creatively for new and better ways to operate and meet the needs of their employees and customers.

Gaining Employee Commitment

A successful business is composed of employees who care about the jobs they do. They are proud of their work, and they feel a sense of commitment to their jobs and to the company. They are dedicated and concerned, not simply going through the motions. Committed employees are motivated to do the best job possible.

Companies have to treat employees well and see that they continue to develop. Progressive, healthy organizations invest considerable time and effort in finding ways to build greater employee commitment. Many have formal programs to provide more opportunities for employee participation and involvement in decision making. Many give employees opportunities for growth through company-supported training efforts. Many offer creative benefits and work options. Many give workers more discretion and more power to do things that were previously done only by their bosses. This process of giving more decision-making authority and responsibility to workers throughout the organization is known as **empowerment.**

One way to build commitment is to use the talents of the workforce to the fullest extent possible. Most employees want to feel needed in their work. Certainly, if people feel that they are asked to do more than they can, they become frustrated and dissatisfied. However, people also experience frustration and dissatisfaction if they feel that their talents and skills are not being used by the business. If the business does not provide employees the opportunity to use their skills and express their contributions, their sense of underutilization can be a major cause of stress. Healthy organizations encourage employees to contribute their talents.

> **empowerment**
> The process of giving more decision-making authority and responsibility to workers throughout the organization.

Employee commitment comes when managers understand their workforce, are attuned to workers' needs, and make an effort to meet those needs. Consider the employee commitment at SAS Institute Inc., shown in Profile 2.3. SAS Institute is one of the best examples ever of a company so committed to its employees that the employees are intensely loyal to the company. The combination of extraordinary on-site facilities and programs for employees and the absolute respect the company shows its workers in their jobs explains why the turnover rate is nearly zero. Although few companies provide as much for their employees as SAS does, SAS executives are convinced that the cost of the programs and facilities is money well spent.

SAS INSTITUTE

PROFILE 2.3

"Trust your employees to balance the demands of work and life—and give them the opportunity and the flexibility to do so." This is a corporate philosophy at SAS Institute, a company known for building employee commitment and loyalty.

SAS, which stands for Statistical Analysis Software, is a software development company and a whole lot more. Its customer base consists of virtually all the 100 largest U.S. public companies, as well as the U.S. government. In 2001, SAS had sales of $1.13 billion. With 8,300 employees, it has 39,000 customer sites in 117 countries. With nearly half of its sales outside the United States, SAS just experienced its 25th consecutive year of revenue gains.

Yet the most interesting thing about SAS is not its excellent software, but its excellent culture, which was developed and encouraged by founder Dr. James Goodnight. Employee benefits abound. Some of those benefits include low-cost day care facilities for 700 kids; a cafeteria outfitted with high chairs so that employees can eat lunch with their children; free access to a 36,000-square-foot gym, a putting green, and on-site massages; and an office with a door for every white-collar employee. This focus on employee commitment seems to pay off. For example, SAS's annual turnover rate generally runs about one-fifth that of the industry. Some employees have reported taking pay cuts to come work at SAS.

The company believes that its stable workforce is one reason it can produce new versions of its data-mining and statistical-analysis software more cheaply and efficiently. "The well-being of our company is linked to the well-being of our employees," says SAS CEO Jim Goodnight. "Employees determine whether we flourish or fail. If we make the effort and invest resources in our employees' professional welfare, everyone wins—the employee, the customer, and the company. If you treat employees as if they make a difference to the company, they will make a difference to the company."

Source: Nicholas Stein, "Winning the War to Keep Top Talent," *Fortune,* May 29, 2000, pp. 132–138; SAS website, www.SAS.com (accessed October 23, 2002).

Assessing the Environment and Its Impact

environment of business

Those factors or influences that affect the business but over which the firm has little control.

Once the indicators of success for a particular business have been determined, the next step in the process is to research and study the firm's environment. This step, shown in Figure 2.5, gives the managers the information they need to make good decisions. The **environment of business** consists of those factors or influences that affect the business but over which the firm has little control. Decision makers must understand the nature of the environment in which their business operates. They must be aware of critical forces in the environment and recognize the shifts and patterns that occur.

Managers must not only be aware of environmental forces but also be able to assess the potential impact of those forces on the business. A business that lacks this environmental sensitivity is severely handicapped. It is unlikely to be able to make good decisions and continue to survive.

Five key environmental forces influence business decisions. They are so important that a separate chapter is devoted to each environmental force. We will begin by looking at *diversity trends and issues.* Then we'll move to *economic forces, financial markets and processes, globalization,* and *legal and regulatory forces.* These chapters together make up Part Three of the book.

THINK ABOUT THIS

1. Look at the five indicators of success we just discsussed. Consider a business that you know well. Which indicators seem most important? Are there some that are not relevant for that business?

2. How would you measure innovation in a manufacturing firm? a retail firm? a service firm?

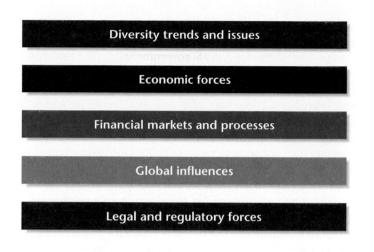

FIGURE 2.5

Assessing the
Environment and Its
Impact

Providing Excellence in Products and Services

Once decision makers have a sense of the business environment, they can begin the process of providing excellence in goods and services. This next stage of the model zeroes in on what the business will do and what approaches it will pursue. These sets of activities and decisions must be performed to get things done and keep the business moving toward the indicators of success. This process is shown in Figure 2.6.

Managers must begin to *think strategically*. A strategic direction does not just happen. For the successful business, this direction follows a careful analysis of the environment, with one eye always on the indicators of business success. This process of strategic thinking and planning is developed in Chapter 12.

To grow, a business must *acquire the resources* necessary to produce products or provide services. Generally, businesses are concerned with four types of resources: human, physical, financial, and information. These resources become the inputs needed to produce the products and services that customers desire. Economists refer to these

FIGURE 2.6

Providing Excellence
in Products and
Services

input resources as the *factors of production* since they are the critical factors needed to produce things. Human resources are the people needed to get things accomplished. Physical resources refer to the land, buildings, equipment, and raw materials that the business uses in producing the product or service. Financial resources are needed to acquire the other types of resources and ensure that the business can continue to operate. Information is needed to coordinate, plan, and measure the performance of the firm. The complexity of acquisition decisions is discussed in Chapter 13.

With the strategic direction of the company in mind and resources planned for, business leaders can turn their attention to *creating value for their customers.* There are two parts to this process, which we will discuss in Chapters 14 and 15. First, leaders must learn about their customers to produce products or services that best meet customer needs. This step requires careful study of their customers (and potential customers), analysis of existing products produced by the firm and its competitors, and a determination of the potential for each product or service. A central focus in product development is the quality of products and the quality of the processes necessary to make the products. Many of the decisions that are made have an impact on quality, and these decisions can affect a firm's ability to compete effectively.

Second, in addition to providing value for customers, managers must communicate that value to the customers. The best possible product will still fail if customers are not made aware of its existence. We will discuss a number of ways to communicate the value of a product or service to the company's customers.

Regardless of the types of products or services provided and the kinds of resources involved in their production, the entire process must be managed effectively. Indeed, even the best resources can be wasted if they are not managed properly. The topic of *integrating activities and encouraging commitment* is the basis for discussion in Chapter 16. Decisions in this area involve how jobs are structured and how business leaders attempt to build commitment within the workforce.

One key issue of contemporary management is the *use of technology,* which is changing at breakneck speed. The prevailing technology in an industry may be obsolete within a few years. If a business is going to succeed, it must remain technologically competitive. It must not only be aware of technological changes, but also be constantly updating. Technology falls into two broad categories: information technology and production technology. Both are necessary for the business to operate effectively and efficiently. In addition, exchanging information and processes between businesses is a growing need. This process, known as e-commerce or e-business, will be discussed in Chapter 17.

The six chapters just noted make up Part Four of the text. They deal with key decisions and actions of the successful business that are necessary to provide excellence in products and services. While each chapter focuses on special areas of decisions, these decisions are related.

Evaluating Results and Making Changes

A business can be successful over time only if its managers carefully evaluate performance results and make necessary changes to improve those results and meet new demands. This stage of the business process is shown in Figure 2.7. Managers must constantly know how they are performing so that they can take corrective action when necessary. This knowledge demands that the business monitor and *measure its performance* against the indicators of success it has previously established.

FIGURE 2.7

Evaluating Results and
Making Changes

Measuring Performance

– Achieving financial performance
– Meeting customer needs
– Building quality products and services
– Encouraging innovation and creativity
– Gaining employee commitment

Change and renewal

Sometimes a manager finds that the business is right on target with the success indicators. However, the business environment is complex and changing. Competitors are always adjusting. Consumer demands shift regularly. Quality standards are constantly being raised. Employee expectations are changing. As a result, adjustments often must be made. Measurement is important because it pinpoints where adjustments are needed. Measurement issues will be discussed in Chapter 18.

If properly done, measurement focuses the business on needed *change and renewal.* Yet that does not mean that change occurs easily. One of the key challenges facing any business is to convert the need for change into action. The healthy business must be willing and able to renew itself. This process is difficult and often involves resistance.

Accordingly, the way the business approaches change is critical. Successful businesses invest in ongoing training and development to facilitate positive change. They encourage creativity and innovation. They understand that change is a process. They approach planned change as a serious set of activities for which management must assume responsibility. Issues of change and renewal are discussed in Chapter 19.

THE BIG PICTURE

We have briefly outlined five key indicators of a successful, healthy business. In many ways, these are the five outcomes a business hopes to achieve as it operates.

Recognize that these outcomes are not independent of one another. In fact, they are interdependent. What happens in one area affects other areas. For example, attention to quality and sensitivity to customers should enable a business to undertake operations and provide products and services that improve its financial performance. Innovation keeps the business on the cutting edge, assuring customer responsiveness and enhancing financial outcomes. Utilizing the workforce and gaining employee commitment build a sense of drive and dedication that may promote quality, customer service, and innovative ideas. A focus on one piece of the success picture without attention to others would yield an incomplete picture and could endanger the long-term success of the business.

Summary

1. Many businesses have vision statements and mission statements to guide them in their operations.

   • What is a vision? What is a mission?

   A vision is a broad statement of a desirable and possible future for the business. A mission spells out why the business exists and what it will do. It includes the company's philosophy.

2. A successful business produces several kinds of desired results. The results are measured by indicators that managers strive to achieve.

   • What are the indicators of business success?

   Five critical indicators of business success are (1) achieving financial performance, (2) meeting customer needs, (3) building quality products and services, (4) encouraging innovation and creativity, and (5) gaining employee commitment.

3. A business does not operate in a completely controllable environment. Numerous forces that affect business success are beyond the control of business managers. Managers must be aware of changes in those forces and must decide how to respond to those changes.

   • What are the external factors that affect business?

   Five key environmental forces influence business decisions: (1) diversity trends and issues, (2) economic forces, (3) financial markets and processes, (4) global influences, and (5) legal and regulatory forces.

4. A successful business is one in which managers make good decisions and follow them with effective actions. The goal of these decisions and actions is to provide excellence in products and services. Many kinds of decisions must be made, and this usually means that many employees must be involved in the decision-making process. Even more employees are usually involved in taking the actions that implement the decisions.

   • What kinds of decisions and actions are required for business success?

   The six categories of decision making and actions are (1) choosing a strategic direction for the business, (2) acquiring the resources, (3) providing value through quality products and services, (4) enhancing value through communicating with customers, (5) integrating activities and encouraging commitment, and (6) using technology.

5. Business is both exciting and challenging precisely because most decisions involve uncertainty. Managers can never be sure that their actions will produce the results they expect. For that reason, every successful business must monitor the results of past actions and constantly look for ways to improve performance. That is, it must evaluate results and make changes.

   • How do measurement and promoting change enable firms to improve performance?

   Measurement permits the business manager to evaluate the results of operations in terms of the indicators of success that were previously established. Measurement should help the business identify where changes are needed. However, making needed changes is difficult. It requires overcoming resistance to change and involves ongoing training and innovation.

Key Terms

continuous improvement, p. 31

creativity, p. 31

customer sensitivity, p. 29

customer service, p. 29

empowerment, p. 33

environment of business, p. 34

expenses, p. 26

innovation, p. 32

learning organizations, p. 33

mission, p. 23

productivity, p. 26

profit, p. 26

quality management, p. 31

revenue, p. 26

vision, p. 23

1. Choose either Dell, Best Buy, or Southwest Airlines. Go to its website. Study the site to find as many examples of excellence in the indicators of business success as possible. Write your results in a three- to four-page paper.

2. Choose one of the indicators of business success. Then choose a small company you are familiar with that does well on that indicator. Prepare to discuss your results in class.

3. Go to *Fortune*'s website at www.fortune.com. Click on the link to the 100 fastest-growing businesses. Select a business that looks interesting, and find out what it does (you can even link to the company's website). What evidence can you locate about the business's performance on our indicators of business success?

4. Some businesspeople argue that a firm's current financial success can be an impediment to continuous improvement, change, and renewal. Why?

5. Think back to the last time you traveled by air. Recall your impressions of that experience. Consider the quality of the service you received, how your needs as a customer were met, and the overall attitude and approach of the airline people with whom you were involved. What suggestions would you make to improve the airline's operations? Be as specific as possible.

Exercises and Applications

3M: A Lab for Growth?

FROM THE PAGES OF

BusinessWeek

Throughout its 100-year history, 3M has had a surefire formula for growth: hire top-notch scientists in every field, give each an ample endowment, then stand back and let them do their thing. That anything-goes approach has yielded thousands of new products over the decades, from sandpaper and magnetic audio tape to Post-it Notes and Thinsulate insulation. Indeed, 3M generated $5.6 billion in sales in 2000—fully one-third of its revenues—from goods that didn't exist just four years earlier.

But that's not good enough for 3M's new boss. Sure, that record of innovation impresses Chairman and Chief Executive W. James McNerney Jr., the first outsider to take the helm. Yet he argues that even with a $1 billion budget and staff of 7,000, 3M's vaunted products laboratory won't be able to achieve the growth he wants. And how much is that? McNerney audaciously predicts he can double the record numbers of 2000 in 10 years or less.

To hit his targets of increasing sales by 11% a year and operating earnings by 12%—nearly twice the rate of the past decade—the newcomer conceded he needs to pull off a string of decent-size acquisitions and plunge into services.

The company's new chairman has launched several initiatives since arriving. 3M is planning to move more manufacturing overseas and to pool its purchases across divisions to get lower prices. Taking a page from GE's playbook, 3M has specially trained "black belts" rooting out inefficiencies in departments from R&D to sales. Product development has always been a 3M strength, but it is now pushing to get goods into the marketplace much faster by focusing R&D spending on the most likely prospects.

McNerney's new course. . . runs the risk of stifling 3M's hallmark creativity. He and his lieutenants are already specifying where research and development dollars are spent and establishing uniform performance standards across 3M. That runs counter to its tradition of giving individual business chiefs free rein. . . 3M old-timers generally back McNerney, conceding that money wasn't always wisely spent. McNerney says he understands the balancing act: "My job is to add scale in a fast-moving entrepreneurial environment. If I end up killing that entrepreneurial spirit I will have failed."

Wall Street is mostly rooting for McNerney because 3M has held up relatively well during the recession. Credit some GE-like cost-cutting measures. Only weeks after succeeding L. D. DeSimone, McNerney announced the layoff of 5,000 of 3M's 75,000 employees. . . The balance sheet shows his handiwork. 3M had piled up almost $440 million in cash as of Sept. 30, up 45% from the start of the year. Overhead expenses, in the meantime, were down 7% in the third quarter on a year-to-year basis. . . Investors appreciate the numbers. . . [S]ince Sept. 21, 3M is up 34% vs. 21% for the S&P 500. . . Unquestionably, however, McNerney's ambitions have been slowed by the economic downturn.

McNerney has vowed no massive reorganization at 3M. That, he says, could be demoralizing. "It's not a matter of machine-gunning the team because I'm new and I think I'm smarter and better," says McNerney. "This is taking a very good company and making it better."

Decision Questions

1. The model discussed in this chapter begins with the company mission. How did McNerney's predecessors define 3M's mission? How does McNerney define it?

2. The model explains that all businesses must identify the indicators of business success and measure company performance against the goals set for each indicator. What indicators of success seem to figure most prominently in McNerney's mind?

3. The model explains how a company must assess the environment to spot opportunities and threats. Name one feature of the global environment that represented an opportunity seized by McNerney. Name one feature of the economic environment that has made it difficult for McNerney to achieve his objectives in the short run.

Source: Michael Arndt, "3M: A Lab for Growth?" *BusinessWeek,* January 21, 2002, pp. 50–51.

References

1. Justin Fox, "What's So Great about GE?" *Fortune,* March 4, 2002, pp. 64–67; and *Fortune* website, www.fortune.com (accessed February 20, 2002).

2. Spiegel website, www.thespiegelgroup.com (accessed February 23, 2002).

3. Southwest Airlines website, www.southwest.com (accessed February 24, 2002).

4. Palm website, www.palm.com (accessed February 23, 2002).

5. "Eight Key Attributes of Reputation," *Fortune,* March 4, 2002, p. 75.

6. Janet Guyon, "Nokia Rocks the Competition," *Fortune,* March 4, 2002, pp. 115–118.

The Scope of Business Today

Can small companies outduel giants? Can small retailers whip Wal-Mart? Can smaller software companies beat Microsoft? Not often, says Liberate Technologies CEO Mitchell Kertzman. "You have to be not just as good as them, you have to be a lot better, and your execution has to be almost flawless." Kertzman's Liberate Technologies is an interactive TV software company that produces simple, easy-to-install, non-Windows software that existing cable TV set-top boxes could run. Its more formidable competitor is Microsoft. However, in spite of Microsoft's $10 billion investment in cable TV software, Liberate has more users than Microsoft.

Kertzman has several rules for smaller companies that want to compete against larger ones. First, do one thing very, very well. Rather than trying to compete across the board, pick one thing you do well and focus intently on it. Another rule is, innovate or die. You must constantly be on the move, developing new and better visions of your product. Palm has the majority of market share, but its failure to innovate has allowed the Pocket PC to steal some of Palm's market share. Lead strongly from the top is another key. You must have dynamic, decisive leadership. It is imperative that the entire company be working on the same plan, and coordination of effort requires strong leadership. Finally, don't try to be Microsoft. Fighting a giant by trying to be just like it or attacking with a frontal assault will seldom work.

Being a small business—or even a smaller business—can be difficult when the competition is a large, dominant force. Smaller companies must recognize that they are not simply small versions of their larger competitors. They must emphasize the advantages of being small and compete on that basis. Small companies can, indeed, coexist with large companies. Sometimes they can even beat the giants. But careful planning is a must.[1]

As you will learn in this chapter and the following chapter, there are many kinds of businesses. You need to understand the scope of business today. It is important to know some of the ways businesses differ. It is also important to understand the impact of those differences. For example, you need to recognize that there are millions more small companies than large companies. In terms of employees, however, almost half of all workers are employed by only about 16,000 firms. It is important that you know the different forms of businesses and the different ownership combinations that are possible.

After studying this chapter, you should be able to:

1. Explain the magnitude of business in our society.
2. Differentiate between a small business and a large business and describe the impact of each.
3. Understand the concept of entrepreneurship.
4. Define *franchising* and explain its advantages and disadvantages.
5. Explain the nature and impact of not-for-profit organizations.
6. Compare and contrast sole proprietorships, partnerships, limited liability companies (LLCs), and corporations.
7. Identify the various types of owners of businesses.

In this chapter, you will learn the significance of business in today's world. That significance is, to a large extent, a function of the vast number of businesses and the great variation in their sizes and scopes. We begin our discussion by noting the number and size of businesses. We follow that with the impacts of large and small businesses and of not-for-profit organizations. We then note the most important legal forms of businesses today. Finally, we discuss who actually owns businesses.

The Number and Size of Businesses

According to the U. S. Small Business Administration (SBA), there are over 25 million businesses in the United States.[2] This number includes approximately 10 million people who have business income, but not as a result of their primary occupation such as a high school teacher who paints houses during the summer for extra income or your next-door neighbor who is a part-time Mary Kay Cosmetics representative. Even the authors of this textbook fall into that category, since all three of us are full-time professors in addition to writing this book. Of the nearly 16 million businesses remaining, approximately 10 million individuals own businesses in which they are the sole employee such as a carpenter who works for a variety of homeowners, a barber or hairstylist who rents space in a salon, and a novelist who writes murder mysteries as her only occupation.

Subtracting out the part-time business owners and the sole-employee owners leaves approximately 6 million businesses with employees. Of those, over 5.8 million have fewer than 20 employees. In fact, less than 2 percent of all businesses employ more than

FIGURE 3.1

Percentages of
Businesses by Number
of Employees

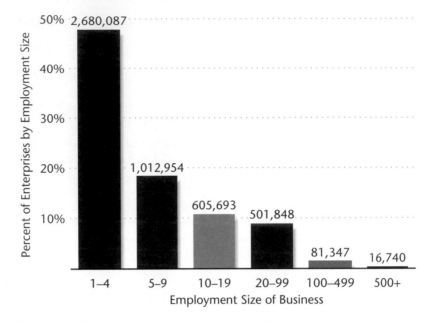

Source: U. S. Census Bureau website, www.census.gov (accessed September 9, 2002).

100 workers. Only about 16,700 businesses have more than 500 employees. Figure 3.1 presents this situation rather dramatically by showing the percentages of all businesses by number of employees.

To realize the magnitude of business today, consider the following: The 6 million firms with employees represent a total of over 90 million workers, or 35 percent of the total U.S. population. If we consider that most of these employees have families or significant others who depend on them for part of their livelihood, the impact of business is certainly substantial.

Over 98 percent of all businesses are small. The SBA defines a **small business** as any business that is independently owned and operated, is not dominant in its field, and meets size standards that vary depending on the industry. A rule of thumb is that any business with under 100 employees is considered a small business, although that number varies from industry to industry.

At the opposite end of the continuum are the large businesses. There are far fewer large businesses than small businesses. But their impact is tremendous. Further, we hear so much about large businesses that they are common knowledge to us.

Even large businesses vary greatly in size and number of employees. For example, General Motors employs over 350,000 workers throughout the world. Southwest Airlines employs 33,000 and Dell has 34,600 around the globe. Best Buy has 90,000 employees, of whom 70,000 work at Best Buy stores, and the rest work in one of its subsidiaries. Although each of these is considered a large business, the differences among them are dramatic. The following two sections discuss the relative impact of large and small businesses.

The Impact of Large Businesses

Consider a single firm—Wal-Mart. Wal-Mart is the world's largest retail business and the largest business of any kind in terms of sales. It had 2001 sales of $218 billion. It employs 1.28 million people worldwide. That number is approximately the same as the

small business
Any business that is independently owned and operated, is not dominant in its field, and meets size standards that vary depending on the industry.

Wal-Mart is the top retailer in the U.S. with over 4,000 stores in 2002. Its stores include Wal-Mart, Super Wal-Mart, Sam's and others. What accounts for its great success?

TABLE 3.1

Facts about Wal-Mart

Number of Suppliers	30,000
Value of 100 shares of Wal-Mart stock purchased in 1970	$11.5 million
Wal-Mart rank in grocery sales	1
Wal-Mart rank in jewelry sales	1
Share of U.S. toothpaste purchased at Wal-Mart	26%
Share of U.S. dog food purchased at Wal-Mart	35%
Total square miles of Wal-Mart occupied space	10.3
Terabytes of data in Wal-Mart's computers	500
Terabytes of data in IRS computers	40
Megawatt-hours of energy used by Wal-Mart	7.8 million
Megawatt-hours of energy generated by Hoover Dam	4 million
Number of daily customers at Wal-Mart worldwide	15.7 million
Number of items stocked by Wal-Mart Supercenter	100,000
Annual advertising budget	$500 million

Source: From "Lord of Things,"*Business 2.0,* March 2002. Copyright © 2002 Time, Inc. All rights reserved.

population of Salt Lake City, Utah, or New Orleans, Louisiana. In 2002, it had 4,382 stores worldwide, and opened over 400 new stores. To get an even better image of the size and impact of Wal-Mart, look at Table 3.1.

Now look at Table 3.2 carefully. Note, for example, that the 10 most valuable firms in the country have total sales of nearly $1 trillion. In addition, the 16,700 largest businesses account for 46.9 percent of the employees and 52.7 percent of the total payroll in the country. As you can see, the impact of very large businesses is tremendous if we consider only sales. Amazingly, as Table 3.3 shows, the revenues of some of the largest U.S. businesses exceed the real gross domestic product (GDP) of many countries. (The GDP is the total value of goods and services produced in a country.)

More to Come

Chapter 8

TABLE 3.2

The Top 10 Most Valuable U.S. Companies, 2001 ($ in billions)

Rank	Company	Value	Sales
1	General Electric	367.8	125.9
2	Microsoft	322.2	26.8
3	ExxonMobil	294.0	191.1
4	Wal-Mart	273.7	210.1
5	Pfizer	252.3	32.2
6	Citigroup	249.6	112.0
7	Intel	204.4	26.5
8	American International Group	185.4	55.5
9	IBM	178.2	85.8
10	SBC Communications	127.3	67.2

Source: "Fourth Quarter 2001 Corporate Scoreboard," BusinessWeek online, www.businessweek.com (accessed March 24, 2002).

TABLE 3.3

GDP of Selected Countries and Revenue of Selected U.S. Companies (U.S. $ in billions)

Country or Company	2000 GDP or 2001 Revenue	Country or Company	2000 GDP or 2001 Revenue
Belgium	259	Finland	118
Egypt	247	Israel	102
Wal-Mart	**218**	**IBM**	**86**
Switzerland	207	Ireland	82
Austria	203	**Phillip Morris**	**73**
ExxonMobil	**191**	**Verizon Communications**	**67**
Greece	181	New Zealand	67
Hong Kong	181	**Boeing**	**58**
General Motors	**177**	Bulgaria	48
Ford Motor Co.	**162**	**Dell**	**32**
Portugal	159	Uruguay	31
Denmark	136		
General Electric	**126**		

Source: *The World Fact Book, 2001,* CIA website, www.cia.gov/publications/factbook (accessed March 24, 2002); and "Industry Rankings of the S&P 500," *BusinessWeek,* Spring 2002 (special annual issue), pp. 87–125.

Adding to the impact of large businesses is the number of industries in which they compete. You may think of General Electric as a producer of appliances or light-bulbs. But it is far more than that. Look at Table 3.4. Note the differences among GE's businesses. They make airplane engines, medical equipment, many kinds of lighting, and appliances. They are also heavily into financial services of all kinds, own NBC, and are significantly into e-commerce. Johnson & Johnson makes baby oil and Tylenol, but it also makes Band-Aids, ACUVUE contact lenses, Reach tooth-

TABLE 3.4

General Electric's Businesses

Aircraft engines	Corporate, commercial, marine, and military engines.
Appliances	Refrigerators and freezers, speedcook ovens, electric and gas ranges and cooktops, microwave ovens, washers and dryers, dishwashers, disposals and compactors, room air conditioners, and water purification systems.
Financial services	All aspects of financing—auto, mortgage, aircraft, health care, leasing, shipping, equity financing, credit cards, real estate.
Insurance	Risk management and insurance for corporations, health, home, and even other insurance companies; personal investments.
Industrial systems	Electric motors, circuit breakers, transformers, switches.
Lighting	Incandescent, fluorescent, halogen, high-intensity, and outdoor bulbs and fixtures.
Medical systems	Computed tomography (CT) scanners, X-ray equipment, magnetic resonance imaging (MRI) systems, nuclear medicine cameras, ultrasound systems, patient monitoring devices, and mammography systems.
NBC	NBC Television, television stations, CNBC, many cable networks.
Plastics	Plastics used in most industries.
Power plants	
Transportation systems	Diesel locomotives, diesel engines for a variety of applications.
GE Supply	Distributor of products from 150 different manufacturers.

Source: GE website, www.ge.com (accessed September 9, 2002)

brushes, Neutrogena skin and hair products, joint replacements, glucose monitoring systems, surgical instruments, and a host of prescription drugs. H.J. Heinz Company sells Ore-Ida potatoes, StarKist tuna, Bagel Bites, Kibbles 'n Bits, and scores of other products in addition to ketchup. Rubbermaid is the familiar maker of containers, but it also makes chair mats, floor cleaning equipment, recycling bins, office furniture, playground equipment, lab coats, shipping containers, wheelbarrows, and workbenches.[3] There is an additional message here. Many large, easily recognized businesses are diversified. A **diversified business** is involved in more than one type of business activity.

Another indication of the size and influence of large businesses deals with mergers and acquisitions. A **merger** occurs whenever two companies join to form a combined company. An **acquisition** occurs whenever one company buys another company.

When one company acquires another, it does so with the idea that the acquisition will increase its overall revenue and profits. Often that is the case, and the value of the combined units is greater than the value of the two companies before the acquisition. If that happens, it is called a synergistic relationship. **Synergy** means that the sum of the two parts combined is greater than the value of the two parts separately before they were combined.

To illustrate the concept of synergy, consider Kraft. Kraft is a diversified food company. It sells products in 145 countries from 218 manufacturing plants around the world. Among its brands are Post cereals, Philadelphia cream cheese, Velveeta processed

diversified business
A business that is involved in more than one type of business activity.

merger
The joining of two companies to form a combined company.

acquisition
The purchase of one company by another company.

synergy
The sum of the two parts combined is greater than the value of the two parts separately before they were combined.

cheese, Maxwell House coffee, Ritz crackers, Oscar Mayer meats, Jell-O, Planters, Cool Whip, Nabisco snacks, and Country Time lemonade. Sixty-one of its brands have revenues of over $100 million each, and six of its brands have revenues exceeding $1 billion each. Synergy is evident because many of the brands are complementary—purchasing one product increases the odds that customers will purchase another. In addition, owning these brands gives Kraft considerable marketing power that they would not have if the brands were each owned by different companies. Having the many brands also allows them to do joint advertising, especially through coupon inserts in your Sunday newspaper. It also allows Kraft to do cross-marketing—putting advertisements for one product on the package of a different, but complementary product. Kraft also publishes recipes which, not surprisingly, call for one or more Kraft products.[4]

Sometimes, however, the acquisition does not go as planned. The acquiring company does not benefit from the acquisition as much as desired. Perhaps the acquiring firm does not know enough about the acquired firm to improve its well-being. Indeed, sometimes, the culture of the acquired company clashes with that of its new parent. The story of Snapple, in Profile 3.1, is an excellent example of an acquisition gone wrong.

The Impact of Small Businesses

The impact of large businesses comes from the sheer size of the individual businesses. Large businesses employ large numbers of people, and they contribute much to the overall economic productivity of the country. The impact of small businesses is different, but certainly no less dramatic. There are four special ways that small businesses affect society and the economy. Each deserves some attention.

The first impact of small businesses is economic and is due to the number of small businesses that exist. As we discussed earlier, over 98 percent of the businesses in this country are technically considered small. In addition, over 600,000 new businesses are started each year. Although the typical small business produces relatively few goods or services, when all small businesses are added together, the economic impact is substantial. Although our economy may be driven by giant businesses, the cumulative impact of small businesses is critical. American small business is an economic power.

The second impact of small businesses is seen in the number of people they employ. Over half of the U.S. private workforce is employed by small businesses. In fact, small businesses have created more net new jobs in recent years than large businesses have. Almost half of the nation's business payroll is now provided by small businesses.[5]

The third impact of small businesses comes from the technological innovations they contribute. Many new products are created in small businesses. One study found that 55 percent of all innovations came from small businesses. Small firms produce twice as many innovations per employee as large firms and obtain more patents per sales dollar. Following are some of the innovations that have come from small businesses.[6]

1. Airplane
2. Digital wireless communication
3. Fiber-optic examining equipment
4. Pacemakers
5. Optical scanners
6. Personal computers
7. Soft contact lens
8. Zippers

From its beginning, Snapple was a fun beverage. Founder Arnie Greenberg and some friends sold the fresh apple drink across New York City, operating from the back of his parents' pickle store in Queens. The labels on the bottles were unique, and its advertisements were quirky and offbeat, including advertising on the Howard Stern and Rush Limbaugh shows. Sales were initially concentrated in delis and small stores, but distributors finally broke into the supermarket segment, and sales ballooned from $4 million in 1983 to $674 million 10 years later. Greenberg and his partners realized that the business had grown beyond their capabilities, and they sold Snapple to Quaker Oats.

Quaker Oats was excited to buy Snapple and willingly paid the $1.7 billion for the company. It had purchased Gatorade in 1983 and had built it from $100 million in sales to $1 billion in just 10 years. But Quaker felt it needed a second beverage company to give it economies of scale. It thought it could market Snapple the same way it had Gatorade.

Quaker's acquisition of Snapple went askew almost from the beginning. Quaker alienated Snapple distributors, replaced the quirky advertising with bland advertising, and assumed that Snapple customers would be just like Gatorade customers. But Snapple's customers were accustomed to single-serving bottles of Snapple in contrast to Gatorade customers, who preferred the large bottles of Gatorade. Gatorade was more associated with sports teams, while Snapple was more of a lunchtime drink.

In three years, Snapple sales had dropped to $440 million. Quaker, which had paid $1.7 billion for Snapple, sold it in 1997 for $300 million. The acquisition had been a fiasco and was part of the reason Quaker Oats, itself, was later acquired by PepsiCo.

A private company, Triarc, bought Snapple. Triarc's culture was as free-wheeling as Quakers had been risk-averse. Triarc brought back much of the advertising that had been in existence before the acquisition by Quaker, and it repaired relationships between Snapple and its distributors. Triarc's success was so great that it was able to sell Snapple to Cadbury Schweppes in October 2000 for an estimated $1 billion—not a bad return for a $300 million investment three years earlier.

Source: John Deighton, "How Snapple Got Its Juice Back," *Harvard Business Review,* January–February 2002, pp. 47–53.

Innovation is important to a society; it is a sign of growth and progress. There are logical reasons why small businesses tend to be so innovative. They are often run with fewer restrictions and more flexibility than larger firms. Accordingly, it is generally easier to bring new ideas into focus. Also, there are fewer layers of bureaucracy to work through, so new ideas are less likely to get buried. Further, small businesses are often run by creative entrepreneurs, who feel comfortable taking risks and grasping new ideas. To a great extent, their businesses probably survive in the tough competitive environment because they operate in this manner. Creativity and innovation are part of the success formula for many smaller operations.

The fourth and final small business impact is significant. Many small businesses serve special segments, or *niches,* of the market that larger firms choose to ignore. The industry may be very fragmented or very localized, so large businesses cannot compete efficiently in the market. Many local service businesses operate in these niche markets. Some industries have more small businesses than others. In construction, for example, 98 percent of the firms have fewer than 100 employees, and 81 percent have fewer than 10. Mining, utilities, and manufacturing are somewhat less populated with small companies, but even in those industries, small businesses make up over one-third of the total.[7]

Starting Your Own Business

entrepreneurship

The act of starting, buying, or expanding a business, often with innovative products or processes.

Each year over 600,000 people start their own businesses. Why? Why are people willing to take a chance, perhaps risking their own savings, to become entrepreneurs? An entrepreneur is a person who starts, buys, or expands a business. At many colleges, you can take courses or perhaps even major in entrepreneurship. **Entrepreneurship** is starting, buying, or expanding a business, often with innovative products or processes. The tasks associated with entrepreneurship include conducting market research, planning product development, writing business plans, identifying means of financing the business, expanding the business, and even considering taking the company public or selling it to someone else at a significant premium.

So why become an entrepreneur? Some do so for the allure of potential wealth. Some do so because they have invented a product or process that has market potential. Some become entrepreneurs because they believe they can do something better than the company they work for. One individual started his own business because he felt his former bosses were unethical, and he thought he could do the same job on his own without the moral dilemmas. Some, such as Kim Farlin in Profile 3.2, want to be their own boss and not be constrained by the corporate world. For some, the allure is not wealth, but the challenge of overcoming the odds and the thrill of the action.

PROFILE 3.2   MS. FIXIT

Kim Farlin is a unique role model. As the owner of Ms. Fixit, a home remodeling and repair business with only one employee, Farlin operates a small business in a field that is almost exclusively the domain of men.

In 1973 Kim Farlin became the first woman carpenter in the United States Air Force. She was a part of an Air Force program to introduce women to trades that have traditionally been dominated by men. Farlin was trained in all aspects of building repair and maintenance and served as a carpenter until 1976.

Farlin, who developed quite a talent and love for carpentry, began working for an apartment complex in Atlanta, Georgia. While working for the apartment complex, she gained training in plumbing, electrical work, appliance repair, heating and air conditioning, and other skills. Farlin soon became a "Jill-of-all-Trades," working on remodeling, maintenance, and repair on anything and everything. Her skills were in demand not only from her employer, but from friends who would frequently call for help. They jokingly called her "Ms. Fixit" because of her knack for fixing almost anything.

Wanting more freedom and excitement, Farlin started Ms. Fixit, her aptly named carpentry business. Ms. Fixit specialized in home maintenance, repairs, and small remodeling jobs. She later moved to be closer to her parents and restarted Ms. Fixit in her new community. Working and owning a construction business as a female in a male-dominated industry has presented many challenges. "Every time I arrive on a job site the men look at me . . . I have to show them that I know what I am doing and they don't have to carry my tools for me," states Farlin.

The key contributor to Kim Farlin's success with Ms. Fixit is her dedication to quality in all aspects of the job. With the combination of quality materials and quality work, Farlin prides herself on getting the job done correctly. "If I can't feel good about a job when I'm finished, it's not a good job." Farlin realizes that she is not going to get every bid, but she feels that is a good thing because of her dedication to not cutting corners. Ms. Fixit has a client base of 60 to 70 customers, most of whom are a result of very positive referrals.

Working as a female in a male-dominated industry could present some challenges, but Kim feels that it is an asset to her business, creating an instant niche in a competitive industry. Farlin and her customers would agree that she operates in a way that sets Ms. Fixit apart from many of her competitors. Both male and female customers feel that Ms. Fixit is more honest and direct than much of the competition. Finally, many of Farlin's female customers feel more comfortable with a woman in the house doing repair work.

Ms. Fixit is an example of the millions of one-person businesses in the United States and Canada. Being a small business owner allows Farlin to give exceptional personal attention to customers and to choose those projects in which her desire for quality shows through.

Kim Farlin has long been an advocate for women's education in the trades and in business. She has taught courses in home repair and ownership at Emory University, educating men and women on the basics of home repair and maintenance. She is a member of the National Association of Women Business Owners, and she has been a speaker for the American Business Women's Association. Farlin is concerned that young people, especially women, are not paying attention to the carpentry trades. "Young girls, teens, and women are capable of much more than cooking and cleaning; it's empowering to know that women are capable of constructing a house."

Source: Personal interview, April 2002.

Small business owners report that they receive personal satisfaction from running their own businesses. Research by the National Federation of Independent Business showed that the average satisfaction level among small business owners is 8 on a 10-point scale, and 40 percent rated their satisfaction a 9 or 10. Owners report that their firms are generally successful. That success comes from offering high-quality products and services and from treating employees, customers, and business associates well. About half of the business owners want their companies to grow, while approximately the same number are happy with the size of the business as it is.[8]

There are four ways to become an entrepreneur. First, you can start your own business from scratch, as Kim Farlin did. Second, you can take over a family business.

Small businesses offer many opportunities and challenges including the chance to be one's own boss and provide personal service to customers. The challenges are different from those offered in large businesses. Would you like to own your own business some day?

Third, you can buy an existing business. Fourth, you can buy a franchise, which is a combination of buying a business and starting your own. Each method has its advantages. Starting your own business allows you to design it however you want. Taking over a family business extends the family legacy into the next generation. Buying a business offers the continuity of an existing business. Franchising, which we discuss next, offers the mix between a large business and a small business.

Should you start your own business? Do the advantages of having your own business offset the risks? Look at Table 3.5. It shows a number of characteristics of entrepreneurs. How many of them describe you?

TABLE 3.5

Characteristics of Entrepreneurs

1. They like freedom and independence.
2. They like challenges and the opportunity to see evidence of what they have accomplished.
3. They are willing to take moderate risks.
4. They are optimistic.
5. They are willing to tolerate uncertainty.

Franchising: A Hybrid of Large and Small Business

It is the day before the prom, and you are busily taking care of last-minute preparations. You stop by Gingiss Formalwear to pick up the tuxedo you rented and Budget Rent a Car to get a clean late-model car. On the way home, you grab some chicken at KFC. Then you stop at Baskin-Robbins for some ice cream. You have just had exchanges with four businesses. All have provided a product or service, and all have something else in common. They are franchises, a special type of business arrangement that is increasingly popular.

In 2000, 40 percent of all sales by U.S. businesses were from franchises.[9] Franchised sales are about $1 trillion each year. From Dairy Queen and Dunkin' Donuts to the Hair Emporium and the Medicine Shoppe, franchises dot the business landscape. Let's examine the attractions of this business arrangement in more detail.

Franchising combines the advantages of both large and small businesses. In a **franchise,** a business that owns a service or trademarked product grants the exclusive right to another (individual or business) to use the franchise name and sell its products or services within a given location. There are two important designations here. The business that sells the franchise is known as the **franchisor.** The person or business that purchases the franchise is known as the **franchisee.**

There are two different types of franchises. The first, and older, is called the *product and trade name franchise.* These companies have agreements with the franchisor to sell products under given trade names. Examples are car dealers, gasoline stations, and soft drink bottlers. This type of franchise is still the largest type of franchising in terms of sales. The second kind of franchise is the *business format franchise,* in which the franchise agreement specifies exactly how the business will be operated. Examples here include fast-food restaurants, oil change shops, business services, firms, and carpet cleaning companies.

To understand the logic of franchising, let's explore the business basis for the franchise arrangement. Why would anyone want to operate a franchise? In other words, what does the franchisee get from the franchise relationship? Three outcomes are important. First, the franchisee gains the advantage of a proven business reputation. The franchising company or product name carries an earned reputation and guarantees instant customer recognition and positive regard. Much of the initial building of customer rapport that is so critical when a new business starts has already been done. The franchisee can count on immediate customer awareness and related sales. Second, franchisors provide franchisees with managerial assistance and training in how the business should be run to assure its success. Most franchisors have regional managers who help franchisees deal with the tough day-to-day decisions that must be made. Further, franchisors often offer advertising and provide accounting and reporting systems that help the franchisee stay on top of the operation. Third, the franchisee gains the rights to an exclusive territory. If you have the Red Lobster franchise for your city, the company assures you that no competing Red Lobster will enter your territory without your having the right to purchase the franchise.

franchise
A business that grants the exclusive right to another individual or business to use its name and sell its products or services.

franchisor
The business that sells the franchise.

franchisee
The person or business that purchases a franchise.

Dippin' Dots franchises sell tiny beads of ice cream in many flavors and colors. A Dippin' Dots franchise currently costs $12,500 plus other costs. You can go to www.dippindots.com for information on how to become a franchisee.

Although this picture looks quite favorable, there is a downside. The franchisee does incur some costs. A franchise fee is paid to the franchisor simply for the right to operate the business. The franchise fee may range from less than $10,000 to more than $50,000. A royalty, often 5 to 8 percent of gross sales, is paid to the franchisor on a continuous basis. Then there's the advertising fee. The franchisor typically handles the advertising for the entire chain. Each franchisee contributes an average of 2 percent of sales to underwrite those costs. The last fee is the investment in the actual building and equipment. This amount varies depending on the nature of the business. Even though the franchise fee itself is usually less than $50,000, the total investment in the franchise may easily exceed $500,000 and may reach $1 million for companies like McDonald's.

Beyond these direct monetary factors, there is another concern for the franchisee. The franchisee sacrifices some owner discretion as a result of the franchise relationship. The franchisor designates the products that will be carried, how items will be arranged or prepared, and how promotions will be run. Much of the independent discretion that some business operators enjoy is lost. This structure and control make sense from the franchisor's perspective. Burger King, for instance, wants to assure customers that they can expect the same quality and similar experiences whether dining at a store in Maine or Montana. Without that consistency, the franchise image loses its appeal. But this control by the franchisor also means an individual franchisee cannot add a special sauce or modify the way the fries are prepared even if local customers would love it. For some businesspeople, this sacrifice of individual discretion is troubling. It is important to understand both the advantages and disadvantages of the franchising arrangement before choosing this business option.

Franchising is experiencing continued growth both domestically and throughout the rest of the world. But keep in mind that it is only one of many kinds of business arrangements. An important issue when considering careers is which kind of business situation appeals to you.

Not-for-Profit Organizations

> **not-for-profit organization**
> An organization that provides benefits to a set of constituents.

In Chapter 1, we said the driving force of a business is to make a profit for its owners. Some organizations, however, do not exist to make a profit, so they cannot, technically, be considered businesses. If an organization does not seek to make profits, what does it do and why does it exist? A **not-for-profit organization,** or *nonprofit organization,* exists to provide value to some set of constituents. Generally, nonprofits provide a set of services. We encounter nonprofit organizations daily. Public schools, most colleges and universities, government agencies, social and human service organizations, some hospitals, religious organizations, and community theater and symphony groups are all nonprofit organizations.

Even though they are not driven by profits, nonprofit organizations are extremely concerned with resources and money. They must rent or buy facilities; pay utilities; hire people; pay salaries; carry out valued programs, activities, or events; and pay a range of expenses in the process. Accordingly, they must find ways to generate enough revenue to allow them to cover expenses while meeting the needs of their constituents. Nonprofits generate revenues in a variety of ways. In some cases, constituents pay directly for part of the services they receive. You do this when you pay to skate at your community's park district skating rink or when you pay tuition to take classes at your college or university. In some cases, constituents pay indirectly for the services they receive. Such is the case with public schools; taxpayers contribute funds that are used to support the schools' educational programs. Some nonprofits, such as the United Way and religious

Habitat for Humanity college chapters exist all over the country. Like these Bradley University and Purdue University students, many chapter members will spend their spring breaks and weekends during school building houses for low-income families. The student members gain building skills while working for a good cause. Does volunteering for a not-for-profit organization such as Habitat for Humanity appeal to you?

organizations, rely mainly on contributions and donations. Other nonprofits rely on membership fees or ticket sales for at least part of their revenues, as is probably the case with your community symphony orchestra. In most cases, not-for-profit organizations rely on more than one type of revenue-generating activity. As you can see, money, cash flow, and careful financial management are critical to the very existence of nonprofits. In fact, most nonprofits of any size have full-time employees whose job is to figure out how to raise and distribute money for the organization.

Nonprofits have unique features that distinguish them from businesses. Their approach to getting funds is one. Another is their reliance on volunteers. Typically, a not-for-profit organization has a number of unpaid workers who contribute their time and talents to the organization. Many nonprofits could not operate without these volunteers. This dependence on volunteers can make management of the nonprofit difficult. Finally, unlike businesses, nonprofits are exempt from paying income taxes.

Just as a business must understand its customers, a not-for-profit must seek to understand its constituents and their needs. One complication of operating a nonprofit is that there are usually many constituents, often with conflicting needs. Let's consider a nonprofit most of you know, public schools. They operate to provide a solid educational foundation for the young people within a community. To accomplish this goal, they receive funds from the government. Most taxpayers contribute to the school system. Who are the relevant constituents? The students, of course. But what about the parents, the taxpayers, the community, even society in general? If funds are to continue to flow to the school system, the needs of all these constituents must be balanced somehow.

This section has provided a brief introduction to not-for-profit organizations. We will refer to nonprofits and use them periodically throughout the book as examples. It is important that we do so, because nonprofits employ millions of people. Some of you reading this text will work for nonprofit organizations. Many of you will do volunteer work, and some of you will even provide leadership and managerial insights. Your business knowledge and background will be quite relevant.

Forms of Business Ownership

Every business is owned by someone and exists in one of a very few forms. There are four major forms of ownership and a few more specialized forms, which are beyond the scope of this book. The four major forms are the sole proprietorship, the partnership, the corporation, and the limited liability company.

Sole Proprietorships

sole proprietorship
A business that is owned by one person.

A **sole proprietorship** is a business that is owned by a single person. This is the most common form of business ownership. In the United States, nearly 70 percent of all businesses are sole proprietorships. One person owns the business and all the assets of the business. We encounter sole proprietorships daily. When the plumbing stops working in your house, you turn to the Yellow Pages and call Sam's Plumbing Service. Sam arrives later in the day. His truck is brightly painted with a giant plunger on the side. Sam enters your house with a rack full of special plumbing tools and equipment. Within an hour he has the problem remedied and you have his bill. As a sole proprietor, Sam owns his truck, tools, and equipment. His goal is to earn enough to cover the cost of these and other expenses and still make a profit.

Sole proprietorships do not have to be run by one person working alone. Instead of Sam's Plumbing, you might have called Royal Plumbing. Royal Plumbing is also a sole proprietorship, owned by Mike Royal. Mike has been in business for 15 years and has a much larger customer base than Sam's Plumbing. He provides 24-hour emergency service and has a staff of 20 plumbers. He has commercial contracts with a number of organizations in the community. He has a manager in charge of residential plumbing and a manager for commercial accounts. As long as Mike is the sole owner, the business is still a sole proprietorship even though he employs 20 people and generates considerable revenue.

Let's look more closely at this form of ownership. Why is it so prevalent, and what are the advantages and risks to this approach? The advantages help explain why this form is so popular. First, a sole proprietorship is easy to start. It requires little effort beyond getting locally required licensing and permits and reporting profits or losses on the owner's IRS 1040 form. Second, and quite significant, the owner receives all the profits of the business and does not have to share them with anyone else. The third advantage is a bit more involved. We call it *owner discretion.* Owners of sole proprietorships have complete control and discretion to do what they want. If Sam wants to take off on Mondays, he

THINK ABOUT THIS

1. Think about your first job after you graduate from college. Would you rather work in a large business? a small business? a not-for-profit organization? What advantages do you see to your choice?

2. How can a small business compete with a large business in the same industry?

3. Look at the characteristics of entrepreneurs in Table 3.5. Would you make a good entrepreneur?

4. Select a not-for-profit organization. Who are its constituents? Who are the benefactors? Why may they be different?

Advantages	Disadvantages
• It is easy to form	• Owner is liable for debts
• Owner has discretion	• Funds are limited
• Owner controls profits	• Business ceases when owner dies

TABLE 3.6

Advantages and Disadvantages of a Sole Proprietorship

can. He calls the shots and makes the decisions. Many people like the freedom and independence this discretion brings.

However, there are some risks and limitations involved with sole proprietorships. First, the owner is liable for the debts of the business. If the firm closes while it owes money or if it is sued, creditors can file a claim against the owner's personal assets. That means they can go after Sam's truck, his home, and even his personal savings. This, clearly, is the major risk to the sole proprietor.

Second, sole proprietorships are limited in the sources they can turn to for funds needed to run or expand the business. The owner has personal savings, perhaps gifts or loans from family and friends, and loans from lending institutions. That is a fairly limited source of funds. If the business is new and very small, lenders (banks) may be quite reluctant to extend much credit. Often the business is constrained by such a shortage of funds.

The final disadvantage is the lack of business continuity. When the owner dies, the business ceases to exist. These advantages and risks are highlighted in Table 3.6.

Partnerships

A **partnership** is a business that is owned by two or more individuals. Although less prevalent than sole proprietorships, partnerships do constitute about 10 percent of the businesses in the United States. The most common form of partnership occurs when family members or friends decide they want to pool their resources and start a business. The partnership may be formed because the partners have unique talents to offer, because the business venture needs more financing than one person can put together, or simply because two or more people want to work together. The financial motive is illustrated by the following example.

You're sitting in your dorm room one night when Dana, your neighbor across the hall, runs into your room full of excitement. Dana has a friend who can get a shipment of 100 sweatshirts at a rock-bottom price. Dana wants to emblazon the sweatshirts with a catchy slogan promoting the upcoming homecoming dance and sell them on campus. She says the cost of purchasing the sweatshirts and having them imprinted will be about $800. The sweatshirts can be sold for $25 each or $2,500 total. Accordingly, there is a $1,700 profit to be made for very little work. The problem, of course, is coming up with the initial $800. Dana knows that students have little extra money but wants to offer you a deal. She will invest $300 and is seeking five friends—including you—to invest $100 each. Each person will own part of the business and, of course, share in the windfall profits that are sure to come. Here, Dana is proposing a partnership with six partners.

Although there are a number of distinctions that can be made regarding partnerships, there are basically two ways a partnership may function. First, each partner may play a role in the day-to-day operations of the business. Such partners are known as **working partners.** Second, some partners may work in the business while others do not. Partners who are not involved in the day-to-day operations of the business are known as **silent partners.** Typically, the silent partner contributes money to the business but does not want to get involved in its ongoing operations. In fact, that is exactly Dana's plan.

partnership
A business that is owned by two or more individuals.

working partners
Business partners who play a role in day-to-day operations.

silent partners
Business partners who typically contribute money instead of being involved in day-to-day operations.

TABLE 3.7

Advantages and Disadvantages of a Partnership

Advantages	Disadvantages
• It is easy to form	• Partners have financial liability
• Partners have claim to profits	• Partner's actions commit other partners
• Additional talents help in running the business	• Partnership dissolves upon death of one partner
• More sources of financing are available	• Interpersonal conflicts between partners may arise

partnership agreement

A document that prescribes the responsibilities and privileges of each business partner.

She will do all the purchasing, printing, advertising, and selling of the sweatshirts. You need only contribute money and do nothing more. Dana is a working partner; you and the four other investors are silent partners.

It is very important for the partners to establish a partnership agreement at the inception of the business. The **partnership agreement** is a document that prescribes the responsibilities and privileges of each partner. The agreement can be quite complex, but it should specify at least three things. First, the agreement should state the percentage of ownership of each partner. Second, it should state how the profits (and losses) will be divided. Often, profits are distributed on the basis of percentage of ownership. However, this method of distribution of profits need not be the case. For example, Dana has contributed 37.5 percent of the funds for the sweatshirt business and thus has a 37.5 percent ownership share. However, because she is the working partner, she expects to get half of the profits, with the remaining 50 percent shared equally among the five silent partners. Such an arrangement may well be fair, but it should not be assumed. These expectations should be spelled out in the partnership agreement. Third, the agreement should state how the partnership can be dissolved. It should specify how partners can *buy out* other partners. More will be said about this provision shortly. The advantages and drawbacks to the partnership form of business are noted in Table 3.7. A major advantage is that it is relatively easy to form a partnership. A second advantage is the partners' claim to profits. As with a sole proprietorship, the partners claim all the firm's profits and report them on their respective IRS 1040s in proportion to their ownership share. A third advantage is the range of backgrounds and skills the working partners bring to running the business. The fourth and probably most significant advantage of the partnership comes from the additional financing it makes available. Each partner can contribute capital to the business, and the presence of additional owners usually increases the business's capacity to borrow funds if needed.

Among the drawbacks to this form of ownership is financial liability. As with the sole proprietorship, creditors can file claims against the owners' personal assets. In fact, each partner is personally liable for the business's debts. A second disadvantage is that any partner can legally commit the entire business without the other partners' consent. Third, if any partner dies, the partnership arrangement is dissolved.

The fourth and final disadvantage is that interpersonal conflicts may arise between partners. A business between friends or family members that sounds great in the beginning may become quite contentious and strained as it struggles through the daily stresses of business life. These situations can get so difficult that work ceases to be enjoyable. Thus it is important to have buyout provisions written into the partnership agreement. Generally, if extensive conflict arises in the relationship, the partners need a way to dissolve their association and still keep the business intact.

Advantages	Disadvantages
• Indefinite life	• Double taxation
• Limited liability	• Laws and regulations
• Ease of raising capital	

TABLE 3.8

Advantages and Disadvantages of a Corporation

Corporations

A **corporation** is a separate business entity owned by stockholders. Corporations make up almost 20 percent of all businesses. A corporation differs in a number of ways from both a sole proprietorship and a partnership. There are a number of advantages to forming a corporation. First, the corporation has an indefinite life. If one of the stockholders dies, the business continues. Second, and perhaps most important, there is **limited liability,** meaning owners are liable for the firm's debts only to the extent of their investment in the business. Therefore, their personal assets are protected. A third advantage is the relative ease of obtaining additional capital. If more money is needed to run the business, shares of stock can be sold to new investors. This option is better than having individuals buy the company's assets, as in the case of sole proprietorships and partnerships.

There are also some disadvantages to the corporate form of ownership. The first deals with taxes. The earnings of the business itself are taxed. Then if those earnings—in the form of dividends—are paid to the stockholders, they are taxed again as the stockholders' income. This situation is commonly referred to as double taxation. A second disadvantage is that the corporation is subject to more laws and regulations than either the sole proprietorship or the partnership. The advantages and disadvantages of the corporate form are shown in Table 3.8.

Virtually all large companies are corporations. As such, they can be publicly held if desired, so they can have thousands of stockholders. The ability to issue stock is important for growth. Consider the case of Southwest Airlines. When Southwest was formed, Herb Kelleher decided on the corporate form of ownership because he knew he would have to raise a lot of money to buy and maintain costly aircraft. Southwest Airlines now has over 760 million shares of stock outstanding.[10]

In many cases, the advantages of the corporation make it a desirable form of ownership. These advantages are particularly true for those who choose the *subchapter S (sub S) corporation,* a variation on the corporate form of ownership allowed by the IRS, which can be taxed as a partnership. The sub S corporation has the protection offered to a corporation without the double taxation, making it a very desirable form of ownership. The sub S corporation is an excellent choice for small- to medium-sized businesses because it allows up to 75 stockholders without the double taxation.

Limited Liability Company

A **limited liability company (LLC)** is a relatively new form of ownership that combines the advantages of partnerships with the advantages of corporations without the limitations imposed by the subchapter S designation. Many advantages are making the LLC an increasingly popular form of ownership. First, there are tax advantages. Since the limited liability company is a company, not a corporation, it is taxed as a partnership. Second, it receives the liability protection accorded corporations. The third advantage is the number and types of owners it can have. For example, a sub S corporation

corporation
A separate business entity owned by stockholders.

limited liability
Liability of a corporation's owners for the firm's debts only to the extent of their investment in the business.

SOUTHWEST

limited liability company (LLC)
A form of ownership that combines the advantages of partnerships and corporations without the limitations imposed by subchapter S.

TABLE 3.9

Advantages and Disadvantages of a Limited Liability Company

Advantages	Disadvantage
• Taxed as partnership • Enjoys liability protection • May have unlimited numbers and types of owners	• Laws and regulations

can have only 75 stockholders, but an LLC can have unlimited numbers of "members." Further, in the sub S corporation, the stockholders must be individuals, but the members of an LLC can be other companies or corporations. This provision is important because it gives the company much more flexibility. Having an unlimited number of owners makes raising capital easier.

The tax provisions are a key to LLCs for both small and large companies, because a limited liability company's profits or losses can be reported on the owners' tax forms. The LLC itself does not pay income taxes. If the owners are individuals, then the impact is shown on their personal taxes just as it would be in a partnership. If the owners are other companies, then the LLC's earnings or losses are reflected on their company tax forms. This allowance is particularly important when the LLC may initially have significant losses.

There is only one major disadvantage of limited liability companies: the laws and regulations that must be followed in qualifying for and forming the LLC. The same type of registration is required for LLCs as for corporations. The limited liability company has now been approved by almost all states. Its advantages and the disadvantage are shown in Table 3.9. Because of its advantages, LLCs may eventually replace both partnerships and sub S corporations.

Who Owns Businesses?

stockholder
Any person who owns at least one share of stock in a corporation.

The preceding section discussed different types or forms of business ownership. In this section, we discuss who actually *owns* businesses. There are at least five primary possibilities regarding the ownership of a business: single owners, partners, stockholders, employees, and other businesses. Keep in mind that our interest here is not on the forms of ownership but on *who* the owners are.

We mentioned earlier that one individual owns a sole proprietorship. Two or more individuals may own a partnership. However, the issue of who owns businesses becomes more complex when we consider corporations. To understand this issue better, let's look more closely at the concept of stockholders. A **stockholder** is any person who owns at least one share in a corporation. Corporations can have any number of stockholders, from one to perhaps millions.

In some cases, a single person may own all the stock of a company even if the business is relatively large. In other cases, a small number of stockholders may own all shares of the corporation and not wish to sell shares to anyone else,

THINK ABOUT THIS

1. How would your decision regarding the form of ownership differ if you were starting a T-shirt business as opposed to a restaurant? Would liability be an issue?

2. Why are there fewer partnerships than corporations and sole proprietorships?

3. Some problems of sole proprietorships relate to the fact that there is only one owner. Some people argue that this can lead to a shortage of management talent. What types of problems might occur if there is a shortage of management talent?

as is often the case in midsize businesses. For example, three or four family members may own all the stock and have no intention of extending stock ownership outside the family, or a handful of investors own a business and are quite comfortable with the arrangement. When there are only a few stockholders and the stock is not open for sale to the public, the company is known as a **privately held corporation.**

By contrast, in many corporations, stock is open for sale to the public. Such businesses are known as **publicly held corporations.** Dell, Best Buy, and Southwest Airlines are examples. Publicly held companies may have millions of stockholders. Each stockholder buys one or more shares in the company.

In recent years, a number of companies have moved toward employee ownership. Companies may become owned by their employees through an **employee stock ownership plan,** commonly known as an **ESOP.** An ESOP is an arrangement in which employees buy ownership in the company. For some companies, an ESOP takes the place of a pension plan or retirement plan. Instead of putting their money into a retirement account, the workers invest in their own company. This arrangement can be a powerful motivating device, since the employees know that their own performance can affect their future benefits. When employees retire, they can sell their shares either on the stock market if the company is publicly held or back to the company if it is privately held.

A final category of ownership occurs when one business owns another business. Best Buy, for example, owns Musicland, Sam Goody, Suncoast, Media Play, On Cue, Magnolia Hi-Fi, and the Canadian subsidiary Future Shop. Each of these store chains is a subsidiary of Best Buy, and Best Buy is the parent company. A **subsidiary** is any business that is wholly or partially owned by a parent company. Conversely, a **parent company** is any company that owns one or more subsidiaries. The parent company provides capital to the subsidiaries just as stockholders would if the subsidiary were publicly held. The parent company may allow the subsidiary to function relatively independently, or the parent's managers may control the subsidiary very closely.

In some cases a business may be owned by two or more companies. This arrangement is called a **joint venture.** Here, the subsidiary is a separate company, but it is owned simultaneously by two or more parent companies. This arrangement often occurs in international situations where a company is owned partially by, say, a U.S. company and partially by a Japanese company. An example is Caterpillar-Mitsubishi in Japan, which is owned half by Caterpillar of the United States and half by Mitsubishi Heavy Industries of Japan. A more dramatic example is the joint venture formed to drill for oil on the North Slope of Alaska. Although the venture included big-name companies such as BP, ARCO, Exxon, Mobil, Amerada Hess, Phillips, and Unocal, none of the companies could underwrite the venture by itself. But by coming together in a joint venture, they were able to develop the potential of this great oil field.

In summary, a company may be owned by a single person, by two or more partners, by any number of stockholders, by employees, or by another company. Although the general public seldom knows who the actual owner of a business is, it is important for you to see these ownership distinctions. Ownership affects business control and ultimate decision making. Table 3.10 illustrates the variety of ownership possibilities.

---

privately held corporation
A business that has a few stockholders and the stock is not open for public sale.

publicly held corporation
A business with stock that is open for public sale.

employee stock ownership plan (ESOP)
An arrangement in which employees buy ownership in the company.

subsidiary
Any business that is wholly or partially owned by a parent company.

THINK ABOUT THIS

1. What is the significance of *who* owns a business compared with the *forms* of business ownership?

2. How would business decisions differ for a corporation owned by one major stockholder compared with one owned by thousands of stockholders?

3. What do you think are some of the benefits of an employee stock ownership plan?

TABLE 3.10

Business Ownership
Possibilities

Form of Business	Ownership
Sole proprietorship	One owner.
Partnership	Two or more individuals, but generally a small number.
Corporation	One or more stockholders in a privately held corporation; often millions of stockholders in a publicly held corporation.
	Other businesses.
	Combinations of individuals and other companies.
Sub S corporation	No more than 75 individuals.
Limited liability company	One or more individuals or other companies.
Joint venture	Two or more other companies.
Not-for-profit organization	No owners.

parent company
Any company that owns one or more subsidiaries.

joint venture
A business owned by two or more companies.

THE BIG PICTURE

Look again at the topics in the chapter, but do it this time from a personal viewpoint. What kind of career do you want to have? Do you want to work in a large corporation in which you will likely be trained very well to become a specialist in an important section of the company? Or do you want to be a larger fish in a smaller pond by working in a small business? In that case, you will be much more of a generalist, often doing many different jobs. You will have the challenge of making everything fit together. Taking that idea a step further, would you want to own your own business so that you could be totally in charge of and responsible for the entire company?

Think also for a moment about the section on who owns businesses. What is the real difference between a business owned by a single person and one owned by two or three partners, or by a million stockholders, or by another company? How are the challenges different? On the one end, a business owned by a single person may be somewhat in peril if the owner is overwhelmed or by chance becomes incapacitated. On the other end, a business owned by another company may be at peril because the parent company serves as the bank, and the managers of the parent may not see the subsidiary in the same light that the subsidiary's managers do. Partnerships pose the possibility of conflict among partners, while publicly held firms are somewhat at the mercy of the stock market. Thus, all the ownership relationships exhibit some kind of risk, but that risk is different for each one.

Summary

1. One way to appreciate the scope of business in American society is to look at the statistics about business.

   • What is the magnitude of business in our society?

   There are over 25 million businesses in the United States. This number includes approximately 10 million people who report business income even though the business is not their primary occupation. It also includes 10 million businesses in which the owner is the sole employee. Of the remaining 6 million businesses, over 5 million have fewer than 20 employees.

2. A striking feature of the American economy is the coexistence of very large and very small businesses.

   • What is the difference between large and small businesses?

   The U.S. Small Business Administration defines a small business as any business that is independently owned and operated, is not dominant in its field, and meets size standards that vary depending on the industry.

   • What are the impacts of large and small businesses?

   The impact of large businesses comes from their size. They employ many people and contribute greatly to the economic productivity of the country. In some communities, a single dominant large business may affect the quality of life.

   Small businesses affect the economy in four ways: (1) When all small businesses are taken together, they account for a large share of the American economy. (2) Over half the American workforce is employed by small business. (3) Many new products are created in small businesses. (4) Small businesses serve special market niches that larger firms ignore.

3. Over 600,000 new businesses are started each year by entrepreneurs.

   • What is entrepreneurship?

   Entrepreneurship is starting, buying, or expanding a business. An entrepreneur is a person who starts, buys, or expands the business. Entrepreneurs may launch a business because of the allure of wealth, the desire for independence, the feeling that they can do something better than anyone else, or the challenge of running one's own business. Entrepreneurs tend to be independent, willing to take moderate risks, optimistic, and willing to accept uncertainty.

4 A popular method of combining the advantages of large businesses and small businesses is franchising. In the past 40 years, franchising has created a host of familiar names, such as McDonald's, Pizza Hut, and Budget Rent a Car.

   • How would you define *franchising?*

   A franchise exists when a business that owns a service or trademarked product grants the exclusive rights to another business or individual to use the franchise name and sell its products and services within a given location.

   • What are the advantages and disadvantages of franchising?

   Advantages are that the franchisee gains (1) the advantage of a proven business reputation, (2) managerial assistance, and (3) the rights to an exclusive territory. Disadvantages are (1) the payment of a franchise fee and other costs and (2) the sacrifice of some owner discretion.

5. A vast number of organizations exist to meet the needs of individuals who are not adequately served by business or government. These organizations are called nonprofit or not-for-profit organizations.

   • What is a not-for-profit organization?

   Some organizations do not operate to make a profit, so they are not technically considered businesses. These not-for-profit organizations exist to provide services to some set of constituents. Even though they are not driven by profits, they are extremely concerned with attracting money to make their operations possible.

Nonprofits have three unique features that distinguish them from businesses: (1) their approach to fund-raising, (2) their use of unpaid volunteer workers, and (3) the fact that they are exempt from paying income taxes.

• What is the impact of not-for-profit organizations?

We encounter nonprofits daily. Most schools, social and human service agencies, religious organizations, and artistic agencies operate on a nonprofit basis, as do some health care organizations. Thus, nonprofits make a valuable contribution to the quality of life of a community.

6. Although all businesses have owners, the legal form in which ownership is held can vary.

• What are the basic forms of business ownership?

The four major forms of ownership are the sole proprietorship, the partnership, the corporation, and the relatively new form of ownership—the limited liability company.

7. The study of business ownership may involve more than examining the legal forms of ownership. When a corporation is involved, the issue of ownership becomes more complex.

• Who owns the business?

There are five basic possibilities: (1) A company can be owned by a single person. (2) A partnership is owned by two or more individuals. (3) A corporation is owned by stockholders, who may number from one to millions. A privately held corporation has a small number of stockholders, and the stock is not open for sale to the public. A publicly held corporation has a large number of stockholders, and the stock is open for sale to the public. (4) In an employee-owned corporation, the majority of the stock is owned by employees. These are usually called employee stock ownership plans (ESOPs). (5) A business may be owned by another business.

Key Terms

acquisition, p. 47

corporation, p. 59

diversified business, p. 47

employee stock ownership plan (ESOP), p. 61

entrepreneurship, p. 50

franchise, p. 53

franchisee, p. 53

franchisor, p. 53

joint venture, p. 62

limited liability, p. 59

limited liability company (LLC), p. 59

merger, p. 47

not-for-profit organization, p. 54

parent company, p. 62

partnership, p. 57

partnership agreement, p. 58

privately held corporation, p. 61

publicly held corporation, p. 61

silent partners, p. 57

small business, p. 44

sole proprietorship, p. 56

stockholder, p. 60

subsidiary, p. 61

synergy, p. 47

working partners, p. 57

Exercises and Applications

1. Consider the following resolutions for debate. Choose the resolution you support, and prepare your arguments for debate.

• Large businesses are more important to society than small businesses.

• Small businesses are more important to society than large businesses.

2. Suppose you are one of three owners of a partnership. What factors might persuade you to change the form of the business to a corporation?

3. Interview the owner of a small business in your community. What challenges does that person face? How are these similar to or different from those a manager in a large business experiences?

4. Think about your career options. Would you prefer to work for a large or a small business? Explain why.

5. Search the Internet for one of the following companies. Determine what its subsidiaries are.

   • General Motors

   • General Electric

   • PepsiCo

   • RJR Nabisco

   • Ford

In Hot Pursuit of the Wi-Fi Wave

FROM THE PAGES OF

BusinessWeek

Sky Dayton is a classic entrepreneur. Shortly after graduating from high school in 1988, he opened two successful businesses, Café Mocha (an L.A. coffee shop) and a graphic-design firm. But that was just the beginning. In 1994 when he was only 23 years old, he started EarthLink Inc. Today EarthLink is the third largest Internet service provider, and Dayton is regarded as a true pioneer of the Web.

Now Dayton has launched a new endeavor, Boingo Wireless Inc. Boingo is built on the principle of wireless fidelity, or Wi-Fi, which allows users to "tap into the Web from anywhere to retrieve e-mail and surf the Web at lightning speed." He's making deals with Wi-Fi operators in hotels, airports, and other hot spots to create a nationwide net. In order for his business to succeed, Dayton has to win over a range of partners such as big phone companies and Internet service providers which can "bundle Wi-Fi with cell-phone or net-access plans."

Dayton's record of accomplishments at EarthLink has helped him get meetings with just about any potential partner he chooses, but that does not guarantee success in what is a highly competitive market. So far, he's had some good fortune, such as his deal with Sprint Corp. that's brought Boingo $15 million in start-up capital.

Like most entrepreneurs, Dayton has a certain flair and risk-taking nature. He's been described as being both laid-back and intense. The intensity applies to just about every competitive activity he undertakes. For example, he's a fearless surfer and a former skateboard racer. Also, like a lot of entrepreneurs, he's experienced and learned from failure. One of his ventures is a business startup incubator named eCompanies. Although it's been around since 1999, the business has failed to launch any real successes, and even Dayton admits that eCompanies "threw money at half-baked ideas." Poignantly and reflectively, the 31-year-old Dayton says, "What I learned is just because you have a great idea, that doesn't mean the world's ready for it." He hopes the timing is right and the world's ready for Boingo!

Decision Questions

1. Some people argue that the leader talents needed to start a small business are different from the talents needed to run a successful firm once it has grown and become a national competitor. What differences do you see in these two situations?

2. In this chapter, we talked about synergy and how business combinations can bring synergy. Explain how Dayton's attempts at partnering for Boingo Wireless can create synergy.

3. Many people argue that Boingo has a big advantage over its competitors because Sky Dayton "lends credibility to Wi-Fi." What do you think? Would you invest in Boingo?

Source: Arlene Weintraub, "In Hot Pursuit of the Wi-Fi Wave," *BusinessWeek,* April 29, 2002, p. 106.

References

1. Erick Schonfeld and Ian Mount, "Beating Bill," *Business 2.0,* June 2002, pp. 36–46.

2. The data in this section are from the U.S. Small Business Administration, www.sba.gov, and the U.S. Census Bureau, www.census.gov (accessed March 10, 2002). Because the Census Bureau and the SBA have different methods of collecting data, the numbers do not always coincide. The important issue is to note the approximate numbers and relative magnitude of small businesses in today's economy.

3. Company websites: www.ge.com, www.johnsonandjohnson.com, and www.rubbermaid.com (accessed September 9, 2002).

4. Kraft website, www.kraft.com (accessed October 25, 2002).

5. "Small Business Frequently Asked Questions," U.S. Small Business Administration website, www.sba.gov (accessed March 24, 2002).

6. "Contribution of Small High-Tech Firms to the New Economy," SBA memorandum, October 20, 2000.

7. U. S. Census Bureau website, www.census.gov (accessed March 26, 2002).

8. *Success, Satisfaction, and Growth,* NFIB National Small Business Poll 1, no. 6, 2001, p. 1.

9. www.franchisesolutions.com (accessed March 26, 2002).

10. Southwest Airlines 10-K Report, December 31, 2001, www.southwest.com (accessed March 26, 2002).

4

How Businesses Fit Together

Few companies compete in as many different ways as Walt Disney Co. while staying in a single broad industry—entertainment. Disney sells a wide variety of merchandise, which it either produces or licenses. It produces movies and television shows. It also distributes those movies and TV shows through its networks and movie distribution companies. Its theme parks provide entertainment to millions of eager customers. It also sells services through its training units.

Disney is in the entertainment industry. Yet that industry is broad. It includes manufacturing of products, distribution of those products, and service businesses such as theme parks. Thus, it competes in a number of different industry sectors.

Consider a sample of Disney's holdings. In the film production area, you are well aware of Disney Studios. But did you know that Disney also owns Buena Vista studios and Touchstone Pictures? In fact, Touchstone was started so that the company could produce films with PG-13 and R ratings without damaging the family orientation of Disney Pictures. In theme parks, Disney owns Disneyland and Walt Disney World—as well as Tokyo Disney and Disneyland Paris. You may not be aware that Disney is heavily into publishing. These ventures include the magazines *Discover* and *Family Fun* and the publications of Disney Press. It owns Capital Cities/ABC, which includes ABC, ESPN, A&E, and a number of TV stations. And—oh, yes—it owns the rights to Mickey Mouse.

It is important for you to understand how businesses like Disney fit together in industries. It is part of the integrative nature of business to be aware of the links among companies within an industry as well as the links among industries. This chapter will help you understand both the similarities and differences among manufacturing firms, wholesale and retail firms, and service businesses.

After studying this chapter, you should be able to:

1. Identify major industry sectors.
2. Explain the characteristics of the manufacturing sector.
3. Describe the important characteristics of the distribution sector.
4. Identify the major characteristics of the service sector.
5. Discuss the relationships among companies in an industry.

This chapter continues the discussion of the nature of business. The previous chapter looked at how businesses vary with regard to size and ownership. This chapter examines how businesses fit within their industries and how those industries work. We are especially interested in important business concepts that are relevant for an entire industry sector. We turn our major attention to three sectors of business: manufacturing, distribution, and service.

Before we begin these discussions, however, it is important to note how industries are classified. Thus, we begin this chapter with a discussion of the North American Industrial Classification System (NAICS). You will see the logic of a classification system that helps organize information about industries and businesses.

How Industries Are Classified

An industry classification system is important because it allows for the collection, storage, retrieval, and analysis of millions of pieces of data about business. A system should be readily accessible so that anyone who wants information about businesses or industries can find it. This information can be used for a vast number of purposes. For example, if you want to know the number of computer manufacturers in the United States, you can look into data sources using the classification system.

The North American Industrial Classification System (NAICS) is designed to catalog businesses in the United States, Canada, and Mexico,[1] thereby giving uniformity to the three countries of the North American Free Trade Agreement (NAFTA). NAICS consists of 20 broad categories of industries, shown in Table 4.1. These categories are then broken into more refined classifications until fairly specific industry groups are determined. Each specific industry group has a unique six-digit NAICS number.

Here's an example of how the NAICS classification system works. Suppose you work at Dell and want to study the printer market. You want to know as much as you can about the printer industry and the companies in it. You consult the Census Bureau website, www.census.gov/naics. By scrolling down the list of manufacturing codes, you find that computers fall into the manufacturing sector (NAICS 334). But you need to know more than that. Checking further, you find that printers are in the industry category of computer and peripheral equipment manufacturing (NAICS 334119). Once you know this information, you can find a substantial amount of information. For example, Dun & Bradstreet, a well-known publisher of industry data, publishes an annual volume called *Industry Norms and Key Business Ratios.*[2] In it, you can find how many companies make printers, average financial data for the industry, and even accounting ratios

More to Come
CHAPTER 10

TABLE 4.1

NAICS Categories

Code	Industry Sector
11	Agriculture, forestry, fishing, and hunting
21	Mining
22	Utilities
23	Construction
31–33	Manufacturing
42	Wholesale trade
44–45	Retail trade
48–49	Transportation and warehousing
51	Information
52	Finance and insurance
53	Real estate and rental and leasing
54	Professional, scientific, and technical services
55	Management of companies and enterprises
56	Administrative and support, waste management
61	Education services
62	Health care and social assistance
71	Arts, entertainment, and recreation
72	Accommodation and food service
81	Other services (except public administration)
92	Public administration

Source: U.S. Census Bureau website, www.census.gov/epcd/www/naicsusr.html (accessed May 22, 2002).

industry sectors
Major groupings of industries with similar characteristics.

manufacturing sector
The broad group of companies and industries that produce tangible objects.

manufacturing firms
Companies that convert raw materials or components into products that may be sold to consumers or to other businesses.

that measure the financial health of companies in the industry. If you want to see how companies compare within the industry, the Dun & Bradstreet publications will tell you.

File this information in your mind for future use. It may come in handy when you are doing a research paper or business case analysis.

The Three Primary Business Sectors

The 20 NAICS codes divide all businesses and government organizations into distinct divisions called **industry sectors.** Three of these sectors—manufacturing (codes 31 through 33), distribution (codes 42 through 49), and service (codes 51 through 81)—make up the majority of businesses. Agriculture, mining, and construction are significant, as is the public sector (NAICS 92). Our discussion here, however, will focus on the three largest sectors.

The **manufacturing sector** includes companies and industries that produce objects. These objects may be anything from microchips to jet airplanes to nuclear power plants as long as they are tangible objects when completed. **Manufacturing firms** convert raw materials or components into products that may be sold to consumers or to other businesses. Thus, manufacturers *add value* to raw materials. Consider the significance of this fact. Iron ore in the ground has little value. Once it is extracted, it has more value.

When it is converted into steel, it has still more value. When it is used to build a vehicle, it has even more value.

The **distribution sector** consists of wholesale and retail firms that move products from the manufacturer to the ultimate customers or users. The distribution sector is the link between the producer and the end user. Without this sector it would be nearly impossible to get products to buyers efficiently.

The **service sector** includes businesses that provide some sort of service to customers. Even though a service may also bring products to the customer, as in the case of a plumber who installs a new faucet in a customer's home, the primary benefit of the interaction is through the service provided. The service sector includes a wide variety of businesses, from movie theaters to consultants.

We discuss each of the sectors in some depth and cover a number of concepts that are important to that sector. We also profile one of our focus companies to illustrate the dynamics of that sector.

> **distribution sector**
> The wholesale and retail firms that move products from the manufacturer to the ultimate customers or users.

> **service sector**
> The broad group of companies that provide some sort of service to customers.

The Manufacturing Sector

Manufacturing industries generate billions of dollars of products each year. Yet as a percentage of gross domestic product in the United States, manufacturing has declined over the past 40 years. Table 4.2 shows the value of durable manufactured goods, nondurable manufactured products, and services over time. *Durable goods* are those products that have a life expectancy of several years and may be used continuously or with great frequency. Cars, appliances, computers, electrical generating stations, and home construction are considered durable goods. Products such as clothing, food, plastics, chemicals, and leather goods are *nondurable goods* because they are either consumed or worn out over a relatively short period of time. Note in the table that the value of services exceeded the total of durable and nondurable goods between 1980 and 1985, and the gap has increased since then.

Who Buys Manufactured Goods?

Manufactured goods may have one of three ultimate destinations. First, they may be purchased by *individual consumers* (those customers who purchase consumer goods for their personal use). Consumer goods include cars, washers and dryers, home construction, apparel, jewelry, and breakfast cereals. Note that although there are great differences between a car and a breakfast cereal, both are consumer goods.

TABLE 4.2

Value of Services and Manufactured Goods ($ in billions)

Industry	1960	1965	1970	1975	1980	1985	1990	1995	2000
Durable goods	43.3	63.3	85.0	133.5	213.5	361.1	476.5	583.5	895.5
Nondurable goods	152.9	191.6	272.0	420.6	695.5	927.6	1245.3	1529.0	1849.9
Total manufactured goods	**196.2**	**254.9**	**357.0**	**554.1**	**909.0**	1308.7	1721.8	2087.0	2745.4
Services	136.0	189.4	291.1	475.0	851.4	**1416.1**	**2117.5**	**2963.4**	**3527.7**

Source: *Economic Report of the President*, February 2002, www.access.gpo.gov/eop (accessed March 21, 2002).

FIGURE 4.1

Representative
Destinations of Raw
Materials

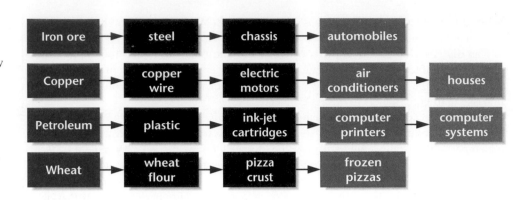

Consider tire maker Goodyear. If you go to a local tire dealer to buy tires for your car, you will have a number of types and sizes from which to choose. These tires are consumer goods because you, the individual consumer, are purchasing them.

The second destination for manufactured goods is to become *components* of products produced by other firms. For example, sheet steel becomes a component in an auto body. Oil may become a component in chemicals. Copper may become a component in wiring. These components may go through several processes and be considered part of several different industries before reaching the ultimate consumer. Figure 4.1 shows examples of component products.

A term that you hear occasionally in relationship to businesses is **original equipment manufacturer (OEM).** A company is an OEM if it makes components for another product. Now consider Goodyear again. We mentioned that this company makes tires for consumers to buy. It also makes tires for car manufacturers to buy. Thus, Goodyear is an OEM for the automotive industry, which puts them on cars as they come off the assembly line.

The third destination for manufactured goods is to become **capital goods,** that is, machinery and equipment used in the production process. Note the difference between this and the previous category, even though in both, goods are sold to other businesses. For example, Caterpillar Inc. produces truck engines as well as large off-road trucks. The truck engines are often sold for installation in on-road trucks manufactured by Ford, GM, Peterbilt, or Mack. These trucks are then bought by trucking firms to use in transporting all kinds of products. The truck engine is an example of one firm's product being an OEM component in another firm's product.

Caterpillar's large off-road trucks are produced entirely by Caterpillar and are sold to mining companies for use in mining excavation. In this case, the product becomes capital equipment that mining companies use in the extraction process. Individual consumers would never purchase these products; they may routinely cost several hundred thousand dollars and are designed for industrial use. We refer to buyers of either components or capital equipment as *industrial customers.*

Companies in virtually every industry sell consumer goods, component goods, and capital goods. Consider the wood products industry. Georgia-Pacific makes paneling

original equipment manufacturer (OEM)

A company that makes components for another product.

capital goods

The machinery and equipment used in the production process.

Some furniture manufacturers still rely on assembly lines. As shown here, Rowe Furniture dismantled the assembly line and let workers make the furniture in the way they preferred. As workers become more self-managed, fewer supervisors are needed. Do you think workers might become more motivated if they are allowed to design their own workplace and use their own processes?

that is sold to individual consumers who want to redecorate the family room of their home. It also sells similar paneling to housing contractors to use in new homes. Finally, if the paneling is part of a large office building, it might be considered capital goods.

Characteristics of Manufacturing Firms

Manufacturing firms often share a number of characteristics unique to manufacturing. For example, large manufacturing companies are often **capital intensive,** which means that the firm relies heavily on expensive equipment and machinery to produce its products. Manufacturing firms often make a significant investment in buildings and equipment as a percentage of their total investment. It is not unusual for a large firm to invest several million dollars to build a new production facility and equip it with high-tech production equipment. Dell, for example, increased its investment in plant and equipment from $342 million in 1998 to $826 million in 2002, thereby more than doubling its investment in production facilities in just four years.[3]

> **capital intensive**
> Relying heavily on equipment and machinery to produce products.

The significance of capital intensiveness is seen in the high investment, which can affect both costs and profit. Companies with a lot of capital equipment have ongoing expenditures related to that equipment. For example, they typically make regular interest payments on the equipment and incur regular maintenance costs to keep the equipment working. They have a lot of money tied up in the equipment that cannot be used for other things. Further, the costs are *fixed costs,* meaning that the company must pay those costs regardless of its level of sales or revenues. If sales are high, the firm can make substantial profits. But if sales drop, the fixed costs can lead to losses quickly. Fixed costs are especially important for small businesses. Since their sales are low, managers of small companies must try to keep capital equipment and fixed costs as low as possible. Failure to watch fixed costs can be fatal.

> **vertical integration**
> The degree to which a firm operates in more than one level of the overal production chain.

A second characteristic that is unique to manufacturing is that many firms are vertically integrated. **Vertical integration** is the degree to which a firm operates in more than one level of the overall production chain. In other words, vertical integration is the control of two or more sequential processes in the production and distribution of a product. A company that only assembles products is less vertically integrated than one that assembles products *and* produces the components that are assembled. If it also produces the materials that go into the components, it is even more vertically integrated.

> **outsourcing**
> Acquiring components or services from outside the firm rather than providing them using company resources.

A trend that has increased in recent years is just the opposite of vertical integration. That trend is toward **outsourcing,** acquiring components or services from outside the firm rather than providing them using company resources. Company managers find that they can reduce their investment in plant and equipment by having other companies produce components or provide services for the firm. This approach allows the managers to concentrate on the core activities of the business.

> **strategic alliances**
> Long-term agreements between firms to work together for the benefit of both.

A final characteristic seen in manufacturing firms today is **strategic alliances,** long-term agreements between firms to work together for the benefit of both. Such alliances sometimes involve outsourcing, but they may also involve joint marketing of products, working with companies in other countries, or sharing technology expertise. The concept of strategic alliances will reappear a number of times throughout the book.

More to Come
CHAPTERS 10, 12, 13

THINK ABOUT THIS

1. Why is it important to note who buys manufactured goods? What is different about how the goods are marketed to customers?

2. We mentioned that many manufacturing firms are capital intensive. But it is often labor costs that convince a company to move to the South or to Mexico. Why would those costs be the deciding factor?

3. Manufacturing firms increasingly outsource nonessential operations, such as cafeterias, human resources, and maintenance. Why is outsourcing cheaper than performing those tasks in-house?

We highlight the manufacturing sector with a discussion in Profile 4.1 of one of our focus companies, Dell. As you know by now, Dell produces and sells a line of computers, network servers, and switches.

PROFILE 4.1   DELL

"Dell, the world's most preferred computer systems company, is a premier provider of products and services required for customers worldwide to build their information-technology and Internet infrastructures. Dell, through its direct business model, designs, manufactures and customizes products and services to customer requirements, and offers an extensive selection of software and peripherals."

These lines from Dell's website underscore the nature of the manufacturing company. Dell's product line includes desktops, laptops, servers, and switches. The company's revenue for the past four quarters (2001–2002) totaled $31.2 billion, 30 percent of which came from Europe and Asia. Its products are made for at least two distinct markets. First is the consumer market. Customers go to the Dell website, configure a computer the way they want it to be, add shipping and credit card information, and click to order. The computer is manufactured to order and arrives at their door within two days. Second is the business market, which works much the same as the consumer market, with Dell building desktops and laptops to order. Eighty-two percent of Dell's revenues come from laptops and desktops.

For larger businesses, Dell provides not only desktops and laptops but also servers that connect individual computers, handle e-mail, and process large databases. Dell is at the forefront of server consolidation. Its multiple servers can be used in company data centers to add efficiency, flexibility, and higher levels of service.

As a high technology manufacturer, Dell outsources many of the components of its products to maintain an advantageous cost structure and maximize its flexibility. But it also does substantial design research to be on the cutting edge in home and office computers, networking, and storage equipment. Dell recently launched powerful new servers, including an innovative modular system that packages the performance of six servers in the space of one to simplify and help lower the costs of enterprise computing for its customers. Composed of high-performance server "blades" designed by Dell, the PowerEdge 1655MC accommodates up to six servers with two Intel Pentium III processors in a single enclosure. This design—the first in Dell's new modular server line—offers dramatically increased density and simplified server management, making it ideal for server consolidation, thin client computing, and high-performance clustering.

Dell does not use intermediaries such as retailers or wholesalers other than its recent foray into "white box" generic computers. Instead, its business is conducted either online or in direct consultation with customers. Half of its business is conducted over the Internet.

Source: Dell website, www.dell.com (accessed May 2, 2000).

The Distribution Sector

The distribution sector consists of businesses that serve as intermediaries, or links, between the producer and the final customer. It would be difficult and costly for manufacturers of most products to sell directly to the customer, and it would be equally impractical for final consumers to buy directly from a manufacturer. We will discuss the process of distribution and then focus on the two primary intermediaries: wholesalers and retailers.

Figure 4.2 shows three possibilities for distributing products from a manufacturer to an end user. The three columns in the figure represent channels of distribution. Note that the information in Figure 4.2 relates to consumer products. If you consider the discussion in the previous section about manufacturers, however, you will realize that a roughly similar distribution system is at work getting materials from suppliers to the manufacturers themselves, which they then convert into consumer or industry goods.

In the first column, a manufacturer ships goods directly to the customer. In an industrial setting, an example would be when IBM ships a large computer system to a customer and installs the unit in the customer's business. Dell also does that when it ships laptops to small businesses. In the consumer products area, an example is L.L.Bean, which ships products directly to customers who have ordered through a catalog or online.

In the second column, a manufacturer ships to a retailer who then sells the product to the end user. Automobiles are a good example here. Customers and car dealers discuss specifications for a car and negotiate the terms of the deal. The dealer either sells the customer a car from the lot or orders one from the factory.

The third column shows two intermediaries, a retailer and a wholesaler. In addition, there may be either manufacturer's representatives or jobbers involved in getting the product through the distribution channel. In this channel, the manufacturer produces products that are purchased by wholesalers around the country. The wholesalers, in turn, sell the products to the retailers, who then sell to consumers.

Several factors affect how many intermediaries are used in the distribution channel. Perhaps the most significant of these is the type of distribution desired.[4] **Exclusive distribution** means that the product is sold only in a single outlet in a market area. Products that are appropriate for exclusive distribution include designer clothes,

> **exclusive distribution**
> The distribution of a product to only a single outlet in a market area.

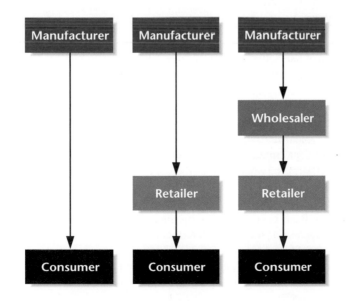

FIGURE 4.2

Channels of Distribution

selective distribution
The distribution of a product to a limited number of dealers or stores.

intensive distribution
The distribution of a product to every possible venue.

automobiles, expensive furniture, and sometimes, major appliances. Usually, these products are upscale and involve significant brand loyalty. These products often use few intermediaries. **Selective distribution** uses a limited number of dealers or stores to sell the product. Examples are sporting goods, some clothing, televisions, home computers, and less expensive furniture. Products with selective distribution may use at least one intermediary besides the retailer. **Intensive distribution** is selling products in every possible venue. Examples are gum and candy, toothpaste, paper clips, and soft drinks. The emphasis here is on convenience. The products are typically inexpensive, routine purchases. They are usually distributed through wholesalers and regional distribution centers before getting to a wide variety of retailers. Consider video sales, for example. Videos may be purchased through Best Buy or other electronics stores. They may also be purchased from video rental stores. Discount stores such as Target and Wal-Mart carry them, and some grocery store chains also sell them. Thus, intensive distribution uses as many outlets as possible to get the widest market coverage.

Finally, the cost of distribution must be considered. Each added intermediary adds to the cost of the product. That cost must be either assumed by the manufacturer or passed on to the customer in the form of price increases. Either way, the cost affects profitability. But keep in mind that trying to minimize costs may result in insufficient market coverage.

Multiple Distribution Methods

It is not uncommon for manufacturers to use multiple distribution methods. Look again at Figure 4.2. Using multiple methods of reaching customers assures wider coverage while possibly reducing costs. Consider Gap Inc., which is primarily a retail store chain selling merchandise that the company has manufacturers produce exclusively for it. Thus, its primary channel is from the manufacturer to the retailer. But it is also possible to purchase Gap clothing online. Lands' End, on the other hand, has done the opposite. Lands' End is primarily a mail-order or online seller of clothes and related items. Thus, it would be an example of a contracted manufacturer producing products for the direct marketer to sell directly to customers. Recently, however, Lands' End has been acquired by Sears to sell its products through retail stores. As you will see in Profile 4.3 near the end of this section, Best Buy also uses both in-store and online selling.

We now consider two big players in the distribution of goods from manufacturers to end users—wholesalers and retailers.

Wholesalers

wholesalers
Businesses that serve as intermediaries between manufacturers and retailers.

A category of merchants that is largely invisible to consumers is **wholesalers,** businesses that serve as intermediaries between manufacturers and retailers. Manufacturers typically cannot afford to call on individual retailers to take orders and transport goods to them. Likewise, most retailers cannot personally contact each manufacturer to find information and order products. This is where the wholesaler comes in.

Think of the typical hardware store. It may stock 10,000 individual products, produced by 2,000 to 4,000 manufacturers. There is simply no efficient way to get the manufacturers and retailers together without the help of wholesalers.

Though unknown to the general public, wholesalers provide major services through their distribution of goods. Figure 4.3 illustrates these important roles. They include storing goods that have been produced by manufacturers, breaking items sent in bulk into smaller shipments for individual retailers or business customers, providing industry and consumer information about products to retailers, providing capital and credit for the purchase of goods, maintaining inventory from which a retailer can draw rather than keeping inventory on-site, transporting goods, and ordering goods on behalf of the

FIGURE 4.3

The Roles of
Wholesalers

retailer. As you can see, the wholesaler accepts much of the risk that individual retailers would otherwise assume. Profile 4.2 illustrates the role of wholesalers by looking at the Fleming Companies, a major wholesaler of food and food-related products.

Remember, wholesalers are intermediaries between manufacturers and retailers or business customers. Intermediaries play more important roles in some industries than others. In some industries, such as automobiles, the manufacturer ships products directly to the retailer. In others, such as heavy equipment or machinery, the producer often ships products directly to the end user. In many other industries, particularly consumer goods, the manufacturer ships products to a wholesaler, who then ships to retailers. There are exceptions. When the retailer is a large chain such as Wal-Mart, Home Depot, or Sears, manufacturers often work directly with the retail headquarters buyer, thereby effectively eliminating the wholesaler because the retail chain is large enough

THE FLEMING COMPANIES   PROFILE 4.2

The Fleming Companies is the number one distributor of consumables to the U.S. retail market. It operates primarily as a wholesaler, but it also is a retailer. Fleming markets food and food-related products by serving more than 3,000 supermarkets in all 50 states, 6,800 convenience stores, and 2,000 supercenters. It also operates 100 company-owned retail stores. It supplies virtually every national brand of grocery products, plus high-volume private-label items and a full line of perishables, including meats, dairy, deli products, frozen foods, and fresh produce. It also provides a variety of general merchandise often found in grocery stores. In 2001, Fleming had $15.6 billion in sales and 23,000 employees.

In addition to distributing food products, Fleming offers retailers a complete range of services to enable them to compete more effectively. It also has a real estate division that sells stores and commercial real estate.

Source: Fleming Companies website, www.fleming.com/ (accessed April 16, 2002).

to perform wholesaler duties. This approach reduces costs and is one of the key reasons that chains such as Wal-Mart can offer lower prices.

Related to wholesalers is the concept of a **manufacturer's representative,** a company or person that sells products to wholesalers or retailers on commission. Think of a manufacturer's representative as the equivalent of a full-time salesperson traveling around the country selling products. The advantage of using manufacturers' reps is that they often represent many manufacturers, each of which may have only a few products to sell. The rep takes catalogs and order forms and calls on wholesalers and retailers to get orders for the products. The products are then shipped directly to the wholesaler or retailer.

Two key differences between manufacturers' reps and wholesalers is that reps work on commission only, and they do not take possession of the product. They simply take orders and communicate those orders back to the manufacturer. This arrangement gives the manufacturer the widest possible coverage for a relatively low cost.

Retailers

The retail industry is the most visible of all industries from the perspective of the individual consumer. **Retailers** are stores that sell directly to consumers. Table 4.3 shows various categories of retail stores.

The competitive structure within retailing is continually evolving. Fifty years ago, there were very few large department stores and certainly no malls. Very few franchises existed. Today, every city of at least medium size has one or more malls. Each is anchored by a national department store chain, such as JCPenney or Sears. A second anchor is a regional department store, such as Carson Pirie Scott in the Midwest and Dillard's or Foley's in the Southwest. The other stores are likely to be smaller specialty store chains, which may be either company-owned or franchised. A very small percentage of stores in malls are locally owned and operated.

The retail scene is dominated by large chains of stores. Many of these chains are owned by even larger corporations. Table 4.4 shows the 10 largest retailers, along with their sales, type of stores, and the subsidiaries they operate. Note the subsidiaries. Most of these are well-known names themselves, but it's surprising to see who owns them. For example, did you know that JCPenney owns 2,900 Eckerd drugstores, or that Lord & Taylor, Famous-Barr, Strawbridge's, Meier and Frank, The Jones Store, Foley's, and Filene's are all owned by the May Department Stores Co.?

As shown in Table 4.4, most of the large retailers are either department store chains or grocery chains. Increasingly, however, chains known as category killers are having a major impact. **Category killers** are large chain stores that specialize in a narrow line of products. They provide great depth in products and offer prices lower than traditional stores can offer. Toys "R" Us in toys, Home Depot in home improvement and hardware,

---

manufacturer's representative
A company or person that sells products to wholesalers or retailers on commission.

retailers
Stores that sell directly to consumers.

category killers
Large chain stores that specialize in a narrow line of products.

TABLE 4.3

Selected Types of Retail Stores

Garden supply stores	Shoe stores
Grocery stores	Radio, TV, and computer stores
Meat and fish stores	Computer and software stores
New and used car dealers	Restaurants and bars
Boat dealers	Used merchandise stores
Motorcycle dealers	Jewelry stores
Women's clothing stores	Optical goods stores

TABLE 4.4

The Top 10 Department Stores, 2001 ($ billions)

Rank	Company	Sales	Store Type	Subsidiaries
1.	Wal-Mart	$218.0	Discount	Wal-Mart, Wal-Mart Supercenters, Sam's Wholesale Club, McLane Company, Wal-Mart International
2.	Kroger	50.1	Groceries	Kroger, gas and convenience stores, jewelry stores
3.	Sears	41.1	General merchandise	Sears, NTB, Sears Hardware
4.	Target	39.9	Discount, general merchandise	Target, Marshall Field's, Mervyn's, Associated Merchandising, Target Financial Services, Dayton's Commercial Interiors
5.	American Stores	39.7	Groceries, drugs	Lucky Stores, Acme Markets, Jewel Food Stores, Osco Drugs, Sav-On
6.	Safeway	34.4	Groceries	Safeway, The Vons Companies, Tom Thumb, Dominick's, Carr's, Genuardi's Pavillions, Randall's
7.	JCPenney	32.0	General merchandise	Penney's, Eckerd Drug
8.	Federated Department Stores	15.6	Department stores	Bloomingdale's, Macy's, Lazarus, The Bon Marche, Burdines, Sterns, Rich's, Goldsmiths
9.	May Department Stores	14.2	Department stores	Lord & Taylor, Foley's, Robinsons-May, Hecht's, Kaufmann's, Filene's, Famous-Barr, Meier & Frank, LS Ayres, Strawbridge's, The Jones Store, David's Bridal, After Hours, Priscilla of Boston
10.	Kmart	8.0	Discount	Kmart, Bluelite.com

Source: Company websites (accessed April 15, 2002); "Industry Rankings of the S&P 500," *BusinessWeek,* Spring 2002, pp. 87–125.

and Staples in office supplies, for example, specialize in wide assortments of products within a specific market and sell at deeply discounted prices. As a result, they are formidable competitors within their particular market.

Although large chains dominate the retail landscape, franchises are almost as significant. As you learned in Chapter 3, a franchise is a business owned by a franchisee that uses the name, standard operating procedures, training, and marketing provided by the franchisor. Over 40 percent of all retail sales are made through franchised outlets.

We have already discussed selling over the Internet, and we will discuss it still further in Chapter 17. It is important, however, to consider an entire category of distribution called direct marketing. Direct marketing occurs when businesses sell directly to the consumer without any intermediaries. Examples include Avon, the Home Shopping Network, and a range of catalog retailers. The number of direct marketing firms and

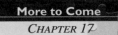
More to Come
CHAPTER 17

eBay began as simply an on-line auction of miscellaneous products that individuals were willing to sell to other individuals. It has now greatly expanded and does business with large manufacturers of products. Are there products that do not sell well on eBay?

Internet retailers grew rapidly during the late 1990s, tapered off somewhat during the 2000–2001 dot-com crash, and resurged beginning in 2002. Internet sales, also known as electronic marketing or e-tailing, were approximately $40 billion in 2002, up from $30 billion in 2001.[5] Companies such as Amazon.com, eBay, J.Crew, and L.L.Bean are either totally or heavily into e-tailing.

Three types of e-tailers are notable. First are the totally Internet-based companies, such as Amazon.com and eBay. Their success or failure is directly dependent on customers' accessing them over the Internet. Second are the catalog marketing companies, such as Lands' End or J.Crew. In this case, the companies existed as direct marketing companies before the Internet became popular. They added Web marketing to their catalog marketing. Third are the companies, often referred to as brick-and-mortar retailers, that are traditional retail store chains. These companies, such as Gap, Abercrombie & Fitch, Eddie Bauer, and even Wal-Mart and Target, have added Web-based marketing as a relatively minor part of their total operations.

E-tailing and other direct marketing methods have the advantage of reaching customers in the comfort of their homes. Customers most likely to use e-tailing are the younger, more savvy shoppers and dual-income couples who do not have the time or interest to shop in stores. As more and more customers become comfortable with Internet shopping, this segment should see continued growth.

The remainder of the retail landscape is populated by numerous small, independent businesses. Some consist of a single store, owned and operated by one person with the help of a few full- or part-time workers. Some are multistore chains operating within a relatively small geographic area. Many are specialty stores that cater to particular demographic or customer segments—for example, exclusive gift stores or apparel stores focusing on a particular niche.

Small, independent retailers must compete against giants in the industry. Large department stores and category killers can provide much wider selection at a significantly lower price. Because of their size and national scope, they can advertise continuously in the media; a small store can afford only a token amount of advertising in comparison. Thus, the smaller store must compete on the basis of personal service or service to a small niche of loyal customers.

Transportation

An integral part of the distribution function is transporting the product to its destination. The cost of transportation is directly related to both speed and flexibility of the transportation method. Using overnight shipping is extremely expensive, but it is quick. Using trucks is slower but less expensive. Using train cars or ships for bulk items is even cheaper but even slower.

In some cases, the nature of the product determines the shipping method used. Coal always has to be shipped by rail or barge; its weight and bulk preclude other methods. Produce for grocery stores is normally shipped by refrigerated trucks, allowing distribution to a variety of sites without loss of perishable food.

Some companies use **contract carriers,** trucking companies that specialize in carrying a particular kind of good for a few customers. For example, if a company has a fleet of refrigerated trucks, its customers may consist of Sara Lee Foods, Johnson Wax, Ore-Ida potatoes, or a small number of similar companies. All these clients need the special handling provided by refrigerated trucks.

Other trucking companies, called **common carriers,** transport a wide variety of products for many clients. When you see a truck on the highway with a name like

> **contract carriers**
> Trucking companies that specialize in carrying a particular kind of good for a few customers.

> **common carriers**
> Trucking companies that transport a wide variety of products for many clients.

Roadway is a less-than-truckload carrier of industrial, commercial, and retail goods in all 50 states, Canada, Mexico, and Puerto Rico. How are they different from UPS or FedEx?

PROFILE 4.3   BEST BUY

Best Buy and its subsidiaries are retail chains. As such, they produce nothing. All their products are purchased either from manufacturers or from wholesalers or distributors. Thus, much of the focus, particularly in discount-oriented Best Buy, is how to get products at the lowest possible cost while ensuring quality. At the same time, Best Buy continues to open 60 stores per year.

Best Buy stores range from 30,000 to 45,000 square feet. The number of actual products carried in each store varies considerably based on seasonality, the arrival of new software and entertainment titles, and other new-product introductions.

The method of getting products to stores varies by the product. Most products, except major appliances, are shipped directly from the manufacturers to one of Best Buy's strategically located distribution centers around the country. In addition, a warehouse is located in Minnesota specifically for entertainment software. Major appliances are shipped to satellite locations in each major market.

Buyers for products are located at Best Buy's new headquarters in Richfield, Minnesota. Vendors (manufacturers) come to Richfield to persuade buyers to buy their products and to negotiate terms, prices, and quantities. Keep in mind that Best Buy is a tough negotiator because the business makes its profits by keeping its costs low.

Source: Best Buy website, www.bestbuy.com (accessed May 2, 2002); and personal communication with Best Buy representatives, Spring 2002.

Yellow Freight or Roadway, chances are you are seeing a common carrier. These businesses often transport trailer loads of packages from one point in the country to another. Their loads may differ each trip.

THINK ABOUT THIS

1. Look around your apartment or dorm room. Consider the products in the room—notebooks, computer, microwave oven, bedding, posters, and photos in frames. How did each arrive at the store in which you purchased it?

2. How can a small retailer compete effectively with a giant company such as Sears or JCPenney?

3. What determines whether a company should have its own trucks rather than ship products on common carriers?

Large manufacturers, wholesalers, and retailers often have their own trucks, which carry only that company's materials. Whirlpool, Deere, McDonald's, Wal-Mart, and Pizza Hut are among the companies that have their own trucks.

The final method of transportation is small-package carriers such as UPS, the U.S. Postal Service, or FedEx. These are technically common carriers since they carry products for thousands of clients, but because they specialize in small packages, they are considered differently. The price per package may be higher than for other forms of transportation, but since the volume sent at a given time or to a given customer is low, it becomes the most efficient method of delivery.

We end the discussion of the distribution sector by considering Best Buy in Profile 4.3. By now you know that Best Buy was started by Richard Schulze in 1983 as the evolution of earlier audio electronics stores. It now owns a number of other chains in addition to Best Buy stores themselves.

UPS is the world's largest transportation company, offering the most extensive range of e-commerce and supply chain solutions for the movement of goods, information, and funds. Headquartered in Atlanta, Georgia, in the United States, UPS serves more than 200 countries and territories. UPS stock trades on the New York Stock Exchange (UPS) and the company can be found on the web at www.ups.com.

The Service Sector

The manufacturing sector produces products. These are things that we can see and touch. We can consume or use them, or we can return them to the seller if they do not work right. The distribution sector delivers those products to customers. Services, as the name implies, provide intangible benefits to their customers rather than products. In other words, the customer benefits from the service but often has few or no physical products to show for it. For example, if my attorney meets with me to discuss a contract, I will have benefited from the service, and I will be charged a fee. Yet I have nothing other than the knowledge gained from the meeting and perhaps a few documents. If I go to a fitness center, I may feel better, but other than possibly sore muscles I have no immediate tangible benefit from that particular session. Table 4.5 shows a small sample of the hundreds of service businesses that exist today. Note that in every case, the primary benefit is the service provided rather than a specific product.

Once a service has been provided, it is difficult to undo it. If I go to the hospital for surgery and I am not happy with it, I may sue the doctor or the hospital, but I can't easily

TABLE 4.5

Selected Service Businesses

Taxicabs	Warehousing	Shipping companies	Marinas
Airlines	Day care centers	Communications	Hotels
Banks	Sanitary services	Insurance agents	Physicians
Photographers	Real estate brokers	Mailing services	Car leasing
Theaters	Computer services	Car repair shops	Consultants
Hospitals	Advertising agencies	Home health care	Plumbers
Pipelines	Fitness centers	Vocational schools	Accountants
Attorneys	Employment agencies	Security systems	Dry cleaners

undo the surgery. If I have a bumpy ride on an airplane, I may complain and may even get some restitution, but I still go wherever the plane is going.

Services cannot be either stockpiled or back ordered. For example, if I own a retail business selling apparel, I can have a substantial stock of inventory on hand to meet the needs of many customers. If a customer wants a product that I do not currently have in stock, I can order it. Service businesses do not have this luxury. Suppose I own a drain-cleaning business. You call me because your basement is backed up with water from a stopped-up sewer line. If I cannot get to your house today, you will not wait until next week. You will call a competitor immediately.

Service businesses have accounted for an increasing share of the economy for decades. While manufacturing goods, including both durable goods and nondurable goods, have been decreasing steadily as a percentage of the total for decades, services have been increasing. This trend will continue as both businesses and consumers decide that it makes more sense to have others provide certain services than to provide those services for themselves. This has usually been the case for essential services such as health care, police protection, education, and government. Today other services are growing as they offer convenience to increasingly busy households, who place a premium on their time. So it makes sense to have the taxes done by H&R Block, the house cleaned by a maid service, the yard maintained by a lawn service, and routine car repairs and maintenance done by the local garage. Limited leisure time is used to the fullest extent, fueling growth in travel and recreational businesses.

Service sector industries can be just as competitive as manufacturing even though they provide no product. Hospitals are now among the most competitive industries in existence. Banking and financial services have gone through major industry changes since they were deregulated, as have airlines. Competition has helped keep the service industries efficient and customer focused.

Like manufacturing, service industries vary widely in the cost a firm incurs to produce and market the service. A day care center operator may have to spend only a few hundred dollars to add a fenced yard and meet health regulations. An airline may spend from $50 million to $200 million for an airplane. A hospital has extraordinarily high fixed costs compared with those of a consulting firm.

A major difference between services and manufacturing is that service businesses do not, as a core part of their business, deal with inventory and cost of goods sold. Thus, the comparison between costs and prices is much different. At the same time, however, service businesses must recognize the need to keep costs at a minimum. Since inventory does not provide a major part of the flow-through of funds for service businesses, these companies must look elsewhere to find avenues for cost containment.

labor intensive

Relying heavily on people as the key to supplying products and services.

Many service industries are highly **labor intensive**—relying heavily on people as the key to supplying products and services—so labor costs and fringe benefits form a major portion of a firm's expenses. Business owners must carefully consider the degree to which controlling the cost of human resources interferes with the effectiveness of those workers.

Characteristics of Service Businesses

Given that services differ from manufacturing in a number of ways, it is important to consider the kinds of concerns that are unique to service businesses. We consider a number of them here.

Quality in services is a function of the direct interaction between the provider and the customer. Since services cannot be returned as products can, it is imperative that the service be done right the first time. Often little can be done to correct service errors other than make some type of restitution—frequently a costly matter. For example, if an airline overbooks flights and all passengers show up, the airline then must offer some type of incentive to get volunteers to take a later flight. A restaurant whose service does not meet the expectations of a customer often simply will not charge that patron for the meal rather than risk having an unhappy customer. Both of these examples can be expensive if the problem occurs frequently. In addition, poor service often leads to lost customers. Think of the number of businesses that you refuse to patronize because you received bad service. You may or may not have complained, but you most likely told your friends about the bad service you received.

The role of the employee is critical in service businesses. Since services depend on the interaction between customers and business representatives, employees must always be well trained both in the technical aspects of the service and in interpersonal skills. Few things are more frustrating to customers than representatives who cannot answer questions or who do not care about customer satisfaction.

A key issue for managers is the trade-off between cost and customer satisfaction. We have probably all complained that a bank was irresponsible because not enough drive-up windows were open. But the bank's managers must decide how many tellers are needed to service the windows properly. Too many tellers means that the bank is paying labor costs for idle workers. Too few tellers means that unhappy customers must wait. Similarly, too many trained dental hygienists in a dentist's office can be costly, but too few means that patients must be turned away. Unfortunately, labor costs increase in large increments. For example, each hygienist can clean 20 patients' teeth per day. But hiring an additional hygienist may bring in only five new patients per day because of insufficient demand. Thus, the owner of the dental business must decide whether the additional business is worth the expense.

Changes in Service through Technology

We have emphasized that service delivery depends on customer contact and that satisfaction with that contact is critical. Yet one trend in the service industry seems to be toward less direct contact between the service providers and customers. For example, you probably have little if any contact with your bank other than through the ATM. You probably use a self-service gasoline station, and you may even pay for the gas by swiping your credit card through a reader on the pump. You may check into and out of hotels without talking to a human being. These lower levels of contact are convenient and in some cases allow providers to offer services at lower prices.

Many improvements in service provision are the result of increasing technology. You couldn't have done banking from your computer 10 years ago. Technology even permits some medical services without going to a doctor. Now some doctors' offices allow patients to ask nonemergency questions via e-mail. This option saves travel and waiting time for the patients and allows the doctors to use their time and resources more efficiently.

We illustrate the service industries with a profile of Southwest Airlines. You have already learned a great deal about Southwest Airlines. Now observe in Profile 4.4 how Southwest does so well in providing services in a tough industry and still consistently makes a profit.

THINK ABOUT THIS

1. Service industries differ from manufacturing in a number of ways. One major way is customer contact. What employee skills are most important for service industries?

2. We mentioned that services cannot be back ordered or stored. Are there any exceptions to this rule?

3. How can technology be used effectively in services such as real estate sales? car rentals?

PROFILE 4.4   SOUTHWEST AIRLINES

The results are in for 2001. United Airlines lost $2.1 billion. American Airlines lost $1.7 billion. Delta Air Lines lost $1.2 billion. But Southwest Airlines had a profit of $511 million. The year 2001 was without question a bad year for airlines. But Southwest still managed to make a profit for the twenty-ninth year in a row, thanks to an unflinching focus on costs and an absolute emphasis on customer service. It even took delivery of fourteen new 737-700 planes in the first half of 2002.

Southwest's net income for the second quarter of 2002 was $102.3 million, down from $175.6 million in the second quarter of 2001. Still, in a time when other airlines were showing losses, Southwest managed to make a profit and did so without cutting routes or service. Costs rose during late 2001 and early 2002 because of added security measures. In addition, Southwest's load factor dropped from 67.3 percent of capacity to 62.9 percent, partially because of a decrease in passengers and partially because the airline actually added capacity.

Southwest Airlines makes a profit based on its ability to provide excellence in service while keeping its costs as low as possible. Its cost per average passenger-mile, the industry measure of airline costs, is the lowest in the industry. It achieves this cost advantage because of its high utilization of the aircraft fleet and high productivity of the employees compared to Southwest's competitors.

Herb Kelleher set the tone for the airline by encouraging employees to work hard while having fun. The employees have a good time in spite of working long hours. This culture, which has been continued by Jim Parker and Colleen Barrett, translates into customer service. Southwest's employees take care of their customers with spirit and enthusiasm. That is why employee turnover is one of the lowest in the industry and why customers continue to fly Southwest Airlines.

Source: Southwest Airlines website, www.southwest.com, (accessed September 11, 2002); and "Fortune One Thousand Ranked within Industries," *Fortune,* April 15, 2002, pp. F-44–F66.

The Relationships among Companies in Their Industries

In each of the preceding three sections, we have discussed the nature of industry sectors. Manufacturers produce goods that are then distributed to customers by wholesalers and retailers or by the manufacturers themselves. Service providers render a benefit to customers by providing a service to them. It is necessary to take one additional step and look at the relationships among companies within a given industry. These relationships affect how companies compete, how they may cooperate, and how they fit together to constitute an entire industry.

Industry Concentration   **Industry concentration** refers to the number of firms in an industry and their relative size. Increasing industry concentration means that there are fewer and fewer firms in the industry. Firms either go out of business as they become noncompetitive or are purchased by larger firms. As firms leave the industry, the remaining firms grow still larger. This causes even more problems for smaller firms and causes even more concentration in the industry.

Industry concentration is measured by the *concentration ratio,* sometimes known as the C-4 ratio. This is the percentage of total industry sales accounted for by the top four firms. Some industries, such as home construction, have very little concentration. These industries are highly *fragmented.* Others, such as aircraft manufacturing, are more highly concentrated; there are very few firms and they are extremely large.

Some companies compete based on the lowest possible price. Others compete based on highest possible value. Either can be profitable. Is one strategy better than another?

> **industry concentration**
> The number of firms in an industry and their relative size; often calculated by the C-4 ratio (the percentage of total industry sales by the top four firms).

Competition within an Industry   We will discuss competition in more depth in Chapter 12. It is important to note here, however, that much of the interaction among firms in an industry relates to how the businesses compete. For example, some businesses like to have the lowest possible price, such as all three of our focus companies—Dell, Best Buy, and Southwest Airlines. Other companies compete on the basis of the quality of their product—Caterpillar, Lexus, Lord & Taylor, and Herman Miller, for example. Still others, such as McDonalds and Marriott, will compete on the basis of having prime locations. Others, such as Procter & Gamble and Kraft, will compete on the basis of the breadth of their product line.

> **More to Come**
> *Chapter 12*

Intensity of Competition   Industries vary according to the intensity of competition. For example, Coca-Cola and Pepsi are fierce competitors, spending millions of dollars on marketing to gain one or two percentage points of market share. In other industries, companies still compete with one another, but the competition is more subdued and friendly. It is not unusual among small retailers for the store owners to refer customers to their competitors if they cannot provide the products or services themselves.

Supplier–Customer Relations   We have discussed how some manufacturers sell goods to other businesses. That, of course, holds for service businesses as well. The term *outsourcing* is used over and over in this book to indicate how companies rely on other companies to provide components, supplies, and services. In many cases, the transfer of goods or services between two businesses is essentially seamless. A casual observer may not realize that one part of a company's operation is being provided by an outside vendor rather than by the company itself. Company cafeterias, for example, are often run by an outside firm, but few people are even aware of that fact.

THINK ABOUT THIS

1. How would you compete differently if you were a small firm competing in an industry full of other small firms versus in an industry where several small firms compete with a few very large firms?

2. Some firms compete fiercely while others compete in a friendly way. Suppose you were manager of a small firm in a relatively small city. Which might be the best way to compete? Why?

THE BIG PICTURE

In the preceding chapter, we considered businesses according to their size, their legal structure, and their ownership. In this chapter, we looked at various industry segments that make up the overall business arena. Let's step back for a minute and consider the big picture.

There are approximately 25 million businesses in the United States. If we choose to look at them by size and ownership, we see that 70 percent are sole proprietorships, owned by single individuals, with the remainder owned by two or more partners or by stockholders. Over 98 percent of businesses are small, with most having either no employees or only a few. Another way of looking at the businesses is to look at what they do rather than what they are. With this perspective, we see that an increasing percentage of businesses provide a service to their customers. These businesses make their money by doing something for someone else. Others make profits by building products, while still others concentrate on getting those products to the users.

Putting these two views together, we can discuss any given business with more specificity. We could say that the ABC Toy Company is a small company, owned by two partners, that builds toys for the preschool market. The XYZ Restaurant is a privately held corporation, a franchise that specializes in seafood. Or Dell is a publicly held manufacturer of computer hardware. These descriptions give us more information about the companies and where they fit in the overall scheme of the business environment.

Look at a business you know well. How many ways can you categorize it? You may want to keep that business in your mind as you continue your journey through this book. Your picture of that business will become increasingly precise as you learn more and more about how businesses work.

Summary

1. All businesses conduct their activities within one or more industries. Understanding the nature of the industry helps us understand more about a business and how it relates to others.

   • What are the major sectors of the economy?

   The three sectors that make up the majority of businesses are manufacturing, distribution, and services.

2. The manufacturing sector is usually the basis of a country's economy. In recent years the impact of manufacturing has declined, but it is still a significant force.

   • What are the major characteristics of the American manufacturing sector?

   Manufacturing is the process of building a product or adding value to raw materials. Manufacturing produces either durable goods or nondurable goods. Manufactured goods have one of three destinations—final consumers, components in other products, or capital goods. Large manufacturers are often capital intensive, relying on equipment and machinery to produce their products. Some manufacturers (for example, carmakers) practice vertical integration. That is, they control two or more sequential processes in the production or distribution of the product. In contrast to vertical integration is outsourcing, an increasing trend toward acquiring components or services from outside the firm. Some manufacturers also engage in strategic alliances, long-term agreements between firms.

3. The distribution sector moves products from manufacturers to customers. Many kinds of distribution are available.

   • What are the characteristics of the distribution sector?

   This sector contains two major groups, wholesalers and retailers. Wholesalers are the intermediaries between manufacturers and retailers. Their roles include storing goods, breaking bulk items into smaller shipments, providing industry and consumer information, financing, maintaining inventory, transporting goods, ordering goods, and assuming risk.

   Retailers sell to the ultimate consumer. Retailing companies come in many varieties and represent names familiar to almost everyone, such as Wal-Mart, JCPenney, Sears, Kroger, Safeway, and Home Depot. The competitive structure within retailing is continually evolving. Fifty years ago there were only a very few large department stores and no malls or national discount chains. Today, the discounters and malls are everywhere. The retail scene is dominated by large chains.

   Today's retail scene is also noticeable for its category killers. These large chain stores specialize in a narrow line of goods, provide great depth in product offerings, and offer very low prices. Toys "R" Us and Home Depot are two examples.

   Franchises are also popular today. A franchise is a business owned by a franchisee that uses the name, standard operating procedures, training, and marketing provided by the franchisor.

   Direct marketing firms sell their products to consumers without going through intermediaries. These businesses increasingly use the Internet to reach their customers.

   Retailing is also characterized by numerous small, independent businesses. To be successful, they must compete against the chains by offering more personal service or serving a small niche of loyal customers.

   Another important concept in distribution is transporting products to their final destination.

4. Whereas manufacturing used to be seen as the major source of growth, the service sector is now looked to for both economic growth and employment growth.

   • What are the main features of the service sector of the economy?

   Service businesses provide intangible benefits to their customers. Some examples are taxicabs, airlines, hospitals, attorneys, real estate brokers, computer services, security systems, and dry cleaners. A major difference between services and manufacturing is that services do not typically deal with inventory. Many services are highly labor intensive, so managers must try to control the cost of human resources without compromising on the quality of employees.

   In recent years, the service sector has been the largest source of new jobs in the American economy. It has also been the source of some changes in the nature of competition. A major cause of that change has been deregulation, of the airline and banking industries, for example.

   Characteristics of service businesses include the need for quality, positive employee attitudes and expertise, and labor costs.

5. In addition to understanding industries, it is also important to recognize the relationship among companies within a given industry.

   • What are the key features to consider as we look at the relationship among companies within an industry?

   Four themes or features were examined. These dealt with industry concentration, different ways of competing within an industry, the intensity of competition, and supplier/customer relations.

Key Terms

capital goods, p. 72

capital intensive, p. 73

category killers, p. 78

common carriers, p. 81

contract carriers, p. 81

distribution sector, p. 71

exclusive distribution, p. 75

industry concentration, p. 87

industry sectors, p. 70

intensive distribution, p. 76

labor intensive, p. 84

manufacturer's representative, p. 78

manufacturing firms, p. 70

manufacturing sector, p. 70

original equipment manufacturer (OEM), p. 72

outsourcing, p. 73

retailers, p. 78

selective distribution, p. 76

service sector, p. 71

strategic alliances, p. 73

vertical integration, p. 73

wholesalers, p. 76

Exercises and Applications

1. Consider a small retail store in your community. Does it provide better service than department stores? Is the level of service important?

2. Do you prefer services to be high-contact, with knowledgeable, friendly, and attentive service providers, or do you prefer technology-based low contact where you don't have to deal with people? What are the advantages and disadvantages of each? Do you think there is a trend toward less human contact in services?

3. Form teams. Interview the owner or manager of a local restaurant to find out how he or she gets needed supplies. Write a one-page paper discussing the various distribution methods you identified.

4. How does the Internet help the retail distribution and service industries? How do the two sectors differ in their use of the Internet? Go to the home page of a major retailer and analyze the user friendliness of the home page.

FROM THE PAGES OF

BusinessWeek

Are There Just Too Many Stores?

During the 1990s American retailers went on an expansion binge that outpaced demand and put weaker retailers at risk in 2002. The industry added 3 square feet of new store space for every man, woman and child in the U.S. . . . That 20% growth rate was double the rate of population growth during the decade . . . As space grew, the industry became less productive. Average operating profit margins for retailers, after rising slightly to 3.97% in 1996, fell each year thereafter . . . even as consumer spending accelerated . . . That was in the good times. But store owners faced a recession in 2001.

This [overbuilding] cycle is dealing out huge gains for a fortunate few. The dominant players are bigger and more aggressive than they were in the industry's last downturn. They will probably emerge holding a far greater share of the market, with two or three undisputed leaders in most sectors. In discounting, the likely winners are Wal-Mart Stores and Target; in consumer electronics, Best Buy; and in home improvement, Home Depot and Lowes. The flip side? . . . There is the potential for a much broader shakeout than last time, as weaker players are gobbled up, and survivors shutter underperforming stores.

The emerging key players are those that have clear and understandable positions in consumers' eyes. Just as important, they have developed logistical and financial systems to deliver the goods more efficiently. Wal-Mart has staked out the turf of price leader, while the slightly more upscale Target stands for cheap chic. Kohl's sells leading casual brands but is cheaper and more convenient than traditional department stores.

Although the strongest players are becoming increasingly dominant, that is not to say there won't be opportunity for newcomers—or for those willing to head in a radically new direction . . . But for those chains that can't deliver on a crisp identity there will be less and less room to maneuver amid the store glut.

Decision Questions

1. We have explained how successful businesses have to be aware of changes in the economic environment of their industry. According to this article, what characteristic of the retailing industry created problems for many retailers in 2001 to 2002? In retrospect, what could the troubled retailers have done in the 1990s to avoid the problems?

2. The model you are studying in this textbook explains how successful businesses develop strategies that are right for their industry. This article suggests that there are several ways to be a successful retailer. What business strategies seem to work in American retailing? What strategy seems to be a guaranteed recipe for failure?

3. The article suggests that some retailers may not survive given the domination of large firms such as Wal-Mart and Target. Consider other industries, such as the manufacturers of the goods sold at retail. How will the changes affect those industries?

Source: Robert Berner and Gerry Khermouch, with Aixa Pascual, "Retail Reckoning," *BusinessWeek,* December 10, 2001, pp. 73–77.

References

1. U.S. Census Bureau website, www.census.gov/naics (accessed May 22, 2002).
2. *Industry Norms and Key Business Ratios,* 2000–2001 (New York: Dun & Bradstreet Information Services, 2001).
3. Dell website, www.dell.com (accessed April 16, 2002).
4. David J. Bloomberg, Stephen LeMay, and Joe B. Hanna, *Logistics* (Upper Saddle River, NJ: Prentice Hall, 2002), pp. 72–77.
5. Heather Green, "Lessons of the Cyber Survivors," *BusinessWeek,* April 22, 2002, p. 42.

Model of the Path toward a Successful Business

2

Making Decisions in Today's Business

Part Two is relatively short, but extremely important. Here, you will begin to see business as a network of people who make critical decisions that shape the direction and competitive stance of their respective organizations.

Chapter 5 introduces you to the various decision makers who affect businesses. You will learn the role that each plays in helping the business. You will also learn about the logical process of decision making that successful businesspeople follow. In addition, you will be introduced to the power of team decisions, and you will learn how creative decision making can be encouraged.

Chapter 6 introduces you to the idea of stakeholders—those people or groups who have some claim on or expectation about how the business should operate. You will recognize how business tries to carry out its responsibilities to these stakeholders. In Chapter 6 you will also study business ethics. You will recognize that sound ethics is the foundation of not only healthy and successful businesses but also a free enterprise system. You will learn some of the ways that businesses help their people determine the right thing to do.

As you study Part Two, you will see the various business players and the roles they play. You will appreciate the importance of sound, ethical decision making. And you will see, in even greater depth, the dynamic and integrated nature of business actions.

5

Decision Makers and Decision Making

Why would they do it? Why would Coca-Cola and Pepsi both make the strategic decisions to introduce new flavors of their flagship brands? Aren't sufficient brands already on the market? Coke has Coca-Cola Classic, Diet Coke, Cherry Coke, Sprite, Mellow Yellow, and a bevy of varieties of those brands, including those that are caffeine-free. Pepsi has a similar lineup, with Pepsi, Diet Pepsi, Pepsi One, Wild Cherry Pepsi, Pepsi Twist, Mountain Dew, and varieties of those brands. Why decide to add yet another flavor? Yet both companies announced new entries in May 2002. Coke introduced Vanilla Coke, and Pepsi introduced Pepsi Blue, a berry-flavored soft drink that some say is the color of Windex.

Both companies reached their strategic decisions as a result of careful analysis of the competition as well as their own brands. Significant in that analysis is the fact that overall soft-drink sales increased only 0.6 percent in 2001 and the traditional brands actually declined in sales. Thus, the companies needed to do whatever possible to increase growth in their core markets.

The decisions to introduce new brands were made carefully. The intense competition within the soft-drink industry is only part of the story. An additional factor is that customers are switching to juices and bottled water. Of course, some of the water and juice brands are also owned by Coke and Pepsi. Still, they cannot afford to let their cola-based soft-drink brands decline.

As part of their decision-making process, the companies did substantial market research aimed at the teen market. They did taste tests, considered bottle designs, and developed marketing plans. All this research required decision-making tasks and took considerable amounts of time. Time will tell whether the decisions were good or not.[1]

In Chapter 1, we made the case that there is a need for business leadership in today's business environment. That need has become more evident in recent years. The collapse of the dot-com industry; the tragedies of September 11, 2001; and the recession of 2001–2002 have created challenges that contemporary managers had not previously experienced. In addition, the activities of Enron, Andersen, Global Crossing, and others have made the role of executives of organizations both more suspect in the eyes of the public and more critical to the survival of business organizations. The public is increasingly expecting managers to act in an ethical manner and make decisions that ensure the long-run vitality of the companies.

In this chapter, we will examine decision makers—the leaders of businesses and other organizations—and the challenges they face. We look at the different types of decision makers and the kinds of decisions they make. You will see how people go about making decisions. As you read this chapter, keep in mind the kinds of decisions that you personally make and how you go about making those decisions.

After studying this chapter, you should be able to:

1. Identify major decision makers in an organization.
2. Understand the decision-making responsibilities of various people within a business.
3. Analyze and explain the benefits of teams in decision making.
4. Discuss decision making in large versus small businesses.
5. Describe the types of decisions managers make.
6. Understand and apply the basic decision-making process.
7. Use the creative decision-making model to generate solutions to problems.
8. Get a feel for how decisions are made in crisis situations.

Business is about decision making. Nothing can get done in a business without someone making a decision. Decisions range from major strategic decisions such as buying a subsidiary, introducing a totally new product line, or possibly even selling the business itself, to very mundane decisions, such as buying office supplies for a department. But the decision-making process is essentially the same regardless of the magnitude of the decision and the location of the decision makers in the organization.

This entire book is about decision making in business settings. It is about people making decisions, gathering information, committing resources, deciding what products or services to provide to customers, and predicting how the business will perform. Managers have to consider the many factors that affect their decisions. They have to study how their decisions will be influenced by forces beyond their control. They have to set goals, and they have to collect information before making decisions. Managers of businesses must make sure their decisions maintain or improve the health of the business.

The significance of studying decision makers and decision making is apparent when you look at the model (Figure 2.1) that is the basis of this book. Note that every aspect of the model requires decisions by managers. The key word here is *managers.* Managers make the most significant decisions in a business. The decisions the managers make determine how the business will perform when measured against the indicators of business success. Managers monitor the environment. They determine the direction of the company, acquire resources, provide value to customers, gain the commitment of workers, and assure that technology and quality are integrated into products or services. With this awareness in mind, we'll look at who the decision makers are and how they make decisions.

Who Are the Decision Makers in Business?

In Chapter 3, we discussed who *owns* businesses. In considering how businesses operate, knowing who *manages* them may be even more important. As you will see in this chapter, the decision makers are not always the same as the owners. This section discusses the various decision makers that are important in the actual management of the company. These decision makers are shown in Table 5.1.

Stockholders

Stockholders are the owners of corporations. It might seem logical that stockholders would also be actively involved in the management of the firm. However, this is seldom the case, especially for large corporations. Stockholders almost never take an active role in a company. They buy and sell their stock, and they may vote on major issues at the annual meeting. They also elect members of the board of directors, although this vote is much more of a formality than one might expect because the existing board nominates new members. Other than these token tasks, stockholders do not make decisions for the company.

   Thus, the role of stockholders is very limited in large corporations unless one person or group owns a significant proportion of the stock. A large ownership allows the key stockholder to play a major role in the selection of board members. In smaller, privately held corporations, stockholders may play a role in managing the firm, usually because they are key managers or family members rather than because they are stockholders.

TABLE 5.1

Decision Makers and Their Responsibilities

Stockholders	• May vote on major decisions. • Generally, have limited involvement.
Board of directors	• Approves major strategic decisions. • Oversees general direction of the business.
Top management	• Makes major strategic decisions.
Middle management	• Implements top management decisions. • Makes decisions within area of responsibility.
Professional staff	• Makes decisions in area of expertise.
First-line supervisors	• Implement higher-level decisions. • Make day-to-day operational decisions.
Nonmanagerial employees	• Make decisions regarding performance of their individual jobs.

Board of Directors

The **board of directors** is elected by the stockholders to oversee the management of the firm. The actual role the board members play depends on the company, particularly the size of the company. In small companies, the directors may be the owners of the firm, and they may be active in day-to-day management. In larger, publicly held companies, the directors perform a strategic role of helping top managers determine the overall direction of the company. However, it is the top managers who make most key decisions.

Boards of directors often meet monthly or quarterly. The meeting may last one or two days and may consist of hearing reports of top management and then discussing and voting on recommendations for major strategic items.

There are no requirements regarding how many board members a company should have. Many large companies have 8 to 15 board members. Some of these members are **inside directors,** meaning that they are also employees of the company. The remainder are **outside directors,** meaning that they are not employed by the company. Often they are active or retired executives of other large but noncompeting businesses. Typically, they are paid (and often paid quite well) for serving on the board. Profile 5.1 shows the members of the board of directors for Dell.

> **board of directors**
> The individuals elected by the stockholders to oversee the management of the firm.

> **inside directors**
> Directors who are also company employees.

> **outside directors**
> Directors who are not company employees.

DELL'S BOARD OF DIRECTORS   PROFILE 5.1

Dell's board of directors is somewhat typical of boards of large companies. Michael Dell is the only inside director—somewhat unusual, but desirable. Look at the outside directors. These individuals were chosen to give the company expertise that may help in determining Dell's future direction. Some of the board members are from financial companies. Others are from well-known companies or organizations and have a wealth of experience in managing large entities. The list below includes the board members' current associations and the board committees they serve on. These committees help ensure that the company's dealings are above reproach, help select new board members, and help make major financial decisions.

Michael S. Dell
Chairman of the Board and Chief Executive Officer
Dell Computer Corporation
No board committees

Donald J. Carty
Chairman of the Board and Chief Executive Officer
AMR Corporation and American Airlines Inc.
Audit

William H. Gray III
President and Chief Executive Officer
United Negro College Fund
Audit, Nominating

Michael H. Jordan
Former Chairman of the Board and Chief Executive Officer
CBS Corporation
Compensation, Finance

Judy C. Lewent
Executive Vice President and Chief Financial Officer
Merck & Co. Inc.
Finance

Thomas W. Luce III
Partner
Luce & Williams, Ltd.
Audit

Klaus S. Luft
Owner and President
MATCH—Market Access for Technology Services GmbH
Vice Chairman and International Advisor
Goldman Sachs Europe Limited
Finance

Alex J. Mandl
Former Chairman and Chief Executive Officer
Teligent, Inc.
Finance

Michael A. Miles
Special Limited Partner
Forstmann Little and Co.
Former Chairman of the Board and Chief Executive Officer
Philip Morris Companies Inc.
Compensation, Nominating

Samuel A. Nunn
Former U.S. Senator
Current Senior Partner
King & Spalding
Audit, Nominating

Morton L. Topfer
Former Vice Chairman
Dell
Managing Director
Castletop Capital
Finance

Source: Dell website, www.dell.com (accessed September 13, 2002).

Regardless of the size of the company or the size of the board, the decisions the board makes are of strategic significance. These decisions will affect the direction of the firm, its culture, and its goals. Although these decisions will be implemented at lower levels in the firm, their impact is significant. In fact, the activities of some well-known companies in recent years leads many critics to believe that boards of directors should take a more active role in the oversight of companies. Many analysts feel that the board should serve as the corporate conscience of the company, making sure that the firm's activities are ethical and legal.

Top Management

Top management refers to the officers of a business who make major decisions for the company and are responsible for the company's performance. The number of positions depends on the size of the firm. For example, a small business may have only one person in top management—the owner, who is also typically the president. Slightly larger firms may have a president (again, often the owner) plus a few vice presidents. Corporations may have a chair of the board of directors plus a president and some vice presidents. At the very top of most large companies are four critical positions: chief executive officer (CEO), chief operating officer (COO), chief financial officer (CFO), and chief information officer (CIO).

The **chief executive officer** is responsible for the long-range, strategic direction of the company. The CEO will work closely with the board of directors and also with external constituencies. This decision maker's focus is on *external* forces on the company as well as the impact the company has on various stakeholders. The **chief operating officer** is responsible for the *internal,* day-to-day workings of the company. Although the CEO and COO will work together, the COO will typically spend more time interacting with other top managers within the company, such as the executive vice president, the vice presidents, and high-level staff employees. The **chief financial officer** is responsible for the company's financial health and strategy. The CFO recommends the proportion of debt and equity the company should use in the future. As part of the necessary financial analysis, the CFO works with financial institutions, the financial committee of the board of directors, and of course the CEO and COO. Finally, the **chief information officer** is in charge of policies relating to the gathering, use, and storage of the firm's information. The CIO will work with staff representatives to determine the optimal arrangement of computer hardware and software, the frequency of upgrading equipment, and even such things as setting policy on use and transmittal of e-mail.

The top positions are not necessarily held by four different people. At Dell, Michael Dell holds the positions of chairman of the board and chief executive officer and Kevin Rollins is president and chief operating officer. At Best Buy, Richard Schulze is the founder and chairman of the board. Bradbury Anderson is chief executive officer, and Allen Lensmeier is president and chief operating officer. At Southwest Airlines, Herb Kelleher is chairman of the board, James Parker is vice chairman and chief executive officer, and Colleen Barrett is president, chief operating officer, and corporate secretary.

Regardless of the particular structure of top management, the people in these positions make decisions that are of major importance to the company. Examples include underwriting major new-product introductions, acquiring or selling subsidiaries, issuing stock, and helping set the strategic direction for the firm. All these decisions may involve millions of dollars of capital and equipment.

A **vice president** is a top manager who generally has responsibility for a specific area of the company. For example, a company may have vice presidents for marketing, finance, operations, and human resources. Other companies may have vice presidents in charge of particular products or geographic areas. It is common for the vice president of

---

top management
The officers of a business who make major decisions for the company and are responsible for the company's performance.

chief executive officer
The individual responsible for the long-range, strategic direction of the company.

chief operating officer
The individual responsible for a company's internal day-to-day operations.

chief financial officer
The individual responsible for the overall financial health and strategy of a company.

chief information officer
The individual in charge of policy relating to the gathering, use, and storage of company information.

vice president
A top manager who is responsible for a specific area of the company.

FIGURE 5.1

Typical Top Management Positions

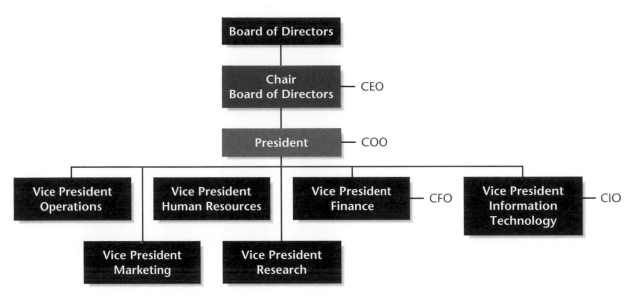

finance to be the chief financial officer of the business. Figure 5.1 presents the typical top management positions. In some companies, two or more vice presidents will report to an executive vice president, who then reports to the president. This is the case at Best Buy, as shown in Profile 5.2.

PROFILE 5.2   BEST BUY'S TOP MANAGEMENT

Best Buy's top management structure recognizes the different aspects of the overall company. From the list, you will see that Richard Schulze is founder and chairman, while Bradbury Anderson is CEO. Both of them have responsibilities for the overall strategic direction of the company. Allen Lenzmeier, president and COO, has overall responsibility for the internal workings of the company. Below them are several other individuals, many of whom are listed as president of either a division or a function within the company. For example, Kevin Freeland is president of Musicland, one of the Best Buy subsidiaries. Marc Gordon is CIO, the chief information officer, in charge of ensuring that information is communicated effectively throughout the organization. John Walden, who is now the executive vice president of human capital and leadership, was previously president of BestBuy.com. It is not unusual for large companies to have several presidents of subsidiaries or functional areas among the officers of the overall company.

Richard M. Schulze
Founder and Chairman

Bradbury H. Anderson
Vice Chairman and CEO

Allen Lenzmeier
President and COO

Michael Kesky
President, Best Buy Stores

Wade R. Fenn
President, Business Development and Strategic Alliances

Philip Schoonover
Executive Vice President, Business Development

Kevin Freeland
President, Musicland

Marc Gordon
Chief Information Officer

Darren Jackson
Chief Financial Officer

Jim Tweten
President, Magnolia Hi-Fi

John Walden
Executive Vice President, Human Capital and Leadership

Source: Best Buy website, www.bestbuy.com (accessed September 13, 2002).

Middle Managers

Decision makers with positions of vice president and higher are typically considered top management. Managers who work at levels from just below vice president down to just above first-line supervisors are referred to as **middle managers.** These people have direct supervisory responsibility over other managers or employees and have significant decision-making authority.

Let's think for a moment about middle managers and what they really do. Middle managers are responsible for translating broad policies and strategies into doable tasks. They receive orders from their own superiors and then must divide those orders into parts for each of their areas to accomplish. They spend much of their time in meetings with their subordinates to explain and gain commitment to plans set forth by their own superiors.

Middle managers sometimes find themselves in difficult situations, particularly in today's world. They depend heavily on those who work for them to achieve the goals that they and their superiors have set. But sometimes those goals were dictated to the middle manager because of the situation at hand—the competitive environment, the wishes of the company's top management, or pressure from outsiders. Middle managers are often held accountable for achieving challenging goals they did not have free rein in

> **middle managers**
> Managers below vice presidents down to just above first-line supervisors; they are responsible for translating broad policies into doable tasks.

developing. At the same time, they may not have been given sufficient resources or have enough latitude in their authority to meet those goals. In addition, subordinates often have demands or requests that middle managers must consider.

Professional Staff

Accountants, market researchers, design engineers, computer analysts, attorneys, and human resources representatives are a few of the hundreds of jobs that are categorized as professional staff. **Professional staff** make decisions within their area of specialty that provide information and advice so other managers and employees can do their jobs. Staff positions illustrate the interrelated nature of most business jobs. The staff employee may spend considerable time interacting with customers, employees, and/or suppliers.

Consider two examples of staff positions. First is Pat, an apparel buyer for a major department store in Los Angeles. She must interact with managers to determine the types and quantities of goods to be carried in the store. She must also work with suppliers to make the needed purchases at the best price. Pat's decisions will affect the company's sales, expenses, and profits.

Second is Kelly, a staff employee in the marketing department of an electronics manufacturer. She has been charged with creating the marketing program for a newly developed camera. Kelly must interact with other marketing professionals to understand the scope of the marketing program. But she must work with her own manager to find out how much money is budgeted for the project. The human resources department will be involved, since more copywriters and artists may need to be hired. The production managers will need to give her input on unique features of the camera to include in her advertising. Both Pat's and Kelly's jobs can be done successfully only if they work with other key people who will affect their projects.

> **professional staff**
> Employees who make decisions within their area of specialty that assist others in doing their jobs.

> **first-line supervisors**
> The lowest level of management; they are directly responsible for overseeing the work of employees who produce products or provide services.

First-Line Supervisors

First-line supervisors are the lowest level of management and are directly responsible for overseeing the work of employees who produce products or provide services. The specific titles of these managers vary broadly from industry to industry. In manufacturing businesses, duties of first-line supervisors include coordinating the arrival of component products, coordinating the flow down an assembly line, motivating workers to produce at their best, and completing paperwork necessary to inform higher managers. In service or retail businesses, the first-line supervisor may oversee the activities of the sales force, make sure inventory is ordered and properly displayed, and deal with special customer problems that other workers have trouble handling.

Supervisors are the direct link between the bulk of the workforce and higher management. Accordingly, they must be able to understand, talk with, support, motivate, and gain the confidence of the workers who are actually creating and selling products and providing services. Supervisors must also understand where their areas are headed and be able to represent their areas clearly and decisively with middle managers. They must be able to translate management directives to the workforce and translate workplace needs and issues to management. Supervisor positions are a key link between management and other employees and are considered by many to be among the most important positions because they are responsible for the actual production of goods or provision of services.

Staff workers are experts in their particular area. Their power over others may be limited to their specific area of expertise. Can this be a source of conflict among departments in an organization?

First-line supervisors may be college graduates with advanced degrees, or they may have only a high school or trade school diploma. In their narrow area of expertise, they can provide valuable input to higher levels of management.

Nonmanagerial Employees

The employees in a business who are actually involved in producing or selling products or providing a service are referred to as **nonmanagerial employees.** They have the most direct responsibility for the product or service. Thus their work is critical to the success of the company. Nonmanagerial employees may work on an assembly line or in an auto mechanic shop. They may work at a computer or travel extensively, selling products to retailers. They may perform highly skilled professional tasks, such as psychological counseling. Teachers in kindergarten, instructors in a community college, and professors in a university are all nonmanagerial workers because they provide a service directly to students.

> **nonmanagerial employees**
> Employees in a business who are actually involved in producing or selling products and providing services.

As these examples show, the term *nonmanagerial* has nothing to do with an employee's skill or education. Nor is there any relationship among the tasks that different nonmanagerial employees do. Both the auto mechanic and the teacher are nonmanagerial employees because they have direct responsibility for the product or service. There is also no relationship between pay rate or payroll method and whether or not the job is managerial. Some nonmanagerial employees are paid minimum wage on an hourly basis. Others are paid a monthly salary that may exceed $100,000 a year.

The reason nonmanagerial employees are so critical is that their decisions and actions directly affect the customer's future trade with the company. They can make the difference between a satisfied customer and a dissatisfied one. In a manufacturing

Dennis Wickersham is a mechanic at Doyle Automotive, an independent car repair shop. He is well respected as an expert in analyzing problems with cars and making decisions regarding what is necessary to repair them. How would decisions he makes differ if he were a part of management?

company, they determine the quality of a given product regardless of top management's actions. In a hospital setting, they can be the key to patient comfort. In a college setting, they are the difference between high enrollment in a class and low enrollment. If the nonmanagerial employee does not do a good job, the customer is likely to go elsewhere. Many companies today, in an effort to demonstrate the critical contribution of these employees, are referring to them as "associates."

You may not have thought of nonmanagerial employees as decision makers. However, as these examples show, they make important decisions every day that affect the business and its operations. Further, there is a movement in business today to give nonmanagerial employees more decision-making power. This movement, called empowerment, involves transferring decision-making authority and responsibility from management to employees at lower levels of the business. Logically, nonmanagerial employees are not empowered to make all decisions. Rather, they make decisions in areas where they have special experience and skill. In other words, these workers have the background they need to make decisions that contribute to the business in meaningful ways.

Teams

Teams exist at many levels of organizations. Top management, as discussed in the previous section, operates as a team. Even though many different positions exist and each has specific responsibilities, most key decisions are made by members of top management operating as a team. In this way, all members of top management are involved in the decision-making process and all know what the decisions are. This arrangement aids in the implementation of those decisions consistently throughout the company.

Teams also are used in middle management and staff positions. In some cases, teams will be specially appointed committees or work groups that work to solve specific problems. In other cases, teams will be ongoing and will work closely together over time.

In addition, many companies have empowered nonmanagerial employees with decision-making responsibilities by placing them in teams that make decisions about the work that is to be done. A typical example is seen in the manufacturing operations of a carmaker that has a team of workers build an engine. The team may be responsible for all assembly activities, including testing and verifying the quality of the engine once it is assembled.

Two types of teams are increasingly popular: self-directed work teams and cross-functional teams. In a **self-directed work team,** team members supervise their own work and are given broad discretion over the direction of their work. As you can see, managers depend on and place high expectations on these teams. Team decisions can have a major impact on the success of the business.

In a **cross-functional team,** members are selected from various areas of the business and brought together to make collective decisions. They, too, may have wide decision-making discretion. Why is this form of team arrangement so relevant today? Businesses are recognizing the importance of the same integrative themes we are stressing in this book. Many key decisions are not just production decisions or marketing decisions or engineering decisions or accounting decisions. Rather, they are complex decisions that should

---

self-directed work team
A group of employees who supervise their own work and are given broad discretion over the direction of their work.

cross-functional team
A group of employees who are selected from various areas of the business and brought together to make collective decisions.

THINK ABOUT THIS

1. What kinds of problems do you think a business might encounter if the same person is the president, CEO, and chair of the board of directors? What advantages might this arrangement provide?

2. We have noted that the first-line supervisor is in a critical position in the business. Why is this so?

3. Consider the position of a neurosurgeon working in a large hospital. Obviously, the surgeon is highly educated and makes life-or-death decisions daily. Yet this surgeon is a nonmanagerial employee. Why?

This team from Meyocks & Priebe Advertising of West Des Moines, Iowa encourages constructive controversy. During team meetings, employees are encouraged to evaluate ideas crtically, and ensure that dominant participants do not overwhelm what can be very spirited meetings. How might this type of "exchange of ideas" get out of hand? What must the team guard against when criticizing?

TABLE 5.2
Advantages of Teams

- Bring together talented people from various areas of the business.
- Break departmental barriers, allowing quicker action.
- Focus on customer service and quality.
- Promote employee involvement and commitment.
- Provide an excellent source of creativity and innovation.

consider expertise and input from many areas and levels of the business. Bringing representatives from each area together to function as a team allows all members, through open discussion, to understand more clearly the needs and concerns of the other areas. Ideally, a better set of decisions will emerge and customers will be better served.

Teams are a very popular form of work arrangement today, thanks to the advantages businesses can gain through the use of well-run teams. Let's consider just a few of the possible gains, as shown in Table 5.2. First, teams bring together talented people from throughout the business. Second, the business can break departmental barriers and get action taken in a timely manner. Third, by focusing on customer service and quality as their overriding goals, teams further these initiatives. In some businesses, team members are even rewarded for the team's contributions to service and quality. Fourth, teams encourage and depend on employees' getting involved in decision making. Workers recognize they have the chance to use their background and talents to make a difference. Often this opportunity helps build employee commitment. Finally, teams are an excellent source of creativity and innovation. When teams are empowered to approach problems in ways that seem best to them, wonderful new approaches and ideas can emerge. As you can see, teams can be an excellent vehicle for fostering the indicators of a successful business.[2]

Interrelationships among Positions

The interrelationships among positions in a business can be thought of as the threads of a giant spiderweb. Each position in the business is an intersection in that web. Thus any task accomplished by one person at one location in the web will affect and be affected by several other members of the organization.

Consider the position of the manager of product development, shown in Figure 5.2. This manager interacts directly with the vice president of research and development and, indirectly, with the president. There is also interaction with other vice presidents regarding issues affecting them. The manager has virtually constant interaction with clerical staff and colleagues in the product design department. But interaction also takes place with people in production, finance, marketing, and human resources, because the characteristics of a new product must be acceptable to those who will produce it, finance it, ship it, store it, and sell it. Product development will also receive input from the basic research department and the testing department. Assuming the product development is successful, the human resources department will be involved in hiring and training employees to produce and sell the product.

Note in Figure 5.2 that only a few of the lines represent **chain of command,** the line of authority that determines the movement of official commands down through the hierarchy of the organization. The rest of the lines are coordinative. For example, individuals within product development must coordinate with those in marketing and production and other areas to produce a product that is best for the customer.

The position of a product development manager is perhaps one of the best to illustrate the dynamic relationship among the positions in a company. Yet all positions interact to some degree. Though positions at the very bottom of an organization rarely

chain of command
The line of authority in a business that determines the movement of official commands down through the hierarchy.

FIGURE 5.2

Relationships among Positions

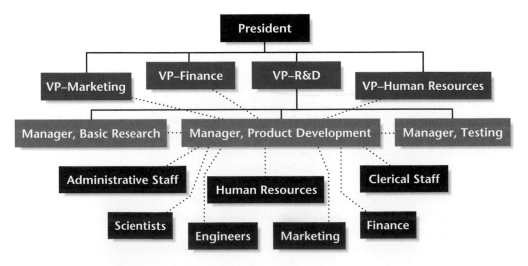

interact with those at high levels, and the president of a large corporation rarely interacts directly with those several layers down, the impact of the president reaches throughout the organization. And even those on the lowest rung interact with their co-workers, their immediate supervisors, and various support staff.

Differences between Large and Small Businesses

The set of interrelated decisions that must be made becomes more complex as the business grows larger. For example, a large organization may have dozens of vice presidents or division presidents. The operating management of General Electric, for example, has 26 people with titles of senior vice president or president or CEO of one of GE's many divisions.[3] In addition to those 26 is the vast number of vice presidents of units within divisions or subsidiaries. A medium-size business, however, may have only a handful of vice presidents, and a very small business may have none.

In a large organization, a vice president may have a very specific set of responsibilities, such as vice president for customer relations. In a smaller company, a vice president may have multiple formal responsibilities, such as vice president of human resources and public relations. The actual tasks performed in small companies are often even broader than the title suggests. A person may be vice president of human resources but may perform duties encompassing human resources, labor relations, customer service, and public relations, as well as serving as the company representative to the local United Way.

Even top managers who have joined a small company with specific skills and talents find that their duties span a number of areas. Hence, the manager of, say, marketing needs to be reasonably well versed in finance and human resources as well. This situation is different from that in a large company, where top managers are much more likely to be specialists.

Construction is a good example of decision making by teams. Construction teams develop the ability to work together to make the pieces of a project fit together. They often have a keen sense of knowing what needs to be done and when, and can make decisions with a minimum of effort. What other examples can you think of where teams work so closely together that decision making seems effortless?

A vice president of a small firm may also perform many of the duties that staff-level individuals would do in a larger firm. For example, in a small company, the VP of human resources may actually interview job applicants. In a large company, the VP of human resources has only general oversight responsibilities for recruiting and may be unaware of who is being interviewed or perhaps even which positions are being filled.

In small companies, a greater percentage of workers may be considered nonmanagerial—that is, directly involved in providing the product or service. As a company grows, it tends to become more top-heavy, with more people in staff and management positions.

Finally, small businesses differ from larger ones in a very important way: how decisions are made. Large businesses tend to be very deliberative. They study issues carefully (sometimes for too long). Committees or teams or task forces are charged with investigating a problem or opportunity and reporting back to some higher level. Decisions often have to go through several layers of management. Small businesses often make decisions faster because they have fewer levels of management and fewer specialists in staff positions. Thus they can adapt quickly to changing environments. Of course, it also means that small business managers may make incorrect decisions sometimes because there has not been sufficient input or analysis in the decision process.

Decision Makers in Not-for-Profit Organizations

Earlier we discussed the various decision makers within a business and the interactions among them. Nonprofit organizations may have somewhat similar structures. Just as there are wide varieties of businesses, there are wide varieties of not-for-profit organizations. A large hospital may be a not-for-profit organization, as are most universities. The United Way and the American Cancer Society are quite large organizations with many paid employees. At the opposite extreme is a local neighborhood development group with no paid employees at all.

A primary difference between a business and a nonprofit organization is the ownership and top management. Businesses are usually owned by individuals, either directly or through stock. Not-for-profit organizations have no such ownership. No one "owns" a nonprofit. They do have top management in the form of a board of directors, although it is almost always a volunteer board. Large nonprofit organizations may have a president, a full set of vice presidents, and many paid staff employees. Smaller nonprofits may have only an executive director and perhaps a secretary as paid staff. Volunteers handle all other work.

THINK ABOUT THIS

1. How large should a business be before adding a new layer of management?

2. There are many benefits from using teams. How large should a team be? If we use cross-functional teams, how do we decide which areas should be represented?

3. Decision making may be faster, yet riskier, in small businesses than in large ones. Explain why this is so.

The Decision-Making Process

So far in this chapter we have discussed who the decision makers are in an organization. We now turn to the process of making decisions and to the various factors that influence how decisions are made. We look first at the types of decisions that are made in businesses and then at the actual decision-making process.

As we've said before, business is about decision making. Indeed, much of every employee's time is spent making some kind of decision. Some decisions are critical, have a long-term impact on the firm, and are made only after months of careful study. Other decisions are relatively simple, such as which kind of label to put on a carton before it is shipped, and can be made quickly.

Consider the following example of rapid decision making. A bar-coding facility for the U.S. Postal Service puts bar codes on letters whose zip codes were not readable by scanners. An employee sits at a machine for hours at a time, looking at envelopes as they move through the machine at about one envelope per second. The employee's job is to look at the zip code, decide what it really is, and enter the code into the machine, which then applies a bar code to the envelope for mailing. Thus, the employee of the bar-coding facility makes one decision per second. These certainly are not high-level decisions, but they are, nevertheless, decisions.

Types of Decisions

Managers and other employees make many types of decisions. We consider three types here: strategic, operational, and problem-solving decisions.

Strategic Decisions

Strategic decisions are those that have a major impact on the general direction of the firm. These decisions are often carefully considered and may involve millions of dollars of investment. They may change the way a business competes. They may involve the introduction of new products or the acquisition of another company. They may require hiring hundreds of employees or laying off thousands. Perhaps the most extreme of all is the decision to sell or close the business. The characteristics of strategic decisions are shown in Table 5.3.

The most significant characteristics in Table 5.3 are that strategic decisions have long-range impact and are made by top management. Others in the organization will have input, but the magnitude of the decision dictates that managers at the very highest level be involved. Strategic decisions involve a structured, analytical process that considers as much information as can possibly be gained. These decisions are typically made slowly, after careful study.

For an example of a strategic decision, consider Southwest Airlines. Southwest was started as a regional airline flying point-to-point routes rather than using hubs. It grew slowly until it was flying to selected cities in the United States even though the key routes were still in the Southwest or connected to cities in the Southwest. Part of Southwest's strategy has always been to fly short hauls into the less-used airports of major cities, such as Love Field (Dallas), Midway (Chicago), and Providence (Boston). In 2002, Southwest Airlines made the strategic decision to offer nonstop, coast-to-coast service for the first

strategic decisions
Decisions that have a major impact on the general direction of the firm.

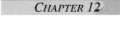

• Have long-range impact.
• Require careful analysis of the firm and its environment.
• Are often the result of a strategic planning process.
• May involve millions of dollars.
• Are designed to capture opportunities or offset competitive weaknesses.
• Involve top management, including board of directors.

TABLE 5.3

Characteristics of Strategic Decisions

time. This decision had both potential and risk. With its budget fare approach, Southwest could take business away from other airlines. On the other hand, the decision could ignite airfare wars with other airlines. To reduce the chances of angering competitors, Southwest decided to move slowly on these long hauls and keep a relatively low profile.[4]

Operational Decisions

operational decisions
Decisions that affect the day-to-day actions of the business.

Operational decisions are those that affect the day-to-day actions of the business. Characteristics of operational decisions are shown in Table 5.4. Operational decisions may or may not involve large amounts of capital, but they tend to deal with specific situations and are made by managers who have considerable experience in the area affected by the decision. Operational decisions might include the volume of products to be produced this month, the selection of a new supplier to replace one whose quality is unacceptable, the selection of new employees to replace those who have left the company or who have been promoted, the amount of money to be budgeted for maintenance of equipment, or the selection of TV stations on which to advertise.

Another characteristic is that operational decisions are frequently made within the boundaries of established policies and procedures. *Standard operating procedures (SOPs)* are often in place to guide the decision making. This structure eases the decision-making process. It means that managers do not need to do a significant study of the situation each time a new decision must be made. Only those decisions that fall outside the purview of the SOP need substantial amounts of analysis.

Problem-Solving Decisions

problem solving
Decision making aimed at correcting an adverse situation that has developed.

Problem solving is decision making aimed at correcting an adverse situation that has developed. The orientation of problem solving is how to fix something that is wrong. Examples abound. A company whose die-stamping machine just broke down is in a problem-solving mode because it cannot use the machine. A key staff employee decides to leave the company abruptly, and the company is left with no one who knows how to do billing correctly. Two employees who previously were cooperative suddenly argue constantly. A firm's accountant presents a department manager with information suggesting that the department's telephone expenses were over budget by 25 percent.

The common element of each of these examples is that the situation is some adverse deviation from the norm. Table 5.5 shows some of the characteristics of problem-solving decisions. Problems to be solved are sometimes of crisis proportions and sometimes minor. The key to problem solving is to reach a decision that leaves the organization in the best possible position, given the situation at hand. The task is to analyze the situation as carefully, but quickly, as possible and find a solution to the problem that is acceptable to all involved.

In some cases, there are no good solutions. Most experienced managers know that occasionally a situation arises that simply cannot be completely resolved. Here the manager must carefully decide which of a set of poor alternatives comes closest to solv-

TABLE 5.4

Characteristics of Operational Decisions

- May or may not involve large amounts of capital.
- Deal with specific situations within an organization.
- Are made by experienced managers in the area.
- Often have standard operating procedures available to guide decision making.
- Require less analysis than strategic decisions do.

- Are aimed at correcting a deviation from normal operations.
- May involve a minor problem or one of crisis proportions.
- Often need to be made quickly while still offering solutions acceptable to all involved.
- May have no easy solutions.

TABLE 5.5

Characteristics of Problem-Solving Decisions

ing the problem, knowing that not everyone will be happy. This situation is unfortunate, but it is the reality of the workplace. For example, suppose your company has a hiring freeze; top management has dictated that absolutely no new employees will be hired. One of your long-time workers decides to take early retirement, thus creating a void in your department. Work will have to be spread among the remaining workers. But the reality is that you will not get a replacement and you must simply live with the problem. You are forced to reallocate work among existing employees to take up the slack.

Sometimes the best decision is to leave the problem unresolved with the hope that conditions may change. For example, suppose you work in a job that requires you to spend hours each day working on a computer. Your computer seems to be increasingly slow and locks up more often than it should. You report this problem to your supervisor, indicating your frustration with the computer. The supervisor could turn in a repair request immediately to have your computer fixed, but your entire department is scheduled to get new computers in two months. Thus, it does not make sense to have your computer repaired. You are told to keep using it, back up files frequently, and hope it doesn't crash completely before the new computers arrive.

A Basic Decision-Making Model

Figure 5.3 shows a simplified model of the decision making process. This model is essentially the same regardless of the type of decision being made. In some cases, the

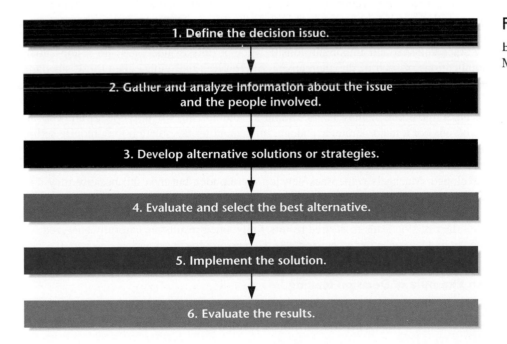

FIGURE 5.3

Basic Decision-Making Model

terminology may change, but the overall process is similar. This process entails six steps.

The first step is to *define the decision issue.* This process can be more difficult than it may appear. Sometimes the real issue is hidden and must be uncovered. It is often difficult to separate the real problem from the symptoms of the problem. Generally, managers must spend a fair amount of time in this first step. Only when we know what the issue really is can we start to address it.

The second step is to *gather information about the issue and the people involved.* If the decision is of a strategic nature, we need to gather as much information about the industry, the competitors, and other parts of the environment as possible. If it is a problem-solving decision, we must gather information about the situation to be objective.

If we are dealing with a conflict, we try to gather as much information as we can about the problem, the people involved, and their motives. Sometimes the problem is more complex than it seems, and substantial study is required to ferret out the truth.

There is often a dilemma in the information-gathering stage. Most managers always want more information. This desire is logical because more information usually provides greater assurance that the right decision will be made. But gathering additional information takes time, effort, and perhaps money. Successful managers recognize that there must be a trade-off. Sometimes we have to step forward boldly and make the best decisions we can with the information available. Sometimes we can't wait for more information.

Once information is gathered, sifted through, and analyzed, managers are ready to begin the third step, *develop alternatives.* These alternatives may be strategies. They may be problem solutions. They may be choices of suppliers or a selection of advertising media or identification of which potential employees to bring back for additional interviews. Several alternatives should be considered. Some will be better than others. Some may seem good but might create other problems.

Once we have a number of alternatives in hand, we must *evaluate them and select the best one.* Sometimes that choice is based on simple judgment, but often detailed analysis will create a number of criteria that must be considered. For example, a strategy to increase sales might seem very good—until we look at the cost of gaining the sales. If the cost of the strategy is as high as the revenues generated, then the strategy is not justifiable.

An additional and important consideration in this evaluation stage is the ethical implications of each of the alternatives. Alternatives that violate the ethical standards and culture of the business should be rejected no matter how attractive they appear.

Next, we must *implement the selected alternative.* If the problem is small, implementing the solution may be as simple as announcing the decision to all who are involved. For a major strategic change, implementing the solution may require selling additional stock or getting a large bank loan. Such complex actions will take considerable time to complete. Alternatives must be implemented as carefully as they were developed. Managers sometimes develop a great idea but then fail because they do a poor job of implementation.

Finally, once a decision has been implemented, it is still necessary to *evaluate* how well the decision leads to desired results. Only when results are carefully analyzed can managers know whether a decision was the best one for the situation.

An Example of Decision Making

Let's consider an example of a decision a manager may face. Lisa is the manager of the customer service department of a large, upscale department store. Five customer service representatives report to her. She has just received reports that one of her people, Ken, has received an unusually high number of complaints. In fact, many customers have expressed dissatisfaction with the way Ken handles their problems. These complaints affect the overall rating of Lisa's unit and could affect their bonuses. Clearly, Lisa has to get to the bottom of this problem.

What exactly is the problem? Lisa begins to investigate. First, she looks at the situation to determine just how severe it is. In talking with other reps and with customers who were unhappy, she determines that the problem is severe enough that the store might actually lose customers because of it. Further, because of the store's policy of quality customer service, a problem of this magnitude cannot be tolerated.

Lisa then begins to study the people involved. Ken is 58 years old and has been with the company for over 25 years. He worked in the catalog department for many years and recently transferred into customer service. This is not the first time problems have surfaced regarding Ken in the six months he has been in Lisa's unit. Apparently he simply lacks the interpersonal skills needed to interact effectively with the public. The problem becomes clearer: Ken is receiving too many complaints because he has weak interpersonal skills.

What are the alternatives? First, Lisa could fire Ken. But that appears to be a drastic and perhaps even legally inappropriate approach for this worker. Although Ken has never been a star performer, he has always done acceptable work. Lisa doesn't think it would be fair or even ethical to dismiss a 25-year company veteran in this manner. Also, she doesn't want to risk his suing the company for age discrimination. A second alternative would be to invest in training to help Ken develop his interpersonal skills. Such training is expensive, and there is no assurance that Ken will change enough to work really well with customers. Finally, Lisa could transfer Ken back to the catalog area, where he did mostly data entry and did not interact directly with the public.

Lisa ponders these options and decides it might be wise to ask Ken what he thinks of the training and transfer options. To her surprise, Lisa learns that Ken does not really enjoy the customer service job; he took it only because he heard there was going to be some downsizing in the catalog area. Armed with this information, Lisa does some more checking. She finds that while reductions in the catalog area were considered at one time, catalog sales have grown substantially and no one will be let go now.

The solution is now evident to Lisa. She should transfer Ken back to the catalog area, where he did an adequate job. However, implementing that solution is not necessarily easy to do. First, there has to be an opening. Further, she wants to find a good person to replace Ken in customer service. After a few days Lisa learns that Maria, who works in catalog sales, would like to transfer to customer service. She is an outgoing, personable young woman who should be quite successful interacting with customers. All the pieces are now in place, and the switch is made.

This decision is a fairly simple example of the day-to-day sorts of issues that managers face. Yet even here you can see that the decision process can become quite involved. The process is often even more complex than the one shown here. Keep in mind that regardless of the level of complexity, the decision-making process remains essentially the same.

A Model of Creative Decision Making

The decision-making model described in Figure 5.3 presents a structured, logical approach to making the kinds of decisions that managers regularly face. This basic approach is based on research, information, and careful evaluation of that information.

Although the basic model is widely accepted, it has certain limitations. Sometimes the nature of the situation and the nature of the real problem are not clear. Sometimes managers do not possess enough information to evaluate alternatives logically. Sometimes obvious or available alternatives are simply not good enough. Sometimes totally new, unique, and unexpected solutions are needed. In short, today's business world is volatile and uncertain. Sometimes a business has to break out of the mold of basic decision making to get the edge on increasingly tough competition. In such cases, creative decision making is needed.

Creative decision making is a process of developing new or different ways to solve problems or capture opportunities. It requires a somewhat different pattern of thinking from rational decision making. The stages of creative decision making are shown in Figure 5.4.

The first stage of creative decision making is the *preparation stage.* Here we must recognize that the true problem may not be what appears at first blush. A decision maker may have to view a situation differently and look for new opportunities. This sensitivity comes not only from careful and reflective study, but also from being open to new perspectives. It is at this stage that new options, alternatives, and creative approaches are encouraged.

It is also important in this preparation stage to look for many possibilities and to defer judgment and evaluation. A popular technique used during this stage is *brainstorming,* where a team of people look at a problem and generate as many alternatives as possible for addressing it. Free association is encouraged. Criticism is forbidden. The goal is to expand possibilities, not limit them.

In short, the preparation stage works when existing assumptions and thought patterns can be suspended and new possibilities can be generated. This stage relies on the view that true creativity usually occurs when people take what is already known and look for new associations, new combinations, and new relationships.[5]

The second stage of creative decision making is known as the *incubation stage.* This stage requires the decision maker to take time to mull over what has been generated during the preparation stage. This is a subconscious mental activity. When a manager takes time simply to let all the information and possibilities sit for a while, the mind will rearrange and search for new linkages that make sense. Who knows what will emerge? Because this step cannot be programmed, nor can it be logically directed, it is a difficult step for many managers. Given the fast-paced nature of business and business decision making, it's hard to allow enough time for incubation to occur.

The third stage is the *illumination,* or *insight, stage.* It is here that a creative or novel idea is recognized. These are the flashes of insight that strike a manager, often in quite unex-

---

creative decision making

The process of developing new or different ways to solve problems or capture opportunities.

FIGURE 5.4

Creative Decision-Making Model

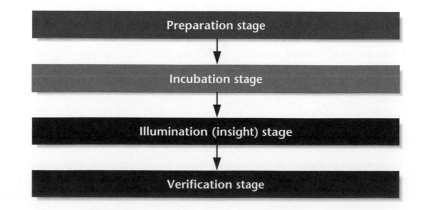

pected ways. In these "aha" experiences, a solution pops up or an idea suddenly comes together, seemingly out of nowhere. Although illumination may appear to be a stroke of unexpected insight, it comes from nonjudgmental preparation and open incubation.

The final step is the *verification stage*. Here the decision maker takes the creative idea and tests it to see if it makes sense. This step may involve talking through the solution with others or even conducting formal research to see if it has merit. It is probably impossible ever to feel completely sure that a creative idea will work, yet verification seeks to gain at least enough sense of acceptance that the manager is not going off the deep end with some wild scheme. This stage verifies that the risks involved in the decision are reasonable and acceptable.

Proposing novel solutions or alternatives may be exactly what the business needs in many situations. Yet formulating new and creative solutions is a difficult task. Many businesses realize that innovation demands developing solutions or alternatives that are *outside the box* and breaking from traditional alternatives. Such creativity can be encouraged in a number of ways. These will be addressed more fully in Chapter 19, when we discuss change and renewal.

> **More to Come**
> *Chapter 19*

Crisis Decision Making

We have discussed a basic decision-making model that can be used for making typical decisions within an organization. We also presented a model for creative decision making when a need arises for decisions based on fresh thinking and innovative ideas. Occasionally, however, a situation arises that does not allow for careful analysis or creativity. Instead, it calls for **crisis decision-making:** a bold response to a unique, unexpected, and potentially devastating situation. Consider the following examples: A fire destroys a critical part of a company's production process. A leak in a company's chemical plant spews toxic fumes into the community. A gunman bursts into the company's office and takes employees hostage. A customer who makes up a majority of your sales declares bankruptcy and shuts down operations virtually overnight. A terrorist bombs the firm's production facilities.

> **crisis decision-making**
> Decision making that requires a bold response to a unique, unexpected, and potentially devastating situation.

Crisis situations have four characteristics that dictate a different decision-making method. First, a short time frame usually exists. Thus, insufficient time is available to do a complete analysis to reach an optimal solution. Second, the situation is often highly visible. Managers must not only act quickly but also realize that many people are watching their decision-making process carefully to see what results will be achieved. A third characteristic is that the decision has significant consequences. A wrong choice may have ramifications that might cause widespread negative publicity or be highly costly. Finally, a crisis situation may be one where at least some risk of survival is at stake. Thus, the decision could become almost a life-and-death situation for the organization.

With these characteristics in mind, how does a manager go about making the best possible decision given the situation? Consider the following caveats, realizing that there may not be a really good answer:

1. The situation must be stabilized immediately, if possible, to prevent it from getting worse.

2. The decision should leave all interested parties no worse off than they currently are. Hopefully, all people involved will be better off, but they should at least not be hurt.

3. Determine whether contingency plans are in place to deal with at least part of the problem. Rarely will textbook answers be readily available, but contingency plans may at least give a starting point for development of a solution.

4. Every effort must be made to inform the company's stakeholders and to gather input for the decision if time permits.

5. Sometimes there is no good answer; in such a case, take the least bad answer.

6. If multiple alternatives exist that are acceptable, take the one that can most easily be changed later if necessary. Often managers simply do not know which solutions will work best because the situation may be in a state of flux. Yet some decision must be made even if it is not the optimal one in the long run. So the best choice may be a decision that does not lock the organization into a single course of action that cannot be changed at a later date.

As this discussion suggests, seldom will easy solutions be readily at hand. Managers must make the best possible decision as soon as they can to make changes to deal with the situation, but often they are working in uncharted territory.

Team Decision Making

We discussed earlier the trend in today's business toward empowerment, the moving of decisions to lower levels in organizations. These decisions are often made by teams. Team decisions tend to take longer to make than individual decisions, but they are often better decisions. More information is brought into the process, and the decisions are better supported by the group once they are made. Team decisions, especially for cross-functional teams, also help assure that the decisions will reflect the broader background of team participants.

More to Come
CHAPTER 16

Selecting team members is an important task. Participants may want team members with whom they feel comfortable, but this should not be the guiding criterion. Members should be selected because they have talents and backgrounds that the team needs to make decisions. This diversity may lead to differences of opinion and conflicts. A well-run team will use those conflicts, however, to spark the creativity that leads to new approaches. This creativity is one of the things that make the team approach so special.

For people to work effectively in teams, they must understand team goals. Members must practice active listening and open communications with one another. Divergent views must be explored to see how they can be used to reach a *team consensus.*

The primary disadvantage of team decision making is the time and effort required to make the decision. Some decisions simply do not need to be made by teams. Sometimes it's a good idea to have one person charged with making decisions for which there is likely to be little conflict. If the decision is not critical, the efficiency of individual decision making may outweigh the benefits of team decision making. As a manager, you must decide when a team effort is better than an individual decision.

THINK ABOUT THIS

1. Consider your decision to attend the college where you are now studying. Use the basic decision-making model in Figure 5.3 to trace how you made your choice.

2. Now use the same model to think about potential career choices. What types of information do you need? What do you need to know about yourself as part of the model?

Decision Making in an International Arena

We have discussed decision makers and decision making throughout this chapter. We presented a basic model of the decision-making process. These decision-making tasks become even more complex as a business operates in the international marketplace. Customs, laws, customer needs, international currencies, and governmental and political influences are additional factors that require attention by skilled decision makers. At times, international decisions create challenges when the ethics of one country differ from those of another.

Return to the model we presented in Figure 5.3. Data gathering is more difficult because of the distances between countries. Possible language barriers make interpreting information difficult. Analyzing the data is also more difficult because many additional points of view must be considered. We will discuss these complexities in more detail in subsequent chapters.

More to Come
CHAPTER 10

THE BIG PICTURE

We all make decisions. When you take your first job after graduation, your decisions may be limited in scope. You may, for example, be working in the computer systems department. Here, your decisions will undoubtedly be limited to the responsibilities within information technology. As time goes on and you are promoted a time or two, the decisions you make will be broader and have greater impact. They may also affect more than one department or area. However, even at the introductory level, your decisions do affect others. When you decide to walk down the hall and help a colleague from another area with a software problem, you are acting in a way that affects other areas. You are allowing a colleague (perhaps from a different department) to work more efficiently, and you are building rapport between your area and that of the colleague. Business decisions never occur in isolation, and they often have a more pervasive impact than we think.

Summary

1. Business is about decision making. Nothing can be done in a business without someone making a decision.

   • Who are the decision makers in business?

   The major categories of decision makers in business are stockholders, the board of directors, top managers, middle managers, members of the professional staff, first-line supervisors, and nonmanagerial workers.

2. Businesses are composed of individuals with varied responsibilities. It is important to understand the relationships among various decision makers for decisions to fit together for the benefit of the entire organization.

   • What are the decision-making responsibilities of the various people within a business?

   Stockholders buy and sell stock. They may also vote on major issues at annual meetings. The board of directors may actively assist top managers in making strategic decisions. The board may also review various aspects of company performance and policy and require corrective actions where necessary. Top management makes the major decisions for the company and is responsible for its performance. Middle managers are responsible for translating broad policies and strategies into doable tasks. Professional staff provide technical support and make decisions in specialty areas. First-line supervisors make decisions related to the direct management of nonmanagerial employees. Nonmanagerial employees make the hourly, daily, and weekly decisions needed in the process of actually producing the firm's product or providing its service.

3. Sometimes decisions are made by a single individual. But in recent years, businesses have increasingly turned to team decision making at all levels in an organization. This type of decision making is done by forming teams and giving them broad guidelines and the authority to make and implement decisions.

   • What are the benefits of team decision making?

   There are five major benefits: (1) Team members bring a variety of talents and perspectives to the business. (2) The business is able to break departmental barriers and get faster action. (3) Teams provide better customer service and higher quality. (4) Teams build employee commitment. (5) Teams are an excellent source of creativity and innovation.

4. Regardless of the size of a business, the basic decision-making process is the same, but the decisions differ depending on the size of the firm.

   • How does decision making differ between large and small businesses?

   There are four major differences: (1) Large businesses have many more decisions to make than do small businesses. (2) The interrelated decisions that have to be made by big businesses are more complex than those in small businesses. (3) Smaller companies tend to have a higher percentage of employees in nonmanagerial positions. Thus, more empowerment of employees may be present. (4) Decision making in large businesses tends to be very deliberative, whereas small businesses tend to make decisions more quickly.

5. Even though vast numbers of decisions are made in any business, it is possible to describe all decisions in terms of a few categories.

   • What are the main types of decisions that managers make?

   Strategic decisions are those decisions that have major, long-range impacts on the general direction of the company. They are made primarily by top management. Operational decisions are those that affect the day-to-day operation of the business. These decisions are often made by people who have experience in the specific area. Problem solving is decision making designed to correct problems that have arisen. Sometimes the solutions to problems are limited.

6. Managers of successful businesses engage in a never-ending cycle of decisions and actions. Regardless of the types of decisions being made, a similar process of decision making is used.

   • Describe the basic decision-making model presented in this chapter.

   The model consists of six steps: (1) Define the issue, (2) collect and analyze information about the issue and the people involved, (3) develop alternative solutions or strategies, (4) evaluate and select the best alternative, (5) implement the solution, and (6) evaluate the results.

7. When normal decision making simply does not provide the kind of decision that is best for a situation, a creative decision-making approach may yield better solutions.

   • Describe the model for creative decision making.

   The creative decision-making model has four stages: (1) preparation, (2) incubation, (3) illumination, and (4) verification. Creative decision making often uses brainstorming to generate ideas. Teams can often produce unique and creative outcomes.

8. Most organizations, regardless of size or type, will occasionally be faced with crises. These unexpected situations require a different kind of thinking than either the basic decision-making or creative decision-making models call for.

   • What characterizes crisis decision making?

   Crisis decision making involves a situation with a short time frame, high visibility, and significant consequences that could affect the survival of the company.

Key Terms

board of directors, p. 97

chain of command, p. 106

chief executive officer (CEO), p. 99

chief financial officer (CFO), p. 99

chief information officer (CIO), p. 99

chief operating officer (COO), p. 99

creative decision making, p. 114

crisis decision making, p. 115

cross-functional team, p. 104

first-line supervisors, p. 102

inside directors, p. 97

middle managers, p. 101

nonmanagerial employees, p. 103

operational decisions, p. 110

outside directors, p. 97

problem solving, p. 110

professional staff, p. 102

self-directed work team, p. 104

strategic decisions, p. 109

top management, p. 99

vice president, p. 99

Exercises and Applications

1. Have someone you know keep a detailed diary, showing 15-minute intervals, for an entire day. What types of decisions were made? Who else was involved?

2. Suppose you need to travel on business from Los Angeles to Miami with a stop for a one-hour meeting at noon at the airport in Tulsa, Oklahoma. Your boss wants you to choose the most economical route. Go on the Internet and decide which flight and which airline to take.

3. Form teams. Using the basic decision-making model, address the following problem:

   A team member in a manufacturing setting frequently calls in sick. You suspect that he is not ill but is spending time enjoying his new swimming pool. Your boss has become aware of the situation. You must resolve this problem.

4. In the same teams, turn to the model of creative decision making. For each of the following products, brainstorm uses that are not its normal use. Break away from old assumptions and look for creative possibilities. Do not make evaluations or judgments.

   • Used tennis balls

   • A brick

   • A rubber band

   • This textbook

FROM THE PAGES OF

BusinessWeek

When Decision Makers Decide to Leave

We discussed in this chapter the importance of the top management team—those with titles such as CEO, COO, CFO, CIO, executive vice president, and others. What happens when a significant number of those officers decide to retire at the same time? Consider the case of Sun Microsystems Inc., one of the key players in the computer hardware industry. Sun's stock dropped from $63 a share in August 2000 to a 52-week low of $6 in May 2002. The company's troubles largely mirror those of the computer industry in recent years.

Is it coincidence, planned change, or a result of recent problems that four key top executives retired on July 1, 2002? The four executives—President and COO Ed Zander; CFO Michael Lehman; Vice President John Shoemaker, who runs the server business; and Executive Vice President of services Larry Hambly—range in age from 51 to 59. According to the Sun executives, they all had planned to leave a year earlier but stayed on until the recession's impact bottomed out. Indeed, the future does look better for Sun as the economy rebounds.

Still, Sun is facing intense competition from IBM and Dell. Its road ahead will certainly not be smooth. CEO Scott McNealy announced that he will reassume the title of president and will not immediately hire a new chief operating officer. The CFO position was filled by Steve McGowan, former finance chief of Sun's server division.

Decision Questions

1. As Scott McNealy takes over more of the day-to-day operations of Sun, how will this responsibility affect his ability to plan strategies?

2. Does the fact that the four executives are all in their fifties concern you? Why?

3. What kind of succession planning should a company have to prevent problems when several executives leave at the same time?

Source: Peter Burrows, "The Leading Lights Leaving Sun," *BusinessWeek,* May 13, 2002, p. 48.

References

1. Betsy McKay, "Pepsi Adds Blue-Hued Beverage to Spectrum of Colored Sodas," *The Wall Street Journal,* May 8, 2002, p. B2; and Betsy McKay, "Pepsi and Coke Roll Out Flavors to Boost Sales," *The Wall Street Journal,* May 7, 2002, p. A1.

2. For an excellent overview of teams and their significance, see the classic work by J. R. Katzenbach and D. K. Smith, *The Wisdom of Teams: Creating the High-Performance Organization* (Boston: Harvard Business School Press, 1993).

3. GE website, www.ge.com (accessed May 1, 2002).

4. Elliot Spagat, "Southwest Air Moves toward Nonstop Trips," *The Wall Street Journal,* May 8, 2002, p. D4.

5. Richard L. Hughes, Robert C. Ginnett, and Gordon L. Curphy, *Leadership: Enhancing the Lessons of Experience* (New York: McGraw-Hill/Irwin, 2002), pp. 189–192.

Understanding Stakeholder Expectations and Ethical Responsibilities

IBM is a leader in the technology industry. With 330,000 employees in over 160 countries, the company is renowned for its cutting-edge research, its history of product innovations, its steadfast focus on quality, and its consistent professionalism. At the same time, IBM has another well-earned reputation. It is an outstanding corporate citizen. The company has a strong commitment to the environment, plays an active role in shaping public policy, and has a stellar record of corporate philanthropy. At IBM, it is all part of their approach to doing business. J. Randall MacDonald, the company's senior vice president of human resources, summed it up well: "Everything we do as a business is the intersection of our relationships with our shareholders, with our customers, with our employees, as well as our communities."

IBM is generous with its contributions. Part of what the company contributes is money, but more important is its contribution of technology products, services, and support. The company is so committed to improving education that about 70 percent of its giving goes to education. Its Reinventing Education program, using technology to transform the way students learn, reaches over 10 million young people from kindergarten through high school in the United States and seven other countries. IBM stresses that it expects its employees to be involved in their communities. In fact, in 2001, IBM employees contributed 4 million hours of time to community projects. IBM backs up its commitment by supporting its people. For over 30 years, the company has offered employees leaves of absence for community service. Stan Litow, vice president of corporate community relations, is emphatic: "Giving is an integral part of the corporate culture. This is a company that has built a culture on being involved in communities as the result of leadership in the company and caring employees."

Make no mistake, IBM encourages and offers such support because the company believes it makes good business sense to do so. Employees feel better about the business, their morale is improved, and they actually may be more committed to their work. IBM's actions also brand it as a good place to work. Commenting on the company's outreach efforts, Mr. Litow comments, "Since we're in competition for the best talent in the world, it makes IBM an attractive place for people to come to work." It seems to be working. The company is a blue-chip giant, and it was ranked as number one on the "best corporate citizen" list for 2002.[1]

Businesses do not operate in a vacuum. Every decision managers make and every action an organization takes affect those around it. In a similar way, the business is affected by those who have contact with it. Some of the interactions are exciting; some are troublesome. Some are easily controllable; some are not. Some have limited impacts; some have significant long-run effects.

After studying this chapter, you should be able to:

1. Explain the concept of stakeholders and list the major categories of stakeholders in business.
2. Differentiate between the primary and secondary stakeholders for businesses.
3. Write an integrated definition of the term *business*.
4. Explain the responsibilities of a particular business to its stakeholders and how those stakeholders affect the business.
5. Describe the role of business ethics in contemporary business.
6. Understand the concept of a moral dilemma.
7. Explain three methods of moral reasoning that can be used to resolve a moral dilemma.
8. Discuss how a business can build an ethical culture.

In Chapter 1, we discussed the definition of *business*. We presented a model for a successful business. In Chapter 5, we discussed the many decision makers in a business and the process of decision making. However, business managers do not make decisions in isolation. Many groups both inside and outside the business affect and are also affected by the decisions managers make. In this chapter, we discuss the interactions between a business and those who have an interest in it. As part of our discussion, we emphasize the responsibilities of a business to each of its stakeholder groups. Finally, we discuss the role of managers in establishing ethical behavior in the organization. We begin these discussions with a concept that may be new to you, that of stakeholders in businesses.

The Concept of Stakeholders

You may not have realized that as a customer of a business, you are one of many key stakeholders of that business. As an employee, you are another. If you become an owner of the business or one of many stockholders, you are yet another. As a resident of the community in which the business operates, you are still another stakeholder of the business, since you are affected either positively or adversely by the actions of the business. So what is a stakeholder anyway?

A **stakeholder** is a person or group that has some claim on or expectation of how a business should operate. Stakeholders include founders and other owners, employees and retirees, customers, suppliers, other businesses, the government, the community, and even society in general. Each of these groups has expectations regarding how a given business should operate. Unfortunately, these stakeholder expectations are often contradictory. Managers must constantly be aware of the conflicting demands of stakeholders. Often, addressing the needs of one stakeholder disappoints another. For example, owners want as much profit as possible, but customers want the lowest possible price and highest possible quality. Providing a low price may conflict with the owner's expectation of a return for money invested. The leaders of a successful business must integrate and reconcile stakeholder expectations. Figure 6.1 lists typical stakeholders of businesses.

Primary stakeholders are those stakeholders whom a business affects and interacts with most directly. At least three stakeholders are commonly considered to be primary stakeholders: the owners of the firm, the firm's customers, and its employees. **Secondary stakeholders** are those whom the business affects in an indirect or limited way. These include strategic business partners, suppliers, former employees, unions, the community, environmentalists, the industry in which the firm operates, other businesses, various levels of government, special interest groups, the media, and society in general. Although the business may not have direct contact with secondary stakeholders

stakeholder
A person or group that has some claim on or expectation of how a business should operate.

primary stakeholders
Those stakeholders whom a business affects and interacts with most directly.

secondary stakeholders
Those stakeholders whom a business affects in an indirect or limited way.

FIGURE 6.1

Typical Business Stakeholders

Primary Stakeholders

– Owners
– Customers
– Employees (and their unions if the firm is unionized)

Secondary Stakeholders

– Business partners
– Suppliers
– Former employees
– The community
– Unions
– Environmentalists environment
– The industry in which the firm operates
– Other businesses
– Government
– Special interest groups
– The media
– Society

on a day-to-day basis, managers must recognize the importance of those stakeholders' expectations.

Primary stakeholders play the major role in how the business operates. The secondary stakeholders play a smaller role—unless a particular issue becomes vitally important to the company or the stakeholder. The importance of a particular stakeholder group varies with the company. A bank, for example, would probably have little interaction with environmental groups, but to a coal mining business, environmental groups might be important stakeholders.

Stakeholders as Part of the Business System

Recognizing the links between the business and its stakeholders is critical to understanding how the business system works. In fact, the idea that businesses and stakeholders interact and affect each other is a unique characteristic of a free market society.

In a free market society, owners provide capital. Customers influence the volume, models, colors, and options that are produced. Competitors affect prices, designs, and distribution. Government is involved in product, employee, and environmental safety. Unions affect wages and working conditions. Suppliers affect costs and, in turn, prices. All these stakeholders interact to constitute the free market business system. Increasingly, as we see in Profile 6.1, businesses are recognizing the importance of considering stakeholders.

PFIZER'S COMMITMENT TO STAKEHOLDERS   PROFILE 6.1

With total revenues exceeding $32 billion, Pfizer is the world's largest pharmaceutical company. Its prescription drugs include everything from Zoloft to Viagra. In fact, of the world's 30 best-selling prescription medicines, 8 are from Pfizer. And its over-the-counter products, such as Visine (eye drops), Listerine (mouthwash), Sudafed (decongestant), and Rolaids (antacid), line most home medicine cabinets.

Behind its formidable success is a firm commitment to sound business practices built around a respect for and attention to a range of stakeholders. Consider the stakeholder focus of Pfizer's new corporate mission—"to become the world's most valued company to patients, customers, investors, business partners, and the communities where we work and live."

Look at some of the specific ways that Pfizer has responded to its stakeholders. First, its attention to its owners is seen in its outstanding financial results. Between 2000 and 2001, its earnings per share grew by 28 percent, the best in the industry. Of course, Pfizer realizes that its performance is only as strong as its products and its people. The company's dedication to researching, developing, and delivering the best products for addressing the needs of patients and customers is unparalleled. And its commitment to employees is just as strong. Pfizer is renowned for its training and development efforts, and the company is perennially listed among the top companies to work for.

But there is much more. Pfizer is recognized as a partner of choice by a number of companies with which it has formed alliances to address major health needs. It has expanded initiatives in developing nations to address HIV infection. One of its dramatic new programs is the Pfizer for Living Share Card. This program provides low-income Medicare recipients who do not have prescription drug coverage a 30-day supply of any Pfizer prescription drug for only $15. In the wake of the September 11 attacks, Pfizer donated medicines and support services, and pledged $10 million for relief and reconstruction programs. Further, the company has worked closely with government authorities to improve protection against bioterrorism.

Pfizer has made a strong statement about its role in society through its commitment to leadership and integrity, backed by policies and procedures to ensure that all aspects of the company's corporate governance are beyond reproach. It's no surprise that Pfizer is always ranked high on the list of America's most admired companies.

Source: Pfizer Annual Report, 2001.

An Integrated Definition of *Business*

> **business (integrated definition)**
> An organization that strives for profits for its owners while meeting the needs of its customers and employees and balancing the impacts of its actions on other stakeholders.

The short definition of *business* (in Chapter 1) said a business strives for profits while meeting the needs of its customers. However, as we consider the nature of stakeholders, it becomes apparent that a broader definition is necessary to sufficiently integrate business with its various publics. Thus, with stakeholders in mind, we now provide an integrated definition of *business*. A **business** is an organization that strives for profits for its owners while meeting the needs of its customers and employees and balancing the impacts of its actions on other stakeholders. This definition captures better the interrelationships between the business and its various stakeholders.

Linking Business and Its Stakeholders: Expectations and Responsibilities

We have established that businesses have links to the stakeholders listed in Figure 6.1. The fact that a business affects and is affected by these stakeholders is an important, complex notion that needs to be discussed more fully. Stakeholders provide businesses with the *capacity* to operate. Owners provide capital necessary for operations. Customers make the purchases that enable the business to generate revenue necessary for survival. Employees are the resources necessary to build products and offer services. Suppliers provide the inputs that allow the business to produce with quality and efficiency. Communities provide the atmosphere and facilities that help the business attract talented people and keep them happy. Without these stakeholders, the business would not have the capacity to do what it does.

But each of these stakeholders has certain *expectations* of the business. Members of each group realize that the business is at least to some extent dependent on them, so they find it reasonable to place certain demands or expectations on the business. Thus, owners expect profits or return on their investments. Customers expect quality products. Employees expect fair payment for their efforts. Suppliers

THINK ABOUT THIS

1. Choose a company with which you are familiar. Identify the stakeholders for that company. Which are primary and which are secondary?

2. How does the integrated definition of *business* differ significantly from the definition provided in Chapter 1?

expect favorable contracts and relationships. Communities expect business support of community programs. The business cannot ignore these expectations. If it does, the stakeholder groups may withhold their part of the capacity formula and make it very difficult for the business to survive.

Accordingly, the business must recognize its *responsibility* to address stakeholder expectations. Of course, not all the expectations of all the stakeholders can be met. Remember, we said that stakeholder expectations often conflict, so the business and its managers must reasonably address and balance the expectations of its various stakeholders. In essence, business decision makers are always looking at the "capacity–stakeholder expectations–business responsibility" framework and trying to determine how best to make all the pieces fit together. In the following sections, we will consider the links between business and some of its key stakeholders. We explore both stakeholder expectations and business responsibilities. We see that management decisions are always subject to the scrutiny of stakeholders.

Owners and Investors

The owners of the firm are obviously primary stakeholders. They are the ones who underwrite the firm. They are the people and institutions who have risked their dollars and support so that the business could operate. They have chosen to invest in the business rather than pursue other opportunities. Surely they deserve to receive a return on their investment for taking such risks. In fact, this notion of a business providing returns to its owners and investors is fundamental to our free enterprise system. Without this focus, there would be no real incentive for anyone to take the risk of investment. Most people agree that a business has a responsibility to its owners and investors to assure a return on their investment.

The real sticking point is, How much return is proper? Some people argue that the most important (many would say sole) responsibility of a business is to maximize return to owners and investors. Milton Friedman, an internationally acclaimed economist, even asserts that it is the social responsibility of business to increase its profits. That means the firm provides the owners and investors as much money as it can. Therefore, managers should focus their energies on enhancing revenues, reducing expenses, and thereby gaining as much profit as possible. Advocates of this view believe that it is *not* the job of business to address social issues or problems. They think other institutions, such as government and nonprofit social service agencies, should deal with social concerns. Do not dismiss this perspective lightly. It is technically sound and is backed by some powerful and well-respected business and economic thinkers.

Others argue that the profit maximization argument is too extreme and fails to recognize that business *does* and *should* have a broader role of responsibility to other stakeholders. Consider, for example, businesses' responsibility to their communities and to society in general. Advocates note that businesses exist in society and are part of society, so being socially responsible is the right thing to do. Business may be in a better position to address social issues than other institutions in our society. Many major organizations have established foundations that provide financial support for an array of social causes. One of the best known is the Bill and Melinda Gates Foundation. Gates, of Microsoft fame, assists health and learning initiatives throughout the world through the foundation's asset base, which exceeds $24 billion.[2] Some business foundations may have even contributed to the college you are presently attending. For example, the Walton family's foundation, funded by Wal-Mart stores, recently gave $300 million to the University of Arkansas.[3]

Some people argue that in the long run, attention to social concerns does benefit the business on the bottom line. For example, if a business helps address public health issues, costs of benefits such as insurance may be reduced. If a business works to provide a less stressful work environment for its employees, they may demonstrate less absenteeism and more overall motivation toward the job. If a business focuses on community issues, it may be able to attract skilled workers to move to the community. If a business addresses important social issues, customers may view it more favorably. The arguments here can be compelling and, as indicated in Profile 6.2, must be communicated carefully. In fact, most people indicate that they would like to know about a company's record on addressing environmental and social issues before they decide whether they want to invest in, buy from, or work for the company.[4]

Today, most business leaders accept that business does have social responsibilities beyond those to owners and investors. However, there should be no doubt that the *first* responsibility of the healthy business is to its owners and investors. They deserve a fair return on their investment. Attention to other stakeholders may require short-run trade-offs for the business. Even if businesses ultimately experience some benefits from these

PROFILE 6.2   A SUBTLE MESSAGE OF SOCIAL ACTION

"They're damned if they do and damned if they don't." Such, say many experts, is the tricky world of corporate giving and good works. Consider two examples: McDonald's gained considerable public attention and warm regard when news programs showed exhausted rescue workers at the World Trade Center receiving free boxes of McDonald's chicken nuggets. The public seemed not only to appreciate McDonald's compassion, but also to accept it as a genuine and sincere effort of help. One housewife even responded that she was impressed "that there wasn't any spin, that McDonald's didn't . . . brag about itself." She further commented that, "I've been buying Happy Meals ever since."

However, Phillip Morris has had a different response from the public. Its recent $250 million advertising blitz heralded the company's commitment to charitable work. Some people saw this as a disingenuous and self-serving publicity move. They argued that if the company was serious about supporting good causes, its huge advertising outlay would have gone to true philanthropic causes. Further, many were struck by the irony of a cigarette producer promoting itself as a socially conscious firm. It seems that Phillip Morris's attempts offended some people.

The message from these examples is that companies have to move carefully. Obviously, businesses want the public to be aware of the good deeds they are performing. However, the publicity can backfire if it's perceived as promotional. So which companies does the public give the highest marks for their philanthropic reputations? According to a recent survey of over 20,000 people, the top firms are Johnson & Johnson, Coca-Cola, Wal-Mart, Anheuser-Busch, Hewlett-Packard, Walt Disney, Microsoft, IBM, McDonald's, and 3M.

Source: Ronald Alsop, "Perils of Corporate Philanthropy," *The Wall Street Journal*, January 16, 2002, pp. B1, B4.

actions, there is still a cost involved. Therefore, the managers of the business must determine how much and how far they will move toward balancing stakeholder expectations. Not surprisingly, there is great variation from business to business.

Customers

Customers are a primary stakeholder since without them, the business could not survive. Managers of successful businesses must be sensitive to their customers if they hope to compete. The business must provide consumers the products they want, when they want, at prices they are willing to pay. However, many people argue that the business's responsibilities to its customers extend beyond this basic competitive focus. Customers' expectations of businesses include quality products and services, choice, communication, safety, and respect. Note as we discuss these expectations that there are trade-offs. Managers must always have an eye on the bottom line. They must ask, What is the relationship between meeting customer expectations and making a profit?

Product and Service Quality

Customers expect an adequate **value–price relationship** from a business. That is, they expect to get the best possible value from the products they purchase, given the price they pay. They also expect the products they purchase to be of good quality, to perform as they are advertised, and to do so with consistency and dependability. But let's think about these expectations more carefully. As a customer, you would like to have the absolute top quality while paying bargain-basement prices. A business simply cannot offer both. It is important for managers as well as their customers to understand the value–price relationship.

> **value–price relationship**
> A relationship in which customers get the best possible value from the products they purchase, given the price they pay.

The value–price relationship does not necessarily mean that the product or service must be of highest quality. Sometimes average quality is sufficient if the price is low enough. For example, customers at Wal-Mart expect no more than average service in their shopping experience, but they expect the lowest possible price. When those same customers shop at Nordstrom's, however, they expect top-quality personal service because that is what they are paying for. Southwest Airlines is an excellent example of the value–price trade-off. Most customers accept the no frills approach of the airline as being reasonable and consistent given the low fares the company charges. Southwest is really respected more for its customer service than its price. Having both excellence in service and low prices produces a very high value–price ratio.

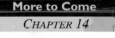

More to Come
CHAPTER 14

SOUTHWEST

Choice

Another area in which customers have expectations is in competitive pricing and selection. Customers expect that companies will compete fairly in terms of both pricing and selection. For the free market to work effectively, companies must not collude in price-fixing and must respect patents and copyrights held by other companies. There are laws designed specifically to protect customers' freedom of choice. Some of these will be presented in Chapter 11.

Communication

Another set of customer expectations has to do with communications in both directions. First, customers expect that businesses will communicate with them—in the form of labels on boxes, instructions enclosed with products, truth-in-lending terms, and complete information regarding what services will be provided and what the real cost is.

Communication is always important, and no more so than with health-related products. Customers expect to know if there are side effects to drugs, how much fat or cholesterol is in food, and whether there are other risks associated with using products.

The second issue regards communication back to the company. If customers have a problem or concern, they expect that someone will answer the phone and give them immediate attention. Some companies do extremely well here in providing hot lines or other mechanisms for contacting them. Others provide websites where customers can interact with the company.

Safety

Consumers expect that products will be safe for normal usage. This issue is critical because consumers typically operate on a *presumption of safety.* Such expectations are reasonable since it is not feasible for consumers to test every product before using it. They assume that the business has done the appropriate tests.

However, the right to safety must be balanced with reality. If, for example, customers use products in a blatantly unsafe manner, it is unfair for them to hold the company liable in the case of accidents. Similarly, if customers have disabled products' built-in safety features, they should not expect remuneration if they are injured.

Respect

Customers expect businesses to treat them with respect. Few things are as frustrating as dealing with a business whose employees seem to feel that the customer is nothing but a necessary evil. This arrogance and insensitivity to customers and their needs risks dri-

Lands' End's policy of accepting returns without question shows great respect for customers. This is critical in a mail order business in order to get repeat business. Is the importance of respect for customers the same in all industries?

ving them away. By contrast, customers appreciate businesses that treat them with care and consideration. Many businesses use their foundation of customer respect as a competitive edge that can pay dividends in terms of repeat sales.

Consider Dell, one of our focus companies. Dell is recognized for its award-winning customer service. For example, if you call Dell with a desktop service or server problem, an expert will walk you through possible troubleshooting options. In the vast majority of cases, this approach works, and the problem is resolved, remotely, in a few minutes. If an on-site technician is needed, Dell's Next Business Day Response Service will provide a certified technician by the following business day.[5]

We have focused here on customer expectations. Does this mean that businesses have an equivalent responsibility for each customer expectation? It means businesses have a responsibility to consider those expectations carefully. To the extent that they can meet customer expectations while maintaining or enhancing profits, they should make every attempt to do so. In those cases where meeting customer expectations is just too expensive, managers must be cautious. They should analyze whether the customer expectations are indeed legitimate and if they can be met profitably.

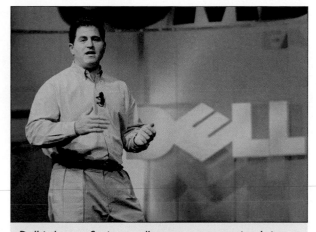

Dell is known for its excellent customer service. It is also known for its charitable work and their contributions to the communities where they are located. Dell strives to be a good neighbor and a careful steward of its communities' natural resources. Is there a relationship between a company's respect for customers and its work with communities?

Employees

Employees are a third primary stakeholder. Their claim on the business is for meaningful jobs that pay an equitable wage or salary. They expect managers to treat them fairly. They expect the business to provide them with a safe place to work. They expect the business to give them sufficient training to do their jobs well. Increasingly, employees expect their work to be challenging and meaningful. The role of employees as stakeholders is particularly significant if they belong to unions. Unions are generally secondary stakeholders because of the impact of unionism on the way the business world operates. But if a particular business is unionized, then the union becomes a primary stakeholder because of the direct interaction between the union and the firm. This relationship is especially true if the union is a major international union that represents workers at several large manufacturing companies (for example, the UAW or Teamsters). The interaction between the business and the union becomes particularly relevant during times of contract negotiation.

More to Come
CHAPTER 16

Businesses recognize these expectations. Yet businesses in today's competitive environment face extreme pressures to ensure that their labor force is as productive as possible. In today's era with a focus on controlling costs, considerable controversy exists regarding the level and extent of a firm's responsibility to its employees. Certainly, some of the traditional employer–employee relationships and expectations appear to be changing. For example, most businesses believe their competitive situations are so fickle that they can no longer guarantee employees' long-term job security.

It is certainly in a company's best interest to treat workers with respect, give them adequate training, provide meaningful work, and pay them a fair wage. Most business

Successful businesses recognize that their people are the foundation of all that they do. These organizations accept and operate under the philosophy that "our people are our most important asset." How does this philosophy affect the way a firm goes about conducting its business?

leaders truly care about their people. Progressive businesses convert this concern into tangible action. Southwest Airlines has a rich history of caring about its employees, treating them respectfully, and taking extra steps to pay attention to its people and their needs. During the tough economic times that hit the airlines during 2001 and early 2002, Southwest put its people ahead of other priorities. For example, while Southwest's competitors were cutting jobs at a dizzying rate, Southwest moved in a different direction. The company delayed the delivery of new planes and canceled renovations to its headquarters to keep employees on the payroll.[6] First Tennessee, a regional bank headquartered in Memphis, also goes the extra mile. Among the benefits its employees appreciate are free checking accounts and financial planning services. The bank even takes the step of publicly stating: "Employees come first. Not customers, not shareholders."[7]

Exactly what are the responsibilities of a business to its people? Four themes seem important. First, the business should operate so that *talent prevails.* People who have talent and skills should be developed, promoted, and compensated regardless of their backgrounds or other differences. Companies must ensure that workers are not unduly harassed or coerced. This responsibility includes preventing sexual and racial harassment, of course, but it also means preventing the coercing of employees to falsify records, knowingly produce inferior products, or commit other unethical or illegal acts. One of the central themes of Chapter 7 is that employees must be utilized to the fullest extent possible.

Second, businesses should ensure that employees operate in a *safe working environment.* Like other stakeholders, the government has an interest in safe working conditions. The *Occupational Safety and Health Administration (OSHA)* is charged with

At Best Buy, community involvement is a central value. Each year, Best Buy dedicates 1.5 percent of pre-tax earnings to charitable programs. Best Buy is the largest sponsor of Dollars for Scholars, helping provide college educations for local students. How many Best Buy stakeholders are affected by the Dollars for Scholars program?

overseeing safety in businesses. The impact of OSHA regulations will be discussed further in Chapter 11.

More to Come
CHAPTER 11

Third, the business should make the work environment as *meaningful and rewarding* as possible. Employees spend a significant portion of their time and often the bulk of their productive efforts and energies at work. In return, the business should try to make that work experience as satisfying as possible.

Fourth, the business should invest in the *training and development* of its people. No business today can guarantee the security of lifetime employment. However, if their skills are consistently being upgraded, employees should feel reasonably secure. They will know that they have talents the business needs. Of course, making sure its people retain marketable and competitive skills should help the business perform better.

Many companies go beyond the minimum. SAS Institute provides a classic example. The company is known for its progressive approaches for reaching out to its people. These include an array of services, such as child care support, a huge fitness center, and a health center that offers free mammograms and other lab tests. SAS is convinced that these services not only are great for their employees, but also make good business sense. Consider the explanation provided by David Russo, SAS's head of human resources. He notes that the turnover rate (the percentage of people who leave the business) runs about 3 percent annually. This rate compares with an industry average of 20%. In other words, SAS has a competitive advantage in the 17 percent of its people who are choosing not to leave. Given the tremendous cost of finding and recruiting talented people in the high-tech field, he estimates a savings to the company of over $50 million. He notes that avoiding the costs of a high turnover rate is how SAS pays for all the extras its employees love. Plus, he adds, "I've got tons of money left over."[8]

Secondary Stakeholders

We listed nearly a dozen groups in Figure 6.1 that could be considered secondary stakeholders. The following paragraphs focus on a few of those to illustrate the links between businesses and these stakeholders.

Unions

unions

Formally recognized organizations that represent a company's or industry's workers.

Unions are formally recognized organizations that represent a company's or industry's workers. Unions are typically considered secondary stakeholders because unionism in general affects how businesses operate. For example, wage rates in a community are affected by unions, even in companies that are not represented by a union. However, unions can succeed only if the business succeeds. If a company's costs are so high that it has trouble competing in global markets, unions may have to make concessions. The union and its members lose if the company is forced to downsize or close a plant. Unions represent about 13.5 percent of the workers in the United States. Government workers are more likely to be members of unions than are workers in private businesses. In fact, the unionization rate of government workers is about 37 percent.[9]

Environmentalists

environmentalism

Efforts and actions to protect the natural environment.

Environmentalism has become a key public policy issue. **Environmentalism** refers to efforts and actions to protect the natural environment. Many people suggest that business must step forward and take a leading role in addressing global warming, landfill contamination, pollution, and other issues of environmental concern. But despite the importance of these concerns, remedies and responsibilities are difficult to establish.

A business can address environmental issues by its policies and actions. Particularly in the areas of air, water, and land pollution, businesses can make decisions and take actions that encourage care of our nonrenewable natural resources. A number of companies are known for their environmental philosophies and activities. For example, Starbucks is committed to environmental leadership in all areas of its business. The company's actions include recycling burlap coffee bags, composting residue organically from its coffee roasting and extract operations, encouraging the use of reusable mugs, and developing a more environmentally friendly disposable cup. The company even has what it calls "The Green Team," a group of partners that provide input and advice on how the company can better meet its environmental responsibilities.[10]

The Community

Many people believe businesses have a responsibility to the communities where they operate. That responsibility may be carried out in many ways. Often businesses support or even sponsor community events, such as the symphony, the opera, the ballet, or special community festivals. These businesses commit their financial support to bring entertainment and cultural enrichment to the community. Many companies have matching gifts programs, in which the business matches employee contributions to charitable organizations.

Many businesses encourage their employees to be actively involved in their communities. It is not unusual to find businesspeople holding key positions as community volunteers. Most social service organizations, from Meals on Wheels to the Boy Scouts of America, depend on such a cadre of volunteers to accomplish their goals. By and large, the business world accepts that volunteerism is important and needs to be encouraged. Often businesses even grant employees some scheduling flexibility so that they can pursue both work and volunteer activities.

Businesses recognize that community involvement is both the right thing to do and good business. Dell provides an excellent example. In addition to the charitable work of the Dell Foundation, the company also has developed a series of corporate community partnerships that directly support the communities in which Dell operates. As part of this program, the company sponsors the Austin Museum of Art (the museum's largest corporate sponsor), the Round Rock Express Baseball Club (the Houston Astros minor league affiliate), the Wilson County Adult Education Center, and a range of other projects and events. Consistent with its commitment to the community, Dell also encourages employee giving and volunteerism.[11]

Society in General

Society places broad expectations on the shoulders of business. The logic is direct and simple. Businesses that are prospering in a society should contribute to the betterment of that society. Many businesses are taking this step.

For example, some businesses are taking a lead in promoting and supporting public health issues. They may contribute funds for basic research aimed at finding answers to troubling health concerns. Corporate sponsorship of muscular dystrophy research (much of it through the very visible avenue of the Jerry Lewis Labor Day Telethon) has enabled important medical advances in dealing with this crippling childhood disease. Research into the most troubling social health concern of our day, AIDS, would be difficult without corporate backing such as that of Pfizer, which we discussed earlier. Tanqueray, American Airlines, and others sponsor AIDSRides each year. In 2002, four AIDSRides, like the one in Profile 6.3, will raise millions for AIDS research.

CYCLING FOR A CAUSE   PROFILE 6.3

The job at the AIDSRides Mobile City each evening was to prepare for 1,700 sore but exuberant bike riders who would be arriving at the end of the day's ride from Minneapolis to Chicago during the week of July 22 to 27: a thousand tents, good food for hungry riders, semitrailers that each held a dozen or more showers with hot water, numerous portable bathrooms, massages if needed, and "butt butter" to apply to appropriate parts of the body at the end of the day's 75- to 100-mile segment. The 500-mile ride from Minneapolis to Chicago raised over $4 million in 2002. Much of the support for the AIDSRides comes from companies that see their assistance as a way to help society.

Companies such as American Airlines, Silicon Graphics, Pallotta Team Works, *Bicycling* magazine, Janus, and Clif Bar joined makers of Tanqueray as primary sponsors of the AIDSRides. The Minneapolis-to-Chicago ride also had local sponsors. Still more companies supported the ride as it progressed through the many small towns of Minnesota, Wisconsin, and Illinois. More support came from companies whose employees spent a week on the ride. Many of these companies allowed the time off without charging it to vacation time.

Source: "AIDSRides USA," www.BeThePeople.com/aidsrides/Landing_ride.htm (accessed May 9, 2002).

Some companies even make strategic business decisions that are guided by their interest in public health concerns. For example, the refusal of Harley-Davidson to continue allowing the name Harley to be used on cigarettes was based on clear evidence of the dangers of smoking. The company did not wish to support such harmful products.

Creating an Ethical Culture

Superimposed on the responsibilities to stakeholders is the need to act ethically in whatever the firm does. This need transcends everything else, and it influences how the firm's managers view their responsibilities to their various stakeholders. The remainder of this chapter discusses the role of ethics in decision making. It introduces the concepts of moral dilemmas and ethical cultures.

Defining *Business Ethics*

business ethics
The search for and commitment to meet appropriate standards of moral conduct in business situations.

Ethics involves a search for standards of moral conduct. Therefore, **business ethics** involves the search for and commitment to meet appropriate standards of moral conduct in business situations. In simplest terms, business ethics means figuring out the appropriate way to act in various business settings. In practice, business ethics is concerned with two issues. First is the difficulty of determining what actions really are appropriate from situation to situation. Second is having the fortitude to carry out those ethical actions.

Why Must a Business Focus on Ethics?

There are many reasons businesses must emphasize the practice of ethical behavior. We will explore four reasons that are key ingredients in the formula of business success and competitiveness:

- The public expects ethical behavior from its business institutions.
- Customers demand ethical behavior.
- Employees want to work for companies that meet high ethical standards.
- Behaving ethically is the right thing to do.

First, the public expects ethical behavior from its business institutions. In fact, the expectation of ethical action is a foundation of our free market system. Unfortunately, in recent years, there has been a breakdown in the general public's confidence in the ethical behavior of businesses. Some analysts have even noted that the public's faith in corporate America is so strained that our capitalist system is struggling with its biggest crisis in decades.[12]

In some ways, this breech of confidence in business ethics is not surprising. Stories of high-profile organizations' moral and legal lapses have dominated the news over the

THINK ABOUT THIS

1. Some people argue that unions have improved the working conditions of all employees over time. How is this so?

2. Can you think of a situation where attention to the interests of *secondary* stakeholders would improve the overall success of the company?

3. What is the benefit of thinking of customers as stakeholders rather than just customers?

4. When does a business know it has gone too far in investing in social causes?

past few years. Although Enron and Andersen may have captured the most initial attention, industry giants such as Oracle, Sunbeam, Global Crossing, WorldCom, Tyco, and Merrill Lynch are among the companies that have also received unwanted attention for questionable behavior. In response, the public has demanded increased scrutiny of business practices and stronger ethical behavior by managers at all levels. Organizational leaders have been challenged to create ethical organizations. Many observers argue that if ethical behavior is to prevail, leaders must be the moral compass for their companies.[13]

Second, businesses must understand and meet the ethical expectations of their customers. Customers demand ethical action and increasingly support businesses' efforts to be good corporate citizens. Many customers are disgusted by the visible examples of poor ethical practice, from companies that pollute or practice discrimination or cut corners on safety in addition to the current concern over financial deals and reporting. Whenever possible, these customers are likely to turn from such businesses.

High ethical standards and public trust are the essence of some businesses. When public trust is lost, the firm's competitive strength is also lost. Certified public accounting (CPA) firms, for example, must adhere to the highest levels of ethics. Reputations for ethical behavior are essential for the confidence clients place in these firms. The same is true for many independent consulting businesses.

Third, employees want to work for companies that have solid ethical reputations. All organizations want to hire and keep the best talent available. These talented employees choose to work for companies where honesty, trust, and ethical behavior are practiced. And they are keenly aware when inconsistent ethical behavior is taking place. According to a national survey of nearly 2,400 U.S. employees, 76 percent reported that they had observed illegal or unethical conduct on the job.[14] Companies whose cultures discourage such behaviors are rewarded with employee confidence and commitment. Consider Edward Jones, a financial services company that is perennially listed among the best places to work. At Edward Jones, 97 percent of its employees reported that they believed the company's management was honest.[15] It's not surprising that people want to be associated with a company like that.

Clear ethical standards and direction foster more favorable and promising work climates. People know what to expect; they know what will and what will not be tolerated. They know that success is not secured at *any* cost. Often this knowledge makes them feel better about their employers and more committed to their work situations.

As businesses become leaner and more streamlined, more and more discretion is being given to employees. The new empowered workforce has been granted expanded decision-making authority. At the same time, there are fewer managers around to act as checks and balances. Increasingly, companies must trust employees to behave ethically on their own. In this environment, clear and consistent ethical standards and practices are fundamental. Empowered workers use these standards and practices as the basis for their actions and decisions.

Fourth, behaving ethically is simply the right thing to do. Most of us know this, and so do most organizations. In fact, the majority of large and midsize organizations have written statements of core values that identify the basic beliefs and standards that the company espouses and strives to meet. In most cases, honesty, integrity, and consistent ethical behavior are set forth in these statements.

It is unclear whether attention to ethical behavior does, in fact, result in higher profits. However, there is clear evidence that businesses that are exposed for corporate crimes such as bribery, tax evasion, and violation of government contracts see a negative impact on their stock prices. Further, there is evidence that socially responsible firms tend to outperform the market average.[16]

The Concept of Moral Dilemmas

At this point, you may question why there is so much concern over ethics. Certainly, reasonable people know the difference between right and wrong. Further, behaving in ways you know are right is pretty straightforward. Figuring out what is appropriate behavior and acting accordingly just cannot be that difficult. But, in fact, the determination of what is appropriate is often quite complicated. And even if you know what should be done, there may be significant pressures nudging you to act in ways different from your personal inclinations. Let's explore these complexities further.

On an episode of the popular TV show "ER," Dr. Benton was faced with a moral decision. He had accidentally discovered that a respected senior surgeon had been excluding certain patients from his research. These exclusions made the senior physician's pioneering surgical procedures appear to have stronger and more successful outcomes than actually was the case. They were inconsistent with the research parameters being touted and even raised questions regarding the overall effectiveness of the surgical procedure. Benton's personal moral standards told him that these discrepancies should be reported. But nearly everyone advised him to say nothing. These colleagues argued that the senior surgeon could destroy Benton's career. Also, the senior surgeon's well-earned reputation brought large financial contributions—contributions that were essential to the survival of one of the few hospitals that cared for patients who couldn't pay. What should be done? As in most real situations, the issues are cloudy and open to different interpretations. Further, the ramifications are perplexing and potentially costly. This story allows us to examine some of the dynamics of ethical decision making.

Dr. Benton is experiencing a **moral dilemma,** which exists when there is a conflict of interests involving ethical choices (see Figure 6.2). A moral dilemma exists because Benton's personal standards of what is right and appropriate conflict with the demands of the situation (strong pressures to say nothing). Like Benton, each of us has personal moral standards, which are known as our **private morality.** Our personal standards, or private morality, are learned. They are developed and refined throughout our entire

moral dilemma
A conflict of interests involving ethical choices.

private morality
Personal moral standards.

FIGURE 6.2

Elements of a Moral Dilemma

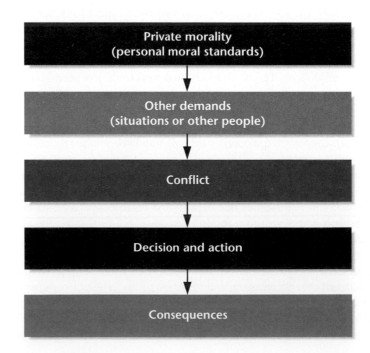

lives. Like anyone else confronted by a moral dilemma, Benton must decide how to act or respond to resolve this dilemma. Consider the possibilities: He may abide by his own sense of what seems to be right (private morality) and file a formal report outlining his charges. He may talk to the senior surgeon and attempt to change the surgeon's behavior. Or he may yield to the pressures of the situation and reason that it is less risky to just forget what he saw.

Whatever action he takes will produce consequences. If a formal report is filed, a surgeon's reputation will be tainted, hospital funding will probably be affected, many meaningful programs may be lost, and many people will be angry with Benton. If he takes a personal approach and talks informally with the surgeon, Benton's conscience may be clear but the action may be devastating to his career. Finally, if Benton does nothing, the lives of innocent patients may be affected. As you can see, identifying and understanding the possible consequences should play a major role in the decision-making process.

The decision that Benton makes—his enacted ethical decision—will contribute to the ethical environment of the organization (hospital) where he works. His decision will affect others' perceptions of him. His actions (or lack of action) may eventually even affect the reputation of the hospital. Ethical decisions have a way of affecting many more people (stakeholders) than might at first appear to be the case. Take a look at the ethical decisions presented in Profile 6.4.

AN ETHICAL DILEMMA?   PROFILE 6.4

Ethical dilemmas are not always dramatic, life-or-death decisions. In fact, they rarely are. Yet most of us do encounter ethical dilemmas from time to time. Often they involve subtleties, and the proper way of acting is not always clear. After all, that's why they are dilemmas. Consider the following examples. What would you do?

You have been asked to serve as a student representative on a college committee that is conducting a search for a new dean for your school. The seven-person committee is composed of six faculty members and you. Although the search has been quite lengthy, the committee has finally narrowed the field to four candidates. All four have visited your campus and have met with faculty, students, administrators, and your committee. You are especially impressed with Dr. Jones. He is a visionary with great ideas. He seems to have a strong student focus, and you surmise he is the students' preferred candidate. All members of the committee have ranked him as their first choice. It is clear that he will do great things to enhance the programs and reputation of the college.

However, in doing final reference checks, the committee has received some troubling input. Dr. Jones's résumé indicates that he served as all-school (student body) president during his senior year of college. The résumé also states that he has served as a member of the board of directors for Focus on Youth, a not-for-profit organization that helps underprivileged youth. Finally, he indicates that he received a prestigious Fulbright scholarship to teach for a year in the Czech Republic. Surprisingly, all three claims seem to be slight exaggerations. The committee has learned that although Dr. Jones was dorm president in college and ran for all-school president, he did not win. Further, although he had done some volunteer work for Focus on Youth, he had never served on the board. Finally, although he taught for a year in the Czech Republic, he never received a Fulbright scholarship. Would you exclude Dr. Jones from consideration? (Recent research indicates that over 90 percent of employers and 80 percent of employees believe that it is unethical to falsify experience on a résumé).

What would you do in the following situation? You've recently started working part-time for Star-Tech. The company provides computer and information systems technical support to a range of midsize businesses in your region. You work the help line. It's tough work. Typically, the calls you handle involve clients who are stressed out because of some technical glitch. You must provide sound answers while trying to calm and soothe the callers. Although the job offers valuable experience (it will look good on your résumé), the place is a pressure cooker. Supervisors really push the help line employees (typically, young people, and often, college students), the pay is minimal, and most of your colleagues hate the job. The company treats its employees with little regard and even less respect. For example, most of your co-workers are incensed at the company's policy prohibiting using company e-mail for personal reasons.

One way a number of your peers have responded is to stretch the perks. For example, nearly everybody takes home office supplies (everything from blank computer disks to computer paper) for personal use. A number of peers have copied some of the company's software for home use. And one employee regularly spends time each day using his business computer to search for other job openings. These practices don't really seem to be hurting anybody, and the work is always done. What do you think of these actions? Would you participate in them?

Again, recent research provides some interesting insights. Most workers do not consider the personal use of company e-mail unethical. In fact, only 34 percent of workers do. However, most do consider taking home office supplies (60 percent), copying company software for personal use (66 percent), and using work equipment to search for another job (66 percent) unethical acts.

Sources: "Ethical Issues in the Employer-Employee Relationship," http://ecampus. bentley.edu/dept/cbe/newresearch/1.html (accessed May 10, 2002); and "Technology and Ethics in Workplace," http://ecampus.bentley.edu/dept/cbe/newresearch/12.html (accessed May 16, 2002).

Many of our most pressing ethical concerns are affected by issues of *exploitation,* which involves taking advantage of someone or something for personal gain.[17] Although exploitation can occur in a number of ways, determining whether or not it exists is tricky. When is an action just good hard-nosed business, and when is it taking advantage? Is, say, corporate downsizing an unethical and exploitative action? Consider a company that eliminates the jobs of thousands of middle managers. These managers may have given years of loyal performance to the business. They have done nothing wrong. Indeed, it may be the strategic errors of top management that have pushed the business into financial disarray. Can it possibly be "right" to crush the lives of thousands who do not deserve it?

On the other hand, the business must survive and its costs must be curtailed. Only the most critical areas and positions can be protected. This is the nature of our contemporary competitive climate. As you can see, there is a conflict of interests. There is a moral dilemma. Whatever decision is made will have consequences that affect the lives of many.

Resolving Moral Dilemmas

Employees at every level must make difficult choices and decisions that represent their best attempts to resolve the moral dilemmas they face. How do people make such choices and decisions? Even more important, how should they? To answer these questions, we must consider some basics of moral reasoning and suggest some approaches for deciding what is the right thing to do.

Return to the question of downsizing. The downsizing decision affects not only the lives of hundreds of employees and their families but also the future competitiveness (perhaps even the survival) of the business. Some ethicists would propose an approach to this dilemma known as utilitarianism. Here is how it works: Decision makers (in this case, business leaders) are asked to consider all possible parties who could be affected by the downsizing decision. These parties are stakeholders, since they have some stake in what happens. Leaders are asked to evaluate the impact of the decision for each of these relevant stakeholders. Sometimes this impact can be determined objectively. Usually it cannot, and a subjective impression must be used. In **utilitarianism,** a decision that produces the greatest good for the greatest number of stakeholders is a morally sound decision. Stated differently, an ethical decision should maximize benefits and minimize harms for stakeholders.

> **utilitarianism**
> An approach to decision making that assumes decisions producing the greatest good for the greatest number of stakeholders are ethical.

In our example, the downsizing decision will affect the hundreds of workers who will lose their jobs. It will affect their families. Their reduced buying power may affect the communities where they reside. Remaining employees (survivors) may feel extra stress and pressure at their jobs. For all these stakeholders—laid-off employees, their families, their communities, and even surviving employees—there are costs or harms from the downsizing decision.

Yet there are other stakeholders whose situations must be considered. If the company continues to lose competitive position and market share, even more workers will be laid off. The business may have to close a portion of its operations, which will be even more detrimental to the community. As competitiveness slips, the company's stock plummets and investors suffer.

A decision maker must consider all these stakeholders and the likely impact of a downsizing decision on each. The advantages of downsizing may truly outweigh the costs, in which case the downsizing decision, from a purely utilitarian perspective, is ethically sound. Decision makers should exercise caution when approaching decisions as utilitarians. They must be careful to consider the full range of stakeholders involved. Further, they must be objective and thorough when weighing the real impact on each stakeholder.

Most business managers feel comfortable with the utilitarian approach. It is the kind of logical, cost–benefit style of decision making that makes sense to them. Despite that comfort level, the use of utilitarianism can be quite complex for decision makers. Many decisions will have positive consequences for some stakeholders and negative consequences for other stakeholders at the same time. Determining how many people will be affected and weighing the actual extent of good or harm can be quite difficult.[18]

Consequently, utilitarian-based decision making may not be enough, and other methods of reasoning may be necessary. Two other methods of moral reasoning are typically emphasized: the theory of rights and the theory of justice.

The **theory of rights** approach to decision making argues that there are certain individual rights that must always be protected. If a decision violates or threatens these rights, it is not ethical. Return to our example of the young doctor faced with the dilemma regarding the senior surgeon. One might argue from a utilitarian view that

> **theory of rights**
> An approach to decision making that assumes there are certain individual rights that must always be protected.

saying nothing is the best way to maximize overall stakeholder benefit while minimizing stakeholder harm. But doesn't every person have the right to life and safety, the right not to be placed in a threatening situation without prior knowledge? By saying nothing, the doctor risks violating the rights of innocent patients. Even though the risks may be small, individual rights may be violated by a failure to disclose information, and patients' well-being may be endangered. Rights to safety, health, privacy, and truthfulness are held in high regard in the American culture. If a decision threatens these basic rights, its moral integrity is suspect.

> **theory of justice**
> An approach to decision making that assumes decisions should be guided by equity, fairness, and impartiality.

The **theory of justice** states that decisions should be guided by equity, fairness, and impartiality. Using this line of reasoning, decision makers should try to be sure that both the benefits and the burdens that result from decisions are shared equitably by those involved.

For example, in recent years, a number of companies have received attention for the multimillion-dollar compensation packages their top executives receive. Is it fair for high-ranking executives to receive such lofty rewards? Is it fair for top executives to receive salary increases while they are downsizing the business and providing only average returns? Sometimes companies have even asked people lower in the organization to make concessions and cut spending to the barest of necessities. There have even been cases, in these same companies, where executives rewarded themselves after they gained a more favorable bottom line by extracting concessions from their employees. According to the theory of justice, these compensation decisions are of questionable morality since not all parties are sharing in the benefits and in the pain and trauma fairly.

Note that the key to the justice approach is *equity,* not equality. Nearly everyone agrees that the CEO deserves to make considerably more than a nonmanagerial employee. But how much more is fair and equitable? This issue points out a basic problem with all theories of ethics: They are based on subjective impressions. When are rights really called into question? When is a discrepancy in pay really inequitable? How do we define *greater good?* Of course, there are no easy answers here. Today most experts in business ethics suggest that decision makers should consider all three approaches when making decisions. In other words, does the decision appear morally sound when weighed against the standards of the utilitarian, rights, and justice approaches? If the answer is yes, the decision is probably ethical. If the answer from any of the forms of moral reasoning is no, then further examination is needed.

Figuring Out What to Do

As the examples here show, it is often quite difficult to know what to do. Even weighing the perspectives of different moral theories helps only so much. However, businesses can guide their employees to determine what is right and proper.

Many businesses include their ethical intentions as part of their missions. Even though such statements are broad and general, they do signify that the practice of ethical behavior is fundamental to the business. This priority underscores the ethical foundation that the business believes is important.

> **core values**
> The specific beliefs that a business makes part of its operating philosophy.

Some businesses go a step beyond the mission statement by defining a set of **core values,** those specific beliefs that the business makes part of its operating philosophy. These statements of core values typically cover honesty, respect, trust, and the overall moral tone of the business. For example, Avnet, the world's largest distributor of semi-conductors and other computer products, holds integrity as one of its key values. As the company notes: "We demonstrate integrity in everything we say and do. Honesty is the foundation upon which we as individuals and Avnet are built."[19]

Another popular way for many businesses to promote ethical behavior is through codes of conduct, sometimes referred to as codes of ethics. **Codes of conduct** are formal, written statements specifying the kinds of things that the business believes should be done and those things that should be avoided. The purpose of such a code is to tell employees how to approach and resolve difficult ethical issues. Usually, the code tries to define and outline common ethical problems or dilemmas that are likely to arise. Codes of conduct can be quite specific. For example, they might tell employees to accept no gifts from any dealers, suppliers, or associates with whom they do business. Presumably, such a directive is intended to reduce the risk of favoritism. Johnson & Johnson is well known for its ethics code, which helped guide the company through the Tylenol poisoning crises in 1982 and 1986. Today company employees periodically evaluate how well the company is doing in meeting its code. If needed, corrective action is taken promptly.[20]

> **codes of conduct**
> The formal written statements specifying the kinds of things a business believes should be done and those that should be avoided.

Although codes of conduct are important, they may not address the range of complex ethical situations managers encounter. In reality, they cannot. Codes of conduct deal with the most common issues and concerns and offer general guidance. They do not help much with the gray areas, the most difficult struggles many managers face. However, codes of conduct do make positive, constructive statements regarding some areas of ethical intent and action.

Some companies provide more detailed policies and procedures than are contained in codes of conduct. Some companies use ethics booklets to offer specific guidelines for dealing with ethical questions that may arise in certain areas. These booklets are usually updated regularly to provide guidelines on how to respond to current ethical concerns. Consider Minneapolis-based Tennant Company. Tennant manufactures and markets industrial and commercial floor-maintenance equipment and industrial floor coats. To help its employees understand and work through ethical dilemmas, the company has established its own *Business Ethics Guide* that clearly lays out expected behaviors and establishes the company's culture. In part, the guide asks employees to consider four basic questions: Is it the right thing to do? Is it the way you would want to be treated? Would you want to see this in tomorrow's newspaper? Will it protect and enhance the company's reputation as an ethical company?[21]

Finally, many companies try to help their employees by providing formal ethics training. This training usually includes background on the utilitarian, rights, and justice approaches to moral reasoning and examples of how they can be used. Real-world business cases allow employees to practice making decisions in difficult ethical situations. The training also provides a detailed overview of the programs and approaches the business has available to provide guidance for handling ethical dilemmas.

Building an Ethical Culture

The idea of business culture is important to the study of business ethics. **Business culture** is a set of unwritten values and beliefs about what is proper, right, and appropriate in a business. These beliefs and values are generally well known and accepted by the

> **business culture**
> A set of unwritten values and beliefs about what is proper, right, and appropriate in a business.

PROFILE 6.5   CLEAR ETHICAL MESSAGES AT SERVICEMASTER

The name ServiceMaster may not ring a bell, but you probably know many of the franchises that are part of its network of service companies. These include Terminex (pest control), TruGreen-ChemLawn (lawn care), Merry Maids (residential cleaning), Service-Master (heavy cleaning), and Furniture Medic. The company is a giant outsourcing service business with more than 12 million customers in the United States and 44 other countries and revenue of $7 billion.

You sense that this business takes ethics seriously as soon as you visit company headquarters in Downers Grove, Illinois. Entering the large two-story lobby, you are in awe of the curving marble wall 90 feet long and 18 feet high. Carved in 8-foot-high letters are the company's objectives—"To honor God in all we do; to help develop people; to pursue excellence; and to grow profitably." The company commits to operating by the highest ethical standards. It notes that its business "recognizes the dignity, worth and potential of each individual" and asserts the belief that "everyone from the service worker to company president has intrinsic value and worth." The company emphasizes its "commitment to truth" and pushes as an organizational mandate "to do the right thing in the right way."

Although the company has an extensive code of conduct, it recognizes that it is impossible to cover every possible situation. Chairman and CEO C. William Pollard comments, "When circumstances make the right course of action unclear, I urge you to seek guidance from your leadership . . . If you are uncertain of the response . . . feel free to contact the Corporate Compliance Department directly. If you feel the matter needs my attention, don't hesitate to write or call me directly."

Source: ServiceMaster website, www.servicemaster.com/overview_conduct.asp (accessed May 20, 2002).

members of the business. It is important to realize that a business culture develops slowly over time. A desired culture does not spring into existence full-grown because a leader dictates it. To nurture an ethical culture, business leaders must take certain steps. As Profile 6.5 shows, building an ethical culture takes dedication and commitment. We emphasize three key steps for building an ethical business culture.

First, leaders must establish clear moral values for the business, removing as much doubt as possible regarding where the business stands on key moral values. In fact, business culture often reflects the personal values of its key managers. This is particularly true in small businesses, where the president of the company has a tremendously strong influence on the culture of the company. The culture of a business is visible in the community in which the firm operates, and it is apparent to customers.

As noted earlier, businesses build culture through mission statements, statements of business philosophy, and statements of core values. Yet responsive leaders do more. They make sure company training efforts address moral values. The orientation programs for new employees feature the moral values of the business. Often there is open and regular discussion about ethical and moral concerns. In short, the leaders of the business go out of their way to elaborate and clarify moral values for their people.

The second step follows logically. Leaders must model the desired ethical standards and behavior. Actions really do speak louder than words. In business jargon, we say that leaders must "walk the talk." The best cue employees have as to how they should behave ethically comes from what they see people in positions of power and responsibility do. When leaders give ethical standards high priority and maintain them consistently, their actions send a powerful signal to the rest of the employees.

The third step in this culture-building process may be the most difficult. The business must support and reinforce employees for adhering to ethical values. This support shows most in the way companies reward employees. In general, people do what they are rewarded for doing. In other words, if the business consistently rewards ethical behavior and disciplines unethical behavior, employees learn how central ethical values are to the company. Logically, it is in their own best interests to practice ethical behavior.

Ethics as a Foundation of Business Practice

Ethics pervades every area of business. When salespeople promise customers delivery of products by certain dates, they are making ethical statements. When engineers design products to have the highest quality and the safest controls possible, they are making ethical statements. When internal accountants follow generally accepted practices without wavering, they are acting ethically. When managers treat their employees with respect and consideration, they are acting ethically.

Every employee in every area of the business is an ethical ambassador of the business. Of course, some employees are more visible than others. Some affect more people with their actions and decisions than others. However, as we discussed in this chapter, the ethical nature of the business resides in the heart of the business. If an ethical philosophy is not felt and practiced by every employee at every level throughout the business, a true ethical culture will not exist. In the future, as a business leader you must be an ethical role model within your business. Ethical considerations should be the foundation from which you start your decision-making process.

THINK ABOUT THIS

1. If you were Dr. Benton in the television show "ER" discussed in this chapter, what would you have done? Why?

2. What do you think business leaders should do to promote the highest levels of ethical behavior in their organizations?

3. In your work experience, have you ever seen actions that you think were unethical? How should the business have responded to those actions?

THE BIG PICTURE

Business does not take place in a vacuum. A business affects a variety of people and institutions. In turn, those people and institutions affect the business. Owners and investors, customers, employees, regulatory groups, consumer advocates, and even communities are all active stakeholders who must be considered when making key business decisions. Failure to recognize and address the expectations of these stakeholders can lead to mistakes and missteps. Some of these missteps, particularly those drawing the ethical and moral foundations of the business into question, can be damaging. Sensitivity toward stakeholder expectations and ethical actions are not luxuries to be pondered. They are realities, fundamental to business success.

Leaders (and future leaders like you) should be engaged in an ongoing process of refining their private morality and developing their own personal code of ethics. These refinements may not always be major or sweeping. More likely, they are subtle and incremental. The key is to keep questions about ethics in the forefront as your style of leadership evolves and you develop your approach to decision making.

Summary

1. Businesses affect many different groups of people, and that fact presents a problem for business leaders. The problem is how to take into account the impact of the business on the affected groups, or stakeholders.

    • What is a stakeholder?

    A stakeholder is a person or group that has some claim on or expectation of how a business should operate.

    • List the major categories of stakeholders.

    The major stakeholder groups are owners, customers, employees, suppliers, former employees, unions, the community, the natural environment, the industry in which the firm operates, other businesses, government, special interest groups, the media, and society in general.

2. Although the list of business stakeholders can be long, it can be divided according to how directly they influence the business.

    • Differentiate between the primary and secondary stakeholders for a business.

    Primary stakeholders are those the business affects and interacts with most directly. The three stakeholder groups commonly considered primary are owners, customers, and employees.

    Secondary stakeholders are those whom the business affects in an indirect or limited way. These include the remaining stakeholder groups, such as unions, environmentalists, the community, and society in general.

3. Some people view the business firm as having only one stakeholder, the stockholders. As a result, they tend to define or view business from a narrow perspective.

    • Give an integrated definition of the term *business*.

    A business is an organization that strives for profits for its owners while meeting the needs of its customers and employees and balancing the impacts of its actions on other stakeholders.

4. Stakeholders provide the business with the capacity to operate; in return, they expect something from the business.

   - What are the responsibilities of each stakeholder group to the business and what does each group expect in return?

   Owners provide capital and expect profits or return on their investments. Customers provide revenue and expect quality products. Employees provide labor and skills and expect fair pay and treatment. Suppliers provide needed inputs and expect favorable contracts and relationships. Communities provide the atmosphere and facilities that help the business attract talented people and keep them happy. In return, communities expect the business to support community programs.

5. Underlying all the relationships between a business and its stakeholders is business ethics. This issue, which regularly appears in the media, is an important business topic.

   - What is the role of ethics in contemporary businesses?

   There are many reasons businesses emphasize ethics. Three important ones are the following: (1) Businesses must understand and meet the ethical expectations of their customers. (2) Clear ethical standards and direction foster better work climates. (3) Clear and consistent ethical standards are crucial in the emerging environment of leaner organizations, where employees have to be trusted to know and do the right thing.

   - How would you define *business ethics?*

   Business ethics involves a search for and commitment to meet appropriate standards of moral conduct in business situations.

6. Addressing ethical issues can be challenging because of the presence of moral dilemmas.

   - Explain the concept of a moral dilemma.

   A moral dilemma exists when there is a conflict of interests involving ethical choices.

7. Managers must have some foundation for reasoning through the moral dilemmas they face.

   - Explain three methods of moral reasoning that can be used to solve a moral dilemma.

   One method is utilitarian reasoning, in which the morally best choice is that which produces the greatest good for the greatest number of stakeholders.

   A second method is the theory of rights, which argues that there are certain individual rights that must always be protected. If a decision violates or threatens these rights, it is not ethical.

   A third method is the theory of justice, which requires that decisions be guided by considerations of equity, fairness, and impartiality.

8. Given the importance of ethics, it is not surprising that many top managers devote substantial effort to helping employees act ethically. Those efforts consist of various specific practices and an attempt to create an ethical culture.

   - Describe some of the methods businesses use to help employees determine what is right and proper.

   They may include stating the company's ethical intentions as part of the mission statement, defining a set of core values, issuing a code of conduct or a code of ethics, and/or providing formal ethics training for employees.

• What is a business culture? What are the steps to building an ethical business culture?

A business culture is a set of unwritten values and beliefs about what is proper, right, and appropriate in the business.

Three key steps for building an ethical culture are these: (1) Leaders must establish clear moral values for the business. (2) Leaders must model the desired ethical standards and behavior. (3) The business must support and reinforce employees for adhering to ethical values.

Key Terms

business (integrated definition), p. 126	private morality, p. 138
business culture, p. 143	secondary stakeholders, p. 124
business ethics, p. 136	stakeholder, p. 124
codes of conduct, p. 143	theory of justice, p. 142
core values, p. 142	theory of rights, p. 141
environmentalism, p. 134	unions, p. 134
moral dilemma, p. 138	utilitarianism, p. 141
primary stakeholders, p. 124	value–price relationship, p. 129

Exercises and Applications

1. Ask three professors to comment on which stakeholders are most important to a business. Select one professor from each of the following disciplines: finance or economics, management or marketing, and sociology or philosophy. Write a brief statement on how these professors agree and differ on the idea of stakeholders.

2. Go to the Ben & Jerry's website (www.benjerry.com). Look at the three-part mission statement. How does it include stakeholders?

3. Consider two arguments of recent debate. One argument assumes that the only relevant goal of a business is to maximize its profits and provide as much return as possible to its owners. The other argument assumes that the successful business must balance the needs and concerns of a broad range of stakeholders, even if that means providing a lower rate of return to its owners. Which argument do you support? Be prepared to defend your view.

4. Consider the following situations. Decide what you think is the proper course of action for each.

• You are the human resources director of a midsize business. You have just interviewed a candidate for an engineering job. Although not the best candidate, he has an interesting background. He has spent the previous 10 years working in engineering and design for your top competitor and has indicated he knows many design secrets that he is willing to share with you and your business. Should you hire him?

• Your business has a strict policy that limits personal absence days to two days a year. However, it allows six sick days a year. You have already taken your two personal days for a ski trip to Vail but have taken no sick days. Last night, a close friend you have not seen in two years called to say he would be in town tomorrow and would like to spend the day with you. Will you call in sick?

- While going through some paperwork, you came across evidence that your company is dumping waste materials into the local river. You bring this to the attention of your supervisor. He tells you to forget you ever saw the documents and implies that your job may be at risk if you pursue this matter. You are young, have a new house in a nice neighborhood, and have just had your first child. Do you forget the event or report it?

5. In teams, discuss the three scenarios in exercise 4. Reach a team consensus on what the appropriate action should be. What arguments presented during the team discussion were helpful in understanding and dealing with the issues at hand?

6. Moral dilemmas are tough to handle. As discussed in this chapter, there are often conflicting interests. Look again at the "waste in the river" scenario in exercise 4. What is the moral dilemma here? Write a one-page analysis of this situation using each form of moral reasoning (utilitarianism, rights, and justice).

Ethics Starts at the Top

FROM THE PAGES OF

BusinessWeek

In the wake of the Enron and Andersen debacles, more emphasis has been placed on the ethical responsibilities of today's leaders. In light of that emphasis, the following comments stand out in a recent *BusinessWeek* article:

"If the challenge for executives in the 1990s was to transform corporate behemoths into nimble competitors, the challenge in coming years will be to create corporate cultures that encourage and reward integrity as much as creativity and entrepreneurship. To do that, executives need to start at the top, becoming not only exemplary managers but also the moral compass for the company. CEOs must set the tone by publicly embracing the organization's values. How? They need to be forthright in taking responsibility for shortcomings, whether an earnings shortfall, product failure, or a flawed strategy and show zero tolerance for those who fail to do the same.

"The best insurance against crossing the ethical divide is a roomful of skeptics. CEOs must actively encourage dissent among senior managers . . . by encourag[ing] opposing viewpoints. At too many companies the performance review system encourages a "yes-man culture" that subverts the organization's checks and balances. By advocating dissent, top executives can create a climate where wrongdoing will no longer go unchallenged."

"No one can legislate or mandate ethical behavior. But leadership must create an environment where honesty and fairness is paramount. If integrity is to be the foundation of competitiveness, it has to begin at the top."

Decision Questions

1. What do you think of the zero tolerance policy toward those managers who fail to meet the company's ethical standards?

2. Should organizational leaders be held to a higher standard than others in the business?

3. The article suggests that "integrity is . . . the foundation of competitiveness." Why is this foundation so important in a free market system?

Source: John A. Byrne, with Louis Lavelle, Nanette Byrnes, Marcia Vickers, and Amy Borrus, "How to Fix Corporate Governance," *BusinessWeek,* May 6, 2002, pp. 68–78.

References

1. "Leading the Way: Profiles of Some of the 100 Best Corporate Citizens for 2002," *Business Ethics: Corporate Social Responsibility Report,* www.business-ethics.com (accessed May 2, 2002); and "A Commitment to Corporate Citizenship," www.ibm.com/ibm/ibmgives (accessed May 2, 2002).

2. "Bringing Innovation in Health and Learning to the Global Community," www.gatesfoundation.org/aboutus (accessed May 7, 2002).

3. Elizabeth Schwinn, "Walton Family Gives $300 Million to University of Arkansas," *The Chronicle of Philanthropy,* http://philanthropy.org (accessed May 7, 2002).

4. Ronald Alsop, "Perils of Corporate Philanthropy," *The Wall Street Journal,* January 16, 2002, pp. B1, B4.

5. "Next Business Day Onsite Support," www.dell.com/us/gen/services/service_nbd.htm (accessed May 7, 2002).

6. "The No-Layoff Policy," *Business Ethics* 16, no. 1, January–February, 2002, p. 7.

7. "The 100 Best Companies to Work For," *Fortune* 145, no. 3, February 4, 2002, p. 86.

8. Reported in Roger E. Herman and Joyce L. Gioia, *How to Become an Employer of Choice* (Winchester, VA: Oakhill Press, 2000), pp. 65–66.

9. "Union Members Summary," Bureau of Labor Statistics, http://stats.bls.gov/news.release/union2.nr0.htm (accessed May 8, 2002).

10. "Environmental Affairs," www.starbucks.com/aboutus/envaffairs.asp, and "The Green Team," www.starbucks.com/aboutus/greenteam.asp (both accessed May 9, 2002).

11. "Community Initiatives" and "Corporate Community Partnerships," www.dell.com/us/en/gen/corporate/vision_initiatives.htm (accessed May 9, 2002).

12. John A. Byrne, "How to Fix Corporate Governance," *BusinessWeek,* May 6, 2002, pp. 69–78.

13. Ibid.

14. "2000 Organizational Integrity Survey," http://ecampus.bentley.edu/dept/cbe/newresearch/2.html (accessed May 10, 2002).

15. "The 100 Best Companies to Work For," p. 72.

16. "Following Your Conscience Is Just a Few Clicks Away," *BusinessWeek,* May 13, 2002, pp. 116–118.

17. Warren A. French and John Granrose, *Practical Business Ethics* (Englewood Cliffs, NJ: Prentice-Hall, 1995), pp. 41–42.

18. Sandra Waddock. *Leading Corporate Citizens* (New York: McGraw-Hill/Irwin, 2002), pp. 131–132.

19. "Core Values," www.avnet.com/corporate/profile/corevalues.html (accessed May 28, 2002).

20. "Johnson & Johnson Credo," www.johnsonandjohnson.com/who_is_jnj/cr_index.html (accessed May 28, 2002).

21. "Leading the Way."

Model of the Path toward a Successful Business

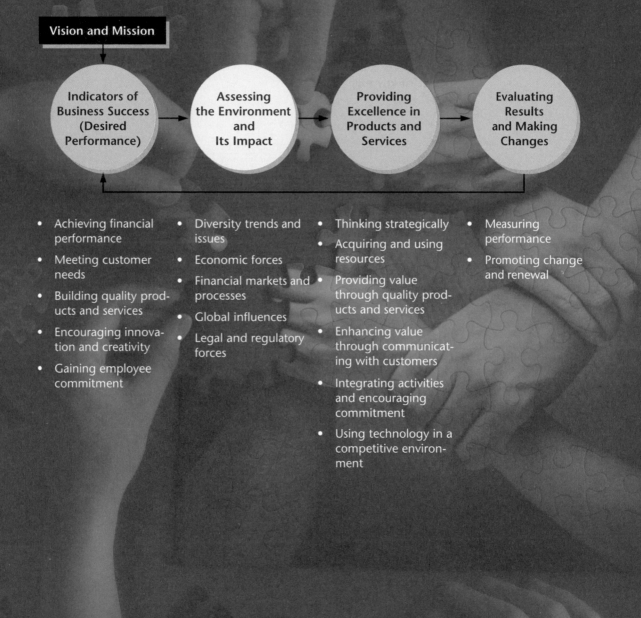

Vision and Mission

Indicators of Business Success (Desired Performance)

Assessing the Environment and Its Impact

Providing Excellence in Products and Services

Evaluating Results and Making Changes

- Achieving financial performance
- Meeting customer needs
- Building quality products and services
- Encouraging innovation and creativity
- Gaining employee commitment

- Diversity trends and issues
- Economic forces
- Financial markets and processes
- Global influences
- Legal and regulatory forces

- Thinking strategically
- Acquiring and using resources
- Providing value through quality products and services
- Enhancing value through communicating with customers
- Integrating activities and encouraging commitment
- Using technology in a competitive environment

- Measuring performance
- Promoting change and renewal

The Impact of External Forces

Part Three examines the impact of key external forces that affect the business and its operation. Business managers who understand these external forces and can devise approaches for capitalizing on the opportunities and minimizing the threats these forces pose will enjoy the greatest success.

Chapter 7 looks at the growing diversity in today's business world. This diversity opens up new opportunities and presents new challenges. We explore how business decision makers can manage diversity and build a supportive and inclusive business culture.

Chapter 8 explores the key economic forces affecting businesses. You will learn how changes in the economy affect business and how knowledge of economic patterns can help business planning and decision making. You will also learn how demand for and supply of products interact.

Chapter 9 examines the impact of financial markets and processes. Here, you will learn how financial markets affect the business firm. You will also gain sensitivity to the role of interest rates and the stock market.

Chapter 10 looks at the global influences on business. You will learn why international business activity makes sense and why its influence has grown. You will also become familiar with some of the ways that businesses can participate in the global economy. The chapter addresses some of the complexity that international activities can bring, such as dealing with cultural differences and sorting through a new range of ethical issues.

Chapter 11 explores legal and regulatory forces. These establish the parameters within which businesses must operate. You will understand how laws and regulations both support and restrict business operations so that the interests of society can be served.

You will learn from the chapters in Part Three that understanding external forces requires awareness, careful scrutiny, and thoughtful analysis.

7

The Impact of Diversity: Trends and Issues

Richard Parsons, Ken Chenault, Andrea Jung, Stanley O'Neal, Alain Belda, Franklin Raines. These are all successful and powerful businesspeople. All lead major corporations. Parsons heads AOL Time Warner; Chenault is CEO of American Express; Jung is at Avon; O'Neal leads Merrill Lynch; Belda is Chairman and CEO of Alcoa; and Raines is the top person at Fannie Mae. And all have one other factor in common— they are all minorities. These leaders spent years working their way up the corporate ladder, using their talents and business expertise to achieve the top leadership positions in their respective organizations. They are part of what some have termed a quiet revolution, where power and credentials are no longer bound by race and ethnicity.

Consider Andrea Jung. In some ways, she is far from the image of the traditional business titan. In her 40s, married, with a young daughter, the 5' 8" Asian American still takes her daughter to the bus stop before she walks to her Manhattan office. However, Jung, as chairman and CEO of the world's largest direct-selling company, exemplifies a smart, savvy, top-level executive with an amazing record of success.

Graduating magna cum laude from Princeton University, Jung gained experience with exclusive retailers such as Bloomingdale's, Neiman Marcus, and I. Magnin. Those lessons were tested when she moved to Avon. When Jung took over Avon in 1999, the company was in deep trouble, with its stock price falling. Some questioned whether the more-than-100 year-old company had become stale and dated and perhaps could not survive. Jung overhauled nearly everything, including the way the company advertised, manufactured, packaged, and even sold its products. Many feel that she not only turned around a sleeping giant, but literally saved the business. Under her leadership, annual sales are now almost $6 billion. Perhaps most impressive, the company maintained excellent financial results during the challenging economic times of the early 2000s.

Jung understands business, but she also appreciates the need for diversity and balance. In fact, she has stated: "I'm very selective in the companies I work for. I started at Bloomingdale's because it was committed to developing women. When I went to I. Magnin in San Francisco, it was to accompany a female CEO, and because there was a strong Asian population in that city, I never encountered a glass ceiling because of my race." Jung takes great strides to balance her career and family life. She sets aside blocks of time to spend with her daughter and husband. The family even makes every effort possible to be home by 7:30 p.m. so that they can have dinner together.

Andrea Jung is not just the first woman to lead Avon. She has reshaped the entire operation with her bold and progressive strategies, and she has emerged as one of the most powerful women in business today.[1]

We stated in earlier chapters that a successful business must understand its customers. It must also bring together talented people and keep them motivated to serve the needs of those customers. One of the biggest trends in today's business world is the increasing diversity of both customers and the workforce. As the model for a successful business shows, diversity is an important element of the environment in which a business operates. This chapter explores the nature of that diversity. It will help you recognize the challenges and opportunities diversity brings to a business. You will also learn how businesses need to respond proactively to diversity issues.

After studying this chapter, you should be able to:

1. Identify the dimensions of diversity.
2. Define *workforce diversity*.
3. Explain the major diversity issues facing business and how those issues affect business.
4. Formulate a definition of *diversity management*.
5. Identify and explain why a business should be concerned with diversity management.
6. Recognize the elements of a strong diversity management culture.

You have probably heard and read about how our society is changing and becoming more diverse. In fact, that diversity is the hallmark of our society. Some societies are homogeneous, meaning that their members share a relatively uniform or standard set of values and backgrounds. Japan, for example, is a fairly homogeneous society. The United States, on the other hand, is a very **heterogeneous society.** It is composed of many dissimilar people with a varied mix of backgrounds, values, needs, and interests. Further, most evidence suggests that the United States is becoming more diverse all the time. Not surprisingly, our domestic workforce mirrors this growing diversity.

Diversity brings with it special issues and concerns, particularly for businesses trying to understand and respond to their environments. Pinpointing trends and emerging consumer interests and demands is difficult, since they may relate to only a small segment of the total market. It is also difficult to manage all the people in a business effectively. No single management style or approach will work. No given set of rewards will motivate all workers, since most businesses have a broad range of employees with unique and quite varied needs. Indeed, diversity and heterogeneity make business a much more complex undertaking.

Yet we must remember that diversity offers many rich opportunities for businesses that understand the dynamics of change and are poised to act. Indeed, such understanding is essential for any business in today's competitive world. In this chapter, we will explore the nature of these changes, discuss how they affect businesses, and look at some of the ways businesses must respond to them.

> **heterogeneous society**
>
> A society composed of many dissimilar people with a varied mix of backgrounds, values, needs, and interests.

Dimensions of Diversity

One of the problems with studying diversity is the complexity of the concept itself. There are so many ways people can be different. Some of these differences, such as gender and race, are easy to recognize. Others are more subtle. To understand the range of diversity better, consider Figure 7.1.

The inner wheel of Figure 7.1 contains the areas of age, race, ethnicity, gender, mental and physical abilities and qualities, and sexual orientation. These six areas are considered the primary dimensions of diversity. They are primary because they represent dominant ways of looking at differences in people. The author of this model, Marilyn Loden, contends that these are the dimensions that shape our basic self-concept and are critical to the way we view and interact with the world.[2]

The outer circle consists of work experience, first language, income, family status, military experience, religion, communication style, work style, geographic location, and education. These 10 areas are considered the secondary dimensions of diversity. Unlike the primary dimensions, these areas can be acquired and changed. The model is certainly not all-inclusive, but it is helpful to anyone seeking to understand diversity issues.

It is important to avoid stereotypes when dealing with the topic of diversity. **Stereotyping** occurs when we place people in broad social groups, generalizing about and labeling them because they are part of a given group. Stereotyping ignores individual variation and difference. It is a shorthand way of categorizing people, but it ignores the uniqueness of each person.

> **stereotyping**
>
> Placing people in broad social groups, then generalizing about and labeling them because they are part of a given group.

Consider your peers in this class. Look at them as they enter the classroom. There are some obvious, primary dimensions of difference. There are both men and women. In many cases, there are individuals from a variety of racial and ethnic backgrounds. Most of the students are probably about your age, but some may be older. There may even be some obvious physical differences.

FIGURE 7.1

Primary and Secondary Dimensions of Diversity

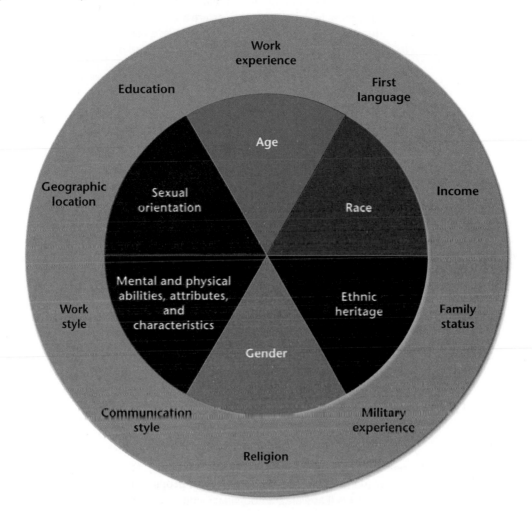

Sometimes we categorize people on the basis of a single area of difference, but doing so can be very misleading. To really understand, appreciate, and value any person, we have to look beyond the obvious elements of difference. For example, to say you are an 18-year-old college student tells us something about you. However, to say you are an 18-year-old Hispanic female who comes from a large family in Miami with professional parents and strong family values tells us a lot more. We begin to get a better sense of what a complex person you are. We begin to understand better the unique background and views you are likely to bring to the class discussion. We begin to see how you may be an important person to have on a class project team. By looking beyond the obvious, we get a richer sense of who you are.

Throughout this chapter, as we talk about differences, we encourage you to keep this beginning notion in mind. Recognize that although the topic of diversity may be studied in discrete sections, people do not fit into easy, simplistic categories. They are quite complex. Generalizations, while convenient, are often misleading. Given this cautionary note, we look at some key diversity themes in greater detail. We do this by dividing this chapter into two parts. In the first part, we look at some important diversity challenges and explore how these challenges are affecting today's businesses. In the second part, we discuss diversity management. How must a business begin to refocus its thinking to address the challenges and opportunities of diversity?

Diversity Challenges and Opportunities

This section deals with some of the important diversity issues that confront contemporary businesses. These issues must be addressed. Businesses have to change some of their traditional assumptions and approaches in the face of growing diversity. As you study this section, you will recognize that these diversity issues can be both challenges and sources of opportunity for progressive and creative businesses.

workforce diversity
The mix of people from differing demographic and ethnic backgrounds and value orientations in an organization.

In some cases, diversity has an impact on the workforce. **Workforce diversity** refers to the mix of people from differing demographic and ethnic backgrounds and value orientations in an organization. For most businesses, this translates into the inclusion of more women, older and younger employees, disabled people, African Americans, Asian Americans, and Hispanics into the workforce. In other cases, diversity points to emerging market issues. We will discuss some of the most important diversity issues, which are shown in Table 7.1.

The Growing Presence of Women in the Workforce

Over the past half century, there has been a steady and significant increase in women working outside the home. In 1955, about 36 percent of the women in the United States were in the workforce. Today, about 60 percent of U.S. women are in the workforce.[3] Women now constitute nearly half of our workforce.[4] Certainly, more work opportunities are available to women than in the past. Further, it has become common for women to pursue careers that were traditionally dominated by males. Just look at your business class. In all likelihood, the distribution of women and men is closely balanced.

This increased workforce participation among women affects society and its businesses in countless ways. One obvious impact, the change in work and family patterns, will be addressed in the next section. At this point, though, let's consider another impact. The increased female presence in the business world creates a different workplace. Accordingly, the successful business must build a work environment where women (and all other workers) can reach the full potential of their talents, where all employees can be comfortable and productive.

Women have made great corporate strides. In 1972, they held about 19 percent of the management positions in this country; today, they hold about 50 percent of all management and professional positions.[5] Many companies, such as Bayer Corporation and Marriott International, have gained

THINK ABOUT THIS

1. Many social commentators argue that the United States is a richer, stronger society because of its heterogeneity and diversity. Do you agree? Why or why not?

2. Look around the classroom or another large group of people. How many areas of diversity can you identify?

3. Some businesses do not employ a diverse group of people. What might be some of the reasons for this situation?

TABLE 7.1

Key Diversity Issues:
Challenges and
Opportunities

- The growing presence of women in the workforce.
- The balance between work and family.
- The growth of racial and ethnic minorities.
- Age and generational influences.
- The accommodation of individuals with disabilities.
- Teams and diversity.
- Global business and diversity.

excellent reputations for advancing women through their corporate ranks. In the past few years, more women have been achieving top leadership positions. Even among very large businesses, it is becoming more common to see the CEO's chair filled by women, for example, Meg Whitman (eBay), Anne Mulcahy (Xerox), Patricia Russo (Lucent), Carly Fiorina (Hewlett-Packard/Compaq), Andrea Jung (Avon), and Carole Black (Lifetime Entertainment Services). And you are already aware of Colleen Barrett, president of Southwest Airlines. You can learn more about Black and Russo in Profile 7.1.

A number of companies have made important strides in having more women on their boards of directors. Among Fortune 500 companies, women account for 12.4 percent of all board seats.[6] That trend represents significant movement and advancement over the past two decades.

While women have achieved more representation in recent years, disparity still exists. While women fill about half of all management and professional positions, they constitute only about 12 percent of the top management positions in the country.[7] Some people argue that as women try to advance to senior management positions, they

Women have made great corporate strides in the last 30 years. What strengths and advantages have businesses gained as more women have entered the workforce?

PROFILE 7.1   WOMEN AT THE TOP

Her achievements are stunning. Since she was named president and CEO of Lifetime Entertainment Services in 1999, Carole Black has transformed Lifetime TV into the number one cable network in prime time. Black's is a classic success story typical of the kind of upbeat portrayals of women that have been the foundation of Lifetime's popularity. Raised by her Armenian grandparents, Black was voted "girl most likely to succeed" at her high school. At Lifetime, she is known as a "tough but loving big sister," a style that shows even in Lifetime's programming. As Black says, "We're not into fantasy. Our shows and our characters have to feel real."

The numbers she has produced have also been real—real winners. Revenue for 2001 was $715 million. That's a 30 percent jump from the previous year. Programming, marketing, and advertising budgets have been dramatically expanded. Although advertisers have generally trimmed their spending throughout the industry, they are more than willing to buy time on Lifetime TV.

Kodak was hoping for the same kind of dramatic progress when it hired a new CEO, Patricia Russo. Russo was hired away from Lucent Technologies to turn around Kodak, a struggling giant in recent years. Russo has a reputation for getting tough jobs done. During the mid-90s, she led a successful turnaround of the business communications division of AT&T and Lucent, a $6 billion business.

She is known for her expertise in telecommunication services and her strong focus on technology. Experts felt she might be just the person to push Kodak's needed transition from traditional photo products toward digital imaging products and services. Unfortunately, Kodak was not the only company to recognize Russo's skills. She was hired back to Lucent in 2002 to become its CEO.

Source: "The Top Managers of the Year," *BusinessWeek,* January 14, 2002, pp. 60, 65; Kodak website, www.kodak.com (accessed March 20, 2002); Lucent website, www.lucent.com (accessed September 20, 2002).

---

glass ceiling
Systematic barriers that prevent women from advancing in the organization.

encounter a **glass ceiling**—systematic barriers that prevent women from rising in the organization. The glass ceiling is so subtle it is transparent, yet so real and so pervasive that it effectively blocks upward mobility.[8] That ceiling may be due to stereotypes, misdirected assumptions, or insensitivity to the unique needs women bring to the workplace. It may be due to underdeveloped career tracks. It may be due simply to a tendency of those in senior positions (usually men) to promote people quite similar to themselves (presumably men). In all likelihood, the reasons are complex, multifaceted, and usually not very clear.

What is more clear is the impact of the glass ceiling. The frustration of continually running into it leads many women to leave the company and seek opportunities elsewhere. This result is especially troublesome when those who leave are among the most talented (and, accordingly, the most marketable) in the organization.

How can the glass ceiling be shattered, and how can a gender-friendly workplace be structured? These are important questions. Some businesses offer mentoring programs and support groups to coach women how to work through the political dynamics of the business. Others take active roles in developing career paths for promising women, making sure that women get access to the training and professional development they need, and moving promising women into positions where they can gain the experience and the exposure necessary for promotion. Increasingly, these efforts mean that women must be provided opportunities for extended international assignments that are important for executive development and advancement. However, the vast majority of these assignments go to men, prompting a new label, the **glass border.**[9]

In many cases, businesses must be more proactive in facing issues that affect women. One example is the area of sexual harassment. Most businesses of any size now have explicit sexual harassment policies designed to encourage a positive tone of interaction between men and women in the workplace and to avoid a hostile environment. The range of possibilities is endless. This movement demands that businesses seek creative responses to better meet employee needs. More will be said about this issue later in the chapter, when we talk about how businesses can build cultures that embrace diversity.

> **glass border**
> The tendency for women not to receive international assignments important for their advancement.

Balancing Work and Family

For most adults, male or female, the two most important areas of our lives are work and family. Not surprisingly, these two areas do not exist independently. They spill over into each other, at least to some extent. Often work and family demands interfere with each other, a condition known as **work–family conflict.** The need for balance is often quite pressing.

This challenge is an outgrowth of two factors. First, as we have discussed, there are more women in the workforce. Second, there seems to be a prevailing attitude, particularly strong among younger workers, that balance is expected. Writer Claire Raines has addressed this point clearly. In discussing workers in their 20s and 30s, she notes that "they have witnessed first-hand a work ethic that eats people up and spits them out and they want something different. They believe work should not be more important than family, friends, and hobbies."[10] This belief does not mean that younger workers are poor performers or unmotivated. It simply means that they have seen what an overfocus on work can do, and they seem to be pushing for a more balanced life.

Consider this demographic phenomenon: In the past, many women entered the workforce only after their children started school. During the 1980s and 1990s, it became more common for women to combine career and family responsibilities, and there was a dramatic surge in the number of working mothers. Today, over 50 percent of married mothers and nearly 60 percent of unmarried mothers (about a quarter of all mothers) with children under a year old were in the workforce.[11]

But we must also consider an important recent development. Although the majority of mothers with infant children are in the workforce, the percentage has fallen since 1998.[12] Some experts argue that this drop is a signal that women are more willing to put their careers on hold to raise young children. Others indicate that this move signals the need for more flexible work schedules and more telecommuting opportunities for talented young women. Still, many families need two incomes to afford the lifestyle they want. In many homes, both the husband and wife are actively pursuing full-time careers. These arrangements are known as **dual-career households.** When both spouses work, family income rises. At the same time, pressures for child care and redistribution of household tasks also increase.

The possible tensions between work and family are issues of great significance for business. First, businesses have to address the potential conflicts between work and

> **work–family conflict**
> The sense that work and family demands interfere with each other.

> **dual-career households**
> Families in which both partners are actively pursuing full-time careers.

Telecommuting offers the advantage of working while staying home at least some days of the week. Employees benefit by spending more time with their families and not having the stress and expense of a daily commute. This helps balance their work and family responsibilities. The downside of telecommuting is that employees have less interaction with others at work. Why is this a problem?

telecommuting
A work arrangement in which workers spend part of each week working at home and communicating with the office via computer.

flextime
A work arrangement that allows employees to adjust work hours, often to meet other responsibilities.

job sharing
A work arrangement in which two or more employees share one job and split all the duties and responsibilities, as well as the compensation of that job.

family. Family leave policies, flexible work schedules, and child care assistance may be solutions. When a business addresses diversity, it is concerned with all these issues. For example, the business may turn to flexible work schedules to attract talented employees and enable them to meet both work and family demands. In fact, when employees were asked which benefits would help provide better balance between work and personal life, 55 percent said flexible work hours, followed by on-site personal services and child and elder care programs.[13]

One approach that has become popular is **telecommuting,** in which workers spend part of their time each week working at home and communicating with the office by means of computer. This arrangement reduces travel time and increases child care options. Of course, telecommuting will not work for every business, particularly where employees must be present to interact with customers. However, where appropriate, it lets employees be productive without being physically present.

More and more companies use **flextime,** which allows a worker to adjust work hours, often to meet other responsibilities. Basically, flextime gives employees discretion over when they start and end their workdays. At DeLoitte and Touche, a large public accounting firm, well-run work–family policies that include flextime and telecommuting help the business retain talented people.[14] Both men and women seem to appreciate the freedom to arrange part of their workday to better meet other responsibilities and needs.

Given that a number of parents prefer part-time work, some businesses have turned to a work approach known as **job sharing,** where two or more employees share one job and split all the duties and responsibilities, as well as the compensation of that job. With this arrangement, two workers can hold an important professional position. One may work from 8 A.M. to noon, handling all areas of the job. The other works from noon to 4 P.M., continuing to carry out all the responsibilities of the job. Or one may work Mondays, Wednesdays, and Fridays while the other works Tuesdays and Thursdays. In job sharing, both employees receive and share all the benefits, such as insurance plans, that go with the job. The job-sharing idea seems to be growing in popularity.

Some businesses recognize that quality child care is so important for working families that they go out of their way to support child care arrangements. Some have benefit packages that cover at least part of the cost of child care. A growing number of businesses have childcare facilities on-site. Johnson & Johnson, the world's largest maker of health care products, has six child development centers serving over 500

THINK ABOUT THIS

1. Our model of a successful business shows that financial performance is the prime indicator of a healthy business. How is the inclusion of more women in the workforce likely to lead to improvements in a business's financial performance?

2. What business opportunities can you think of that may come from the changing family structure and the increased spillover between work and family?

children of employees. It also has centers at other J&J facilities throughout the country.[15] Proponents say that parents who know their children are being well taken care of and who can drop in on them during the workday are more productive employees.

Businesses support flexible work schedules and child care arrangements because these programs give them a better chance of employing talented workers who might otherwise find it difficult to be in the workforce or might go to work for a more understanding company. Also, employees who have more say over their lives and time feel better about their work, which may improve their morale and commitment toward their employer. Businesses hope that added flexibility will lead to better performance.

The Growth of Racial and Ethnic Minorities

An important impact of diversity for all businesses today relates to changes in the racial and ethnic composition of our population. Racial and ethnic minorities are growing as a percentage of the U.S. population and should exceed 30 percent of the population by 2005.[16]

Today in the United States, African Americans are the largest minority group. However, it is projected that by 2005, Hispanics will grow to 13.3 percent of the population and become the largest minority cohort.[17] The term *Hispanic* encompasses various ethnic groups, including Mexicans, Puerto Ricans, Central and South Americans, and Cubans. The majority of Hispanics (60 percent) are of Mexican descent.[18] Table 7.2 offers a further look at some of the key population and workforce numbers and projected changes.

Minority groups are growing in both size and affluence. For example, in recent years, African Americans have seen a sharp rise in household income, prompting a 50 percent rise in purchasing power among African Americans since 1996. About 51 percent of married African Americans have incomes of $50,000 or higher.[19]

Let's return to an earlier theme. Since people differ in many ways, it is dangerous and misleading to look at minority groups as if all members exhibit the same characteristics and behaviors. It makes no more sense to treat Hispanics, African Americans, or Asian Americans as uniform groups than it does to treat Caucasians as a single group. Consider Hispanic use of the Internet, and look at a single variable—the language Hispanics prefer to speak. Hispanics as a group use the Internet slightly less than non-Hispanics. But primarily English-speaking Hispanics use the Internet far more than primarily Spanish-speaking Hispanics and even more than non-Hispanics. Similarly, far more primarily English-speaking Hispanics own computers than primarily Spanish-speaking Hispanics. Hence, computer manufacturers might be well advised to market

	Population		Workforce	
	2002	**2005**	**2002**	**2005**
White (non-Hispanic)	70.6	69.3	72.5	71.2
Black	12.9	13.1	12.0	12.3
Hispanic	12.4	13.3	11.2	12.0
Asian	4.3	4.6	5.3	5.6

TABLE 7.2

Percentage of Resident Population and Workforce by Race and Ethnicity, 2002 and 2005 (projection)

Source: "Projections of the Total Resident Population by Race, Hispanic Origins, and Nativity: Middle Series, 2001 to 2005," U.S. Census Bureau website, www.census.gov (accessed March 18, 2002); and Civilian Labor Force, Bureau of Labor Statistics website, www.bls.gov (accessed March 18, 2002).

computer upgrades and enhancements to English-speaking Hispanics while marketing entry-level computers to Spanish-speaking Hispanics.[20]

Because of the growth in minority populations, many companies are developing strategies for better reaching and serving those markets. That often means being more understanding and sensitive to the needs of minorities. Consider the following examples: Southern New England Telecom (SNET) went to great lengths to figure out why Hispanic customers had delinquency rates (failure to pay the phone bill) so much higher than other cultures. What it found were cultural differences that clashed with the company's typical customer service system. SNET found that the average Hispanic customer felt a need to develop rapport with the service representative before he or she was comfortable getting down to business. The somewhat abrupt style that SNET had taught its reps caused many Hispanics to be hesitant to call the company to work out a problem. By getting to know its customers better, SNET and its reps were able to adjust their approach and significantly lower the delinquency problem.[21]

Other companies have focused their business efforts on promising minority markets. For example, McDonald's tested a Cuban sandwich in its South Florida restaurants. And taking a cue from the popular Latino dessert, Mars has test-marketed *dulce de leche,* chocolate and caramel–flavored M&Ms. Many advertisers produce Spanish versions of their commercials for distribution to certain areas of the United States.

Businesses are coming to realize that racial and ethnic minorities increasingly represent the base from which they draw prospective employees. But there are still shortcomings in their efforts to include more minorities in the workforce. Let's look at two issues.

First is the reality of the glass ceiling. Although originally conceived to describe a lack of opportunity for women, the glass ceiling appears to be even more prevalent for ethnic and racial minorities. Minority employees are still quite uncommon in the managerial ranks.

Second, and quite important, a recent survey found that 44 percent of blacks felt that blacks are treated unfairly on the job.[22] The impact of such perceived unfairness is significantly affected by how the business chooses to respond. If it does not redress inequities, minority employees may reasonably feel frustrated and may seek to leave the organization.

Organizations can positively, aggressively, and firmly address these issues and concerns. One business that has done so is Xerox, which has been a leader in the diversity arena for over a quarter of a century. Xerox is known for its Balanced Work Force (BWF) process. The goal of the balanced workforce strategy is to gain equitable workforce representation in all areas of the company.

One vehicle Xerox uses to further its diversity goals is caucus groups—for example, a women's caucus group and a black caucus group. These **caucus groups** are made up of employees who get together and address key concerns relating to members of their particular group. They then communicate these perspectives to upper management at Xerox. In addition to being a communication link, the caucus groups are a wonderful way for group members to network and offer support for one another. Thus, promising young African Americans can find role models and mentors through the caucus system. Importantly, Xerox has created a culture that is highly supportive of and responsive to these caucus groups. This attention to diverse groups is one reason Xerox is recognized as a model of effective employee utilization.[23]

caucus groups
Groups of employees who get together to address key concerns relating to members of their particular group.

Age and Generational Influences

As we try to understand and respond to diversity, we see that some of the most dramatic effects come from age and generational influences. Profiling the population according to age leads to a better understanding of customer needs, as well as to areas of business opportunity.

Baby Boomers

The generation of Americans born between 1946 and 1964 is known collectively as the **baby boomers.** This generation, since its arrival, has been a major force for businesses, basically because it is such a significant proportion of the population. For example, in the 1970s and 1980s, most baby boomers were in their 20s and 30s. As a group, they valued health and fitness. It is not surprising that entire industries, such as the home fitness industry, grew around the demands of this generation.

> **baby boomers**
> The generation of Americans born between 1946 and 1964.

Today, as the boomers age, their impact is still dramatic. From 1980 to 2000, the number of people between the ages of 40 and 59 increased by more than 20 million. During that period, the fastest-growing age group, in total numbers, was 50- to 54-year-olds.[24] As baby boomers moved into their 50s, demand for goods and services reflected their new needs. Consider the following series of developments: During their younger years, boomers pushed the fitness movement and were at the heart of the running craze. As boomers aged, they still wanted to stay fit, prevent health problems, deal with stress, and just feel better about themselves. So where did they turn? How about health clubs? Over half of current health club and fitness center members are 40 and older, and "seniors"—those 55 and older—are the fastest-growing age group at health clubs.[25]

The business possibilities are endless. Investment and retirement planning services should benefit. Vacation and travel services should grow. Products ranging from bifocals to electronic planners offer considerable sales potential.

The Aging of the Workforce: The Baby Boom Effect

Another factor that is important for businesses is the aging (what some refer to as the "graying") of the workforce. As shown in Table 7.3, the average age of the workforce is rising and the proportion of workers who are older is increasing. The number of workers in the 55–64 age group will increase by nearly 52 percent by 2010.[26] Part of this movement is driven by the demographics we've discussed. As the baby boom generation ages, their sheer numbers mean more older workers over the next few years. Part of this phenomenon arises because people are living longer and simply wish to work longer. This trend may be due to concerns over the costs of early retirement, as well as a shortage of younger, skilled workers.

Age Group	2000	2010	Percent Change
Under 25	22.7	26.1	14.8
25–34	31.7	34.2	8.1
35–44	37.8	34.0	−10.2
45–54	30.5	36.8	20.7
55–64	14.0	21.2	51.7
65 and older	4.2	5.4	29.6

TABLE 7.3

Percentage of Workforce by Age Group, 2000 and 2010 (projection)

Source: Peter Francese, "The American Workforce," *American Demographics,* February 2002, pp. 40–41 (reporting Bureau of Labor Statistics data).

There are a number of business implications to this trend as well as a number of open questions.[27] For example, some experts argue that an older workforce will be experienced and stable and thus more productive than a younger workforce. Others predict that older workers may be less open to change, which may reduce their productivity. Both views have some merit. Older workers do bring important backgrounds and experiences that can be extremely beneficial in business practice. Yet if their experiences are not relevant to the changing demands of contemporary business, they are of limited value. For this reason, we expect employee retraining to become even more important with an aging workforce. **Employee retraining** involves regularly providing employees the education and training they need to expand their base of skills so that they meet the needs of businesses.

Older workers also raise competitive issues. Businesses are extremely concerned with reducing or controlling costs. They recognize that cost considerations are critical to their long-run competitiveness. In many ways, older workers do represent higher costs for the business. Since older workers have usually been with a business longer, their pay is often higher. They also represent higher health care costs and higher pension charges. Yet older workers represent talent and experience. Often the business has invested a lot of money in their development. They are important resources. It's a dilemma. How should a business respond? What makes sense? What seems fair? There are no easy answers here. Some businesses offer incentives for older employees to take early retirement. But they must be cautious so that they don't lose key talent in the process of reducing costs.

> **employee retraining**
> The practice of regularly providing the education and training workers need to expand their base of skills so that they can meet the needs of business.

Generation X

Generation X refers to those who were born between 1965 and 1980. While much has been written about the uniqueness of this generation, a few themes are coming into clear focus as this generation ages. The majority of Gen-Xers are now married (55 percent), and a majority of Gen-X women have children. Growing up in an era where violence, divorce, and corporate downsizing are prevalent, Gen-Xers have a fundamental concern for security. This generation seems to emphasize the value of education strongly, and they are better educated than previous generations.

As we noted earlier, in the section on balancing work and family, Gen-Xers seem to reject the notion of sacrificing family for career. Although they are willing to work hard and be productive leaders, they place strong values on family, friendships, and social causes. They tend to be less enamored with loyalty and allegiance to one particular company than was the case with their parents. Gen-Xers are more loyal to their professions. They want careers where they can experience professional growth, be challenged, do work that is meaningful and significant, and still have balance in their lives. Gen-Xers create key challenges for organizations that are trying to motivate and retain the best and the brightest. As we see in Profile 7.2, Gen-Xers will be the new cadre of organizational leaders.

> **Generation X**
> The generation of Americans born between 1965 and 1980.

Generation Y: The Net Generation[28]

Generation Y, including today's teenagers, comprises those born between 1981 and 1999. This generation is more than three times the size of Generation X and is the largest group since the baby boomers.[29] They are a racially diverse generation (one in three is not Caucasian), are likely to have working mothers, and have strong buying power. That buying power makes Generation-Yers a special challenge for today's businesses. Trying to understand and read the inclinations and preferences of this group is critical to the success of a number of firms. The Internet has become a powerful tool for

> **Generation Y**
> The generation of Americans born between 1981 and 1999.

They have been called the "next generation of minority business leaders." Even at their relatively young ages—all under 40—their accomplishments and leader potential are already noteworthy. These men and women come from companies that support them because of the unique talents and perspective they bring to their work.

Consider Alicia Fernandez-Campfield of Xerox. Alicia is national billing manager, charged with ensuring the accuracy of Xerox's XBS billing information system. Additionally, she is president of the Hispanic Association for Professional Advancement, an organization within Xerox that works to increase Hispanic representation at all levels of the company. Or consider Martha Salinas of Compaq Computer Corporation. Martha, who just turned 30, is responsible for Compaq's targeted e-mail marketing program for all of North America. And there is Mary Beth Stone West of Kraft Foods. Mary Beth is an executive vice president responsible for leading Kraft's meals division. Rene Hernandez is associate counsel in the law and regulation department of the Allstate Corporation. He plays a key role in reviewing and developing a range of functions that include national advertising campaigns and new-product introductions. Or what about Greg Watson, vice president for Olive Garden brand marketing. A former Marine helicopter pilot and the recipient of the 2001 Central Florida YMCA Black Achiever award, Greg creates national advertising and promotion programs for Olive Garden restaurants.

Alicia, Martha, Mary Beth, Rene and Greg are all young (each is under 40), well educated (each has an MBA), and hardworking. All seem poised to take on more and more responsibilities at their respective organizations. All have strong commitments to diversity, and their companies support their efforts. Keep these names in mind. They may well be, just a few years down the line, the next generation of presidents and CEOs.

Source: Chris A. Enstrom, "Generation Next," *Minority MBA,* Winter–Spring 2002, pp. 12–17.

reaching this market—a generation that grew up with home computers and instant technology. As one marketing executive noted, "They all have Internet addresses. If a company can't communicate via e-mail, the attitude is 'What's wrong with you?'"[30]

Nearly 17 million Gen-Yers have been labeled "tweens" (10- to 13-year-olds). Although they have money to spend, they are an advertising challenge. They don't respond to ads that are too sarcastic or edgy. But they do like and seem to be influenced by musicians. In 2000 and 2001, Britney Spears was their idol, and she pitched everything from Pepsi to Skechers footwear.[31]

Many companies recognize the opportunities available by tapping into the buying power of Gen-Yers. They also recognize how important it can be to build brand loyalty in this generation. For example, Toyota has launched a new car line, Scion. This youth-targeted car is aimed directly at Generation Y.[32]

I DON'T WANT YOUR PITY.
I WANT THE JOB.

Millions of talented people seek something more from life. And they're ready and able to earn it. That's why wemedia.com has teamed up with HotJobs.com to offer access to the best jobs for people with various disabilities. It's part of how wemedia.com serves the needs of the more than 54 million Americans with disabilities, enabling them to pursue their potential without compromise.

Cary Fields, President/CEO

we media.com

Over 20% of the U.S. population has some level of disability. These may range from difficulties seeing or hearing to the use of a wheelchair. This ad for wemedia.com promotes the fact that they have a unique job search section for people with various disabilities.

Accommodating Individuals with Disabilities

More than 54 million Americans have some level of disability, ranging from difficulty seeing or hearing to the use of a wheelchair. The *Americans with Disabilities Act* (ADA) has required businesses to be more responsive to the unique needs of disabled workers. Progressive businesses have understood the talents that workers with disabilities can bring, so they have already made their work environments more accessible and accommodating. Further, ongoing advances in assistive technology are helping bridge the gap between what disabled workers can and cannot do.

Consider Target Corporation. The Minneapolis-based retailer has a great reputation for seeking out and hiring people with disabilities. It is also highly regarded for its commitment to and practices of accommodating employees with special needs. The company was the first retailer to use models with disabilities in its print advertising. In 2002, Target was named employer of the year by the National MS Society.[33]

In recent years, there has been concern that employees with disabilities are particularly vulnerable to job loss during economic downturns. In fact, U.S. Census data indicate that the disabled are the demographic group with the highest unemployment rate. Many observers argue that despite the legal foundations of the ADA, the disabled are the last hired and the first to be dismissed.[34]

Teams and Diversity

As we noted earlier in the text, businesses typically use teams of employees to do part of the work that needs to be done. Ideally, teams are the best option when a decision, project, or task requires multiple skills, perspectives, or experiences.[35] Since differing talents and backgrounds are needed, effective teams include a diverse makeup of people. At times, teams may include employees from different areas of the business so that their views can be represented on a project. At times, teams purposely bring together people who have different views so that new ideas and creative approaches can be explored.

Of course, when employees with such differences are brought together on teams, the chances for clashes and conflicts are greatly increased. Progressive companies realize that when handled respectfully, conflicts and disagreements can be powerful stimuli for exploring new thinking and coming up with novel solutions. This outcome is one of the reasons strong organizations realize they need more diver-

THINK ABOUT THIS

1. Have you ever visited a foreign country where you were different from others because of appearance or language? How did you feel? What responses of others made you feel more comfortable?

2. Have you ever been in a situation where you felt as if you were being put down or discriminated against because of some difference? How did you feel? Did the discriminatory behaviors of others motivate you to prove yourself, or did it make you withdraw?

3. What difficulties is a business likely to face as it trains and retrains its workforce to deal with diversity?

Diverse work teams have become a key feature at progressive organizations. These companies feel that bringing together people with different backgrounds and points of view adds to the richness and quality of team decisions. What specific advantages do companies gain by using more diverse teams?

sity in their boards of directors (which really function as top-level teams), among their top executives (who meet regularly in team settings), as well as throughout the rest of the organization.

Successful companies train team members how to appreciate, respect, and work through the differences they experience on teams so that better decisions can result.

Global Business and Diversity

In chapter 10, we will discuss the extent and impact of a rapidly developing global economy. The global focus of business creates a number of opportunities. Yet this global focus also creates a number of issues that must be understood and addressed. One of these issues is the need for sensitivity to the cultures of other countries and to the backgrounds of people beyond our domestic borders. This sensitivity is important for doing business outside American borders, especially when you are working with people from parts of the world where values, assumptions, and approaches differ and may even clash.

Experts point out that there is a need for cross-cultural literacy—an understanding of how cultural differences affect the way business is carried out. This literacy is based on respecting the values and norms of a given culture. Business leaders must be aware of and sensitive to the keys that define a culture. These keys include the political philosophy, the economic philosophy, the educational systems, the language, the social structure, and the religious and ethical systems.

Sometimes cross-cultural literacy means understanding what the culture appreciates and respects. Consider the recent experience of computer giant Microsoft. Microsoft is known for its tough and aggressive negotiating approach to capturing new business. Yet the company found that this style met with resistance as it tried to persuade Japanese video game software businesses to create games for Microsoft's Xbox. The financial

More to Come
CHAPTER 10

muscle that Microsoft commanded did not sway the Japanese, known for their creativity as game developers. Kazumi Kitaue of Konami Corporation expressed a unique stance regarding Microsoft: "They are the newcomer and have to approach each software maker humbly. We're the elders. We know this business."[36]

Diversity Management

You now have some facts. You have seen some demographic profiles and projections. You have what we call an intellectual awareness of diversity. In other words, you have an educated sense of some of the key workforce changes that are occurring. But the big challenge of diversity has not yet been addressed. How do we convert what we know into meaningful organizational action? In other words, how do we manage diversity?

Today, most businesses are aware of the diversity challenges we have already discussed. Yet, as Susan Jackson notes in her classic book *Diversity in the Workplace: Human Resource Initiatives,* there is a big difference between knowing what is changing and responding to the demands of change.[37] That is the challenge before us.

Look at the case of Advantica, owner of Denny's restaurants. Faced with a series of discrimination lawsuits in the early 1990s, the company responded by demonstrating a strong commitment to minorities. For example, 48 percent of its new hires are minorities, and now 31 percent of the company's officials and managers are minorities. In both 2000 and 2001, the company was rated as the best company in America for minorities. In Jackson's words, Advantica certainly has responded to the demands of change.[38]

Defining *Diversity Management*

diversity management
An approach to management that puts together a well-thought-out strategy for attracting, motivating, developing, retaining, and fully using the talents of competent people regardless of their race, gender, ethnicity, religion, physical ability, or sexual orientation.

Diversity management is putting together a well-thought-out strategy for attracting, motivating, developing, retaining, and fully using the talents of competent people regardless of their race, gender, ethnicity, religion, physical ability, or sexual orientation. It is important to realize that diversity management moves beyond the traditional legislative approaches to workforce equity that have been in place in this country for years. Those approaches were aimed largely at addressing discrimination in the workplace. You have probably heard of two of them. The *Equal Employment Opportunity (EEO) Act* specified that a business cannot deny a person a job because of race, gender, ethnicity, age, or sexual preference. Its well-known companion, *affirmative action,* directed businesses to take positive steps to hire and promote members of the classes noted in the EEO Act. These government efforts have been important.

assimilation
The assumption that women and minorities should blend in and learn how to work within the existing organization and its culture.

However, many of today's diversity leaders realize that these approaches have not gone far enough. In fact, EEO and affirmative action were based on a view of diversity known as **assimilation,** which presumes that women and minorities should blend in and learn how to work within the existing organization and its culture. It places the responsibility for changing and accommodating on the employee, not on the business. This approach loses much of the true value of diversity.

inclusiveness
The assumption that it is the business's responsibility to make decisions and take actions so that the talents of all employees can be fully realized.

Diversity management is broader. While some degree of assimilation is required, progressive organizations that understand diversity focus on the concept of **inclusiveness.** Inclusiveness assumes that it is the business's responsibility to make decisions and take actions so the talents of all employees can be fully realized. With its emphasis on inclusiveness, diversity management has as its goal creating and maintaining a culture where individual uniqueness is valued and respected. Further, diversity management helps build a culture where all workers feel welcome and supported and have the opportunity to work up to their potential. This is the type of culture Advantica created. The goal was to have a broader, more diverse group of people at all levels of the company. The company enacted carefully developed strategies to see that its goal was met. Do not be misled here. Diversity management does not mean that organizations capitulate on their performance goals in an effort to meet employee demands. It does mean that businesses are more flexible and tolerant in how they go about meeting goals and achieving results.

Many companies have taken bold steps to attain meaningful diversity action. More than 75 percent of the Fortune 1000 companies have diversity initiatives in place. Many of these businesses even have a chief diversity officer (CDO) as part of their executive team.[39]

Why Should a Business Be Concerned with Diversity Management?

There are good, logical, bottom-line reasons businesses should be serious about putting a diversity management approach in place. However, unless senior managers recognize and see value in diversity efforts, little meaningful diversity action is likely to occur.

There are seven basic reasons diversity management makes sense. These arguments are shown in Table 7.4 and discussed here.

First is the *resource acquisition* argument. Businesses need topflight talent. Accordingly, a business must do everything it can to attract the best and the brightest minds. Barbara (Bobbi) Guttman, a diversity planner at Motorola, spoke clearly to this issue. She noted: "We're not interested in getting more blacks, more women, more Hispanics, per se. What we're interested in is taking away any barrier between us and the best minds in the country. And it just doesn't make sense to us that the best minds in the country all look the same."[40]

Businesses that are serious about diversity and have implemented a diversity management plan should be better able to attract some of the best minds from diverse groups of prospective employees. Bright young minorities will want to come to work for companies that will support their growth within the business.

The second argument is *resource retention*. Attracting a diverse talent pool to a business is only part of the equation for success. To be competitive and successful, a business has to keep that talent. But turnover rates for women and minorities have historically been higher than those for white men. Turnover represents a drain of talent from the organization. It is also quite expensive. The business has to recruit, select, replace, and orient new people and bring them up to speed. Such efforts take time—and a lot of money. Businesses that can avoid such costs gain a competitive cost advantage over rival firms.

Third is the *resource utilization* argument. This view asserts that in a global, competitive environment, a business must use its human resources as effectively as possible

Resource acquisition	Attract a skilled and talented workforce.
Resource retention	Keep the talent of the workforce.
Resource utilization	Build an environment where everyone can contribute fully.
Customer sensitivity	Better understand and respond to a broad base of customers.
Innovation and creativity	Bring fresh ideas and novel approaches.
Legal requirements	Respond to and avoid legal problems.
Ethical stance	Do the right thing.

TABLE 7.4

Arguments for Diversity Management

if it is going to be successful. Notice the complexity of this statement. A business may attract and keep talented people, yet still not fully tap their potential. Organizations that embrace the philosophy of diversity management go further. They seek to understand the unique needs of their workers, and they are willing to help those workers be as productive and fulfilled as possible.

Fourth is the *customer sensitivity* argument, one of the most direct and strongest points in building the business case for diversity. This view contends that a business is better able to understand and respond to the needs of a diverse customer base when the organization contains people who mirror the diversity of that population. This sensitivity may have gender, racial, and ethnic connotations. Consider SBC Communications, a phone company that is based in San Antonio. Since 35 percent of its customers are people of color, SBC realizes that its workforce must mirror the population it serves.[41]

Sometimes the issue is not about gender or minority status. Rather, it is about putting people in key positions in which they are in touch with the customer. For example, Maryland National Bank found that its branches that had the best customer retention records recruited and hired locally. This practice allowed tellers to swap local gossip and made it easy for managers to show interest in local customers. No doubt this type of relationship led to feelings of comfort and commitment among the bank's customers.[42]

Fifth is the *creativity and innovation* argument. The wide range of attitudes, values, perspectives, and interests a diverse workforce brings with it often results in conflicts and tensions. Yet this diverse mix may be exactly what a business needs as it attempts to find fresh and novel ways to operate and serve customers. It's probably not surprising that research indicates that diverse groups tend to outperform homogeneous ones.[43]

Sixth is the *legal requirements* argument. There is little doubt that some companies' concern for diversity is prompted by a desire to avoid the legal tangles that can arise when diversity issues are left unattended. Research suggests that many diversity efforts are focused on legal concerns. Developing sexual harassment policies, providing access to employees with disabilities, and abiding by equal employment opportunity and affirmative action requirements are often the thrust of the diversity movement.

There is nothing wrong with this approach. Dealing with legal issues proactively is a reasonable and sound advantage of diversity management. Ideally, of course, the company's interest in diversity extends beyond this single issue to embrace some of the other arguments we have noted.

Seventh is the *ethical stance* argument. In today's business environment, diversity management is simply the right thing to do. All three ethics theories discussed in Chapter 6—utilitarianism, rights, and justice—indicate that diversity management is appropriate. Responsive businesses must take this ethical stance.

Dell's approach to diversity is based on a number of the themes we have just discussed. Michael Dell notes that Dell's commitment to diversity is both the right thing to do and a key business performance strategy. To compete, the company must attract and retain talented men and women who represent a range of backgrounds. Further, Dell realizes that its diverse workforce fosters innovation, creativity, and new solutions that help the bottom line.[44]

Building a Diversity Management Culture

We have identified some of the workforce changes that are facing businesses, defined *diversity management,* and explained why diversity management makes good business sense. Yet the most critical component of the diversity puzzle is still missing. How does a business respond to the challenges of diversity? How does it build a culture that really values, supports, and manages diversity? There is no easy answer, no blueprint that will work in all situations. Yet some businesses seem to make better strides than others. For example, Kodak, Xerox, BellSouth, Advantica, and Dell have all earned reputations for progressively addressing diversity needs. There are certain common actions these businesses take. When we study these businesses, a general strategic approach to diversity management begins to emerge. This strategic approach has four elements:

- Top management champions
- A diversity audit
- Goals and accountability
- Education, training, and support

Top Management Champions

Most businesses that have enacted successful diversity strategies have individuals at the very top of the company who are willing to champion the cause of diversity. These leaders are not simply saying the right words at the politically appropriate time. To them, diversity is a value that becomes part of their vision for the business. As champions, they are willing to take the lead in convincing others that diversity makes sense. They actively spread support for the diversity movement throughout the management ranks. Remember, diversity management represents a fundamental cultural change and most people tend to resist change. These changes are generally most effective when they start at the top.

Fannie Mae is a large mortgage financing company based in Washington, D.C. Its diversity record is remarkable. Nearly half of its new hires are minorities, and nearly 30 percent of its managers are minorities. Women make up nearly 40 percent of the company's officers. Yet there is little doubt that chairman Franklin D. Raines is the driver behind these impressive numbers. As Raines proudly notes, "Fannie Mae's record of diversity is no accident; it is a business priority.[45]

Assessment: The Diversity Audit

It is critical for a business to perform a diversity audit as it begins to get serious about diversity management. A **diversity audit** is a snapshot of how good a job the business is doing in the area of diversity management. It should tell the business where its diversity needs exist.

There are three things the audit should reveal. First, it should crunch the numbers to show what sort of representation exists at all levels of the company, especially at the professional and managerial levels. More importantly, these numbers should help managers see the movements and changes that are occurring. In other words, a business may be underrepresented in the number of women and minorities who hold management positions. But if great strides have taken place over the past few years, the trend is positive.

Second, the audit should reveal underlying assumptions and attitudes about diversity within the company. Third, the audit should uncover the actual behavior toward diversity and diverse groups that is occurring. Steps two and three are absolutely critical, yet often avoided. That tendency is not hard to understand; it is considerably more difficult to uncover attitudes and behaviors than to focus on the numbers. Yet the numbers may be meaningless if the attitudes and behaviors do not support diversity.

For example, a business may be meeting its affirmative action numbers. That is, the number of employees of diverse groups is consistent with the proportion found in the general population. Further, there is reasonable representation throughout the various levels of the company. But that does not guarantee that the workplace is "diversity-friendly."

> **diversity audit**
> A snapshot of how good a job a business is doing in the area of diversity management.

The numbers alone are not enough. Perhaps the women and minority members in the managerial ranks are quite dissatisfied. They may feel that they do not get much attention from their bosses; are overlooked for the challenging, developmental job assignments; and receive inadequate performance feedback. Further, they may encounter sexism and racism in the workplace.[46] Thus, if one looks only at the numbers, the business may appear quite progressive. However, a closer look at attitudes and behaviors reveals some major concerns.

To uncover attitudes and behaviors, a business may have to rely on written, anonymous surveys of employees; focus groups where small numbers of employees are encouraged to discuss their experiences openly; and perhaps even in-depth interviews with some employees to gain further understanding. To reassure employees and reduce their fears about discussing these matters openly, businesses often turn to outside consultants to conduct this portion of the audit. As you can see, the audit is comprehensive and quite detailed. It takes time, money, and a willingness on the part of the business to openly confront what is going on. Yet the audit is the most logical method of determining what issues the business should confront and what approaches seem to be most reasonable.

Goals and Accountability

The audit should point the business in the direction it needs to move to build a culture of diversity. The needs and concerns it identifies should be converted to diversity goals. Goals give managers something to work toward and a way of measuring progress. They are tangible yardsticks used to help the business move continually in the desired direction.

Accountability is also a key. Someone, usually someone in management, must be held accountable for meeting the diversity goals that are established. There is evidence that this accountability becomes more meaningful when managers are rewarded for meeting the goals. At Xerox, for example, diversity efforts were greatly advanced and diversity goals were given far greater attention when management compensation was tied in part to success in achieving goals of diversity. Today at Consolidated Edison (Con Ed), part of every manager's performance evaluation is based on diversity goals.[47] There is a basic truism in business life: People do what they are rewarded for doing.

Education, Training, and Support

The diversity audit should help determine the type of education and training the business needs to help deal with issues of diversity. Education and training may take many forms. They may be oriented toward increasing awareness of issues. Training may attempt to provide needed information and guidelines so that employees can understand and deal with certain problem areas of diversity. For example, when a business provides training in how to identify and eliminate sexual harassment, the focus is on information and guidance. A business may want to probe further and actually attempt to address attitudes and preconceptions, especially if the audit reveals deep pockets of prejudice or misunderstanding. Obviously, this step requires a greater depth of training. Role plays, simulations, and focus groups may be used. Again, the choice of educational and training approach depends on the diversity audit and what it reveals about the needs of the group.

If a company's diversity management efforts are going to have any real impact, support programs must be put in place. If the audit indicates unmet employee needs, the business must take programmatic steps to meet those needs. It is easy to talk about diversity and espouse all the right positions. It is tougher to walk the talk, to set up the programs that support what you say you want to do. Businesses must be very cautious here. There is often a tendency to want to implement the latest, trendy, high-profile diversity program, but that may not be what the business needs. A program that does not meet the specific needs of the business can become an inefficient expenditure. Good diversity management support programs are tailored to the particular business in question, based on the needs uncovered by the audit.

Consider the following examples. The diversity audit may indicate that one of the major issues facing the business is the need to increase minority representation. Specific programs should be formulated to address this issue, perhaps special recruiting efforts to attract minorities to the business, or scholarships or internships that are earmarked for select minorities. If the audit shows that the organization is having difficulty promoting women and minorities, special mentoring programs or the formalization of support groups may help. Perhaps the audit reveals trouble retaining women with the best qualities for the job. Further, the audit may suggest this is due in part to work–family conflicts. Flextime, telecommuting, or company-sponsored child care may be the kind of support necessary to address this issue.

More and more companies are recognizing the importance of support groups that provide understanding, guidance, and even mentoring of segments of the minority workforce. For example, BellSouth sponsors affinity groups, where people associate on the basis of a common ethnicity, religion, or gender.[48]

All training and education and certainly all support programs take money. That monetary commitment can be hard to sell in a business environment that is overwhelmingly concerned about cost containment. That is why the business reasons for diversity that we developed earlier are so important. A business will commit to training and support programs only when it is convinced that business value will result. The business leaders must recognize they will gain some advantage from diversity management.

THE BIG PICTURE

Managers must understand demographic and behavioral dynamics. Diversity efforts will be most effective when everyone understands that diversity is about inclusiveness. It is about creating a business where all talent can be used and maximized.

Diversity is also about tolerance and respect. Although many themes of tolerance and respect are important, two are at center stage. First is the need for better harmony across racial, ethnic, and gender boundaries. Despite social movements for greater equality and rights, tensions persist. Because businesses operate within society, they are not immune to the tensions and their consequences. Second is the need for greater respect for lifestyle differences. Sensitivity to sexual orientation issues is as important as sensitivity to the needs of single parents and the willingness to overcome the challenges faced by disabled workers.

Appreciating diversity, respecting others, and accepting differences is simply the right thing to do. In addition, however, it is in the best interest of businesses to be inclusive both within the marketplace and the workplace.

Summary

1. The concept of diversity is complex. Yet it is an important area for managers to consider.

   - What are the dimensions of diversity?

   The six areas considered primary dimensions of diversity are age, race, ethnicity, gender, mental and physical abilities, attributes and characteristics, and sexual orientation.

   The 10 areas considered secondary dimensions of diversity are work experience, first language, income, family status, military experience, religion, communication style, work style, geographic location, and education.

2. As more women, racial and ethnic minorities, and both younger and older workers enter the job arena, the workplace is becoming increasingly diverse.

   - How would you define *workforce diversity?*

   Workforce diversity refers to the mix of people from differing demographic and ethnic backgrounds and value orientations in the organization.

3. Contemporary businesses face a number of opportunities and challenges with the diversity they encounter.

   - What are the major diversity challenges facing business?

   Seven major areas of challenge are covered in this chapter: (1) the growing participation of women in the workforce, (2) work and family balance, (3) the growth in workforce participation of racial and ethnic minorities, (4) age and generational issues, (5) the accommodation of individuals with disabilities, (6) teams and diversity, and (7) global business and diversity.

4. The first step in dealing effectively with diversity issues is for the business to recognize their existence. The next step is to develop and implement a diversity management plan.

   - How would you define *diversity management?*

   Diversity management is putting together a well-thought-out strategy for attracting, motivating, developing, retaining, and fully utilizing the talents of competent people regardless of race, gender, ethnicity, religion, physical ability, or sexual orientation.

5. Diversity has important implications for a business. Attention to diversity can also yield favorable outcomes for the business.

   - Why should businesses be concerned with diversity management?

   There are seven reasons diversity management makes sense: (1) Resource acquisition: With needed skills in short supply, a business must do everything it can to attract the best and brightest minds. (2) Resource retention: To be competitive and successful, a business has to keep that talent. (3) Resource utilization: In a global, competitive environment, a business must use its human resources as effectively as possible in order to succeed. (4) Customer sensitivity: A business is better able to understand and respond to the needs of a diverse customer base when its employees mirror the diversity of that population. (5) Creativity and innovation: A diverse mix of employees helps the company find fresh, novel ways to operate and to serve customers. (6) Legal reasons: A diversity management program will help the company avoid the legal problems that can arise when diversity issues are left unattended. (7) Ethical stance: Diversity management is the right thing to do.

6. Because the issue of diversity is so complex, it is not easy for a company to implement an effective diversity management program. There are no simple models that can be copied from others and be expected to work without difficulties. Instead, diversity management programs must be tailored to the specific situation of each business. To do that effectively, the company must build a culture that values, supports, and manages diversity.

   • What are the elements involved in building a strong diversity management culture?

   Four elements are involved in the general strategic approach to building an effective diversity management program: (1) the presence of top management champions, (2) assessment—the implementation of a diversity audit, (3) the establishment of diversity goals, and (4) the installation of a program of diversity education, training, and support.

Key Terms

assimilation, p. 170

baby boomers, p. 165

caucus groups, p. 164

diversity audit, p. 173

diversity management, p. 170

dual-career households, p. 161

employee retraining, p. 166

flextime, p. 162

generation X, p. 166

generation Y, p. 166

glass border, p. 161

glass ceiling, p. 160

heterogeneous society, p. 156

inclusiveness, p. 170

job sharing, p. 162

stereotyping, p. 156

telecommuting, p. 162

work–family conflict, p. 161

workforce diversity, p. 158

Exercises and Applications

1. Suppose you work for the marketing department of a large compact disk distributor. Develop ideas on how you will market your CDs to Gen-Yers.

2. Working in teams (diverse, if possible), advise the marketing department of the CD distributor in exercise 1. As a team, develop a plan for marketing the CDs to Generation Y and a separate plan for marketing them to baby boomers. How do the experience and the results of the team exercise differ from what you did when working by yourself?

3. Interview a business owner who is either a woman or a member of a minority group. Ask whether this person has experienced discrimination as he or she pursued a career. If so, how did the business owner respond?

4. Consult the U.S. Census website (www.census.gov) for information about the city where your school is located. Check the demographic profile of that city. What diversity challenges and opportunities does it suggest for businesses in the city? How will those challenges differ for large companies versus small businesses?

5. Look at the demographic makeup of your class. What can your school's admissions office do to create a more diverse demographic mix of students? Do you think it is important to have a diverse mix? Why or why not?

6. Regardless of your career, each of you will encounter an increasingly diverse business world. Write a brief position paper (one-half to one page) describing what you can do to embrace and value diversity.

FROM THE PAGES OF

BusinessWeek

A CEO and His Son Face Depression

Howard Solomon is the CEO and chairman of Forest Laboratories Inc., a modest drug company based in New York City. When his 31-year-old son, Andrew, fell into a deep depression in 1994, their lives and Howard's business were changed forever.

Howard, a widower with two sons, "became Andrew's nurse, advocate, and companion. He woke Andrew every morning; he ate dinner with him every night, cutting up his son's food when Andrew couldn't."

Prompted by this very personal encounter with severe depression, Howard decided to act. He knew that millions of Americans (estimates today say about 19 million each year, or 1 out of every 10 adult Americans) suffered from some form of depression, but those figures now had a very personal face—that of his son. While researching treatments for his son, Howard learned of a promising drug produced by a Danish company. Howard set out to license the antidepressant since it was unavailable in the United States. The drug, known in Europe as Cipramil, was renamed Celexa. "It was a decision that would change the fortunes of Forest . . . Its antidepressant, Celexa, is the fastest-growing of its class of drugs, which includes Prozac, Paxil, and Zoloft; its share of new prescriptions is 17.5%. Since its U.S. launch in September 1998, Celexa has accounted for almost 70% of Forest's overall sales . . . Profits have grown from about $37 million in 1998 to $338 million [in 2001–2002]."

The Solomons have been remarkably open and straightforward about their battle with depression. In fact, Andrew won the National Book Award for nonfiction for his book, *The Noonday Demon: An Atlas of Depression,* which chronicles his struggles with the disease. And Howard today "tells his son and all those who suffer from depression that there is nothing to be ashamed of." But his efforts have gone further. "Forest has introduced a comprehensive Employee Assistance Program. And it began providing the same amount of health insurance for mental illness as for other maladies," a contentious point for many companies trying to contain health care costs.

Decision Questions

1. How can an issue like depression be considered a part of diversity as discussed in this chapter? Can a business ignore an issue that affects as much as 10 percent of its workforce?

2. Do you feel that Forest's decision to include mental illness as part of its insurance coverage is a sound business decision?

3. Following the September 11 crisis, Howard Solomon considered offering free antidepressants to those in need. If you were advising him on this matter, what would you counsel him to do? (Incidentally, the company decided against it.)

Source: Susan Berfield, "A CEO and His Son," *BusinessWeek,* May 27, 2002, pp. 72–80.

References

1. Ellis Close, "Rethinking Black Leadership," *Newsweek,* January 28, 2002, pp. 42–49; "Executive Sweet," www.goldsea.com (accessed March 15, 2002); and Avon website, www.avon.com (accessed September 18, 2002).

2. Marilyn Loden, *Implementing Diversity* (Burr Ridge: IL: Irwin Professional Publishing, 1996).

3. "Civilian Labor Force Participation Rate and Employment/Population Rate, 1955–2001," Department of Labor, Bureau of Labor Statistics, www.bls.gov (accessed September 18, 2002).

4. "Employment Status of the Civilian Noninstitutional Population by Sex and Age," Department of Labor, Bureau of Labor Statistics, www.bls.gov (accessed September 18, 2002).

5. "2000 Catalyst Census of Women Corporate Officers and Top Earners," www.catalystwomen.org (accessed September 18, 2002).

6. "2001 Catalyst Census of Women Board of Directors of the Fortune 1000," www.catalystwomen.org (accessed September 18, 2002).

7. "2000 Catalyst Census of Women Corporate Officers and Top Earners."

8. The classic work in this area remains Ann M. Morrison, Randall P. White, Ellen Van Velsor, and The Center for Creative Leadership, *Breaking the Glass Ceiling: Can Women Reach the Top of America's Largest Corporations?* (Reading, MA: Addison-Wesley, 1987).

9. "Passport to Opportunity: U.S. Women in Global Business," (New York: Catalyst, 2000).

10. Claire Raines, *Beyond Generation X: A Practical Guide for Managers* (Menlo Park, CA: Crisp Publications, 1997), p. 46.

11. "Employment Characteristics of Families Summary," U.S. Bureau of Labor Statistics, www.stats.bls.gov (accessed September 18, 2002).

12. Rifka Rosenwein, "The Baby Sabbatical," *American Demographics,* February 2002, pp. 40–41.

13. Hewitt Associates, 2000, reported in "The Laboring Masses," *American Demographics,* November 2001, p. 56.

14. "Flexible Work Arrangements," www.deloitte.com (accessed September 18, 2002).

15. "Balancing Work and Family," www.jnj.com (accessed September 18, 2002).

16. "Projections of the Total Resident Population by Race, Hispanic Origin, and Nativity: Middle Series, 2001 to 2005," www.census.gov (accessed September 18, 2002).

17. Ibid.

18. Joan Raymond, "The Multicultural Report," *American Demographics,* November 2001, pp. S3–S6.

19. Ibid.

20. Ken Greenburg, "Does Not Compute," *Brandweek,* April 1, 2002, pp. 5–9 to 5–14.

21. John P. Fernandez, with Jules Davis, *Race, Gender, and Rhetoric: The True Story of Race and Gender Relations in Corporate America* (New York: McGraw-Hill, 1999), p. 223.

22. Jack Ludwig and Vijay S. Talluri, "To Leverage Diversity, Think Inclusively," *Gallup Management Journal,* Winter 2001, www.gallupjournal.com (accessed September 18, 2002).

23. "Diversity at Xerox," www.xerox.com (accessed September 18, 2002).

24. Alison Stein Wellner, "The Census Report," *American Demographics,* January 2002, pp. S3–S6.

25. Sandra Yin, "Grandpa Gets Fit," *American Demographics,* November 2001, pp. 13–14.

26. Bureau of Labor Statistics, as reported by Peter Francese, "The American Workforce," *American Demographics,* February 2002, pp. 40–41.

27. For an excellent discussion of the impact of an aging America, see Richard W. Judy and Carol D'Amico, *Workforce 2020* (Indianapolis, IN: Hudson Institute, 1997).

28. For a good overview, see John B. Izzo and Pam Withers, *Values Shift: The New Work Ethic and What It Means for Business* (Vancouver, BC: FairWinds Press, 2001).

29. Ellen Neuborne and Kathleen Kerwin, "Generation Y," *BusinessWeek,* February 15, 1999, pp. 80–88.

30. Ibid., p. 84.

31. John Fetto, "Caught in the Middle," *American Demographics,* July 2001, pp. 14–16.

32. Norihiko Shirouzu, "This Is Not Your Father's Toyota," *The Wall Street Journal,* March 26, 2002, p. B1.

33. Caryn S. Kaufman, "Target Corporation Receives Employer of the Year Award from the National MS Society," www.wemedia.com (accessed September 18, 2002).

34. Suzanne Robitaille, "For the Disabled, It's Always a Depression," *BusinessWeek Online,* December 5, 2001, www.businessweek.com/bwdaily/dnflash/dec2001/nf2001/25_8727.htm (accessed September 19, 2002).

35. See the classic work, Jon R. Katzenbach and Douglas K. Smith, *The Wisdom of Teams: Creating the High-Performance Organization* (New York: Harper Business), 1993.

36. Robert A. Guth and Khanh T. L. Tran, "In the Battle for the Future, Microsoft Must Woo Japan's Game Makers," *The Wall Street Journal,* March 26, 2002, pp. A1, A8.

37. Susan E. Jackson and Associates, *Diversity in the Workplace: Human Resource Initiatives* (New York: Guilford Press, 1992), p. 13.

38. "America's 50 Best Companies for Minorities," *Fortune,* July 9, 2001, pp. 122–28.

39. Cora Daniels, "Too Diverse for Our Own Good," *Fortune,* July 9, 2001, p. 116.

40. "The Pursuit of Diversity at Motorola," *AAHE Bulletin,* March 1995, pp. 3–7.

41. Jeremy Kahn, "Diversity Trumps the Downturn," *Fortune,* July 9, 2001, pp. 114–16.

42. Susan E. Jackson and Associates, p. 14.

43. Patrick Mirza, "Diversity Adds Value to Organizations," *HR News Wire Story,* www.shrm.org/hrnews (accessed July 17, 1999).

44. Dell website, www.dell.com (accessed March 27, 2002).

45. "Diversity: A Letter from Frank Raines," www.fanniemae.com/careers/diversity (accessed September 18, 2002).

46. For an excellent review of approaches to the diversity audit, see Lee Gardenswartz and Anita Rowe, *Managing Diversity: A Complete Desk Reference and Planning Guide* (Burr Ridge, IL: Irwin Professional Publishing, 1993).

47. "America's 50 Best Companies for Minorities," p. 126.

48. Ibid., p. 123.

The Impact of Economic Forces

The long expansion of the American economy in the 1990s ended with the recession of 2001. It turned out to be a very short and mild recession. Nevertheless, a wide range of American firms and industries experienced declines in sales and profits. Telecommunication firms, such as AT&T, Lucent Technologies, and Qwest, were already suffering from overly optimistic expansion and the resulting excess capacity when the recession worsened the situation. Virtually all computer producers—IBM, Dell, Gateway, Compaq, and Hewlett-Packard—saw significant declines in sales. In fact, this decline was a major impetus for the eventual merger of Compaq and Hewlett-Packard. Even otherwise profitable firms, such as Cisco Systems, were caught off guard by the recession and had to claim a loss on inventories that had been built up in anticipation of sales that failed to materialize. In March 2001, Cisco announced it would write off a $2.5 million loss on the inventories. Shortly afterward, it announced that it would eliminate 3,000 to 5,000 regular jobs.[1]

As gross domestic product began to grow again at the end of 2001, other companies and industries experienced the negative aftereffects of the recession. Banks began to report loan losses stemming from the recession, and commercial real estate firms experienced increased vacancies and pressure to lower rental rates to hold on to customers. Companies in a wide range of industries found it difficult, if not impossible, to raise prices to profitable levels in the environment of postrecession excess capacity.

Experienced managers, those who had been around for more than a decade, had seen this series of circumstances happen before. They were confident that the economic environment would eventually improve and boom times might return for a while. But they also expected future episodes of excess capacity, recessions, and renewed competition. In short, experienced managers know that the economic forces beyond their immediate control will present an ever changing set of threats and opportunities. They know that one of management's major responsibilities is to be prepared for these changes and to respond quickly as each economic challenge appears.

Every business is subject to economic forces. Sometimes those forces threaten the profitability of the business. At other times they present the business with unique opportunities. In either case, the challenge facing a business manager is to identify the threats and opportunities and take actions to deal with them. This chapter will help you understand how economic forces affect a business.

After studying this chapter, you should be able to:

1. List the major economic forces beyond the immediate control of a business that affect the firm's success.

2. Use simple macroeconomic concepts to explain how growth, inflation, unemployment, and interest rate changes occur and how they affect the way a business competes.

3. Explain the concept of the business cycle and list the threats and opportunities each phase of the cycle creates for a business.

4. Explain how prices are determined and why they change.

5. Explain the concept of price elasticity of demand and demonstrate how a business can use the concept to increase profits.

6. List the types of competition a firm may face.

7. Discuss the role of economics in management decision making.

Economic forces are the second of five environmental forces that have an impact on business. Like the others, these forces are largely beyond the control of the firm. Although managers must anticipate and react to changes in the economy, they have little power to control them. Economic forces include the macroeconomic forces of unemployment, inflation, interest rates, and growth, as well as the microeconomic forces of supply and demand, and competition. We describe these forces and give examples of how each can help or hurt a business. As you read this chapter, you need to understand the concepts and how they relate to the model of a successful business used throughout this textbook. More importantly, you need to understand how the economic forces affect businesses. We begin with a discussion of macroeconomic forces.

Macroeconomic Forces

Macroeconomics studies the entire economy of a nation. Macroeconomics deals with four factors that concern a business: economic growth, inflation, interest rates, and unemployment. These factors affect businesses in general, so a particular business will be affected because all businesses are affected.

macroeconomics
The study of the entire economy of a nation.

Suppose you manage a Best Buy store in Atlanta, Georgia. How can macroeconomic variables affect you? Certainly, *economic growth* will have an effect. As the nation's and Georgia's economy prospers, people will have more money to spend. They may spend some of that on the electronic equipment and other products you sell. If *inflation* increases rapidly, the costs of the products you sell will go up. If the incomes of your Atlanta customers don't keep up with inflation, those customers will have to cut back their spending somewhere. Since you sell items that consumers can postpone buying in a pinch, your sales will probably suffer. If *unemployment* increases in the Atlanta area, your sales could decline as people hold on to their money in case they get laid off. Finally, if *interest rates* are high, the cost of buying from you will go up for those customers who charge purchases on their credit cards. In addition, there will be an increase in the earnings they can obtain by investing their money rather than buying your products. They may decide to postpone making a purchase at Best Buy and, instead, invest some of their money. Finally, the increased interest rates will increase the cost of the inventory of goods that your store carries.

We will discuss the four factors just mentioned as well as three other concepts of macroeconomics: gross domestic product, monetary and fiscal policy, and business cycles. We begin with gross domestic product.

Gross Domestic Product

The modern concepts of macroeconomics originated in the writings of John Maynard Keynes in the 1930s. Keynes, introduced in Profile 8.1, conceived of the entire economy as composed of a limited number of variables. Modern versions of his theory give the name **gross domestic product (GDP)** to the entire economy. Gross domestic product is the market value of all final goods and services produced in a country in a given year. Today it is customary to think of the GDP as consisting of the following four parts:

> **gross domestic product (GDP)**
> The market value of all final goods and services produced in a country in a given year.

1. Personal consumption expenditures.
2. Gross private domestic investment.
3. Government consumption expenditures and gross investment.
4. Net exports of goods and services (the value of exports minus the value of imports).

Table 8.1 shows the preliminary estimates of the value of each of the components of GDP for the second quarter of 2002.

Increases or decreases in any of these variables affect the overall GDP. For example, when government increases its spending, GDP increases. When the private business sector increases its investment expenditures, GDP increases. Can you predict what

TABLE 8.1

The Value of GDP in The United States, Second Quarter 2002 Preliminary ($ in billions)

1. Personal consumption expenditures	$6,544
2. Gross private domestic investment	1,585
3. Government consumption expenditures and gross investment	1,703
4. Net exports of goods and services	−494
Total GDP	$9,389

Source: U.S. Bureau of Economic Analysis, www.bea.doc.gov/bea/niptbl-d.html#realgdp (accessed September 19, 2002).

would happen if consumer expenditures increased? If exports increased while imports remained the same? What do you think would happen if investment spending declined? Would the same thing happen to GDP if consumption expenditures, government spending, or exports declined?

In addition to the direct impact of each of the four variables, Keynes suggested that the variables interact and, as a result, have further effects on GDP. Keynes argued, for example, that a fall in investment would cause a subsequent decline in consumption. This would result in a further decline in GDP. On the other hand, an increase in investment would cause an additional increase in consumption expenditures, which would cause an additional increase in GDP. Keynes called this interaction the *multiplier effect.* We now know that through the multiplier effect, a given decline in investment can eventually cause GDP to fall by two or more times the original decline in investment.

JOHN MAYNARD KEYNES   PROFILE 8.1

The British economist John Maynard Keynes originated the modern field of macroeconomics. He did it with a new theory of economic growth and unemployment, explained in his book *The General Theory of Employment, Interest and Money,* published in 1936. It took another 10 years for his ideas to earn widespread acceptance by economists. But when the U.S. Congress passed the Employment Act of 1946, his ideas became an official part of American policy and economic education.

Keynes argued that recessions are usually caused by declines in investment spending, so government should increase spending or cut taxes to fight recession. He also argued that inflation is caused by excessive government spending financed by borrowing. To fight inflation, the government should raise taxes, cut spending, or raise interest rates so that investment spending would decline. These Keynesian viewpoints led to the belief that government can control inflation and unemployment. The Employment Act of 1946 stated that the federal government could and should fight inflation and unemployment and promote economic growth.

Prior to the Keynesian revolution, economists had concerned themselves with only one macroeconomic issue—inflation. They explained inflation in terms of the *quantity theory of money.* In simplest terms, that theory says inflation is the result of the money supply growing too fast. The policy prescription for controlling inflation was to control the rate of growth of the money supply.

Modern macroeconomics has advanced greatly beyond the basic ideas presented by John Maynard Keynes. Today's models are far more complex, and today's policy conclusions sometimes differ from his. Furthermore, today's economists are not nearly as optimistic about government's ability to use government spending and taxes to fight inflation and unemployment. In fact, as pointed out in the discussion of Milton Friedman in Profile 8.2, one influential group of modern economists believes that Keynesian thinking is dangerously misleading. Nevertheless, Keynes's idea of a macroeconomic approach to the economy is a major part of modern economics.

Economic Growth

economic growth
An increase in total spending in the economy.

Economic growth refers to an increase in total spending in the economy and is reflected as an increase in gross domestic product. Economic growth can mean an increase in sales for the average business. When that happens, the business can produce more, provide more profits to owners, and employ more workers. But economic growth can be a two-edged sword. Too much growth in a short period of time can eventually lead to production bottlenecks, runaway costs, and even problems with maintaining product quality. Indeed, if growth is too rapid in the economy as a whole, an overall increase in prices will occur. This is what we all know as inflation. Fear of such an occurrence is the major reason the Federal Reserve Board occasionally raises interest rates to slow down the rate of growth.

Economic growth is caused by investment in factories, equipment, and other capital goods. Growth is also caused by technological change and innovation. Much of the investment takes the form of new and improved production facilities and products. Sometimes the growth process is driven by major innovations that change the way the nation works and lives. The invention of the mass-produced automobile was just such an innovation, and it propelled American growth in the 1920s and again after World War II. Another example is the period you have recently witnessed—the great investment boom propelled by the computer revolution, followed by the Internet revolution, and further heated up by the globalization revolution. A popular name for this revolution is the "New Economy."

The rate and direction of economic growth are also affected by population changes. Consider the case of the baby boom we discussed in Chapter 7. The sharp increase in the number of births after the war led to sharp increases in the demand for goods and services needed to raise the children (including new homes and new schools in the suburbs). That need spurred an investment boom that made the 1950s and 1960s a period of steady growth. As the baby boomers age and retire from the labor force, there should be a sharp increase in the demand for the kinds of goods and services desired by the elderly. Astute business planners can often do a good job of forecasting the direction of future demand for their products by analyzing population trends.

Population changes also have an impact on the supply of labor available to businesses. As Figure 8.1 indicates, the growth rate of the American labor force will slow down significantly in the next several decades. This slowdown may create labor shortages, and employers will have to respond with such policies as these:[2]

- Offering more flexibility to working mothers.
- Hiring more minority workers.
- Enticing older workers to retire later or to return to work.
- Recruiting and training hard-to-place workers.
- Increasing company spending on training and education.

per capita economic growth
The difference in GDP per person from one year to the next.

Because of the relationship between GDP growth and population growth, business leaders need to distinguish between overall economic growth and **per capita economic growth.** Overall annual growth is calculated by comparing last year's GDP with the current year's GDP. Per capita GDP is calculated by dividing the GDP in each year by the population in that year. The per capita growth rate is then determined by comparing the GDP per person in the preceding year with the GDP per person in the current year. When businesses see that economic growth is largely a matter of per capita growth, then they must try to figure out what consumers will want to buy as their incomes increase.

FIGURE 8.1

Compound Annual Labor Force Growth by Decade, 1950s–2010s

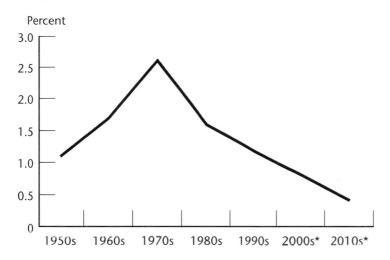

*estimates

Source: "Too Many Workers? Not for Long," *BusinessWeek*, May 20, 2002, p. 126; data from Watson Wyatt Worldwide.

Inflation

Inflation refers to a general increase in prices or an increase in the prices of most goods and services. The most popular measure of inflation is the *consumer price index (CPI)*. Published by the U.S. Department of Labor every month, the CPI measures the price level of consumer goods and services. The overall index represents a weighted average of the prices of a wide variety of consumer goods and services. Table 8.2 gives you an idea of the major categories that are currently used and shows how the rate of change differs for the various items in the index. Figure 8.2 shows the Consumer Price Index changes from 1992 to 2002.

> **inflation**
> A general increase in prices or an increase in the prices of most goods and services.

Item	Percent Change
Food	1.3
Housing	2.3
Apparel and upkeep	−1.7
Transportation	−1.0
Medical care	4.6
Recreation	1.0
Education and Communications	2.7
Other goods and services	3.2
Average of all items	1.5

TABLE 8.2

Annual Changes in the Major Components of the U.S. Consumer Price Index, September 2001–September 2002

Source: State of the Nation, www.stat-usa.gov (accessed November 10, 2002).

FIGURE 8.2

Consumer Price Index
(Urban), 12-Month
Changes, 1992 to 2002

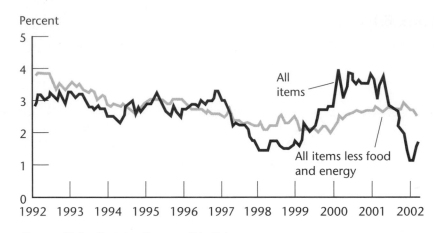

Source: Bureau of Labor Statistics, Consumer Price Index.

A low rate of inflation can be good for business if it makes raising prices easier. But high rates of inflation create a number of problems. Inflation leads to an overall increase in the cost of living, causing people to buy less of everything. Of course, this affects a particular business since there will be a reduction in the demand for the company's products. A decrease will also occur if the company's sales are sensitive to interest rates. Since higher inflation rates usually lead to higher interest rates, inflation can result in lower sales of products, such as homes and automobiles, that are bought with borrowed money.

Another problem with inflation is the uncertainty it causes, especially if inflation rates are high. Because prices are increasing rapidly, managers do not know how to react. Should they buy more inventory now because prices may rise later? Should they buy inventory even if they have to borrow money to do it? Should they raise their own prices or try to hold the line? If all businesses raise their prices to offset their own increasing costs, it will cause even more inflation. Should they put any available funds in short-term investments in hopes of higher returns, or should they use the same funds to buy capital equipment now rather than pay higher prices later? Since inflation can affect both sales and costs of doing business, an astute manager will watch inflation data closely and be prepared to react when necessary to offset inflationary cost increases.

The opposite of inflation is **deflation.** Deflation is a general decrease in prices or a decrease in the prices of most goods and services. When deflation occurs, any person or business that has borrowed money finds it more difficult to pay back the loan. That is because the prices of the goods sold by the business are falling while the amount of the loan that must be repaid remains at the original level. Deflation has been rare in American experience. Inflation has been the rule. But in the late 1990s, one of America's major trading partners, Japan, found itself stagnating because of deflation. The general price level began to fall in Japan. Japanese businesses found it more difficult to pay off loans. Japanese households cut back on spending because of the uncertainty about the future of the economy and because products could be bought at lower prices if one waited. In that atmosphere, Japanese businesses were reluctant to invest, and without investment increases, Japan's GDP stopped growing. Even though North America has not experienced an actual deflation in recent times, business leaders should consider the possibility of deflation some time in the future.

deflation

A general decrease in prices or a decrease in the prices of most goods and services.

Unemployment

In macroeconomics, unemployment means wanting to work but not having a job. Unemployment is usually measured by the **unemployment rate.** This is the ratio of the number of people classified as unemployed to the total labor force.

There are several types of unemployment, as shown in Table 8.3. One is *frictional unemployment.* This refers to people who are looking for work and will eventually find it because jobs are available for which they are qualified. These unemployed people will find work if they keep looking. Suppose that when you graduate from college, you choose to wait until you return to your hometown to look for a job. If it takes you a few weeks to actually find one, you are an example of frictional unemployment.

A second form of unemployment is *structural unemployment.* This refers to people who cannot find work because the skills they possess are not appropriate for the available jobs. In this case, the unemployed people must learn new skills or relocate to get a job. Now suppose that you graduate from college with a degree in art education. There are no openings for art education teachers in the community where you live, but there are vacancies for people with computer science training. Thus, you are structurally unemployed until you get the computer training. The ironic aspect of structural unemployment is that some people are unable to find work while companies are searching in vain for employees with the skills they need.

A third form of unemployment is *seasonal unemployment.* This refers to situations where the job is available only at certain seasons of the year. An employee in a construction firm is an example, because most road or house construction occurs during warmer months. In this case, the employee may earn enough during the construction season to cover living costs during the off-season. Yet, if the person cannot find a job in the winter months, he or she is an example of seasonal unemployment.

A fourth form of unemployment is *cyclical unemployment.* This refers to people who can't find jobs because a decline in the economy has caused employers to cut back on hiring. Many of these people will have to wait for the economy to improve before they can find jobs.

Some unemployment will always exist because of the combinations of frictional, seasonal, structural, and cyclical unemployment. A certain rate of unemployment is even desirable for the economy at large, since extremely low rates of unemployment can lead to inflation. This condition occurs as employers bid up wages to attract the limited supply of employees. At the same time, since more people are employed, there is more money for them to spend, again pushing up prices.

Let's consider the impact of rising unemployment on businesses. The bad news is that increases in unemployment result in reduced income for the unemployed, which in turn means smaller sales for the businesses that serve them. Higher unemployment rates also mean that people currently holding jobs will be less likely to take a chance on new, higher-paying jobs for fear that they might also end up unemployed if the new job does

Form of Unemployment	Cause
Frictional unemployment	The time required to find a job.
Structural unemployment	Inappropriate skills.
Seasonal unemployment	Seasonal nature of jobs.
Cyclical unemployment	Insufficient growth in economy.

TABLE 8.3

Forms of Unemployment

not work out. The good news is that businesses can take advantage of higher unemployment rates by being very selective about whom they hire. If many people are looking for work, the recruiter has a wider selection of qualified workers.

Now let's consider the reverse situation—the impact of very low unemployment rates. This situation occurred in the United States from 1998 to 2001, when it was not uncommon in some communities for unemployment rates to be under 4 percent—an extremely low rate given the four possible types of unemployment. Extremely low unemployment also occurred in some industries and some occupations. Computer-related industries, for example, saw virtually zero unemployment until 2001.

Low unemployment rates mean more people have income to spend, so demand for the goods and services of most businesses is higher. Low unemployment rates also mean less need for government payments to support the unemployed, and that means potentially lower taxes. But low unemployment also means that businesses will find it harder to hire qualified workers. The firms may have to accept applicants with lower skill levels than desired. Furthermore, low unemployment means that workers can shop around for better pay. That possibility puts many firms at risk of losing some of their best workers.

All these outcomes mean that managers should monitor the unemployment rate to see how it will affect both demand for the firm's products and the firm's ability to recruit and hold qualified workers. Structural unemployment may be of concern to businesses that hire large numbers of technical workers or highly skilled workers. Frictional and seasonal unemployment may actually benefit employers, since large numbers of potential workers will be available. Finally, cyclical unemployment will almost always affect a business adversely, since the declining general economy will reduce demand for the firm's products.

Interest Rates

interest
The price that individuals or businesses pay to borrow money.

Interest is the price paid by individuals or businesses to borrow money. The *interest rate* expresses that price as a percentage per dollar of funds borrowed. Interest rates affect businesses in three significant ways. First, rising interest rates increase the total price paid by customers who use credit for products and services. So as interest rates rise, the demand for products will likely decrease.

Second, most businesses borrow money to run their daily operations. Higher interest rates mean higher costs of doing business. Managers must either raise the prices of their products to cover this cost of doing business or accept lower profits.

A third effect of interest rates is on the expansion of a business. Since a company must sometimes borrow money to finance new equipment, the interest rate is of great concern to the manager. Lower interest rates may mean that it is a good time for the business to borrow to invest in an expansion. Higher rates will make a manager consider delaying expansion until the cost of borrowing decreases. We will discuss this issue in more depth in Chapter 9.

More to Come
Chapter 9

Business leaders need to know what is happening to the macroeconomic factors of growth, inflation, unemployment, and interest rates. This knowledge enables them to take advantage of favorable changes in the economic environment and protect themselves against adverse changes.

Monetary and Fiscal Policy

Keynes's thinking led to a revolution in public policy. His models showed how government could intervene to promote economic growth, reduce unemployment, control inflation, and adjust interest rates. In the United States, the government agency that implements economic policy is the Federal Reserve Board, often called the Fed. The Fed will be discussed in Chapter 9.

The group of policies emphasized by Keynes involved raising or lowering taxes or government spending in order to influence growth, unemployment, and inflation. Those policies are called **fiscal policy.**

In the 1960s, a movement began among economists to pay more attention to a second group of policies involving the role of money in the economy. This group of policies involved changing the money supply to change interest rates directly, thus influencing inflation, growth, and unemployment. These policies are called **monetary policy.** The leader of that movement was University of Chicago economist Milton Friedman, whose background is shown in Profile 8.2.

Sometimes monetary policy can do most of the work by itself. Such was the case in the 2001 recession and the 1990–1991 recession. The 1990–1991 recession was triggered by the Federal Reserve Board to forestall what was expected to be a serious inflation problem. Why was an inflation problem expected? The prospect of a war against Iraq was the culprit. Of course, the Fed could hope against all odds that it would be able to slow the economy without actually causing a recession. But it was more likely that a recession would occur, and the Fed was willing to accept that prospect to stop inflation

More to Come
CHAPTER 9

fiscal policy
The raising or lowering of taxes or government spending to influence growth, unemployment, and inflation.

monetary policy
The changing of the money supply to change interest rates directly, thus influencing inflation, growth, and unemployment.

MILTON FRIEDMAN   PROFILE 8.2

After World War II, the ideas of John Maynard Keynes became very influential among economists. As a result, American and European economists proposed the frequent use of fiscal policy to improve the performance of an economy. A revolt against this type of thinking arose in the 1960s. The most prominent figure in that revolt was University of Chicago economist Milton Friedman, founder of the monetarist school of economic thought.

Monetarists believe that the money supply is the most important determinant of the GDP as well as prices. They also believe that a competitive free market economy will tend naturally to produce full employment as long as government does not disrupt the economy with unwise policies. Milton Friedman was especially pessimistic about the ability of government to manage the economy. In his writings and TV interviews, he argued that government decision making tends to be inefficient and ineffective and reduces individual freedom. He therefore recommended that the public sector be made as small as possible and that government avoid trying to manage the economy through monetary and fiscal policy. To learn more about Friedman's views, read *Capitalism and Freedom* and (with Rose Friedman) *Free to Choose*. You will also learn more about the monetarists' views on economic policy when you take your first course in economics.

Source: Milton Friedman, *Capitalism and Freedom.* (Chicago: University of Chicago Press, 1962); and Milton Friedman and Rose Friedman, *Free to Choose* (New York: Harcourt Brace Jovanovich, 1980).

early. If the Fed had waited longer, it probably would have been required to "cause" an even longer and deeper recession to kill what would have been an even higher rate of inflation.

Once the recession of 1990–1991 succeeded in heading off the anticipated inflation, the Fed then used monetary policy to stimulate a new expansion. That expansion continued until March 2001, setting a new record for the length of a post–World War II expansion. That 120-month expansion was made possible by a masterful exercise of monetary policy by the Fed.

A good argument can be made that monetary policy is often sufficient to pull the economy out of a recession. The expansions beginning in 1991 and 2001 certainly support that view. But you must remember that both expansions followed very mild recessions. If either of those recessions had been significantly deeper or longer, it might have been necessary to use fiscal policy in the form of increased government spending or tax cuts to pull the economy out of the recession. The lesson in all this? Government needs to have available both monetary and fiscal policy to deal with the ups and downs of the business cycle.

Monetary and fiscal policies are now firmly established parts of the macroeconomic environment in which businesses operate. Managers must learn to anticipate the monetary and fiscal policies government will use. Doing so will let them prepare for possible periods of rapid growth, recessions, inflation, and changes in interest rates.

The Business Cycle

One of the major benefits of Keynesian theory was that it told the government how to measure the economy. In the 1930s, the American government began to compile estimates of what we now call the gross domestic product and its components. Once those numbers became available, economists began to study how GDP changed over time. Soon they discovered a somewhat regular pattern of ups and downs in aggregate production, measured by fluctuations in real GDP, known as the **business cycle.**

The business cycle has four parts, or stages, as illustrated in Figure 8.3. One stage is the recession (contraction). This is the period during which GDP is falling. A common rule of thumb is that if GDP falls for at least two quarters (six months), then a recession has occurred. Although it is common practice to look at GDP numbers to identify a recession, the official designation of the starting date of a recession is done by the National Bureau of Economic Research (NBER), which uses a panel of economists to make the decision. The NBER determines the month the recession began as well as the month it ended.

Eventually, the decline in GDP stops. At that point the business cycle reaches the next stage, which is called the trough. This is usually a very short period. It is followed

business cycle

A somewhat regular pattern of ups and downs in aggregate production, as measured by the fluctuations in real GDP.

FIGURE 8.3

The Business Cycle

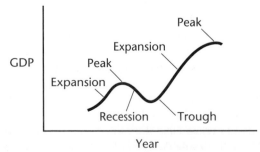

The stage of the business cycle will affect demand and sales. What decisions might an auto maker make if a recession seems likely? How might that auto maker respond to encourage sales during a recession?

by a period of time during which GDP rises. This period of economic growth is called an expansion.

Sooner or later the growth stops and GDP reaches the fourth stage, which is called the peak. This stage is usually very short and is followed by a recession, which marks the beginning of a new business cycle.

A recession begins when one or more elements of the GDP declines. Usually it is investment that falls. Sometimes, however, government spending is cut or taxes are raised, causing consumption expenditures to fall. It is even possible for a drop in net exports to trigger a recession. Once the recession has started, GDP continues to decline for a while as a result of the multiplier effect.

Since a decline in investment is the most common reason for a recession to begin, it is important to understand why a decline might occur. One major cause is an increase in interest rates. Interest rates tend to rise naturally during an expansion as the demand for loanable funds grows faster than the supply. Sometimes the federal government responds by increasing the money supply. But that action creates the danger of inflation, so sooner or later the government will probably let interest rates rise and risk triggering a recession.

The expansion phase of the business cycle is similarly triggered by an increase in investment spending, government spending, or net exports. That increase causes an initial increase in GDP, which leads to the multiplier effect. As the process of expansion continues, the economy enters a potential inflationary period.

No two business cycles are identical. Recessions can last for as little as six months or as long as several years. Expansions show similar variations. Table 8.4 shows you the time spans for peaks and troughs in the United States since the 1920s. Figure 8.4 then shows the quarterly detail, starting in 1994.

As you can see from Figure 8.4, 2001 and 2002 were years of uncertainty, with a recession lasting three quarters in 2001, followed by two quarters of significant growth in 2001-IV and 2002-I, and very modest growth in the second quarter of 2002.

TABLE 8.4

Business Cycle Peaks
and Troughs in the
United States

Date of Trough	Date of Next Peak	Number of Months from Trough to Peak
November 1927	August 1929	21
March 1933	May 1937	50
June 1938	February 1945	80
October 1945	November 1948	37
October 1949	July 1953	45
May 1954	August 1957	39
April 1958	April 1960	24
February 1961	December 1969	106
November 1970	November 1973	36
March 1975	January 1980	58
July 1980	July 1981	12
November 1982	July 1990	92
March 1991	March 2001	120

Source: National Bureau of Economic Research, "U.S. Business Cycle Expansions and Contractions," www.nber.org/cycles.html (accessed September 14, 2002).

To understand how the business cycle works, consider the following famous historical example. A monetary policy action in 1979 caused a recession in the U.S. economy. In October of that year, the Federal Reserve decided to fight a worrisome inflation rate by cutting back the growth of the money supply. That action drove up interest rates and caused the GDP to begin falling by the end of January 1980. The decline in GDP was not particularly large, so the inflation problem continued and GDP began to increase at the end of July 1980. Determined to bring down inflation, the Fed continued to reduce the growth of the money supply. Interest rates rose so high that they caused a very sharp drop in investment and consumer installment purchases. The GDP fell again, beginning in July 1981. This time the drop was quite large, and the unemployment rate increased dramatically. But the inflation rate also began to decline.

Then, in the midst of the worst recession since the 1930s, fiscal policy came to the rescue. Ronald Reagan had been elected president in 1980. Once in office, he persuaded Congress to enact both tax cuts and increased spending (primarily for military purposes). The result was a sharp increase in *deficit spending* (the government was spending more than it was taking in through taxes). Keynesian theory tells us that large-scale deficit spending is the way to pull an economy out of a recession. And that is exactly what happened. The GDP began to rise by the end of November 1982 and continued to grow until July 1990.

That turnaround illustrates some basic features of the role of government policy as it affects the business cycle.

THINK ABOUT THIS

1. John Maynard Keynes thought that government should actively try to manage the economy. Milton Friedman disagreed. What do you think?

2. Should top management of a business be more concerned about a rising rate of inflation or rising interest rates?

3. Which seems like the better way to affect the economy, monetary policy or fiscal policy? Which policy has Alan Greenspan pursued in recent years?

FIGURE 8.4

Gross Domestic Product Quarterly Change, 1994–2002 (Percent change, seasonally adjusted annual rate)

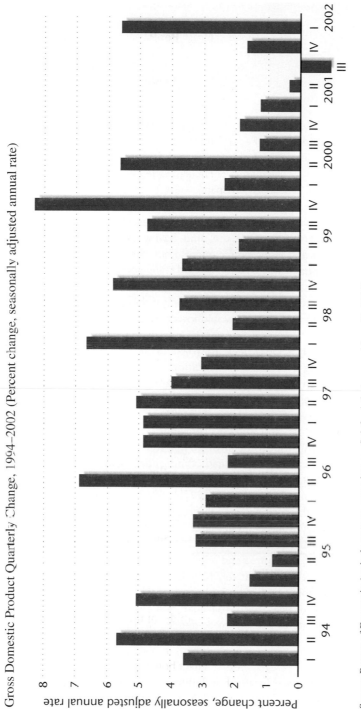

Source: Bureau of Economic Analysis website, www.bea.gov/briefrm/gdp (accessed June 11, 2002).

PROFILE 8.3   ALAN GREENSPAN

With just a few simple words, Federal reserve Board Chairman Alan Greenspan has the ability to affect markets and monetary policy across the globe, not just the United States. His recommendations regarding the U.S. economy can have significant effects on economies in Europe and Japan. Have you ever noticed the stock market on days when he is supposed to make an announcement? Even days before or just after?

John Maynard Keynes and Milton Friedman (and others) provided the theoretical framework used by the Federal Reserve System to implement monetary policy. But the actual implementation requires a fair amount of judgment by the Fed in general and by its chairman in particular. One chairman who has handled that job particularly well is Alan Greenspan.

Greenspan was a respected private consulting economist when President Reagan appointed him chairman of the Federal Reserve Board in 1987. The U.S. economy was performing well at the time, having experienced five years of growth, falling inflation, and rising employment. Thus, the task for Greenspan and his Federal Reserve Board was to keep a good thing going. Their best method of accomplishing that was to raise or lower interest rates by small amounts to head off problems they thought might be emerging. If they saw the economy slowing down too much in the future, they would lower rates to stimulate it a bit. If they feared that the inflation rate might start to rise in the foreseeable future, they would raise rates. With a lot of luck, they would be able to manipulate interest rates without causing a recession. In addition to luck, however, a leader was needed who could keep the data analysis sharp and who would refuse to bow to short-run political pressures.

For three years the Greenspan team kept the economy growing while unemployment rates fell and inflation remained low. When it began to look like the United States might become involved in a war with Iraq, Greenspan convinced the Fed to raise interest rates to head off potential inflation. Raising rates created the risk of a recession, and that is exactly what happened. A recession began in July 1990 and continued until March 1991. It was a mild recession, and it was shortened by the Fed, which reduced interest rates to stimulate recovery.

The recovery that began in March 1991 continued until March 2001, setting a record for the longest peacetime expansion. What made that record expansion so special was that both inflation rates and unemployment rates fell to exceptionally low levels while GDP growth was relatively high. Low unemployment and high GDP growth are usually accompanied by higher inflation rates, but that did not occur in the 1990s because of the skillful way that Greenspan and the Fed raised and lowered interest rates by small amounts to accelerate or decelerate the economy as needed.

Monetary policy was used to attack inflation and in the process caused a recession by driving up interest rates. Fiscal policy was used to pull the economy out of the recession. These are typical developments. The skillful use of government policy was particularly effective in managing the economy in the past decade. Much of the effectiveness was due to the actions of chairman of the Federal Reserve Board, Alan Greenspan, discussed in Profile 8.3.

Even though no two business cycles are alike, it is important for business leaders to understand the concept and its history. Knowledge of the cycle can help a business take actions to minimize the damage done by recessions or inflation. Such knowledge can also be used proactively to take advantage of expansions, inflation, and sometimes, a recession. Managers can use their knowledge of the business cycle to prepare themselves for periodic booms and busts.

Industry Cycles

Some industries are subject to their own cyclical fluctuations in sales and profits. Such cycles are most likely to occur in industries in which a high percentage of the cost of production is incurred at the time production capacity is created. Consider the cases of the telephone, airline, or electricity generation industries. The major cost of telephone service lies in the equipment that has to be in place before customers can buy service; the major cost of air travel is the aircraft which must be purchased before any sales are made; the major cost of electricity is the cost of building the generating capacity and transmission lines. In all three cases, if there is competition, it is likely that the industry will build too much capacity during times when demand is growing rapidly. Once that excess capacity is available for service, the competing firms will be tempted to charge extremely low prices to use the excess capacity. The low prices will cover the short-run costs of serving the customer but will in all likelihood not be high enough to cover the costs of building the original capacity. So the firms will report losses for a while. Of course, the firms will stop adding capacity. If demand continues to grow, it will eventually catch up with capacity and then the firms will raise prices to cover all costs. But as demand continues to grow, the danger arises that the industry will go through another episode of excessive increases in capacity.

One way of dampening this kind of cycle is for government to regulate firm pricing as well as entry into and exit from the industry. If the cycle becomes a matter of significant public concern, such regulation is likely to be imposed on the industry. But regulation can lead to inefficiency and a decline in innovation. When the inefficiencies of such regulation become a matter of public concern, it is likely that government will deregulate the industry. You will learn more about this issue in Chapter 11.

More to Come
CHAPTER 11

Microeconomic Forces

The previous section discussed the role of forces in the macroeconomic environment that affect businesses. **Microeconomics** studies the behavior of individual people and firms in particular markets. It studies the interactions of buyers and sellers. The place where buyers and sellers meet and bargain over goods and services is called a **market.** So microeconomics studies how markets work. The two major microeconomic forces that affect business are (1) supply and demand and (2) competition.

microeconomics
The study of the behavior of individuals and firms in particular markets.

Supply, Demand, and Market Price

We introduced the concept of *revenue* in Chapter 1. Remember, a business gains revenue when customers pay for the goods or services the business provides. A business firm's revenue is determined by two factors: (1) the prices customers pay and (2) the total amount of goods and services that customers purchase. This simple but important relationship can be expressed as follows: Price multiplied by the quantity sold equals total revenue, or

market
The place where buyers and sellers meet and bargain over goods and services.

$$P \times Q = TR$$
where P = price, Q = quantity sold, and TR = total revenue

FIGURE 8.5

A Supply and Demand Model

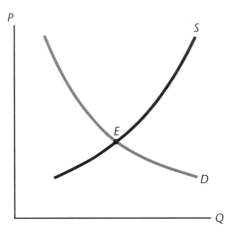

demand

The quantity consumers are willing and able to buy at different prices.

supply

The quantity businesses are willing to provide at different prices.

equilibrium point

The point on a graph where the demand curve intersects the supply curve.

The price and the quantity sold are determined by bargaining that takes place between buyers and sellers in the market and leads to our notions of demand and supply. **Demand** is the quantity consumers are willing and able to buy at different prices. **Supply** is the quantity businesses are willing to provide at different prices. Buyers are usually willing to buy more of a seller's good or service if the price is lower. Sellers are willing to provide more of the good or service if the price is higher. If the price is too high, the amount the sellers have to offer is greater than the amount buyers will purchase. If the price is too low, the amount the buyers want to purchase is more than sellers have to offer. So the buyers and sellers bargain back and forth until they arrive at a price where the amount sellers have to offer is exactly equal to the amount buyers want to purchase.

Economists explain this relationship between buyers and sellers by drawing demand and supply schedules, as shown in Figure 8.5. The curve labeled *D* is called the demand curve. It shows how much of a good or service buyers will purchase at each possible price, assuming other factors such as tastes and incomes remain the same. The curve labeled *S* is called the supply curve. It shows the amount of a good or service that a business will offer at each possible price, assuming other factors, such as technology and the prices of various inputs, remain the same. The point where the demand curve intersects the supply curve is called the **equilibrium point.** This is where the bargaining between buyers and sellers causes the quantity demanded to exactly equal the quantity supplied. This point (*E*) tells us the market price (*P*) and the market output (*Q*). All business firms that serve this market would sell their goods or services at the market price (*P*). All firms together would share in the market output (*Q*). The share of each firm would depend on various competitive factors, which we will discuss later in this chapter.

A typical business firm sells goods or services in more than one market. Thus, its total sales revenue is determined by the prices and outputs in all the firm's markets.

Price Equilibrium Processes

equilibrium processes

Processes by which the price moves toward its equilibrium point.

A very important feature of the market is the notion of **equilibrium processes,** which move the price toward its equilibrium point. We explained how demand and supply tend to determine a price in the market. This equilibrium price is a valuable concept because it tells you where the price is heading and where it will settle. However, the market rarely arrives at equilibrium (or stays there) because demand and supply are constantly shifting. In fact, a typical situation is one where the price has temporarily moved away from the long-run equilibrium value and is in the process of moving back. Therefore, the real usefulness of the concept of equilibrium is to tell business leaders where the price is going in both the short and the long run.

Every year the major daily newspapers and the nightly television business news programs carry numerous reports of prices that appear to be above or below equilibrium. The knowledgeable businessperson, consumer, or student can use that information to buy before prices rise or to refrain from buying until prices fall. Thus, if new home prices are very high by historical standards, you can be fairly certain that builders will eventually respond by increasing supply and the price will fall to more normal levels. But if new home prices fall below the historical trend, you can be sure that builders will reduce production and prices will eventually rise. If automobile prices have recently gone up significantly, you can be fairly certain that automobile makers will increase production this year or next and prices will return to their historical trend. If the pay for a profession such as nursing goes up significantly because of a reported shortage, you can be somewhat confident that eventually the supply will increase and bring nurses' pay back to where it would be if it followed its normal upward trend. If coffee prices triple because of a freeze in Brazil, you can be certain that the supply will eventually increase and bring the price back down to a more normal level. If stock prices soar to extremely high levels that cannot be justified by earnings, you can be sure that eventually the stock prices will fall. But if stock prices are much lower than would be expected given the earnings of firms, there is a good chance that the prices will eventually rise. Hence, the simple stock market rule: Buy low and sell high!

In all the examples above, economic analysis can be used to estimate what an equilibrium price would be for a product or service. If the actual price is significantly higher or lower than the estimated lower price, then the businessperson will study the situation to determine whether or not there are plausible reasons to expect supply or demand to shift and bring the price back to a more normal level.

Demand and supply curves shift frequently. As a result, market price and output are always changing. Sometimes these changes are caused deliberately by a business firm, as in the case when a major advertising campaign makes more people aware of the firm's products. More often, they are caused by forces beyond the firm's control such as changes in consumer tastes and preferences or changes in prices of competitive products. The macroeconomic forces we discussed earlier are major causes of supply and demand shifts. Shifts in demand are also caused by changes in customer tastes and prices of competitive products. Shifts in supply are also caused by changes in technology and changes in the prices of capital, labor, or raw materials.

To develop an idea of how the supply and demand model can help businesses think about future prices, consider the six versions of the model in Figure 8.6. Panel A shows the simple equilibrium situation. The price (P_1) and output (Q_1) are determined by the intersection of the demand and supply curves. Panel B shows what happens when supply increases while the demand curve remains in place. As you can see, the increase in supply causes the price to fall to P_2 and the quantity sold to increase to Q_2. This kind of shift is common and is often driven by technological change such as the development of faster and cheaper computer chips. Panel C shows a drop in supply (the curve shifts to the left), which causes the price to rise to P_2 and the quantity sold to fall to Q_2. Among the reasons this situation might occur is a crop failure caused by a drought or a restriction in oil production caused by deliberate action on the part of the oil-producing states.

Changes in demand can have similar effects, also illustrated in Figure 8.6. Panel D shows the effect of an increase in demand (shift of the demand curve from D_1 to D_2), with the supply curve remaining in place. As you can see, the price rises from P_1 to P_2 and the quantity sold increases from Q_1 to Q_2. Changes in consumer tastes, increases in income, and changes in interest rates are common causes of this kind of change. Panel E shows the effects of a drop in demand. For example, as more and more companies have moved toward business casual attire, the demand for suits has dropped significantly. Some suit manufacturers have even been struggling to survive.

FIGURE 8.6

Six Versions of Demand and Supply Models Showing Shifts

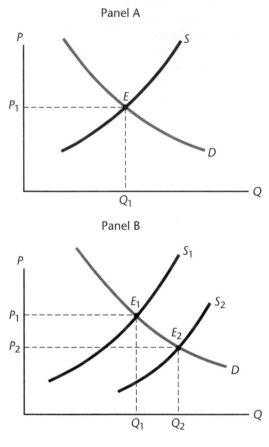

Panel A

Panel B

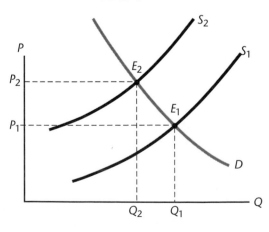

Panel C

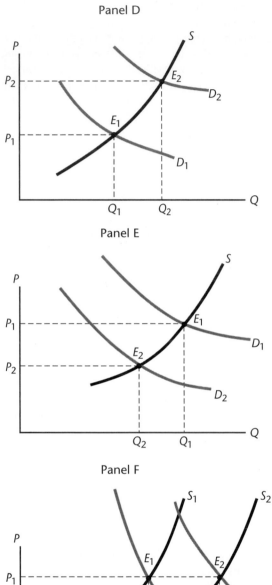

Panel D

Panel E

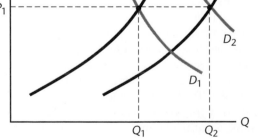

Panel F

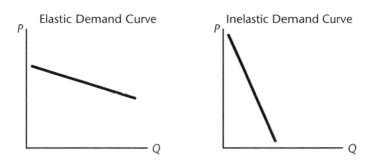

FIGURE 8.7

Elastic and Inelastic
Demand Curves

Finally, Panel F shows one of many examples of what might happen if both demand and supply increase. In this case the demand curve and the supply curve shift to the right at the same rate, so the price remains the same. It is more likely that one of the curves will shift faster than the other, so the price will either rise (if demand increases faster than supply) or fall (if supply increases faster than demand).

Price Elasticity of Demand

Business depends on revenue for survival. As we've seen, revenue depends on market price and the quantity sold. Therefore, business managers must constantly be thinking about price changes and their impact on the firm's future revenue. The concept that explains the relationships among price, quantity, and revenue is the **price elasticity of demand.** Economists measure it by dividing the percentage change in the quantity of a product or service demanded by the percentage change in its price. An elasticity greater than 1.0 is an elastic demand; less than 1.0 is an inelastic demand.

Business history has several illustrations of the price elasticity concept. Profile 8.4 describes some of these, and Figure 8.7 illustrates the concept. Note that products that have an elastic demand curve, which is relatively flat, are price sensitive. Examples of price-elastic goods and services are clothes, glassware, furniture, stereo equipment, restaurants, and relatively low-priced luxury goods. Products that have an inelastic demand curve, which is relatively steep, are not price sensitive. Examples of price-inelastic products include medicine and hospital services, alcohol, legal services, auto repair, and gasoline.

> **price elasticity of demand**
> The percentage change in the quantity of a product or service demanded divided by the percentage change in its price.

Personal Computers: Steve Jobs and Michael Dell

In the mid-1970s IBM dominated the computer market. Most customers were business-people, because the computers were large and expensive. IBM did not think there was a market for inexpensive personal computers. Steve Jobs disagreed. He believed that the demand for home computers would be price elastic if the computer was easy to use. He and Steve Wozniak invented just that kind of computer and formed Apple Computer to sell their invention. They were right. Demand turned out to be price elastic. Because

Apple's prices were so low and the computers so easy to use, the company was able to sell to an entirely new group of people who had never before considered buying a computer. IBM responded with a personal computer of its own and its version became the market leader. But neither IBM nor Apple took full advantage of price elasticity of demand. That job was left to a group of new computer makers who manufactured computers that used the same operating system and software as IBM but were sold for a lower price. By 2002 it was clear that the most successful of these makers of IBM clones was one of our focus companies—Dell.

Discount Airlines and Herb Kelleher

In the 1970s most airline executives thought demand for their service was price inelastic, so they did not try to cut costs and fares. But Herb Kelleher disagreed. He was convinced that demand for air travel was price elastic. He formed Southwest Airlines to prove his point. By offering extremely low fares, Southwest proved that there was a huge potential market of airline passengers just waiting for prices to fall low enough to enable them to switch from their automobiles to a commercial airline. After Congress deregulated the airline industry in 1978, other discount airlines followed the example of Southwest. One interesting example is JetBlue Airways, which started service on February 11, 2000. JetBlue tried to combine low fares with some touches of luxury, such as live satellite television offered free at every seat.

Sam Walton and Discount Retailing

Sam Walton pioneered discount retailing in rural America when he opened his first Wal-Mart store in Arkansas in 1961. In disagreement with the experts, he was convinced that demand for the services of general merchandise retailing was price elastic in rural areas. He was right. Customers poured into Wal-Mart stores in rural America, and total revenue grew rapidly. Eventually, of course, Wal-Mart spread into urban areas throughout the United States and into foreign countries. While Wal-Mart was conquering the general merchandise segment, other specialty retailers successfully introduced a format combining low prices and a huge assortment of merchandise. Best Buy and Circuit City did this in consumer electronics; Home Depot and Lowe's did it in hardware and building supplies; Toys 'R' Us did it in toys.

In the examples above, the initial benefits of discount pricing are due to the creation of a whole new class of customers. In other words, the total market expands significantly. Once that new customer base has been fully developed, further price-cutting will come only from taking business away from other firms in the industry. The economist's concept of price elasticity of demand refers only to the case where the total market expands significantly.

Let's consider how price elasticity might work for a company like Best Buy. Suppose your local Best Buy store has been selling a particular brand and style of computer for $600 and that it has been selling on average 1,000 per year. In other words, this store receives $600,000 per year total revenue for selling this product. Now Best Buy headquarters tells the manager of the store to lower the price by 10 percent to $540. Is this a good idea? It is if demand is price elastic. In other words, it is a good idea if a 10 percent reduction in price will cause more than a 10 percent increase in unit sales. Suppose in this case that the price cut causes sales to increase by 15 percent. Then total revenue will equal 1,150 units multiplied by $540, or a total of $608,100. Consumer price sensitivity as reflected through price-elastic demand caused total revenue to increase.

Now consider the case of a price-inelastic demand. What would happen to total revenue if the price reduction of 10 percent caused unit sales to increase by 9 percent? The store would receive less revenue on each of the 1,000 units it had been selling. It would receive $60 less per unit, for a total reduction of $60,000. On the other hand, it would sell an additional 90 units (1,000 units multiplied by 9 percent). Each of those would sell for $540, so total revenue gained from the sale of new units would equal $48,600 (90 units multiplied by $540). By lowering the price, Best Buy gains $48,600 from the sale of additional units but loses $60,000 that it would have earned by keeping the price at $600 and selling the original 1,000 units.

The message should be clear. Reduce the price only if demand is price elastic. On the other hand, consider raising the price if demand is price inelastic. Why? Because the increased revenue you will receive from the units you sell at the higher price will more than offset the revenue lost by the reduction in the number of units sold if costs are constant.

Keep in mind that price elasticity is not the only factor at work here. Competitors' models and prices are important. Costs of production and marketing capabilities are also important. Managers must balance a number of factors to reach a final decision on pricing.

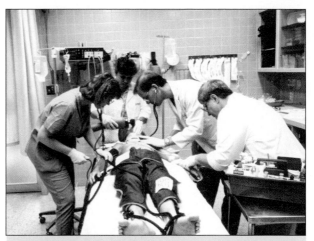

Prompt care centers, such as the one pictured here, are growing in number across the country. They provide needed, urgent care without waiting for a doctor's appointment. Can you use your knowledge of demand and elasticity to explain the rapid growth of these centers?

Competition

We now turn to the second major microeconomic force affecting business, the concept of competition. Most managers can readily give you the names of their major competitors. Table 8.5 shows a partial list of competitors for each of our focus companies. Furthermore, astute managers can tell you what their competitors do well and where they have weaknesses in competing for customers. But there are some difficulties involved in correctly assessing the firm's competitive situation. Sometimes it is hard to define competitors accurately because the industry is quite diversified. The company may have a number of competitors, but each competitor will overlap only a portion of its products or services. Some competitors are fierce competitors, while others are less aggressive. This section discusses the force of competition and how it affects businesses.

THINK ABOUT THIS

1. Gasoline prices seem to have a habit of going up just before holiday travel begins. Can you explain why in terms of demand and supply curves?

2. Why are many of Southwest Airlines' customers leisure travelers? Why do many airlines have cheaper fares if the customer agrees to stay over Saturday night?

3. Why is the price of strawberries high in early summer?

TABLE 8.5

Selected Competitors of Focus Companies

Southwest Airlines	Dell	Best Buy
United Airlines	Gateway	Circuit City
Delta Airlines	Hewlett-Packard	Office Depot
JetBlue	Apple	Staples
Continental Airlines	Sony	Sears
AirTran	Matsushita	Independent electronics stores

Types of Competition

There are two generic types of competition, direct and indirect. The most obvious competitors are direct competitors. These are the firms that sell the same goods and services and compete for the same customers.

Direct Competition

Economists group directly competing firms into one of four categories: pure competitors, monopolistic competitors, oligopolies, and monopolies.

Pure competition is a situation in which all firms sell identical products and no one firm can raise its price without losing its customers. Since the individual firm cannot raise prices on its own, it has to accept the market price. Agriculture is a good example of a purely competitive industry.

Monopolistic competition is a situation in which there are many firms and relatively easy entry, but each firm sells a somewhat differentiated product or service. There are a number of ways that firms can differentiate themselves from rivals. They may offer different formats, styles, designs, or models. They may offer unique services. Even the way they package their product may be differentiated. Or—and we see this frequently—they may use advertising to convince customers that they are indeed different.

Within a limited range, price is demand inelastic. That is, up to a point, each firm can raise its price without experiencing a decline in revenue because some people will be willing to pay a little bit more for the firm's preferred product or service. Merchandise retailing, retail services, and food retailing exemplify this kind of competition. The casual-dining segment of the restaurant business is a good example. You will find local restaurants competing with such chains as Chili's, Cheddars, Perkins Family Restaurants, Red Lobster, Applebee's, and others. Each caters to similar customers, but their food offerings, their theme and décor, and even their hours of operation provide some differentiation.

Firms engaged in monopolistic competition will not earn exceptional profit in the long run. Any temporary advantage will be eliminated by a combination of price-cutting by existing competitors and entry of new competitors. So management in this type of industry must look for ways of finding a competitive advantage that cannot be copied by competitors. An excellent example of such a success is Starbucks. It is not too much of an exaggeration to argue that Starbucks created a different kind of coffee shop that no rival has really matched on a national level.

pure competition
A market situation in which many firms sell nearly identical products and no one firm can raise its price without losing most of its customers.

monopolistic competition
A market situation in which there are many firms but each has a slightly different product.

An **oligopoly** is a situation in which a few firms, with or without differentiated products, dominate the market. The reason for the small number of companies is the extremely high cost of entering the industry. Because there are only a few firms, there is little incentive to compete on the basis of price. Since intense price competition would hurt them all, companies in an oligopoly situation tend to compete in other ways, such as advertising and new-product development. The steel and automobile industries are good examples of oligopolies.

A **monopoly** is a situation in which there is only one firm selling a product or service. As such, it can set the market price subject to the constraints of the demand curve. Many monopolies are regulated by the government. Electric power companies have traditionally been good examples of a regulated monopoly. Today, their monopolistic position is being challenged. The ability to sell power across geographic areas is now changing the industry from a monopoly toward an oligopoly.

It is important for business leaders to know which category applies to their business situation because the principles for successful competition differ from one category to the next. For example, in purely competitive industries, the firm has to compete strictly in terms of cost. Management must concentrate on lowering costs so that the firm can make a profit at the existing market price. In oligopoly situations, management competes by differentiating the product, perhaps through advertising or new-product development.

Indirect Competition

Before leaving our discussion of competition, we must consider the impact of indirect competition. Indirect competitors sell different goods and services than you do, but your customers perceive the products as acceptable alternatives. You may also hear indirect competitors noted as providers of substitute products or services.

Interestingly, Southwest Airlines was established to compete with automobile travel between the Texas cities of Dallas, Houston, and San Antonio. Thus, it was established as a substitute for, or indirect competitor of, ground transportation rather than as a competitor for airlines. Another interesting example is the role of the Internet as a substitute for the U.S. Postal Service. Whereas UPS and FedEx are considered competitors of the U.S. Postal Service, the Internet is a substitute, or indirect competitor.

One reason businesses must be concerned about indirect competition is the way these competitors can affect price. If customers believe they can get similar value from a substitute at a lower price, they are likely to switch products. New substitutes come on the market frequently. If a business is considering raising the prices of its products, it may inadvertently be pushing its customers toward substitute products. Managers must be aware of the impact those substitutes may have on revenues of their own products.

oligopoly
A market situation in which a few firms, with or without differentiated products, dominate the market.

monopoly
A market situation in which only one firm sells a product or service.

SOUTHWEST

There is probably a street like this close to your college. Different businesses appear and others close with relative frequency. Given this competitive scene, how much price variation would you expect across businesses? How do these businesses try to truly distinguish themselves from the others?

The Role of Economics in Management Decision Making

We have discussed the impacts of both macroeconomic forces and microeconomic forces on businesses. Let's return now to the decision-making process discussed in Chapter 5. How do the economic forces really affect decisions? Indeed, does the typical business leader really use the economic concepts and considerations we have highlighted in this chapter? The answer is yes, both in the abstract and in making specific decisions.

Managers must observe and predict what will happen in the overall economy to ensure that their decisions match their best guesses of the future. Large publicly held companies in particular must look at the economy because they know their performance and stock price will be affected by forces beyond their control. Stockholders will want to see continually rising stock prices or at least valid reasoning if stock prices do not meet expectations. Top managers in these large companies may make acquisitions, sell divisions, or even sell the company itself depending on their assessment of the economy and how their firm can compete.

An example illustrates one such approach. H.J. Heinz recently sold its pet foods division and its StarKist tuna product line to Del Monte. Why would the company do this? Its reasoning was that those product lines were not adding enough to the bottom line—the profits. Since the economy was in a state of uncertainty, Heinz decided it would be prudent to divest those lines that were not tied closely to its core products and use the funds from that divestiture to enhance the company's ability to become a faster-growing, more focused, international food company.[3]

Smaller companies will also be affected by economic forces. In particular, their ability to hire highly qualified workers may depend on the unemployment in their local area since large companies can afford to outbid them for the top candidates available. With low unemployment, smaller firms may have to be content with less-qualified workers. Interest rates will also affect small firms' ability to compete. Rising interest rates will make borrowing more expensive. Owners of these firms may have to consider carefully whether expansion is the correct strategy, especially if the economic situation as a whole is somewhat tenuous.

THINK ABOUT THIS

1. Suppose you want to start your own retail bakery. What types of competition will you expect to encounter?

2. Will the impact of indirect competition be as great as that of direct competition? Could it be greater?

THE BIG PICTURE

Economics is perhaps the most integrative of all topics covered in this book because it affects virtually every department and functional area within a business. For example, the marketing department may want to lower prices of a product or service. But if that service is price inelastic, lowering the price would be ill-advised. The need to control costs throughout the company, particularly in producing the product, may depend on what type of competitive situation the company faces. Cost savings is far more important in a purely competitive situation than in, say, an oligopoly because the firm cannot raise prices effectively.

Thus, economics and competition are critically important to how a company operates. Management must use the basic tenets of economics as part of the decision-making process. As you read the remaining chapters in the book, remember how these forces can affect each part of the business.

Summary

1. A major responsibility of a manager is dealing with economic forces external to the firm.

   • What are the major economic forces that affect a firm's success?

   The two major economic forces that affect how a business operates are macroeconomic forces and microeconomic forces. Macroeconomic forces deal with economic growth, inflation, unemployment, and interest rates. Microeconomic forces deal with supply and demand and competition.

2. It is impossible to forecast changes in the macroeconomic forces accurately. However, business managers can try to anticipate their occurrence by understanding some simple macroeconomic concepts and then using them to interpret economic reports commonly reported in the business press.

   • What are the macroeconomic concepts managers should understand?

   Managers should understand the concept of gross domestic product (GDP). This is the market value of all final goods and services produced in a country in a given year. It is the sum of four types of spending: consumption, investment, government, and net exports. Economic growth is measured by increases in GDP.

   It is important to distinguish between GDP and per capita GDP, since GDP may increase simply as a result of a population increase. In fact, population change is an important variable that businesses need to monitor.

   The multiplier effect refers to the idea that when one component of GDP increases, that increase causes an additional increase in one of the other components.

   The most popular measure of inflation, the consumer price index, measures the prices of consumer goods and services. Inflation is important because it affects the cost of products or services provided and the demand for the product.

   The unemployment rate is published monthly by the U.S. Bureau of Labor Statistics, which calculates it by dividing the number of people classified as unemployed by the total labor force. Unemployment includes frictional, structural, seasonal, and cyclical unemployment.

   Interest is the price paid by businesses to borrow money, and the interest rate measures that price as a percentage of the amount borrowed.

The concepts of monetary and fiscal policy can be used to anticipate possible government actions in response to the most recent reports on GDP growth, inflation, unemployment, or interest rates. Monetary policy refers to government efforts to change the money supply and interest rates. Fiscal policy refers to changes in government spending and taxation.

3. Managers can look at the relative growth or decline in the economy and can watch for changes in government policy that may affect the economy.

   • What is the business cycle, and how does it work?

   Managers should be familiar with the concept of the business cycle. This concept refers to the historical fact that GDP exhibits periodic increases and decreases. The business cycle consists of four stages: recession (contraction), trough, expansion (recovery), and peak.

4. Perhaps the single most important determinant of business success is the price received for the company's product or service. If the price is too low, the firm will eventually go out of business or have to abandon the unprofitable product line. If the price is sufficiently high, then the firm can earn profits. If the price is too high, the firm will lose customers. Managers need to be able to forecast the prices they are likely to receive for their products.

   • How are prices determined, and why do they change?

   Prices are determined by the interaction of demand and supply in the market. Prices may change because of a shift in demand, because of a shift in supply, or because of simultaneous shifts in demand and supply.

5. In the long run, the price of a product or service is determined by the interaction of buyers and sellers in the market. The impact of prices on revenues depends in part on the price elasticity of demand.

   • What is price elasticity of demand, and how can knowledge of it be used to increase profits?

   Price elasticity of demand refers to how the quantity of a product or service demanded changes in response to a change in price. To measure elasticity, divide the percentage change in quantity demanded by the percentage change in price. If the percentage change in quantity demanded is greater than the percentage change in price, then demand is said to be elastic. If the percentage change in quantity demanded is less than the percentage change in price, demand is inelastic.

   A firm can increase revenues by raising prices in markets where demand is price inelastic or by lowering prices in markets where demand is price elastic.

6. Competition is the key to the success of the capitalist economic system. Society as a whole benefits from the rivalry of business firms. However, firms themselves are under constant pressure to cope with the competition. To do so effectively, managers must first understand what types of competition they are facing.

   • What are the major types of competition that businesses face?

   There are two generic types of competition, direct and indirect.

   Economists break direct competition into four basic categories: (1) pure competition, in which all firms produce identical products and there are so many firms that no one firm can raise its price without losing its customers; (2) monopolistic competition, where there are many firms but each has a slightly different product, so each firm can raise its price without losing its customers; (3) an oligopoly, where a few firms dominate the market; and (4) a monopoly, where only one firm serves the market.

Indirect competition refers to firms that sell different goods or services but sell to the same customers. For example, steel companies face indirect competition from producers of plastic and aluminum.

7. Managers must use knowledge of economics in decision-making.

• What must managers do?

The typical manager must use the economic concepts and considerations highlighted in this chapter during the decision-making process. Managers must observe and predict what will happen in the overall economy to ensure that their decisions match their best guesses of the future.

Key Terms

business cycle, p. 192

deflation, p. 188

demand, p. 198

economic growth, p. 186

equilibrium processes, p. 198

equilibrium point, p. 198

fiscal policy, p. 191

gross domestic product (GDP), p. 184

inflation, p. 187

interest, p. 190

macroeconomics, p. 183

market, p. 197

microeconomics, p. 197

monetary policy, p. 191

monopolistic competition, p. 204

monopoly, p. 205

oligopoly, p. 205

per capita economic growth, p. 186

price elasticity of demand, p. 201

pure competition, p. 204

supply, p. 198

unemployment rate, p. 189

Exercises and Applications

1. Search the Internet for government sources of economic data. Look up the consumer price index over the past decade and interest rates over the same period. What is the relationship between the two?

2. Select one or more products, and estimate the relationship between prices and quantity sold. For example, how many PayDay candy bars would you buy at 60 cents each? 50 cents each? 40 cents each?

3. Redo exercise 2. This time, however, survey a large number of people. Calculate the elasticity of the demand for the product by dividing the change in number sold by the change in price. Was the elasticity greater than 1.0? Remember, elasticity greater than 1.0 is an elastic demand, and elasticity less than 1.0 is an inelastic demand.

4. Interview the owner of an auto repair shop near campus. Ask how sensitive customers are to changes in price. Are they as price sensitive for repairs as they are for a simple oil change? Ask the owner how business has been affected by the advent of the quick-lube businesses. Write your findings in a one-page paper.

5. Go to Figure 8.4. Update that figure to the present time by going to the Bureau of Economic Analysis website. Now go to Table 8.4. What is the latest trough or peak?

6. Pick a product that is familiar to you. What type of competition is the manufacturer of that product facing?

FROM THE PAGES OF

BusinessWeek

Tough Times for a New CEO

In 2001 Kenneth I. Chenault became CEO of American Express. Between 1991 and 2000 Chenault had rescued American Express from mediocrity by first formulating a comeback strategy and then implementing the plan.

For most of its history, American Express had provided charge card services to a niche of high-income customers who were expected to pay all their charges within 30 days. The customers used the cards primarily for travel and entertainment and paid a hefty fee for the privilege. As the credit card revolution gained strength in the 1980s, AmEx found itself faced with a serious competitive threat. "In 1991 [American Express] was losing market share to Visa and MasterCard. Restless merchants were in revolt over the high so-called discount fees they had to fork over to American Express on every charge—as much as 4% compared with less than half that for Visa." Chenault soothed relations with merchants; he eased payment terms for cardholders and made the card attractive to customers outside the high-end niche where American Express had been stuck. "He aggressively signed on retailers like gas stations, discounters, and supermarkets. And he launched a credit-card version of a frequent traveler program." The results were impressive. The number of cardholders rose from 36.6 million in 1991 to 54.3 million in 2001; charge card revenue rose from $111 billion in 1991 to $297 billion in 2000.

However, this outstanding performance occurred during a period of steady and outstanding growth of the American economy. When economic growth slowed and the economy entered a short recession in 2001, American Express encountered some serious problems. Significant numbers of card-carrying customers stopped making payments, and write-offs on bad card debt reached 5.7 percent, a level higher than the 5.2 percent average for all credit cards. To make matters worse, competition from other credit card issuers was forcing American Express to lower interest rates and fees. And the faltering economy caused bankruptcies of firms whose bonds were part of the American Express investment portfolio. That, in turn, forced American Express to report losses on the money management side of the company's business.

Chenault acted decisively. In the middle of 2001, he twice announced write-offs of hundreds of millions of risky, high-yield junk bonds. The second announcement, in July, caused the company's second-quarter income to fall 76 percent. Chenault also announced employee layoffs as part of an aggressive effort to reduce costs. Simultaneously, he moved to strengthen the charge card network, to expand the company's international presence, and to broaden product offerings. To employees and investors, he communicated his conviction that American Express would be well positioned to prosper when the recession ended.

How does Chenault himself see the leader's role? In his words, "The role of a leader is to define reality and to give hope."

Decision Questions

1. The experience of American Express during the upturn and downturn phases of the business cycle is common for a majority of businesses. During the upturn every business faces the danger of making decisions that will cause problems for the company when the next recession occurs. What actions did American Express take in the 1990s that caused problems for the company during the recession of 2001?

2. What does this case tell us about actions a company may have to take when a recession has an impact on its income?

3. This case illustrates opportunities and threats that a company faces in deciding whether to compete in a mass market or specialize in a smaller niche. What niche was historically the source of AmEx success? Was the company wise to move out of that niche? What changes did it have to make to serve the mass market?

Source: John A. Byrne and Heather Timmons, "Tough Times for a New CEO," *BusinessWeek,* October 29, 2001, pp. 68–70.

References

1. John K. Waters, *John Chambers and the Cisco Way.* (New York: John Wiley, 2002), pp. 151–62.

2. Aaron Bernstein, "Too Many Workers? Not for Long," *BusinessWeek,* May 20, 2002, pp. 126–30.

3. "Best Buy," *Value Line Investment Survey,* May 17, 2002, p. 1713.

4. "Heinz Announces Transformative Transaction to Become Faster-Growing, More Focused Company," Heinz website, www.heinz.com (accessed September 20, 2002).

The Impact of Financial Markets
and Processes

What was the most successful Internet company during the long stock market boom that ran from 1991 to 2001? Cisco Systems would certainly be one of the top candidates for that honor. Cisco benefited from its position as the leading supplier of the infrastructure equipment that made the Internet possible. Demand for that equipment enabled Cisco's core Internet business to grow at a rate of 70 percent per year. The company managed that growth so well that it was able to meet or beat stock market analysts' profit growth expectations for 45 straight quarters prior to the January 27, 2001 quarterly report (when earnings fell short of analysts' expectations by one cent per share).

The stock market rewarded that impressive performance by pushing the company's stock price from $5 per share in 1995 to its peak of $82 in 2000. Cisco, in turn, used its highly priced stock as the means of paying for a large number of acquisitions of other Internet-related companies. It acquired 41 such companies from 1999 through 2000. Those acquisitions fueled Cisco's growth enough to make it the most valuable company in the world for one brief moment in March 2000.

Then the financial and economic environment became Cisco's foe. Telecommunications companies stopped buying equipment because their industry had developed excess capacity. The Internet industry entered a recession of its own as one dot-com company after another declared bankruptcy or sold itself to avoid such embarrassment. The stock market began a sharp decline, and Cisco's stock fell sharply from its high of $82 to a low of $35.20 in 2000 and an even lower $11 per share in 2001. It was only marginally better in the middle of June 2002. With its stock having lost so much value, Cisco was no longer in a position to continue its acquisition binge at the old rapid rate. It made only 2 acquisitions in 2001. CEO John Chambers did hope to make 8 to 12 acquisitions in 2002, but that would still be quite a comedown from the glory days of the late 1990s.

The role of the stock market in first fueling and then stalling Cisco Systems' growth illustrates one way the financial environment can affect a business. In this chapter you will learn what managers need to know about important financial relationships that create opportunities and pose threats for business managers.[1]

Financial markets are the enablers of growth for businesses. In simplest terms, businesses cannot grow substantially without funds available from outside sources. Without access to financial markets, a firm can grow only as far as its sales generate enough funds to support both current and future needs. Financial markets are important not just for big, thriving businesses; new, start-up businesses also rely on these markets. Small businesses often need to tap into banks and other financial institutions. Therefore, it is important for you to understand the nature of financial markets and processes.

After studying this chapter, you should be able to:

1. Explain the nature of financial markets and identify the major financial institutions
2. Describe the major ways financial markets affect businesses.
3. Understand the concepts of interest, interest rate, and real rate of interest.
4. Explain why interest rates change over time.
5. Explain how stock prices are determined.
6. Explain the ethical and practical issues related to financial reporting by business firms.

In Chapter 8, you learned about the role that competitive markets play in the daily affairs of business. There the emphasis was on the markets where the business sells its goods or services. In this chapter, you will learn about another set of markets that are vitally important to business firms—financial markets. As the model of a successful business in Chapter 2 showed, financial markets are a major part of the environment.

This chapter will introduce you to four important aspects of financial markets. First, you will learn about the six ways financial markets influence businesses. Second, you will explore the basic features of interest rates. Third, you will become familiar with stock market fundamentals. You will also learn about several types of government policies that have important influences on financial markets. Finally, you will become aware of the ethical issues that a business faces when presenting its financial reports to the public. When you finish this chapter, you will not be an expert in finance, but you will have a good general understanding of the various opportunities and threats financial markets present to the healthy business.

For most of us, commercial banks are the most recognized financial institution. However, even traditional banks differ in their focus. For example, some emphasize commercial loans, while others focus more heavily on housing and real estate loans. Banks are also involved in a growing array of financial services. What bank services do you use?

The Nature of Financial Markets

Businesses need money for a variety of purposes over the course of time, including starting the business, financing expansion, underwriting day-to-day operations, and acquiring other businesses. Every business hopes to generate money from the sale of its products or services, but in many cases those funds are insufficient. Then the manager must go outside the firm for additional funds. The most likely outside sources are financial markets.

Financial markets are places where businesses that need to acquire capital are brought together with financial institutions that help provide the funds. There are many financial institutions available, including commercial banks, venture capital firms, insurance and pension fund companies, investment banking houses, and nonbank lenders.

The most common type of financial institution is banks. Commercial banks deal in the lending and borrowing of funds. Banks make loans to businesses and charge interest on the loans. As you learned in Chapter 8, interest is the cost of borrowing money. Banks often require some kind of collateral to guarantee the loan. **Collateral** is any asset owned by the borrower that is pledged to the lender in case the loan is not repaid. If the business defaults on the loan, the bank can take possession of the asset.

Keep in mind that what you and I would consider lending and borrowing are precisely the opposite for banks. Thus, when we make a deposit in a bank, we are actually lending that money to the bank. The money is a liability for the bank. Conversely, when we borrow money from a bank, that loan is an income-producing asset for the bank, an asset on which it earns interest. The success of a bank depends on its ability to lend its money at a higher rate than it pays for it.

Banks are involved in a range of consumer services. In addition to the normal checking and savings accounts, certificates of deposits, and a variety of loans, banks can now sell mutual funds, stocks, and other investment instruments.

A second type of institution is **venture capital firms,** corporations that invest in risky businesses with high growth potential, usually in exchange for a considerable share of the ownership. They know they will lose money on many of these ventures, but they make high returns on others.

A third type of financial institution is *insurance and pension fund companies.* Insurance companies allow businesses to shift risk, as we will discuss later in the chapter. Perhaps more important, insurance and pension fund companies invest premiums in stocks and bonds of other companies. Thus, these companies are the largest single owners of many companies, and they can put significant pressure on firms to perform adequately.

An **investment banking house** is a financial institution that works with businesses to get large amounts of financing when they need it. Investment bankers are usually involved in growth-oriented businesses, particularly those that anticipate going public.

Finally, recent years have seen the growth of nonbank lenders, such as the financial services units of General Electric and the Boeing Company. A **nonbank lender** is a financial services unit of a large company, which makes loans to other businesses.

financial markets
The places where businesses that need to acquire capital are brought together with financial institutions that help provide the funds.

More to Come
CHAPTER 13

collateral
Any asset owned by the borrower that is pledged to the lender in case the loan is not repaid.

venture capital firms
Corporations that invest in risky businesses with high growth potential, usually in exchange for a considerable share of the ownership.

Percent

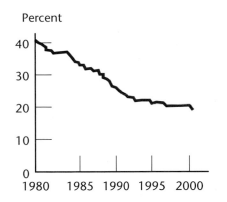

FIGURE 9.1

Traditional Banking Institutions' Share of the Credit Market, 1980–2000

Source: From *The Wall Street Journal,* Eastern Edition. Copyright © 2002 by Dow Jones & Co., Inc. Reproduced with permission of Dow Jones & Co., Inc. via Copyright Clearance Center.

Consider the following example: Peake Printers, Inc., a commercial printer based in Cheverly, Maryland, was facing some tough challenges. Several firms whose annual reports it had expected to produce had gone out of business, meaning that a big chunk of its revenues would not materialize. Things got even worse when Bank of America said that Peake would have to repay a $3.2 million loan by year-end. Two other banks refused to lend the business money. With the 125-employee firm's survival at stake, the CEO finally found an eager lender: General Electric Capital. Though Peake had to put up printing equipment, a building, accounts receivable, and $1 million of the owners' cash as collateral, it got the loan it needed.[2]

The financial services arm of General Electric illustrates how nonbank lenders are taking over from banks as suppliers of credit to big slices of the U.S. economy. As shown in Figure 9.1, the percent of total lending made by traditional banking institutions has dropped from 40 percent in 1980 to 20 percent in 2000.

In addition to these financial institutions, businesses are also influenced by the stock and bond markets. **Stocks** are shares of ownership in companies that are sold to individuals or financial institutions. Stock ownership gives investors voting rights on certain major issues affecting the business. The nature of the stock market will be covered in more detail later in the chapter. A **corporate bond** is a loan sold to the public by a business. The bonds are sold in an organized market where the buyers are various financial institutions as well as individuals.

> **investment banking house**
> A financial institution that works with businesses to get large amounts of financing.

> **nonbank lender**
> A financial services unit of a large company, which makes loans to other businesses.

> **stocks**
> Shares of ownership in companies that are sold to individuals or financial institutions.

> **corporate bond**
> A loan sold to the public by a business. Buyers may be individuals or financial institutions.

Six Ways Financial Markets Affect the Firm

Financial markets and institutions play a variety of roles in the operation of successful businesses. Six of the most important roles are shown in Table 9.1, and you will learn about them in this section.

Providing Funds to Start and Expand the Business

When a business is launched, its founders can raise funds from a variety of sources, which are shown in the first column of Table 9.2. Note that, especially for start-up situations, entrepreneurs typically cannot make good use of financial markets. The most common source for start-ups is personal or family savings. Such funds are relatively easy to

TABLE 9.1

The Impact of
Financial Markets

1. Providing the funds needed to start a business and expand it.
2. Providing funds to operate the business.
3. Influencing customer demand for the firm's products.
4. Pressuring management to focus on short-term profits.
5. Providing opportunities to reduce operating risks.
6. Providing opportunities to supplement operating earnings by wisely investing the company's surplus cash.

TABLE 9.2

Sources of Funds for
Start-ups and
Expanding Firms

Start-ups	Expanding Firms
Nonfinancial market sources	**Nonfinancial market sources**
Personal savings	Additional owner contributions
Families and friends	Partners
Partners	Suppliers
Suppliers	
Financial market sources	**Financial market sources**
Banks	Banks
Personal finance companies	Private investors
Credit card companies	Venture capitalists
	Investment bankers
	Nonbank lenders
	Bond market
	Stock market

More to Come

CHAPTER 13

acquire, and no formal ties or contracts are needed. The owner may have personal funds or count on family members or acquaintances to contribute the funds in the form of either a loan or an investment. Sometimes a partner may join the firm and contribute capital. Suppliers may also provide goods or services on credit.

These personal sources are not considered financial markets. Remember, financial markets include only those formal institutions that provide capital to businesses. Generally, the most common financial institution used for start-up is a commercial bank. Even in the case of banks, the new business owner will probably have to put up collateral. A common source of collateral is the business owner's home. Personal finance companies and credit card companies may also be used if banks will not lend the money.

Once firms are launched and show promise of succeeding, more sources of financing become available, as shown in the second column of Table 9.2. As you might expect, growth-oriented firms and relatively large companies that need substantial infusions of capital to achieve their goals are most likely to use financial institutions other than banks. The crowning stage in such an evolution is the moment when the company first raises funds from the general public through an offering of its stock. That action is called an **initial public offering,** or IPO.

initial public offering (IPO)
A company's first-time issuance of stock to the public.

Dell's early history illustrates the process of a start-up advancing to the initial public offering stage. While in high school, Michael Dell started buying cheap components, which he used to build upgraded computers that he sold to people he knew. He used *personal savings* to finance the business. When he entered the University of Texas in 1983, he expanded that activity and continued to use personal savings and *retained earnings* as his source of finance. In 1984 he incorporated the business and moved it out of his two-bedroom condominium into a small business center in North Austin, Texas. In 1986 the company was growing too fast to be financed out of profits. So Dell obtained a *loan* from Texas Commerce Bank. In 1987 Dell obtained an additional $21 million in financing through a *private placement of company stock.* That is, stock was sold to a small group of investors instead of being registered for sale to the general public. Then, in 1988 Dell raised $30 million through its *initial public offering.*[3]

One interesting way a firm can use the stock market to raise funds is by paying for the aquisition of another firm with the company's stock. As you learned at the beginning of this chapter, that was the main way Cisco Systems paid for its numerous acquisitions in the late 1990s. The Cisco example reminds us that this technique is useful primarily when a company's stock has a high value.

Profile 9.1 discusses Southwest Airlines' early efforts at financing. Its situation is unusual because of the magnitude of funding required to start an airline. The profile shows how many different financing sources and financial institutions were involved.

If a company tries to raise funds through any of the financial markets except banks, it may need to have one or more financial specialists on staff. The complicated legal and financial knowledge needed to make key financial decisions may be beyond that possessed by the typical company founder or nonfinancial manager. At this point in the company's evolution, most managers will want to have a top-level management

SOUTHWEST FLIES HIGH ON BORROWED FUNDS

PROFILE 9.1

The history of Southwest Airlines provides an interesting example of fund-raising in the early stages of a company's growth. The initial capital was provided from personal funds by founders Rollin King and Herb Kelleher, as well as from a group of investors contacted personally by King and a few other early investors. The total amount raised was $543,000. Most of that was spent fighting legal roadblocks placed in Southwest's way by existing competing airlines. After the legal battles were won, Southwest had $142 left in its bank account—and $80,000 in unpaid bills.

Nevertheless, the company was able to hire a retired airline executive named Lamar Muse as the new CEO. Muse immediately went to work raising the capital needed to get the airline off the ground. He invested $50,000 himself and was able to raise another $250,000 from friends and from contacts in the airline industry. Muse then called on a wealthy business friend who invested $750,000. Next he arranged a public stock offering after finding a brokerage firm that agreed to take a large share. (The first stock was sold on June 8, 1971.)

The public offering, plus the earlier private investments, gave Southwest $7 million of start-up capital. That made it possible for Muse to turn to a supplier for the final slice of funding needed to get into the air. Muse then convinced Boeing to sell Southwest three new jet planes on an installment plan.

Source: Kevin Freiburg and Jackie Freiburg, *NUTS! Southwest Airlines' Crazy Recipe for Business and Personal Success* (Austin, TX: Bard Press, 1996), pp. 18–22.

employee who is a financial specialist. Two common titles for such a person are treasurer and chief financial officer (CFO) as we discussed in Chapter 5.

One of the most important tasks of the company's top financial manager is to determine the best time and terms for seeking funds from financial markets. Trying to sell stock at the wrong time or for the wrong terms can harm a company's performance. Sometimes bad timing can so cripple a company that it loses its ability to compete effectively.

Providing Funds to Operate the Businesses

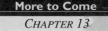

The amount of money available in a business changes continuously. Sometimes a business has more money than it needs, so it invests that money in financial markets. At other times, however, a business needs additional funds from other sources to handle daily operating expenses. For example, the business usually needs money to pay suppliers before customers make their payments to the business. Occasionally the week's or month's sales fail to provide enough cash to pay employees their weekly or monthly wages. Money set aside or used for operating the business is called **working capital.**

working capital
The money set aside or used for operating a business.

It is possible for the business to generate part of its working capital out of its earnings. But it is also possible to obtain the working capital by taking out a bank loan. The interest rate the company has to pay for its working capital loan depends on several factors. One of the most important is the bank's cost of obtaining the funds it is lending to the business. The bank's cost of funds is determined by the general level of interest rates in financial markets. Since that rate changes frequently, the business can expect its interest expense to fluctuate over time.

Because working capital represents a cost, a business must constantly search for ways to reduce the need for working capital. One firm that excels at this is Dell. A key component of Dell's original strategy was to build to order to reduce the need for working capital. In other words, the company would not build a computer until it had an order. This strategy made it possible to avoid holding an inventory of completed orders ready to be sold. Since Dell did not have to hold such an inventory, it did not need to acquire working capital to pay the costs of holding the inventory. Of course, Dell's recent foray into no-name PCs that are sold to dealers raises some questions. Dell counters that the impact will be minimal, there will be no inventory, and their lean operating strategy will not be disrupted.[4]

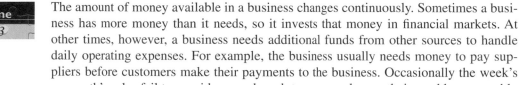

Best Buy is another company that has done well in reducing working capital costs. Best Buy's working capital as a percentage of sales has been consistently much lower than the average for the specialty retailing group. In 1998, for example, Best Buy's working capital represented 6.7 percent of total sales, compared with the 12.2 percent average for the entire industry. In 2002 Best Buy had reduced the ratio of working capital to sales to 1.7 percent, compared with the specialty retailing industry average of 8.4 percent.[5] The declines for both Best Buy and the industry reflect one of the benefits of the information technology revolution. That is, businesses have better information on sales and inventory on hand and can move more quickly to increase or decrease inventories in response to sales fluctuations.

Influencing Customer Demand for the Firm's Products

Some businesses sell products that customers purchase using borrowed funds. For example, cars and homes are typically purchased on an installment plan. In such cases, the customer has to consider not only the selling price but also the interest expense to be incurred. When interest rates are very high, many households postpone making the purchase to avoid the high interest charges on the installment loan. On the other hand, when interest rates are very low, many households are motivated to make the purchase right away.

Thus, interest rates become a matter of some concern to those businesses whose customers borrow the funds to make purchases. High interest rates mean that such businesses can expect a drop in demand. Low interest rates usually mean an increase in demand.

Many retailers provide credit to their customers both as a sales tool and as a source of extra income. As a source of income, this can be an attractive strategy. In 2002 operating profit on company-provided credit cards was about 11 percent, compared with a 7 percent operating profit on retail operations.[6] As a way of stimulating sales, providing credit can also be a method of establishing stronger bonds with customers. An interesting example in Brazil today is the case of Casas Bahia, presented in Profile 9.2.

BRAZILIAN RETAILER BUILDS AN EMPIRE BASED ON CREDIT

PROFILE 9.2

Samuel Klein's Casas Bahia chain is Brazil's largest nonfood retailer, and Klein has been favorably compared to Wal-Mart's Sam Walton. Their backgrounds are certainly different. Klein had only four years of schooling, is a survivor of the Holocaust, and began his business career after World War II as an immigrant peddler in Brazil. Walton was a star economics graduate of the University of Missouri, spent World War II in the American military stationed in the United States, and started his business career as a Ben Franklin franchisee with a loan from his father-in-law. But both men had a touch for selling to

Businesses like Brazil's Casas Bahia depend on credit sales and installment payments. What other businesses or industries do you know that are heavily reliant on credit sales?

common people. In Klein's case, the use of credit has been a key to selling to low-income Brazilians. About 90 percent of Casas Bahia sales are on credit. That strategy explains how Klein was able to sell $1.5 billion of furniture, household goods, and appliances in 2001, including one-third of all new TV sets sold in Brazil. The following vignette illustrates how Klein's approach works:

> *"Maria Pereira visited a Casas Bahia store recently to pay a $38 monthly installment on a music system that she bought last year. On her way out, a set of five cooking pots on sale for $25 caught the housewife's attention, and she purchased it as well, in four installments. 'I hadn't thought of buying anything, actually,' says Mrs. Pereira, whose husband earns $167 a month as a security guard."*

Doesn't Casas Bahia run a high risk of nonpayment by its low-income customer base? Not in Klein's view. Klein feels that poorer customers are more punctual with their payments because they know they need to guard their reputations to protect their ability to buy on credit.

Source: Miriam Jordan, "A Retailer in Brazil Has Become Rich by Courting the Poor," *The Wall Street Journal,* June 11, 2002, p. A1.

Pressuring Management to Focus on Short-Term Profits

Financial markets encourage managers to be very attentive to the need for short-term profits. This is especially true in publicly held companies. Some experts argue that this kind of pressure is good for a company. They say stockholder pressure forces managers to be more efficient and competitive. Managers who don't meet the challenge will be forced out of office and "better" managers will be brought in. This move can be made by the existing board of directors, or it can be accomplished through a takeover.

If a publicly held company consistently performs below its potential, the business becomes vulnerable to a takeover. A **takeover** occurs when investors (including other companies) purchase enough of the company's stock to control the company. In some cases, the price of the company's stock under the old management may fall until it becomes attractive to outsiders. In other cases, the takeover process triggers an increase in the price of the company's stock before the takeover has taken place. This rise in price occurs because the takeover group believes the company could be much more profitable than it is, and the outsiders are willing to pay a higher price for the chance to prove they are right. Once the outsiders gain control, they will introduce more efficient methods of operation and make the firm more competitive. These actions by outsiders mean that earnings will increase, just as the takeover group expected. Again, proponents argue that financial markets can provide a useful public service in this manner.

Some observers believe financial markets create undue pressure for short-term performance. These critics fear that firms will cut back on R&D expenditures because of the long time necessary for these kinds of investments to produce a profit. Similarly, firms may underinvest in training and in developing new markets if the payoff will be too far in the future. They argue that even though the business may look financially sound, it is not paying enough attention to the other, longer-term measures of business success that we have discussed throughout the text.

To avoid the problem of short-term stock market pressures, many privately held firms adamantly avoid going public. Similarly, publicly held firms may convert to a privately

takeover

A situation in which investors (including other companies) purchase enough of a company's stock to control the company.

held status to gain freedom of action. A privately held corporation reduces pressures by simply not making its stock available on a stock exchange.

Take the example of Cargill, Inc., one of America's largest privately held corporations. In 2002 it reported earnings of $50.8 billion and employed 97,000 people in 59 countries. One of Cargill's many foreign businesses supplied seed and fertilizer in India and milled flour there. It took the company seven years to earn a profit in India, and company officials doubt that Cargill could have persisted if it had been publicly held. Referring to the Indian situation and numerous other slow-to-develop projects, chairman of the board Ernest Micek once commented: "It takes patience to be in our business. We can't worry about some analyst's expectations for the next quarter." That view was echoed by Thomas Urban, chair of Pioneer Hi-Bred Interval, Inc., a publicly held competitor. Urban's company had to close a potentially profitable oilseed plant in Egypt because it did not become profitable fast enough. Urban said, perhaps with a touch of jealousy, "Cargill can take risks a publicly traded company can't."[7]

Providing Opportunities to Reduce Operating Risks

We have discussed how financial markets affect the way a business operates on a day-to-day basis. Financial markets can also help managers deal with the risks associated with operating the business. The risks of operating a business cannot be completely eliminated; indeed, risk taking is a primary function of business. Nevertheless, managers use a variety of methods to reduce or shift risks. A few of those are found in specialized financial markets. More specifically, managers can use the following financial markets to reduce risks:

1. Commodity markets
2. Foreign exchange markets
3. Insurance markets

Commodity markets are financial institutions that offer businesses an opportunity to guarantee the future prices of certain agricultural products and raw materials. In commodity markets, sellers guarantee that an agreed-upon volume of a particular commodity will be available at a specified price at a future date. Buyers get the right to buy the commodity at that price at that date.

Buying the right to *sell* a product at a set price in the future can be important for an agricultural or raw materials business that wants to reduce the risk of an unexpected fall in the price of a product it is selling. For example, wheat farmers might want to guarantee the price they will get for their next wheat crop by selling a wheat contract in a commodities market. Buying the right to *buy* a product at a specified price in the future can be important to a business that wants to avoid the risk of an unexpected increase in the price of a raw material that is an important input into its production process. For example, a candy company might want to use the commodity markets to guarantee the future price of the cocoa beans that it buys to make chocolate.

Foreign exchange markets are financial institutions that offer businesses an opportunity to avoid potential losses when money earned from foreign sales is exchanged for home currency. For example, Canadian dollars differ in value from U.S. dollars. Thus, Canadian firms sell products in the U.S. with an exchange rate of 1 US$ = 1.5873 CAN$ as of September 24, 2002. However, the exchange rate has ranged from 1 US$ = 1.5122 CAN$ to 1 US$ = 1.6125 CAN$ over the past twelve months. Although one-tenth of a dollar may not sound like much, if you consider that Canadian firms may export millions of dollars of products to the U.S., the potential loss (or gain) simply through foreign

commodity markets
Financial institutions that offer businesses the opportunity to guarantee the future prices of certain agricultural products and raw materials.

foreign exchange markets
Financial institutions that offer businesses an opportunity to avoid potential losses when money earned from foreign sales is exchanged for home currency.

More to Come
CHAPTER 10

Many managers consider the cost of speculation in foreign currency a normal cost of doing business in international markets. They treat it as an expense just as much as they do advertising. What do you think are the pros and cons of speculating in the currency markets?

exchange is dramatic. Thus, Canadian companies who do not wish to speculate on what might happen on the U.S./Canadian foreign exchange markets can offset that risk by buying future U.S. dollars on the foreign exchange markets. In this way, changes in the exchange rate will not affect profits (or losses) on the sale of the product.

Insurance is a contract in which one party agrees, for a fee, to reimburse the other for financial damages incurred. Insurance policies allow a business to shift the risk of losses. If you drive a car, you are already familiar with the insurance concept. You know that, for a price, insurance companies will agree to assume the risk of paying the cost of repairing your car if it is damaged in an accident, within certain limits. The fee you pay to shift risk to the insurance company is called a premium. This insurance principle applies to a wide variety of risks. Businesses can buy insurance to protect against losses due to fire, windstorms, floods, theft, lawsuits by injured workers or customers, and other hazards.

insurance
A contract in which one party agrees, for a fee, to reimburse the other for financial damages incurred.

Insurance companies are financial institutions. The fees they collect from policyholders provide funds that can be invested at a profit. They then use these funds to pay claims to those who have incurred losses under the terms of the contract. Insurance companies pool the risk of loss of tens of thousands of businesses, so it is often cheaper for a business to buy insurance than to set aside money to cover its own losses. On the other hand, there may be occasions when the business determines that insurance is too expensive and it will be cheaper to set aside company funds to cover some of the risks. The potential for such situations appeared recently. Insurance rates had already been increasing for two years prior to the terrorist attack on New York's World Trade Center on September 11, 2001. That event added to the pressures for increases in insurance rates, and there were reports of some insurance premiums increasing by 200 percent or more.[8] Some companies determined that they could fund their own insurance more cheaply than they could pay premiums to insurance companies, perhaps retaining only high-deductible catastrophic coverage.

Providing Opportunities to Invest the Firm's Surplus Cash

A sixth important function of financial markets is to provide businesses with ways of supplementing earnings by investing a temporary surplus of cash in financial instruments that earn interest or dividends. This surplus cash is money the company is holding temporarily and plans to spend to cover future operating expenses.

Suppose a local furniture store knows that it will have to pay local property taxes in the amount of $48,000 once a year. The store's owner decides to set aside $4,000 per month out of earnings. Thus, nine months before the taxes are due, the company will have set aside $12,000; and six months before the taxes are due, the owner will have accumulated $24,000.

What should the owner do with those funds? The obvious answer is to put them in some kind of income-earning investment. Possibilities include a savings account in a bank, a certificate of deposit (CD), or a six-month U.S. Treasury bill. All these short-term investments would generate some interest income while at the same time guaranteeing the store owner the ability to get the original investment back in time to pay the taxes. Thus, the financial markets have provided the furniture store with an opportunity to supplement earnings.

Most companies invest their temporary surpluses in this manner. In larger companies there is often so much money involved that the company employs people who specialize in managing investments. In fact, some of you may decide to major in finance and end up doing this type of work for a large corporation or for a financial institution that manages the corporation's funds.

Interest Rates

By now you know that interest rates have an important impact on businesses. You can see why managers need to watch for changes in interest rates. In this section, you will learn some important concepts about interest rates.

The Concept of Interest

Interest, as you learned in Chapter 8, is the price a borrower pays a lender in return for receiving a loan. What interest do you pay if you borrow $1,000 for one year and agree to pay the lender $1,100 at the end of the year? The answer, of course, is $100. Another way of expressing the cost to the borrower is as the amount of interest paid divided by the amount of the loan. In our example, this would be the $100 in interest divided by the $1,000 loan, or an interest rate of 10 percent. It is customary to report this interest rate in terms of the annual percentage rate.

There are many different types of loans. For example, there are long-term loans and short-term loans. There are government loans and private loans. There are loans made by banks in return for a signed promise to repay the loan with interest. There are loans made by government agencies and large businesses in the form of bond sales. Just as loans differ, so do interest rates. A large, well-known business may be able to get loans with a low interest rate and with no collateral other than the company's name. A small, start-up business will pay considerably higher rates because of the risk of business failure.

One of the most important interest rates is the **prime rate.** This is the interest rate that large commercial banks charge their best corporate customers for short-term loans. The interest rates that business borrowers are charged usually reflect the prime rate. You may know of a small business owner who obtained a loan for two points over prime. This means that the owner paid two percentage points more than the rate given to the best corporate customers.

prime rate
The interest rate that large commercial banks charge their best corporate customers for short-term loans.

THINK ABOUT THIS

1. Which of the six impacts of financial markets on a business are probably most critical for the owners of a small, start-up restaurant? Which are most critical for a midsize software company that needs to expand quickly?

2. On balance, is the U.S. economy better off or worse off because of the short-term pressures that the stock market puts on publicly held companies?

3. How do you as an individual reduce or shift risks? How are your techniques similar to or different from the ways businesses deal with risks?

Interest Rate Changes over Time

One of the most important features of interest rates is the way they vary, or fluctuate, over time. The pattern is cyclical. That is, interest rates rise for a period of time, then they fall for a while, and later they begin another period of expansion. Looking at Table 9.3, for example, you see that the prime interest rate rose from 8.33 percent in 1986 to

TABLE 9.3

Real Rates of Interest in the United States, 1986–2002

Year	(1) Prime Interest Rate*	(2) Inflation Rate†	(3) Real Rate of Interest (1 − 2 = 3)
1986	8.33%	1.1%	7.22%
1987	8.21	4.4	3.81
1988	9.32	4.4	4.92
1989	10.87	4.6	6.27
1990	10.01	6.1	3.91
1991	8.46	3.1	5.36
1992	6.25	2.9	3.35
1993	6.00	2.7	3.30
1994	7.15	2.7	4.47
1995	8.83	2.5	6.33
1996	8.27	3.3	4.97
1997	8.44	1.7	6.74
1998	8.35	1.6	6.75
1999	8.00	2.2	5.80
2000	9.23	3.4	5.83
2001	6.41	1.6	4.81
2002	4.25	1.3‡	2.95

*Prime rate.
†Consumer price index year-to-year changes.
‡The 2002 inflation rate is from April 2001 to April 2002.

Source: *Economic Report of the President* (Washington, DC: U.S. Government Printing Office, 2002); Bureau of Labor Statistics, Tables B-63 and B-73; Federal Reserve Board press release, November 6, 2002.

10.87 percent in 1989. Then it began a period of decline, falling to 6 percent in 1993. At that point a period of increases began, peaking at 9.23 percent in 2000. Then the prime rate began to fall again, reaching 4.25 percent in November 2002, the lowest rate since May 1959. Keep in mind, however, that the prime rate is for preferred customers, generally larger, better performing companies. Newer or smaller companies may pay two percentage points or more above that rate.

Managers know that interest rates tend to fluctuate. How does this knowledge affect their decision making? Keeping in mind that interest is the cost of borrowing money, managers may decide to borrow for expansion when they anticipate that interest rates are at the low end of the cycle, such as they were in late 2002, and may increase in the not-too-distant future. Conversely, they may decide to delay borrowing and expanding if they think interest rates will decline later. But remember that costs are only one factor businesses take into account when making an investment decision. Another important factor is whether or not there will be increased demand for the output that results from an expansion. Thus, in the middle of 2002, interest rates were low and expected to rise. But businesses were not investing nearly as much as might be expected. Concerns about a possible lack of demand for additional production seemed to be a likely explanation for the low rate of investment.

Here is a hypothetical example that further illustrates the complexity of the investment decision. Suppose that at the beginning of 2003, a business owner was considering whether or not to replace old equipment. She would have to borrow $500,000 to replace it. The interest rate for her small company was 10 percent. So the cost of interest payments the first year alone would be $50,000. The old equipment was still operable and the owner believed, based on news reports, that interest rates would be lower in 2004. So she decided to wait. By the beginning of 2004 the interest rate she would have to pay had fallen to 5 percent and the owner took out the loan. Now the interest payment the first year would be $25,000 rather than $50,000. The owner saved $25,000.

Or did she? The business owner's decision seems logical if only the interest cost is considered. But other factors are involved. Since the equipment was old, the cost of repairs during the one-year delay (between 2003 and 2004) might have eaten up much of the $25,000 savings. In addition, the price of the new equipment might have gone up during the year delay. Then there is the possibility that during the delay, the business would not have access to the latest technology that would be incorporated into the new equipment. Staying with the old equipment might have reduced efficiency, offsetting more of the interest expense saved. As you can see, business decisions are complex and always involve trade-offs.

One reason for the rise and fall in interest rates is increases and decreases in the supply of loanable funds as a result of actions taken by the Federal Reserve (which is discussed below). Another is shifts in demand for loanable funds. Demand increases periodically when large numbers of businesses decide to borrow to finance expansion of their operations. Demand falls periodically after businesses complete their expansions or if they experience a significant decline in sales (actual or expected). In other words, when customers stop buying, businesses stop borrowing.

Inflation and Interest Rates

A second reason for rising and falling interest rates is inflation. In the long run, interest rates tend to consist of two parts. The first is the amount necessary to cover the risk that the loan will not be repaid, plus an amount necessary to cover the lender's forgone alternative uses of the funds that are loaned. The second is the expected rate of inflation.

An example should make the relationship between inflation and interest rates clear. Suppose a lender needs to earn an interest rate of 5 percent to cover the risks of a loan to a particular borrower. If the inflation rate is expected to be 2 percent over the life of the loan, then the lender will require the borrower to pay an interest rate of 5 percent plus 2 percent, or a total of 7 percent. If our lender expects the inflation rate to be 10 percent, then the borrower must pay an interest rate of 5 percent plus 10 percent, or a total of 15 percent.

Table 9.3 gives a few more examples to help you understand this point. The examples are taken from the actual experience of the U.S. economy between 1986 and 2002. Notice the column called the **real rate of interest,** the rate the borrower actually paid minus the rate of inflation. In the table, you can see that the real rate of interest varies over time.

Understanding the concept of the real rate of interest can benefit businesses whether they are borrowers or lenders. As a borrower, a business that understands the concept will be ready to take advantage of bargain-basement low rates that aren't obvious to those who do not understand the concept. For example, suppose a bank has an aggressive campaign to attract new customers and is offering a one-time rate of 3 percent. Suppose, further, that the inflation rate expected for the next year is also 3 percent. You

> **real rate of interest**
> The rate the borrower actually pays minus the rate of inflation.

know immediately that these interest rates are only temporarily low. Why? Because interest rates are supposed to reflect expected inflation. The real rate is supposed to be positive at a level of about 3 percent. Yet in this situation it is zero. The 3 percent interest rate just equals the inflation rate. Therefore, you should borrow now before the bank adds another 3 percent to its interest charges to take inflation into account.

Businesses that make loans (including extending credit to customers) can also improve performance by using knowledge of the real rate concept. What the business must do is determine the interest to be charged to the customer by first determining the real rate of interest desired and then adding the inflation rate. Suppose, for example, that management decides that any credit granted to customers must earn a real rate of return of 2 percent. Suppose, in addition, that the expected inflation rate is 3 percent. Then the interest charged the customers should be the sum of 2 percent and 3 percent, or a total of 5 percent.

The Fed, Monetary Policy, and Interest Rates[9]

In a strict economic sense, interest rates are determined by the demand for and supply of loanable funds. Further, the supply of loanable funds is determined by the amount of saving that takes place in the economy and by the government's monetary policy. Accordingly, it is important to take a brief look at how government exercises its influence. It acts primarily through the Federal Reserve Board, which is highlighted in Profile 9.3.

Monetary policy was discussed in Chapter 8. The Federal Reserve System is in charge of our monetary policy. The actions taken by the Fed's Board of Governors influence the economy, primarily by influencing interest rates. The main method the Federal Reserve Board uses to influence interest rates is to increase or decrease the money supply. The primary reasons the Fed takes such actions are (1) to change the rate of growth of the overall economy and (2) to reduce the rate of inflation.

PROFILE 9.3   THE FEDERAL RESERVE SYSTEM AND ITS BOARD

The Federal Reserve System was created in 1913 to stabilize the U.S. banking system. This was to be done by lending money to banks when they needed reserves to meet depositor demands. The Federal Reserve System was also expected to regulate the nation's money supply to prevent inflation from becoming a problem.

The Federal Reserve System consists of 12 regional Federal Reserve banks and a seven-member Board of Governors. Each governor is appointed by the president for a nonrenewable term of 14 years, which gives the Fed a significant degree of independence from Congress and the president. The chairman and vice chairman of the board are named by the president and confirmed by the Senate for a 4-year term. These appointments are renewable. Alan Greenspan has been appointed to his fourth term, extending to 2004.

The most important decision-making body in the system is the Federal Open Market Committee, which consists of the seven members of the Board of Governors plus 5 of the 12 presidents of the regional Federal Reserve banks. The Open Market Committee meets regularly to determine whether or not to tighten or loosen monetary policy and thereby push interest rates up or down.

You may be wondering how the actions of the Fed relate to the job of managers of businesses. The answer is that astute managers pay attention to the actions of the Federal Reserve to form a better idea of what is likely to happen to interest rates. For example, Federal Reserve Board chair Alan Greenspan appears regularly before Congress. The business community pays careful attention to Greenspan's statements. Business leaders try to get a sense of whether the Fed might reduce or increase interest rates. If you were the head of a major corporation, you would take this information to the next meeting of your top executive group and all of you would discuss the likelihood of future cuts or bumps in interest rates. If you all agreed that such cuts were likely, you would postpone some of the borrowing you had planned to do in the next few weeks so that you could take advantage of the lower interest rates that Greenspan suggested were coming.

The Global Economy and Interest Rates

In the past two decades, the emergence of the global economy has caused two important changes in the interest rate environment in the United States. First, it has become possible for American businesses (and our government) to borrow from foreign lenders or in foreign financial markets. Thus, managers can shop around the world for the best possible terms on a loan. If they can get a better deal in London or Tokyo than in Chicago or New York, they will borrow their funds in England or Japan. Of course, their main competitors will be doing the same shopping around. Therefore, companies today need to shop worldwide for loans to stay competitive, in addition to reducing their own costs as much as possible.

The second important change is that American monetary policymakers have to pay more attention to the flow of loanable funds into and out of the United States. This is a concern because of the differences between interest rates here and abroad. In essence, if the Federal Reserve allows a large-scale inflow of foreign funds, the demand for the dollar will rise and the foreign exchange rate will rise. An increase in the foreign exchange rate means American businesses will face stiffer competition from imports because imports will be cheaper in terms of the dollar.

Such movements are why the Federal Reserve Board has to be concerned about keeping interest rates at just the right level. The rates need to be high enough to keep the value of the dollar from falling but low enough to keep the value of the dollar from being pushed up by the inflow of foreign investment funds. Once you understand this situation, you will be better able to predict the Fed's moves with respect to interest rates.

By now, you should understand how interest rates are determined, why they are important, and how business leaders can try to assess what is likely to happen to them. You should also be aware of the high degree of uncertainty involved in forecasting future rates. That should lead you to have even more respect for the ability of top-level managers to continue to produce good performance despite the turbulent environment in which their businesses operate.

The Stock Market

Earlier in this chapter you learned how the stock market affects business. You learned that the stock market can be a

THINK ABOUT THIS

1. Why do banks charge higher interest rates for loans to small or new companies than to large, established companies?

2. We discussed how interest rates can affect the economy. Suppose a recession occurs. What will the Federal Reserve do to help out the economy?

3. As the owner of a small retail clothing store, you are convinced that interest rates will rise over the next six months. What business decisions can you make to respond to this movement?

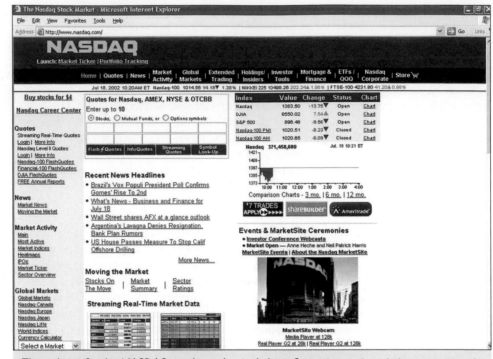

The website for the NASDAQ stock market includes information on its mission statement, its history, and investing. What kinds of stocks (or companies) are found on the NASDAQ that accounted for its growth in the late 90s? Why were there such volatile swings in the NASDAQ in early 2000?

source of funds for a business. You also learned that the stock market can be a source of discipline for a business. Once a company's stock becomes widely held by public investors, the business feels pressured to produce steady and growing profits. We now take a closer look at a few basic features of the stock market.

Stock Exchanges

Stock is bought and sold through organizations known as stock exchanges. By handling these buying and selling transactions, a stock exchange plays a key role for companies that need to raise funds and for individuals and organizations that wish to invest in those companies. You should really think of stock exchanges as securities exchanges because they buy and sell both stocks and bonds. There are a number of stock exchanges. Three major exchanges that you probably know are the New York Stock Exchange (NYSE), the American Stock Exchange (AMEX), and the over-the-counter market. The over-the-counter market is actually an electronic network of brokers throughout the country. The network is referred to as NASDAQ (National Association of Securities Dealers Automated Quotations system).

You may often hear people talking about having a "seat" on the stock exchange. A company or individual who has a seat has met standards set by the exchange and has the right to buy and sell stocks on the exchange. On the NYSE, for example, the number of seats has remained constant at 1,366 since 1952. The NYSE is the largest U.S. stock exchange, and the AMEX is the second largest.

In addition to the three noted above, the United States has a number of regional exchanges. Further, there are a number of foreign stock exchanges. If you listen to the business news some evening, you'll hear reports from the Nikkei in Tokyo, as well as the Financial Times Stock Exchange (FT-SE or "Footsie") in London, and the Hong Kong Stock Exchange.

Going Public

Going public has become a very popular practice for growing companies. **Going public** means that for the first time in its history, a company offers to sell its stock to the general public. If the company has never sold stock before, this is called an initial public offering (IPO). Logically, a company can have only one IPO. To go public, the company typically hires an investment banking firm to arrange the initial sale. Once the sale has been made, the company's stock can be bought or sold on a daily basis through one of the various stock markets that handle such sales.

There are several reasons for a company to go public. However, the key reason is to provide new investment funds the firm can use to expand its operations. One of the more interesting and successful recent IPOs was that of Krispy Kreme, highlighted in Profile 9.4.

At times, a business may go public to enable the original investors (founders and venture capitalists) to get back their original investment plus some profit. This was a major factor for Cisco Systems that we featured in the introduction to this chapter.

The New York Stock Exchange has served investors for more than 200 years. How are the transactions of the exchange affected by the laws of supply and demand?

Another reason for going public is to make it possible to use stock options as a tool to motivate managers. To understand this reason, consider the following situation, which you may well find yourself in. You are about to graduate from college. You have two job offers. One is from a well-established company that will pay you $50,000 a year plus fringe benefits. The other is from a new company, which has ambitious plans but not much of a track record. That firm has offered to pay you $25,000 a year plus the right to buy 10,000 shares of company stock at the current market price of $2 per share. You don't have to buy the shares now. Instead, you have an option to buy any time in the next five years. The company expects the price of the stock to rise to $100 within the next three years. If that were to happen, you could exercise your option, buy 10,000 shares for $20,000 and then sell the same shares for $1 million.

Which job would you take? In the 1990s, many college graduates as well as seasoned business managers took the gamble involving the stock options. As reported by *BusinessWeek,* stock options became a popular method of recruiting and keeping top managers. They became "the juice that helped fuel what was then called the dot-com revolution. They were a powerful magnet that few could resist. Thus, there was a torrent of seasoned executives at old-line companies who left solid career tracks for the potential gains from stock options at tiny, unproven entrepreneurial companies. Large companies, too, doled out options in ever-increasing quantities to keep their bright execs from fleeing to greener pastures."[10]

going public
Offering to sell the company's stock to the general public for the first time.

PROFILE 9.4   KRISPY KREME'S IPO IS A HIT

Krispy Kreme Doughnuts was founded in Winston-Salem, North Carolina, in 1937. Each store produced its doughnuts on the premises. In 2002, each individual store had the capability of producing 4,000 dozen to 10,000 dozen doughnuts a day. Many customers swore that no other doughnut could match the Krispy Kreme product, and the company developed an almost cultlike customer base. Yet as late as 2001, Krispy Kreme was a regional business that had not truly realized its potential. Then management decided it was time to expand and to do so rapidly. To obtain the capital needed for rapid expansion, Krispy Kreme made an initial public offering in April 2000. The IPO placed 13.8 million shares in the hands of the public at a price of $5.25. The stock was an immediate success; the price reached a high of $27.10 per share in 2000 and an even higher $46.90 per share near the end of 2001. It then settled in a range of $33 to $47 per share for the first half of 2002. The infusion of capital enabled Krispy Kreme to open new stores, to step up marketing Krispy Kreme doughnuts through supermarket chains, and to plan expansion into foreign markets, beginning with Australia. Together, these initiatives led to an increase in revenues from $220.2 million in the fiscal year ending February 2, 2000 (just before the IPO) to $394.4 million in the fiscal year ending February 2, 2002. Sales were expected to rise to $515 million in 2003.

No wonder the Krispy Kreme IPO was so successful. Plans call for the company to nearly triple its number of North American stores and to move aggressively in international markets. There is even a recent craze of serving Krispy Kreme doughnuts at weddings. Would you buy stock in Krispy Kreme?

Source: "Krispy Kreme," *Value Line Investment Survey,* June 14, 2002, p. 309.

Stock options, thus, can be a powerful tool to attract talented new employees without having to pay large salaries. Stock options can also be a motivational tool. Managers holding stock options have an extra incentive to work hard to increase earnings so that the stock price will rise and their stock options will become more valuable. But, of course, if a company is going to use stock options, it needs to go public so that the stock can be easily bought and sold.

You should be aware of the fact that stock options can be abused. They create the risk that managers will focus on short-run results to the detriment of the long-run health of the company. Worse yet, stock options may create incentives for executives to misrepresent the true financial performance of the company by making the firm seem to be more profitable in the short run than it really is. Many examples of this practice began to appear following the Spring 2001 drop of the average stock price on the major stock markets.

Factors That Affect the Firm's Stock Price

Once a company has sold its stock to the general public, the firm's environment changes. The new stockholders bought shares in the company with the expectation that profits would grow and the price of the stock would rise over time. If the stock price fails to rise, the stockholders can become quite unhappy. They will show their displeasure by selling the stock. Large-scale sales of the stock will cause its price to fall. If the situation becomes bad enough, the board of directors may even decide to replace the existing management team with a new group of executives. Worse yet, as we noted earlier, the poor performance of the stock may cause outside groups to attempt a hostile takeover.

Because of the problems that can arise if the stock does not perform adequately, it is important for top management to take preventive measures. Managing the price of the company's stock requires a thorough understanding of the forces that influence stock prices, among them earnings, opportunity costs, general stock market conditions, and speculation.

Earnings

The most basic determinant of the price of a company's stock is the company's earnings. In general, stock prices tend to rise or fall with the rise or fall of the company's earnings. However, market expectations must also be considered. If earnings rise, but not as much as expected, then the company's stock price may fall. Similarly, if earnings fall, but by less than expected, the stock price may rise. You need only study the volatile stock market swings in 2002 to understand how this could happen.

Earnings expectations are influenced by a variety of factors. A few typical examples are rumors of a new product under development, the hiring of a key new manager, the report of a stock market analyst, or a change in the macroeconomic environment, such as interest rates or the inflation rate.

Because the price of a company's stock is so sensitive to changes in earnings reports, the top managers of publicly held companies bear a burden they would not have if they were privately held. That burden is the need to try to manage earnings reports so that the price of the stock will neither rise too fast nor rise too slowly (or fall). In the United States, publicly held companies strive to report profits every quarter. Thus, managers have to spend time and effort making sure that profit growth is on target every three months.

Opportunity Cost

Whether or not a firm's earnings are considered good or poor is a relative matter as far as investors are concerned. They are good if they are higher than the investor's next best alternative investment. They are poor if the investor could earn more by investing in an alternative stock or in a bond or in a certificate of deposit. In other words, investors decide whether or not to purchase a stock on the basis of the value of the best available alternative. This line of thinking is based on the concept of **opportunity cost,** that is, the value of the best alternative that is sacrificed to pursue another option. For example, the opportunity cost of buying $5,000 of stock is the earnings that could have been obtained by putting the $5,000 in the next best available investment. If you have narrowed your choice to either a $5,000 purchase of stock or putting $5,000 into a certificate of deposit (CD) paying 5 percent per year, then the one-year opportunity cost of purchasing the stock is the forgone interest on the CD, or $250 (5 percent of $5,000). If the stock does not pay a dividend and if you don't expect its price to increase over the next year, then the opportunity cost exceeds the benefits of the stock purchase. You should put your $5,000 into the CD.

opportunity cost
The value of the best alternative that is sacrificed to pursue another option.

General Stock Market Conditions

A third factor influencing a company's stock price is the general trend for all stocks. Stock prices tend to go through cycles of increases and decreases. A period when prices in the market are generally increasing is known as a **bull market.** A period when prices in the market are generally decreasing is known as a **bear market.** Not all stocks follow the trend, but most do. In a bull market, the price of a company's stock may tend to rise faster than earnings increases alone would dictate. In a bear market, the price of the company's stock may actually fall even though earnings continue to increase as expected. There is nothing a company's management can do to influence the general stock market, but fortunately, stockholders tend to forgive managers for changes in the company's stock price that appear to be a reflection of the general trend of a bear market. Study the stock prices of Dell, Southwest Airlines, and Best Buy in Figure 9.2. Note, for example, the swings in prices within a given year as well as differences from year to year.

bull market
A period when prices in the stock market are generally increasing.

bear market
A period when prices in the stock market are generally decreasing.

The impact of stock market conditions shows clearly in the cases of our three focus companies. If you look carefully at the graphs for each company you will note similarities between two or more of the companies throughout the five year period. First, all three experienced large price increases in the 1990s. That was the period of a strong bull market.

Second, two of the three—Dell and Best Buy—showed a significant drop in price through 2000, the beginning of a general market downturn. This was especially notable in high tech stocks. Southwest Airlines fortunately was able to buck that trend throughout 2000. Looking at mid-2001, you will see the beginning of a downturn as the economy began to slide into a recession. This was exacerbated by the September 11, 2001 attacks. However, all three of the stocks began at least a modest upturn in late 2001, even though Dell's rise was stymied somewhat by the continuing technology stock malaise.

Finally, the climb that Southwest Airlines and Best Buy experiencd in late 2001 lasted only until March or April of 2002 when the stock market as a whole began another steep decline. Fortunately, Dell's stock, which had never recovered from late 2000, did not fall further.

The bull market of the 1990s was replaced by the bear market of the early 2000s. What financial and economic events led to the emergence of this bear market?

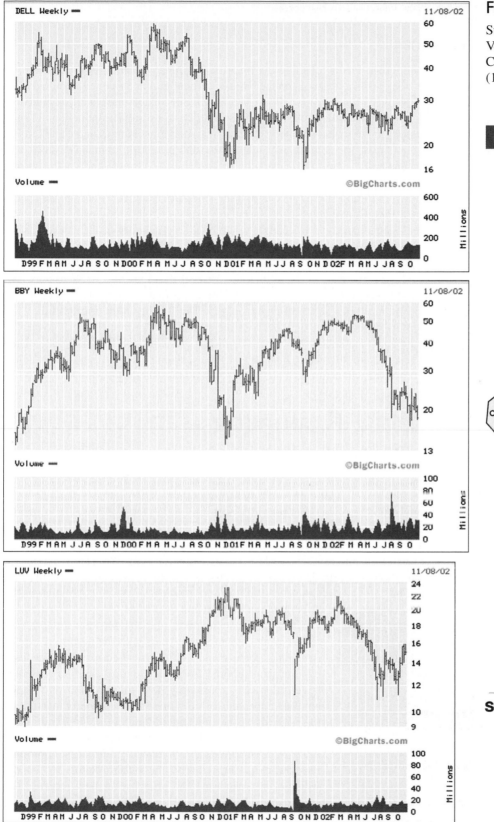

FIGURE 9.2

Stock Prices and
Volume of Focus
Companies
(1998–2002)*

*Weekly stock prices through November 10, 2002.
Source: chart.bigcharts.com, accessed November 10, 2002.

speculation

A situation in which a company's stock is bought or sold on the basis of a belief that its price will soon go up or down.

Speculation

A fourth important factor affecting the price of a company's stock is **speculation,** in which the stock is bought or sold on the basis of a belief that its price will soon move up or down. This type of investor is called a *speculator.* Speculators have a different investing strategy from most other investors, who hold stocks for a significant period of time.

Speculators aim to make a profit by outguessing short-run changes in the market. For example, a group of speculators may suspect that the price of a company's stock will soon fall. They actually borrow a large number of shares, sell those shares at the current price, and plan to buy back the shares after the price falls and return them to the lender. This is known as selling short. Of course, if the stock price actually goes up, the speculator takes a loss. Conversely, if the speculators suspect that a company's stock will soon increase significantly in price, they will buy a large quantity of the stock, wait for the big price increase to occur, and then sell the stock at the higher price.

Speculators add an element of instability to the stock market. An initial speculative sale or purchase can create the belief that the price of the stock will move as they suspect. Such speculative sales or purchases can influence many other investors to follow their lead. The result is a self-fulfilling prophecy. That is, the stock price will move as the speculators expected but only because the speculators prompted the followers to make it happen. Once such a movement begins, it can continue until the price of the stock has reached unrealistically high or low levels. Eventually, the market will adjust and the stock price will return to a normal level that is justified by earnings.

Financial Reporting and Business Ethics

A healthy financial environment is crucial for a country's economic development. A healthy environment is one that provides accurate and extensive financial information to all participants. In this way, there is assurance that investment decisions are based on information that is credible. These conditions of accuracy and credibility are fundamental to an efficient and successful market economy. They encourage investment. In general, the United States leads the world in providing such an environment, with other countries aspiring to match the American performance.

But America's financial markets are not perfect. That fact became clear in recent years with the disclosure of evidence that some major companies filed seriously misleading financial reports. Some accounting firms appeared to have been lax in approving those reports. And some stock analysts appeared to have biased their reports to promote the interests of the investment banking or brokerage firms for which they worked. When such events occur, the credibility of other reports and financial information is brought into question. Importantly, the public begins to wonder whether they can trust the information they receive. The corporations receiving the most criticism in this regard were Enron and WorldCom, the accounting firm receiving the strongest criticism was Arthur Andersen, and one of the leading brokerage firms under attack was Merrill Lynch.

THINK ABOUT THIS

1. Many factors affect the price of a company's stock. Will the factors be the same for a discount retailer like Wal-Mart as for a high-tech company like Motorola?

2. Why is it difficult to take small companies public?

3. Initial public offerings are very popular. Why would an investor be interested in placing funds in an IPO rather than in an old, established stock?

It could be argued that a combination of the market and government regulations handled the problem appropriately. After all, Enron was forced into bankruptcy by the market, and Arthur Andersen was the subject of a federal government lawsuit. Furthermore, Andersen lost a huge share of its business as company after company stopped using Andersen as an auditor for fear that the public would not trust the results of an Andersen audit. When the government won the lawsuit in the trial court, Andersen was put in the position of losing its remaining audit business unless it was able to have the decision reversed by an appeals court.

Finally, the New York attorney general threatened to force Merrill Lynch to pay investors for losses incurred as a result of bad investment advice and to spin off the firm's research department. Merrill Lynch reached an out-of-court settlement by paying a $100 million fine and promising that its investment banking business would stop influencing how much research department analysts were paid.[11]

It is likely that Congress, state legislatures, and regulatory agencies will impose new financial reporting rules on businesses in an attempt to prevent a recurrence of these financial problems. Thus, it is in everyone's best long-run interest to encourage a high standard of business ethics as the front line of defense in avoiding financial reporting abuse while preventing excessive loss of freedom resulting from strict government regulations.

THE BIG PICTURE

What is the difference between managers who fully understand the financial environment of business and those who lack such knowledge? Knowledgeable managers will be able to raise funds more cheaply and in greater quantity. The knowledgeable CEO will be better able to use financial vehicles to acquire other resources. Knowledgeable managers will be better able to motivate employees through creative use of available financial incentives. A knowledgeable CEO will be better able to evaluate investment opportunities and measure the firm's profitability. These managers will be better able to anticipate and avoid ethical slips that could, in extreme cases, lead to customer losses and even a government lawsuit. In short, full knowledge of the financial environment will help managers handle most of the business functions that are the topics of the other chapters in this textbook.

Summary

1. It can be argued that the success or failure of a business depends ultimately on its ability to deal effectively with financial markets.

   • What are financial markets, and what are the major financial institutions that affect business?

   Financial markets are places where businesses that need to acquire capital are brought together with financial institutions that help provide the funds. The major financial institutions that affect business are commercial banks, venture capital firms, insurance and pension fund companies, investment banking houses, and nonbank lenders.

2. Financial markets affect businesses in many ways. Decisions made by managers are frequently influenced by financial markets.

• What are the major ways financial markets affect a business?

This chapter discussed six major functions: (1) providing funds to start a business or expand it, (2) providing funds to operate the business, (3) influencing customer demand for the firm's products, (4) pressuring management to focus on short-term profits, (5) providing opportunities to reduce operating risks, and (6) providing opportunities to supplement earnings by investing the company's surplus cash.

3. Many businesses operate with borrowed money. Consequently, their cost of doing business is influenced by interest rates. Managing those costs of borrowing can be a major management function. In addition, the demand for the company's products is affected directly or indirectly by interest rates. Consequently, managers need to be able to forecast interest rates to predict future demand.

• How would you define *interest? interest rate? real rate of interest?*

Interest is the price a borrower agrees to pay a lender in return for receiving a loan. The interest rate is the amount of interest paid divided by the amount of the loan. This ratio is usually expressed in terms of the amount of interest paid per year as a percentage of the amount of the loan. The real rate of interest is the rate the borrower actually pays minus the inflation rate.

4. One of the key decisions that managers must make is the decision to borrow money and pay the interest that goes along with it. But interest rates go up and down over time. Managers must attempt to forecast changes in interest rates to make appropriate borrowing decisions.

• What determines changes in the interest rate over time?

Managers should be familiar with three major reasons for changes in interest rates over time: (1) shifts in demand for and supply of loanable funds, (2) inflation, and (3) the federal government's monetary policy.

5. Many companies are privately held. As companies grow, however, they may realize the benefits of going public. Once a company's stock becomes publicly held, its price becomes an important management issue.

• What factors determine the price of a stock?

Four factors influence the price of a company's stock: (1) the company's earnings, (2) opportunity cost, (3) general stock market conditions, and (4) speculation.

6. A healthy financial environment is crucial for a country's economic development.

• What is a healthy financial environment?

A healthy environment is one that provides accurate and extensive financial information to all parties.

Key Terms

bear market, p. 232

bull market, p. 232

collateral, p. 214

commodity markets, p. 221

corporate bond, p. 215

financial markets, p. 214

foreign exchange markets, p. 221

going public, p. 229

initial public offering (IPO), p. 216

insurance, p. 222

investment banking house, p. 215

nonbank lender, p. 215

opportunity cost, p. 232

prime rate, p. 223

real rate of interest, p. 225

speculation, p. 234

1. You and your teammates have just been given $100,000 to invest. Choose five stocks to purchase, and decide how much of each to buy. Record your decision-making process. Hold your stocks until the end of the semester. Each week, check one of the Internet financial quote services and plot the movement of the stock price. Suggestion: Pick at least one stock that is likely to be highly volatile and one that is considered an established, blue-chip stock.

2. Assume that your team is about to start a new restaurant that emphasizes unique vegetarian dishes. Your team is convinced that there is a strong market for your service. You need at least $200,000 to get started in business. Drawing from the individuals on your team, determine how you will secure the needed capital. Write a one-page report of how you will finance the start-up of the restaurant.

3. From exercise 2, assume you have been able to secure $100,000 of the needed capital from family and friends. You will need to borrow the additional $100,000 from a commercial bank. Find out what a local bank requires to make such a loan (background on the business, collateral, interest rate, and any other relevant information). Will you qualify for this loan?

4. Get a recent copy of *The Wall Street Journal*. Go to the summary headlines called "What's News" on the first page. Choose a company of interest. Describe what it is doing and how financial markets are involved.

5. You can buy and sell stock over the Internet. A number of companies, such as the Charles Schwab Corp. and Fidelity Investments, offer this opportunity. Go to the Schwab home page (www.schwab.com) to determine what would be required to buy or sell stocks online. Write your findings in a one-page report.

Schwab vs. Wall Street

The ability of companies to raise funds through the sale of stock depends in part on the existence of secondary markets where the buyers of the stock can resell it if and when they wish to do so. America's major stock markets perform that valuable function.

The companies that perform the actual buying and selling for the public are called brokers. Together, they form an industry subject to the same basic forces that other industries confront. One of those forces is the potential entry of a new firm that puts competitive pressure on the existing firms. Such a firm entered the industry in 1973. Its name? Charles Schwab Corporation. Its founder? Charles R. "Chuck" Schwab.

Schwab's original business strategy was to be a discount broker. He would charge lower commissions than the larger established firms (often referred to as Wall Street). He would be able to make a profit on the lower commissions by operating with lower costs. For example, his firm would not offer investment advice and would not employ high-priced sales personnel. This was the beginning of the discount broker revolution in the brokerage industry.

In 1992 he broadened his services by offering a mutual-fund supermarket where customers could buy fund shares without paying a sales commission (load) or management fees. Then in 1996 he took advantage of the Internet and began offering online trading. By 2002 Schwab's e-business accounted for 37 percent of the company's account assets. This was the beginning of the online trading revolution in the brokerage industry.

In 2002 Schwab introduced what he hoped would be yet another revolution in the brokerage industry. He launched Schwab Private Client and Schwab Equity Rating stock-picking systems. The target market for both services was the customer who wanted investment advice. The strategy behind both services was to provide advice that was not colored by the advisor's opportunity for personal gain through recommending a security that wasn't truly in the client's best interest. Thus, the Schwab investment advisor would not earn a commission. And the stock rating service would not be related to the sale of stocks for which Schwab would receive an investment banking commission (a payment for distributing an initial public offering).

Why did Schwab adopt this new strategy? It was a matter of both threats and opportunities in the economic environment of the brokerage industry. The major threat was a sharp drop in revenue. Following the tech stock bust in the spring of 2000, Schwab's mainstay online trading fell sharply, slashing its revenues and operating margins. The decline in revenue forced Schwab to fire nearly one-fourth of its employees in 2001 (26,000 workers).

The major opportunity was the crisis of confidence that was rocking Wall Street in 2002. Corporations and wealthy individuals were blaming the advising services of the major investment advice firms for troubled mergers, lackluster new equity offerings, and trillions of dollars lost in the dot-com bust. Schwab saw an opportunity to take substantial business away from such advice-giving establishment firms as Merrill Lynch, Morgan Stanley Dean Witter, Salomon Smith Barney, and UBS Paine Webber.

But the new strategy could cause problems for Schwab. It will put Schwab into even more direct competition with the independent financial advisers whose clients provided one-third of Schwab's client assets in 2002 (Schwab began to compete with the independent advisors when it acquired U.S. Trust Corp. in 2000). Existing employees hired mainly as order takers won't be qualified to give financial advice and will have to either be upgraded or let go. Schwab will be entering a very competitive field without the historical experience that may be needed to be competitive. It may not be able to find the qualified staff it needs at pay rates that make the service profitable for Schwab.

Decision Questions

1. Which of the six functions of financial markets will Schwab's new effort address?

2. Who appear to be Schwab's main competitors in the market for financial services to business firms and wealthy individuals?

3. What actions can Schwab take to ensure that they are meeting current ethical expectations?

Source: Louise Lee and Emily Thornton, "Schwab vs. Wall Street," *BusinessWeek,* June 3, 2002, pp. 64–71.

References

1. John A. Byrne and Ben Elgin, "Cisco behind the Hype," *BusinessWeek,* January 21, 2002, pp. 55–61; John K. Waters, *John Chambers and the Cisco Way* (New York: Wiley, 2002); and *Value Line Investment Survey,* April 19, 2002, p. 1106.

2. Greg Ip, "Alternative Lenders Buoy the Economy but Also Pose Risk," *The Wall Street Journal,* June 10, 2002, p. A1.

3. Michael Dell, *Direct from Dell* (New York: Harper Business, 1999), pp. 9–32

4. Gary McWilliams, "In About-Face, Dell Will Sell PCs to Dealers," *The Wall Street Journal,* August 20, 2002, pp. B1, B4.

5. Calculated from data in *Value Line Investment Survey,* May 17, 2002, pp. 1705, 1713.

6. Robert Berner, "Target Takes a Gamble the Markets Don't Like," *BusinessWeek,* April 1, 2002, p. 78.

7. Cargill website, www.cargill.com (accessed September 23, 2002); and Scott Kilman, "Giant Cargill Resists Pressure to Go Public as It Pursues Growth," *The Wall Street Journal,* January 9, 1997, p. A1.

8. "Insurance (Property/Casualty)," *Value Line Investment Survey,* March 29, 2002, p. 591.

9. An excellent overview and tutorial is available through the Internet at http://woodrow.mpls.frb.fed.us/info/policy (accessed June 1, 2002).

10. David Henry, Michelle Conlin, Nanette Byrnes, Michael Mandel, Stanley Holmes, and Stanley Reed, "Too Much of a Good Incentive?" *BusinessWeek,* March 4, 2002, pp. 38–39.

11. Emily Thornton, "Research Should Pay Its Own Way," *BusinessWeek,* June 3, 2002, p. 72.

10

The Impact of Globalization

What is the largest cable network? CNN perhaps? Not really. Try MTV. MTV dominates the global audience by reaching twice the number of people who are able to see CNN. This global channel reaches over one billion people in over 164 countries and speaks 18 different languages. And how about this fact about MTV, the channel revered by American teens? The majority of MTV viewers—8 out of 10— live outside the United States, and the fledgling network that revolutionized pop music in the 80s has now become the poster child for globalization.

Bill Roedy, MTV's CEO, is the driving force behind MTV's vast globalization. He has sold the idea to former Israeli Prime Minister Shimon Peres, Chinese leader Jiang Zemin, and a number of other leaders. Even Cuba's Fidel Castro wondered if MTV could help Cuban children learn English. Roedy comments, "We have had very little resistance once we explain that we're not exporting American culture." MTV owes its success to appealing to local cultural and musical trends, not just piping American culture around the globe.

MTV appeals to the 2.7 billion people between the ages of 10 and 34 by offering American music, but the real reason for MTV International's success is offering local talent. The policy calling for 70 percent local talent has caused an explosion in viewers. It has also jump-started the careers of many local musicians and has led to some innovative programming.

In Brazil, MTV created a month-long soccer championship called "Rockgol" that pitted record executives against musicians. Russian MTV created a show called "Twelve Angry Viewers," in which teens discuss the latest videos and then spontaneously dance around the colorful stage or hit each other with giant inflatable lollipops. The Russians love the program and voted it one of Russia's top three talk programs. Hindi Film Music has boosted MTV India's ratings by 700 percent. In Japan, the animated Veejay, video jockey, has a huge following. In China, where MTV is seen in over 60 million homes, a recent audition for veejays had over 10,000 Chinese teens flocking to the auditions. In Scandinavia, MTV recently premiered MTV Live, which goes to homes with broadband cable and allows viewers to play virtual games. Every thing from Mexican hip-hop to a global televised summit with Colin Powell is fair game on MTV International.

While international viewers are flocking to MTV in droves, so are the advertisers, and the profits keep coming. Revenues increased 19 percent in 2001, and operating profits grew 50 percent to $135 million. Analysts expect these numbers to double by 2004. This globalization-fueled growth and the resulting profits make MTV networks a feather in parent company Viacom's hat. The goal is brand recognition. "Everyone that has a TV knows there's something called MTV," states Chantara Kapahi, a 17-year-old Bombay student.[1]

There is no doubt that business has moved into an era of global competition. That movement brings new opportunities and avenues for growth. It also brings enormous complexity to the business landscape. Business leaders must be aware of and sensitive to a number of important global forces and influences. These forces, influences, and the business response to them are the focus of this chapter.

After studying this chapter, you should be able to:

1. Understand the meaning and implications of globalization.
2. Explain why globalization is important in today's businesses.
3. Identify the economic, government, cultural, and ethical issues that affect globalization.
4. Discuss the major ways businesses participate in the global economy.

The Meaning and Implications of Globalization

Today's businesses operate in a highly competitive global economy, and the level and extent of global focus will continue to grow. Businesses are involved in a variety of global activities. For example, manufacturers of everything from computers to cars to lawn sprinklers buy components from all over the world. For many U.S. businesses, the global environment offers new potential and opportunity for the sale of their goods and services. Of course, global markets work both ways. Companies based in other countries have become major competitors in the U.S. home market. A number of foreign-based businesses have even acquired ownership of some well-known American brands and companies. Consider the following:

- The family Jeep and other Chrysler vehicles are made by the German company DaimlerChrysler.
- Your former Amoco gasoline station is now called BP and is owned by British Petroleum.
- Holiday Inn is owned by Britain's Six Continents hotel company.
- Movie producer Universal Studios is owned by a French company, Vivendi.
- Snapple is owned by the British firm Cadbury Schweppes.

globalization
A way of thinking in which a business regards its operations all over the world as part of one integrated business system.

Companies headquartered in one country, such as the United States or Japan, operate manufacturing plants and sales facilities all over the globe. Similarly, when consumers go shopping in their local communities, they are able to choose products imported from a variety of countries. This is the essence of globalization. **Globalization** is a way of thinking in which a business regards its operations all over the world as part of one integrated business system. For many companies, becoming more global is a major strategic challenge.

Look at the firms listed in Table 10.1. All are major firms based in the United States. Yet many derive half or more of their revenue from foreign sales and operations. Note how both high-technology firms and low-tech businesses have established strong global presences. Also realize that a major challenge that some companies face is to become more global. For example, compare General Motors' global presence (17 percent of sales) with that of its Japanese rival, Nissan. At Nissan, 61 percent of sales come from outside Japan, and 39 percent of sales come from the U.S. and Canada alone.[2] Does this suggest that GM may need to expand its global operations?

global strategy
A strategy in which a business sells a uniform product or service throughout the world.

Businesses take two approaches to the issue of globalization: a global strategy or a multidomestic strategy. The distinction between these approaches is important. A **global strategy** occurs when a business sells a uniform product or service throughout the world. The product that is sold in Indonesia is the same as the product that is sold in Brazil. Consider a commodity such as wheat. A grain marketing company buys wheat from a farm in Kansas and sells that wheat in several different countries. No attempt is made to modify the product from one country to another.

TABLE 10.1

International Sales as a Percentage of Total Sales in Selected Companies

Coca-Cola	62	Dell	35
Procter & Gamble	48	McDonald's	51
Caterpillar	51	Yum Brands (formerly Tricon)	35
DuPont	49	(Taco Bell, Kentucky Fried Chicken, Pizza Hut, Long John Silvers, and A & W)	
General Electric	50		
General Motors	17		

Source: Value Line Investment Survey, www.valueline.com/dow30/index.cfm (accessed September 23, 2002); Dell Annual Report and Form 10-K for Fiscal Year Ending February 1, 2002, p. 9; and "Tricon 2001 Annual Report," Yum Brands website, www.yum.com/investors/annual_report.html (accessed September 23, 2002).

A **multidomestic strategy** occurs when a business modifies its product or service to address the special needs of local markets. For example, most restaurant chains must adjust their offerings to the tastes and preferences of each area in which they operate. Sometimes the changes are subtle. Sometimes they are striking. When McDonald's entered India, it had to introduce a vegetarian burger to accommodate Indian religious objections to eating beef. We will discuss the need for a multidomestic strategy later in this chapter when we consider the impact of culture on global firms.

For peak effectiveness around the world, many businesses use a combination of global and multidomestic strategies. They produce a standardized product but make some adjustments for local needs. Consider the automotive industry. Generally, cars are the same throughout the world. Yet in different countries they are driven on different sides of the road. So both left- and right-side driver options must be available.

Some businesses are engaged in **exporting,** which occurs when a business sells its products and services to customers in other nations. Businesses from all over the world are involved in exporting activities. Businesses of all sizes can be involved in exporting. That may surprise you. Yet many small businesses have excellent, high-quality products that are in demand throughout the world.

Other businesses are importers. **Importing** occurs when customers purchase products and services from producers in other countries. If you purchase a Canon camera from Wal-Mart, that camera is an import because it was produced in Japan. Canon is a Japan-based business that sells popular, high-quality cameras in many countries, including the United States. It does so, of course, because consumers in those countries like the features and quality that Canon offers. The number of potential camera buyers in any country is limited. If buyers purchase an import, they have chosen to forgo the purchase of competing domestic products. Thus, importing affects all domestic manufacturers to some extent.

The same reasoning can be applied to businesses of all sizes and even to entire industries. Consider, for example, the consumer electronics industry. At one time, U.S. businesses dominated this field. No longer. Successful imports, often from Japanese firms, such as Sony, changed the competitive landscape. Today the United States is virtually a nonplayer in this industry. Even small businesses that sell only within their own country can be affected by global imports. Few businesses are totally untouched by global competition.

The United States trades with more than 100 other countries. But the bulk of the nation's trade is concentrated among a small number of countries. Table 10.2 shows where U.S. imports and exports were concentrated in 2000. Note that the top 15 countries accounted for 75 percent of American exports and 74 percent of imports. Canada, Mexico, and Japan were the top three trading partners in both cases. China was a distant tenth place for U.S. exports but a close fourth place for imports. Notice that the United States imports more than it exports. This situation is known as a **trade deficit.** When a country exports more than it imports, there is a **trade surplus.** Recognize that the gap between imports and exports is particularly large in the cases of China and Japan. Could this imbalance represent opportunities for U.S. businesses to increase exports to these two countries in the next decade? The potential for China is explored in Profile 10.1.

Note also that some of the world's largest countries in terms of population are not on the list. India, which is almost as large as China, is missing. So is Indonesia. Will these countries become attractive markets for American exports or sources of imports in the future? The point of asking these questions is to make it clear that the global business environment is subject to change and with that change will come new opportunities and threats for American businesses.

---

multidomestic strategy
A strategy in which a business modifies its product or service to address the special needs of local markets.

exporting
The situation in which a business sells products and services to customers in other countries.

importing
The situation in which customers buy products and services from producers in other countries.

trade deficit
A country imports more than it exports.

trade surplus
A country exports more than it imports.

TABLE 10.2

The Top 15 Countries for U.S. Exports and Imports, 2000

Country	Exports Value of Exports ($ in millions)	Percent of All Exports	Country	Imports Value of Imports ($ in millions)	Percent of All Imports
Canada	174,616	22.4	Canada	229,191	18.2
Mexico	108,751	13.9	Japan	149,520	11.9
Japan	64,538	8.3	Mexico	135,080	10.7
United Kingdom	41,361	5.3	China	106,215	8.4
Germany	29,217	3.7	Germany	59,481	4.7
Korea	27,338	3.5	United Kingdom	43,677	3.5
Netherlands	21,694	2.8	Korea	40,911	3.2
France	20,398	2.6	France	30,084	2.4
Singapore	17,497	2.2	Italy	26,001	2.1
China	15,964	2.0	Malaysia	25,990	2.1
Brazil	15,183	1.9	Singapore	19,630	1.6
Hong Kong	14,567	1.9	Venezuela	18,612	1.5
Belgium	13,874	1.8	Thailand	17,161	1.4
Australia	12,332	1.6	Ireland	15,825	1.3
Malaysia	10,830	1.4	Brazil	14,393	1.1
Top 15 total	588,160	75.3	Top 15 total	931,771	74.0
All others	192,940	24.7	All others	327,529	26.0
Total exports	$781,100	100.0	Total imports	$1,259,300	100.0

Note: Percentages are rounded to nearest tenth.

Source: From International Monetary Fund, *Direction of Trade Statistics Quarterly,* March 2002. Reprinted with permission.

PROFILE 10.1 CHINA COMES ON STRONG

Twenty years ago China's economy was basically closed to the rest of the world. Since then, China has begun to adopt the principles of a market system and the economy has boomed. That boom has been fueled by massive foreign investment. Initially, the payoff for that investment came from the fact that China offered a low-cost place to manufacture products that were then exported back to the United States and other developed countries.

Of course, there is another reason that businesses are attracted to China. The Chinese market is huge, and its potential is just beginning to be tapped. Today there is a major U.S. presence in China. McDonald's is there. So are Wal-Mart, Motorola, Boeing, Dell, and many others. Some of the foreigners are already making a decent profit there. Others expect to eventually make significant profits as the incomes of more and more of China's nearly 1.3 billion people rise high enough to make them viable customers. The question for many firms is not *if* they should move to China but *how soon*.

Make no mistake, though. China is not just a rich potential market for foreign investors. Today China is a formidable exporter with a massive labor pool. Chinese workers are industrious, and their wages are low. Just a few years ago, China was known for producing low-tech goods, and the country's poor transportation system hampered efficient operations. There were even concerns about the quality of the workforce. Today those problems are being solved rapidly, and China is becoming capable of producing high-quality and high-technology products. Many countries, even traditionally low-wage East Asian countries, face the prospect of losing production jobs to China. China's trade surplus with the United States is huge, and China may soon overtake Japan as America's number one trade rival.

Source: Bill Powell, "It's All Made in China Now," *Fortune,* March 4, 2002, pp. 121–128.

Why Globalization Is Important

Global concerns are a timely issue for contemporary American business. Prior to World War II, most American firms produced primarily for the huge U.S. market. A few manufacturers exported products that they produced in the United States, although their primary market was within the United States. Only a few large companies, such as IBM, actually conducted significant manufacturing operations abroad. Even then, their foreign operations were not integrated with their domestic operations. This approach has changed. Businesses are going global in their thinking. They are increasingly being involved in world markets, and the American economy is heavily influenced by international trade.

The initial question that must be addressed is, What prompts a business to take a global perspective? There are three prominent influences. First is the rise of foreign competition. Second is the need to control costs. Third is the opportunity for substantial market growth.

The Rise of Foreign Competition

Increasingly, foreign businesses are competing in U.S. markets. Domestic businesses often see imports invade their home markets. These imports are a concern because they take business away from domestic firms. A classic example is the U.S. automobile industry. In the 1970s and 1980s, U.S. manufacturers realized that customers were turning to foreign competitors. Suddenly, Toyota and Honda were no longer minor annoyances. They were capturing market share and threatening U.S. competitiveness. Like it or not, Ford, General Motors, and Chrysler were forced to begin thinking globally. Chrysler, of course, is no longer a U.S. company, having merged with Daimler-Benz of Germany in 1999.

American retailers play a role in bringing foreign competition to the American marketplace. Check the origin of a sampling of products in Wal-Mart or Target, for example, and you will find that a significant number are imported. Or consider the following partial list of foreign companies whose merchandise is sold in America by Best Buy: Acer, Aiwa, BASF, Blaupunkt, Canon, Daewoo, Ericsson, Fujitsu, Goldstar, Hitachi, Konica, Matsushita, Mitsubishi, Nokia, Philips, Samsung, Seiko, Sony, Toshiba, and Yamaha.

The Need to Control Costs

Many foreign competitors become strong rivals because they can produce goods much more cheaply than U.S. firms. There are many reasons for this situation, but two are prominent. First, low-cost labor is available in their countries. Second, many governments *subsidize* businesses, especially in certain industries. These two factors allow foreign companies to produce products and ship them to American customers more cheaply than firms in the United States can produce them. Historically, Japanese steel firms could import iron ore from abroad, convert it into steel, and ship it to the United States at a lower cost than U.S. steel plants could make it themselves. In addition, Japanese automakers could use that steel to produce cars, transport them to America, and still sell them for less than U.S. carmakers could. Thus, U.S. steel and automobile industries were forced to respond to the competitive thrusts of foreign firms.

More to Come
CHAPTER 13

U.S. businesses have to find ways to get access to cheaper labor and lower costs of production. One way is by importing raw materials. In other words, they can shop all

Because of saturation of the U.S. market, many businesses that seek substantial growth are looking beyond our borders into emerging markets for potential new customers and worldwide sales. This Starbucks shop in Tokyo was its first to open overseas. What other relatively "new" companies do you think would benefit by capturing international markets?

over the world and purchase supplies wherever they are cheapest. They can also contract part of their production operations to countries with low labor costs. This practice is an example of *international outsourcing.* Additionally, they can even locate their own production facilities in the foreign country. Whatever tactic businesses choose, their global movement is often motivated by the need to control costs.

Opportunities for Market Growth

The U.S. market for many products is becoming increasingly saturated. Businesses that seek substantial growth may be limited if they confine themselves solely to the U.S. market. There are about 285 million people in the United States. There are about 6.3 billion potential customers in the rest of the world. The world is open for business! The United States will see its population grow to 351.3 million by 2030. By contrast, the population of India will grow to 1.4 billion, Indonesia to 312.6 million, Brazil to 203.4 million, and Nigeria to 222 million. These and other emerging markets are critical areas of growth.[3]

The soft drink industry is a good example. As American baby boomers age, they drink fewer soft drinks. Therefore, in the past two decades, major producers have become increasingly aggressive in capturing international markets. They realize that their future growth and competitiveness depend on worldwide sales.

Issues Affecting Globalization

In this section, we consider four major influences on globalization. Keep in mind that these influences may serve as barriers for those firms wanting to explore globalization for the first time. They may also affect *how* a firm chooses to participate in the global market. And they illustrate both the complexity and the tenuous nature of relationships among companies and among countries in the global arena. The four major influences we discuss below are economic issues, government issues, cultural issues, and ethical issues. Keep in mind that even these four categories of issues are intertwined as each country attempts to maximize the advantages for its companies.

Economic Issues

Economic issues affect a company's ability to compete across borders. They do not prohibit a company from competing in the global market, but they may have an impact on how successful the firm will be. Further, as you will see, they affect the method of competing a firm chooses. The most important of these influences is the exchange rates among countries. These rates are, in turn, affected by a number of factors, the most notable of which are a country's balance of payments and, to a lesser extent, its balance of trade.

Exchange Rates, Balance of Payments, and Balance of Trade

Foreign exchange rates, which we discussed earlier, are very important to managers involved with any aspect of global competition. An **exchange rate** is the value of a domestic currency compared with a foreign currency. An exchange rate tells us how much of a foreign currency can be purchased for one unit of our domestic currency. If one U.S. dollar will buy two German marks (the symbol for German marks is DM), then the exchange rate of the dollar in terms of marks is two.

> **exchange rate**
> The value of a domestic currency compared with a foreign currency.

Let's look at the effects of a strong and a weak dollar on American businesses. The U.S. dollar is said to be *strong* if its value is rising or has reached a level higher than in the relatively recent past. A strong U.S. dollar benefits companies that import goods into the United States. Why? A strong dollar is worth more than a weak one, so each dollar will buy more products on international markets. Thus, imports are relatively cheap. At the same time, a strong dollar works against U.S. exporters because U.S.-produced goods are more expensive in foreign markets. The weaker foreign currencies won't buy as many products. Therefore, foreign businesses and consumers will be less inclined to purchase from U.S. companies.

Conversely, a *weak* U.S. dollar buys fewer imported goods than a stronger one. Thus, it hurts importers by making imported goods and services more expensive. At the same time, however, the weak dollar helps exporters, since foreign currencies can buy more U.S. products than they could previously. The rule of thumb is: Exporters like weak dollars; importers like strong dollars. The same situation would exist for businesspeople in any other country, substituting that country's currency for dollars.

Consider the case of Borland Software Corporation. Its Delphi Studio 7 package is being exported to Germany. Borland wants to receive $3,000 for each package sold. Let's assume that one dollar equals two German marks. Therefore, Borland will charge DM6,000 for the software, plus freight and other handling charges. Now suppose that the value of the dollar falls so that one dollar is worth only one German mark. Now the company can cut the price in Germany in half and still make a profit. The software can be sold for DM3,000 and those marks will be converted into the $3,000 that Borland wants. As you can see, changes in the exchange rate can have a significant effect on foreign sales.

Changes in exchange rates have two important effects on a business. First, as discussed above, exchange rate changes affect the competitiveness of imports and exports. Second, exchange rate variations affect the profitability of earnings on foreign sales. Let's take a closer look at the second of these effects again from the viewpoint of Borland. Suppose that after the value of the dollar fell to one mark, Borland continued to sell in Germany for a price of DM6,000 per package instead of dropping the price to DM3,000. The company can take those 6,000 marks and convert them into $6,000. A quick look would suggest that Borland's sales revenue has doubled, but it has not. With the increase in the value of sales in dollars, there was an increase in profit that had nothing to do with increased sales. Instead, it was due strictly to the decreased value of the dollar.

It should be clear to you now that businesses with foreign sales need to monitor changes in exchange rates and to be prepared to act in response to such changes. American newspapers periodically report on the response of American firms to "cheaper" foreign goods. Here is an example illustrating how one firm responded. Recently, Caterpillar Inc. announced that it planned to move some production from the United States to Europe because of the strong dollar. The company said that the strong dollar gave offshore rivals a "tremendous advantage." The plan was to increase production of some parts in Europe. The parts would then be shipped back to Caterpillar's North American plants. Although the action would increase jobs in Europe and reduce them in the United States, Caterpillar did not plan to close an American plant and open one abroad because of the exchange rates changes. Doing so would

With over half of its sales occurring outside of the U. S., the exchange rate and the strength of the dollar are important issues for international companies like Caterpillar. Do you think Caterpillar would favor a stronger or weaker dollar?

be quite expensive. The implication is, of course, that when the value of the dollar falls in the future, Caterpillar will move some of its production back to the United States.[4]

You should also realize that businesses could gain a competitive edge if they could forecast changes in exchange rates. Unfortunately, such forecasting is not usually very reliable. However, governments do provide some information that firms find helpful in making educated guesses as to the future direction of exchange rates. That information is contained in the balance of payments report.

The **balance of payments** is a record of the inflows of money into a country and the outflows of money from that country. It is a report of all international transactions of a country with the rest of the world. The most common component of the balance of payments is the **balance of trade,** which is the difference between the value of a country's imports and exports of goods and services. Other contributions to the balance of payments are tourism, military spending, various unilateral transfers of money from one country to another, and net investment income from abroad. For example, if a wealthy business person from Europe buys hotels in New York, that purchase affects the balance of payments. Figure 10.1 shows the trade balance for the United States in recent years.

How can balance of payment information indicate changes in exchange rates? It does so by showing us the overall demand and supply for our currency. Recall from our discussion of microeconomics (in Chapter 8) that if the demand for a product goes up, the sellers can command a higher price. If demand for a product falls, the price will drop. Currencies work the same way. If a country has a balance of payments deficit, that is a sign that the quantity of the country's currency being supplied to pay for imports exceeds the quantity demanded for foreigners to pay for exports. In other words, if there is a balance of payments deficit, conditions are favorable for a fall in the value of the country's currency. On the other hand, if there is a balance of payments surplus, conditions are favorable for an increase in the exchange rate.

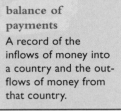

balance of payments
A record of the inflows of money into a country and the outflows of money from that country.

balance of trade
The difference between the value of a country's imports and its exports of goods and services.

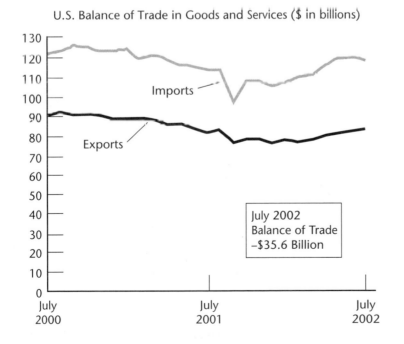

U.S. Balance of Trade in Goods and Services ($ in billions)

Imports

Exports

July 2002
Balance of Trade
−$35.6 Billion

July 2000   July 2001   July 2002

FIGURE 10.1

U.S. Balance of Trade in Goods and Services ($ in billions)

Source: U.S. Census Bureau website, www.census.gov/indicator/www/img/ustrade.gif (accessed September 26, 2002).

Keep in mind that using the balance of payments to forecast exchange rate movements is an inaccurate science. A variety of forces can intervene to prevent an expected exchange rate change from occurring. Not the least of those is intervention by a government that does not want to have the value of its currency fall.

Government Involvement in Global Issues

All governments want to increase the wealth, stability, and standard of living of their societies. To achieve that goal, they often implement policies that affect international trade. These policies may consist of tariffs and other trade barriers or of overt support of businesses as they compete worldwide.

Tariffs and Other Trade Barriers

free trade
A situation in which there are no government-imposed barriers to trade—no tariffs, quotas, or nontariff barriers.

The effectiveness of free trade policies has been debated for decades. **Free trade** refers to a situation in which there are no government-imposed barriers to trade—no tariffs, quotas, or nontariff barriers. One of the most common arguments for free trade is that it increases competition, which causes prices and costs to fall, benefiting consumers in all countries. It also encourages firms to develop new products and more productive ways of doing business. Again, consumers in all countries benefit. While most economists and many government leaders espouse free trade, most governments of the world regularly depart from it to protect domestic production of goods and services that would be imported under free trade. Further, some industries (those that export significant amounts) are more likely to support free trade than other industries (those that must constantly fight imports).

tariff
A tax on an imported product.

How does the government of a country protect its businesses from imports? The three basic tools are tariffs, quotas, and other nontariff barriers. A **tariff** is a tax on an imported product. The tax raises the price that customers have to pay for the imported good. If the tax is large enough, it will cause the price of the import to be higher than the price of the locally produced good or service. Accordingly, customers will be more likely to buy the locally produced products.

Nontariff barriers encompass a variety of ways other than tariffs that governments use to restrict imports. One of the most common nontariff barriers is the **quota,** which is a government's restriction on the amount of a specific foreign product it allows into the country. For example, France might impose a quota restricting the number of cars imported from Japan to 10,000 per year. This keeps the French markets from being flooded with Japanese cars.

quota
A government's restriction on the amount of a specific foreign product it allows into the country.

There are other nontariff barriers governments can use to protect their home industries. One is for the home government to establish rules and regulations that take away the competitive advantage of the imported goods. Another technique is to use social pressure to discourage local buyers from purchasing imports.

Free Trade and Free Trade Areas

Since World War II, the United States has been the leader of a movement to reduce tariffs, quotas, and other nontariff barriers. The long-run goal is to create a world system of free trade.

The United States' primary free trade initiative has been undertaken through an international agreement called the *General Agreement on Tariffs and Trade (GATT).* GATT is an agreement between the United States and 22 other countries to get together regularly to negotiate the reduction of trade barriers. Over the past four decades, GATT

TABLE 10.3

Free Trade Agreements

Agreement	Member Countries
NAFTA	Canada, Mexico, United States.
Mercosur	Argentina, Brazil, Paraguay, Uruguay.
Andean Pact	Bolivia, Colombia, Ecuador, Peru, Venezuela.
European Union	Austria, Belgium, Denmark, Finland, France, Germany, Greece, Ireland, Italy, Luxembourg, Netherlands, Portugal, Spain, Sweden, United Kingdom (others expected to be added soon).
ASEAN	Brunei, Cambodia, Indonesia, Laos, Malaysia, Myanmar, the Philippines, Singapore, Thailand, Vietnam.
Free Trade Area of the Americas (proposed)	All of Central, North, and South America.

Source: Council of the Americas website, www.counciloftheamericas.org (accessed June 21, 2002); Charles W. L. Hill, *International Business: Competing in the Global Marketplace,* (Burr Ridge, IL: Irwin/McGraw-Hill, 2000), Chapter 8.

has held a series of negotiations that led most of the nations of the world to agree to make drastic reductions in tariffs and quotas. A significant agreement was completed in 1994 when the U.S. Congress approved it. Called the Uruguay Round, that agreement resulted in an overall reduction in tariffs of 39 percent. It also created a global regulatory body called the World Trade Organization (WTO), which has the authority to determine whether or not a country is violating the terms of the GATT agreements. In 2001, a new round of negotiations began in Doha, Qatar.

Many countries are forming **free trade areas** based on agreements with other countries to allow shipment of goods across borders without tariffs. These free trade agreements encourage trade among the nations within the area while discouraging imports from nonparticipating countries. Table 10.3 shows some of these agreements.

The North American Free Trade Agreement (NAFTA), adopted in 1993, created a free trade area comprising Canada, Mexico, and the United States. Free trade areas have also been created for 15 countries in Europe, in the southern part of South America (Mercosur), in the northern part of South America (Andean Pact), in Southeast Asia (Association of Southeast Asian Nations, or ASEAN), and in other locations throughout the world.

Members of the European Union (EU) have gone a step further by adopting a common currency, the euro. They have also eliminated or reduced border checks for people and goods moving between the countries, making commerce among those nations virtually seamless.

The experience with NAFTA has been generally favorable. Neither the view that NAFTA would destroy U.S. businesses nor the view that these businesses would see major domestic growth as a result of NAFTA has been supported. The agreement continues to make movement of goods and services among the three countries more efficient. The proposed Free Trade Area of the Americas offers the potential to be the most significant trade group in the world. It proposes free trade from northernmost Canada to Tierra del Fuego in Argentina. Experts are divided on whether it will actually be approved by all the countries involved.

What are the implications for businesses of the movement toward free trade and free trade zones? First, managers should be aware of the competitive dynamics caused by free trade. A business that wants to remain globally competitive must sharpen its

> **free trade area**
> A geographic area where free trade is permitted among the member countries but imports from nonmember countries are limited.

competitive skills and possibly move production to locations that offer cost advantages. For example, after NAFTA, some U.S. firms moved some of their operations to Mexico to take advantage of the lower wage while being able to import the products back into the United States with little or no tariffs. Similarly, U.S. businesses that export to Canada or Mexico now have fewer restrictions on the movement of the goods between countries. Companies operating in the European Union have similar benefits.

Second, while some businesses benefit from free trade zones and policies, managers should recognize that total free trade is not yet a reality. Thus, managers of internationally oriented firms must be willing to consider establishing plants in countries that restrict exports.

Finally, business leaders should stand ready to work with their governments to ensure that foreign companies are not given unfair advantages or to make sure that U.S. firms gain competitive advantages abroad. Lobbying in favor of particular laws—either increasing free trade or protecting home industries—should be the norm for large companies and industry organizations.

Government Support of Business

The level of government support of international business varies from country to country. In tightly controlled economies, the government regulates virtually all the businesses and influences how much production should occur and what prices should be charged. Other countries take a more *laissez-faire* approach and give business much more freedom. Yet even this approach usually offers considerable government support.

Look at the United States as one example. The United States has typically been toward the laissez-faire end of the continuum. However, businesses work within a legal environment that regulates anticompetitive actions and promotes social welfare. Additionally, the federal government, mostly through the U.S. Department of Commerce, provides international experts or trade specialists to help small and medium-sized businesses learn about and navigate the ropes for doing business abroad. Most states also have their own agencies for promoting and supporting global trade. Here, businesses receive information, export assistance, and in some cases even receive funds to help underwrite the costs of their international activities.

There are even times when the U.S. government has agreed to help a struggling American industry. For example, in the 1960s, the government began to restrict the importation of textiles to protect American producers. In the 1980s, it convinced the Japanese to "voluntarily" limit their automobile exports to the United States. In the 1960s and 1970s, it restricted imports of steel. In 2002, President Bush raised tariffs on imported steel to help the struggling American steel industry. As you can see, the U.S. government certainly does not assume a completely "hands-off" policy regarding its support of U.S.-based businesses.

Some governments do go further in their support efforts than the United States. For example, Japan's economic development strategy promotes exports and actively protects their home market from foreign competition. The government identifies industries that have the most potential to stimulate overall economic growth if the country can find a way to establish those industries. Examples have been steel, automobiles, and computers. The government helps the chosen industries by protecting the Japanese market from

THINK ABOUT THIS

1. Explain why it is important for businesses in today's world to go global. Is this move more important for some industries than others?

2. We mentioned that some industries are far more eager for free trade than others. Predict how each of the following feels about free trade: (a) airplane industry, (b) textile industry, (c) steel industry, (d) earth-moving equipment industry.

3. China is an emerging economic giant. Some experts argue that China is now the number one trade rival with the United States. Why is China such a force?

import competition and denying foreign firms the chance to locate in Japan. The government also helps by providing various subsidies for exports and by insisting that the protected firms learn to compete successfully in export markets.

The Japanese also have extensive policies and rules that are generally less formal than tarrifs or import quotas. Their purpose, nonetheless, is to limit imports into the country. In a classic example, Japanese customs inspectors examined each imported tulip bulb by slicing it down the middle, and thereby ruining the bulb. Is this an effective trade barrier? Apparently, it has the desired effect. The Netherlands exports tulips to nearly every country in the world with one exception—Japan.[5]

Japan's approach is especially important because the value of Japan's exports to the United States has been far greater than the value of its imports. The U.S. government believed that a major reason was that the Japanese unfairly restricted imports from America. Demonstrating another form of support, the United States was able to convince Japan to open its home markets to American telecommunication equipment in 1986. In 1995, Japan agreed to do the same for American cars.

However, as you will recall from Table 10.2, the trade deficit with Japan is not as large as that with China. In 2000, the U.S. trade deficit with China was a staggering $90.2 billion. China has the potential for soon becoming the world's most vibrant economy. It may surprise you to know that there are thousands of Chinese companies in the United States right now, many of them owned and supported by the Chinese government. What does this suggest about U.S. policy and support?

Cultural Differences

Understanding differences between the cultures of countries can be important to a firm that tries to export to or establish a production facility in a foreign country. Problems can arise because of differences in language, customs, values, and lifestyles. Stories of business miscues in the international markets are legend. General Motors' attempt to market the Chevrolet Nova was unsuccessful in South America because GM failed to realize that *no va* means "won't go" in Spanish. Gerber found little success in marketing its baby foods in some third world countries until it realized that their tradition was to put a picture of the product on the label. Thus, having a picture of a baby on the label of baby food was clearly unacceptable. Hand gestures that mean "OK" or "well done" in the United States may be obscene in other countries.

Culture is the result of many factors in a society. As shown in Figure 10.2, political and economic philosophies play a large role. Russia is an example of a country trying to change the culture of its country through its political and economic systems. Changing from a communist ideology to a more capitalist economy and democratic political system has been challenging indeed. Religion also plays a significant role in a country's culture. Countries with different religious bases often find it difficult to be trading partners because the religious mandates influencing their cultures are intertwined with their methods of doing business. Language, educational differences, and social structure also have important effects. Doing business in countries with different languages is far more difficult than trading with international partners speaking the same language.

Businesses often have to adjust their products and approaches to customers to meet the unique perspectives of foreign cultures. Domino's Pizza has been in international markets since the mid-1980s and now has over 2,000 stores outside the United States. However, its one-pie-fits-all approach was modified for the Japanese market. Local franchisees in Japan were permitted to experiment with their own toppings; a popular seller is squid and sweet mayonnaise. The strategy worked. Foreign sales grew from $16 million to $503 million in 10 years.[6]

Understanding the differences among the cultures of countries can be important to a firm. Consider McDonald's, like this one in Manila or consider the placement of a McDonald's in India where a cow is considered sacred and no one eats beef. What other cultural differences can you think of that might affect a business like McDonald's? How could they be overcome?

FIGURE 10.2

The Determinants
of Culture

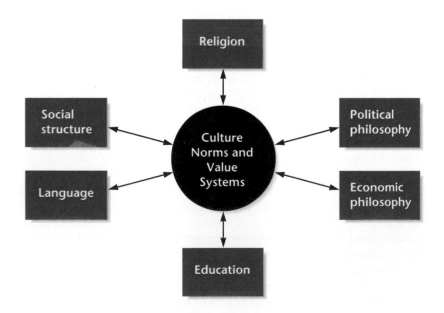

Sometimes multinational companies must work with their local counterparts to develop new ways of operating in the local environment. When McDonald's of Canada decided to put its first McDonald's in Moscow, it realized that Russian potatoes were not suitable for making french fries. It had to import potatoes to plant in Russia to ensure a continuous supply of french fries. It also had to build huge manufacturing facilities to make buns and to process meat and vegetables.

In some cases, a business may attempt to modify some aspect of a country's culture to ensure that employee talents are used to their fullest extent. An example occurred when Motorola established a factory in Malaysia. Motorola places heavy emphasis on employee involvement and wanted a group of workers who would speak out when there were problems or opportunities for improvement. However, the Malaysian women employed in manufacturing operations were initially uncomfortable with that approach because the Malay culture does not encourage women to speak out. Motorola had to either adapt to Malaysian ways or change this small part of the culture. Roger Bertelson, Motorola's local manager at that time, encouraged involvement by listening to the women, providing positive reinforcement, and encouraging peer recognition.[7] In that case it was possible to make modest changes in the local culture. More often, however, the multinational company must adapt to local culture.

Ethical Issues

Successful competition in the world economy may on occasion create moral dilemmas for business leaders. Of course, ethical concerns and moral dilemmas arise in local competition too, as we discussed in Chapter 6. However, when a company does business in foreign countries, it encounters different cultures. Those cultures may have different standards of right and wrong behavior. Those cultural differences may create unique expectations for business interactions and negotiations. There may even be occasions when a business leader from one country is asked to do something that is considered unethical back home but perfectly acceptable in the country where the request is made.

Ethics, the search for appropriate standards of behavior, can be quite complex in a global environment. Two competing ethical views are relevant when we examine global ethics: cultural relativism and universalism. **Cultural relativism** argues that what is right or wrong depends on the culture of the country where business is taking place. Thus, an act may be considered improper in one culture but quite acceptable in another. By contrast, **universalism** holds that there are commonly shared business standards and principles that are accepted throughout the world. In other words, most people in most places would consider certain actions to be wrong.

An example will clarify the differences between these two views. Sometimes managers may feel pressure to bribe foreign government officials in order to make a sale. Such bribery is a common practice in many countries. Prior to 1977, significant numbers of U.S. firms apparently made such bribes. Most Americans were probably uncomfortable doing so but felt they had to go along with the particular country's customs. They may even have reasoned, from a cultural relativism point of view, that such bribes were acceptable because they were accepted in the host country.

Conversely, universalists argue that bribery is simply wrong. They point out that bribery is "officially" prohibited in nearly every country in the world. The United States provided additional incentive for managers to refuse to make such payments by passing the Foreign Corrupt Practices Act of 1977, which made it illegal to pay bribes abroad.[8] Some firms and individual managers routinely refuse to make bribery payments even without the encouragement from the law. Of course, they risk losing business to less ethical competitors.

cultural relativism
The belief that what is right or wrong depends on the culture of the country where business is taking place.

universalism
The belief that there are commonly shared business standards and principles that are accepted throughout the world.

Motorola is an example of a company that comes close to the universalist view. Its key beliefs— "constant respect for people" and "uncompromising integrity"—apply to the international arena as well as at home. These key beliefs are supplemented by the Motorola Ethics Renewal Process (MERP), which allows discussion of ethical issues encountered by Motorola employees.[9]

Another common ethical issue involves the working conditions provided by employers. This issue is of particular relevance to U.S. firms because of their high standards of plant safety and protection of workers' health. American standards are normally much higher than those practiced in less developed countries, so U.S. firms locating factories in such countries could get by with much lower expenditures on worker health and safety. Cultural relativists may be tempted to accept the lower standards and enjoy the cost savings. Universalists argue that such actions are clearly unethical. They contend that the truly healthy business will resist those temptations, even if it means not being able to do business in the country in question.

A third common ethical issue is whether or not to reduce employment in the home country and move production to foreign countries with cheaper labor. This is a different twist on global ethics, but it is an issue that faces many firms, including many in the United States. In some cases, the company doesn't really have a choice. To get its costs down to competitive levels, it will have to move production to lower-cost locations. But in other cases, options are available. Staying in the home country is often an option if the company can differentiate its product so that it doesn't have to match its competitors' lower prices. It is also an option if the company can use proprietary technology to offset its higher labor costs. Nevertheless, the decision not to move takes courage. A fine example of such courage is the story of New Balance Athletic Shoe Inc., which is presented in Profile 10.2.

PROFILE 10.2   NEW BALANCE TRIES TO KEEP THE JOBS IN THE USA

Do American manufacturers have to move low-skilled jobs to cheap-labor foreign countries to stay competitive? Many people used to argue that they did. And the recent experience of a long list of American companies that have moved production offshore certainly supports the case.

But Maine-based New Balance Athletic Shoe has been an exception. Owner Jim Davis bought the company in 1972 and then watched as his rivals moved production out of the United States. Reason suggested that he, too, should move; but as the son of immigrant parents who had prospered in America, he had an emotional desire to keep the jobs at home. So he looked for reasons and ways to keep production in Maine. His reason was the common argument that by staying in the United States, the company would be able to respond more quickly with new styles and new orders from American customers. But that legitimate advantage would permit only a somewhat higher price for New Balance shoes. Without some other ways of holding prices down, there would be no way for Davis to pay his workers the expected $14 per hour while competitors in China were paying labor 20 to 40 cents per hour.

Davis's solution to the high wage problem was to use technology and training. Employees were taught a variety of skills and put to work in high-productivity teams. Management committed itself to a constant search for new technologies and to adapting them to the company's needs. Combined with new technologies, the new skills and teamwork boosted worker productivity. Today, New Balance workers can produce a pair of shoes in 24 minutes, compared with 3 hours in China. Therefore, New Balance can produce a pair of shoes for $4 versus $1.30 in China. That still makes China the low-cost production location. But the gap is narrow enough to make New Balance competitive when customers figure in the advantages of faster New Balance response time. For the time being, Jim Davis has maintained his ethical mindset to keep the jobs at home.

Source: Aaron Bernstein, "Low-Skilled Jobs: Do They Have to Move?" *BusinessWeek,* February 26, 2001, pp. 94–95.

As with any situation that involves ethical issues and moral reasoning, it is impossible for us to prescribe what you should do. It is critical, however, that you think through and understand the ethical implications of each situation. You can use the forms of moral reasoning we discussed in Chapter 6. Moral reasoning does become more complex in the global arena, if only because there are more stakeholders involved.

How Businesses Participate in the Global Economy

As we discussed earlier, there are logical, bottom-line reasons why businesses become involved in global activities. This section considers several of the ways businesses can take when they become involved in the global economy.

Domestic Firms That Compete with Imports

We define a *domestic firm* as a firm that does business only in its home country. A domestic firm's involvement with the world economy consists of competing with imports in the home market. Although imports may compete in a number of ways, the strategic approach that is usually most threatening is price competition.

There are three types of foreign price competition. The first is price competition based on the foreign firm's lower costs of production, as we discussed earlier. American firms are particularly vulnerable to this threat because many developing countries have low-wage workers who are as skilled as American workers. It may be difficult for a U.S. firm to compete under such conditions.

THINK ABOUT THIS

1. Do you think a country should discourage its manufacturers from moving manufacturing facilities to another country? Discuss the pros and cons of such a move.

2. If you were the head of a multinational corporation, would you contract with a foreign firm that you knew was going to use child labor to fulfill your contract?

3. Many restaurant chains try to have consistent menus in all their restaurants. This strategy provides them greater control and consistent quality. In this section, we noted that many restaurants must modify their menus to appeal to global markets. What should these chains do to ensure continued high quality?

The second type of price competition occurs when the value of the home currency increases. We discussed this under the topic of exchange rates. Such a threat was actually faced by American businesses between 1980 and 1985, when the value of the dollar increased by 63 percent. The prices of imported products fell, forcing American companies to make some tough decisions. Some cut their prices and eventually went out of business. Some cut their prices and found ways to cut costs and restore profitability before they went out of business. Some cut their prices and sustained losses until the value of the dollar fell in 1987. One American firm that successfully met this challenge was the motorcycle manufacturer Harley-Davidson. When it was faced with extinction, the U.S. government provided temporary protection and the company used the breathing period to regain its competitiveness. Profile 10.3 summarizes that story.

The third type of import price competition is lower prices due to a practice known as dumping. Technically, **dumping** occurs when imports are sold at prices that are below the cost of production and distribution. Why would a foreign competitor do this? If a foreign firm can flood a market with very inexpensive products, it may be able to drive local competitors out of business. Dumping is a common practice in international trade, probably because it is hard to determine if a business truly is dumping. U.S. businesses

> **dumping**
> Selling imports at prices that are below the cost of production and distribution.

PROFILE 10.3   HARLEY HOGS THE MARKET

In 1903, William Harley and the three Davidson brothers (Walter, William, and Arthur) made and sold their first motorcycle in Milwaukee, Wisconsin. Over the next 60 years, the Harley-Davidson motorcycle became America's most famous brand and the company prospered. Harley-Davidson was acquired by American Machine and Foundry (AMF) in 1969. As a subsidiary of AMF, Harley-Davidson declined in production efficiency and quality, and Japanese imports began to take customers away. AMF finally concluded that Harley-Davidson was no match for the Japanese and put the motorcycle division up for sale.

Surprisingly, a group of top managers in the Harley-Davidson division bought the company in 1981. They were convinced that they could compete with the Japanese imports. Soon after the purchase, the Japanese competitors launched a price war, which threatened to bankrupt the American firm before the new management could turn things around. In desperation, Harley-Davidson appealed to the federal government for temporary relief from imports. In 1983, the government agreed to impose a tariff on imported Japanese motorcycles for five years. After that, Harley would have to compete without any protection from imports.

Given this opportunity, Harley-Davidson's management completely changed the company by modernizing manufacturing methods, dramatically improving quality, and changing the model line in response to customer demand. That effort was so successful that Harley's management asked the government to remove the tariff on Japanese bikes in 1986, a year before it was set to expire.

Operating without the tariff protection, the revived Harley-Davidson continued to gain market share. In 1985, it had 16 percent of the U.S. market for "heavyweight" motorcycles. By 1987, its share was up to 25 percent; by 1990, it had 45 percent; and by 1994, it had 56 percent.

Harley sold 234,461 motorcycles in 2001, of which over 45,000 were shipped abroad. Its 2001 results—$336 billion—marked the 16th consecutive year of record revenues and earnings. This was especially notable since 2001 was a recession year. Harley-Davidson was named "Company of the Year" in 2002 by *Forbes* magazine and was listed as one of the nation's "Most admired Companies" by *Fortune* magazine. In addition Harley-Davidson is the number one selling heavyweight motorcycle in Japan.

Source: Gary Hammel, "Killer Strategies That Make Shareholders Rich," *Fortune,* June 23, 1997, pp. 70–84; Hoover's Online, www.hoovers.com (accessed August 11, 1999); Harley-Davidson 1998 annual report; Jonathan Fahey, "Love into Money," *Forbes,* January 7, 2002, pp. 60–65; 2001 Harley-Davidson Annual Report, www.harley.davison.com (accessed October 1, 2002).

have charged a number of times that Japan engages in dumping. Presumably, Japanese firms could do this because their government subsidized the businesses, which would otherwise have had major losses.

Most countries, including the United States, have provisions to stop dumping when it is discovered. Those provisions typically require a complaint from the domestic firms that are being victimized. Of course, the victimized firm has to have enough proof to file a credible complaint. Further, it must have enough resources to survive until the government acts on the complaint.

Import-Oriented Firms

Imports represent an opportunity as well as a threat. A firm that does business in a single country can still take advantage of the world economy by purchasing its supplies from all over the world. As discussed earlier, this approach may be prompted by a need to control costs—though that is not always the case.

Many American firms are import-oriented. Nike built its leadership in the athletic footwear industry on the importation of shoes manufactured in Japan and Korea. The Limited and other retailers built huge retailing empires based on importing clothing manufactured abroad. Pier 1 Imports was built on the concept of importing unusual items produced in other countries. Pier 1 imported 34 percent of its merchandise in 2001 from China alone.

Globalization has caused many American firms to turn increasingly to imports, some made in their own offshore factories and some made by independent contractors. Bicycle maker Huffy Corporation, a major

Oshkosh B'gosh depends on imports as a key source of merchandise. While these imports help lower costs, what are some of the new challenges these arrangements bring to the business?

producer of bicycles and bicycle products, ceased manufacturing in the United States in 1999 and now imports its merchandise from Mexico, Taiwan, and China. In 1999 Russell Corporation, maker of leisure apparel and fabrics, moved its sewing operations to a combination of owned and contractor locations in Central America and Mexico. Oshkosh B'gosh imported 75 percent of its merchandise in 2000. It used a combination of company-operated facilities and third-party contractors. The dress, pants, and shirt maker Haggar imported 92 percent of its merchandise in 2000. Of that total, about 25 percent came from company-owned factories in Mexico and the Dominican Republic. To stay competitive, these and many other firms have turned increasingly to imports.[10]

Imports affect more than just retailers or apparel manufacturers. For example, Boeing is actually one of the United States' largest exporters. Yet, as shown in Profile 10.4, it also has to consider import decisions with regard to the components for Boeing airplanes.

PROFILE 10.4   MANAGEMENT FOCUS: MAKE-OR-BUY DECISIONS AT THE BOEING COMPANY

The Boeing Company is the world's largest manufacturer of satellites, commercial jetliners, and military aircraft. In terms of sales, Boeing is also the largest U.S. exporter. About 75 percent of the commercial jetliners in the world are built by Boeing. Despite its size, in recent years Boeing has found it tough going competitively. The company's problems are twofold. First, Boeing faces a very aggressive competitor in Europe's Airbus Industrie. The dogfight between Boeing and Airbus for market share has enabled major airlines to play the two companies off against each other in an attempt to bargain down the price for commercial jet aircraft. Second, several of the world's major airlines have gone through some very rough years during the past decade, and many now lack the financial resources required to purchase new aircraft. Instead, they are holding onto their used aircraft for much longer than has typically been the case. Thus, while the typical service life of a Boeing 737 was once reckoned to be about 15 years, many airlines are now making the aircraft last as long as 25 years. This practice translates into fewer orders for new aircraft. Confronted with this new reality, Boeing has concluded that the only way it can persuade cash-starved airlines to replace their used aircraft with new aircraft is if it prices very aggressively.

Thus, Boeing has had to face up to the fact that its ability to raise prices for commercial jet aircraft, which was once quite strong, has now been severely limited. Falling prices might even be the norm. If prices are under pressure, the only way Boeing can continue to make a profit is if it also drives down its cost structure. With this goal in mind, in the early part of the 1990s, Boeing undertook a companywide review of its make-or-buy decisions. The objective was to identify activities that could be outsourced to subcontractors, both in the United States and abroad, to drive down production costs.

When making these decisions, Boeing applied a number of criteria. First, Boeing looked at the *basic economics* of the outsourcing decision. The central issue was whether an activity could be performed more cost-effectively by an outside manufacturer or by Boeing. Second, Boeing considered the *strategic risk* associated with outsourcing an activity. Boeing decided that it would not outsource any activity that it deemed to be part of its long-term competitive advantage. For example, the company decided not to outsource the production of wings because it believed that doing so might give away valuable technology to potential competitors. Third, Boeing looked at the *operational risk* associated with outsourcing an activity. The basic objective was to make sure Boeing did not become too dependent on a single outside supplier for critical components. Boeing's philosophy is to hedge operational risk by purchasing from two or more suppliers. Boeing has also considered whether it makes sense to outsource certain activities to a supplier in a given country to help secure orders for commercial jetliners from that country. This practice is known as *offsetting* and is common in many industries. For example, the cooperation between Boeing and China is extensive. Today, over 3,000 Boeing planes are flying the world's skies with parts and assemblies built in China. One of Boeing's hopes is that pushing subcontracting work China's way will help it gain market share. The stakes are high. Boeing estimates a market of jetliner sales in China that will be worth $144 billion over the next 20 years.

Source: Boeing company website, www.boeing.com (accessed September 30, 2002); Stanley Holmes, "Is Boeing Cutting Too Close to the Bone?" *BusinessWeek,* November 26, 2001, p. 108; and Charles W. L. Hill, *International Business: Competing in the Global Marketplace* (New York: Irwin/McGraw-Hill, 2000), p. 517.

Export-Oriented Domestic Firms

A third way to take advantage of the world economy is to get involved in exporting goods and services that are produced in the home country. Japan's famous big businesses are excellent examples. Sony, Toyota, Yamaha, and many other well-known Japanese firms started manufacturing for the Japanese market and then enlarged their scope of activities by exporting to other countries. Their export business has long been a very important part of their total business and a key to their overall success.

Many American firms have also profited handsomely from exporting. Perhaps the most famous is Boeing, featured in Profile 10.4. Exports account for almost half of Boeing's sales.

Exports can be the source of significant additions to earnings for smaller firms, too. In 2000, glassmaker Libbey generated 12 percent of its revenue from exports to 80 countries through the use of independent agents and distributors. Small-engine maker Briggs & Stratton obtained 21 percent of its sales from exports. International sales accounted for 15 percent of footwear manufacturer Timberland's revenue. In each case, the opportunity to export clearly enriched a firm that was producing primarily for the home market.[11]

Multinational Firms

The step beyond exporting is locating manufacturing facilities in foreign countries. Many businesses have done so, transforming themselves into multinational businesses. **Multinational firms** are businesses that have major production and sales operations in more than one country.

When U.S. companies first began manufacturing abroad, their intent was to use their foreign factories primarily to serve foreign markets. In most cases, differences in tastes, high transportation costs, and difficulties of communication made it unprofitable to export from those factories back to the United States. Over time, foreign tastes and American tastes began to draw closer together. Transportation costs fell, and it became much easier to communicate between U.S. headquarters and the foreign branches. Eventually, it became possible to profitably export products or parts from the foreign facility back to the United States. As a result, a number of American multinational firms began to regard their production facilities all over the world as part of one interrelated system.

multinational firms
Businesses that have major production and sales operations in more than one country.

One of our focus companies illustrates how a multinational strategy might arise. In 1986, Dell scanned the environment for opportunities and decided that if the company was going to continue its outstanding growth, it would have to expand outside the United States. At the time, the company was only two and one-half years old. Since Dell was short of capital, it decided to start in the United Kingdom and expand into the rest of Europe from there. The launch was made in June 1987. A plant was eventually built in Ireland to handle that business. Next was Japan in 1992. Most of the computers sold there were eventually manufactured in Malaysia. The Malaysian plant also provided the platform for sales to other Asian nations, including China. Once the Chinese market proved to be substantial and China proved to be a reliable location for a manufacturing facility, Dell opened a factory there. That then became the place from which to provide computers for the Japanese market. Why? Because Dell was able to cut manufacturing and shipping costs by one-third from the Chinese location.[12] For the rest of the story of Dell in China, read Profile 10.5.

> **international partnerships**
> Arrangements between two or more businesses from different countries that enable those companies to do business more successfully.

International Partnerships

Another way of doing international business, which has developed in recent years, is the international partnership. **International partnerships** are arrangements between two or more businesses from different countries that enable those companies to do

---

PROFILE 10.5   DELL IN ASIA

In 2002, Dell targeted Asia in general and China in particular as the corporation's next big growth opportunity. To achieve that growth, Dell made several major moves. First, it established a factory in the Chinese city of Xiamen. That action was expected to substantially reduce its costs.

Second, it decided to develop a locally designed PC called Su Ma (translation: Speedy Horse). Dell's normal practice was to offer its customers hundreds of PCs in hundreds of configurations. This was a major advantage of Dell's build-to-order model. But China's per capita income is still very low, so Dell saw a need to reduce costs even lower than the low-cost model it sold elsewhere. To further reduce costs and, therefore, consumer prices, Dell offered Speedy Horse in only three versions. Dell's move caused the leading Chinese competitor, Legend, to invest heavily in its own build-to-order business.

The establishment of a factory in China also created the opportunity to lower the cost and price of Dell computers sold in the Japanese market. This posed a threat to the Japanese competitors both at home and in China. They responded by shifting some of their own production to China to reduce their costs and remain cost-competitive with Dell.

Globalization had forced the Americans, Japanese, and Chinese to modify an aspect of their business model with no certainty that there would be a payoff in terms of increased market share or profitability. But consumers in China and Japan clearly emerged as winners in this particular example of globalization at work.

Source: Bruce Einhorn, Andrew Park, and Irene M. Kunii, "Will Dell Click in Asia?" *BusinessWeek*, May 20, 2002, p. 132B.

business more successfully. These arrangements include licensing, contract manufacturing, management contracting, joint ventures, and strategic alliances.

Licensing is an arrangement in which a domestic manufacturer permits a foreign company to manufacture and sell its product. The foreign company pays a fee and obtains the right to use the domestic company's trademark, patent, production process, or other valuable property. For example, bottlers around the globe sign licenses with Coca-Cola and get the secret syrup from Coke. And under a licensing agreement, Kirin breweries in Japan make Budweiser beer.[13]

Contract manufacturing occurs when a domestic company contracts with manufacturers in a foreign market to produce its product or service. Levi Strauss is an example of this type of arrangement, and so is Nike. Both companies outsource the production of much of their products to foreign manufacturers to remain competitive. *Management contracting* refers to a situation in which one firm provides management know-how to a partner who provides the capital. Some hotel companies, such as Hilton and Marriott, use this approach. *Joint ventures* occur when a domestic and a foreign firm create a separate company, which they own together. Kentucky Fried Chicken used a joint venture with Mitsubishi to enter the Japanese market (Mitsubishi was one of Japan's largest chicken producers).[14]

Strategic alliances involve long term agreements between businesses to work together for their mutual benefit. A strategic alliance may involve cooperative pricing, as when an airline joins with a hotel or a rental car company to give customers joint discounts. A strategic alliance may involve one company's providing distribution services for another. For example, Nissan sells Volkswagens in Japan while Volkswagen sells Nissan vehicles in Germany. Whatever the specific form of the arrangement, the underlying strategy is to pool the different strengths of the two companies in a long-term, cooperative effort to achieve joint competitive advantage.

More to Come
CHAPTER 12

THE BIG PICTURE

There was a time in American history when most businesses paid little attention to the international business environment. Those businesses that did some exporting or importing did so through an international department that was largely ignored by top management. That time has passed. Today's international environment contains opportunities and threats of such magnitude that top management must pay attention to them—and do so constantly.

The most important threat posed by the international environment is competition. Low-cost competitors already abound in the global economy, and new ones appear every day. There is the ever-present risk of a change in exchange rates that will give competitors a price advantage. Technological transfer is proceeding rapidly, often through the arrival of multinational firms in low-wage countries. When one multinational firm makes such a move, the others have to respond or find themselves at a cost disadvantage.

The most important long-term opportunity is the huge market that will slowly emerge as per capita incomes grow in less developed countries and as countries such as China and India become more open to foreign firms. But competition for those potential new customers will be fierce. So firms will need to redouble their efforts to achieve excellence in products and business practices.

In short, globalization increases the pressures on businesses to master the principles discussed in the other chapters of this textbook.

Summary

1. Business managers today must look beyond their domestic borders and see the opportunities of globalization.

   • What is globalization?

   In globalization, a business regards its operations all over the world as part of one integrated business system.

   • What is meant by the terms *exporting* and *importing*?

   Exporting occurs when a business sells its goods and services to customers in other nations. Importing occurs when customers purchase goods and services from producers in other countries.

2. Today's managers enter the global arena for a number of reasons. In some cases, they do so because of opportunities. In other cases, it is a protective or defensive move.

   • Why is globalization an important consideration for today's businesses?

   There are three prominent reasons: (1) the rise of foreign competition, (2) the need to control costs, and (3) opportunities for market growth.

3. To make effective decisions regarding global operations, business leaders need to be familiar with certain basic economic influences.

   • What are the most important economic influences on globalization?

   The major economic influences are (1) the exchange rate—the value of a currency compared with foreign currencies; (2) the balance of payments—a record of the inflows of money into a country and the outflows of money from that country; and (3) the balance of trade—the dollar amount of goods exported from a country minus the dollar amount imported.

4. Every country will attempt to affect trade through establishing government policies.

   • What are some of the important government methods of affecting trade?

   Government influences could include the following:

   (1) Tariffs and other trade restrictions. A tariff is simply a tax on an imported good. Other trade restrictions are quotas and nontariff barriers.

   (2) Free trade areas. A free trade area involves a geographic territory within which there are no government-imposed barriers to trade.

   (3) Government support of business in global competition. One example of this is the economic development policy practiced by Japan.

5. Firms that do business in foreign countries sometimes make the mistake of thinking that what works in the home country will work abroad.

   • What are some of the ways cultural differences might hamper a firm's efforts to compete globally?

   Different countries have different customs. The culture of a country influences both what motivates employees and why customers purchase certain products. Products that appeal to customers in one culture may be totally rejected by those in another.

6. In a global economy, a firm may encounter ethical concerns.

   • What are some basic ethical issues that arise in the context of globalization?

   This chapter identified three issues. The first is the question of cultural relativism versus universalism. Cultural relativism argues that what is right or wrong depends on the culture of the country where the business is taking place. Universalism holds that there are commonly shared business standards that should be accepted throughout the world. A second issue is a specific application of the first. It has to do with whether or not the global firm is ethically obliged to meet the same high standards of working conditions for foreign workers as for domestic workers. A third ethical issue is whether or not to reduce employment in the home country and move production to locations abroad with cheaper labor.

7. Once a business recognizes that it must deal with global competition, the company's leadership must decide how to deal with globalization's threats and opportunities.

   • How might a business deal with the threats and opportunities of globalization?

   This chapter highlighted five possibilities for a firm:

   (1) Simply compete aggressively against imports.
   (2) Become an importer itself, searching abroad for products that it can bring back to the home country and sell for a profit.
   (3) Decide to export from its home base.
   (4) Become a multinational firm by establishing production facilities in foreign countries.
   (5) Establish international partnerships. Such arrangements include licensing, contract manufacturing, management contracting, joint ventures, and strategic alliances.

Key Terms

balance of payments, p. 249

balance of trade, p. 249

cultural relativism, p. 255

dumping, p. 258

exchange rate, p. 247

exporting, p. 243

free trade, p. 250

free trade area, p. 251

globalization, p. 242

global strategy, p. 242

importing, p. 243

international partnerships, p. 262

multinational firms, p. 261

multidomestic strategy, p. 242

quota, p. 250

tariff, p. 250

trade deficit, p. 242

trade surplus, p. 242

universalism, p. 255

Exercises and Applications

1. In teams, discuss the pros and cons of protectionism versus free trade. Based on your discussion, which argument seems more compelling?

2. Suppose you own a business that makes umbrellas. You think your sales are tapering off, and you are considering exporting the umbrellas. What do you need to know before you make that decision?

3. Go on the Internet and find the recent exchange rates for the U.S. dollar, the Japanese yen, and the Russian ruble. (Several websites provide this information.) Compare these with the rates six months ago. Given our discussion of exchange rates, how is this information important to U.S. exporters and importers?

4. Interview at least two people with cultural backgrounds different from your own (they may be professors, friends, or other students). What frustrates them most about American culture? How can a business use this information to respond better to customers from that culture?

5. What is the impact of using universalism rather than cultural relativism as your company's ethical model? Is the impact the same for small companies as it is for large ones? Write your conclusions in a two-page paper.

FROM THE PAGES OF

BusinessWeek

Cool Korea

"Swing by the high-fashion enclave of Changdamdong on any Saturday night, and you'll see the affluent twenty-somethings of Seoul chattering away on their pastel-colored mobile phones. Chic Korean women float by, bedecked in Chanel, Hermes, and Gucci." There is no doubt. Korea has bounced back from the economic trauma it faced in 1998. Today's Korea is fast-paced, and its economy is booming.

"The country of 48 million has become a model for developing nations everywhere . . . Korea has already made the transition from authoritarianism to democracy and from a low-end, exporting economy sealed off from the world to one that is plugged-in, dynamic, and increasingly high-tech." Korea has a budget surplus, a low unemployment rate, one of the best-performing stock markets in the world, and over $50 billion of direct foreign investment that has poured into the country in just the past four years.

Content in the past to produce cheap knockoffs, the new Korea has an innovative business environment. Businesses make cutting-edge products such as digital televisions, liquid crystal displays, Internet-surfing mobile phones, and MP3 players (where Korea has garnered 55 percent of the global market).

Korea's leaders want to make Korea a "North Asian global trade and export platform for foreign multinationals. One big edge is Korea's proximity to the fast-growing Chinese market. Another is the billions that the government and private sector have poured into wiring the nation with broadband fiber optics . . . And Korea's manufacturing capacity and chip expertise add up to the 'perfect environment' for Korea to emerge as an information-technology research and development center . . . Dare we say it? Korea is cool."

Decision Questions

1. Given the head start that Korea has on China, which country do you think will have the biggest impact on the world's economy over the next five years? Explain.

2. Given Korea's sophisticated technology and the government support, what would you predict would be Korea's balance of trade position over the next two years?

3. How will the recent changes that are discussed above affect foreign businesses' inclinations to outsource to Korea?

Source: Brian Bremner and Moon Ihlwan, "Cool Korea: How It Roared Back from Disaster and Became a Model for Asia," *BusinessWeek,* June 10, 2002, pp. 54–58.

References

1. Kerry Capell, Catherine Belton, Tom Lowry, Manjeet Kripalain, Brian Bremner, and Dexter Roberts, "MTV's World," *BusinessWeek,* February 18, 2002, pp. 82–84.

2. "Nissan Global Annual Report, FY 2001," www.nissan_global.com (accessed September 23, 2002).

3. Sources for this section include the U.S. Bureau of the Census, Population Division, http://eire.census.gov/popest/data/national.php (accessed June 10, 2002); CIA World Fact Book, www.cia.gov/cia/publications/factbook (accessed November 11, 2002).

4. James P. Miller, "Caterpillar's Europe Production Up," *Chicago Tribune,* March 22, 2002, sect. 3, pp. 1–2.

5. Charles W. L. Hill, *International Business: Competing in the Global Marketplace,* 3rd edition (Burr Ridge, IL: Irwin/McGraw-Hill, 2000), p. 157.

6. "Think Globally, Bake Locally," *Fortune,* October 14, 1996, p. 205.

7. William Greider, *One World, Ready or Not* (New York: Simon & Schuster, 1997), pp. 82–83.

8. Charles W. L. Hill, *International Busines,* p. 70.

9. E. Brian Peach and Kenneth L. Murrall, "Establishing and Maintaining an Ethical Posture in a Global Multicultural Environment: A Case Study—Case B," Paper presented at the Academy of Management meeting, Chicago, August 9, 1999.

10. Standard and Poor's, *Standard and Poor's Small Cap 600 Guide, 2002 Edition* (New York: McGraw-Hill, 2002).

11. Ibid.

12. Michael Dell, *Direct from Dell* (New York: Harper Business, 1999), pp. 27–29; and Bruce Einhorn, Andrew Park, and Irene Munii, "Will Dell Click in Asia?" *BusinessWeek,* May 20, 2002, p. 132B.

13. Philip Kotler and Gary Armstrong, *Principles of Marketing,* Activebook Version 1.0 (Upper Saddle River, NJ: Prentice Hall, 2001), p. 472.

14. Ibid, pp. 472–73.

11

The Impact of Legal
and Regulatory Forces

Microsoft is one of the most recognized business success stories in the world. The company's market value placed it second behind General Electric on *Fortune*'s 2002 list of the 500 largest corporations, and they rank 8th in terms of profits. Microsoft ranked 28th on *Fortune*'s 2002 list of the best companies to work for in America. And the company ranked fourth on *Fortune*'s list of "America's Most Admired Companies (behind General Electric, Southwest Airlines, and Wal-Mart). [1]

Yet both Microsoft's reputation and its managerial effectiveness have been tarnished and hampered by issues in the company's legal environment. For the most part, Microsoft's problems have been placed in the public spotlight through the work of the Anti-trust Division of the U.S. Department of Justice. The Department of Justice (and 19 states) sued Microsoft, alleging it monopolized the market for PC operating systems and engaged in anti-competitive practices to maintain its monopoly position. The suit and the publicity surrounding it have been embarrassing and costly for the company.

Microsoft was found guilty of monopolizing. The government considered requiring a breakup of Microsoft but finally settled for an agreement whereby Microsoft would change various practices. Among monopolistic practices Microsoft agreed to eliminate were bundling its software products with Windows to exclude rival software products and failing to give competitors the technical data they needed for their software to run smoothly with Microsoft products. Although the federal government and Microsoft reached agreement, nine state governments and the District of Columbia refused to accept the accord. They thought that the decision was too easy on Microsoft. Consequently, in the summer of 2002, the federal court was still hearing arguments before making a final decision.

Microsoft's legal entanglements don't end there. The company recently settled a dispute with the Securities and Exchange Commission over accounting practices. That settlement followed earlier settlements of a number of other lawsuits involving temporary workers, competitors, and customers.

Microsoft's CEO Steve Balmer viewed these legal environment challenges not only as a business expense to be avoided if possible but also as a dangerous diversion of management time. He also has realized that the company's legal woes have led to skepticism and distrust within the industry. In response, he has started communicating with critics and even rivals such as Larry Ellison of Oracle. He's even listed as one of his goals for the company to "learn to be respectful and open and honest." It's a goal that some observers feel was prompted by the tenacity of the legal and regulatory environment.[2]

Modern businesses deal with an elaborate system of laws and regulations. Business owners cannot survive without basic knowledge of these laws and regulations. Therefore, it is important for you to understand the basic legal and regulatory forces that affect business.

After studying this chapter you should be able to:

1. Describe the basic philosophy underlying the legal environment of a capitalistic society.
2. Explain how government regulations actually support business.
3. Explain the various ways government regulates business in the United States, and especially the legal and regulatory impacts on the following issues:
   - Monopoly and antitrust.
   - Industrywide regulations.
   - Employee relations.
   - Financial.
   - Consumer relations.
   - Environmental.
   - City, county, and state regulations.
4. Explain the impact of taxes on business.
5. Discuss the effect of the legal environment on the firm's global competitiveness.
6. Explain the relationship between business ethics and the legal environment of business.

This chapter is divided into six sections. The first helps you understand the basic relationship between government and business. The second explains some of the ways government supports business. The third helps you understand the major ways government regulates business. The fourth discusses the impact of taxes on business. The fifth points out the relationship between the global environment and government regulation within a country. The last discusses the relationship between the legal environment and business ethics. Together, these elements constitute the legal and regulatory forces that are among the environmental influences on a successful business, as shown in the model in Chapter 2.

To understand the essence of this chapter, consider an analogy between business and a basketball game. The competing business firms are like the competing basketball teams. The CEOs are somewhat like the coaches. The game is played with a number of rules. Many of the rules are well known and cannot be violated, such as the number of minutes in the game, the number of allowable fouls per person, and the dimensions of the court and its markings. Other rules encourage players and coaches to act in certain ways even though they do not have to—for example, shooting from behind the three-point line and taking the opportunity for time-outs. Players do not have to shoot from beyond the three-point arc, but they can earn higher scores if they do. Similarly, the coach does not have to call time-outs but can if desired. Other rules control the flow of the game and the behavior of players. Unwarranted contact between players elicits a foul call from the referee. Taking excessive steps before shooting results in a turnover. However, as long as they operate within the rules, the teams are allowed considerable discretion in how they play the game.

Business operates in much the same fashion. Some rules and regulations simply define the nature of business and are freely accepted by all involved. Some regulations penalize businesses for infractions or inappropriate behavior. Other regulations encourage certain types of behavior. For example, tax regulations allow businesses to deduct expenses from their revenues. The managers do not have to deduct the expenses but can reduce their taxes if they do. The government is analogous to the referees. However, you will also learn from this chapter that some of the rules and regulations are designed so that businesses can do things without government involvement.

Freedom, Property Rights, Risk Taking and Responsibilities

freedom

The power to make one's own decisions or choices without interference from others.

property rights

The freedom to possess and regulate the use of tangible items (such as land and buildings) and intangible items (such as a copyrighted piece of music or a patented invention).

Before we discuss various parts of the legal environment, we will review the basic philosophy of a capitalistic society. Four concepts are important. The first is **freedom,** the power to make one's own decisions or choices without interference from others. Freedom is one of America's most cherished values. The Constitution of the United States and the accompanying Bill of Rights were designed to promote and protect freedom for all individuals and, by extension, for the businesses they choose to operate. Consequently, many of the laws we will be reviewing in this chapter are designed to restrict the actions of the few to protect the freedom of the many.

Second is the concept of **property rights,** the freedom to possess and regulate the use of tangible items (such as land and buildings) and intangible items (such as a copyrighted piece of music or a patented invention). The right to hold and use private property is one of the freedoms protected by the Constitution, and it is a key feature of the American business system. Private property is also a key feature of the economic system within which business operates, and it differentiates a free market economy from a socialist economy. A major purpose of the American legal environment is the protection of property rights.

A third concept is **risk taking,** which means that businesses are willing to undertake actions without knowing for sure what the results will be. Risk taking is necessary for economic growth to take place. Managers are willing to take risks because they are confident that, if their gambles succeed, they will make a profit. The legal environment of business has an important role to play in encouraging risk taking through entrepreneurship.

The fourth concept is responsibility. Along with the property rights of the businessperson is the requirement that the property be used in a socially responsible manner. **Responsibility** means using one's property (both tangible and intangible) in a manner that does not unduly infringe on the freedom of others. Rights and responsibilities go together. Just as the law upholds property rights, it also encourages the property owner to behave responsibly.

Much of this chapter will discuss laws that seem to limit the freedom of business. In a broader sense, however, the law generally encourages managers to behave responsibly so that freedom will be protected in the long run. Furthermore, some laws explicitly expand the freedom of business with the expectation that responsible businesspeople will use that freedom to better serve their customers and other stakeholders.

> **risk taking**
> The willingness to undertake actions without knowing what the results will be.

> **responsibility**
> The use of one's property (both tangible and intangible) in a manner that does not unduly infringe on the freedom of others.

Government Support of Business

We begin with a discussion of five legal situations that encourage business investment and risk taking. These regulations actually benefit businesses by encouraging them to take risks associated with operating a business. They are listed in Table 11.1.

Supporting Business through Limited Liability

Chapter 3 discussed four ways to form companies: the sole proprietorship, the partnership, the limited liability company (LLC), and the corporation. Two of these, the limited liability company and the corporation, have as their most salient characteristic limited liability for the owners. You may recall from that discussion that creditors of sole proprietorships and partnerships can seize both business and personal assets of the owners if necessary. However, the LLC and the corporation do not have that risk; the owners can lose only as much as they have invested in the company. This limitation on personal liability encourages owners of high-growth or risky businesses to invest in the businesses without fearing the loss of their personal assets. Recall, too, that LLCs provide this limited liability protection while allowing the owners to report the business taxes on their own tax forms.

1. Limiting ownership liability.
2. Limiting losses through the use of bankruptcy laws.
3. Protecting innovation through copyrights, trademarks, and patents.
4. Providing structure through establishment and enforcement of rules and industry standards.
5. Encouraging competition by limiting monopoly power.

TABLE 11.1

Ways Government Supports Business

Assisting Business with Bankruptcy Laws

bankruptcy
A situation in which a firm does not have the money to pay its debts.

One of the risks of doing business is the possibility of going bankrupt. In **bankruptcy,** the firm does not have the money to pay its debts. Bankruptcy laws give business owners a second chance to succeed.

There are two major types of bankruptcy provisions. One type deals with liquidation, and the other deals with restructuring. A Chapter 7 bankruptcy (called that because its rules are set out in Chapter 7 of the bankruptcy regulations) frees the owner of a failed business from liability for all debts beyond those that can be paid out of the sale of the firm's assets. In other words, the business owners can keep personal assets, but the business assets must be liquidated and the business ceases to exist. The owner's business assets are given to a bankruptcy trustee, who sells them and divides the proceeds among the creditors. Again, the owner keeps personal residence, car, personal and household items, and tools of the trade. That makes it possible for the bankrupt owner to start over in business.

In a Chapter 11 bankruptcy, the business reorganizes and reaches agreement with its creditors about repayment of debts. The business is not forced to cease operations. It continues in hopes of turning the situation around. This approach is possible if the business has a long-term prospect of being able to pay its obligations, even though it cannot do so in the short run. A repayment plan must be approved by the court and the creditors. Some companies emerge from Chapter 11 bankruptcy and eventually become competitive and successful again. That is the hope of Kmart, which sought bankruptcy protection on January 22, 2002. The company cut expenses and planned to close 283 of its 2,105 stores. But it continued to operate most of its stores while it proceeded to reorganize under court supervision. The reorganization will have to give first consideration to satisfying creditors to whom Kmart owes substantial sums of money—bankers, landlords, suppliers, and bondholders. But shareholders held out hope that there would be something left for them, and Kmart's stock continued to trade on the New York Stock Exchange.[3]

Encouraging Risk Taking with Copyrights, Trademarks, and Patents[4]

copyright
The exclusive right to the use of intellectual property such as books, photographs, music, or cartoons.

We began this chapter by pointing out that risk taking is a major function of the successful business. We also said government reduces risks by providing for organizational forms that limit liability. Copyrights, trademarks, and patents are other methods that government uses to encourage risk taking.

A **copyright** gives the holder the exclusive right to the use of intellectual property such as books, photographs, music, or cartoons. This protection encourages individuals or companies to produce products without the fear that someone else will duplicate them. A copyright lasts for the life of the author plus 70 years.

trademark
The exclusive legal right to the use of a name, symbol, or design.

A **trademark** gives exclusive right to the use of a name, symbol, or design. Companies make extensive use of trademarks to identify their goods and services. Trademarks are good for 6 years and may be renewed for an indefinite number of 6-year periods.

Look at Profile 11.1. How many trademarks do you recognize? As you study them, you should get a sense of why they are so important and why companies vigorously protect them.

patent
A government-protected legal monopoly on a product or product design.

A **patent** is a government-protected legal monopoly on a product or product design. Knowing that their products are protected for an extended period of time (20 years) and that other companies cannot produce identical or virtually identical products encourages firms to engage in research and development.

SOME WELL-KNOWN TRADEMARKS   PROFILE 11.1

Trademarks are a valuable marketing tool. Successful trademarks are widely recognized. How many of the famous trademarks below can you recognize? Answers: Top row, left to right: Boise Cascade, Delta Airlines, United Airlines. Second row, left to right: Sprint, Adobe, DaimlerChrysler. Third row, left to right: United States Postal Service, Honda, Best Buy. Bottom row, left to right: Toyota, Southwest Airlines, Dell.

All of our focus companies use trademarks. (The logos we use for our focus company examples are trademarks, and we use them with the permission of the companies.) All of them have invested heavily in establishing a reputation that customers know and trust. It is important to them that no competitor be able to sell competing products or open a competing airline or run a competing retail business that uses the same name. This may seem like a trivial point since you probably never see that type of competition. But that is because trademark protection makes it illegal to use a business name or logo that is the same or essentially the same as that of another firm. From time to time you may read about an unknown firm that has been illegally using the name of a well-known trademarked firm. Some firms are absolutely relentless in searching out and stopping such activities. They will contact the offending company and threaten (or take) legal action if the practice is not stopped immediately.

Some companies base their business model on patent protection. Most large pharmaceutical firms fall into this category. They rely on a small number of patented drugs for current income and on the development and patenting of new drugs for their future income. Merck has been an outstanding example of such a firm. Patent protection motivated Merck to produce such recently successful drugs as Pepcid (antacid drug), Vasotec and Prinivil (hypertension drugs), and Vioxx (anti-inflammatory pain-killing drug). But in 2002, the large profits provided by these drugs were threatened by patent expiration, competition, or (in the case of Vioxx) concern over side effects.[5] Patent protection doesn't eliminate business risks, and it doesn't last forever, but it does increase the supply of new products. Check out Profile 11.2 to see another example of a company working with its patents.

PROFILE 11.2   ASTRAZENECA STRETCHES A PATENT'S LIFE

The American patent system is based on the expectation that the firm holding the patent will legally charge a high price during the patent's life. That is the reward thought to be necessary to motivate research and development for new products and processes. But once the patent has expired, it is also expected that legal, copycat versions of the product or process will be introduced by competitors, and the price will fall sharply.

That scenario often does occur. But in some cases, significant competition fails to develop immediately. AstraZeneca's handling of its best-selling heartburn drug, Prilosec, is an example. The patent on the high-priced drug expired in April 2001. A year later no generic competing drugs had been introduced. AstraZeneca was still selling Prilosec for the high price of $4 per pill.

How did AstraZeneca manage that feat? Six years before the patent expired, the company formed a team of lawyers, marketing experts, and scientists, and instructed them to develop a strategy to prevent post-patent competition. The team considered dozens of options and finally settled on a two-part strategy. First, AstraZeneca would develop an improved successor product, Nexium, and convert Prilosec users to the new heartburn drug. Second, the company would extend the life of the existing patent by making minor changes in the product, such as adding a layer of coating, and then re-patenting the product.

The first part seems consistent with the spirit of patent law philosophy. But the second action might be considered an abuse of the patent system. What do you think?

Interestingly, AstraZeneca has an additional strategy in the works. The company has appealed to the Food and Drug Administration (FDA) for permission to sell Prilosec as an over-the-counter antacid medicine. If FDA permission is granted, AstraZeneca will then have Nexium as a prescription drug and Prilosec as a similar nonprescription drug.

Source: Gardiner Harris, "As a Patent Expires, Drug Firm Lines Up Pricey Alternative," *The Wall Street Journal,* June 6, 2002, p. A1, A10; and Jill Carroll, "FDA Advisers to Review AstraZeneca's Prilosec," *The Wall Street Journal,* June 21, 2002, p. B2.

Encouraging Business with Rules and Industry Standards

Industry standards can promote business investment by encouraging product standards, process standards, or other rules of competition for a given industry. Working relationships between government and industry are not new. Safety standards for many consumer products are a result of cooperation between the relevant industry groups and the *Consumer Product Safety Commission (CPSC)*. These standards are designed to protect consumers and to give manufacturers opportunities to develop new products that are safe as well as competitive.

It might appear that establishing and enforcing rules and industry standards would not be conducive to business operations, but doing so may actually be one of the greatest services that government provides. The establishment of clear sets of rules and guidelines, coupled with their fair enforcement, provides a structure, much as the rules regarding fouls and substitutions provide structure for a basketball game. When managers know what the rules are and how they will be enforced, they are more likely to continue investing in a given industry. Consider the free trade agreements we discussed in Chapter 10. Rules that govern movement of goods across borders let businesses know exactly how imports and exports will be handled. In addition, the regulations of NAFTA, for example, encourage American businesses to increase production of products for export to Canada and Mexico.

Southwest Airlines' struggle to get started illustrates both how a set of rules can help a business and how established firms can use the rules to suppress innovation. As soon as Southwest received its charter from the Texas Air Commission, one of its competitors, Continental Airlines, went to court and obtained a temporary order forbidding Southwest to fly until a trial had been held to determine whether a charter should have been granted. The trial took place in the district court in Austin, Texas, and three established airlines—Braniff, Texas International, and Continental—argued that Southwest should be denied the right to fly. Southwest was represented by its co-founder and company attorney, Herb Kelleher. The trial court ruled that there was not enough traffic to support more than the existing carriers, so it denied Southwest permission to fly. Southwest appealed to the appellate court, where it lost. It appealed again to the Texas Supreme Court, and this time Kelleher won. But the established airlines then appealed to the U.S. Supreme Court. That court refused to consider the appeal, leaving Southwest Airlines the winner, with full rights to fly passengers between the three Texas cities.[6]

When Southwest entered the airline business, Kelleher knew the rules of the game well enough to anticipate the possibility of legal opposition by the established carriers. However, he also knew the rules well enough to know he would get several opportunities to present his case in court. He had enough faith in the basic fairness of the process that he expected to win because the economic facts were on his side.

Encouraging Business by Protecting Competition

In the next section, we will discuss how government regulates the behavior of businesses. One important aspect of regulation is the regulation of monopolies. We will see that in some cases monopoly power hinders consumers, while in other cases monopoly power harms competition among businesses. This second type of situation might involve a single firm's gaining too large a share of the market. Or it might involve several firms trying to eliminate or at least cripple a potential rival. Southwest Airlines faced just such a situation. Even after it won the suit allowing it to fly, other airlines kept up the pressure. Braniff and Texas International Airlines (TIA) wanted Southwest's underwriters to back out of their agreement to manage Southwest's first public stock offering. Southwest found another underwriter. Next Braniff and TIA obtained a court order to keep Southwest from scheduling flights opposite theirs. Kelleher appealed to a higher court and won. The competitors then attempted to keep Southwest from participating in the airline credit card system, pressured suppliers to refuse to sell to it, and kept it from using the fuel hydrant in Houston. Eventually, the other airlines were indicted by the U.S. government for conspiring to restrict competition and put Southwest out of business. The government used the antitrust laws to punish the rivals, and they were each fined $100,000.[7]

Government Regulation of Business

antitrust laws
Laws that prohibit companies from unfairly restricting competition.

Up to this point you have been learning about the ways government and the law make it easier for firms to do business. However, businesses must also comply with laws and regulations imposed by the federal government as well as those created by states, counties, and cities. This chapter focuses on some of the key federal laws. Keep in mind, however, that firms must be alert to all the legal requirements wherever they do business including state and local requirements. Let's take a look at some of those key federal laws and regulations.

THINK ABOUT THIS

1. Many people don't think the government does much good in its efforts to support business. How would you respond to someone who is critical of the government's role?

2. Government rules and regulations help business because they provide stability and limit business because they impose restrictions. Is one role more important than the other? Why?

3. Copyrights owned by businesses last for 70 years. Patents are good for 20 years. Are these limits too long? Why do you think the government set such long limits?

Regulation of Monopoly

One of the social problems created by some large corporations is monopoly power. Recall that a monopoly exists when there is only one firm selling a product or service. All countries show some concern for this problem, but no country has attacked it more enthusiastically than the United States. Table 11.2 presents an overview of some of the key laws in this area.

The most significant monopoly-related regulations deal with antitrust issues. **Antitrust laws** prohibit companies from unfairly restricting competition. The first major American antitrust law was the 1890 Sherman Antitrust Act, which was expanded by the Clayton Act of 1914 and further enhanced by the Federal Trade Commission Act of 1914. These laws are enforced by the U.S. Department of Justice and the Federal Trade Commission (FTC). There have been various changes to the antitrust laws over the

TABLE 11.2

Key Laws Regulating
Monopolies

Interstate Commerce Act (1887)

- Established the Interstate Commerce Commission (ICC).

- Outlawed price-fixing and discrimination practices in the railroad industry.

Sherman Antitrust Act (1890)

- The first federal antitrust act (indeed, the term *antitrust* comes from this act).

- Aimed at preventing big businesses from combining, concentrating their power, and blocking the competitiveness of smaller businesses.

- Because of vague language and problems with enforcement, the act was not very effective.

Clayton Act (1914)

- Prohibits specific actions that hurt competition.

- Established remedies, such as injunctions, to stop actions that harm competition.

- Allows for remedies, such as suits and damages, for violation of the act.

Federal Trade Commission Act (1914)

- Established an independent agency, the Federal Trade Commission (FTC), to enforce antitrust laws.

Robinson–Patman Act (1936)

- Strengthened the Clayton Act by prohibiting price discrimination.

- Prohibits predatory pricing, specific pricing practices designed to restrict or exclude competition.

Wheeler–Lea Amendment (1938)

- Made "unfair or deceptive acts or practices," such as deceptive advertising, unlawful.

Cellers–Kefauver Act (1950)

- Prohibits mergers that hurt competition.

years, but the basic principles and enforcement agencies have remained the same. Among the several ways that companies may be affected are three that deserve further comment—monopolization, price-fixing, and mergers.

Monopolization refers to a situation in which a single firm controls all or most of a market. Although occurring infrequently, monopolization cases grab headlines when they do occur. You may have already studied the 1911 monopolization case that caused the breakup of Standard Oil Company of New Jersey. More recently, IBM was the target of an antitrust suit that dragged on for 14 years before ending in 1982. The government finally dropped that case because technological change and new competition was thought to have destroyed IBM's monopoly position. The experience of Microsoft in the introduction to this chapter is an even more recent example.

Many businesses periodically become frustrated by the stiff price competition of their rivals. On occasion, those frustrated businesses consider **price-fixing,** which occurs when rival firms agree to charge the same price for their competing products. Their argument is that they all make more money if all competitors agree to raise their prices. Fixing prices, however, hurts customers because they no longer have a choice among variously priced products.

monopolization
A situation in which a single firm controls all or most of a market.

price-fixing
A situation in which rival firms agree to charge the same price for their competing products.

A dramatic example of price-fixing involved Archer Daniels Midland (ADM), one of the world's leading processors of oilseed and corn. The company announced that it was being investigated for engaging in price-fixing in three of its product lines. Various reports that followed indicated that ADM had encountered sharp price competition from an oligopolistic rival and had attempted to convince that rival that it was in the best interests of all competitors to agree to refrain from price competition. ADM pled guilty to charges of price-fixing in two product areas, citric acid and an animal feed supplement called lysine, and agreed to pay $100 million in penalties for violating the law. That was the largest price-fixing fine ever won by the U.S. Department of Justice.[8]

ADM's troubles are still not over, however. In 2002, the seventh U.S. Court of Appeals reinstated a lawsuit from the earlier case, this time focusing on corn sweetener that is used in everything from soft drinks to candy. This suit contends that Archer Daniels Midland and co-conspirators rigged prices in what is now a $2.4 billion market.[9]

Although price-fixing is illegal, it still happens occasionally. The government periodically uncovers examples and puts a stop to them. But it is likely that many other cases go undetected. Price-fixing is not only a legal matter but also an ethical issue. Ethical business managers refuse to participate in price-fixing schemes on both legal and moral grounds.

Another area in which the government antitrust agencies affect businesses is that of mergers and acquisitions. As you learned in earlier chapters, a merger occurs when two firms join to become a single firm. An acquisition occurs when one firm buys a second firm. Sometimes a merger or acquisition is between firms that compete with one another (a horizontal merger), sometimes the merging firms are in unrelated lines of business (a conglomerate merger), and sometimes the merger is between a firm and its supplier or customer (a vertical merger). Two of our focus firms have used mergers as part of their expansion strategy. Southwest Airlines acquired a small discount airline named Morris Air to add new routes to its offerings. Best Buy acquired Sam Goody music stores.

A merger is one way for a firm to expand, but it can also be the source of increased monopoly power. Antitrust laws attempt to stop mergers that will lead to monopoly power by significantly restricting competition. This is especially true in the case of horizontal mergers. Whether or not a merger does pose enough of a threat to be stopped by the government is a judgment call by either the Justice Department or the Federal Trade Commission. Consequently, before a business undertakes a merger, its management should consult with legal experts regarding whether or not the intended merger is likely to be challenged by the government.

> **industrywide regulation**
> A situation in which a local, state, or federal government controls the entry of firms into an industry, the prices they charge, they way they operate, or even their exit from the industry.

Mergers and acquisitions are ways businesses can grow and strengthen their competitive positions. They can also signal antitrust concerns. Do you think Best Buy's acquisition of Sam Goody threatens to create monopoly power that significantly restricts competition?

Industrywide Regulation and Deregulation

Industrywide regulation refers to a situation in which a local, state, or federal government controls the entry of firms into an industry, the prices they charge, the way they operate, or even their exit from the industry. In the United States, this form of legal restriction has historically been found in such industries as electrical and gas utilities, telephone service, banking, railroads, trucking, and the airline industry. This kind of regulation began in 1887 when the federal government created the Interstate Commerce Commission to regulate the railroads.

American experience with regulation has produced mixed results. It can be argued that the regulators prevented potential abuses of monopoly power, which some of the regulated firms would have naturally enjoyed. It can also be argued that in some industries, such as trucking, there would not be monopoly power even without regulation. Furthermore, even in those cases where economies of scale or other factors justified monopoly, it often seemed that regulation encouraged inefficient practices by the firms' managers.

Because of these inefficiencies, the U.S. government began a process of deregulation in the late 1970s. Deregulation usually occurred in situations in which it was possible to introduce genuine competition.

In some industries, the expected competition failed to appear or was short-lived and the possibility of reregulation arose. This situation occurred in the local cable TV industry. Cable subscription prices rose sharply under deregulation, consumers complained, and the federal government reinstated local price regulation. In the airline, electric, and telecommunication industries, as reported in Profile 11.3, deregulation is now under review partly because of failures of competition to work as expected.

THE DEREGULATION ISSUE: EFFICIENCY AND INNOVATION VERSUS STABILITY AND SECURITY   PROFILE 11.3

During the 1990s, three major American industries were freed from a host of regulations, and expectations were high for lower prices and a faster pace of innovation. But unexpected problems emerged in 2000 through 2002. In California, deregulation of the electricity industry led to temporary capacity shortages and price hikes, which led to calls for a return to regulation. The financial health of most of the nation's airlines was jeopardized by suicidal price wars. Additionally, the major firms in the telecommunications industry were suffering large financial losses and huge layoffs as a result of serious overbuilding.

The problems encountered by these three formerly regulated industries suggested that America may need to rethink its approach to deregulation during the next few years. Economists had an explanation for the problems of the airline, electricity, and telecommunication sectors. All three industries were so-called increasing returns businesses. This means that they incurred heavy capital costs before they started selling their services; but once capacity was in place, they could cut prices drastically as sales increased and still make a profit. That is, they could still make a profit since there were no competitive pressures. But deregulation meant there was competition. Firms rushed to build more capacity than their competitors in the hope of being the profitable, surviving firm. Firms made temporary price cuts below costs to capture more of the market. They expected to raise prices once their rivals had been driven into bankruptcy. This combination of economic forces was causing concentration of ownership (tending toward monopoly), huge price differences for customers in competitive market segments versus those in areas that offer no choice, and violent swings in investment. At the same time, technological progress had picked up.

In summary, America's deregulation experience through 2002 shows that deregulation brings two benefits (efficiency and technological progress) but forces society to give up two other benefits that come with regulation (stability and security of supply). Government's challenge in the next few years is to find ways to get a better balance of the conflicting benefits of regulation and deregulation.

Source: Peter Coy, "Deregulation: Innovation vs. Stability," *BusinessWeek,* January 28, 2002, pp. 108–109.

Regulation of Employee Relations

The U.S. government has developed an extensive array of laws and regulations that affect companies' relations with their employees. These fall into three broad categories: discrimination, working conditions and compensation, and unionization. In addition, many state governments have similar laws.

Employment Discrimination

Many federal, state, and local laws are designed to prevent employment discrimination. Perhaps the best known of these is Title VII of the 1964 Civil Rights Act, which prohibits employment discrimination based on race, color, religion, sex, or national origin. Subsequent federal laws also prohibit discrimination based on pregnancy, age (for those over 40), and disability. State and local laws may create additional protected classes. These laws are designed to keep businesses from discriminating in hiring, pay, promotion, or termination procedures. Table 11.3 gives an overview of some of the important laws that address discrimination in employee relations.

TABLE 11.3

Key Laws Dealing with Employment Discrimination

Equal Pay Act (1963)
- Protects men and women who perform substantially equal work in the same establishment from sex-based wage discrimination.

Title VII of the Civil Rights Act (1964)
- Prohibits employment discrimination based on race, color, religion, sex, or national origin.

Age Discrimination in Employment Act (1967)
- Protects individuals who are 40 years of age or older from age-related discrimination.

Sections 501 and 505 of the Rehabilitation Act (1973)
- Prohibit discrimination against qualified individuals with disabilities who work in the federal government.

Title I and Title V of the Americans with Disabilities Act (1990)
- Prohibit employment discrimination against qualified individuals with disabilities in the private sector and in state and local governments.

Civil Rights Act (1991)
- Provides monetary damages in cases of intentional employment discrimination.

The purpose of affirmative action programs is to create a level playing field for all individuals regardless of race or gender. However, in recent years, these programs have come under fire because they give preference to women and minorities in hiring decisions. Some states are moving to either remove or reduce the impact of affirmative action programs on businesses. This issue will likely be a topic of consideration for courts and legislatures for a number of years.

Another important issue facing businesses today is sexual harassment. Although it is not specifically covered in Title VII, the courts have since ruled that sexual harassment constitutes a form of sex discrimination that violates Title VII. The most explicit sexual harassment occurs when hiring, promotion, or benefits are contingent upon sexual favors. But sexual harassment also encompasses the presence of a *hostile work environment*. This includes unwelcome comments and conduct, as well as behaviors that are seen as offensive.

To appreciate the range and nature of federal job discrimination regulations, consider the following three examples.[10] On September 19, 2001, the U.S. Equal Employment Opportunity Commission (EEOC) announced that a Florida jury had found Outback Steakhouse guilty of sex discrimination against a female employee and had ordered the company to pay the victim $2.2 million in damages. The employee held an administrative position, which she lost to a male employee after personally training him. When she complained, Outback transferred her to a clerical position. She later discovered that Outback had hired the male employee at twice her salary, so she complained again. This time Outback fired her.

On March 6, 2002, the EEOC reported that a federal court had approved a $1.245 million settlement of a class-action race discrimination lawsuit against McKesson Water Product Company and Groupe Danone (which acquired McKesson in 2002). The EEOC had accused McKesson of paying African-American drivers less and increasing their compensation at a slower rate than it did for white drivers. In addition to paying damages, McKesson agreed to implement new antidiscrimination policies, to train employees on equal opportunity law, to institute a formal job bidding system, and to develop new, nondiscriminatory criteria for determining route assignments, compensation, promotions, and performance evaluations.

On May 8, 2002, the EEOC announced a settlement with the Burlington Northern and Santa Fe Railway Company (BNSF) in a case involving the genetic testing of 36 employees. The employees were covered by the Americans with Disabilities Act and had not consented to the tests. The tests were implemented after the employees had filed claims for on-the-job injuries. BNSF agreed to pay up to a total of $2.2 million to the employees and to cease such testing. As employers are increasingly held accountable for their actions, we assume that they will work harder to create discrimination-free and harassment-free workplaces.

Working Conditions and Compensation

Several laws are designed to deal with working conditions and compensation. Table 11.4 gives a brief review of some of the more important laws in this area. Perhaps the best-known law in this area is the federal Occupational Safety and Health Act, passed in 1970 to reduce job-related accidents, injuries, and health problems by requiring all employers to institute preventive measures. The act created the *Occupational Health and Safety Administration (OSHA)* to be the watchdog over workplace safety issues. OSHA recently suggested safety measures, such as bulletproof glass partitions, to help protect retail clerks such as those in convenience stores. These workers, often victims of robberies, are in jobs that OSHA has found are among the most dangerous in the United States.

TABLE 11.4

Laws Dealing with Working Conditions and Compensation

Fair Labor Standards Act (1938)

- Established minimum wage.
- Guarantees employees overtime pay if they work more than 40 hours a week.

Occupational Safety and Health Act (1970)

- Designed to ensure safe and healthful working conditions.
- Created the Occupational Safety and Health Administration (OSHA) to conduct workplace inspections and protect workers against safety and health hazards.

Employee Retirement Income Security Act (ERISA) (1974)

- Established standards for business retirement, pension, and other employee benefit plans.

Family and Medical Leave Act (FMLA) (1993)

- Requires businesses with 50 or more employees to give unpaid leave for family and medical emergencies.
- Businesses must offer up to 12 weeks of unpaid leave after childbirth or adoption without loss of job seniority.
- Businesses must continue health care coverage during the leave.

A series of laws attempts to protect the financial security of workers. Perhaps best known is the Fair Labor Standards Act, which, among other things, established that employers must pay their workers a minimum wage and pay higher wages for overtime work.

In addition to these regulations, federal and state governments require businesses to share responsibility for dealing with certain potential social problems, such as injuries on the job, unemployment, medical care, and retirement. They require firms to make payments into funds that are used to help injured and unemployed workers, to provide for medical care, and to make monthly payments to retired workers and/or their dependents. From the standpoint of the business, such payments are part of the cost of employing each worker. These employment costs can be significant.

Unionization

In addition to the laws already listed, other important laws allow employees the right to join unions and bargain with employers. Some of the key laws in this area are covered in Table 11.5.

Employees usually join a union for one of three reasons. First, they may be dissatisfied with some aspect of their jobs, such as wages, benefits, or working conditions. Second, they may fear management. They feel the union gives them greater security and protection from arbitrary management actions. Finally, a union often represents employees who feel relatively powerless to deal with problems with the employer on their own. They hope the power and clout of the union will get management's attention.

The law gives employees the right to form unions and to engage in **collective bargaining,** the process through which company and union representatives work together to negotiate a labor agreement. That agreement or contract covers many things, including terms of employment, how relationships between employees and the company will take place, and how grievances will be handled. The union represents employees in collective bargaining in exchange for dues the workers pay into the union fund.

collective bargaining

The process through which company and union representatives work together to negotiate a labor agreement.

TABLE 11.5

Laws Dealing with Employees' Rights to Unionize

National Labor Relations Act (Wagner Act) (1935)

- Established the legal right of employees to join unions.

- Requires businesses to bargain collectively with unions representing their employees.

- Established the National Labor Relations Board (NLRB) to enforce the act.

- Prohibits unfair labor practices by employers.

Labor–Management Relations Act (Taft–Hartley Act) (1947)

- Prohibits unfair labor practices by unions.

- Lists the rights employees have as union members.

- Lists the rights of employers.

- Gives the president of the United States the right to temporarily stop a strike that will harm the national interest.

Labor–Management Reporting and Disclosure Act (Landrum–Griffin Act) (1959)

- Protects union members from abusive activities by their union.

Sometimes you will hear of a company and union engaged in collective bargaining but unable to reach an agreement. The collective bargaining process can break down, and unions can go on strike. This right to strike is protected by law. Although strikes get a lot of media attention when they occur, the vast majority of contract negotiations, over 95 percent, reach a settlement without a strike.

Labor–management relations are overseen by the *National Labor Relations Board (NLRB),* which was authorized by the National Labor Relations Act. The NLRB employs a staff of experts who investigate cases in which either a union or a company believes the other party has violated the contract. In most cases, it is the union that files an unfair labor practice case with the NLRB on behalf of a represented employee or group of employees. The NLRB also certifies elections conducted by employees who want to form a union for the first time.

Financial Regulation

When an American business attempts to raise financial resources, it runs into a variety of laws and regulations. Some make the process of acquiring capital easier or safer; others make it slower and more expensive.

One set of regulations deals with raising capital by issuing stocks or bonds. Before a business can offer stocks or bonds for sale, it must satisfy the legal requirements of federal and state security laws. Another set of regulations deals with financial reporting. Publicly traded American businesses are required to report information so that existing and potential investors in a firm's stocks and bonds can make informed

Strikers create public attention and attempt to pressure the company into responding favorably to union demands. The Taft-Hartley Act allows the U.S. president to declare a "cooling off" period that temporarily stops a strike when national health and safety are threatened. What businesses or industries seem most likely to have this cooling off provision used?

decisions whether to sell or hold the securities. These reporting requirements and provisions are covered by the Federal Securities Act of 1933 and the Securities Exchange Act of 1934. The Securities Exchange Act established the *Securities and Exchange Commission (SEC),* which oversees the trading of securities. Preparing such reports takes time, but they can be an important factor in potential investors' decisions to provide a business with capital funds. The availability of accurate financial information is one of the factors that make U.S. financial markets so strong.

When American companies enter the global market, operations become far more complex. Laws are different in other countries, so it is often difficult to deal with laws and customs in other countries without running afoul of U.S. regulations. A law that was passed to give structure to international business is the Foreign Corrupt Practices Act of 1977, which (among other things) prohibits the payment of bribes to foreign officials to get business.

Regulation of Consumer Relations

If consumers were all-knowing and all businesses were totally committed to providing full and accurate information, there would be little need for consumer legislation. Experience shows, however, that consumers do not always have adequate knowledge. Thus there are situations in which legal protection may be justified. Some regulations help ensure that consumers receive needed information about products and services they buy. Other regulations help ensure product safety. Still others guard against businesses using deceptive or unfair practices.

Table 11.6 identifies the major consumer protection laws in the United States. Each law has resulted in a plethora of government enforcement actions. To get a feel for what the business community experiences as a result of these laws, consider the following actions announced by the Consumer Product Safety Commission in June 2002.[12] The

TABLE 11.6

Key Consumer
Protection Laws

Food, Drug and Cosmetics Act (1938) plus amendments

- Charge the Food and Drug Administration (FDA) to set and enforce standards for safety, purity, production cleanliness, efficacy, and labeling of drugs, cosmetics, and food products.

National Traffic and Motor Vehicle Safety Act (1966) and related acts

- Give the National Highway Traffic Safety Administration authority to set and enforce standards for motor vehicle safety and fuel economy.

Fair Packaging and Labeling Act (1966)

- Requires the manufacturer to clearly state the contents of a package in a prominent place and use a unit of measurement appropriate to the product.

Truth-in-Lending Act (part of the Consumer Credit Protection Act) (1968)

- Applies to consumer credit loans; requires the lender to disclose the amount of the finance charge and the annual percentage rate of interest.

Consumer Product Safety Act (1972)

- Gives the Consumer Product Safety Commission authority to set consumer product safety standards, ban hazardous consumer products, and require manufacturers to report defects and dangers in their products.

Brinkmann Corporation of Dallas, Texas, agreed to recall 45,000 outdoor tabletop propane heaters that emitted high levels of carbon monoxide. Graco Children's Products of Elverson, Pennsylvania, agreed to recall 152,000 toy tracks attached to children's activity centers. The tracks posed a choking hazard to young children. The CPSC publicized the availability of portable heaters with safety devices that reduced the danger of carbon monoxide poisoning. Luxo Corporation of Port Chester, New York, agreed to recall 18,300 portable fluorescent lamps that could overheat and cause a skin burn hazard to consumers. Peg Perego USA of Fort Wayne, Indiana, agreed to pay a $150,000 civil penalty to settle allegations that the company had failed to report serious defects in its battery-operated ride-on toys. The CPSC alleged that the defects posed both a fire hazard and an injury hazard due to failure to stop.

The government requires producers of food products to put labels on their products that list the ingredients as well as nutrition information, such as the amount of fat, sodium, cholesterol, and sugars. Why is this information important to consumers? Should it be required?

As you can see, these regulations really address the responsibilities that a business should logically have toward its customers, as discussed in Chapter 6. These topics are governed by state and federal legislation and enforced by agencies within the executive branch of the appropriate governments. With respect to federal laws, the Federal Trade Commission and the Consumer Product Safety Commission are the two most prominent agencies. Notice that in this area the government's role seems to be to force businesses to tell the truth, the whole truth, and nothing but the whole truth.

Another area of consumer protection, tort law, is governed by the state and federal court system. A **tort** is either intentional or negligent behavior that harms another person. Tort law makes businesses potentially liable for wrongfully harming a consumer. Under this law, the injured customer can sue the seller, and the settlements can be quite large.

> **tort**
> A behavior, either intentional or negligent, that harms another person.

Consumer protection is also provided by the agencies regulating specific industries. In the airline industry, for example, safety is regulated by the Federal Aviation Administration (FAA). The Federal Communications Commission (FCC) regulates the communications industry. The Nuclear Regulatory Commission (NRC) regulates power plants. Transportation is regulated by the Interstate Commerce Commission (ICC).

Regulation of Environmental Issues

By the 1960s, many parts of the United States suffered from air and water pollution. The problem became so serious that the government stepped in with regulations that reduced the pollution and raised the quality of the nation's air and water. Once the public became aware of government's ability to protect the environment, other environmental issues arose. Among those of greatest concern to business are the issues of solid waste disposal and the protection of endangered species. Some of the legislation designed to address environmental problems is shown in Table 11.7.

Three areas of environmental regulation—air pollution, water pollution, and toxic substances—affect substantial numbers of businesses. Federal regulation of air pollution began with the Clean Air Act of 1963, which set broad goals for cleanliness. Regulation was substantially toughened by the Clean Air Act Amendments of 1970, 1977, and 1990. Water pollution regulation received significant federal support with the Clean Water Act of 1977 followed by the Safe Drinking Water Act of 1986. Elimination of unregulated disposal of toxic substances was the target of the Toxic Substances Control Act of 1976.

TABLE 11.7

Key Environmental
Laws

National Environmental Policy Act (NEPA) (1970)

- Requires that an environmental impact statement be prepared for business actions that could affect the environment.

Clean Air Act (1963, amended 1970, 1977, and 1990)

- Provides broad standards of air quality.

Resource Conservation and Recovery Act (RCRA) (1976) and Toxic Substances Control Act (1976)

- Regulates handling and disposal of hazardous waste.

Clean Water Act (formerly Water Pollution Control Act) (1977)

- Establishes goals and timetables to eliminate water pollution.
- Emphasizes control of toxic pollutants.

Comprehensive Environmental Response, Compensation, and Liability Act (CERCLA) (1980)

- Creates superfund for environmental cleanup of hazardous waste.

Safe Drinking Water Act (1986)

- Regulates quality of drinking water.

Chemical Safety Information, Site Security, and Fuels Regulatory Relief Act (1999)

- Covers reporting of information regarding flammable fuels.

The Environmental Protection Agency (EPA) was created in 1970 to enforce the nation's environmental laws. The EPA is an active and far-reaching federal agency. For example, it has been involved in restricting the use of pesticides for many fruits and vegetables. Its primary focus of concern is children, who it fears may incur neurological disorders caused by pesticide exposure. Federal laws require business to incur the costs of reducing or eliminating the emission of contaminants that affect our air, water, and land.

A representative example of the Environmental Protection Agency's enforcement efforts is the May 29, 2002, announcement of a settlement with Boston Sand and Gravel Company for a Clean Water Act violation. Boston Sand and Gravel was found to have discharged waste concrete material into the Millers River without a permit and to have discharged storm water into the Island End River and Mystic River without a permit. The Millers River pollution was alleged to pose a risk to wildlife and to the government goal of making the river swimmable by 2005. Boston Sand and Gravel agreed to pay a fine of $897,983 and to complete an additional environmental protection project which would cost the company $445,000.[13]

City, County, and State Regulations

There are many other regulations and restrictions that can affect businesses at the city, county, and state levels. Sometimes, state regulations are so severe that the company's managers consider moving to a more business-friendly state. Cities and counties have

FIGURE 11.1

States with Right-to-Work Laws

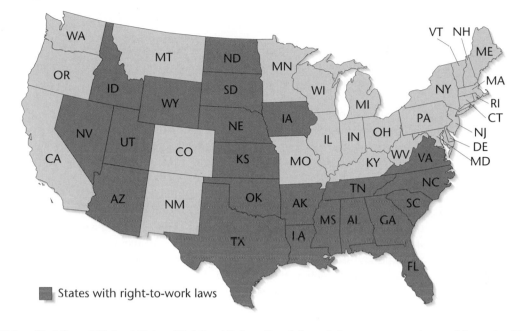

Source: "Right to Work States," National Right to Work Legal Defense Foundation website, www.nrtw.org (accessed September 28, 2002).

unique zoning laws that restrict where a business or one of its units can locate. Many cities and states require taxes of one form or another in addition to those collected by state and federal agencies. For example, a city might levy a 2 percent sales tax on restaurants and hotels to underwrite the building of a civic center complex.

A state regulation that affects many businesses has to do with unions. We said earlier that laws allow individual employees to join unions. However, 22 states and Guam have passed *right-to-work laws* that significantly restrict a union's ability to organize workers. These states are shown in Figure 11.1. Right-to-work laws state that it is against the law to force a worker to be a member of a union as a condition of employment. In other words, employees have the right to decide for themselves whether or not to join a union. Industrial states in the northern United States have traditionally not passed right-to-work legislation, preferring a stronger union presence in their manufacturing firms. Other states, especially in the South and West, have right-to-work legislation. As a result, the past two decades have seen a major migration of plants and entire businesses to the right-to-work states because companies that are not unionized can pay lower wages.

Although cities often make rules or establish taxes that discourage businesses, sometimes the opposite occurs. A large business considering moving into a city may be able to negotiate favorable concessions from the city government. This situation is especially likely to occur if the business intends to hire thousands of the city's residents. In fact, large companies considering building a new manufacturing plant often communicate their intentions to a number of cities. The cities (and sometimes even states) then compete to develop a favorable package, which may include tax relief, the construction of *infrastructure*—roads, sewer lines, and utilities—at no charge, and low-interest loans with favorable payback terms.

Taxes, Social Overhead Capital, and Subsidies

Taxes, like regulations, can be a source of irritation for businesses. Yet, like regulations, taxes often have a positive impact. Local, state, and federal governments use some of their tax revenue to provide goods and services that make it easier for businesses to function.

Some of those goods and services can be considered a form of capital investment that is made by government to increase the productive capacity of businesses. **Social overhead capital** is a term used to describe this form of government spending. Examples include roads and bridges, public education, police protection, and air traffic control service.

In addition to social overhead capital, all three levels of government use some of their tax revenue to encourage business expansion or retention by providing subsidies of various types. An example of a subsidy is a city providing water and sewer service at no charge to a company that agrees to build a new factory in that town. Government research and development grants to businesses are another example. And, of course, some industries, such as those producing military equipment, earn most or all of their revenue by selling to the government.

Tax considerations are a necessary element of business planning. Investment decisions must take into account the tax laws and consider ways the investment can be made in a manner that legally reduces the taxes the firm will have to pay. Location decisions will often involve tax considerations. Lower taxes may be a reason for choosing one city, state, or even nation over another as the location for a new facility.

> **social overhead capital**
>
> The purchase of goods and services by government to increase the productive capacity of business.

THINK ABOUT THIS

1. Consider the following statement: Companies are supposed to compete aggressively, but if they are extremely successful, they must fear being regulated as a monopoly. How would you reconcile those two ideas?

2. Does antitrust policy really serve a useful purpose? If we did not have such a policy, wouldn't competition eventually break up any monopolies or price-fixing agreements that might develop?

3. Some people contend that government regulation itself is a problem. Think of some examples of how this belief could be true. Is the real problem government regulations or overzealous administration of them?

Global Competition and The Legal Environment

One of the major issues raised by the globalization of the U.S. economy is the differences between the legal environments in the United States and those in other countries. The basic question is whether or not government regulations in the United States make it overly difficult to compete. If they do, then the business may find it necessary to move production facilities to countries with less costly legal environments. The company's executives may agonize over such a decision because of the harm it may do to the American workers who will lose their jobs and the American communities that will lose a valuable taxpayer and community supporter. But in some cases, a failure to move could mean such a loss of competitiveness that the firm will go out of business. In other words, moving to a foreign location may be required for sheer survival.

There are two sides to this debate. One side argues that within limits, a tough legal environment can be a source of competitive advantage, not disadvantage.[14] Tough legal standards can produce a competitive advantage for two reasons. First, tough standards will force a firm to make continuous efforts to improve its operations to meet the standards. In the process, the continuous improvement habit will spread to other areas of the business. This outcome will give the firm a competitive advantage in terms of operating efficiency and a commitment to continuous improvement. Second, tough standards in one location often represent the standards that will eventually become the norm everywhere else. So the firm that learns to meet the standards early will have an advantage when firms everywhere have to meet them.

The other side of the debate suggests that countries with less costly legal standards will have an advantage when competing with countries that have more stringent restrictions.[15] Therefore, restrictions on international trade and other global rules can help ensure that companies worldwide compete on a level playing field. As suggested by Profile 11.4, global businesses themselves are beginning to push for global rules.

WHILE COUNTRIES DEBATE WORLD STANDARDS, COMPANIES WRITE THE RULES — PROFILE 11.4

The member countries of the World Trade Organization agree that continued expansion of world trade will require global rules regarding labor, environmental, and other social standards. But the member countries have not been able to agree on the actual rules.

In the meantime, some global corporations and their developing-country suppliers are taking the initiative to set some standards. By 2002, more than 240 codes of conduct regarding the environment and labor relations had been established voluntarily in the United States and Europe. Many were initiated by individual companies and represented no more than the companies' promises to abide by the rules they had set. But at least 26 codes involved associations of companies and required the members to allow independent inspection of their facilities. For example, clothing makers in Bangladesh agreed to a set of rules restricting the use of child labor, prohibiting forced labor, and guaranteeing the right to form labor unions. The agreement included a provision to have inspections conducted by the International Labor Organization.

Why the hurry? Constant pressures from consumer and human rights groups were certainly one factor. The possibility of obtaining higher U.S. import quotas was another. In addition, some business leaders saw self-imposed standards as a way of competing with lower-cost countries. Here is how the president of the Employers Confederation of the Philippines put it when explaining why 1,000 Philippine garment factories had agreed to abide by higher labor standards: "We want to make it clear in everyone's mind that if they buy Philippine products they know they're not made in a sweatshop."

Source: Aaron Bernstein, "Do-It-Yourself Labor Standards," *BusinessWeek,* November 19, 2001, pp. 74–76.

Business Ethics and the Legal Environment

It is important to end our review of the legal environment of business with a brief consideration of the relationship between ethics and the law. You have already encountered ethical issues in earlier chapters. Here we want to make you aware of the difference between law and ethics.

Lawful behavior represents the minimum standard of conduct that a society finds acceptable. Firms that fail to meet the minimum standards run the risk of being punished. Failure to meet legal standards may even lead to bankruptcy. Firms that fail to meet the minimum standards of the law may lose the trust of customers, employees, suppliers, and competitors.

However, the mere fact that some action is not legally required of the business or specifically prohibited by the law does not mean it is right or proper. A firm that is genuinely committed to high ethical standards may do more than the law requires. Sometimes that requires structuring the business so that management has the freedom to operate by high ethical standards. Sometimes maintaining a high standard of ethics leads to lower profits in the short run. Sometimes a firm may have to pull out of certain markets to abide by high standards of ethics.

Although ethics is a higher standard of behavior than the law, there is often a close relationship between the two. In a democratic society, laws represent the desires of the people. They map out a collective expression of what is proper and right for that society. Ethics, the search for what is proper and right, is the basis for law. Ethical concerns can lead to the development of laws; some laws that affect business are responses to alleged or real ethical shortcomings. For example, the National Traffic and Motor Vehicle Safety Act of 1966 was passed after the publication and widespread discussion of the book *Unsafe at any Speed,* written by consumer advocate Ralph Nader. Nader alleged that the carmakers produced cars that they knew were unsafe and decided not to take steps to reduce the possibility of serious injuries. The ethical discussions that surrounded this situation raised enough concerns that laws were enacted to prescribe adequate safety in automobiles.

In late 2002, a similar situation was developing with regard to ethics in the financial services industries. The failure of some highly visible firms to employ a publicly acceptable standard of business ethics led to a loud and widespread call for corrective legislation in 2002. Congress began hearings to consider such changes while, at the same time, some government agencies announced plans to issue new rules to force firms to behave better. This is an important public policy issue, and there clearly are opportunities for positive regulatory actions. But there is also the danger of overreacting. As *The Economist* put it in June 2002, "The biggest mistake would be to sacrifice the benefits of well-functioning capital markets. All the evidence is that deep and liquid capital markets constitute one of America's biggest competitive advantages."[16]

In summary, laws are a minimum foundation. Many businesspeople move beyond that foundation because they feel it is right and proper to do so. These actions, when collectively felt and expressed, can lead to changes in the law to reflect higher standards for all.

THE BIG PICTURE

The legal and regulatory environment affects every aspect of the business. Every aspect of business planning and operation requires legal knowledge. That means incurring costs of legal advice and compliance with the law. Large firms will usually have a legal staff to help them sort through the relevant laws and encourage legislation favorable to their operations. Small firms will seek outside legal assistance from time to time and support trade association efforts to pass favorable legislation. Both large and small firms will, if they are farsighted, bear the cost of training employees to be aware and observant of the laws affecting their operations. The wisest of firms will go the extra mile and instill a high standard of ethics.

While legal issues and regulations impose costs on businesses, they also provide benefits. Clear laws and consistent enforcement provide the best methods for ensuring a healthy environment where businesses, consumers, and society all emerge as winners.

Summary

1. Human institutions are based on assumptions regarding the way the world works, or at least ought to work. If the institutions are going to work effectively, the people working in them and with them must understand and accept this underlying philosophy.

    *   What are some of the basic philosophical concepts underlying the legal environment of a capitalistic society?

    This chapter identified four crucial concepts: (1) freedom, (2) property rights, (3) risk taking, and (4) responsibility.

    Freedom is the power to make one's own decisions or choices without interference from others.

    Property rights are the freedom to possess and regulate the use of tangible items such as land and buildings and intangible items such as a copyrighted piece of music.

    Risk taking means that businesses (and individuals) are willing to undertake actions without knowing what the results will be.

    Responsibility in the business context refers to using property in a manner that does not unduly infringe on the freedom of others.

2. A healthy capitalistic economic system requires a government that not only regulates business but also encourages business investment and risk taking.

    *   What are some of the ways government supports business?

    This chapter identified five ways government encourages business: (1) limiting ownership liability; (2) limiting losses through bankruptcy laws; (3) protecting innovation through copyrights, trademarks, and patents; (4) providing structure through rules and industry standards; and (5) encouraging competition by limiting monopoly power.

3. Most businesses can be counted on to act responsibly most of the time. But there will always be glaring exceptions. And even many basically honorable managers may from time to time be tempted or pressured to engage in socially irresponsible behavior. Consequently, governments in all capitalistic economies find it necessary to regulate business in a variety of ways.

- What are some of the major ways government regulates business?

This chapter identified the following seven forms of government regulation: (1) regulation of monopoly; (2) regulation and deregulation of industry; (3) regulation of employee relations; (4) financial regulation; (5) regulation of consumer relations; (6) regulation of environmental issues; and (7) city, county, and state regulations.

4. All businesses pay taxes to the government.

- What are some of the benefits that government provides to business in return?

This chapter identified two benefits. One is social overhead capital, which consists of such capital investments as roads and education. The second is direct subsidies used to encourage business expansion or retention.

5. All nations engage in government regulation of business, but the regulations differ from one country to another. This situation creates a potential problem for firms involved in global competition.

- What is the basic conflict that can emerge between global competition and a nation's system of business regulation?

The basic conflict is that some of the nation's business regulations and taxes may make it difficult for domestic firms to compete in a global economy. If the regulations raise the cost of doing business in the home country, the domestic government may be under pressure to relax its regulations in order to lower the costs of doing business and thereby improve the competitiveness of domestic firms.

6. If all businesses operated on a high ethical plane all the time, there would be no need for many existing government regulations.

- What is the relationship between business ethics and the law?

Laws represent the minimum standard of behavior a business should maintain. A firm that is genuinely committed to operating by a high ethical standard will do more than the law requires.

Key Terms

antitrust laws, p. 276

bankruptcy, p. 272

collective bargaining, p. 282

copyright, p. 272

freedom, p. 270

industrywide regulation, p. 278

monopolization, p. 277

patent, p. 272

price-fixing, p. 277

property rights, p. 270

responsibility, p. 271

risk taking, p. 271

social overhead capital, p. 288

tort, p. 285

trademark, p. 272

Exercises and Applications

1. Form teams. Half of the teams will take the view that government regulation is basically helpful to business. The other half will take the view that government regulation is overly restrictive. Outline your arguments and be ready to present your case to the class.

2. Check out the website for the U.S. Patent Office (www.patent.gov). What is required to get a patent? Now do the same thing for trademarks and copyrights. What are the differences? Write your results in a one-page report.

3. Interview a local business owner about the specific government regulations that she or he encounters. Pick one issue of law noted by the owner. Look up information on the law and decide whether the stated purpose of the law and its value outweighed the cost and inconvenience to the owner.

4. Prepare to debate the following statement: Local and state regulations are more troublesome for most businesses than are federal regulations.

5. Can there ever be a situation in which a business or a business manager behaves ethically but illegally? Explain.

Southern: The New Power in Power

FROM THE PAGES OF

BusinessWeek

Companies can and do try to influence the rules of the legal environment in which they operate. Take the lobbying efforts of the electric utility Southern Company. "In recent years, Southern Co.'s strategy in Washington hasn't been terribly different from that of other successful corporations: lavish millions on politicians and hire a battery of A-list lobbyists to make sure its voice was heard in the corridors of power. Trouble was, as hard as it tried, the Atlanta-based utility giant kept running into fierce resistance from a colossus named Enron Corp., whose views on energy deregulation and other issues were diametrically opposed to Southern's agenda." Southern wanted to keep government regulation of electricity. Enron was the nation's premiere promoter of deregulation.

"Now, with Enron having collapsed in scandal, Southern is emerging as the new power in power: And the company that provides electricity to 4 million customers in the Southeast intends to use that clout to win concessions as Congress completes action on an energy package and clean-air legislation . . . The utility's seven political action committees have [already] spent more than $1 million since 1999 . . . Southern's lobbying activities don't stop at the federal level. In its four states, Southern, its affiliates, and its employees donated $116,430 to candidates in the latest elections.

"What is Southern getting for its money? At the state level it has staved off deregulation. And on White House policies from energy to air pollution, the utility has found a sympathetic ear.

"The influence of Southern . . . will be tested again in coming weeks as the energy debate heats up. Legislation nearing completion on Capitol Hill includes several measures pushed by Southern, such as research and development funding for clean-coal technologies. In addition, the House version provides $3.3 billion in tax credits over 10 years for clean-coal investment and production—another item on Southern's wish list."

Decision Questions

1. This case illustrates the fact that different groups of businesses mount opposing lobbying efforts. Can you think of other groups of businesses that would be likely to disagree regarding laws affecting their legal environments?

2. This case illustrates some of the ways the legal environment affects a business. Name them. Can you think of others that might affect an electric utility company?

3. This case reminds us that our elected officials receive financial support from businesses and that businesses expect something in return. Do you consider this relationship a problem? Should contributions from business be made illegal?

Source: Laura Cohn, "Southern: The New Power in Power," *BusinessWeek,* June 3, 2002, pp. 62–63.

References

1. "Fortune 500 Largest Corporations," *Fortune,* April 15, 2002, pp. F-1 to F-20; "The 100 Best Companies to Work For," *Fortune,* February 4, 2002, pp. 72–90; and Matthew Boyle, "The Shiniest Reputation in Tarnished Times," *Fortune,* March 4, 2002, pp. 70–72.

2. Jay Greene, Steve Hamm, and Jim Kerstetter, "Balmer's Microsoft," *BusinessWeek,* June 17, 2002, pp. 66–74; Mike France and Jay Greene, "Commentary: Settlement or Sellout?" *BusinessWeek Online,* November 19, 2001 (accessed October 1, 2002); Rebecca Buckman and Gary McWilliams, "Microsoft Adjusts Windows' Features," *The Wall Street Journal,* May 24, 2002, p. A3; and "Microsoft," *Value Line Investment Survey,* May 31, 2002, p. 2200.

3. "Kmart," *Value Line Investment Survey,* May 17, 2002, p. 1682; and "Kmart Trustee Plans Shareholders Panel," *The Wall Street Journal,* May 29, 2002, p. A2.

4. For additional information on patents and trademarks, see the United States Patent and Trademark Office website www.uspto.gov. For information on copyrights, go to www.copyright.gov.

5. Amy Barrett, "Merck Could Use a Few Pep Pills," *BusinessWeek,* December 17, 2001, pp. 128–29.

6. Kevin Freiberg and Jackie Freiberg, *Nuts! Southwest Airlines' Crazy Recipe for Business and Personal Success* (Austin, TX: Bard Press, 1996), pp. 17–18.

7. Ibid. pp. 20–25.

8. Nancy Millman, "$100 Million Fine in ADM Guilty Plea," *Chicago Tribune,* October 15, 1996, sec. 1, pp. 1, 14.

9. Scott Kilman, "Court Reinstates Suit Alleging Archer Rigged Sweetener Market," *The Wall Street Journal,* June 19, 2002, p. D2.

10. These are three of a number of cases reported in the press release section of the EEOC website in June 2002, www.eeoc.gov/press (accessed June 5, 2002).

11. Randall Smith and Aaron Lucchetti, "How Spitzer Pact Will Affect Wall Street," *The Wall Street Journal,* May 22, 2002, p. C1.

12. These examples come from the U.S. Consumer Product Safety Commission's website, www.cpsc.gov/cpscpub/prerel/prerel/junos (accessed June 16, 2002).

13. "EPA and U.S. Attorney Announce $1.3 Million Enforcement Settlement for Clean Water Act Violations," *EPA New England Press Releases,* May 29, 2002 (accessed through the EPA website, www.epa.gov/region1/pr2002, June 17, 2002).

14. Michael E. Porter, *The Competitive Advantage of Nations* (New York: Simon and Schuster, 1989).

15. John Cobb and Herman Daly, *For the Common Good* (Boston: Beacon Press, 1989).

16. "The Wickedness of Wall Street," *The Economist,* June 8, 2002, p. 12.

Model of the Path toward a Successful Business

Vision and Mission

Indicators of Business Success (Desired Performance)

Assessing the Environment and Its Impact

Providing Excellence in Products and Services

Evaluating Results and Making Changes

- Achieving financial performance
- Meeting customer needs
- Building quality products and services
- Encouraging innovation and creativity
- Gaining employee commitment

- Diversity trends and issues
- Economic forces
- Financial markets and processes
- Global influences
- Legal and regulatory forces

- Thinking strategically
- Acquiring and using resources
- Providing value through quality products and services
- Enhancing value through communicating with customers
- Integrating activities and encouraging commitment
- Using technology in a competitive environment

- Measuring performance
- Promoting change and renewal

Providing Excellence in Products and Services

Part Three of the text stressed that managers must be aware of environmental forces and recognize how they will likely influence business activities. The chapters in Part Four address the decisions that must be made so the business can provide its customers with excellence in products and services. These decisions include, among others, setting the strategic direction for the business, getting the resources to start a new plant, using the latest technology to build superior quality products, and working with employees to develop a more motivated and committed workforce.

Chapter 12 explores the strategic activities necessary for successful businesses. You will see how businesses establish areas of competence and build these into competitive advantages.

Chapter 13 discusses how businesses get the resources they need to operate. The acquisition of human, physical, financial, and information resources will all be considered. You will see that resource acquisition always involves trade-offs, since no business can have all the resources it ideally desires. Deciding how to handle those trade-offs is part of the challenge and excitement of business decision making.

Chapter 14 discusses how quality products are designed, produced, and delivered to the customer. We emphasize the process that is used to create products or services.

Chapter 15 focuses on enhancing value through effective marketing communications. The basic premise of this chapter is that the best possible product is of little value if the customer does not know about it.

Chapter 16 talks first about how businesses try to organize all of their activities into some logical pattern or structure so that they can operate effectively and efficiently. The second part of the chapter looks at how businesses build strong commitment in their employees.

Chapter 17 looks at the dramatic role technology plays in business. You will learn of some important ways businesses are using technology to gain competitive strength.

You will enjoy Part Four. You may even see an area of business that appeals to you as a possible business career.

12

Thinking Strategically about the Business Operation

Who is the world's largest watchmaker? Did the names Seiko, Bulova, or Timex come to mind? Well, here's a hint: It's a Swiss company. And it has 18 different brands of watches that range in price from its basic Flik Flak model, selling for $30, to its luxury-oriented Breguet, which sells for over $310,000. With annual revenues of $2.5 billion, the surprising winner is Swatch.

Started in 1982 by Nicolas Hayek, Swatch exploded on the market. The first plastic Swatch watches were a "must-have" for teens and preteens. Selling 2 million watches in its first two years, Swatch was the fad of the early 80s. While the early plastic Swatches flooded the market, they carried an unwanted image—cheap. As high-end retailers, weary of the Swatch image, dropped Swatches from their stores, a new Swatch strategy seemed warranted. Hayek responded. Through a series of expansions and acquisitions, the company moved upscale. Today, 45 percent of sales and 60 percent of operating profits come from watches that sell for more than $1,500.

Enter Nicholas Jr. Taking over as CEO, the younger Hayek has a new idea and a new strategy. The Swatch group commands about a 15 percent share of the luxury market for expensive watches, just behind Rolex and LVMH. Nicholas thinks there's room for growth in this market. His strategy is bold. He wants to pull the Swatch brand from U.S. department stores and have Swatch watches sold exclusively at Swatch-owned stores. These stores will be sleek, boutique-like, stand-alone stores. He plans to add 35 new Swatch stores in 2002 alone, at a cost of about $10 million. Limited-edition watches, such as the $3,000 Swatch Diaphane One, will be added to spruce up the brand.

But his plans for the company don't end there. Nicholas is convinced the company must diversify beyond watches. His intended goal is to have a Swatch line of jewelry that will be sold, you guessed it, in the Swatch stores. Will all this work? Many industry insiders are skeptical. But with operating income slipping, Hayek Jr. knows some serious strategic thinking and action are needed.[1]

In Part Three of this book we focused on five key environmental forces: diversity trends and issues, economic forces, financial markets, global influences, and legal and regulatory issues. With this information in mind, business decision makers must begin to think strategically about their operations. This chapter looks at the ways managers determine where the business is going and how it intends to get there. This chapter will show you how a business strategically plans and positions itself in a competitive market to gain the greatest possible success. You will learn how business leaders think through their environmental readings and put together effective strategic actions to achieve the indicators of business success (as defined in Part One). Most students find the strategic issues and action ideas of this chapter quite interesting. After studying this chapter, you should be able to:

1. Establish the importance of the business profile and the role SWOT analysis can play.

2. Be familiar with the concepts of distinctive competence and competitive advantage, understanding why they are critical and how they can be achieved.

3. Gain a sense of business strategy and identify some of the general strategies that businesses typically pursue.

4. Recognize some of the important keys to competitive success.

5. Discuss some of the basic approaches a business might use to pursue a strategy of global operations.

6. Demonstrate a working knowledge of the strategic planning process.

Managers of businesses must be sensitive to changes in any of the five forces in their environment. You will recall that although those five forces have strong impacts on the company, the firm in general cannot exert much influence on them. Diversity patterns affect how the company hires and works with its employees and how it interacts with its customers. Economics has a big impact on businesses because of the magnitude and interaction of the economic forces at work. Financial markets affect a business as it tries to raise capital, take the company public, or make effective use of its financial resources. Global issues increasingly influence how a business operates, even if the business itself is not directly involved in foreign markets. Laws and regulations affect many day-to-day operations, since government both encourages and regulates companies in many ways.

The chapters in Part Three were analytically oriented. That is, they were aimed at analyzing the impacts of the environmental forces. We turn now to chapters oriented toward the actions the company must take to compete in a dynamic marketplace. This chapter discusses the need to think strategically. The first step in thinking strategically is to develop a meaningful **business focus,** the general direction in which top managers plan to take the business. Chapter 13 will then consider the resources necessary to put strategies into action. Succeeding chapters will look at additional pieces of the action thrust, as shown in the highlighted portion, "Providing Excellence in Products and Services," in our model of successful business shown at the introduction of Part Four.

business focus
The general direction in which top managers plan to take a business.

The Need to Look Both Outward and Inward

Environmental sensitivity is important for two reasons. First, managers must understand what is happening in the environment. They must recognize changes that are occurring or are likely to occur. Second, they must anticipate how environmental events and changes are likely to affect their businesses. A firm's environment can hold both opportunities and threats. A manager's task is to identify those opportunities that can be exploited and counter those threats that may do damage.

Simply being aware of opportunities and threats facing the business is not enough, however. Managers must take a hard and objective look at the firm's internal operations and determine how it is positioned to address both environmental opportunities and threats. This process of looking inward is commonly known as developing the business profile. The **business profile** is an assessment of the firm's strengths and weaknesses. For example, a company's strength may reside in the excellent facilities and technology it has available. Its strength may lie in its strong customer orientation and the consumer-focused reputation it has built. Or strength may be in its people, who are both highly skilled and dedicated to their work. A single company may even have all these strengths. Its weaknesses may also cover a range of areas. The company may be in an unstable financial position. Costs may be rising. The possibility of taking on additional debt financing may be quite remote. The business profile is an internal reality check.

business profile
An assessment of a firm's strengths and weaknesses.

The business profile suggests two things to management. First, it helps determine which areas of business focus are possible to pursue. Wonderful opportunities for growth or expansion into promising new markets may exist in the environment, but the profile may indicate that the business simply does not have the resources to take advantage of those opportunities. Thus, not every environmental opportunity is a real business opportunity. Second, the business profile reveals the problem areas that must be addressed if the business is to be competitive and successful.

Many techniques are available for drawing interpretations about the external and internal condition of the business. One of the most direct and most common is known as the SWOT analysis. SWOT stands for *s*trengths, *w*eaknesses, *o*pportunities, and *t*hreats. The **SWOT analysis** provides an assessment of the firm's key strengths and weaknesses compared with the opportunities and threats it faces. The SWOT assessment may be quite basic in a small business; perhaps a group of leaders get together to think through the various areas and assess what has been happening. Or the SWOT analysis can be complex, relying on quantitative analysis of trends and using a variety of sophisticated techniques to project into the future. Regardless of the level and nature of complexity, every business uses some form of analytical model that provides information similar to a SWOT analysis. This assessment gives the business a feel for both movements in its environment and its internal capacity to respond.

SWOT analysis
An assessment of a firm's key strengths and weaknesses compared with the opportunities and threats it faces.

The SWOT analysis is the beginning of the firm's efforts to establish a meaningful business focus. Armed with the awareness and sensitivity gained through the SWOT analysis, the manager must decide how to act to best position the business in the environment. Those decisions are never easy. Uncertainty and risk are always involved. Despite these difficulties, the manager must outline a direction for the business.

Let's consider an example of how a small business used the SWOT approach informally. Bob and Len Gorgan had been operating a small restaurant since they graduated from college with degrees in restaurant management four years ago. Located only one block from the main gate of a midsize university, their Handlebar Cafe had experienced modest success at best. The brothers knew that their business had some areas of strength and competence. For example, they were close to campus, and there was no other walk-in restaurant within a two-block area. Both owners had solid training and backgrounds. There was a ready supply of bright and energetic college students to serve food. The Gorgans were willing to try new things; they were always tinkering with menu items and themes.

Unfortunately, the Handlebar Cafe also had certain weaknesses. The restaurant was in an old building that lacked any real restaurant ambiance. Good cooks were hard to find and their turnover rate was exceptionally high. The most glaring weakness, however, was money. The business lacked capital. Cash flow was always tight. Any growth opportunity that required much investment would be beyond its capability. The cafe was pretty much tapped out.

One winter morning, the Gorgans were forced to begin to think strategically about their business. On the way to work, Bob walked past the vacant corner lot only a half block from the Handlebar. A gas station had been there but had gone out of business about a year ago. On this morning, Bob was shocked to read the sign on the lot: "Future site of a new 24-hour McDonald's!" As Bob and Len sat at a corner table drinking coffee, they recognized the significance of this threat. McDonald's would be more popular with the students because it was fast and cheaper, even though the quality did not match theirs. Its presence could capture Handlebar's customer base and drive the Handlebar out of business.

In the midst of their discussion, Len brought up an idea he had been thinking about for some time. He knew coffeehouses were growing in popularity across the nation. Could this be an area of opportunity for the Handlebar? The brothers explored this idea. They became convinced that a coffeehouse with a very limited breakfast, lunch, and dinner menu could work. Local performers or students playing music and doing skits in the evening just might be a popular draw with the college crowd. Could they pull it off? Little extra needed to be done to turn the cafe into a coffeehouse; the old building already had a coffeehouse feel. They had the background, talent, and basic facility to capitalize on this opportunity. In the process, they could sidestep the threat of McDonald's. Within a year, the new Handlebar Cafe had a steady following of loyal customers, with packed houses for the evening performances.

What the Gorgan brothers did was not magical. You might argue that it wasn't even proactive management, since they were forced into making a change. But however awkward it may have been, they did do some systematic strategic thinking. They carefully thought through the relevant strengths and weaknesses and opportunities and threats. They performed a basic SWOT analysis.

SWOT analysis is performed by most businesses. Larger firms will have quite sophisticated approaches, often with extensive quantitative information and analysis. Yet the fundamental idea is the same as we have just described. To gain another view of how SWOT is used, take a look at Dell in Profile 12.1.

PROFILE 12.1   A BOLD, NEW STRATEGY FOR DELL

DELL

Dell has been very successful in the personal computer (PC) market. However, the boom days of PC growth are gone. With little opportunity for growth in its traditional market, a company like Dell faces a real competitive threat. In the face of these prospects, Michael Dell and his leaders are embarking on a new strategic direction that is based on careful SWOT analysis.

First, although PC sales will never see the 50 percent annual growth days of just a few years ago, the overall market for technology is still enormous. In fact, industry experts peg the technology market at $1 trillion, and that is a lot of potential opportunity.

Dell has taken a careful look at its competitors in the PC arena. Major players like Compaq have had tough going. In fact, many experts feel that Compaq was forced to merge with Hewlett-Packard because it could not compete against Dell. Gateway has experienced big losses recently and even higher-end manufacturers such as Sun Microsystems and SGI have experienced big dips in sales. Dell's cost-cutting, low-margin approach appears to have been quite successful. Only IBM has been able to respond to Dell's cost-cutting strategy.

So now, given its financial strength, its proven success in the PC market, the troubles of its major competitors, and the untapped opportunities in the technology market, Dell has decided to expand. That is a bold, new strategy. Dell plans to enter every phase of the technology market, including desktop PCs, servers, storage devices, switches, and even mainframe systems. As one expert noted, "Michael Dell wants to thrust his company into every corner of . . . enterprise computing . . . all the stuff you need to assemble and run computer networks. If he could do that, he would double revenues to $60 billion in the next four to five years."

Of course, there are some big threats and caveats here. The focus of the company will undergo a significant shift. The firm will change from being an assembler of PCs, which it learned to do efficiently and at a low cost. It will have to broaden its scope and hire new talent. Some people believe that Dell will have to spend billions hiring engineers, service, and support personnel. It will have to move much more strongly into research and development (R&D) than it ever has. Take switches, for example. The technology involved is complex and ever expanding. As one expert has noted, "There's a reason Cisco [the leading switch manufacturer] spends 18% of its revenues on R&D, compared with a puny 1.5% for Dell." It's only after weighing all these factors (as well as a number of other related issues) and analyzing the opportunities and risks, that the decision to pursue expansion was pursued. Only time will tell if this strategy will work.

Source: Daniel Fisher, "Pulled in a New Direction," *Forbes,* June 10, 2002, pp. 102–12.

Vision and Mission

We discussed the ideas of vision and mission in Chapter 2. These themes are important when considering the strategic thinking and direction of the business. Remember that the vision is a desirable and possible future that the business believes in and strives to attain. The vision is drawn from a careful, reflective, and honest view of the competitive environment and the business profile. A good vision can become a rallying point, providing focus for the business and motivation for its people.

Consistent with the vision, the mission sets out with greater clarity why the business exists and what it seeks to do. The mission often highlights the core values of the business. Mission statements are seen as important for today's businesses because they set the basic course of business direction and activities. You will often hear business leaders talk about staying true to their mission. This statement reflects a concern that the business should not stray into too many fragmented areas that can deplete its resources and threaten its competitive position.

Core Competence, Distinctive Competence, and Competitive Advantage

The environmental assessment and the business profile provide the background for framing the vision and mission statements. These assessments and business profiles also provide the information managers need to determine the **core competence** of the business. A core competence is some activity or set of activities that a business performs very well or a quality it possesses in abundance. Core competences can cover a number of themes. One business may feel that the way it serves customers is its core competence. It may have an excellent sales force and expert maintenance and repair personnel. A manufacturer may feel that quality and technological innovation are its core competences. It may hire expert technicians and engineers and use state-of-the-art technology. Although Dell emphasizes quality and technological leadership—qualities certainly important to its success—the company's core competence seems to be in its competitive pricing and best-in-class service. These are the areas in which Dell performs exceptionally well. Of course, while looking for ways to operate more efficiently, Dell must maintain the quality and technological features demanded in the market. However, as noted in Profile 12.1, the business has learned to be an efficient, low-cost producer, enabling it to hold down prices. And its customers regard Dell's after-purchase service and follow-up as being top-notch.

There is a fine but important distinction between core competence and distinctive competence. A **distinctive competence** is some skill, activity, or capacity that the business is *uniquely* good at doing in comparison with rival firms. These are the themes that make the business special and distinguish it from others in its industry. In a competitive market, these themes are used to persuade customers to choose one business over another. Like core competences, distinctive competences can cover a number of themes. Consider Southwest Airlines. Southwest has established a distinctive competence through the way it handles ordinary organizational processes and routines, such as ticketing, gate turnaround time, and relationships between employees and customers.

core competence
An activity or set of activities that a business performs very well or a quality it possesses in abundance.

distinctive competence
A skill, activity, or capacity that a business is uniquely good at doing in comparison to rival firms.

*Bose Corporation is known for its reputation for high-quality audio equipment, more specifically stereo speakers. The first sentence of the ad promotes the research the company does "into new technologies for better sound reproduction." Bose emphasizes this research as one of its **core competences**. Do you think this research and the technology it produces also gives Bose a **competitive advantage?***

While it is certainly true that every airline has to attend to these same things, Southwest handles them better than others. Other airlines have tried to duplicate Southwest's processes, but they have not been able to achieve Southwest's level of performance. These processes distinguish Southwest from its rivals and give it a competitive edge.[2]

Distinctive competence can be developed. Consider the car dealerships in your community. One may have built a reputation for offering the best deals. In fact, it may even be one of the emerging car dealerships that offers a low, nonnegotiable sticker price. Its low price and hassle-free approach to customers may indeed be unique in the community and therefore be a distinctive competence. Another dealership may have a reputation for the excellent service it provides once the purchase has been made. It may even have developed a special set of procedures and services for customers while their cars are undergoing maintenance. To the extent that its approach is unique or special, this business may have a distinctive competence.

Look at the example of Eclipse Aviation Corporation in Profile 12.2. Eclipse is trying to build a distinctive competence by building a special aircraft that will help reduce the hassles involved in short-distance air travel. The company is part of a new concept in air travel, and its planes are not for everyone. But for businesses and families desiring point-to-point, low-hassle travel, Eclipse offers a unique option.

Ultimately, a business wants to possess competences that are real competitive advantages in the marketplace. A competence becomes a **competitive advantage** when two conditions are met. First, the competence must represent some skill, activity, or capacity that consumers really value and care about. Second, the business must be capable of exploiting its area of competence.

competitive advantage

An area of competence that consumers value and the business is capable of exploiting.

Consider Dell again. Dell emphasizes low-cost quality and service. It believes its focus on these areas provides an advantage over rival businesses, which makes the areas both core competences and a competitive advantage. Dell has convinced customers that these qualities bring real consumer value.

Having a competence and being able to deliver on it do not always go hand in hand. Consider the case of EMI, Ltd., which developed the modern CAT (computerized axial tomography) scanner. In fact, the EMI research engineer who invented the CAT scanner won a Nobel Prize for it. Initially, EMI was the only company that knew how to make CAT scanners. Clearly, it had technological know-how that was special. However, EMI lacked the background to market the product effectively and lacked the service and support staff to build customer confidence in such a complex machine. It had the competence but lacked the capability to bring the scanner to market successfully.

GE took the idea, built an imitation (to avoid patent infringement), and marketed the product successfully. Within eight years, EMI was out of the CAT scanner business and

TAXI, ANYONE?   PROFILE 12.2

In recent years, the airline industry has struggled, and it has faced changing attitudes from its customers. Air travel has become a painfully slow process. Security checks, scan searches, two-hour preflight arrivals, and long lines have led a recent NASA study to conclude that for journeys of 500 miles or less, you might as well drive. Into this fray comes Vern Raburn, president and CEO of Eclipse Aviation Corp. He has envisioned a new approach to air travel—the air taxi. An air taxi is designed for short flights. A business team or even a family flies from point to point on the chartered air taxi. You fly at typical air speeds, pay typical air fares, but avoid the hassles. There are no lengthy check-ins, no extensive security checks, and no cancelled or bumped flights. You fly in and out of tiny airports, thus avoiding major congestion. There are over 5,000 suitable airports, located conveniently across North America. Efficiency is the key.

Of course, a unique plane is needed to make this unique approach work. That's where Eclipse steps in. The company hopes to revolutionize the industry by designing and building small jet planes that will be safer and easier to handle, and that will cost a fraction of the price of competing aircraft. The Eclipse 500 is a six-seat twin-engine plane that flies at 408 miles an hour. It costs a bargain-basement $837,000, and that's the key. A similar jet, such as the Cessna CJ1, is more than four times as expensive. To keep prices low, Raburn has to sell thousands of these planes over the next decade. Raburn has raised $220 million to fund this venture, and his investors include such luminaries as Bill Gates.

Source: Hesh Kestin, "The Plane Truth," *Inc,* June 2002, pp. 64–72; and Eclipse website, www.eclipseaviation.com (accessed July 11, 2002).

GE was in the driver's seat. Although EMI had a competence (unique technology), it lacked the capability to build a competitive advantage.[3]

You may wonder whether all businesses possess distinctive competences and competitive advantages. The answer is no. Further, you may wonder how important it really is to have these features. That question is not easy to answer. If consumer demand for a product or service far outstrips the available supply, then any business that offers the product or service will make sales and generate profits. There may be no special competence required. Yet in a competitive market, this condition is likely to be short-lived. Remember the discussion of microeconomics in Chapter 8. If demand outpaces supply and existing businesses are making money, new competitors will seek to enter the market. Eventually the shortage of supply will be eased. In the process, competition will increase. Market battles will occur as businesses try to secure a hold on the market. Some businesses will not survive. Which are most likely to succeed? In all likelihood, it will be those businesses that have established strong competences and competitive advantages.

One final piece that should be considered in this initial look at how a business thinks strategically is the concept of a sustainable competitive advantage. A **sustainable competitive advantage** is one that is not easily duplicated by competitors. It is special

> **sustainable competitive advantage**
> A competitive advantage that competitors cannot duplicate easily.

Core competence	A strength; anything that the business does very well.
Distinctive competence	A unique core competence; something that the business does better than its rivals.
Competitive advantage	A distinctive competence that customers value and that the business has the resources to exploit.
Sustainable competitive advantage	A competitive advantage that the business can continue to exploit over time.

and can remain unique to the business for some period of time. Logically, every business would like a sustainable competitive advantage. One way of accomplishing this is to secure trademarks and patents, as we discussed in Chapter 11. These legal means provide some protection against a rival's directly pirating your ideas or technology. Another way to ensure a sustainable competitive advantage is to remain on the cutting edge of the industry, offering the latest and best innovations. Table 12.1 summarizes the concepts we've just discussed. Notice that each concept builds on and is more beneficial than the previous one.

The reality of business is that most competitive advantages are very difficult to sustain. In fact, bright competitors are always looking for ways to invade and minimize another firm's competitive advantage. Of course, in a free enterprise system, this is exactly what we expect. Let's return to Southwest Airlines. It certainly has had a competitive advantage in the airline industry. But what about JetBlue and other airlines that are trying to emulate Southwest's strategy? Given these competitive moves, do you think Southwest's competitive advantage is sustainable?

We now turn to the discussion of business strategies. These are the actions business managers take to take advantage of their competences in order to successfully reach their vision.

competitive strategy
The specific approach a business chooses to pursue for addressing its competitive environment.

Foundations of Business Strategy

THINK ABOUT THIS

1. Conduct an informal SWOT analysis of your campus bookstore. From this analysis, how could the bookstore improve?

2. Look at your college or university. In your mind, what is the core competence of the school? Do you feel the core competence is a distinctive competence? Is there a real competitive advantage?

3. Consider some of the businesses in your community. Which do you feel have a true distinctive competence? Why?

In a competitive environment, a business must continually try to develop ways to compete more effectively. Businesses try to identify strategies that will give them an edge over the competition. The search for strategies for business success is one of the most interesting areas of business.

Some of the early work done in the area of competitive strategy came from Harvard University professor Michael Porter, who contends that when businesses compete, they must pursue some strategic approach to gain an advantage over their rivals.[4] They must use some type of competitive strategy. In other words, **competitive strategy** is the specific approach the business chooses to pursue for addressing its environment. According to Porter, there are three broad and rather basic competitive strategies that can be pursued: the low-cost leader strategy, the differentiation strategy, and the focus strategy. A business may emphasize one or a combination of these strategies.

Low-Cost Leadership Strategy

The first general strategy that some businesses pursue is known as a **low-cost leadership strategy.** Here a business looks for ways to reduce the cost of providing a product or service and pass the savings on to the customer. A business may reduce costs in many ways. It may find more efficient ways of operating, be able to get supplies or products at reduced rates, or find cost-effective ways to distribute its products. One of the best-known companies that pursues a low-cost leadership strategy is Wal-Mart. Its ability to buy name brand products in bulk and pass the cost savings on to customers through lower prices has made it the leading discount retailer in the country. Although its scope of retailing is more limited, Best Buy uses an approach similar to that of Wal-Mart. Specializing in consumer electronics, PCs, entertainment software, and appliances, it provides a range of products at low prices.

Both manufacturers and service businesses can pursue a low-cost leadership strategy. When manufacturers use this approach, they attempt to reduce production costs every way possible. All unnecessary steps are eliminated and every phase of the operation is made as efficient as possible.

In service industries, the low-cost leadership strategy works if the company can reduce costs to the minimum while still providing quality service. Southwest Airlines is immensely successful using the low-cost leadership strategy. As we've said, it uses a single type of plane that is efficient over short hauls. It uses less-congested airports than other major airlines. Its employees are more flexible and more productive, thereby reducing labor costs. The efficiency of Southwest's operations allows each employee to handle 2,300 customers a day, which is twice as many as any other airline.

> **low-cost leadership strategy**
> A competitive strategy that entails finding ways to reduce the cost of providing a product or service and pass the savings on to customers.

Differentiation Strategy

The second general competitive strategy is differentiation. A business that is pursuing a **differentiation strategy** is providing a product or service that has some unique feature. That unique feature can cover a broad range. Perhaps the company's products are known for being of higher quality than those of competitors. Perhaps the business provides superior service once a purchase has been made. Perhaps the business has such friendly, knowledgeable workers that customers feel comfortable with the help and support they receive.

The competitive strength of the differentiation strategy comes from what the unique feature allows the business to do. In theory, the unique feature should enable the business to sell more of its products because customers value the uniqueness provided. Many companies look for creative ways to differentiate themselves from competitors. For example, New Balance is the only company in the athletic-shoe industry that produces its entire line of shoes in a full range of widths. Customers can choose shoe widths from AA to EEEEEE. The extra comfort and fit this feature provides give New Balance an edge over its rivals.[5]

In some cases, a business may even be able to charge higher prices than competitors because the unique feature is valued so highly. Consider the example of Caterpillar Inc., which manufactures off-road earth-moving equipment. The equipment is known for its high quality. The firm is also known for having a superb dealer network, so parts and service are readily available. These features allow Caterpillar to charge a premium over competitors whose reputation and dealer support are inferior.

Let's look at the fiercely competitive restaurant industry. Restaurants are always looking for ways to differentiate themselves. Romano's Macaroni Grill uses the differentiation strategy. It patterns itself after restaurants in Italy, with an open-market feel and a menu that includes fresh vegetables, choice meats, and various pasta choices. Meals are prepared in full view of customers. Jugs of wine are placed on tables, and customers

> **differentiation strategy**
> A competitive strategy that is built on providing a product or service that has some unique feature.

serve themselves. Customers even report on an honor system how many glasses of wine they have consumed. Macaroni's tries to create a different sort of dining experience for its customers and seems to have a passion for ensuring customer satisfaction. Company president John Miller emphasizes the customer commitment when he says, "If a guest wants samples of all the dessert offerings, that is what the guest will get."[6]

Litespeed is also a good example of the differentiation strategy. Its bikes are certainly not cheap; even the lowest-priced models sell for over $5,000. The top-of-the-line Ghisallo model can easily exceed $10,000. The company's real strength is in the quality of its bicycles. Through the use of excellent design and titanium frames, Litespeed produces bikes that are in high demand among hard-core riders. World-class riders from around the world compete on Litespeeds. Customers are willing to pay the premium price because they know the name and the quality it represents.

Focus Strategy

> **focus strategy**
>
> A competitive strategy that is built on positioning a business to serve the needs of some unique or distinct customer segment that is not being fully served by the competition.

In the **focus strategy,** the business positions itself to serve the needs of some unique or distinct customer segment that is not being fully served by the competition. The market may be segmented in a number of ways. For example, the unique segment may be a distinct group of customers, a geographic area, or some specific need that has not been fully addressed by any other competitor. Often the focus strategy is the natural and most reasonable approach pursued by small businesses and entrepreneurs. These creative people look at the business environment and see areas of consumer need that are not being tapped. They are convinced that if they offer products and services to meet these market needs, they can be successful. They are searching for a gap between what is currently available in the market and what consumers want. They organize their businesses to serve this niche.

The stories of successful focus strategies are legendary. For example, Dave Thomas entered a market that nearly everyone thought was already laden with too many competitors. In many ways, he extended the market by focusing on a unique set of consumers. The hamburger fast-food market was dominated by McDonald's and Burger King. Thomas believed that neither of these competitors appealed directly to the adult consumer. He committed his efforts to providing a quality hamburger for adult customers. This focus paid off, and his company, Wendy's, experienced unprecedented growth in its early years.

Privacy Technologies provides innovative products and services to protect people's right to privacy. Its latest product, created to meet a unique but growing customer need, is called the TeleZapper. The TeleZapper is not for everyone. It's aimed at that niche of people who are so frustrated with being bombarded by telemarketing calls that they are willing to do something about it. The TeleZapper jams any incoming calls that are dialed by the automatic-dialing machines that telemarketers use, thereby blocking most telemarketing calls without interfering with normal calls. The TeleZapper is relatively small, plugs into your phone line, and sells for just under $50 at consumer electronics retailers such as Best Buy or Radio Shack.[7]

Many small businesses use a focus strategy. They realize that carefully selecting a niche in the market is their avenue for competing against bigger rivals.

Keys to Competitive Success

The key to success with each of Porter's three general strategies is attention to the specific emphasis. In the low-cost leadership strategy, the key is attention to the *production process.* Managers must be singularly focused on how to wring costs out of the production process to provide products or services at the lowest possible price.

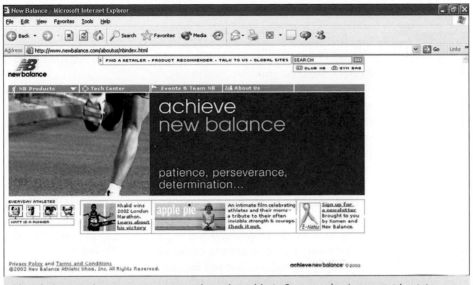

New Balance takes a unique approach to the athletic footwear business, emphasizing quality manufacturing and fit over high profile marketing and fashion. The company makes shoes in multiple widths; adheres to an "endorsed by no one" policy; and builds strong bonds with its retail partners. Do you think these actions have allowed New Balance to differentiate itself from its rivals?

A business that wants to be the low-cost producer should be aware of two important economic concepts that govern costs of production. One is the concept of **economies of scale.** Often a firm can lower its average cost of production by increasing the size of its production facilities and its overall volume of production. It can then offer volume discounts to its customers.

The second cost-related concept is the **experience curve** (also referred to as the learning curve). Without increasing the scale of operation, a business can nevertheless lower costs as a result of increasing efficiencies gained from experience in making the product. To take advantage of efficiencies, management has to deliberately try to learn how to cut costs as the company gains experience in producing the product. In short, the company learns how to handle the production process in a more efficient and less costly way. Later in this textbook, you will learn about the process of continuous improvement and the Six Sigma approach, which are popular methods many companies are using to increase efficiency.

In the differentiation strategy, managers pay attention to how they can improve the *product.* Product teams are charged with finding ways to make the product more valuable to customers. They constantly strive to add visible value that customers will be willing to pay a premium for.

One major way a business can differentiate itself is through the quality of its products. Competing on the basis of quality is popular for several reasons. One is that it is more difficult for a competitor to match another firm's quality than to match its price. Another is that customers are usually willing to pay more for quality.

A high-quality strategy can be the basis of prolonged competitive success. But it does have risks. The business can be a target for competitors who try to get their quality close enough so that their lower price will capture customers from the quality leader. An example is Korea's Samsung Electronics. Samsung began its business making cheap,

economies of scale
Reductions in a firm's average cost of production that are achieved by increasing the overall volume of production.

experience curve
A concept whereby costs are lowered as a result of a firm's increasing efficiency through experience in making the product; also called the learning curve.

More to Come
CHAPTER 14

12-inch, black-and-white televisions under the Sanyo label. Today, with over 30 years of experience in the industry, Samsung has learned how to produce world-class quality products ranging from cell phones and flat-screen TVs to ultrathin laptop computers and memory chips. Understandably, traditional quality leaders such as IBM, Sony, Toshiba, and Matshushita, are concerned.[8]

Quality as a competitive tool is not restricted to large companies. Entrepreneurs often start their companies with a quality strategy. Sometimes the quality concept is good enough to lead to substantial growth. Today's outdoor sportswear market offers three examples. Patagonia, North Face, and Columbia have all established national brand recognition by producing clothing of distinctive quality.

Some businesses find that they can beat the competition by developing new and improved products or services. If the change represents a new product or a verifiable improvement in a product, then the development is known as an *innovation*. HDTVs and DVD players would be examples. If the changes are largely cosmetic, such as changing the exterior look of a car, then the development is a change in *fashion*. In either case, the business is competing by giving the customer something new or different.

Most companies will engage in both fashion and innovation from time to time. In some cases, a company may resort to innovation when fashion changes are insufficient to gain the revenue or market share desired. General Motors is an example. In recent years, GM has seen its market share decline substantially as its cars seem out of step with buyers' tastes. Minor style changes did not seem to work. Importantly, GM found that younger buyers were especially turned off by GM's styles. Determined to recapture the younger market, GM introduced a number of new cars, each designed to be stylish while being moderately priced. We can watch the performance of the flashy sport wagon, the Pontiac Vibe, as well as the new Saturn Ion and the redesigned Cavalier to see how this approach works.

In the focus strategy, attention must be given to better serving a special set of *customers*. The managers place great importance on interacting with specific customers, since providing value to that unique customer niche determines their success.

Let's consider a couple of examples. The next time you are at a hockey game, you'll see an example of a company that has had dazzling success by focusing on a unique segment of customers. Whether the ice rink's users are a group of ten-year-olds or the Detroit Redwings, in all likelihood, the ice will be resurfaced by the same product—the Zamboni ice resurfacing machine. The Zamboni machine, developed over 50 years ago, is still going strong today. Although there are other brands of resurfacing machines, the Zamboni machine is available only from Frank J. Zamboni & Co. Inc. Another example is Arthur's Wine Shop in Charlotte, North Carolina. Of course, there is nothing special about selling wine, and competitors extend all the way from grocery stores to wine outlet centers. But Arthur's is different. The business caters to the wine enthusiast. In fact, Arthur's specializes in bringing to the shop rare and hard-to-find wines from throughout the world.[9]

Frank J. Zamboni & Co. focuses on a unique product. Why would a local recreation center purchase a Zamboni rather than a rival ice resurfacing machine?

© Zamboni Company

Other General Strategic Considerations

A business can make many other strategic moves. You will likely study these when you take a course in business strategy, probably during your senior year. Here we limit discussion to three additional strategic considerations you should understand: diversification, acquisition, and cooperative strategies.

Diversification

Joe Russell has been in the bicycle business for a quarter of a century. Over those years his retail store, Russell's Cycle, has developed a reputation for its unique focus and expertise in biking. The business appeals to biking enthusiasts—those with a real passion for the sport. Russell's sells and services top-quality bikes, such as Cannondale, Specialized, Schwinn, and Bianchi. Of course, the business depends on trends. For example, BMX built the business during the first seven years. As BMX's popularity waned, mountain biking began to soar. Today, BMX is back and so is road biking, fueled by enthusiasm from strong U.S. performances at the Tour de France.

Ten years ago, Russell's embarked on a new strategy. While biking was always the business's bread and butter, biking revenues were seasonal. Business was brisk between March and September, but fell dramatically in the late fall and winter. Even with a slight blip for Christmas sales, cash flow during the winter was typically bleak. In response, Russell's decided to expand its business into fitness products. The company now has a broad line of high-quality fitness products designed to "provide fitness solutions to improve the quality of life." Exercise equipment, treadmills, and stationary bikes are popular. Major manufacturers such as Spirit and Startrek are carried. Even the name of the business has been changed to Russell's Cycle and Fitness Center. This logical move helped the store cope with the seasonal downturn that always occurred in the bicycle business. This is an example of **diversification,** which occurs when a business decides to get into an additional area (or areas) of business.

Usually, a company diversifies for one of three reasons. First, it may diversify to deal with the seasonal nature of its main business. Second, a company may feel the need to diversify if its traditional business is losing market attractiveness. Third, a company may diversify simply as a way to grow and enhance its profits. Businesses often diversify into other businesses that are closely related to their traditional business focus.

This is the case with Best Buy. Look at the range of operations, retail stores, and commercial websites that are all part of the Best Buy family: Best Buy, Futureshop, Magnolia Hi-Fi, Media Play, On Cue, Sam Goody, Suncoast, and BestBuy.com. Although each business has a slightly different focus, all are retail-oriented, operate in the consumer technology fields, and use the same basic business approaches.[10]

Consider Darden Restaurants Inc., the largest casual-dining restaurant company in the world. All its 1,200 restaurants are company-owned. Its diversified portfolio of businesses includes Red Lobster, Olive Garden, Bahama Breeze, and Smokey Bones. Although each chain has a different theme, all are in the restaurant business.[11]

Some businesses diversify into what seem to be completely unrelated businesses. Consider the Walt Disney Company, the second largest media conglomerate in the world (just behind the AOL Time Warner Company). As you may recall from Chapter 4, Walt Disney's interests include both movies (Miramax Film Corporation and Touchstone Pictures) and television (Buena Vista Television and the Disney Channel). The company owns the ABC network and several TV stations. But it is also in other forms of entertainment. For example, Disney owns the Anaheim Mighty Ducks professional hockey team. Of course, all these businesses are in addition to Disney's traditional core

diversification
A strategy that entails branching out into an additional area (or areas) of business.

Companies like Honda have diversified into a broad range of product offerings. Does Honda seem to be pursuing a related or unrelated diversification strategy?

business—theme parks. The theme park empires include Disneyland (now in Anaheim, Paris, and Tokyo) as well as Disney World in Orlando.[12] But be careful. All these businesses may not be as unrelated as they first appear. In fact, all have the common tie of being in the entertainment business and building on the Disney brand name.

Sometimes a business's diversification is so broad and far-reaching that it's hard to recognize the parent company at all. For example, the same company that makes Butterfingers also makes Alpo dog food, PowerBars, Coffee-Mate, and Perrier bottled water. And that's just a sampling. This company employs over 200,000 people throughout the world, making it the world's largest food company. One last hint—it's the largest industrial company in its home base of Switzerland. Or try this one. You may have seven different products of this company in your garage today. The company makes lawn mowers, snowblowers, marine engines, generators, motorcycles, ATVs, and its bread and butter—cars. Did you guess the names of these two diversified giants? Nestlé and Honda.[13]

Acquisition

You have already read about acquisitions—when one company buys another company. In fact, barely a day goes by without news of some new acquisition or merger that alters the business climate. One of the most heralded recent deals was Hewlett-Packard's $19 billion acquisition of Compaq. The acquisition created a giant in the high-tech industry with annual sales of $82 billion. Why does a company undertake such a massive move? The answer: competition. The new Hewlett-Packard company now has the size and the depth of products and services to compete more effectively with industry leader IBM. At the same time, it is better positioned to respond to low-cost competitors such as Dell. Why wouldn't a pioneering company such as Hewlett-Packard simply work to further build its own size and enhance its own products and services? The answer: Acquisition allows quicker movement. It takes a lot of time, expertise, and money to expand on your own. Given that HP and Compaq had been experiencing recent struggles, the deal was beneficial to both.[14]

Let's look at another deal. Cadbury Schweppes (with brands such as Dr. Pepper and Snapple) is buying Dandy's chewing gum business. Dandy is the fourth largest chewing gum maker in the world. Combined with its current business, this deal will suddenly make Cadbury Schweppes second in the European market and first in some profitable countries such as France. That's an instant jump in market share that should convert to profitability.[15]

Cooperative Strategies

> **cooperative strategies**
> Situations in which two or more businesses decide to work together for their mutual benefit.

Cooperative strategies exist when two or more businesses decide to work together for their mutual benefit. These cooperative strategies have become quite prevalent in recent years. We have already discussed some forms of these strategies in earlier chapters. One form is the strategic alliance, in which two or more organizations decide to share resources or competences so they can better achieve their business purposes.[16] You may frequently hear the terms *partnerships* and *strategic partnerships*. These terms refer to the same type of relationship as the strategic alliance.

Alliances are very popular in industries in which change is rapid and innovation is critical. Although the average large business has about 30 partnerships and alliances, it is not uncommon for businesses to have many more.[17] Major manufacturers such as Microsoft and IBM generally have alliances with a number of smaller suppliers who provide the level and quality of parts and components that are needed. See Profile 12.3 to learn about the unique partnering links that are present at the College Television Network.

CTN ON THE SCENE   PROFILE 12.3

With an audience of over 8 million college students on 800 campuses across the country, there is a good chance you are already aware of CTN, the College Television Network. Started in 1995, the network had a simple plan. Place TVs in high-traffic areas, such as cafeterias, gyms, and lounges. Then pipe in only CTN, 24 hours a day, 7 days a week, to a captive audience unable to change the channel. CTN offers unique programming for students, a continuous stream of music, news, sports, and fashion. But it also provides a public address system for the college and a captive audience for advertisers. And all this comes free of charge to the participating school. CTN has found an innovative way to tap into the lucrative college-age demographic.

CTN is built around a series of partnerships in which everybody benefits. That begins with knowing its viewers. Sixty percent of the programming has music-related content. The other 40 percent comes from two- to four-minute segments tied to CTN's partnership arrangements. For example, there is a partnership with CNN to provide news coverage. Additionally, CTN has partnered with the History Channel to provide segments such as "This Week in History," "Time Tunnels," and "Moments in Time." There's also a partnership with ESPN in which ESPN produces three-minute segments of sports news. In exchange, CTN broadcasts promotions for ESPN's popular "Sports Center" program.

There's even a partnership with Conde Nast Publications, publisher of *Glamour.* Through this arrangement, CTN presents "Glamour on Campus." Airing several times each week, it's a great market for *Glamour.* In fact, of the magazine's 12 million readers, 2 million are college students. *Glamour* staff members even tour 10 CTN campuses in the fall and spring and one spring-break location, distributing gift baskets and hosting auditions for the chance to be a guest host of CTN.

Of course, CTN finances its business by selling advertising on its network. Not surprisingly, advertisers are flocking to buy time on the network. Big names such as Coca-Cola, Hershey's, Nike, AT&T, Best Buy, Visa, Clairol Herbal Essences, and the United States military, helped account for the 61 percent increase in advertising business that CTN experienced from 2001 to 2002. Given that college-age students are hard to reach with traditional advertising (for example, they don't usually watch much TV), CTN has tapped a formula for success for a number of interested players.

Source: "College Television Network Viewership Reaches New Highs among 18–24 Target Audience," www.collegetelevision.com (accessed January 30, 2002); Kate Fitzgerald, "College Television Network: Ann E. Brown," *Advertising Age,* October 8, 2001, p. S20; and Jane Gottlieb, "Selling College Students, Via Niche TV," *Multichannel News,* June 11, 2001, www.tvinsite.com/multichannelnews/index (accessed October 2, 2002).

A joint venture is a more formal arrangement. Here, two or more organizations combine their strengths to create a new business.[18] Each organization will have partial ownership of the new joint venture. Recall from Chapter 10 that strategic alliances and partnerships are often used in the global arena.

Global Strategic Thinking

In Chapter 10, we discussed the global forces affecting today's businesses. We said competitive forces often encourage a business to go international with its operations. For example, global operations can provide access to cheaper labor, lowering the costs of production and reducing the firm's overall costs. Of course, one of the most basic reasons for going global is purely strategic—the business believes it can expand sales by having access to larger markets and expanded customer bases. In this section, we look at global strategy and explore some specific global entry strategies that businesses pursue.

Competing Globally

The main difference between being globally and domestically competitive is that in the case of global competition the firm's performance is measured against international standards. Management must identify the best companies in the world and use their performance as the standards to meet or beat.

The healthy global business must adopt an attitude of relentless improvement. It must deliberately seek pressures for innovation. It must monitor industry change. In these categories of competitiveness, globalization merely forces the firm to broaden its horizons.

Global Entry Strategies

export management firm

A firm located in the United States that sells products abroad for another business.

Although this thinking makes sense, a major issue remains unanswered. Once a business makes the strategic decision to go global, how is it done? How does the business go about moving from a domestic to an international operation? The answer is indeed complex. Here, we will address four common entry strategies that a business may use: an export management firm, licensing, a foreign sales office, and manufacturing abroad.

Export Management Firm

Some businesses, particularly small and midsize ones, have sound products that sell well in the United States. There may also be a market for these products in select foreign countries, but there is a problem. The business and its managers have no idea how to do business in the international arena. In simplest terms, no one in the firm has sufficient expertise to take the firm's products international. This is a real dilemma. The business has a great product with real global potential, but it doesn't have enough skill to make the transition happen. One answer for such a business is to use an **export management firm,** a company located in the United States that sells products abroad for another business.

Why would a small business use an export management firm? It gives the small business entry to international markets it could not otherwise reach. The export management firm does a lot of the tough work. Of course, the business makes two significant sacrifices. First, the export management firm gets a cut of the profits. Second, the business loses some control, particularly over how the product will be sold.

Licensing

A second entry strategy a business might use is **licensing,** whereby a business allows its products to be produced and distributed in other countries by a foreign company. There are many advantages to this approach. Like export management firms, licensing gives a business a fairly easy, low-cost entry into a foreign market. Further, much of the legwork is being done by a business that knows the country and knows the markets it wants to serve. There are two big concerns, though. First, the U.S. business must share its profits with the foreign business. Second—and this can be a major concern—the U.S. business must share certain sensitive information with the foreign business. For example, it must disclose special processes or ingredients so that production can take place. This disclosure can be dangerous; once the licensing arrangement ends, a possible competitor knows some of the U.S. firm's secrets.

licensing
An arrangement in which a business allows its products to be produced and distributed in other countries by a foreign company.

Foreign Sales Office

Some businesses sell directly in foreign markets by establishing **foreign sales offices** in the countries where they operate. The products are not produced in the foreign country, but they are sold and serviced by special operations there. Caterpillar is a good example of this approach. It has an extensive worldwide network of dealers who sell the large earth-moving equipment it makes. Caterpillar produces a machine in Illinois and ships it to its dealer in Lima, Peru. The local dealer handles the sales and service needs of customers in the Peruvian market. Caterpillar maintains control but works with the local dealer, which facilitates more sensitive and timely responses to the needs of customers in the foreign country.

foreign sales office
A special operation in a foreign country that sells and services products that were made domestically.

Manufacturing Abroad

Manufacturing abroad can be a demanding entry strategy for a U.S. business to take, so it is generally used by large companies. A U.S. business decides to both produce and sell its products abroad. Sometimes it establishes a separate operation in the desired foreign country and treats it as one of the businesses of the large (parent) company. When the foreign operation is owned as part of the larger business, it is known as a **wholly owned subsidiary.**

A second approach to manufacturing abroad that is frequently used is the joint venture route, which we discussed earlier. Remember, a joint venture is really a cooperative strategy in which companies (in this case from different countries) join to form a new business. There may be many strategic reasons for doing a joint venture. It gives companies a chance to share costs and risks, thus taking on projects too big to approach without support from more than one company. There are two other important strategic reasons for joint ventures. First, when a U.S. business forms a joint venture with a foreign business, it gains the knowledge of the market and how to deal with it that the foreign business has. This know-how helps break through some of the bottlenecks and mistakes that companies make

wholly owned subsidiary
A business that is owned as part of a larger business; may be a foreign subsidiary of a domestic firm.

THINK ABOUT THIS

1. Porter's general strategies apply to businesses as they engage in global operations as well as their domestic ventures. Which strategic approach do you think Sony has taken in the consumer electronics industry? Explain.

2. Which approach has Toyota taken in the automobile industry? How about Mercedes-Benz? Justify your reasoning.

3. When should a company planning a global strategy use a joint venture instead of setting up its own manufacturing facilities without help from a foreign partner?

when they don't know the people, customs, and markets fully. Second, in some cases, a joint venture is the only possible route of entry to a country. Some governments demand it as a condition of manufacturing in their countries.

Strategic Planning

In this chapter, we have discussed a number of important areas of business that must be addressed as decision makers begin to think strategically. We have noted that vision, mission, areas of competence, competitive advantage, and strategic approach must all be considered. In fact, these areas fit together to form the strategic planning process of the business.

strategic planning
A systematic way of analyzing and responding to a competitive environment.

Strategic planning is a systematic method of analyzing and responding to a competitive environment. The need for well-thought-out strategic planning has never been greater than it is in today's dynamic, ever-changing world. Strategic planning should be viewed as an ongoing process. It provides an overview and analysis of the business and its relevant environment. Then it prescribes an outline or action plan of how the business will proceed to capitalize on its strengths and minimize its weaknesses or threats.

There are many advantages to strategic planning. One advantage dominates: As an ongoing and active process, strategic planning keeps the business focused on change. It encourages the business to continually assess its business environment and search for ways to operate more effectively. By its very nature, strategic planning is future-oriented and proactive. While strategic planning helps the business map out a direction for the future, the process is fluid and flexible enough to deal with unpredictable events. In many ways, strategic planning is one of the most powerful tools in a businessperson's arsenal.

You will use strategic planning throughout your business career. You will refine and gain expertise in applying the ideas presented. You will build on the foundations of this model that we have discussed in this chapter.

Who in the business should be involved in strategic planning activities? Certainly, strategic planning is the unique responsibility of upper management. They have the broad, overall view of the business needed to provide a real strategic perspective. However, upper managers are increasingly realizing that they need input from people throughout the business as they develop strategic plans. They need information, outlooks, and insights from those employees who are closest to their customers, products, and services. Further, when employees have a hand in establishing strategic plans, they feel active ownership of the plans. They understand the reasons for objectives and may work harder to achieve them.

THE BIG PICTURE

The chapter you have just studied is perhaps the most central to the entire business operation. Consider where we have been so far in this course and what is left to do. We started the book by discussing what businesses are and how they fit together. Then we discussed decision makers and the stakeholders that depend on good, ethical decisions. We then moved to the mounds of information that can be gathered and assessed. In this chapter, we began the action phase of business planning and operation by discussing the kinds of strategies that are available. The next few chapters will get more involved in making those strategies work and ensuring that desired performance is achieved.

But consider this scenario: There are perhaps 25 million businesses in the United States today. Most are small, a few are medium to large, and a very small percentage are gigantic organizations operating in many different countries. There are also thousands of not-for-profit organizations that provide services to constituents. Is there a common tie among these millions of organizations? Indeed, there is. That common tie is that all businesses and organizations operate on the basis of some strategy that the organization's leaders have determined to be best for them. Of course, many of those strategies are the result of only informal planning, and perhaps no formal analyses or written strategic plans exist. But the strategies are in the minds of the business leaders that are owners or managers of the organizations. Even though the sizes and types of businesses vary widely, and the strategies used are diverse, the process of arriving at those strategies is essentially the same. Regardless of whether we are considering the corner laundry or General Motors, the process of strategic management exists and has common roots.

Summary

1. Successful businesses are those that match the abilities of the firm with the opportunities in the business environment. The business profile and the SWOT analysis are starting points for developing such a business focus.

   - What is a business profile?

   A business profile is an analysis of the strengths and the weaknesses of the business.

   - What is a SWOT analysis?

   A SWOT analysis is an assessment of the firm's strengths and weaknesses in comparison with the environmental threats and opportunities it faces. SWOT stands for *s*trengths, *w*eaknesses, *o*pportunities, and *t*hreats.

2. A successful SWOT analysis must be brutally honest in identifying ways the firm can realistically aspire to compete. In other words, the analysis must identify the firm's core competence, distinctive competence, and potential competitive advantage.

   - What is a core competence?

   A core competence is some activity or set of activities that a business performs very well or a quality that it possesses in abundance.

   - What is a distinctive competence?

   A distinctive competence is a core competence that the business is uniquely good at in comparison with rival firms.

   - What is a competitive advantage?

   A competence becomes a competitive advantage when consumers value it and the business is capable of exploiting it.

3. After the firm has successfully completed its SWOT analysis, it must determine how best to take advantage of the findings. This step requires the development of a competitive business strategy.

   - What is a competitive strategy?

   A competitive business strategy is the specific approach the business chooses to pursue for addressing its environment.

- What are the basic strategies a business might pursue?

There are three general strategies: (1) a low-cost leadership strategy, (2) a differentiation strategy, and (3) a focus strategy.

4. There are, of course, a range of other strategic approaches that contemporary businesses use on a regular basis.

- What are some of the popular strategic considerations being used today?

Three popular strategic approaches discussed in this chapter are diversification, acquisition, and cooperative strategies. Diversification can be closely related to the firm's core business, or it can be unrelated. Acquisition is often used to expand the scope of operations and provide quick entry into new markets. Finally, cooperative strategies, such as strategic alliances, partnerships, and joint ventures, are important options.

5. Many companies decide to compete in global markets in addition to their domestic market.

- How does a decision to compete globally affect the development of a business strategy?

The main difference is that the firm's performance is measured against international standards. Once that comparison has been completed, the firm must choose its global entry strategy. This chapter discussed four possible entry strategies: (1) using an export management firm, (2) licensing, (3) establishing foreign sales offices, and (4) manufacturing abroad.

6. Earlier in this text you learned about the large number of decision makers in business. Top management is one of those groups. Perhaps the most important decision-making role of top management is to direct the development of the SWOT analysis and the resultant strategy and objectives. When those activities are combined with a review of their results, we refer to the entire process as strategic planning.

- What is strategic planning?

Strategic planning is a systematic way of analyzing and responding to a competitive environment. It prescribes an action plan of how the business will proceed to capitalize on its strengths and minimize its weaknesses.

Key Terms

business focus, p. 300

business profile, p. 300

competitive advantage, p. 304

competitive strategy, p. 306

cooperative strategies, p. 312

core competence, p. 303

differentiation strategy, p. 307

distinctive competence, p. 303

diversification, p. 311

economies of scale, p. 309

experience curve, p. 309

export management firm, p. 314

focus strategy, p. 308

foreign sales office, p. 315

licensing, p. 315

low-cost leadership strategy, p. 307

strategic planning, p. 316

sustainable competitive advantage, p. 305

SWOT analysis, p. 300

wholly owned subsidiary, p. 315

1. Contact the president of a campus fraternity, sorority, or club. Meet with him or her and do an informal SWOT analysis of the organization.

2. Southwest Airlines has decided to extend its routes nationally. Given our discussion of its strengths, weaknesses, competences, and competitive advantages, what concerns do you have with this move? Write your analysis in a one-page report.

3. In teams, brainstorm and choose a business that you think would be fun to start and could be profitable. What environmental and competitive information do you need to know to help ensure success?

4. Use one of the Internet search engines to find as much information as you can for exercise 3. Outline the information and include the address for each website you used.

5. Find a small business in your locality that competes with large national chains or franchises. Casually visit the business. How do you think it competes in the shadows of the larger firms? In other words, what strategy does it seem to be pursuing? Outline your analysis.

6. Interview the owner of the business from exercise 5 to determine the impact of the large competitors on the smaller firm.

Exercises and Applications

Striking the Right Chord

In 1997, Edward Steele, CEO of Singing Machine Co. faced a bleak picture. Annual sales were only $6 million and falling. The company had already filed for Chapter 11 bankruptcy protection, and many experts questioned whether the business would survive. But that was then. Today, the business is thriving, and it was even selected as number one on *BusinessWeek*'s list of hot growth companies for 2002.

How did Steele alter Singing Machine's prospects? The company's "fortunes turned around after Steele made the decision in the late 1990s to sell home-karaoke machines instead of $2000 nightclub models." These home versions "play special compact disks that let users connect the machine to TV sets and read lyrics on the screen." It was a clever and well-timed marketing move.

But there was another key piece to the strategic turnaround—a partnership with MTV. Singing Machine targets the music teens and young adults enjoy, and it adds this youth-oriented image by placing the MTV logo on its machines. In fact, Singing Machine's best-seller is the MTV-brand model, complete with built-in TV screen which sells for $199.99. Singing Machine appears to have found its niche. The partnering strategy has been so effective that Singing Machine has now reached an agreement with Nickelodeon, hoping to tap an even younger (under age 10) market. The Nickelodeon-brand karaoke machine carries a low price tag of $49.99.

Some experts worry that the company's recent success is simply riding the wave of a fad. Accordingly, they argue that Singing Machine's growth will soon fade. Steele, however, believes that he can double sales by introducing some innovative product concepts. One is a "$119.99 portable karaoke with a tiny built-in camera that records a singer's performance." Steele also "envisions karaokes with chips that record and change a singer's voice from male to female, machines with DVD players, and others that can process MP3 files." Steele believes that the only thing that can block Singing Machine from becoming a major company is if "people stop singing."

FROM THE PAGES OF

BusinessWeek

Decision Questions

1. Sometimes creative strategic thinking is "born out of desperation." Discuss how the Singing Machine example demonstrates this idea.

2. Given your reading of the article summary and your understanding of the market, do you feel Singing Machines products are simply fads?

3. Singing Machine's leaders believe that the home-karaoke market in the United States alone may be $150 million a year. However, if the market becomes too attractive, major companies will be tempted to begin competing. If that happens, what strategy would you advise the leaders of Singing Machine to pursue?

Source: Aixa M. Pascual, "Striking the Right Chord," *BusinessWeek,* June 10, 2002, www.businessweek.com/magazine/content/02_23/b3786606.htm (accessed July 3, 2002).

References

1. Melanie Wells, "On His Watch," *Forbes,* February 18, 2002, pp. 93–94.

2. Mary Coulter, *Strategic Management in Action,* 2nd ed. (Upper Saddle River, NJ: Prentice Hall, 2002), p. 126.

3. Charles W. L. Hill and Gareth R. Jones, *Strategic Management: An Integrated Approach,* 4th ed. (Boston: Houghton Mifflin, 1998), p. 217.

4. Michael E. Porter, *Competitive Strategy: Techniques for Analyzing Industries and Competitors* (New York: Free Press, 1980).

5. "Width Sizing," www.newbalancewebexpress.com/width_sizing.htm (accessed June 24, 2002).

6. "The Right Stuff," www.macaronigrill.com (accessed October 1, 2002).

7. Walter S. Mossberg, "A Device That Stops Telemarketers?" *The Wall Street Journal,* May 8, 2002, p. D4.

8. William J. Holstein, "Samsung's Golden Touch," *Fortune,* April 1, 2002, pp. 89–94.

9. Zamboni website, www.zamboni.com/about.html (accessed July 11, 2002); and Arthur's Wine Shop website, www.arthurs-wine.com/aboutus2.htm (accessed July 11, 2002).

10. "Investor Relations," Best Buy website, www.bestbuy.com (accessed October 2, 2002).

11. "Darden Restaurants," www.darden.com/darden.asp (accessed June 28, 2002).

12. "The Walt Disney Company," http://bsuvc.bsu.edu/~JRBROWN/profile.html (accessed June 28, 2002).

13. Nestlé website, www.nestle.com/all_about/at_a_glance.index.html (accessed June 28, 2002); and Honda website, www.hondacorporate.com (accessed June 28, 2002).

14. Pui-Wing Tam and Scott Thurm, "Married at Last, H-P, Compaq Face Real Test," *The Wall Street Journal,* May 8, 2002, pp. A1, A4.

15. "Cadbury Schweppes Acquires Dandy's Chewing Gum Brands for 201 Million Pounds Sterling," www.prnewswires.com (accessed October 2, 2002).

16. Coulter, p. 268.

17. Arthur A. Thompson, Jr., and A. J. Strickland, Jr., *Strategic Management: Concepts and Cases,* 12th ed. (Boston: McGraw Hill-Irwin, 2001), pp. 172–74.

18. www.strategic-alliances.org/pubs/BPWpreview.pdf (accessed July 1, 2002).

13

Acquiring and Using Resources

Lands' End, the clothing retailer of choice for millions of Americans and Europeans, recently merged with Sears. Why? From Sears' viewpoint, adding a line of Lands' End clothes upgrades the image of the department store chain, and the merger also brings in the talent to do online marketing of Sears' products. But why would Lands' End want to merge with a large chain in which it risks becoming just another brand in the clothing department? The answer may be that Lands' End wanted to grow more rapidly than it could with the resources it had available. Although Lands' End has been successful with its direct marketing via the Internet and catalogs and has a dozen or so outlets, achieving major growth requires a different kind of strategy and far more resources than the company has available.

Obviously, Lands' End would need financial resources to underwrite its growth strategy. But if the company wanted to expand its brick-and-mortar exposure, it would require major fixed assets or leases of stores across the country. In addition, selling in a fixed market such as Denver or Atlanta would require intensive marketing in those cities. Further, a greater number of people would need to be hired to staff the stores. Sears has agreed to introduce Lands' End clothes in 870 stores in 2002. There is no way Lands' End could grow that fast without the resources Sears provides.

In Chapter 12, you learned that businesses have a wide range of strategies to use in competing in their industries. However, regardless of the strategy adopted, implementing that strategy will require substantial resources. In the case of Lands' End, needed resources for an independent growth strategy would have included physical resources such as buildings, human resources to staff stores, information resources to use in determining locations for stores and marketing, and perhaps most important, a quantum increase in financial resources.

No business can operate without resources. Resources are the fuel for businesses just as gasoline is the fuel for automobiles. If a business has insufficient resources or an inappropriate mix of resources, it will operate just as poorly as a car with not enough or the wrong kind of fuel. Businesses rely on four major fuels: human resources, physical resources, financial resources, and information resources. Business managers must be able to balance the need for each resource and plan how to acquire each one. This is a challenging responsibility and an important aspect of building a successful business, as indicated in the model of a successful business.

After studying this chapter, you should be able to:

1. Explain the integrative nature of resource acquisition and use.

2. Identify the two major challenges a manager must overcome in acquiring and using resources.

3. Identify the three major challenges in human resources management and briefly explain some of the issues involved in each challenge.

4. Explain the major issues involved in the acquisition of physical resources.

5. Describe the major characteristics of the acquisition and use of financial resources.

6. Identify uses for and sources of information resources.

The Integrative Nature of Resource Acquisition and Use

Resources are the lifeblood of a company. They provide the basic ingredients it needs to succeed. **Resources** are the people, physical materials, financial assets, and information the firm's managers use to produce a product or service. Business managers spend much of their time acquiring resources, providing an appropriate mix of resources, managing them, and using them in the firm's operations.

Resource acquisition and use is one of the most integrative topics confronting managers. Resource acquisition demands that managers work with a host of people throughout the company to create an acceptable balance. A manager cannot decide to hire 10 more employees without consulting with those in charge of financial resources. Similarly, acquiring new equipment not only takes financial resources but also may require extra training of employees in order to use the equipment effectively. Even those in charge of financial aspects of the firm cannot simply decide to issue more stock or invest excess cash without checking with managers of other areas.

The integrative nature of resources is evidenced by two sets of relationships. The first is synergy. The second is opportunity cost.

> **resources**
> The people, physical materials, financial assets, and information a firm's managers use to produce a product or service.

Synergy

If a business adds financial resources, it can purchase new technology-related equipment. In turn, this equipment may help employees work more efficiently. Thus, a change in one resource ripples through the business. It affects physical resources such as technology, and it enhances the productivity of human resources. The same is true for other investments. If a business invests capital to increase the number of trained employees, productivity will go up. These examples illustrate **synergy,** the combined action of two resources so that their total effect is greater than the sum of the effects taken independently. Simply defined, synergy means 2 plus 2 equals 5.

Consider Dell, which we already know is a manufacturing firm. Dell has millions of dollars of equipment, thousands of employees, and of course, substantial financial resources. Its processes are highly automated, as you can see by going to the Dell website. Suppose Dell's top management decides to further automate a particular process. That plan will take additional financial resources to buy the equipment. But increasing the amount of investment in equipment will make existing employees more efficient and capable of producing more computers per day. This increase will, in turn, generate additional revenues, which will more than replace the resources that were invested in the first place.

The integration of resources is just as real in service firms as in manufacturing firms. A business that provides a service will likely have fewer physical resources than a goods-producing firm. Still, if managers invest financial resources in the purchase of more technology, that technology may help employees perform more efficiently and effectively. If the employees do indeed become more efficient, the business can avoid having to hire additional employees, even as additional services are delivered.

Consider a small company that does termite inspection and treatment. The owner has 20 technicians who call on customers to inspect their houses. If the owner does nothing more than buy them pagers or cellular phones, efficiency may increase since technicians can now communicate with their boss regarding which house to inspect next. This capability reduces their time on the road since they do not have to return to the shop for their next instructions. If a handheld computer is added to each truck, technicians can call up the history of a house to see when the last treatment was done and where problems have been in the past. This knowledge allows the technicians to provide better service and increases the revenues of the business. Further, because the technicians are more efficient, the increase in revenues need not be accompanied by an equivalent increase in staff.

These examples illustrate the interrelated nature of resources. Increasing one resource may increase the capacity of another resource. Enhancing technology enables people to operate more efficiently. Business managers look for ways to build synergy, and they make decisions with that concept in mind.

Opportunity Costs and Trade-Offs

Although the addition of one resource often makes another resource more productive, the integrative nature of resource acquisition also requires trade-offs. A useful concept in understanding the trade-offs that are necessary in resource acquisition is that of opportunity cost, which we introduced in our discussion of financial markets in Chapter 9. If a manager uses funds for one activity, the manager gives up the opportunity to use those funds for some alternative activity. Some opportunity is forgone, or lost. The value of the best alternative that a firm sacrifices to pursue a different option is known as the **opportunity cost.**[1]

You encounter the idea of opportunity costs and other trade-offs fairly often. For example, if you use all your discretionary money to buy a car, you will not also be able to buy a computer system. The value you could have received from that computer is your opportunity cost. If your college uses its library funds to purchase books, those same funds cannot also be used to order magazines or journals. The value that could have been derived from those magazines and journals is the opportunity cost. If a business purchases a new conveyor belt system to move packaged parts from one part of the plant to another, it may not have funds to replace an aging drill press. The value (such as higher quality and fewer breakdowns) that a new drill press could have provided is the opportunity cost.

It is important for managers to understand the concept of opportunity costs and trade-offs when considering the acquisition and use of resources. For example, a manager may want to hire a new staff person in the training department and also equip a new multimedia training room. Yet the new training facility may cost as much as the annual salary plus benefits of the staff person. The manager must choose between personnel and equipment. Each has value, and either decision will result in some value being forgone. The manager must decide which option contributes the greater value as the business pursues its goals and strategies. The manager must balance the trade-offs that occur when choosing resources.

Note that synergy and opportunity cost work against each other. Synergy suggests that adding one resource may make another resource more productive. Opportunity cost, on the other hand, suggests that adding one resource may preclude adding another. Both of these concepts are the result of the interrelatedness of resources.

The Flow of Resources

Another concept that is important for both resource acquisition and use is the flow or movement of resources. For example, when a business purchases raw materials, those raw materials move from suppliers into the operations area of the business. In turn, cash moves from the business to the suppliers as payment for the materials. As the business hires additional employees, the employees enter the firm in exchange for wages or salaries, which leave the firm. As the business adds new equipment, funds leave the business to pay for that equipment. Accordingly, resources are added that increase the capacity of the business to perform. Other resources, in this case money, leave the business.

The movement of resources does not stop here. The materials, people, and equipment that have been gained are used to produce products. Those products leave the business as they are sold to customers. Customers pay for the products, which returns cash to the business. This process of resources moving into, through, and back out of the firm is a dynamic and continual process.

Resource Challenges

There are two important challenges that managers face in dealing with resource acquisition and use. The first is to have an adequate *amount* of resources. The second is to have the *right mix* of resources.

The Total Amount of Resources

Managers almost never have sufficient resources. Even in the best of times, more staff would be desirable, additional equipment would increase productivity, and more and better raw materials would lead to better products. Consider the class for which you are reading this book. It would be nice if the class were small and were taught in a comfortable classroom with plush seats and state-of-the-art multimedia equipment. If you are indeed in one of these rooms, count yourself lucky.

However, limited resources often dictate that the course be taught in large lecture sections. Further, many buildings are not equipped for optimal learning. If the school had all the resources it desired, it could have excellent facilities and still have funds to offer scholarships and pay faculty members high salaries. Since it does not, administrators must make trade-offs. Perhaps by keeping the size of your class large and not investing in the latest technology, the school was able to offer additional financial aid packages that permitted you or your friends to attend the college.

Capital is always limited. It must be generated through sales or acquired from external sources. These sources may not be adequate: Banks may refuse to lend as much as requested, investors may not be willing to underwrite additional equipment, or sales may not reach desired levels. Any of these events may cause the amount of resources available to be less than desired. It is important for managers to understand that funds may be scarce. It is also important for lower-level workers to understand that the firm cannot generate additional funds just by asking someone for more capital.

The Right Mix of Resources

Even though the overall amount of resources is perhaps a more severe problem, a second challenge is to have the right resources in place at the right time. Physical resources, for example, are not easily reallocated from one area to another. Falling demand for a product produced at one plant may suggest that resources should be reallocated to a plant that produces a different product that is in high demand. However, since physical resources are fixed, they cannot be transferred easily from plant to plant. In fact, it may be impossible to get the desired efficiency.

Even human resources can reflect this problem. Dell, for example, has major production facilities in Austin, Texas and in Nashville, Tennessee. If products produced in Nashville surge in demand while a product made in Austin tapers off, Dell may find that it has the right total number of employees, but too many of them are in Austin and too few are in Nashville. Thus, the company has adequate resources, but they are in the wrong place.

Managers struggle to predict production, marketing, and distribution needs so that resources can be available in the proper mix when they are needed. Sometimes they can rely on past trends to help in this determination. However, when they are dealing with new products or new markets or undertaking new strategies, predicting the needed resource mix is very difficult.

THINK ABOUT THIS

1. If synergy suggests that 2 plus 2 equals 5, what does opportunity cost suggest?
2. Consider the resource challenges just discussed. How are they interrelated?
3. Think of additional examples or resource challenges at your college. How can they be addressed?

Human Resources

CEOs and presidents often say their most important asset is their people. Chapter 16 will discuss how to maximize the productivity of workers. Our intent here is to consider how to acquire the quality and quantity of human resources necessary for the efficient operation of a business.

As we wrote in Chapter 5, human resources consist of top management, middle managers, professional staff, first-line supervisors, and nonmanagerial workers. It is important that each position be staffed with the best people possible given the constraints of budgets. To achieve quality and quantity goals, managers should address three challenges:

1. Accurately forecasting human resources needs.
2. Recruiting potential candidates.
3. Selecting the best talent possible.

Forecasting Human Resources Needs

Forecasting human resources needs follows the logical process outlined in Figure 13.1. First, managers must determine the firm's strategy and the impact that strategy will have on human resources needs. For example, they must decide how many employees the business will need to make its strategies succeed. They must also decide the type of backgrounds and skills those employees will need to possess. Managers ask a basic question: What type of workforce do we need to have a successful strategy?

Second, managers must analyze the characteristics of their available workforce. They must examine the number of workers they have now, their skills, and their abilities to perform needed tasks. Managers must also determine whether this available workforce will be sufficient to meet the needs of the future. To make that determination, they must predict the number of retirements, promotions, and terminations of employees. They also try to gauge whether the existing workforce can be trained in the needed new skills. Through this process, managers are trying to answer this question: Is there a gap between the available employees and skills we have and those we will need?

Finally managers ask: If there is a gap, what types of people do we need to bring to the business? The answer may simply be that the business needs more people, but increasingly, the answer is that the business must bring in people with new talents, skills, and backgrounds.[2]

This forecasting challenge is especially difficult when the business is growing rapidly or is facing a turbulent environment. It is also difficult when technologies are changing rapidly and skill sets must be continually upgraded. Even the task of hiring lower-level workers is more difficult today than in the past because of the changes in equipment, software, and networking among workstations.

Businesses that are experiencing mergers or acquisitions or those facing extremely tough, competitive times may face another problem. They may need to downsize if they find that their current level of business is insufficient to support the staff they now have. The recent recession caused many firms to consider whether or not they should downsize. **Downsizing** is reducing the number of employees in a business. This process is painful for all involved. Accordingly, businesses want to be sure that they downsize

> **downsizing**
> Reducing the number of employees in a business.

FIGURE 13.1

Overview of Human Resources Forecasting

carefully. Downsizing often eliminates those functions and people that are least critical to a business's success. Downsizing may also involve outsourcing of some jobs. The determination of how downsizing should proceed depends on the success of the human resources forecasting the business has done.

Recruiting Potential Employees

The challenge of recruiting potential employees changes with the times and with industry situations. Changing demographics and economic forces affect the pool of available talent. For example, hiring fast-food workers used to be a simple task when the number of teenagers searching for jobs far exceeded the number of jobs. But now fast-food restaurants are hiring retirees and other older workers because there are simply not enough teenagers around who are willing to work there. College graduates in the early 1990s faced a very tough job market. In the late 1990s, a very promising market provided many jobs, especially in technology-related areas. By 2002, jobs had become scarce again. Look back at Figure 7.3. What would you predict will be the situation in 2015, especially as baby boomers retire in greater numbers?

Employees can be recruited from many different sources, ranging from ads in newspapers to employment agencies, trade associations, and other companies. Employees may also come from within the organization when someone is either promoted or transferred to a new position. Table 13.1 illustrates both internal and external sources of employees for a few selected positions.

Internal sources of employees are individuals within the company who are interested in and qualified to fill the job. Note that in virtually every position listed, the internal candidates include others at the same level and employees one level down. This situation

College job fairs, like the one pictured here, can be an excellent way for students to meet a wide array of employers. Why do you think businesses find it valuable and important to attend college job fairs?

TABLE 13.1

Sources of Employees for Selected Positions

Position	Internal Sources	External Sources
Nonmanagerial		
Administrative assistant	Other assistants or other positions with clerical skills.	Newspaper ads, employment agencies, recommendations.
Machine operator	Operators of similar machines, apprenticeship programs.	Newspaper ads, employment agencies, recommendations, trade schools.
Salesperson	Production or service workers, professional staff, sales personnel in other territories or products.	Newspaper ads, employment agencies, colleges and universities, recommendations.
Supervisory		
First-line supervisor	Other supervisors, related staff positions, promotion from nonmanagerial ranks.	Newspaper ads, employment agencies, vocational schools, recommendations.
Midmanagement/ professional staff		
Middle manager	Other middle managers, promotion from staff, sales, or production supervisor positions.	Newspaper ads, employment agencies, colleges and universities, recommendations.
Professional staff	Related professional staff, promotions from lower-level positions in same area.	Newspaper ads, employment agencies, colleges and universities, trade associations, recommendations.
Top management		
Vice president (VP)	Other VPs, high-level managers in headquarters or divisions.	Specialized newspapers, trade associations, headhunters, recommendations.
Executive vice president	VPs.	Specialized newspapers, trade associations, recommendations, headhunters.
President	VPs or executive VPs.	Specialized newspapers, trade associations, recommendations, headhunters.
Board member	Top levels of management, including controller and general counsel.	Contacts in high levels of other companies, headhunters.

allows for both lateral transfers and promotions. A *lateral transfer* means a transfer from a position at one level in the company to another position at the same level but with different responsibilities. Many individuals want this extra experience. Even though the position is not a promotion and may not pay more, the experience often prepares them for later promotions. Filling a position through promotion means advancing one of the people who holds a lower-level position into the open position.

Companies often look for candidates internally before looking externally. There are compelling reasons for filling job openings from within. First, promoting someone from a lower level is psychologically rewarding. It serves as reinforcement and recognition for the good work that person has done. Further, it signifies management's confidence that the employee will continue to perform well. Second, filling the job with someone at the same level (a lateral transfer) has the advantage of broadening an employee's experience base. Third, selecting someone from either the same or a lower level creates an opportunity for someone else to advance. Fourth, an employee promoted or transferred from within already knows the organization, its culture, and its method of operation. This knowledge makes training faster and easier.

Searching externally is often a wise decision when higher-level positions are being filled. Outside candidates can bring a fresh perspective to the position and may have experience that internal candidates simply do not have. An external search may also be needed if there are no highly qualified candidates inside the firm.

Now look at the external sources of employees in Table 13.1. Note the differences in sources as the positions move from lower to higher levels of responsibility. Nonmanagerial candidates are often found simply through ads in the local newspaper or contacts with a local, state, or private employment agency. Companies filling sales positions sometimes find applicants through ads in newspapers, but many companies prefer to recruit on college campuses. Candidates for technical and supervisory positions may be found in trade schools. Managerial and staff positions are still advertised in newspapers, but other sources such as colleges and universities are also tapped. Higher-level management people, such as vice presidents or presidents, may be located through specialized newspapers such as *The Wall Street Journal* and through contacts in trade associations. Some trade associations even run placement services for their members. Organizations filling the highest-level positions may also use specialized employment agencies that focus strictly on upper-level employees. These agencies are often referred to as *headhunters*.

An increasingly popular source of candidates for many jobs is the Internet. For example, you can consult the Southwest Airlines website to find what jobs are open. The listings include the requirements for each position and the benefits offered. Southwest has over 35,000 employees, 81 percent of whom are unionized. It received 194,821 applications in 2001, and it hired 6,406 new employees. Table 13.2 shows a typical job listing for a customer service position.[3]

To ensure a broad and diverse pool of candidates, a company should take steps to advertise and recruit candidates in all logical markets. In addition to expanding the pool of candidates, these actions help make sure that the company stays within the legal frameworks dealing with recruiting. The business should generate a set of qualified candidates who meet the needs of the business while reflecting the demographic makeup of the relevant labor market. (For more about the benefits of employee diversity, refer to Chapter 7.)

Selecting the Best Candidate

Once enough qualified job candidates have been identified, the next task is to identify the best candidates. The selection process must be done carefully. Managers must screen candidates on the basis of predetermined criteria for the job.

Return to the Southwest Airlines listings in Table 13.2. Note that the requirements of the job are listed, as well as its duties. The customer service representative needs to have great communication skills, have a high school diploma, and be able to work well under time pressures.

Managers interviewing potential employees must be careful to focus the interview on job-related issues. It is against the law to ask questions related to race, gender, religion, marital status, or age—and if you are the interviewee, you do not need to answer such questions.

TABLE 13.2

Job Opening at
Southwest Airlines

Southwest Airlines Ground Operations Department—Customer Service Agent

Updated January 15, 2002

Position title: Customer service agent

General purpose: Customer Service Agents provide friendly service to customers by selling airline tickets, issuing boarding passes, checking baggage, and providing general flight information in airport locations.

Locations: All Southwest Airlines Airports

Qualifications and requirements:

- At least 18 years old.
- High school diploma or GED.
- Excellent communication skills.
- Well groomed and physically fit.
- Typing ability or keyboard skills.
- Ability to work efficiently under time constraints.
- Able to lift up to 70 pounds repetitively.
- Available to work shifts, weekends, holidays, and overtime.
- Weight must be of such proportion to height that a neat appearance is maintained and physical ability to perform all functions is not hindered. Only standard uniform sizes are available. Men's uniforms range in waist size from 27 to 42 inches. Women's uniforms range in size from 0 to 18. No tailor-made uniforms are permitted. If hired, you must sustain compliance with the Appearance and Physical Performance Standards Policy throughout your employment.
- Able to attend 2 1/2 weeks of unpaid training in Dallas (expenses paid).
- Able to read and write English, bilingual skills encouraged but not required.
- Must be a U.S. citizen or have authorization to work in the United States as defined in the Immigration Reform Act of 1986.

Pay:

	1st Year	2nd Year
California and Baltimore	$9.29/hr.	$9.91/hr.
All Other Locations	$8.50/hr.	$9.29/hr.

All pay rates are contingent upon current contracts.

Source: Southwest Airlines website, www.southwest.com (accessed October 2, 2002).

Managers must ensure that the business does not discriminate or otherwise violate laws relating to the hiring process. For example, all those who interview candidates must be careful to restrict questions to job-related issues. It is illegal to ask questions on application forms or in interviews about a candidate's race, gender, marital or family status, religion, or national origin. In addition, a business should keep its diversity goals in mind when making selection decisions (as we discussed in Chapter 7).

The selection process becomes more rigorous as the business recruits for higher-level positions. Lower-level workers may be given skills tests and then be interviewed by a single manager or by members of the human resources department's recruiting team.

Higher-level positions demand more in-depth analysis of the candidate. A number of people may be involved in interviewing and in selection decisions. Candidates may be invited back for second or third interviews or may spend a full day or two at the firm to assess whether there is a good match between their qualifications and the needs of the business.

Application forms routinely ask for references. Managers should always check those references to verify the information provided. This task should be done for all positions at all levels. Talking to references will also help determine if there is a good fit between the person and the position.

After the analysis of the application, the interview, and the reference checks, managers are ready to choose the best candidate. They should consult with everyone who has been involved in the selection process, particularly those who will be working with the successful candidate. Only when all concerned are in general agreement should an offer be made.

Outsourcing Human Resources

In the next section, on physical resources, we will note that materials can be either produced in-house or outsourced (purchased from another company). These two options are also true of human resources. We have discussed obtaining human resources through schools, other companies, employment agencies, and ads in the media. A remaining method is to outsource human resources.

Human resources outsourcing means contracting with temporary help agencies or with consulting firms to provide the people a firm needs. The individuals technically work for the outside company, but they do their work at the host company's location. They are paid by their own company, and the amount of benefits (such as vacations and sick leave) they receive comes from their own company rather than the host company at which they work.

Consider the following example. Nims & Associates is a California-based computer consulting firm. It specializes in providing staff to do computer training for large companies. Nims' employees are college graduates who are well trained in computer information systems and who can communicate well with other employees. Companies contract with Nims to provide training for their workers over an extended time period. This approach saves the companies from having to hire their own trainers. When all of a firm's employees have been trained on the prescribed software, Nims' employees move on to the next client—or, as often happens, begin teaching the next version of desired software to the large firm's employees.[4]

The advantage of outsourcing workers is that they are totally contract labor. The company does not have to go through the hiring process, provide benefits, or worry about promotion and retirements. Outsourcing personnel also provides a smoothing effect in regard to the size of the workforce. Since contract labor has no long-term arrangement with the company, outsourced workers can provide assistance only when needed. When the extra workload ends, no permanent employees are laid off.

In addition to outsourcing individual workers, companies are increasingly outsourcing entire functions or departments. The trend in business today is to outsource everything that can be done more efficiently outside the company, including both products and services. For example, many companies—and perhaps even your college—contract out their cafeteria operations. Many companies outsource their maintenance or repair services and their security services. Some even contract out some human resources functions, such as the administration of employee benefits. Profile 13.1 describes Hewitt Associates, which specializes in designing employee benefit systems for clients. If the client so desires, Hewitt can also operate the system.

human resources outsourcing
Contracting with temporary help agencies or with consulting firms to provide the people a firm needs.

OUTSOURCING WITH HEWITT ASSOCIATES   PROFILE 13.1

Hewitt Associates was begun in 1940 by Edwin (Ted) Hewitt as an insurance brokerage firm. He and his associates soon decided to change from selling insurance to consulting in the area of benefits administration. Today the firm has over 13,000 associates (employees) in 80 offices in 37 countries. Its clients include more than half of the Fortune 500 companies and a host of smaller companies. It handles 53 million human resources-related transactions a year for more than 13 million employees of client companies such as Johnson & Johnson, Nokia, Continental Airlines, and the Royal Bank of Scotland.

Hewitt's activities include several unique aspects of human resource management. One is benefits administration consulting. In this part of the company, consultants work with clients to develop administrative systems for their employee benefits. Computer specialists and others work with the client to design an information system that automates as much of the information as possible. They carefully check the system to make sure it works for the client. Once the system is totally operable and has been fully tested, the consultants move on to another client.

The second part of Hewitt Associates' business actually operates a system that the consultants have designed. This group of people will work for a specific client over an extended period of time to answer questions and enter decisions from individual employees in the client company. Employees who need information about their benefits call a number that is answered in Lincolnshire, Illinois, not at their own company. They may not even know that the person on the other end of the line is not in their own corporate headquarters building.

The benefit to the client company of having Hewitt design and operate its benefits administration system is that the company can go about its primary mission and outsource a complex but secondary part of the firm's overall operation.

Source: Hewitt Associates website, www.hewitt.com (accessed October 2, 2002).

Some companies take outsourcing even further. One company advertises to small businesses that it "wants to become your human resources department." Its ad observes that most small businesses do not have the expertise to handle their own human resources issues. For a fee, the specialist firm will contract with the client to perform all its human resources activities, from payroll processing to benefits administration to providing temporary employees and helping recruit employees throughout the firm.

THINK ABOUT THIS

1. Why is the geographic labor market so much broader for higher-level jobs than for lower-level positions?

2. What changes in hiring practices might we expect as the baby boom generation ages?

3. Why is outsourcing human resources appealing to large companies? to small businesses?

Physical Resources

At the start of this chapter, we noted that businesses use four important types of resources: human, physical, financial, and information. This section focuses on the **physical resources,** which include fixed assets, such as land, buildings, and equipment; raw materials that will be used in creating the firm's products; and general supplies used in the operation of the business.

The key to effective acquisition of all four types of resources is planning. Planning is especially important in the acquisition of physical resources, both fixed assets and the raw materials used in production. As you read this section, keep in mind our discussion at the outset of this chapter about trade-offs and the interrelatedness of the different kind of resources.

Fixed assets are extremely capital intensive. A large amount of capital is required to build or purchase the facilities, and they may be used for more than 20 years. Overestimating or underestimating the amount of fixed assets needed can be a fatal flaw in the operation of a business. Thus, it is extremely important to forecast fixed-asset needs accurately. This forecast is certainly true in manufacturing industries because of the production equipment needed. It is also true for some service businesses. Recall, for example, that Southwest Airlines is considered a service business even though its airplanes may cost over $30 million each. Even a smaller service business, such as a doctor's office or a consulting firm, will have significant fixed-asset purchases when it is first started.

Careful planning for the acquisition of raw material and other production-related purchases is also important because of the need for scheduling. The production of products can move no faster than the availability of raw materials. Yet too much raw material at one time means excessive inventory, which must be paid for, stored, insured, protected, counted, moved around a warehouse, shipped to other plants, and possibly discarded if the company's needs change. Holding materials in inventory represents a major cost for business.

The Make-or-Buy Decision

One of the most critical decisions facing firms that produce goods for sale is the **make-or-buy decision.** The managers of a business must decide whether to manufacture a product in-house or buy it from a supplier. There are two types of make-or-buy decisions. First, managers must decide whether to make a given product in-house or have other people make it for them. Second, for any product they do produce themselves, they must decide what percentage of the total process they want to do in-house.

A business can make an entire product and package it, market it, and ship it to customers, or it can outsource the product. **Product outsourcing** means that the firm purchases a product or component of a product from another company. Thus, the make-or-buy decision is a decision about whether or not to outsource.

If the manager chooses to outsource the product, the business purchases the product already completed and possibly already packaged with the firm's name and logo. In the extreme, managers can arrange to have another firm build a product to their specifications, package it, and ship it directly to their customers. That way, they need not invest in production facilities at all. They can concentrate their efforts on marketing the product. If a business decides to outsource production of a product, it may have to pay more for the product than it would cost to make it in-house. However, the managers do not have to tie up money in capital equipment. In some cases, they may even save money because the other firm can produce the product more cheaply than they can. Many large companies, especially those that are unionized, are finding that outsourcing is both more efficient in the short run and less capital intensive in the long run.

Outsourcing is a good example of the interaction between financial, human, and physical resources. Although outsourcing requires considerably fewer human resources and a smaller investment in physical resources, it does require close cooperation and coordination between the finance department, the human resources department, and the operations area of the firm. Issues of quality, timeliness, and total cost must be resolved before a final decision can be made.

The second type of make-or-buy decision relates to the purchase or manufacture of components that go into manufactured products. General Motors, for example, has hundreds of suppliers producing thousands of products that become parts of its cars. These products range from seat belts and windshield wiper blades to tires, batteries, windshields, and seats. It might be possible for GM to make all these components. Yet it would be economically unwise because of the investment needed to develop the factory capability.

Acquiring Fixed Assets

Manufacturing firms own millions of dollars of fixed assets. These are the buildings and equipment that are used to produce products. Acquiring major equipment or facilities involves a number of people within a firm. Building a new factory requires the combined efforts of financial managers, production managers, legal staff, human resources managers, site acquisition experts, public relations staff, and many others. Top managers are involved in the decision to build new facilities due to the great cost involved and the impact the building will have on the community. Many people in the community are also involved. Local government must provide infrastructure, the combination of roads, sewers, utilities, fire and police protection, and other services necessary to build and operate a plant. Local chamber of commerce representatives may help get tax relief and other enticements to encourage the company to build the plant.

Locating the Facilities

Locating sites for new manufacturing plants—or for other businesses such as retail shopping malls—is a very involved process. Site location decisions must be made at the regional, local, and individual site level. Some factors to consider are the proximity to customers, closeness to suppliers, total cost of construction, available infrastructure, availability of quality labor, government regulation or encouragement, and the overall business climate.[5]

Once a decision has been made to build or expand in a community, managers must decide whether to build on a new site, remodel the current plant, or purchase an existing building. A totally new site is sometimes referred to as a greenfield site. The term *greenfield* comes from the fact that many new manufacturing sites, such as the Mitsubishi Motors plant in Illinois, were built where cornfields had been. For new sites, managers must purchase the site and get building permits—an onerous task, to say the least. Residents of the area may resist the company's attempts to purchase or rezone the property. They may fear a decline in their property values and worry about the possibility of hazardous waste production.

It is frequently controversial when a company like Mitsubishi buys producing farmland to build its plant. What advantages does a community gain by having a Mitsubishi plant in its locale?

Companies may decide to purchase or remodel existing facilities rather than build on a greenfield site. This option is often faster and may be cheaper, but the decisions are no less critical. If the site is currently being used by the company, arrangements must be made to move production to other facilities while remodeling this one for its new use. That, of course, will trigger extensive planning at the other affected site. If the company decides to purchase a plant, then it must negotiate with the current owner to determine the appropriate price, the amount of equipment that stays with the plant, and the method of payment. This series of events again illustrates how interrelated the resource acquisition decisions are.

Building the Facilities

Once the company gets permission to build, the site must be designed, equipment must be purchased and moved in, a parking lot must be built, and a host of ancillary arrangements must be made. Will the cafeteria be run by the company or outsourced? What level of technology will be used in the plant? Will the plant be built for the minimum possible cost and contain the absolute minimum amount of equipment, or will it be built as a state-of-the-art facility with the latest technology and substantial room for expansion? These questions and decisions are complex.

One utility company, for example, built a new generating plant on a greenfield site. It designed the facility in modules. It purchased enough land and received permission to build three modules of generating units. It needed only one module immediately and expected to need the second in a very few years. It completely constructed the first module and made plans to build the second. The third would be built decades later, so no investment in construction was needed at that time.

In some cases, the equipment must be specially designed and made for the particular use at that site. Hence, the company may spend over $1 million on one piece of equipment. Tremendous coordination is required for all parts of the facility to be operational at the same time.

The types of decisions made by a manufacturing firm are typically more detailed than those of service firms, but you should not assume that the task is easy for service firms. With the growth in service industries, the need for facilities is tremendous. You need only drive along interstate highways in or around large cities to witness the growth in corporate facilities in recent years. Most of them are service firms. Like manufacturing firms, service firms must give considerable attention to the location, design, technology, parking, and ancillary services to be provided.

Acquiring Raw Materials

Once managers have acquired facilities, they must begin the task of acquiring raw materials to use in the production process. There are many different sources of raw materials. Each has particular benefits, each requires a different type of coordination, and each uses a different type of contractual arrangement. Table 13.3 shows various types of suppliers for manufacturing firms.

Independent contractors are typically small businesses that may range from a small carpentry business to a machine shop specializing in a few products. This kind of supplier often provides personalized service and may produce for only a very few customers. Sometimes it produces, under contract, for a single large customer. For example, a small company might make only the cabs for John Deere tractors. In that case, the small company works very closely with the larger manufacturer and is almost an extension of the larger firm. Incidentally, although our focus here is on physical resources, keep in mind that independent contractors are a prime source of services to other businesses.

		TABLE 13.3
Independent contractors	Local producers with only a few customers.	Types of Suppliers
Regional producers	Medium-size producers that sell within a several-state region.	
National or international producers	Large producers that routinely sell to a large number of customers, often internationally.	
Specialty goods producers	Producers that make a single product that is used by a number of customers nationwide or worldwide.	
Foreign producers	Producers in other countries that build under contract for individual companies or sell to a broad market.	
Competitors	Producers that make a product for other companies but also make similar products to sell under their own brand name.	

Regional producers market their goods or services in a larger geographic area, which may cover a few counties or perhaps several states. They often have either a single plant or a small number of plants. They usually sell to a number of customers, which may be either industrial or final consumers. Some may have a product line or service that they sell in a limited area plus a small segment of their business that reaches a larger market. An example is an architectural firm that designs office buildings in a tricounty area, designs hospitals in a multistate region, and designs prisons for construction anywhere in the United States.

National and international producers are those companies that typically make a number of products for sale throughout the United States and in international markets. The items they make may range from components to entire products. An example is Cummins Engines, which produces truck engines that may become part of trucks built by Peterbilt, Mack, GMC, or Ford. Since these companies make major components, they may have plants in a number of states and other countries. Lear Corporation, featured in Profile 13.2, is a supplier that operates in both the domestic and international markets.

Specialty goods producers are companies that produce a single product, which may be sold worldwide. For example, Potash Corp. of Saskatchewan Inc. (PCS), a potash mining company headquartered in Saskatchewan, Canada, is the world's largest producer of potash (which is used in fertilizer). Until recently, potash was essentially the only product sold by PCS. Today, through acquisitions, it produces nitrogen and phosphate in addition to potash and is now the world's largest integrated fertilizer company.[6]

Foreign producers make an item and ship it to the United States either for sale to the public or for use in products. Use of foreign suppliers may lower costs since wages are often lower in developing countries than in the United States. In some cases, the U.S. company owns the foreign producer and therefore has a direct supply channel. In other situations, the foreign company is separately owned but has contracts with the U.S.-based firm to provide the desired products. Nike, for example, sells a wide range of athletic shoes and apparel. Most of the products are made in Southeast Asia and shipped to Nike to sell.

A final source of physical resources may surprise you. In several industries, it is not unusual for companies to purchase goods from their competitors. For example, in the home appliance industry, Sears does not produce any of its products. Instead, it contracts with suppliers to produce goods for marketing under one of the Sears brand names, for

PROFILE 13.2   LEAR SEATING IS IN YOUR CAR

Regardless of what kind of car you rode in last, the odds are high that you sat on seats made by Lear Corporation. Although Lear Corporation has been in the automotive parts business since 1917, it sold its first automotive seats in 1984. Through 300 facilities in 33 countries, Lear's 120,000 employees serve the global requirements of Ford, General Motors, DaimlerChrysler, Volvo, Saab, BMW, Volkswagen, Jaguar, Isuzu, Subaru, Ferrari, Peugeot, Renault, Audi, Mercedes-Benz, and Honda. Lear products are in over 300 different models of cars. Lear is the largest independent automotive interior supplier in North America and Europe. As the leading player in the $50 billion global automotive interior market, it generated almost $14 billion in sales and $680 million in profits in 2001.

Lear Corporation produces components for all portions of a car's interior, including the seating system, floor, acoustic system, instrument panel, doors and trim, overhead material, and electronic equipment systems. Approximately 61 percent of the products go into cars, with the remaining 39 percent going into light trucks such as the Ford Explorer.

Lear's growth, with current annual sales, has been the result of several trends—outsourcing, globalization, supplier consolidation, greater design and engineering responsibility given to suppliers, and increasing sophistication of seat systems.

In addition to producing car interiors, Lear Corporation is involved in the design of the systems and even in R&D into ergonomics and passenger safety. Its people work closely with automotive manufacturers to provide the most appropriate seating.

Source: Lear Corporation website, http://www.lear.com (accessed May 12, 2002).

example, Kenmore. Often the supplier also markets similar products under its own brand. Sears buys its refrigerators from Whirlpool—which also makes refrigerators that it sells under the Whirlpool brand. Why would Whirlpool sell to a competitor? The answer is simple. Sears is an extremely large retailer that sells hundreds of appliances a day. It is a ready market, then, for thousands of units a year that Whirlpool would not be likely to sell under its own brand name. Companies can also use idle capacity to produce for competitors' needs.

The Acquisition Process

The process of acquiring physical resources typically takes one of two forms, both of which require negotiation between buyer and seller. These are the traditional bidding system and the increasingly popular just-in-time system.

In the *traditional bidding system,* a manufacturer solicits bids from a number of suppliers to produce desired components. One or more suppliers are selected to provide the needed goods in large batches. The selection is often made on the basis of the lowest-cost bid. In some cases, the company may have a number of suppliers producing the same product for it, so if one supplier cannot provide the product, others will likely be able to take up the slack. The contract is rebid periodically to ensure the lowest possible prices. Suppliers have to keep careful track of their bidding history and also keep an eye out for new customers in case they are underbid by a competitor. Companies using the traditional bidding method carefully calculate the order quantity that will minimize ordering costs while also minimizing the cost of storing materials.

Just-in-time (JIT) is an integrated set of activities designed to achieve high-volume production using minimal inventories of raw materials, work in process, and finished goods.[7] The logic of JIT is that nothing is produced until it is needed. The supplier provides the component at precisely the time it is needed in the customer's manufacturing process. This system eliminates the need to stock inventory, reduces setup times for assembling the end product, and eliminates waste.

The just-in-time system of acquiring resources changes much of the relationship between buyers and sellers. Whereas in the traditional philosophy, the supplier and buyer were adversaries, the JIT system develops long-term relationships and strategic alliances that both create and rely on interdependency between the two companies.

Profile 13.3 continues the discussion of Lear Corporation, emphasizing its relationship with its customers.

Our discussion of acquisition of physical resources has keyed on manufacturing firms since they require the most physical resources to produce the products. Keep in mind, however, that acquisition of physical resources is also important in service organizations. The resources to be acquired are typically either fixed assets (such as computer systems, furniture, and buildings) or supplies. Even here, JIT and close relationships with suppliers are important. State Farm Insurance, for example, is a service firm; it produces no physical products for sale. Yet because of its size, it requires

> **just-in-time (JIT)**
> An integrated set of activities designed to achieve high-volume production using minimal inventories of raw materials, work in process, and finished goods.

LEAR CORPORATION (CONTINUED)   PROFILE 13.3

As a key supplier, Lear Corporation is responsible to the automotive manufacturers for the design, development, component sourcing, manufacturing, quality assurance, and delivery of interior systems on a just-in-time basis. Now it has taken JIT to a higher level. In what is called sequential parts delivery, Lear not only delivers the interior systems to customers just in time, but delivers them to the actual point of assembly in the precise color and trim sequence requested. This level of service means Lear must build high-quality seats and work especially closely with its customers.

To provide the highest possible quality in the shortest possible time, Lear has developed a system in which interior assembly is performed in modules by highly skilled teams of workers, and quality is inspected often. Also, Lear's assembly plants are strategically located within 20 miles of its customers' facilities.

An interior system order is sent from the customer's assembly plant, usually as the vehicle enters the paint department. The order is received by Lear's computers, which signal the sequencing and loading of the component systems. The system is often delivered to the automotive plant within 90 minutes after the customer sends the order.

Source: Lear Corporation website, www.lear.com (accessed May 12, 2002).

considerable office space in headquarters and regional offices. Even items such as paper and printer toner are consumed in giant proportions. Acquiring those resources requires the full-time attention of many employees, not to mention considerable warehouse space. JIT agreements with suppliers significantly reduce the cost to State Farm.

Financial Resources

cash flow

The movement of cash into, through, and out of a firm.

Financial resources are valuable in that they can be used to acquire other resources as well as invested to earn more resources. In contrast, physical resources are used for a single purpose. Further, if they are not being used, physical resources just sit idle. Financial resources can be used to purchase equipment, pay workers, buy advertising, or acquire another company. Excess financial resources can be invested to add to the company's earnings. Therefore, the acquisition and use of this type of resource is very important.

cash inflow

The movement of cash into the business from owners, lenders, or customers.

Financial resources can be discussed best in terms of the concept of cash flow. **Cash flow** refers to the movement of cash into, through, and out of the firm. Cash inflow is the movement of cash from somewhere outside the firm into the firm. Cash outflow is the movement of cash back out of the company to acquire services, materials, or labor; to pay taxes; to provide a return to owners; or to purchase other companies. Table 13.4 illustrates the inflows and outflows.

equity financing

The money invested in a business by the owners.

Cash Inflow: Acquiring Financial Resources

Cash inflow may come from three primary sources: owners, lenders, and customers. These sources, commonly called equity financing, debt financing, and revenues, are shown in the first column of Table 13.4.

A first source of cash is the owners of the company. Any money invested in a business by its owners is called **equity financing.** In small firms, individual owners may put some of their personal funds into the company. Company owners can also raise equity money by taking in a partner. Corporations can raise cash by selling stock to investors. These stockholders become part owners of the company in exchange for the cash they pay. Companies wishing to raise substantial funds may do an initial public offering (IPO). You will recall from Chapter 9 that an IPO offers stock to the public for the first time. Once the IPO is made, the firm can raise more cash by issuing more stock.

debt financing

The money a company borrows from outsiders, such as individuals, banks, or other lending institutions, or raises by selling bonds.

The second source of funds is money loaned to the company by outsiders, such as individuals, banks, or other lending institutions. Large corporations may also issue bonds, a special type of loan that outsiders buy in much the same way that stockholders buy stock in the firms. Cash lent in these ways is called **debt financing.** There are two significant differences between debt financing and equity financing. First, debt financing *requires* the borrower to pay interest on loans to the business. The loan contract is a legally binding agreement that the business will pay back the principal of the loan plus any interest. Equity financing does not require paying back the investment. Second, the providers of debt financing are called *lenders.* These lenders do not become owners. Thus, if a bank lends a business $100,000, the bank has a legal agreement with the firm, but it is not an owner of the firm.

THINK ABOUT THIS

1. What is different about the process of acquiring fixed assets compared with acquiring inventory or supplies?

2. Why are more and more firms moving toward outsourcing components or products? Is your answer the same for physical resources as for human resources?

3. Describe the relationship between Lear Corporation and its customers. How is it beneficial to both?

TABLE 13.4

Cash Inflows and Outflows

Cash Inflows	Cash Outflows for Operations	Cash Outflows for Financing and Investments
Equity financing	Production	Cash to creditors
Debt financing	Raw materials	Principal
Revenues	Labor	Interest
Cash sales	Other expenses	Cash to owners
Payments on accounts receivable	Utilities	Acquisition of other companies
	Supplies	Investments
	Rent	Acquisition of land, buildings, or equipment
	Marketing	
	Wages and salaries	
	Taxes	

The most critical source of funds is revenue. **Revenue** is the cash generated from the sale of goods or services to customers. As customers purchase goods or services from the firm, they pay for those purchases with either cash or credit that is later turned into cash. Revenues are the most critical source of funding because they are a continual source of new funds. As goods or services are sold, more money flows into the business, money that can then be used to create still more items to sell. If a company is successful, revenue-generated funds will be sufficient to underwrite day-to-day operations. Revenue will also provide returns for the owners and allow excess funds to be reinvested in the business.

Revenue-generated funds may not be enough to keep the firm running at the time of start-up, during seasonal fluctuations, or when the firm is growing rapidly. In these cases, either additional debt or equity financing may be required.

revenue
The cash generated from the sale of goods or services.

Cash Outflow: Using Financial Resources

Cash outflow is cash that moves out of the business for any reason. Outflows may be as simple as dividends paid to stockholders or checks written to a TV station for advertising. Or outflows can be quite complex, such as a combination stock swap and cash purchase of another publicly held company. Generally, outflows fall into two categories. The first is outflows related to the production of the goods or service; we call this simply outflows for operations. The second is outflows for financing and investments.

Cash outflows for operations consist of all those uses of cash that deal with production and sale of the firm's products or services. These expenditures may be for raw materials or inventory that will eventually be processed or sold. Major amounts go to pay the people who work in the production process. Significant amounts of funds are used to purchase utilities, supplies, and miscellaneous items necessary for the operations aspect of the firm.

Once products or services are produced, there is still the task of marketing them to customers. This part of a company's operations requires a large amount of cash. It is not uncommon, for example, for a large company to spend $10 million on marketing just to introduce a single new product. In addition to production and marketing, much of a firm's cash outflow goes to the general administration of the firm. If you think of all the clerical staff, accountants, janitorial staff, researchers, and attorneys, it becomes apparent that much of the cash outflow goes simply to pay people. Of course, you must add

cash outflow
The movement of cash out of the business for any reason.

the computers and communications equipment necessary to operate the firm. Then add in the office furniture, supplies, and travel needed to manage a business. Administrative costs are often 40 percent of the entire cost of the product. Much of the downsizing among large businesses today is the elimination of administrative staff.

The final category of operations-related outflows is taxes. Some taxes, such as sales taxes, are simply pass-throughs from the customer to the taxing bodies. Other taxes, such as income taxes, are a real part of the cost of doing business. Still others, such as real estate taxes in some communities, are an expense the business must incur even though they are not directly related to its operations. The business manager who forgets to include the outflow for taxes in financial planning may make a mistake that is fatal to the business.

Cash outflows for financing and investment include the investment of funds for acquisition of additional fixed assets, the payment of the principal and interest on loans, the payment of dividends to stockholders or returns to the owners (if sole proprietors or partners), and the investment of funds in either typical financial instruments or the acquisition of other companies.

We noted earlier that land, buildings, and equipment are known as fixed assets. Acquiring these fixed assets constitutes a major use of funds. For example, General Motors spent over $1 billion just to build and equip its state-of-the-art facility in Spring Hill, Tennessee, to produce Saturn cars.

We mentioned that two of the three *inflows* of cash deal with debt or equity financing. Similarly, cash *outflows* must be made to return that cash to lenders, bondholders, and owners. In debt financing, the business must pay back the amount borrowed plus interest. Regardless of whether the debt comes from bonds, individuals, or banks, the business still must pay the holders of the debt the agreed-upon interest plus the principal. In equity financing, the business pays the owner or owners part of the profits of the business. In the case of stock companies, the company may pay dividends to stockholders (although many public companies do not pay dividends) plus the occasional repurchase of company stock. In the case of sole proprietorships, partnerships, and LLCs, the payment is that portion of the cash the owners take out of the business.

Companies with excess cash would be ill-advised to simply let it sit in the firm's checking account. It is common to invest excess cash beyond what the business needs to reinvest in the company. Excess cash may be invested in any form that an individual might use. Thus, a company's investments could range from certificates of deposit and savings accounts to stocks or bonds of other companies.

Profile 13.4 shows the cash flow statement for Best Buy. Note that Best Buy had both inflows and outflows of millions of dollars.

PROFILE 13.4 BEST BUY'S CASH FLOWS

The financial document that illustrates the movement of cash into and out of an organization is known as the *cash flow statement*. It is important because it focuses on the movement of cash rather than on income and expenses. For many companies, especially small businesses, this movement of cash is more important than income and expenses since it is cash that is used to pay bills. In addition, many purchases and many sales are made on credit. The cash flow statement acknowledges funds movement when the flow occurs rather than when the sale or purchase occurred. Also, some aspects of a company's expenses are noncash expenses. For example, depreciation is an expense related to the declining value of assets as they are used up. That expense is a noncash expense.

This cash flow statement below shows the cash inflows and outflows of Best Buy. Note that some of the entries offset noncash expenses. Note also that the statement is broken into cash flows related to operations and cash flows from investments and financing. Finally, some of the entries are clear only in light of the "notes of consolidated financial statements," which we have not included here. Items in parentheses are outflows. Those without parentheses are inflows.

Best Buy Co., Inc.
Consolidated Statements of Cash Flows
Fiscal Year Ended 2001 ($ in thousands)

Operating Activities	
Net earnings	$ 395,839
Adjustments to reconcile net earnings to net cash provided by operating activities:	
Depreciation	167,369
Deferred income taxes	42,793
Other	20,609
Changes in operating assets and liabilities, net of acquired assets and liabilities:	
Receivables	(7,434)
Merchandise inventories	(143,969)
Other assets	(16,018)
Accounts payable	16,186
Other liabilities	198,721
Accrued income taxes	134,108
Total cash provided by operating activities	808,204
Investing Activities	
Additions to property and equipment	(657,706)
Acquisitions of businesses, net of cash acquired	(326,077)
Increase in recoverable costs from developed properties	(31,076)
Increase in other assets	(14,943)
Total cash used in investing activities	(1,029,802)
Financing Activities	
Long-term debt payments	(17,625)
Issuance of common stock	235,379
Total cash provided by (used in) financing activities	217,754
Increase (Decrease) in Cash and Cash Equivalents	**(3,844)**
Cash and Cash Equivalents at Beginning of Period	**750,723**
Cash and Cash Equivalents at End of Year	**$ 746,879**

Source: Best Buy website, www.bestbuy.com.

A final form of capital outflow in the investment category is the acquisition of other companies. Businesses may use their current cash plus other funding to purchase another company. These acquisitions often add to a company's product line, reduce competition, or allow the company to expand abroad. For example, in 2001, Best Buy completed its acquisition of Sam Goody and Magnolia Hi-Fi.

Information Resources

It is hard to think of information as a resource, but it is one of the fuels that powers an organization just as much as human resources, physical resources, and financial resources are. Without sufficient information, managers cannot make appropriate decisions.

Managers need two broad categories of information, strategic and operational. **Strategic information** is information about a firm's competitors, customers, and markets that affects its ability to compete. **Operational information** is information relating to the internal workings of the company that helps it run more efficiently. There is obvious overlap between the two types of information. For example, marketing-related information can be both strategic and operational. So can some financial information. So can some manufacturing information. The difference between the two categories of information is the focus. Strategic information has an external focus whereas operational information has an internal focus.

strategic information

Any information about a firm's competitors, customers, and markets that affects its ability to compete.

operational information

Any information relating to the internal workings of the company that helps it run more efficiently.

Strategic Information

Strategic information consists of information about the firm's environment. The chapters in Part Three of this book all dealt with external information that is relevant to businesses. Table 13.5 lists examples of strategic information. Note that the strategic information parallels the environment forces listed in our model of a successful business discussed in Chapter 2.

Managers use strategic information to develop strategies that help the business excel in a dynamic marketplace. For example, they need information about their customers to understand the customer trends that will affect their sales. The more information they have, the better they can position their product or service in a way that maximizes their chances for success.

Information regarding the economy and financial markets is important for assessing the future demand for products. This kind of information is also useful in making expansion decisions because of the effect of interest rates on a company's expenses.

Information on foreign markets is important if the company plans to enter those markets. Even if the business sells only domestically, information about foreign companies exporting to the United States is also important. Information about the size of competitors, exchange rates, and export procedures is critically important.

THINK ABOUT THIS

1. What are the advantages of equity financing compared with debt financing? the disadvantages? How would the advantages and disadvantages differ for small firms compared with large ones?

2. What are the impacts of using too much debt? Are there problems with using too little debt?

3. How might sources of financing differ for small companies compared with large ones?

TABLE 13.5

Samples of Strategic
Information

Demographic Information

Age of customers

Education level of customers

Income of customers

Economic Information

Gross domestic product

Unemployment rate

Inflation rate

Industry performance

Sales compared with price (demand)

Financial Market Information

Trends in interest rates

Stock and bond prices

Amount of consumer debt

International Information

Global sales of products

International competitors

Imports/exports of products

Currency exchange rates

Market reports from other countries

Legal Information

Relevant government regulations

Trends in industry-specific regulation

Operational Information

Operational information is any information that will make the organization run more efficiently. Operational information encompasses at least the following six categories:[8]

1. Marketing information
2. Manufacturing information
3. Accounting information
4. Financial information
5. Product development information
6. Human resources information

Each kind of information helps managers assess how the company is doing and helps it adjust for the future. For example, quality control information within manufacturing allows companies to determine how well they have been doing in terms of product defects. It also points to possible solutions to problems. Human resources information allows managers and employees to assess salaries, benefits, vacation days, bonuses, stock options, and a host of other issues.

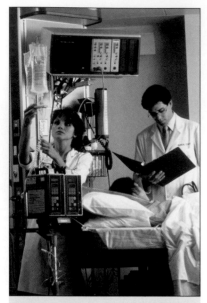

Medical facilities must have both the latest technologies and the skilled staff to operate the equipment. Both the technology and staff are quite expensive. Do you think the demand created by an aging and health-conscious population will support the rising costs that must follow?

Sources of Information

In each of the prior sections, we discussed sources of the relevant resource. We noted different sources of human capital, sources of equipment and raw materials, and sources of debt and equity capital. Here, we mention a few of the many sources of information.

The Internet

There may be no better external source of information for businesses than the Internet. Note, for example, the number of company links listed on this book's website. Many of the sources we cite in this book are websites from companies, the U.S. government, or other organizations. The amount of data available from the Internet is simply mind-boggling. The ease and low cost of getting the information also make it a first-choice source. The use of search engines to find information makes data gathering easy from any personal computer connected to the Internet. Government data are particularly useful and easily accessible. Almost every large company and many small ones have websites. Information can be accessed and then either printed or downloaded into computer files and stored for future use.

Annual Reports

Every publicly held company is required to prepare annual reports, which are routinely sent to stockholders. Publicly held companies are also required to file financial reports with the Securities and Exchange Commission (SEC). These reports are available from the companies, at many libraries, and at most company websites. The availability of the reports allows managers to access significant information about their competitors. Most of the information is provided for multiple years, which lets you see trends or changes in financial conditions.

Trade Association Data

Much information can be gleaned from trade associations, which most industries have. For example, the International Franchise Association (www.franchise.org) has information related to franchises. The National Federation of Independent Business (www.nfib.com) is an advocacy organization for small business. NFIB has a wealth of information available for small businesses regardless of industry.

Internal Databases

The best source of internal information is the broad set of company databases that exist in any business. Like Internet information, these are often readily available and accessible from desktop computers. Most companies have databases for financial information, human resources information, marketing information, manufacturing information, and others. Most of the databases are in searchable form if you have the appropriate authorization. The information is easily retrievable and can be analyzed using statistical software.

THINK ABOUT THIS

1. How do managers know when they have gathered enough strategic information?
2. What internal information would a company need to determine if their quality is sufficient?

We have only skimmed the surface of information sources here. Most managers today have more information available to them than they can use effectively. The key to effective use of information resources is to identify what information is needed, what form it is needed in, and where to find it.

THE BIG PICTURE

When a large company is considering buying another company, one of the key considerations is the concept of strategic fit. In other words, does the new company fit in with the overall strategy and culture of the buying firm? Managers must consider this issue before committing to an action that could turn out to be disastrous.

Considering resources is much the same. Managers must ask: Do the resources we currently have at our disposal fit with the overall strategy of the firm? Further, if we are considering a new strategy—especially a growth strategy—do we either have or can we get the resources we need to make that new strategy work? If we have insufficient resources or the wrong mix of resources, the new strategy could end badly.

In the 1970s, McDonald's grew far faster than either Hardee's or Burger King. Why? It was because McDonald's had the financial resources to underwrite the expansion and the associated national advertising that would be needed. Its fast-food competitors did not have those resources.

As you read the next few chapters, which deal with product development, marketing, technology, and people, keep in mind that each of the four types of resources we discussed in this chapter will be involved. The role of managers is to integrate those resources so that the overall strategy can be successful.

1. This book emphasizes the importance of integrative thinking in business.

   • What are some of the issues of integration you must consider when dealing with resource acquisition and use?

   Resource acquisition demands that managers work with many people throughout the company to acquire and use resources in the most effective and least expensive manner. This strategy is important because changes in one resource can affect the use of others. It is also important because of the concept of trade-offs. Trade-offs mean that using funds for one thing precludes using them for another. Opportunity costs, the value of activities that are sacrificed, must also be considered. Resource acquisition and use involve the movement of goods, equipment, inventory, money, people, and information from outside the organization to inside and back.

2. Resource acquisition provides two major challenges to a business.

   • What are two major resource challenges?

   The two challenges are (1) acquiring an adequate amount, and (2) acquiring the proper mix.

3. CEOs of most companies are quick to tell you that their people are the key to their company's success. What they do not tell you is how they happen to have such superior employees.

Summary

- What are the three challenges of human resources management?

Successful companies must be able to (1) accurately forecast the company's human resources needs, (2) recruit a pool of candidates, and (3) select the best individuals according to the needs of the company.

- What are some of the major issues involved with each of the three major human resources challenges?

(1) Forecasting human resources needs requires managers to predict where the company is going and what kinds and number of employees will be required. It requires predicting changes in the current workforce, such as retirement, promotions, and terminations. It requires forecasting demographic and lifestyle changes and determining how they will affect the firm's ability to find and attract future employees.

(2) Recruiting candidates involves the use of many different sources, ranging from ads to employment agencies, trade associations, hiring from other companies, and internal promotions.

(3) Once candidates are found, they must be carefully screened to make sure their capabilities meet the company's needs. Before actually deciding to hire a new employee, managers should consider the possibility of outsourcing.

4. One important determinant of employee productivity is the nature of the physical resources workers use. The right plant, equipment, raw materials, and supplies will enable workers to achieve peak performance. Inadequate or inappropriate physical resources will prevent even dedicated workers from doing their best.

- What are some of the major issues related to the acquisition of physical resources?

(1) Planning is crucial.

(2) A major issue that must be considered in the planning stage is whether to make the product in-house or buy it from a supplier (outsource it).

(3) For fixed assets, a major issue is whether to build on a new site, remodel, or purchase an existing building.

(4) In choosing suppliers for physical resources, the firm must consider such alternatives as independent contractors, regional producers, national or international producers, specialty goods producers, foreign producers, and competitors.

(5) The process of actually acquiring the physical resources requires the firm to consider two possible forms of negotiation with the seller, traditional bidding and the just-in-time approach.

5. Both human and physical resources have to be purchased with financial resources. So acquiring financial resources is also a continuous challenge for the firm.

- What are some major characteristics of the acquisition and use of financial resources?

Financial resources can best be understood in terms of the concept of cash flow, that is, to the movement of cash into, through, and out of the firm.

(1) Cash inflow refers to the movement of cash into the firm. The issue facing the firm is how to acquire the cash. The three major alternatives are equity financing, debt financing, and revenues.

(2) Cash outflow refers to the movement of cash out of the business for any reason. Cash outflows are caused by expenditures for production of the firm's products and services or by financing activities such as the acquisition of additional fixed assets, payment of dividends to stockholders, and investment of excess cash.

6. Information is much more readily available today than it was even 10 years ago.

   • What sources of information exist, and how can they be used?

   Information is available from a vast array of sources, both inside a business and outside. The most usable source of information today is the Internet, where information from government agencies, other companies, and industry can be found. Company annual reports and information from trade associations are also valuable. Internal information about a company can be gathered from company files and databases.

Key Terms

cash flow, p. 340

cash inflow, p. 340

cash outflow, p. 341

debt financing, p. 340

downsizing, p. 327

equity financing, p. 340

human resources outsourcing, p. 332

just-in-time (JIT), p. 339

make-or-buy decision, p. 334

operational information, p. 344

opportunity cost, p. 324

physical resources, p. 334

product outsourcing, p. 334

resources, p. 323

revenue, p. 341

strategic information, p. 344

synergy, p. 324

Exercises and Applications

1. The Internet sources www.reportgallery.com and www.sec.gov can be used to access company annual reports. (Other Internet sources can also be used.) Go to one of these sources and find Best Buy's annual report. What kinds of information does the report contain about Best Buy?

2. Form teams. Your team is to identify and hire a student to serve as a reporter for the campus newspaper. Outline what must be done to find, interview, and select the best person to fill this job.

3. We discussed outsourcing twice in this chapter and earlier in the book. Assume the role of a staff employee in the manufacturing department of Dell. Prepare a one-page memo to your boss outlining the pros and cons of outsourcing for your department. Make sure your memo is specific to your department rather than a generic essay.

4. Suppose you have just started your own business, a small consulting company that focuses on training other firms to be more customer sensitive. Which resources (human, physical, financial, or information) will be most critical for you as you begin the company? Would your answer be the same if your company were 5 years old? 15 years old?

5. You are the president of a firm that manufactures a line of ceramic vases used in floral shops. Because of growth, you need to add $200,000 more capital. Write a two-page report on the benefits of using equity financing rather than debt financing for the $200,000. What sources of equity financing are most likely available?

6. Search the Internet for as much strategic information as you can find about an independent toy store. Now pool your answers with four other students. How many sources did you have in common?

FROM THE PAGES OF

BusinessWeek

Don't Be Fooled by the Name on the Box

Compaq Computer, now a part of Hewlett-Packard, sells a sleek, handheld computer called the iPAQ. But Compaq not only did not produce the iPAQ, it did not even design it. The product is a result of an increasingly popular outsourcing strategy that uses original design manufacturers, or ODMs.

PC makers have been using contract manufacturing for years, and even IBM is beginning to use foreign manufacturers for some of its products. But the significance of the new moves is that companies are now outsourcing the design as well as the manufacturing. In some cases, the ODM designs and manufactures the complete product, and the U.S. company simply sticks its name on the product.

Consumers generally do not care who actually makes the products. The ODMs are reliable, and companies such as HP and Dell have their own quality assurance people on-site to make sure the quality is acceptable. The downside is that the ODMs make products for a number of different companies at the same time. Thus, the Gateway 200 and the Dell Latitude X200 are essentially identical because both are made by Korea's Samsung, which, incidentally, also sells a look-alike under its own brand. The only differences between the Dell and Gateway machines are the warranties and a few components.

If consumers are buying essentially identical machines, what choices do they have in their purchases? The answer is that companies are competing more on warranties, service, and prices than they are on the machines themselves.

Decision Questions

1. Should you as a consumer care whether a computer is made by a U.S. company in the United States or by a foreign company in Korea or Taiwan?

2. What determines the choice of brands of computers? quality? warranties? service? price?

3. How would your answer to question 2 change with the following information? Quality is quite good regardless of who makes the machines. Service is rarely needed, and warranties are rarely invoked. In fact, retailers make a high percentage of their profits selling extended warranty contracts to customers, knowing full well that they will seldom be used.

Source: Stephen H. Wildstrom, "Don't Be Fooled by the Name on the Box," *BusinessWeek,* June 17, 2002, p. 18.

References

1. William McEachern, *Microeconomics: A Contemporary Introduction,* 5th ed. (Cincinnati, OH: South-Western College Publishing, 2000), p. 26.

2. This forecasting approach is adapted from Gary Dessler, *Human Resource Management,* 8th ed. (Englewood Cliffs, NJ: Prentice Hall, 2000) pp. 122-23.

3. Southwest Airlines website, www.southwest.com (accessed October 8, 2002).

4. Nims and Associates website www.nimsassociates.com (accessed May 2, 2002).

5. Richard B. Chase, Nicholas J. Aquilano, and F. Robert Jones. *Operations Management for Competitive Advantage* (Burr Ridge, IL: Irwin/McGraw-Hill, 2001), pp. 374–76.

6. Potash Company of Saskatchewan, www.potashCorp.com/overview (accessed July 12, 2002).

7. Chase, Aquilano, and Jones, p. 395.

8. Uma G. Gupta, *Information Systems: Success in the 21st Century* (Upper Saddle River, NJ: Prentice Hall, 2000), p. 34.

14

Providing Value Through Quality Products and Services

Since you would never want to be late for class, you slip on your backpack and unfold your Xootr electric scooter to ride from your dorm room or parking lot, gliding quietly by your less ingenious classmates who are . . . walking. After class, you go to your part-time job in the parts distribution warehouse, where you travel around on a Segway Human Transporter, a personal transportation vehicle. You walk into the office area, where the boring taupe-colored cubicles have been replaced with high-tech multifunctional cubicles whose colors can be changed by pushing a button. You notice that the information technology department has just installed a new Dell Power Edge server. Later, you relax your muscles in the comfort of your circulating bathtub spa while listening to one of over 1,000 songs on your Apple iPod and then go into the living room to watch the wall—a flat-panel TV with surround-sound speakers. Another tough day as a college student!

What is the common feature in this eclectic array of products? All have won awards from the Industrial Designers Society of America for their innovative product designs. Other winning products include the 2002 Ford Thunderbird, an iMac whose base looks like the top half of a volleyball, a handheld computer from Handspring, a modernistic-looking chess set with multicolored circles instead of squares, and a portable DVD player from Samsung. In all, there were 174 winners from 17 countries. Each product exemplified ingenuity in product design, functionality, and aesthetics.[1]

This chapter illustrates the integrative nature of business decision making. We begin the chapter with a discussion of market research and market segmentation—two topics that traditionally fall within the purview of the marketing department in large companies. We then move to a discussion of product development and quality—topics that are often discussed when considering the production or operations part of a business. We finish the chapter by discussing distribution of the product, which is an integral part of both traditional marketing and operations areas. As you read this chapter, you should keep in mind that the central focus is on providing the most value to the customers. Chapter 15 will continue this line of reasoning by discussing how we communicate that value to customers.

After studying this chapter, you should be able to:

1. Explain the basic principles of learning about customer needs.

2. Discuss some of the methods used to segment a market.

3. Understand the process of product development.

4. Demonstrate an understanding of quality in product development.

5. Use the key aspects of product distribution to increase the value of a product.

One of the keys to maximizing value to customers is the development of quality products and services. Our concept of customer value is a broad, encompassing one. Successful businesses understand the needs and expectations of their customers. They build products and offer services that meet or exceed those needs. They provide their customers with consistent quality. They ensure that the product or service is delivered where it is needed, how it is needed, and when it is needed. They supply service and follow-up in a timely manner. A business provides value for customers by doing all these things and doing them well.

In today's markets, customers are very demanding. If customers are going to surrender their hard-earned dollars, they demand products and services that offer them what they want. In other words, they are exchanging dollars for value. Customers have choices in the products they buy and the companies they buy from. Thus, it is important that companies understand how to provide the highest possible value to their customers.

Flip back to Chapter 5 and look at the decision-making model we presented. Note that we start by defining the problem. Then we gather and analyze information to develop possible strategies or solutions to implement and review. Keep that model in mind as you read the next few paragraphs. You will see a strong similarity between decision making in general and decision making as it relates to developing quality products and services.

There are four basic steps in providing quality products and services to customers, as shown in Figure 14.1. The first step is to learn what customers need or want. This step entails the tasks of market research. Once a customer's needs are understood, the product development process begins. Product development is an integrated process involving a

FIGURE 14.1

Providing Value through Product or Service Development

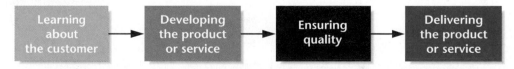

number of different departments or units within a business. Part of this process is assuring that quality is built into the product or service. Quality is both a process and a philosophy within the overall business operations. Finally, the product must be delivered in a timely manner to a location suitable for the customer.

Using Market Research to Learn about Customers

The first step in providing quality products and services for customers lies in learning what they really want and need. There are both a short answer and a long answer to the question, How do we find out what the customers want? The short answer is, Ask them. This answer, of course, is simplistic, but it captures the spirit immediately. Far too many businesses make a product that they *think* customers will want. Then they build a marketing plan to convince customers that they do, indeed, want what the manufacturer built. It would be much better if managers first asked customers what they wanted and then proceeded to build it. Then the task would be simply to communicate that the product is available and to accentuate those parts of the product that particularly meet the customer's needs. Learning about customers can involve a number of approaches, most of which fall under the heading of market research.

market research
The tasks of collecting and analyzing information about the market or potential market for a product or service.

Market research deals with the tasks of collecting and analyzing information about the market or potential market for a product or service. Information is critical because it communicates what products are in demand, what features are desirable, and how the product is best delivered to the customer. Whatever form market research takes, it involves the effort to learn about customer needs and how best to meet those needs.

research design
A plan for determining whom to study and how to collect and analyze information.

Determining the Research Design

The first step in collecting information about customers and their needs is to determine how to actually collect and analyze the information. The **research design** is a plan for determining whom to study and how to collect and analyze information. Figure 14.2 shows a simplified model for designing a research project. The first step is to decide

FIGURE 14.2

Simplified Research Model

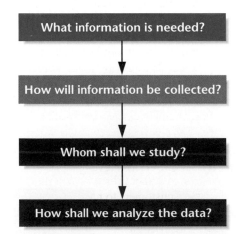

Source: Condensed from Carl McDaniel and Roger Gates, *Marketing Research: The Impact of the Internet* (Cincinnati, OH: South-Western, 2002), pp. 63–67.

what we want to know. That means we must decide *what information* we want to collect from customers or potential customers. How specific does the information need to be? How fast do we need it? What kind of analysis can we do? Second, we must decide how *to collect* the information. We need to decide whether to use surveys, use a focus group, have informal discussions with customers, gather information from competitors, gather only numerical information rather than subjective information, hire a consultant rather than do it ourselves, and a number of other issues. Third, we need to determine *whom to ask.* How many people? All our customers or only a small sample? Only our best customers? Only our Internet customers? Finally, we must decide *how to analyze* the data. Should we do high levels of statistical analysis or should we just summarize the data? Information can be of two types: secondary data and primary data.

Secondary Data

Business decision makers rely heavily on secondary data. **Secondary data** are any data that have already been published. A number of databases contain excellent information— such as census data, trade association reports, economic forecasts, online information services, and the vast amount of other information on the Internet. Secondary data are relatively easy to find, and they can give a wealth of general information about customers, the economy, and trends.

> **secondary data**
> Any data that have already been published.

Some secondary data is almost literally at our fingertips. Much of the data that we need is in our own company. It may be in file folders. It may be results from earlier products. It may be in sales and profit figures from previous quarters or from certain geographic locations or market segments. Most companies have databases of information, which have been collected in the past, about their products and their customers. This information is good by itself, but it is particularly good when compared with more recent information to identify changes.

Primary Data

Customer information may be gained through **primary data,** which are data the business collects directly from customers and potential customers. A popular way to collect primary data is with surveys. You may have participated in a market research survey at some time in your life. Researchers may survey people by telephone, in a mall, by mail, by e-mail, or by visiting with customers in the marketer's store. This kind of information is often more difficult, costly, and time consuming to gather and analyze than is secondary data, but it provides very direct and relevant information if done well. Surveys offer the advantage of tailoring questions to provide specifically needed information and probing for reasons behind the answers.

> **primary data**
> Data that a business collects directly from customers and potential customers.

When developing surveys to collect primary data, managers must first answer these questions: What is it that we need to know, and what will we do with the information? The answers to the questions help managers design the survey and identify the target sample. They can then determine how much accuracy and specificity they need. Are extensive details important, or are general answers acceptable? Should they use a mail survey, which is relatively inexpensive but has a low response rate, or do they want to talk with people personally or by phone to get better response rates and more detailed answers?

Surveys are not the only way to gather primary data. Many companies use their websites on the Internet to encourage customers to provide ideas and thoughts on their products or overall activities. For example, Cannondale, one of the leading bicycle manufacturers, has its website in six languages and has links on its website for customers and others to send e-mail queries or comments. Many of the messages received are comments by Cannondale bicycle owners about their experience with Cannondale bikes.[2]

A particularly rich source of information is a company's own sales agents. These are the people who are actually selling the products or services to the retailers or the end users. They have a wealth of knowledge because they are where the action is. They have heard the complaints and the accolades. They know how competitors' products sell compared with ours. They know the little idiosyncrasies of our product that make it better or worse. Textbook companies such as McGraw-Hill, for example, instruct their sales representatives to collect information on which books are being used at each college they visit. They routinely collect information from professors about the textbooks being used and why the ones used are better than competitors' books. The representatives fill out field reports, which are sent back to the company for review.

Some businesses gain primary data through **focus groups,** small groups of people who are invited to sit as a group and respond to questions posed by a researcher. For example, a dentist wanted to know whether there was a market for specialized dentistry aimed at senior citizens. He commissioned a consultant to assemble a panel of 10 residents of the community who were between the ages of 55 and 65. The dentist provided a list of topics to cover. The consultant then brought the panel together, provided sandwiches and soft drinks, and led a group conversation in such a way as to collect the information. The consultant videotaped the focus group so the dentist could refer to it later. A similar focus group was held by the owners of One World Coffee and Cargo, a unique international restaurant. The restaurant had an excellent lunch crowd, but the dinner hour did not generate the amount of revenue desired by the owners. They decided to reorient their evening operations to a more traditional, casual-dining restaurant. Before making that decision, the owners held a focus group to solicit ideas for the new restaurant concept.

You should note the differences between surveys and focus groups. Well-done surveys provide data that can be extrapolated to the larger population being studied. Suppose, for example, that you own a restaurant and want to know what people really like or don't like about the restaurant. You create a well-worded survey and present it to perhaps every 100th customer for a week. At the end of the week, you analyze the surveys. You can predict with some accuracy that the rest of your customers will feel approximately the same as the sample you collected. Focus groups are not designed to collect statistically accurate results. Their purpose is to allow the researchers to gather in-depth information about a topic, along with reasons why opinions are what they are. They allow participants to bounce ideas off each other as the researcher encourages free interaction on selected topics.

Focus groups and surveys are also examples of qualitative and quantitative research. **Qualitative research** is research whose results are not subject to quantification or quantitative analysis. Focus groups, informal discussions with customers, and judgment panels of experts are all examples of qualitative research. Qualitative research may use fewer than a dozen respondents. **Quantitative research** uses mathematical or statistical analysis to reach conclusions. Quantitative research typically uses larger sample sizes and is concerned with choosing samples so that results can be generalized to a broad population.[3]

Throughout our discussion of market research, we have assumed that the data that are gathered can be meaningfully analyzed. This represents an additional step. **Data analysis** is the study of information with the goal of helping a manager reach a conclusion about some aspect of the company.

---

focus groups
Small groups of people who are asked to respond to a researcher's questions.

qualitative research
Research whose results are not subject to quantification or quantitative analysis.

quantitative research
Research that uses mathematical or statistical analysis to reach conclusions.

data analysis
The study of information to help a manager reach a conclusion about some aspect of the company.

THINK ABOUT THIS

1. Is knowledge of customer needs more critical today than it was 10 years ago? Why?

2. How could you use a focus group to develop a new logo for your college?

3. Why do small business owners often fail to do adequate market research?

Sometimes in-depth statistical analysis is needed. Sometimes the manager can just look at information and interpret it. Regardless of the method of analysis used, the final result will be a set of information that tells the manager something about how customers think and act, what they like and dislike, and how they perceive the company's products or services.

Collecting and analyzing data about a company's customers is important, but a final step must still be taken. You must still make conclusions based on the analysis. It is not enough just to look at the information. Decisions must be made regarding how to reach specific customer groups, how the final product should look, how it should work, how it will be produced and what equipment will be needed, how it can be packaged, and even how it can be shipped.

Identifying and Targeting Market Segments

The previous section focused on how to do market research—how to collect information about customers and potential customers. In this section, we look at a key link between the data collection and the product development process. This link entails using the collected information to segment markets and identify groups of people most likely to use our products or services. We then use that information to adapt products to the targeted groups or to adapt our communications with those unique customers (Chapter 15) to better meet their needs. A **market segment** is an identifiable group of customers or potential customers that have common characteristics. Thus, market segmentation is identifying groups of customers with common characteristics with the goal of better meeting their needs.

> **market segment**
> An identifiable group of customers or potential customers that have common characteristics.

The Benefits of Segmentation

It is not absolutely necessary to break current or potential sets of customers into distinct groups. A seller could simply produce a product or service, advertise it using every possible medium, and sell to whoever walks in the door. And certainly, we would not refuse to sell to any customer who wants to give us money. But the idea behind market segmentation is that marketing costs money. To ensure that our marketing is effective, we should invest our marketing dollars in only those media that best reach our primary customer group. In addition, we can design products or services for more and more precise markets. These changes may be functional changes or simply style changes. But by identifying precise customer groups, we can be more cost-effective in both our production and our communication processes.

Look at Figure 14.3 as an example. Suppose a maker of upscale camping equipment wants to know how large the market is. The total population can be successively segmented to result in a specific subset that is of interest to the business. Notice how each bar has a smaller number of people, but a more precise set of potential customers. By looking at the last bar in Figure 14.3, the business now has a better clue of how large its specific target market is. Most of this information can be obtained from census data. The only piece of information missing is the percentage of families who go camping at least once a year, and that information is likely available from trade associations.

Dell does market segmentation well. Since most of Dell's computers are made to order, it can collect information about each individual user. This information helps Dell target customers based on the type of product purchased, as well as general demographic segments. Dell segments its market for marketing purposes by recognizing the differences between the consumer market and the business market and between the individual business computer purchaser and the buyer of servers.

FIGURE 14.3

Identifying a Market for Camping Equipment: Screening Criteria and Size of Segment

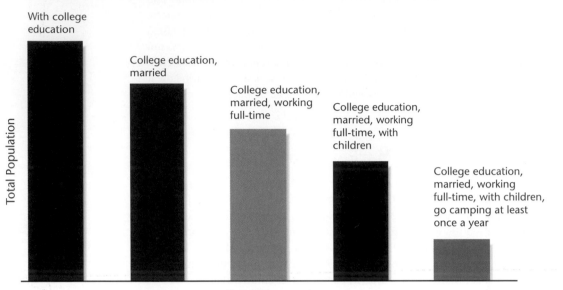

Source: Tom Duncan, *IMC: Using Advertising and Promotion to Build Brands* (Burr Ridge, IL: Irwin/McGraw-Hill, 2002), p. 240.

Market Segmentation Strategies[4]

There are many ways to segment markets. One is by income. For example, General Motors could sell Cadillacs to the affluent market, Buicks to the less affluent, Chevrolets to the still less affluent, and Saturns to the most modest income segment. But you should immediately recognize that segmenting by income alone is insufficient. Perhaps the company could segment by age, selling Buicks and Cadillacs to the over-60 crowd, sport utility vehicles to the younger customers with families, and sports cars to Generation-X or Generation-Y customers. Again, the segmentation seems overly simplistic. We need to do more.

Figure 14.4 presents a common model that shows four different segmentation strategies: segmentation by demographic group, by psychographic group, by relationship level, and by benefits received. We discuss each of these in turn.

Demographic segmentation identifies groups of potential customers on the basis of age, education, income, gender, family size, ethnicity, religion, and the like. You may recall from our discussions of diversity that different age groups behave differently and that different racial, ethnic, and gender groups may react differently to a single piece of advertising. Thus, recognizing demographic differences allows companies to target their marketing more precisely.

The second type of distinction for segmenting a market involves psychographic variables. Psychographic segmentation categorizes people on the basis of their attitudes, interests, and opinions, as well as their lifestyle activities. This type of categorization relates to people's personalities, their hobbies, their stage in life, their social class, their values, and even their clubs and hobbies.

Relationship variables are those variables that address how we interact with others. Here, we may segment markets on the basis of the loyalty of customers to a product. In

Customer Profile Variables

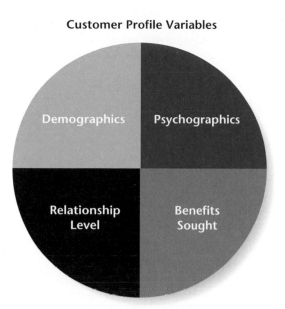

Source: Tom Duncan, *IMC: Using Advertising and Promotion to Build Brands* (Burr Ridge, Il.: Irwin/McGraw-Hill, 2002), p. 248.

FIGURE 14.4

Four Basic
Segmentation Variables

limited loyalty situations, customers switch brands often. Companies have to concentrate on keeping those customers and reattracting those who were former customers. Very loyal customers, on the other hand, will come back again and again with little prodding.

Finally, benefit variables relate to why a customer purchases the product. In some cases, we buy products not because they are highly needed, but because we want to make a statement with the purchase. Consider the purchase of automobiles, for example. Most cars will get a person from point A to point B. But if we consider the differences between a Ford Focus and a Ford Expedition, we can easily see that customers purchase the two vehicles for quite different reasons and with quite different benefits in mind. Those of you who are wearing Abercrombie & Fitch clothing purchased it with benefits in mind different from those of people who bought their clothes at Target.

Using Market Segmentation

Once market segments have been identified, companies can then tailor their products to the specific segments. As you will learn in the next chapter, companies can send different messages to different segments according to the particular segment's interest in a given product. For example, a pharmaceutical firm with a new drug may send a message to doctors saying how effective the drug is, to insurance companies emphasizing how inexpensive the drug is, to patients noting how trustworthy the drug is, and to hospitals describing the training necessary to administer the drug.[5]

We now turn our attention to how products are developed, how we ensure quality, and how we get the products to the end customer. But keep in mind the ideas of market

THINK ABOUT THIS

1. Think about the styles of clothes that you buy compared with those your parents buy for themselves. In how many ways might your parents be in a different market segment than you are? In particular, how would their psychographic classifications differ from yours?

2. Consider the benefits of a segmentation strategy. How would you perceive the benefits of this textbook compared with how your professor would perceive them?

research and market segmentation and consider the impact those issues have on creating total value for the customer. Maximizing value to the customer is, of course, the key to everything in this chapter and, indeed, in the entire book itself.

Developing New Products and Services

Before getting into the process of product or service development, we need to first define what we mean. **Product or service development** is a broad term referring to the creation of a product or service that provides greater value to customers than previously existed. Product development efforts, if successful, will result in a new or modified product that better meets customer needs. There are actually five types of new products.[6]

1. A new-to-the-world product.
2. A new category entry.
3. A new product added to an existing line.
4. An improved product.
5. A repositioned product.

New-to-the-world products refer to totally new products never before seen by customers. These are actually rather rare. In the vast majority of cases, new products are simply variations on existing products. An example of a new-to-the-world product is the Segway Human Transporter, shown in Profile 14.1.

PROFILE 14.1   SEGWAY HUMAN TRANSPORTER

One of the few truly new products in recent years is the Segway Human Transporter (HT). Designed by Dean Kamen, the device combines self-balancing gyroscopes and electronics to create a "battery-powered urban person-mover." Lean forward; it goes forward. Lean back; it stops. The Segway HT is the first self-balancing, electric-powered personal transporter designed to enhance the productivity of people by increasing the distance they can travel and the amount they can carry. It is designed for use in pedestrian environments, providing a nonpolluting, low impact, short-distance travel solution.

Weighing 80 pounds, the Segway HT could be used for limited commuting, but its real value is in outdoor areas and within buildings. Imagine a librarian riding the Segway through book stacks, or warehouse workers moving through the stacks of inventories to retrieve a particular piece for a customer, or perhaps a grocery store stocker riding the Segway HT with a small trailer attached.

Some customers are trying out models now. The U.S. Postal Service, for example, is trying them for their urban mail carriers. The National Park Service is testing the Segway HT at the Grand Canyon's south rim. It allows park rangers and tour guides more mobility that, in turn, allows them to interact better with visitors and to patrol areas better.

The Segway Human Transporter is a radical innovation that provides a fast, convenient way to transport a person over short distances. Where would this product be most useful?

Currently, the Segway HT costs about $3,000. This appears to be a formidable price, but consider the impact on productivity as users can move faster on the Segway than they can walk. Obviously, they can also travel for longer periods and carry heavier loads. Thus, productivity should increase. Segway has received venture capital funding from two sources in the Boston area.

Source: Segway LLC website, www.segway.com (accessed July 19, 2002); Industrial Designers Society of America website, www.idsa.org (accessed July 19, 2002); and "The Best Product Designs of the Year: Winners 2002," *BusinessWeek,* July 8, 2002, pp. 82–94.

New category entries are products developed by a company that did not produce them before, even though other companies did. Such products or services allow the company to compete in new markets. Sometimes the product or service is ancillary to the main mission of the company. Boeing, for example, has a financial services division. Financial services are not closely connected to airplanes, so moving into financial services would count as a new category entry. Adding the financial services division helps Boeing work with its current customers as well as with customers who are not buying airplanes.

A company's new category product may not only be sold to new customers but also attract existing customers. Dell is a good example. Dell has recently entered the

DELL

microportable projector market. The microportable projector is a unit that is designed to be either carried around by a user who might be making a conference presentation, placed on an audiovisual cart that is wheeled from room to room as needed, or affixed permanently to the ceiling. The projector is compatible with notebook PCs and supports most multimedia applications. Dell's unit has a built-in speaker and a remote control with laser pointer. The microportable projector is a new market for Dell and puts Dell in competition with Panasonic, Philips, and Canon.[7]

A less radical method is to add a *new product to an existing product line.* A company develops a product it has never had with the goal of expanding its current product line. When General Mills brought out MultiGrain Cheerios, it was adding a new product to go with its regular Cheerios, Honey Nut Cheerios, and Frosted Cheerios products. Thus, it added a new product to the Cheerios line of cereals.

The firm may also improve or revise an existing product to make it more appealing to customers. *Product improvement* does not create a new product, but it makes a significant improvement on an existing product or product line. Product improvement may include bringing out new models or adding features that make the product more valuable—for example, a faster, more powerful computer chip. The Nova Cruz Xootr eX3 electric scooter designed by Lunar Design is an example of product improvement, although some might feel that it is so different that it could be better classified as a totally new product. The Xootr scooter takes the basic concept of the scooter and adds a small electric motor to the back of it. The Xootr can travel up to 17 miles per hour and up to 16 miles per charge, and weighs less than 20 pounds. As a result, the Xootr, which is really designed for older teenagers and adults, can be a source of short-range transportation as well as an entertaining ride.[8]

Sometimes a firm may reposition a current product. *Product repositioning* means taking an existing product and finding ways to market it to new customer groups. Arm & Hammer, known for decades for its baking soda, has adopted this strategy. In addition to its traditional use in baking, Arm & Hammer's baking soda is being marketed as a refrigerator deodorant, a carpet freshener, and a drain deodorizer, among other uses.[9]

Service development is essentially the same as product development, with the base being a service rather than a product. Thus, a service firm may bring out a new-to-the-world service, introduce a service in a category new to the firm's existing services, add new services, improve or revise its services so that they are more appealing, or reposition its services to appeal to other markets.

Often at this stage, the organization is concerned with **product or service differentiation.** Differentiation means developing a product or service that differs enough from existing products that customers can distinguish the new product from existing ones. Obviously, the hope is that customers will prefer the differentiated product over currently available options. If the product is really different, the business may attract new customers.

> **product or service differentiation**
> The development of a product or service that differs enough from existing products or services so that customers can distinguish the new product or service from existing ones.

The Development Process

At the beginning of this chapter, we said that meeting customer needs begins with assessing those needs and then developing services or products that meet them. In many cases, ideas for new products do come directly from customers. However, employees, distributors, and even competitors may generate ideas that seem worthy of development. The specific process companies use when developing products or services involves concept evaluation, business analysis, development, test marketing, and commercialization.[10]

Concept Evaluation Stage

The first step is **concept evaluation,** which means analyzing the overall idea to see if it fits with the firm's strategy and existing product or service mix. In other words, does the concept seem to make sense for the business? Concept evaluation is a broad-brush analysis that is completed before in-depth analysis occurs. It looks at the big picture of how the idea fits with the existing products or services.

> **concept evaluation**
> An analysis to determine if the overall idea fits with the firm's strategy and existing product or service mix.

Business Analysis Stage

Once the concept has been evaluated favorably, the idea must be subjected to **business analysis,** which compares projected demand for a product with the firm's ability and cost to produce it. The company considers how the product would affect existing products, what investments in production facilities would be required, and what additional marketing staff might be needed. The analysis is ultimately aimed at predicting how much profit can be expected from the product. A concept may look promising, but if it fails to pass the scrutiny of the business analysis, it should not be pursued further.

> **business analysis**
> A comparison of projected demand for a product with the firm's ability and cost to produce it.

Development Stage

If a product idea passes all the business analysis tests, then the actual product development begins. Often a **development team** is used to create the product or service. A development team is a group of individuals from various parts of a company who have an interest in the product or service and are selected to develop it into a profitable activity. The best development work occurs when the development team consists of an integrated mix of employees from research and development, engineering, marketing, accounting, and production, and perhaps even suppliers. There are a number of reasons to use an integrated development team. One is that the various departments that may be involved in either producing, advertising, or selling the product will be more committed to the product if they have input into its design. Second, the probability of customer acceptance increases if those employees who interact directly with customers are involved. A third reason for integrated development teams is to reduce development time, or cycle time.

> **development team**
> A group of people from various parts of a company who have an interest in the product or service and are selected to develop it into a profitable activity.

Product development works best if teams are an integral part of the process. Creating high-performance, cross-functional work teams is not easy, and the process fails if the team members do not trust one another or the company bureaucracy causes problems. A recent research study found, however, that collaborative behaviors emerge when participants agree on a common agenda, openly share concerns and power, and commit to building trust. Work environments and company cultures that encourage risk taking and tolerate failure appear to improve the odds that cross-functional product development teams will be successful.[11]

> **test marketing**
> Selling a product or service in certain select markets to find out what customers think.

Test Marketing Stage

This stage may involve building a prototype that can be studied to make sure the product is sound and feasible. This stage may also include **test marketing,** which involves piloting a product or service in certain select markets to find out what customers think. If customers in the targeted locations do not buy the product or do not respond favorably, some changes or modifications may be necessary. The entire product idea may even have to be scrapped.

THINK ABOUT THIS

1. McDonald's has test-marketed its new made-to-order burgers. How will McDonald's use the information gained from its test site in Colorado Springs to determine whether this product will be a winner? Will the test results apply to New England or California?

2. Why do businesses invest so much money in the product or service development process?

Some businesses do extensive test marketing before introducing products to customers on a broad scale. In 1997, Procter & Gamble began test-marketing a new product called Bibsters, disposable bibs that consumers use when feeding babies. P&G reasoned that disposable bibs would be just as desirable for today's families as disposable diapers were when they were test-marketed 35 years ago. P&G selected cities that met a number of stringent requirements for the test marketing. The cities needed to be medium-size with fairly well defined geographic boundaries so that marketing could be pinpointed. They also needed to have demographic characteristics similar to those of the rest of the country. Test marketing indicated that Bibsters was a solid idea. Today, Bibsters are part of the Pampers product line.[12]

Commercialization Stage

The decision to commercialize a product leads to many tasks: designing or obtaining production equipment, obtaining raw materials, starting production, building inventories, and shipping the product. At the same time, other marketing-related activities occur, such as announcing the new product in trade journals and advertising to potential customers.

Ensuring Quality in Products and Services

Pause for a moment and consider where we have been and where we are headed in this chapter. The title of the chapter is "Providing Value through Quality Products and Services." We began by focusing on the need to know who our customers are. Once we have studied our customers, we can categorize them into one or more market segments, which allows us to focus our products or services more precisely on their needs. We can also orient our marketing communications more directly toward the specific group of customers.

Making quality products requires a primary focus on quality. Can a quality inspector ensure that adequate quality is included in a product?

We then turned our attention to the product development process to illustrate how we develop products and services. Keep in mind that product development should occur only after sufficient market research has been done to assess what needs are currently unmet. The research should also give us a clue about the level of quality that customers expect from our products or services. All these processes are focused on providing value to our customers.

The need for quality surfaced in the 1980s as the Japanese, who, ironically, learned their approach to quality from an American quality guru named W. Edwards Deming, produced products that far surpassed the quality of American products. In response, American manufacturers turned to Deming, Joseph Juran, and Philip Crosby—all noted quality consultants—to help build quality into American products. Manufacturers realized that the cost of poor quality far exceeded the cost of programs designed to teach employees how to build quality into products.

A number of quality management programs have gained in popularity over the years. Among the most recognized are total quality management (TQM), continuous improvement (CI), benchmarking, and Six Sigma quality. We first introduce the dimensions of quality and then briefly discuss each of these programs. We then end by discussing quality certification.

Dimensions of Quality

Quality is a broad term that encompasses a number of issues. In its most basic sense, quality refers to the ability of a product or service to consistently meet or exceed customer expectations. Quality has eight dimensions, as shown in Table 14.1. *Performance* relates to how well a product performs or how well a service is provided. *Features* are those extras that affect performance but are not standard on all competing products or services. *Reliability* relates to the consistency of performance. Can the product always be expected to perform the way it should? Is the service provided always good? *Durability* relates to the life of the product. Is the life expectancy logical? For the amount of money paid, does the product last as long as customers think it should? *Serviceability* relates to ease of repair. *Response* is timeliness. How long does it take to get action, and how competent is the action? *Aesthetics* is the look, sound, or feel of the product. *Reputation* is the past performance of the product or service.

Note in Table 14.1 that these eight dimensions are important whether we are discussing products or services, whether we are talking about for-profit businesses or not-for-profit organizations, whether the customers are end users or other businesses, and whether the business is large or very small. For example, suppose you take your lawn mower in for service at the beginning of the season, partially because it was not running right when you put it away last fall. You get the mower back. In considering whether you will take the mower back to the same shop next time, you might ask yourself the following questions: Did the mower run right when you got it home? (performance). Did someone clean it in addition to servicing it? (features). Was the mower ready when the service manager said it would be? (response). Did it continue to run throughout the season? (reliability, durability). Was the shop neat and clean or did it

> **quality**
> The ability of a product or service to consistently meet or exceed customer expectations.

TABLE 14.1
Dimensions of Quality

Dimension	Product Example: Stereo Amplifier	Service Example: Bank Checking Account
Performance	Signal-to-noise ratio, power.	Time to process customer requests.
Features	Remote control.	Automatic bill paying.
Reliability	Mean time to failure.	Variability of time to process requests.
Durability	Useful life (with repair).	Keeping pace with industry trends.
Serviceability	Modular design.	Online reports.
Response	Courtesy of dealer.	Courtesy of teller.
Aesthetics	Oak-finished cabinet.	Appearance of bank lobby.
Reputation	Market leader for 20 years.	Endorsement of community leaders.

Source: From Richard Chase, Nicholas Aquilano, and Robert Jacobs, *Production and Operations Management,* 9th ed. Copyright © 2001 The McGraw-Hill Companies, Inc. Reproduced with permission from The McGraw-Hill Companies.

The benefit is crystal clear.

The crystal of a Rolex Oyster is no ordinary watch-glass. Perfectly flat, except for the addition of the magnifying Cyclops lens, and a mere millimeter or two thick, it is sliced from a synthetic sapphire—an incredibly hard and virtually scratchproof material.

Then it is fitted to the Oyster case with a seal whose efficiency actually improves with increasing water pressure down to 330 feet for the Datejust styles shown above. Clear proof why, for Rolex, no other material comes up to scratch.

Rolex Datejust in stainless steel and 18kt gold with matching Oyster bracelet. For the name and location of an Official Rolex Jeweler near you, please call 1-800-36ROLEX. Rolex, ®, Oyster Perpetual, Cyclops, Datejust and Oyster are trademarks.

ROLEX

Rolex is known for its quality in watchmaking, priding itself on aesthetics, performance, and reputation. The first line of this ad, "The crystal of a Rolex Oyster is no ordinary watch-glass," differentiates its glass from its competitors by highlighting the glass' special materials. Is high quality always synonymous with high price?

look like a junked-up firetrap? (aesthetics). Did the shop owner check back later to see if the service had been provided well? (reputation). These dimensions are not difficult to understand, nor are they difficult to implement. They do require time and attention and, most important, a focus on quality.

Quality Management Programs

Total Quality Management

Total quality management (TQM) is a systematic method for addressing quality issues. Although TQM programs vary depending on each company's individual approach, one theme is common to all successful TQM programs. They require a total, integrated, companywide commitment to quality. TQM may begin with careful market research to assess customer needs, but quality goes far beyond market research. Designers, development staff, and engineers must be able to take customer desires and translate them into winning, high-quality product designs. Manufacturing must be able to produce these quality products at reasonable cost. Finally, the products must be delivered in a timely and convenient way so that customers receive satisfaction.

TQM involves everything the business does, from initial customer contact through delivery to customer follow-up. It is a fallacy to assume that quality is the job of any single area or function in the business. In TQM, quality is everyone's job. Thus teams are often used in TQM. People from different areas of the business come together to address customer needs and learn how everyone can help deliver customer satisfaction.

total quality management (TQM)

A systematic approach to addressing quality issues that involves a total integrated, companywide commitment to quality.

Continuous Improvement

The second quality management concept, **continuous improvement (CI),** is a mandate to the business and all its people to continually look for ways to improve everything. Continuous improvement truly covers all facets of the business, and all employees should be involved in the effort. Production methods, work flow, equipment, and procedures are all examined and altered where appropriate. Relationships with customers and suppliers are explored to determine where changes can be made to improve the contacts and interactions. Again, teams of employees from different areas of the business are used to help meet this need. Even upgrading employee skills and developing new training opportunities may be areas to target. The possibilities for improvement are endless.

You now have a general sense of what quality management is all about. However, a practical question remains. How do businesses actually go about achieving continuous improvement? What strategies and techniques do they use? One of the most popular techniques is benchmarking.

continuous improvement (CI)

A process in which a firm and all its people continually look for ways to change and improve all facets of the business.

Benchmarking

A key approach to continuous improvement and a strategy for overall quality management is benchmarking. In **benchmarking,** managers compare their practices with the practices of recognized leaders to determine where and how improvements can be made. Managers search out companies that are recognized as "best-practice companies" in one or more aspects of the company's operations.

Typically, the businesses selected for study are in different industries so that they are not competitors, but they have similar practices. For example, Xerox, in its desire to deliver products quickly, studied how mail-order company L.L. Bean handles its product shipping.[13]

Keep in mind that the goal of benchmarking is almost always to improve efficiency, add quality, or reduce cost of operations. Companies that use benchmarking are indeed serious about improving their own operations and are willing to invest the time and effort necessary to work with a best-practice company.

> **benchmarking**
> Comparing one's practices with those of recognized leaders to determine where and how improvements can be made.

Six Sigma Quality

One of the best-known programs in quality management is called Six Sigma. This program was first developed by Motorola as a way of reducing defects in its products. **Six Sigma** is a rigorous, focused, and highly effective implementation of proven quality principles and techniques. Incorporating elements from the work of many quality pioneers, Six Sigma aims for virtually error-free business performance. Quality is enhanced through a performance improvement model known as DMAIC, or **D**efine-**M**easure-**A**nalyze-**I**mprove-**C**ontrol. DMAIC can be described as follows:

> **Six Sigma**
> A program that uses proven quality principles and techniques to make business operations as efficient and error free as possible.

1. *Define* the goals of the improvement activity.
2. *Measure* the existing system. Establish valid and reliable metrics to help monitor progress toward the goals defined in the previous step.
3. *Analyze* the system to identify ways to eliminate the gap between the current performance of the system or process and the desired goal. Apply statistical tools to guide the analysis.
4. *Improve* the system. Be creative in finding new ways to do things better, cheaper, or faster.
5. *Control* the new system. Institutionalize the improved system by modifying compensation and incentive systems, policies, procedures, and other aspects of the company's operations.[14]

Consider Caterpillar Inc., a maker of truck engines and earth-moving equipment. At Caterpillar, Six Sigma is a key to the company's quest for quality, excellence, and bottom-line growth. Six Sigma is driving the company's efforts to make major strides in quality improvement throughout the business. Six Sigma is applied to everything from new-product development through the production process. It even encompasses product support activities and administration.[15]

A very powerful feature of Six Sigma is the creation of an infrastructure to ensure that performance improvement activities have the necessary resources. In Six Sigma programs, a small number of employees are assigned to develop significant improvements in quality. These full-time change agents, known as Six Sigma Blackbelts, are the catalyst that institutionalizes change. Six Sigma programs are now in use in many large companies, such as Motorola, Caterpillar, Johnson & Johnson, Honeywell, and General Electric.

The Baldrige Award is one of the top awards for quality given U.S. companies. The award is a symbol of excellence in all phases of quality. Do you find an award like this to be useful?

Baldrige Award
The highest quality governing recognition that a U.S. business can receive.

ISO 9000
Quality management and assurance standards published by the International Standards Organization; a common denominator of business quality accepted around the world.

Recognizing and Certifying Quality

We have said there are real business advantages to having a focus that emphasizes quality. There are also advantages to a business in being recognized for its quality leadership. The highest quality recognition that a U.S. business can receive is the **Baldrige Award,** given by the federal government. To give you an idea of how good a business has to be to win the Baldrige Award, consider that a maximum of six U.S. businesses win it each year. It is a tremendous honor and a real spark to a company's reputation.

Although companies that enter the Baldrige Award competition must do extensive analysis and paperwork, the effort can be well worth it. The award has had a dramatic impact on awareness of the need for quality. It has also provided examples of how quality can be achieved. Adding to the award's significance is information suggesting that high-quality companies typically also perform better financially.

Another quality designation that businesses seek is ISO 9000. **ISO 9000** is a worldwide set of standards administered by the International Standards Organization (in which 91 countries participate). These standards are critical to doing business in international markets; most overseas manufacturers require their suppliers to be ISO 9000 certified. ISO 9000 certification indicates that the business has documented procedures to ensure the highest standards for quality. To earn ISO 9000 status, the business is visited by an outside certifying agency, which conducts a detailed, comprehensive on-site audit of the business, carefully scrutinizing every aspect of the quality process. Often the agency notes changes and improvements that must be made before it will grant certification.

Today many businesses have received ISO 9000 certification, and many others are working toward it. This certification is important for reasons beyond image. ISO 9000 lets all customers know that the firm has the highest quality standards. Many companies prefer dealing with businesses that have achieved ISO 9000 certification. Many large businesses that have already been certified demand certification (or a plan of progress toward certification) from their smaller suppliers. This requirement makes sense. The larger business figures its quality is only as good as the quality of the input it receives from its suppliers. It wants the best quality assurance possible from these suppliers. Accordingly, ISO 9000 certification tends to snowball in actual practice.

Quality Issues Unique to Service Industries

Opportunities to improve quality may be greater in manufacturing firms since they deal with a tangible product and a definitive process that produces the product. However, quality is also important in service firms. Recall from Chapter 4 that service firms differ significantly from manufacturing firms.

Because services are partly intangible, it is more difficult to measure or assess service quality than product quality. Service quality is often based on customer perceptions. One person may feel that service is inadequate while another may find the same level of service acceptable. Some customers are more likely to complain than are others who are equally displeased. Thus, it can be difficult to know whether high-quality service has been provided or not. In addition, unless communications between the provider and the customer occur, the business may not even know when there is a problem.

For example, if a movie theater is dirty or patrons are noisy, the vast majority of customers will not complain to the management. They will, however, complain to each other and go to a different theater next time. The theater management may be unaware of the magnitude of the problem and may even think the few people who do complain are simply whiners. How many times have you gone to a restaurant, had less than desirable food or service, and said nothing to management? Perhaps you left no tip or left a token tip for the server, but you probably did not complain to the very people who could affect the quality of the service.

Another quality-oriented issue for service firms is that the service provider and the customer interact. This interaction gives service providers the opportunity to build rapport with customers—who become repeat customers if the service is provided well. Of course, the service provider must be willing to listen carefully to the customer and respond to specific requests. If good rapport is not established, interaction can become strained and the customer's specific needs are ignored.

Clearly, it can be hard to achieve a quality focus in service industries. Measuring service quality is also difficult. Look back at Table 14.1 and key on measures of service quality. Leaders in service businesses may need to develop indicators of quality that apply to their particular business. In a restaurant, indicators of quality could include the friendliness of the table server, the length of time from placing the order until the food arrives, the correctness of the food compared with the order, and the cleanliness of rest rooms. An airline could have the willingness of flight attendants to assist in storing carry-on luggage, the length of time to load a plane and take off, the number of lost pieces of luggage, and the number of flights canceled because of equipment. A hospital could use the completeness with which a nurse attends to a patient's needs, the time from the push of a call button until a nurse arrives, the number of errors in administering medicine, and aesthetics of the patient's room.

As we have said, providing service quality is complicated by the interactions between the customer and the provider. For example, a disorderly airline passenger can cause problems not only for the flight attendants but also for other customers. A diner in a restaurant who gives an incorrect order and then blames the mistake on the server can affect both timeliness and human factors. Emergencies on a hospital floor may confuse staff to the extent that they make an error with another patient. Thus, managers studying quality of service must do careful analyses.

You may have heard the saying that there are only two rules in customer service: Rule 1: The customer is always right. Rule 2: If the customer is not right, see Rule 1. This saying suggests that the customer calls the shots in anything relating to customer service. Many companies have this policy and would rather lose money on a transaction than have an unhappy customer. They reason that the unhappy customer will tell a number of friends and may cause other problems for the company that outweigh the loss it incurs by giving in.

On the other hand, sometimes a customer is simply wrong. Sometimes the customer is either intentionally or accidentally taking advantage. This situation creates a dilemma for the company. Should it give in when it is obvious that the customer is wrong, or should it hold its ground? There is no right answer here, but often communication is the key. If the server (clerk, nurse, flight attendant, bank teller) can pleasantly but completely communicate the issue to the customer, the misunderstanding may be resolved and the customer satisfied.

THINK ABOUT THIS

1. Define *quality.* What is the real significance to a business of receiving the Baldrige Award? of receiving ISO 9000 certification?

2. Quality management is both a process and a philosophy. Is a formal program, such as TQM, CI, or Six Sigma, necessary to gain a quality focus?

3. Is reliability more important for some service businesses than others?

The key to solving customer problems is to address the human factors involved, usually communication, and make every attempt to solve the issue immediately before it gets out of hand. Many companies empower their customer representatives to solve problems, within limits, without needing approval from a higher authority. This policy makes customers happy and gives the employees responsibility and control over their own jobs.

Providing Value through Distribution of Products and Services

We have discussed how to provide value by finding out what customers want. Managers then take that information and develop products or services that best meet those wants. We have discussed how firms must always be aware of the need for quality. We now turn to providing value by delivering the service or product to customers *when* it's needed, *where* it's needed, and in the *form* that is needed. When making decisions, a manager must be sure these three criteria are met. If any of the three is missing, customers will be unhappy, and ultimately, the manager will be unhappy.

We consider here the distribution of products to two segments of the market: the business segment and the consumer segment. In the business segment, we are interested in what is called supply-chain management. For the consumer segment, a key element is the channels of distribution. It is important to consider, however, that important aspects of distribution apply equally well in the business-to-business segment as they do in the business-to-consumer segment.

Business-to-Business Distribution: Supply-Chain Management

supply-chain management

Management of the movement of products or components through all the stages involved in the production and delivery of final products to an end user.

You may recall from Chapter 4 that products have different destinations. One of those destinations is other businesses that purchase products either for their own use or for conversion into finished products. Consider Figure 14.5. Raw materials are used to manufacture components. Those components become inputs for another business, which then incorporates those components into its own manufacturing process. This cycle of outputs of one firm becoming inputs for another may be repeated until the final product is produced. The final product is then distributed to that company's customers—either another business or intermediaries that eventually sell to an end user. Managing this movement of products or components through all the stages involved in the production and delivery of final products to an end user is called **supply-chain management.** Figure 14.5 shows a simple supply chain that includes only four steps. In actuality, a supply chain may have hundreds of relationships among various producers or intermediaries.

FIGURE 14.5

Simple Supply Chain

Business-to-Consumer Distribution

Providing value to consumers through distribution recognizes that products must reach consumers where needed, when needed, and in the form needed. A simple example illustrates this aspect of distribution. Suppose you are busy reading this chapter late at night when hunger strikes. You have some choices. You can get on some decent clothes, gather your friends, find transportation, and go out to a pizza or burger restaurant. Or you can simply dial a local provider—with the number probably already in your phone's speed-dial memory—and order a pizza to be delivered to your dorm room or apartment. You may have to pay a delivery charge. But the point is that the pizza has more value to you delivered to your door than if you have to go get it late at night.

As you recall from Chapter 4, different products use different distribution channels. Whereas Dell uses a direct-from-the-manufacturer-to-user channel, a business that produces VCRs would find that method inefficient at best. Retailers such as Best Buy provide value to products by making a large number of products available in a single store. Customers then have the capability of purchasing a number of products from a single store, as well as the opportunity to interact with store personnel for advice and assistance.

Let's return to the pizza example. For that delivery to have value for you, three things must happen. First, the pizza should be delivered within 30 minutes. Second, it needs to be delivered where you asked for it to be delivered. Third, it needs to be hot when it gets there. Those three requirements introduce the three key elements of providing value through distribution: timeliness, location, and form.

Timeliness

We discussed timeliness in Chapter 2 as one of the critical measures of a successful business. Our interest here is in two areas. First is the minimization of time from placement of the order or request to delivery to the customer. Second is the commitment to providing the product precisely when it is promised. Thus, timeliness is the provision of products when promised and in the minimum amount of time. Most industries are becoming increasingly time sensitive.

Mail-order companies especially understand the need for timely shipping of goods; some guarantee arrival in two days. They also know of the need for timeliness in order taking, so many have order takers available 24 hours a day, seven days a week.

Some companies have found that, in today's hectic world, timeliness is even more important than face-to-face communications. Thus, banks have moved heavily toward the use of ATMs, which allow customers to make transactions 24 hours a day.

A few years ago, hotels began to allow customers to check out by way of the TV in their room. Guests check their bill on the TV screen and indicate their acceptance by telephone or perhaps just by leaving. Some hotels are now using the equivalent of ATMs for check-in in response to studies that found one of the greatest frustrations of travelers is waiting in line to register. ATM check-ins reduce the average registration time from many minutes to the seconds required to pass a credit card through a reader and punch in a few keys or touch spots on a monitor. This method is particularly handy when many guests arrive at the same time.

Airlines are also discovering the role of timeliness in flight reservations and boarding. Southwest Airlines and most other airlines now use the convenient practice of ticketless travel. Travelers can make their reservations over the Internet, pay for them with a credit card, and go directly to the gate if they have no baggage to check. The gate attendant verifies the traveler's identity and issues a boarding pass. Even those

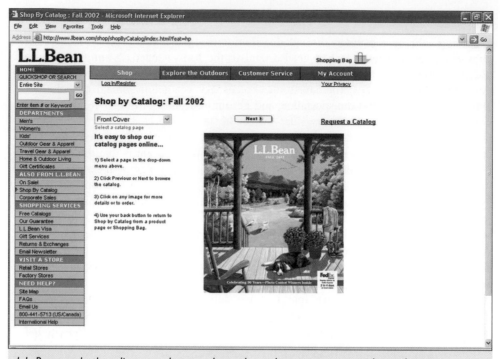

L.L. Bean and other direct marketers rely on the web as a way to provide products to customers in a timely manner. What value does the web site provide that catalogs could not?

customers who make reservations in traditional ways have the option of flying ticket-less. Ironically, Southwest's policy of first-come, first-served has encountered problems since increased security procedures have been installed in airports. Southwest has struggled with the new procedures and, as a result, has seen its on-time performance drop to eighth place among major airlines.[16] Thus, its timeliness has suffered because of the mandated changes.

Managers must guard against going to extremes with automated processing. Customers must be polled periodically to determine which method gives them the greatest value. In most cases, they prefer the option of choosing either automation or face-to-face interaction.

The second area in timeliness is for companies to provide service precisely when it is promised. This issue is especially important for service businesses, whether they work with consumers or with other businesses. Consider the following example: Suppose I am the president of a small company and I have just hired a consultant to do a job analysis to find out how I can make my workers more efficient. I have arranged for the consultant to interview each of my 50 employees over a one-week period beginning June 10. I have scheduled each employee to visit with the consultant for 30 minutes at prescribed times throughout the week. On June 9, the consultant calls me to tell me he can't start until June 15. As a result, I have to change the entire schedule of appointments. I am not happy, the employees are not happy, the production schedule is wrecked, and my own customers may become unhappy. Someone failed to deliver the service as promised and others were inconvenienced. Even if the problem was beyond that person's control, the failure to deliver in a timely manner detracted from the value normally associated with the service.

Location

Creating value through delivery of products to specific locations can be lucrative if done well. Lear Corporation, which we discussed in Chapter 13, is a supplier of interior assemblies to most carmakers. Customers like Ford and GM are demanding. Lear has perfected the value-through-location concept so well that it provides seat assemblies not only to the building where they are needed but to the actual assembly-line position where they are inserted in a car or van.

Providing value through location ensures that customers get products delivered in a convenient manner. Mail-order firms, for example, deliver products to the customer's front door, making shopping a simpler and less time-consuming process. Companies sometimes have options with regard to how or where products can be delivered. Business supply houses, for example, can deliver supplies to the central receiving station for a company or directly to the office that ordered them. The latter method is more time consuming for the supplier, but it provides better value. The key is making sure that the product is at the desired location.

Form

The final way to provide value through product distribution is to provide it in the form that is needed. **Form** refers to the specific design, size, or model of a product that a customer needs. The desired form will, of course, vary from situation to situation. An auto mechanic may want to have motor oil delivered in 55-gallon drums rather than in quart cans. That way the mechanic can pump what is needed from the drums and may also be able to get the oil at a lower price. A business may request specially designed invoice forms to bill its customers rather than using standard forms. A buyer of computer equipment may order a computer with specific software preloaded rather than having to load software after the computer arrives. As these examples show, a company that can customize its products for others can add value to the product through attention to form.

Some progressive and successful companies compete, at least in part, through their efforts to provide value to their customers by emphasizing both form and delivery. For example, Dell builds quality PCs and other equipment that many customers, including a number of large businesses, have selected. Customers order from Dell either by calling a toll-free number or by using the Internet. Once a customer chooses the basic model desired, the features, options, and software needed can be added. All this is done electronically, without face-to-face contact. Even though each machine is custom built, the company can usually build, ship, and promise delivery within a week of the initial order.

A final important aspect of form is the packaging. As you will learn in Chapter 15, packaging plays an important role in communicating value to the customer. Packaging also provides value to the product itself. Packaging protects the product from damage. It provides space to include directions or suggestions for product use. Packaging can even make the product easier to use. Consider a ketchup bottle, for example. Adding a flip-top lid with a small hole provides a mechanism to get just the right amount of the condiment on the hamburger with a minimum of mess. Jelly manufacturers have followed that lead in recent years by offering squeezable plastic bottles.

> **form**
> The specific design, size, or model of a product that a customer needs.

THE BIG PICTURE

Think value. Why do we conduct market research to find out what customers want? Why do we spend considerable time developing new products for either our current or potential customers? Why are we concerned that products get where they are needed, when they are needed, and how they are needed? The answer: value. We are providing value for the customer.

Customers are willing to pay for value, but that value must be in terms of the price that is being paid. A customer may be willing to pay FedEx charges to get a product shipped overnight because timeliness has value to that customer. A cheap, used car may provide sufficient value for the price if the car is for a teenager to drive to work, but a Lexus certainly provides better value and perhaps better value for the price for that teenager's parents. It is the responsibility of business leaders to assess and determine how to provide value to the company's customers.

The "think value" concept is an important principle for business leaders to instill in their employees throughout the organization. As new products are developed, for example, it is important to use teams representing several departments in the business to get input about what value means to individual areas of the firm. Only when we can get broad input from a variety of perspectives can we develop products and services with high levels of value for customers.

Summary

1. Companies cannot maximize value to their customers unless they understand what their customers want. It is important to communicate with customers as part of the product or service development process. This form of communication is known as market research.

   • What is market research?

   Market research is collecting information about the market and potential market for products or services. This task can be accomplished through either secondary research or primary research. Secondary research is studying already existing information. That information may be found on the Web, in trade journals, or in other printed media. Primary research requires collecting new information through surveys of customers, focus groups, or observations. Surveys may be done by mail, by telephone, or by using the Web.

2. Part of learning about customers is placing them in groups with similar characteristics. This strategy allows companies to tailor their products to more specific segments of the market.

   • What is market segmentation?

   Market segmentation is the process of differentiating customers on the basis of a number of possible dimensions. Four were suggested: demographics, psychographics, relationships, and benefits. Once this process is completed, companies can fine-tune their offerings to better meet the needs of specific customer groups.

3. Once a company knows what new products its customers want, the next step is to develop the product. Product development usually requires five steps.

   • What are the five steps of the product development process?

Product development begins with concept evaluation to see whether a new product fits within the general strategy of the company. Business analysis examines the cost of the product and compares it with the demand for the product. Then a sample of the new product—a prototype—is constructed. If information is still favorable, limited production may begin with products being test-marketed in a small region of the country. Finally, if the test marketing is successful, full production and commercialization of the product begins.

4. Beginning in the 1980s, competition from Japanese imports prompted U.S. businesses to pay increased attention to the issue of quality. This focus on quality continues today.

   • What is quality?

   In its most basic sense, quality refers to the ability of a product or service to consistently meet or exceed customer expectations. Specifically, quality can refer to any of the following characteristics of a product: (1) performance, (2) features, (3) reliability, (4) durability, (5) serviceability, (6) response, (7) aesthetics, and (8) reputation.

   When the quality movement began, it centered on the thinking of a few well-known quality experts, such as W. Edwards Deming. Two concepts emerging from the quality movement are total quality management (TQM) and continuous improvement (CI). Other programs include benchmarking and Six Sigma.

   • What are total quality management, continuous improvement, benchmarking, and Six Sigma?

   TQM is a systematic approach for addressing quality that requires a total, integrated, companywide commitment to quality. CI is a mandate to the business and all its people to continually look for ways to improve everything. Benchmarking is comparing one's practice with recognized leaders to determine where and how improvements can be made. Six Sigma is a program that implements proven quality principles and techniques to make operations as efficient and error free as possible.

   • What is the highest quality recognition that a U.S. company can receive?

   The Baldrige Award is the highest recognition for quality achievement awarded to businesses by the government of the United States.

   • What is the most prominent international program for certifying a company's dedication to high quality standards?

   The ISO 9000 certification program is the largest and most prominent international quality certification program. It consists of a worldwide set of standards developed and evaluated by the International Standards Organization.

5. Even the best product or service is of little value if it is not provided at the time and location needed by the customer. Delivery of services is just as important as delivery of products. Both require attention to at least three aspects of distribution.

   • What are the three keys to effective distribution?

   The three keys to effective distribution are timeliness, location, and form. Products and services must be provided when needed, where needed, and in the form needed. Timeliness refers to when a product or service is provided and the response time by the company once an order has been received. Location is the delivery of a product or service where it is needed by the customer. Form deals with the size, design, and packaging of a product so that it can be best used by customers.

Key Terms

Baldrige Award, p. 368

benchmarking, p. 367

business analysis, p. 363

concept evaluation, p. 363

continuous improvement (CI), p. 366

data analysis, p. 356

development team, p. 363

focus groups, p. 356

form, p. 373

ISO 9000, p. 368

market research, p. 354

market segment, p. 357

primary data, p. 355

product or service differentiation, p. 362

product or service development, p. 360

qualitative research, p. 356

quality, p. 365

quantitative research, p. 356

research design, p. 354

secondary data, p. 355

Six Sigma, p. 367

supply-chain management, p. 370

test marketing, p. 363

total quality management (TQM), p. 366

Exercises and Applications

1. You have probably come into contact with several forms of market research. You may have participated in market research efforts. Drawing from your experiences, identify as many forms of market research as you can.

2. Pick a product or service with which you are familiar. Develop a market research questionnaire that could be used to solicit feedback from customers. What questions should you ask to determine how well the product provides value to customers?

3. In teams, consider one or more of the products discussed in the introduction to this chapter. Determine which individuals should be involved in designing the product for the company. Why is each important?

4. Choose a fast-food restaurant in your area. Visit it and analyze the level of service quality you see there. Use the criteria for service quality discussed in this chapter as the basis for your evaluation. Prepare a one-page report of your findings.

5. Form teams. All team members should name a product that they purchased but with which they were dissatisfied. Compare experiences. Which dimensions of product quality were missing?

6. Prepare a chart listing the best methods of distributing the following products or services. Then discuss the methods in a small group.

   • A product purchased from eBay.com.

   • A tax return prepared by H&R Block.

   • This textbook.

   • A bottle of aspirin.

   • A meal from Chili's or another casual-dining restaurant.

Meet the Uber Mercedes

FROM THE PAGES OF

Mercedes-Benz's $116,000 S600 sedan should be enough for the most discerning driver. Its features—a navigation system, self-activating windshield wipers and others—meet or exceed that of competing luxury sedans. But just in case the S600 sedan is not enough, Mercedes is now bringing out a superluxury, super-high-priced brand that sells for a mere $300,000. The Maybach is an 83-year-old name plate that is being relaunched with high-tech gadgets and personalized accoutrements. One customer, for example, wanted a Maybach paneled with wood from a favorite but dying tree in his garden. Maybachs can come with a state-of-the-art cell phone, a DVD player, a flat-screen TV, a fax, and a "liaison manager" to handle any problems. It will have climate controls for each passenger, and some versions even come with rear seats that recline and have a pop-out footrest. Owners will be able to reach a sales agent 24/7 by pressing a button on the car-phone keypad. The Maybach has a 12-cylinder engine that produces 500 horsepower.

Mercedes thinks it can sell 1,000 of the Maybachs and already has 200 orders, including one from King Abdullah II of Jordan. Other luxury car companies—Cadillac, Bentley (owned by Volkswagen), and Rolls Royce—all have plans in the works.

Is there a demand for these superluxury cars? Perhaps. Buyers of these cars are not concerned with changes in the economy. Ferrari, for example, had a three-year waiting list for its cars in the middle of the most recent recession. One Mercedes sales executive mused that the people who buy these cars have the tough choice of whether to buy a yacht, an apartment in Paris, or another car. Mercedes thinks they will buy the car.

Decision Questions

1. What kind of market research would need to be done to confirm the market for the Maybach?

2. Quality is important in many products. But is this much quality necessary?

3. Is Mercedes bringing out the Maybach as a profit generator since it is very difficult to make a profit with only 1,000 vehicles per year? If not, why else might the company be bringing out the car?

Source: Christine Tierney, "Meet the Uber Mercedes," *BusinessWeek*, May 27, 2002, p. 71.

References

1. Industrial Designers Society of America website, www.idsa.org (accessed July 19, 2002); and "The Best Product Designs of the Year: Winners 2002," *BusinessWeek*, July 8, 2002, pp. 82–94.

2. Cannondale website, www.cannondale.com (accessed July 19, 2002).

3. Carl McDaniel, Jr., and Roger Gates, *Marketing Research: The Impact of the Internet* (Cincinnati, OH: South-Western, 2002), pp. 122–25.

4. Much of this information is taken from Tom Duncan, *IMC: Using Advertising and Promotion to Build Brands* (Burr Ridge, IL: Irwin/McGraw-Hill, 2002), chap. 7.

5. Duncan, p. 261.

6. C. Merle Crawford and C. Anthony Di Benedetto, *New Products Management* (Burr Ridge, IL: Irwin/McGraw-Hill, 2003), pp. 12, 13.

7. "Dell Introduces Microportable Projector to Complement Notebooks," *T.H.E. Journal,* June 2002, p. 54.

8. Nova Cruz website, www.novacruz.com (accessed July 19, 2002).

9. Crawford and Di Benedetto, p. 10.

10. Charles W. Lamb, Jr., Joseph F. Hair, and Carl McDaniel, *Marketing* (Cincinnati, OH: South-Western, 2000), pp. 349–53.

11. Avan R. Jassawalla and Hemant C.. Sashittal, "Building Collaborative Cross-Functional New Product Teams," *Academy of Management Review* 13, no. 3 (1999), pp. 50–63.

12. Pampers website, www.pampers.com (accessed October 8, 2002).

13. Mark M. Davis, Nicholas J. Aquilano, and Richard B. Chase, *Fundamentals of Operations Management,* 4th ed. (Burr Ridge, IL: Irwin/McGraw-Hill, 2003), pp. 167–171.

14. Thomas Pyzdek, *The Six Sigma Revolution,* Quality America, Inc. website, www.QualityAmerica.com (accessed August 5, 2002).

15. Caterpillar Annual Report, 2001.

16. Melanie Trottman, "Vaunted Southwest Slips In On-Time Performance," *The Wall Street Journal,* September 25, 2002, pp. D1, D2.

Enhancing Value through Effective Marketing Communication

The company's marketing campaign has been described as creative, humorous, and even irreverent. But one thing is irrefutable. The campaign and particularly the colorful ads have helped catapult the business from the brink of extinction into one of the world's largest manufacturers of outdoor apparel.

You may have already guessed the business—Columbia Sportswear. Gert Boyle was a housewife with three children when her husband died of a heart attack. The sportswear company he left her was deep in debt, and Gert knew practically nothing about managing the troubled family business. But with a keen sensitivity to customers, some creative communication, and a straightforward work ethic, Gert and her son Tim have transformed Columbia Sportswear into a hot corporate giant. Today, Gert still serves as chairman, while Tim holds the CEO reins.

Certainly, Columbia was in the right place at the right time, as the outdoor sportswear business experienced explosive growth over the past two decades. But Columbia's approach has been special, and the Boyles have made some astute business decisions. They began by listening to their customers and being open to change and innovation. Tim highlights the company's approach: "Our research doesn't rely on a design ivory tower or lab. We talk to our customers about what they want to buy, and we make it." The resulting innovations have produced such highly successful products as Columbia's Quad jackets for hunters and its now famous Bugaboo ski jackets. Importantly, Columbia decided to produce high-quality garments but price them lower than those of its major competitors, Patagonia and North Face.

The public centerpiece of the company is its unique advertising, featuring both Gert and Tim. Its famous "Mother Boyle" ads portray Gert as a "tyrant who makes sure the company's jackets and pants can stand up to her tough standards as well as Oregon's legendary bad winters." The ads may show a stern-faced Gert noting that "old age and treachery will overcome youth and skill," or "Mother has kept many a man warm on a cold winter's night." The ads are a hoot. And they are highly successful. Since the Mother Boyle campaign started, Columbia's annual sales have skyrocketed from $3 million to over $780 million.

Today, with industry growth tapering off, Columbia is innovating. It is moving into footwear and general sportswear in an effort to reduce its reliance on cold weather items. Columbia is also expanding internationally. And what about Mother Boyle, now approaching 80? She has no intention of retiring, and as Tim says when asked how the company will respond if its driving force dies, "We'll just have her stuffed."[1]

In Chapter 14, we discussed how to create value through developing and delivering quality products. We covered important concepts in the product development process. We discussed how to ensure that the desired quality does, in fact, become part of the product or service. We even explored important issues in getting the product to the customer. But producing and being able to deliver quality products is not enough. Products do not provide value for the customer if the customer is unaware of their existence.

This chapter addresses how to communicate the value of a product or service to the customer. Communication with the customer enhances the value that was created through the product development process. Communication with customers also gives opportunities for even more value as the customer provides feedback to the business.

After studying this chapter, you should be able to:

1. Discuss the impact of communication on value to the customer.
2. Describe branding and brand equity.
3. Discuss the various methods of communicating with customers, such as advertising, direct marketing, personal selling, sales promotions, and pricing.
4. Demonstrate the need for a consistent message across all communications with customers.
5. Recognize the value of customer feedback and how to obtain it.

The Impact of Communications on Customer Value

Enhancing value is an important part of the exchange between the provider of a product or service and the company's customers. Value can be created or enhanced in a number of ways. In Chapter 14, you learned how producing a product that customers want creates value for the customer. In service businesses, increasing the quality of a service builds value for that service.

Our interest in this chapter is to continue the discussion of value creation. In particular, we are interested in how companies can enhance the value of a product or service through communication. Communication enhances value if it provides the customer with information about the product and where to buy it. Value is enhanced if guarantees or warranties are stated clearly. Value is enhanced if brands associated with a product are desirable. Value is even improved if pricing is appropriate. Throughout this chapter, we will highlight different ways of communicating value to customers, including communicating through mass media, the Internet, one-on-one interaction, and the product itself. As you consider the different ways to reach customers, the important thing to remember is that all methods of communication must be consistent. That is, they must all present similar messages that communicate the same overall theme.

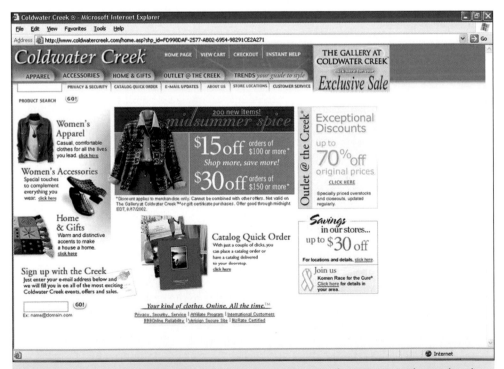

One way that websites create value for customers is by giving them variety with merchandise selection that might not be achievable in a store. What are some of the negative aspects of selling on websites, especially where the consumer is concerned?

A concept that underscores the focus of this chapter is **integrated marketing communications (IMC),** the process of developing and implementing various forms of persuasive communications that send a consistent message over time. The key to IMC is that all communications programs must present a consistent theme and establish a consistent image of the business in the minds of its audiences. The goal of IMC is to influence or directly affect the behavior of the selected communications audience. IMC makes use of all forms of relevant communications. The process starts with identifying target customers and works backward to define the kinds of communications that will be most effective in reaching those customers.[2] For example, if the target market is teenagers, the communications methods will be far different from those used in reaching their parents.

Southwest Airlines exemplifies the concept of integrated marketing communications. Its entire image is built around the idea of a no-frills airline that has excellent customer service and is fun to fly. All Southwest communications tell that story. Its advertisements are well made and always have a bit of humor. Some of its aircraft are painted in unique colors that might represent Shamu the whale or perhaps the state of Texas. Southwest's recorded on-hold message for a customer calling for reservations is humorous. The required safety message given by flight attendants is done in a professional but enjoyable way. Southwest's founder Herb Kelleher is known as a fun-loving guy, and President Colleen Barnett is known as a real "people person." These factors, coupled with Southwest's frequency in achieving best on-time delivery, baggage handling, and customer service ratings in the industry, give the airline a well-delivered and distinctive message that is integrated throughout its operations.

Companies can communicate with customers in a number of ways, and most companies use several of these simultaneously. For example, a company may advertise on television and in the print media (newspapers and magazines) and may hire a number of salespeople to further carry the company's message to the customer. From an integration standpoint, all the media must provide a similar message.

Consistency from one medium to another is a key to integration within marketing communications. Consider the following example: Lippmann's Furniture and Interiors is an upscale retail furniture company with locations in two neighboring cities. Although it is possible to purchase modestly priced furniture from Lippmann's, most of its furniture appeals to upper-middle-class customers. Furniture brands include Pennsylvania House, Henredon, Lane, Hickory Chair Company, and others. Lippmann's advertises on television, occasionally on radio with spots featuring special sales, in newspaper advertisements and inserts, and through some direct mail pieces. Most of this advertising is co-op, paid partially by Lippmann's and partially by the manufacturers. The key to all these advertisements is the professional quality Lippmann's is known for. There are no screaming, in-your-face, television ads nor print ads touting the latest in a series of clearance sales. Instead, the advertisements feature a few excellent products along with an invitation to come to the store for a free consultation. Lippmann's sales representatives are impeccably dressed and are professional in their dealings with customers. Even the company's website has a professional tone and includes links to the fine-furniture manufacturers that supply it. Thus, every method of communicating with its customers is consistent with Lippmann's quality theme.

integrated marketing communications (IMC) The process of developing and implementing various forms of persuasive communications that send a consistent message over time.

SOUTHWEST

THINK ABOUT THIS

1. Is there a difference between creating value and enhancing value?
2. How can a company ensure that all its communications are sending a consistent message?

Communicating Value by Building Loyalty and Brand Equity

Customer loyalty is a key to business success. Customer loyalty is an asset. That loyalty is a result of effective communication with clientele who increasingly come to the business because of the quality products or service provided. For example, Gionne's is a successful Italian restaurant in the heart of a midsize city. Patrons love the food and the atmosphere. The intimate setting seats only 85 people. Weekend reservations are needed a week in advance. Leo and Lisa Gionne are enjoying their work and enjoying their success. But the picture has not always been so positive. Fifteen years ago, the Gionnes operated a sandwich shop at the same location. They catered to the downtown lunch crowd. Their evening clientele consisted of stragglers from downtown events who would occasionally stop in for drinks after a play or sporting event. Gionne's looked like a dozen other restaurants in the area. It was losing money. Leo and Lisa even considered selling the business.

The Gionnes were perplexed. The business, they thought, *should* be more successful. Their location was great. There was plenty of traffic. The downtown area was active with businesspeople during the day and hopping with potential evening customers who attended theater, musical, and sporting events at the civic center only two blocks away. Why aren't we doing better, the Gionnes wondered? In desperation, they began to question people who wandered in. They asked simple questions: What are you looking for in a restaurant? What sort of environment do you want? What sort of menu? How expensive? What drink selections are important? They learned that most evening patrons wanted a nice experience to complement their night on the town. Although price was not unimportant, most people were willing to pay for reasonable value. They wanted a nice, quaint, intimate atmosphere. They wanted good ethnic food. And, most surprisingly, they wanted a good selection of wines.

The Gionnes listened. They remade their restaurant in the image of the customer wishes they received. Small tables for two or four were purchased to replace booths. Candlelight dinners became the norm. The menu was limited to a small selection of Italian favorites that Lisa had perfected over the years. Leo began delving into the best moderately priced wines he could find. And he never stopped talking to patrons. You could expect Leo to visit your table once or twice during each meal, usually to be sure that the wine you selected met your expectations and again to be sure you enjoyed your meal. Leo learned the names of customers. He would greet return customers by name and suggest new wine selections they might enjoy. Soon the word was out: The place was intimate and cozy, it had great food, and it offered a super wine list. In a few short months, Gionne's became the place to go. Visiting celebrities would often stop by before or after a performance. A thriving, healthy business had been born. The Gionnes have tapped the secret of customer service and the foundation of customer loyalty.

Building Customer Loyalty

Businesses want to build a base of loyal customers for at least two reasons. First, they want current customers to remain their customers, choosing their products and services over those of the competition. Companies need that repeat business. It makes good sense financially. It costs significantly less to keep a customer than to get a new one. Second, loyal customers are excellent sources of free positive communication that is likely to lure additional customers to the business. Loyal customers are likely to refer their friends and acquaintances.

Although customer loyalty can be built in many ways, relationship marketing is one of the most important. **Relationship marketing** occurs when the business gets to know its customers, establishes rapport, and develops long-term relationships with them. Relationship marketing emphasizes meeting customer needs over time. It rejects the notion of exploiting customers to make quick sales and gain one-time profits. In our earlier example, Leo and Lisa Gionne practiced relationship marketing by being sensitive and responsive to their customers.

Consider another example: Weiland's Lawn Mower Hospital is in the competitive business of providing sales and service for outdoor power equipment. In many of its product lines—lawn mowers, riding mowers, snowblowers, hedge clippers, and gas grills—the company must compete with large retail outlets offering lower prices. But Weiland's is different from the large retailers. If you enter Weiland's retail center to purchase a riding mower, it's likely that one of the associates will spend considerable time talking with you about your property and its unique features. The associate will recommend product options and may even bring a couple of your final choices to your home for you to try out before you make a purchase decision. But the relationship does not end there. Weiland's goes the extra mile for customers. One year, as an impending winter storm threatened, Weiland's extended its hours and associates worked around the clock to service customers' snowblowers. In short, Weiland's knows its customers and makes every reasonable effort to serve their needs. Accordingly, when customers need additional outdoor equipment or want to learn about the new models, they venture back to Weiland's. In addition, Weiland's customers freely recommend the business to friends in need of power equipment.

On a larger scale, Dell's success is grounded in its commitment to relationship marketing. The company views its customers as unique individuals. Dell's marketing efforts are focused on establishing relationships with its customers.[3] Dell does not simply sell a computer and forget the customer. Instead, the company stays in contact with the customer through e-mail announcements and print advertisements.

Communicating through Branding

Another way to communicate value and build customer loyalty is through branding. A **brand** is a name, term, symbol, design, or image that identifies the products or service of a business and differentiates it from its competitors.[4] A brand is not only a name but also a set of images that the seller attempts to communicate to the buyer. Through the brand, the company communicates to the customer that the product or service embodies a certain set of desirable qualities.

Brands may suggest quality, performance, reliability, prestige, or some other image that customers value. The brand may enable the company to attract customers, and it may even allow the company to charge higher prices. For example, do you buy that generic can of tuna fish and save some money, or do you go with the Chicken-of-the-Sea brand because you know it will be high quality? Consider your choice of camera film. A number of brands will produce excellent pictures, but you know the Kodak name and feel comfortable with the brand. One study, using identical TV sets, found that those with the Hitachi brand sold for $75 more than those with the GE brand.[5]

Brands become important when they are so well recognized that they suggest value to customers who think of them when they need to purchase the product. The importance of brands is captured in the concept of **brand equity,** the value attached to a brand. Are you willing to pay more for a particular brand than for its generic counterpart? If so, that choice is due to brand equity. The brand, then, is a way of communicating value about the company's product. Brand equity may come from sources such as brand name awareness, perceived quality, patents and trademarks, and brand loyalty.[6]

brand
A name, term, symbol, design, or image that identifies the products or service of a business.

brand equity
The value attached to a brand.

PROFILE 15.1   DISNEY AT THE BREAKFAST TABLE

Ok, so you know Mickey and Minnie, Winnie the Pooh, and the other Disney characters. You watched the cartoons and read the books when you were much younger. Perhaps you even have a Mickey sweatshirt or a Disney World hat. You are aware of the theme parks, and you know from our earlier discussions that Disney owns ABC, ESPN, a hockey team, movie production studios, and a cruise line. But would you like to sit down to a bowl of Mickey's Magix, Buzz Blasts, or Hunny Bs cereal from Kellogg's? Or perhaps you would enjoy a bottle of juice from Coca-Cola's Minute Maid with Disney characters on it.

Disney, Kellogg's, and Coca-Cola believe that the Disney brand communicates value for products, and those products can include food products as well as sweatshirts, books, and motion pictures. Kellogg's is so sure of Disney's value that the company priced its cereals at a premium compared with traditional corn flakes. Kellogg's feels that parents—with encouragement from their children—will pay extra for cereal that is kid-friendly and carries both the Kellogg's brand and the Disney brand. Both of these brands communicate an image of value, and combining the two should enhance the value of the cereal as well as the bottom line of each company.

Interestingly, sales have not met expectations. Kellogg's officials worry that the premium price may have overridden the enhanced brand equity associated with Disney. If parents have the choice of a high-priced, Disney-connected cereal versus a low-priced, generic cereal, they may opt for the low-priced version. Keep in mind that both brands and prices can communicate value, but value is subject to interpretation.

Source: Stephanie Thompson, "Disappointment for Disney Extensions," *Advertising Age,* August 12, 2002, p. 12.

Some brands have far greater brand equity than others. Profile 15.1 shows how some companies take advantage of their brand equity and extend it to products not normally associated with the brand. Companies with high brand equity routinely license their brand to other companies to produce a plethora of products. You may, for example, have a pair of Caterpillar hiking boots. Were they made by Caterpillar, whose specialty is engines and earth-moving equipment? Of course not. But the Caterpillar brand and logo have so much brand equity—suggesting a tough, hard-working, quality image—that the producer of the boots was willing to pay Caterpillar a licensing fee to affix the Caterpillar logo to its boots.

Some companies have established their brands so effectively that most people identify the brand with an entire product category. Consider the following scenario: As you leave for your late afternoon entertainment, you grab some Fritos, strap on your Rollerblades, and head down a sidewalk. In your haste, you lose control, take a nasty fall, and gain an unsightly case of road rash on both knees. A classmate offers a Kleenex to clean the mess, while another offers you a Band-Aid. Fritos, Rollerblade, Kleenex, and Band-Aid are brands so well established in customers' minds that they are synonymous with their product categories—corn chips, in-line skates, facial tissues, and adhesive bandages. In fact, there is a danger of the name's becoming generic for the product. For example, the words *aspirin* and *escalator* used to refer to brands, but now are generic words for a painkiller and a power-driven set of stairs. Listen carefully the next time you hear an advertisement from Frito-Lay or Kimberly-Clark Corporation or Johnson & Johnson. The ad will mention Fritos brand corn chips or Kleenex brand facial tissues or Band-Aid brand sterile pads in an attempt to separate the brand from the product and prevent the company's unique brand from becoming a generic term for the product.

Some brands project a specific image. For example, Gucci, Rolex, and Lexus connote quality and prestige. Others, such as Best Buy and Wal-Mart, send the image of good value and low prices. Some, such as McDonald's and Subway, suggest an image of speed and consistency. And, of course, when you want a cold and refreshing drink, what do you order? In all likelihood, you ask for a Coke or a Pepsi rather than simply a soft drink. Brands also carry their own special personalities. Denim jeans are basic clothing, but the image and personality of Calvin Klein, Wrangler, Tommy Hilfiger, and Lee may be quite different.

Methods of Communicating Value to Customers

advertising
Any paid form of presentation and promotion of ideas, goods, and services by an identified sponsor to a targeted audience.

Table 15.1 shows ways that companies communicate value to customers. In the sections that follow, we will discuss a number of these types of communications and how they are used. Then we will bring them all together to show how they should be integrated to be totally effective.

Communicating Value through Mass Media

Mass communications media are excellent methods for communicating a company's message to a large number of people simultaneously. As a result, advertising is the most frequently used method of communicating with customers. It is also the one in which the most money is spent by companies that want to get their messages to their customers. **Advertising** is any paid form of presentation and promotion of ideas, goods, and services by an identified sponsor to a targeted audience and delivered primarily through the mass media.[7] Advertising can range from a Super Bowl advertisement that costs over a million dollars a minute to a classified advertisement in a newspaper advertising a carpenter's business. Advertising helps sell products and build brand recognition. It can help the overall reputation of the company as customers hear planned messages about the firm's quality and reliability.

Advertising typically is one of two types: institutional advertising or product advertising. **Institutional advertising** is communication about the company itself, rather than about the company's specific products. The goal of institutional advertising is to create a positive image of the company. For example, a recent advertisement in *The Wall*

institutional advertising
A communication about the company itself, not its products.

TABLE 15.1

Selected Methods of Communicating Value to Customers

Branding	One-on-one interaction
Mass media	Personal selling
Newspapers	Informational packaging
Radio	Sales promotions
Television	Indirect communication
Yellow Pages	Sponsorships
Direct marketing and the Internet	Publicity
Direct mail	Pricing
Websites and e-mail	
Television	

Street Journal shows a business executive gazing at a city skyline, and offers the caption: "Ever heard of anyone dreaming of making it to the middle? On the way to the top you can rarely mix business with pleasure. But that doesn't mean the journey can't be pleasurable. We know what it takes." The advertisement is for Intercontinental Hotels and Resorts and suggests that Intercontinental offers quality and comfort, even though no specific features are ever mentioned.

Another full-page ad pictures waves about to wash-out a message scrawled at the edge of the beach. The caption: "It's not how many ideas you have. It's how many you make happen." The advertisement's sponsor is Accenture, a consulting firm. Again, there is no mention of the specific services Accenture offers. The message communicated is that Accenture can make ideas and innovation happen. These are clearly institutional rather than specific product advertisements.[8]

Product advertising encourages customers to buy specific products or services. The idea is to get them to buy the company's products or services rather than those of competitors. Product advertisers often use catchy slogans or subjects with a strong visual impact to get the customer to remember—and be influenced by—the advertisements. Phrases such as "Did somebody say McDonald's?" are easily recognized and can be coupled with information about the latest menu item. The challenge for product advertisers is to get customers to remember the advertisement, tie it to the sponsoring company, and then buy the product. Some slogans are easily recognized and tied to the product or company. Most people know that "the breakfast of champions" is Wheaties, that Maxwell House coffee is "good to the last drop," and that Nike encourages people to "just do it." Remember that integrated marketing communication wants to present a consistent message and image that favorably affects the business. This task isn't always easy. For example, most of you have seen the Aflac commercials with the duck chanting "Aflac" in various situations. But do you know what Aflac is or what it does?

The top 100 national advertisers spent $81 million on advertising in 2001. Table 15.2 shows the top 10 advertisers in the United States, all well-known companies with well-known products. Why are they so well known? Because they produce commonly accepted products and commit millions of dollars to communicating with customers. Keep in mind, however, that most of the firms listed in Table 15.2 have many products that are included in their promotion budgets. For example, Ford advertises for a bevy of Ford cars, plus those of its subsidiaries, which include Jaguar, Volvo, and part of Mazda.

Some media lend themselves to one type of company more than another. For example, the top 10 spenders on newspaper advertising in 2001 included four retail

> **product advertising**
> Advertising that encourages customers to buy specific products or services.

TABLE 15.2

The Top 10
Advertisers, 2001

Rank	Advertiser	Total Annual U.S. Ad Spending ($ in billions)
1	General Motors	$3.37
2	Procter & Gamble	2.54
3	Ford	2.41
4	PepsiCo	2.21
5	Pfizer	2.19
6	DaimlerChrysler	1.99
7	AOL Time Warner	1.89
8	Phillip Morris	1.82
9	Walt Disney Co.	1.76
10	Johnson & Johnson	1.62

Source: "100 Leading National Advertisers," *Advertising Age*, June 24, 2002, p. S-2.

chains and five telecommunications companies. Magazines were more populated by car companies—General Motors, Ford, DaimlerChrysler, and Toyota—and by product companies such as Phillip Morris (which includes Kraft Foods), L'Oréal, Johnson & Johnson, and Pfizer. Network TV has GM and Ford, but it also has Procter & Gamble, Johnson & Johnson, Phillip Morris, PepsiCo, two drug companies—Pfizer and GlaxoSmithKline—and Walt Disney. Some businesses, such as General Motors and Ford, advertise in virtually every medium: magazines, newspapers, national newspapers, network TV, outdoor advertising, and Yellow Pages. General Motors is even the second largest advertiser on the Internet.[9]

Some product companies are finding that mixing branded products with entertainment is a viable method of communicating with their target market. A documentary in 2001 entitled "Road to Paris" featured Lance Armstrong's successes. And what emblem was displayed prominently on Armstrong's uniform? The Nike Swoosh. Nike is also underwriting a Broadway musical called "Ball" that includes, of course, Nike basketball attire.[10] An even better example comes from the summer 2002 hit movie "My Big Fat Greek Wedding." Anyone who has seen that movie knows the answer to the question, What product was featured prominently in the movie? The answer: Windex. Advertisers are discovering that product placement in entertainment can reach an identifiable target market and be more believable than the same exposure in an advertisement.

Some companies are best served simply by advertising in the Yellow Pages of telephone books. The Yellow Pages contain advertisements for the vast majority of businesses, many of whom also use other types of advertising. But the Yellow Pages are particularly well suited for small contractors and other service providers. Consider a local plumber, for example. This business owner most likely could not afford television advertising, which would be of limited effectiveness in any case, because customers are not tuned in to plumbers until they have a plumbing problem. At the same time, when plumbers are needed, they are often needed immediately. Thus, the normal course is to pick up the telephone book and turn to the Yellow Pages category labeled "plumbers." There, a resident can find a listing of all the plumbers in town and can study the advertisements of those plumbers who choose to advertise. They can see immediately what plumbers' strong points are, where they are located, if they are bonded and insured, if they work on weekends and evenings, and perhaps whether they offer discounts to senior citizens.

Communicating Value through Direct Marketing and the Internet

direct marketing

Any attempt to sell a product directly to customers without going through intermediaries such as dealers or other retailers.

Communicating through **direct marketing** is any attempt to sell a product directly to customers without going through intermediaries such as dealers or other retailers. Direct marketing can use direct mail, the Internet, or television.

Direct mail is the use of catalogs and other materials sent specifically to the homes or businesses of potential customers. Catalogs have been around for decades, but their use has increased dramatically in recent years. This trend tries to capture the one thing that many consumers find most lacking—time. With catalogs, shopping time is reduced and the hassle is lessened. Customers receiving catalogs can order at their leisure by returning an order blank, calling the company toll-free number, or going to the website.

direct mail

The use of catalogs and other materials sent to the homes or businesses of potential customers.

The advantage of direct mail is that it can target specific customers. Catalogs are typically sent to customers who have previously purchased a product through direct marketing, because these customers are more likely to buy than those without a record of direct mail purchasing.

The key to direct marketing using catalogs is the database. Most direct marketers have a database containing millions of names, addresses, and characteristics of would-be customers. These databases can then be accessed so that particular characteristics determine who will receive a catalog.

Internet marketing

The communicating of product information through a company's website, encouraging customers to order online.

The other major direct communications medium is the Internet. **Internet marketing** is communicating product information through the company's interactive website and encouraging customers to order online. Although few companies sell solely over the Internet, many use the Internet in conjunction with their other marketing activities. In many cases, Internet marketing is more efficient for both the customer and the company than either mail or telephone marketing. For example, airlines now encourage customers to book airline tickets over the Internet using secure links. This option is more convenient for many people than working through a travel agent or calling the airline, and it is cheaper for the airline. The Internet allows the user to shop for the best flights that are either most convenient or least expensive. Profile 15.2 shows Southwest Airlines' success with its website.

More to Come

Chapter 17

PROFILE 15.2 SOUTHWEST.COM

Southwest Airlines is well known for its low-priced fares and its outstanding marks in on-time arrivals, baggage handling, customer service, and friendliness of employees. It has also received recognition for using its website as an interactive communications media. Consider the following. Southwest was the first airline to have its own website and to allow online reservations. In the first quarter of 2002, Southwest sold $500 million in reservations through its website—46 percent of its total sales. The cost of booking an airline reservation through a travel agent is $6 to $8. The cost is somewhat less for telephone reservations. But the cost of an online reservation is only a dollar. Do customers like Southwest's website, online reservations, and Internet fares? Apparently so. Over 3.5 million users subscribe to Southwest's "Click 'n Save" e-mails. Southwest's website gets over 50 percent more hits than the websites of other airlines.

Southwest.com has received a number of recognitions. According to research conducted by Nielsen/NetRatings and Harris Interactive, Southwest's website has been named the top-ranking website for customer satisfaction among major travel sites. In the June 11, 2001, issue of *InternetWeek,* Southwest's website was named one of the top 100 e-businesses in the United States, as determined by the 2001 *InternetWeek* 100 survey. On May 30, 2002, the Jupiter Media Metrix named Southwest the airline that best utilizes the Internet and provides brand synergy between its mainline and online presences.

Source: Southwest Airlines website, www.southwest.com (accessed August 14, 2002).

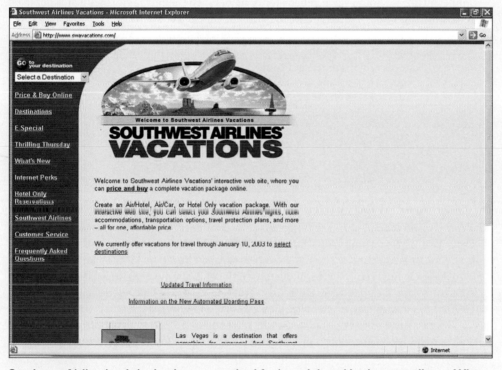

Southwest Airlines' website has been recognized for its web-based business excellence. What are some of the things that need to be on a company's website for it to be an effective communication tool?

Businesses can communicate with customers with either one-way or two-way communication. In one-way communication, companies provide static information on websites. Customers can go to the site, read the information, and then make decisions. This level of communication is relatively inexpensive, and it provides an easy way to get information to customers who actively seek it. The downside of using one-way communication on the Web is the difficulty of getting customers to actually go to the site. In addition, unless a tracking mechanism is used, the company has no way of knowing how many people accessed the site and what their response was after visiting the site.

Two-way communication gives users the option of interacting with the site provider. This includes searching the site by requesting information in fill-in blanks and being provided specific information. Another version allows site visitors to submit information to the site provider. For example, change of address information may be submitted electronically to magazines, government agencies, and Internet retailers. Often included in two-way communication is the ability to purchase products or services via the website. Many of you may have used this method if you applied online for admission to the college you are now attending. Southwest Airlines, in Profile 15.2, is another good example. Customers can search the Southwest site for schedules and fares. They then have the option of purchasing tickets online using a credit card, calling Southwest's reservation line, or moving on to united.com, Americanairlines.com, jetblue.com, or other airlines' websites.

Companies often have facilities or stores plus a significant online business. These businesses are sometimes referred to as **bricks and clicks retailers.** Retailers such as Gap, Inc. (including Old Navy and Banana Republic), Sears, J.Crew, Eddie Bauer, and Borders are examples. Most are primarily brick-and-mortar stores with a significant online business. Some have retail stores in one geographic region with online sales across the rest of the United States and abroad. Others, such as L.L. Bean, are primarily catalog and Internet marketers with a few brick-and-mortar stores. Bookstores are interesting because of how the Internet marketing and traditional marketing relate. Three bookstores are discussed in Profile 15.3.

> **bricks-and-clicks retailers**
> Companies that have both facilities or stores and a significant online business.

PROFILE 15.3   SELLING BOOKS WITH BRICKS AND CLICKS

While some companies are Internet-only providers, other companies are better described as bricks-and-clicks companies. Consider booksellers. In the Internet-only category, Amazon.com is a prime example. Amazon began in 1995 as an Internet-only bookseller. It now has millions of customers from 220 countries. In addition to books, Amazon's site includes free electronic greeting cards, online auctions, CDs, videos, DVDs, toys and games, electronics, kitchenware, and computers.

The two most notable bricks-and-clicks bookstores are Barnes & Noble (www.bn.com) and Borders (www.borders.com). Borders Group, Inc., is a leading global retailer of books, music, movies, and other information and entertainment items. Headquartered in Ann Arbor, Michigan, Borders Group operates 385 Borders Books and Music stores in the United States, as well as 25 international Borders stores, approximately 800 Waldenbooks locations, and 36 U.K.–based Books etc. stores. Borders Group employs more than 32,000 people worldwide and posted revenues of approximately $3.4 billion in 2001. Borders.com is a strategic alliance between the Borders Group, Inc., and Amazon.com.

Barnes & Noble is the nation's largest bookseller, employing more than 32,000 booksellers in approximately 900 stores in 49 states under the Barnes & Noble and B. Dalton names. Barnes & Noble.com is a separately run, publicly held company. Barnes & Noble.com's stock consists of 40 percent ownership by Barnes & Noble, Inc.; 40 percent by Bertelsmann, AG, a leading international media company; and 20 percent that is publicly held.

Source: amazon.com; borders.com; bn.com (accessed August 14, 2002).

Another combination of communications methods is joining direct mail using catalogs with Internet marketing. A good example of a catalog marketing company that is increasingly using the Internet is Lands' End. Lands' End's revenues were $873 million in fiscal 2002, of which $299 million was from landsend.com. Lands' End sends out millions of catalogs a year, often one a month to recent customers. In addition, its website allows customers to look at clothes online and even develop a personal mannequin that approximates the customer's measurements. By making a few clicks, customers can "try on" the clothes to see how they look on a body similar to their own.[11]

Lands' End, however, also illustrates the risks of moving too fast toward the new medium. In 1999, Lands' End made the strategic decision to focus more heavily on Internet sales than on its catalogs. It beefed up its website, including the digital mannequins discussed above. In exchange for that, Lands' End reduced the number of catalogs it sent to customers. Unfortunately, many customers preferred to peruse the catalogs rather than look at images on a computer screen. The result was significant. Lands' End sales dropped approximately 14 percent for the holiday season. The financial markets reacted dramatically, dropping the company's stock from a 52-week high of over 80 to as low as 35. The results from this strategic error most likely influenced Lands' End's decision to merge with Sears in 2002.

A third method of communicating through direct marketing is really a hybrid of mass media and direct marketing. This method is the selling of products on television channels such as the Home Shopping Network and QVC. Here, the products are advertised on television, but individuals purchase the products over the phone with a credit card. Since the products are not sold through a retailer, they fit the characteristics of direct market products.

Communicating Value through One-on-One Interaction

personal selling
The face-to-face communication between a company representative and the customer.

A company communicates with its customers in a number of ways. We have already discussed mass media, direct mail, the Internet, and television-based direct marketing. We have also made the case that the message must be consistent regardless of the media used. This same caveat is necessary when the communication changes from communicating with many people simultaneously to communicating with customers one at a time.

One-on-one communication with customers is often referred to as personal selling. **Personal selling** is the face-to-face communication between a company representative and the customer.[12] This method can be expensive because individual sales representatives must be hired to promote the company's products. On the other hand, personal selling can be very effective when a product is complex or includes installation. Personal selling is particularly effective in business-to-business selling, in which the rapport between the buyer and seller is important.

Effective personal selling requires a number of steps. First, the salesperson must learn about the customers and their needs. Since salespeople are typically paid a salary plus a commission, it is costly to have a representative who has not learned as much about the potential customers as

THINK ABOUT THIS

1. Communicating through mass media can be either very expensive or relatively inexpensive on a per-customer basis. What determines the difference?

2. How do you think customers' responses to Web-based communications differ from responses to traditional advertising?

3. Will Web-based advertising eventually replace direct mail advertising? How can direct mail companies ensure that customers will surf to their websites?

qualifying the customer

Determining whether the customer is likely to purchase the product or service.

possible. As part of learning about the customer, the salesperson should qualify the customer. **Qualifying the customer** is determining whether the customer is likely to purchase the product or service. It is wasteful to make presentations to customers who will not or cannot purchase the product or service. Once the customer is qualified, the salesperson must make the presentation to the customer, answer any questions, and overcome any resistance to the purchase. Finally, the sale must be closed and follow-up actions must be taken. This step includes getting the customer's signature on the line, doing necessary paperwork, and arranging for the delivery of the product or service.

In personal selling, companies can either hire their own representatives to communicate with customers and potential customers, or they can contract with an outside sales force to push their products. In retail and wholesale situations and in some manufacturing companies, the representative is the traditional salesperson. In some manufacturing situations, however, this approach is very inefficient. In these cases, the companies turn to outsiders known as manufacturers' representatives. As we noted in Chapter 4, manufacturers' representatives are independent sales representatives who may sell products for more than one manufacturer. They are particularly useful for small companies that cannot afford to have their own sales force spread across the entire country. Instead, the manufacturers' reps, as they are frequently called, carry literature about each of the products and each of the manufacturers they represent. They visit customers throughout a large geographic territory and explain the value of the products they represent. If the customer decides to purchase a product, the representative transmits the order back to the manufacturer, who then ships the product directly to the customer. The manufacturers' rep then receives a commission on the sale.

Communicating Value through Informational Packaging

We have already discussed the importance of branding as it contributes to communicating value to customers. An integral part of that brand communication is the package that holds the product. Packaging creates value—brand equity—through communication using the words or logos that appear on the package. Packaging gives companies the opportunity to describe the product and its uses. Through graphics, it can show a number of possible benefits from buying the product. The packaging can also show warnings, warranties, nutritional values in food products, and other information. All this information helps the customer make a decision on whether to purchase the product.

Packaging also enhances the value of a product by protecting the product. It can make the product easier to carry or use. Companies can also reduce shoplifting by placing the product in a larger package. A product can be shrink-wrapped to a card that can be hung on a rack hanger, making it more visible and attractive. Packages for products can vary in shapes and colors that identify brands and varieties. In some cases, the package itself has value. An example is a small paint roller that comes packaged in a tray with a lid. The package becomes the roller tray that holds the paint.

Influencing Customers through Sales Promotions

Much, if not most, of the communication between a business and its customers is encouraging the customer to purchase a product. This holds true for mass communications and advertising, direct mail and Internet marketing, one-to-one communication through personal selling, and even the packaging. Sometimes, however, all that communication is insufficient to get the customer to respond as desired. In that case, an additional incentive is provided to encourage the exchange. These incentives to encourage customer response are called **sales promotions.** A number of types of sales promotions exist, including coupons in newspapers, end-of-the-aisle displays in retail stores, magnets or pens with a company's logo and phone number, and samples. Sometimes manufacturers include incentives within the package itself, such as General Mills did recently when it included movie DVDs inside Cheerios boxes.

Think back to the first day of classes. As you left the bookstore with your load of books, you may have noticed that the bags the bookstore used had a batch of coupons or advertisements in the bottom for everything from credit cards to subscriptions to *The Wall Street Journal.* You may have also had an activities fair the first week of school where local restaurants either gave away food or sold it very cheaply. Why would they do this? They know that if you sample their restaurant food and it is good, you will likely stop by the restaurant later for a meal.

Although you are most acquainted with customer-oriented incentives, you should realize that there are also incentives for salespeople. Trips to Las Vegas, dinner theater tickets, golf clubs, company jackets, and many other products can be incentives for the sales force to exert higher levels of motivation in gaining sales. You will learn more about this approach in the next chapter when we talk about performance-based incentives for employees.

> **sales promotions**
> Additional incentives provided to encourage customer response.

> **More to Come**
> *CHAPTER 16*

Indirect Communications with Customers

The communications methods we have discussed so far use direct methods of getting the company's message to customers. In addition, however, there are at least two ways to reach customers indirectly. These methods, while seldom having a measurable relationship between the communications and company sales, do help in maintaining the image of the company in the minds of customers. The two most significant of these are sponsorships and publicity.

Sponsorships

Anyone who watches sports on television is quite familiar with sponsorships. Similarly, anyone who works with a not-for-profit organization knows the importance of sponsorships as a funding mechanism. **Sponsorships** are investments in special events or causes for the purpose of building awareness of the company and its products. They provide companies with significant exposure in a venue where thousands of people might watch an event. In addition, the event often includes participants or celebrities who may wear the sponsor's clothes, or have the sponsor's logo splashed across a race car or bicycle, or have the logo on an arena wall or the outfield fence of a baseball stadium. This advertisement makes an impression that the sponsor hopes will linger until customers purchase its product.

Look at the websites for bicycle manufacturers such as Trek, Cannondale, and Specialized. In each, you will find references to races, marathons, or bike rides for charity. These events give the bicycle companies considerable exposure. In some cases, a particular company may underwrite an entire event. In others, it may sponsor certain parts of the event, such as an evening meal, or provide free T-shirts, water bottles, or other paraphernalia. The company name or logo will, of course, be prominent on the product.

> **sponsorships**
> Investments in special events or causes for the purpose of building awareness of the company and its products.

THINK ABOUT THIS

1. If you were in charge of a company's overall marketing communications budget, how would you allocate dollars to advertising, personal selling, and sales promotion?

2. How would your answer to question 1 differ if your business were a retail apparel store, a hospital, an income tax service, or a manufacturer of nails?

Publicity

All the communications concepts we have discussed have one thing in common. They cost money. **Publicity,** on the other hand, is communication to a mass audience that is not paid for by the company.[13] This type of communication relies on other media to tell a story about the company; it is free exposure. Companies routinely issue newsworthy information about the company in press releases, hoping that news media will pick it up.

The downside of publicity is the same as that of any other unpaid exposure. A company may not be able to control what actually appears in print or on the nightly news. In addition, bad news is picked up more often than good news. United Airlines, for example, recently announced that it was having financial difficulties, and its stock dropped precipitously because of the negative publicity.

Communicating Value through Pricing

We have discussed how to create value through product development and how to enhance that value through branding, advertising, packaging, sales promotions, and personal selling. Each enhancement method communicates something to the customer. Pricing shares this characteristic. Although setting a price for a product certainly is an economic issue, as you will see, pricing is also a form of communication. Pricing can tell a customer if the product is competitive with those of other companies. Sale pricing communicates that the end of the season is near or that the company is overstocked or that a particular model has been selected for featuring. As we noted in Chapter 12's discussion of business strategies, pricing can signal that the company wants to be the low-price leader or that it wants to be differentiated from other companies on the basis of some aspect of quality other than price. Price can be used to indicate and drive new business approaches and strategies. For example, America West Airlines and Frontier Airlines recently lowered their ticket prices on last-minute, unrestricted, walk-up fares. These fares are typically favored by business travelers, who prefer the flexibility of such tickets. At the same time, the airlines raised the prices on most leisure fares. What's going on? This strategy appears to be an attempt to trade cheap-ticket vacation travelers for more lucrative business travelers. The pricing choice may even help these smaller airlines lure business travelers from their larger competitors.[14] In the following paragraphs, we will highlight some of the more common pricing strategies and how they impute value.

An economics-based pricing method is **cost-based pricing.** Here, the company determines all the costs associated with producing the product, adds a measure for profit, and arrives at a price for the product. This method of pricing is useful because it ensures that the company will make a profit. Two things, however, can get in the way. First, we are making the assumption that the company accurately determines all the costs associated with the product. This calculation often is not done well, especially in smaller companies that have a relatively low level of sales or do not have sufficiently expert staff to make the sometimes complex calculations. Managers may mistakenly omit fixed costs or administrative costs from their calculations or may not apply an appropriate factor to arrive at total cost. The second problem is that relying on cost-based pricing ignores other issues, such as competition and the need to clear out the current season's merchandise to make room for the newly arriving materials.

A second method of pricing is **value-based pricing.** Here, the firm determines what customers are willing to pay for the products it sells. This method of pricing is the essence of communicating value, which we have discussed in this chapter and in Chapter 14. The business determines through market research the products customers want, the features they desire, and the amount they are willing to pay for them. Although the business certainly has to keep an eye open for costs and competitors, it is setting the price that is appropriate for the target market.

Keep in mind that the value-based price may indeed be higher than the cost-based price. Consider the 2002 Ford Thunderbird. This retro car, which looks very much like its 1950s-era predecessor, hit the market like a storm. Ford priced the car at a premium that certainly should provide the company a hefty profit for this limited-production-run car. The demand for the car far exceeded production. Dealers found that customers were willing to pay not only the sticker price, but even hundreds of dollars over the sticker price. Even with a higher price, there were still too few cars to meet demand.

In some cases, the value-based price is lower than cost-based pricing would suggest. If that's the case, the company has a problem. The product will not sell for the cost to make it. The company must find ways to reduce the cost of the product, enhance the value of the product with features, or devise advertising communication to persuade customers to buy the product at a higher price. None of these strategies can be adopted overnight.

Some restaurant chains discovered this problem and adjusted their offerings accordingly. Casual-eating chains, such as Applebee's and Red Lobster, found that their prices were creeping up beyond what customers were willing to pay. When surveying customers, they also found that customers complained about being served too much food. The cost of food, of course, was a major por-

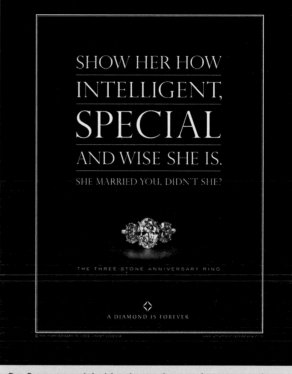

De Beers is a global leader in diamond mining and marketing. Their diamonds, sold exclusively through De Beers stores, are known for their style and quality. How is the De Beers image of having the world's finest diamonds affected by price?

tion of the cost associated with the meal. The restaurants' response was to create half-size meals or value meals in addition to the regular-size entrées. This approach allowed customers with smaller appetites to order smaller portions at a lower price. The prices of ancillary products, such as soft drinks and desserts, remained the same. Some restaurants, realizing that many of their patrons were senior citizens, created early-bird menus with smaller portions at a lower price. This practice not only brought in more customers, but also moved the first round of customers to earlier in the evening so that there was room for a second round of customers who wanted the full-size, full-price meals.

A third method of pricing is **image pricing.** Here, the business sets prices high to indicate the exclusive, upscale nature of the product or service. This approach often enhances the value to the customer in spite of the higher price because the customer realizes some status from buying from the upscale provider.

A somewhat opposite strategy from image pricing is **penetration pricing.** Penetration pricing involves setting the price temporarily low, often below cost, to gain a large market share. In many cases, penetration pricing is used with new products. Prices are set low to get customers to try out the product. Some independent software developers do this. When the software is initially marketed, early buyers are given extremely low prices to try out the software. If the results are favorable, prices are then raised. Penetration pricing is a short-run strategy. The firm normally expects to raise the price in the long run after it has achieved market acceptance.

image pricing
A situation where a business sets prices very high to indicate the exclusive or high status nature of the product or service.

penetration pricing
Temporarily pricing below competition to gain market share.

competitive pricing
Pricing based on competitors' prices for similar products.

In **competitive pricing,** companies set their prices on the basis of the prices competitors charge. The prices may be just higher, just lower, or as near the same as possible, but whatever strategy is used, the price will stay proportionately the same. Gasoline prices illustrate this method. Gasoline at self-serve stations will always be a few pennies below the price at full-service stations and usually the same as the price at other self-serve stations.

discount pricing
A strategy of pricing low to increase sales volume.

Another pricing strategy is **discount pricing,** such as Wal-Mart uses. The company knows that its competitively low prices will increase sales volume. What it loses on margin—the difference between price and the cost of the product—it makes up for in volume. End-of-season pricing is also used by businesses to clear out current-season merchandise to make room for next season's products.

The common theme with the pricing strategies discussed here is that they are methods of communicating with customers. Each pricing strategy sends a message to customers as well as to competitors. Each strategy addresses the concept of value to the customer, taking into account that the definition of value changes over time and from customer to customer.

Integrating the Marketing Communications

At the outset of this chapter, we noted the importance of integrated marketing communications for successful businesses. We now return to that topic to reinforce its importance and note some ways to ensure that such integration happens.

Each method of communicating with customers adds value to the product or service being provided. Regardless of whether the communication is on the package, in instructions, in advertising that illustrates the benefits of the product, or in interaction between a salesperson and a customer, the communication helps customers make choices about whether to purchase the product or how to use it. This consistency enhances value for the customer. But all messages must be integrated throughout a company's attempts to communicate with customers.

Consider an example of the failure to integrate communications: A car dealer advertises on television and in the newspaper that it promises to have the best deals in town. In addition, it challenges customers to bring in offers from competing dealers, which it promises to beat by $200. Once a customer walks in the door with a competing deal, the sales representative tells the customer that the cars aren't exactly comparable or that additional charges will apply beyond the negotiated price. Here, two different types of communication with the customer contradict each other and leave the customer puzzled and disgruntled at the treatment by the dealer.

The key to integrated marketing communications is consistency. The messages to customers must all say the same thing. They must reinforce each other in the minds of the customer. They must be consistent with each other, and they must be consistent with the overall strategy of the company.

THINK ABOUT THIS

1. Look back at Profile 15.1, in which Kellogg's was using the Disney brand to sell premium-priced cereal. How do pricing and branding relate? In other words, how much more would you be willing to pay to get a well-known brand—5 percent? 10 percent? 25 percent? How would your answer vary for different products?

2. What is the risk of using a penetration pricing strategy?

3. Cost-based pricing and value-based pricing are two very different strategies. Is there any relationship between the two, or are they totally independent?

Soliciting Feedback from Customers

We began Chapter 14 by noting the need to find out what customers want. We noted the importance of obtaining this information before new products could be developed. It is important to add that this communication from the *customer back to the company* is often just as important as communication from the company to the customer. **Feedback** from customers tells the company how it is doing. It tells the company when it has problems and when it is doing well. Companies should encourage and solicit feedback from customers.

Consider the importance of feedback for restaurants. Managers of restaurants need to know when customers have bad experiences. To encourage feedback, many restaurants leave comment cards on the table for customers to complete there or to mail back to the restaurant company. In addition, good managers will spend at least part of their time carefully discussing the quality of service and food with patrons. This attempt must involve more than the perfunctory "How was everything, OK?" that some servers and managers are noted for. It means taking the time to visit with customers to get their opinions. Applebee's and Red Lobster, both casual-dining chains, occasionally give customers a number to call to respond to a telephone survey in exchange for a few dollars off a meal or a free dessert at their next visit. The information helps the restaurants analyze their menu, cleanliness, and service.

Some auto dealers call customers a few days after their car has been serviced to get information about the service provided. In addition to simply finding out information about the quality of service, the call sometimes uncovers problems of which management was unaware. Suppose the service technician got grease on the steering wheel. The call from the dealer allows it to offer an apology and perhaps a free total car cleaning to make up for the inconvenience. This is good customer service, which can be provided only if the dealer solicits communication from the client.

Even in an information age, there are times when personal selling is an important and needed approach. What situations have you encountered where personal selling is essential?

feedback
Communications from customers that tell a company how it is doing.

THE BIG PICTURE

We have preached the value of effective communications throughout this chapter. It is important, however, to end the chapter with a discussion of how communicating with customers affects other areas within a business.

Sometimes a department makes a decision that helps that department but ultimately hurts the company as a whole. This problem is especially severe in the area of communications. Consider the connection between customer communications and the production function of the business. If, for example, the marketing department does an excellent job of communicating value through setting low prices, it may stimulate demand for the product beyond the manufacturing department's ability to produce the product. This imbalance, in turn, will result in lost sales and lost customers.

The concept of integrated marketing communication should be considered on two levels. First, within the marketing function, the message must be consistent. But the communication between a company and its customers should also be considered from the perspective of the overall image of the company. Marketing communications must be thoroughly integrated into the overall strategy of the firm. Just as the quality of a company's products must fit its strategy, so too must the quality of communications fit and enhance that strategy.

Summary

1. The best product in the world is of little value if that value is not communicated to the customer.

   • How does communication with customers enhance value?

   Communicating with customers enhances value by providing information about the product, where to buy it, its warranties, and how to get the product to the customer.

   It is important that communications be consistent by telling the same message all the time. Doing so involves integrated marketing communications.

   • What is integrated marketing communications?

   Integrated marketing communications is using all available means of communicating with the customer to persuade the customer to buy the firm's products or services. Consistency is the key to successfully integrating communications between the company and customers.

2. Building and maintaining customer loyalty is fundamental to business success. Loyalty is especially valuable as competition intensifies.

   • What are the keys to building customer loyalty?

   Relationship marketing and brand equity are two key themes. Relationship marketing involves the process of getting to know customers and developing rapport and long-term relationships with them. Brand equity is the unique value a business gains because of its brand.

3. There are many ways of communicating with customers. Businesses must consider which method is best.

   • How can businesses communicate with customers?

   Communications with customers include mass communication and advertising, direct marketing and the Internet, one-on-one interactions, informational packaging, sales promotions, indirect communication, and pricing.

   One of the most effective ways that a business can communicate with its customers is through mass media. Mass media include television, radio, magazines, newspapers, and telephone directory Yellow Pages.

   • How is advertising used as a method of communicating with customers?

   Advertising is any paid form of presentation and promotion of ideas, goods, and services by an identified sponsor to a targeted audience and delivered primarily through the mass media. It includes institutional advertising, which provides general information about a company, and product advertising, which gives specific, value-oriented information about one or more products.

   Communicating through direct marketing provides customers with information with the hope that they will respond by purchasing products directly from the company without the use of dealers or other retailers.

• What are the two major types of direct marketing?

Direct marketing is typically done either through the use of catalogs or over the Internet. The use of catalogs requires effective use of huge databases of names and addresses. Internet communication provides information to customers. These sites can also allow customers to choose products and purchase them by completing online purchase arrangements.

Although the most efficient methods of communicating in terms of cost per customer reached are through mass media and direct marketing, one-on-one communication is more effective in some situations.

• What is one-on-one communication?

One-on-one communication consists primarily of personal selling, in which a sales representative talks directly to a potential customer. This method is especially effective in business-to-business selling.

Most communication from a company to its customers is direct, either through some media or through one-on-one communication. Additionally, however, companies can communicate with customers indirectly.

• What are some examples of indirect communication?

Two excellent examples are sponsorships and publicity. In these cases, the company does not control the final message, but the message can sometimes be used effectively to enhance the firm's image.

Businesses use various pricing approaches or strategies to communicate value to customers.

• What are the main pricing strategies that companies commonly use?

Six commonly used strategies are cost-based pricing, value pricing, image pricing, penetration pricing, and competitive pricing.

4. It is important that each method of providing information to customers be done in a way that is consistent with other methods and with the firm's overall strategy.

• How can a company ensure that a consistent message is being presented?

The way a firm coordinates its messages is through the use of integrated marketing communications. The key to integrated marketing communications is consistency.

5. In addition to providing information *to* customers, it is important that the company solicit information *from* customers.

• What is customer feedback, and how is it obtained?

Customer feedback is information and opinions gathered from customers regarding how well the company has performed. It can be gained through comment cards, discussions with customers, or contact with customers after a service has been provided.

Key Terms

advertising, p. 387

brand, p. 385

brand equity, p. 385

bricks-and-clicks retailers, p. 392

competitive pricing, p. 398

cost-based pricing, p. 396

direct mail, p. 390

direct marketing, p. 390

discount pricing, p. 398

feedback, p. 399

image pricing, p. 397

institutional advertising, p. 387

integrated marketing communications (IMC), p. 383

Exercises and Applications

1. Pick five Internet websites that do (or could do) Internet marketing. These might include Lands' End, J.Crew, United Airlines, hotels, and car rental companies. Compare the sites for ease of use. What is difficult about some of them?

2. Form teams. Pick a product that is appealing to your team. Design a print advertisement for the product. Then write a script for a radio advertisement for it. Which type of advertisement is easier to do?

3. Choose three brands that you regularly purchase. Compare the prices of the brands with their generic equivalents. Discuss brand equity by looking at the value of each brand.

4. How did your college communicate value to you before you chose to attend? How does your experience compare with the information provided in earlier attempts to persuade you to attend? Discuss the experiences with your classmates. Did they have the same experiences?

5. Suppose you work in the marketing area of a bank. How could you use sponsorships to increase revenues? Write a two-page paper that outlines how you might choose a nonprofit organization as your partner and how you could help that organization while creating good publicity for your bank.

6. In teams, develop a website to advertise and get people to buy a dormitory room cleaning service. Decide how much to charge, how you would link the website to others, and how you would advertise the site itself.

7. Go to the Best Buy website. What kinds of value do the messages on its website provide?

FROM THE PAGES OF

BusinessWeek

Everyone Loves a Freebie—Except Dell's Rivals

It's not the lottery, but Dell gave away $50,000 a day during July 2002 to some lucky customers whose names were drawn from a pool of buyers of Dell equipment. That is indeed an incentive to buy Dell equipment. But Dell isn't the only company that offers incentives to buyers. Apple offered computers on credit with no payments for several months. Gateway gave away printers or scanners with selected models of PCs. Hewlett-Packard offered $400 rebates on Compaq and H-P machines. Retailers such as Best Buy and Circuit City also offered rebates and savings deals.

The use of incentives to buy computers is a marketing tactic borrowed from the automobile companies, which have offered no-interest financing for the second straight year. The reason for the incentives offered by computer companies? Computer sales have tanked as a result of a soft economy and a feeling among some users in the consumer sector that a two- or three-year-old computer is good enough.

Dell's rivals have some cause for concern. Whereas Dell typically makes computers to order and therefore has little inventory in stock, many of its competitors have several weeks of inventory sitting on their shelves. With Dell already being the computer of choice for many buyers and with its being one of few firms in the industry that actually made a profit, Dell is forcing the competitors to scramble to meet its deals. Since the competitors have weaker financial conditions, the sales promotion strategy of providing expensive incentives is indeed expensive.

Some forecasters are predicting an equally dismal outlook for 2003. This could mean that computer companies, like the automobile companies, are "buying customers" this year who, then, are not likely to be in the market next year. Thus, computer companies are in trouble this year if they do not use incentives, but they will be in trouble next year if they do offer incentives.

Decision Questions

1. Is offering incentives an ethical issue or simply an economic issue?

2. Is the use of incentives the best way to communicate enhanced value to customers?

3. Would incentives be as effective in industries other than computers or automobiles? How about the utility industry? the restaurant industry? your college cafeteria? the textbook publishing industry?

Source: Cliff Edwards, "Everyone Loves a Freebie—Except Dell's Rivals," *BusinessWeek,* July 22, 2002, p. 41.

References

1. Stanley Holmes, "Gert Gets the Last Laugh," *BusinessWeek,* June 10, 2002, p. 100.

2. Adapted from Terence A. Shimp, *Advertising Promotion: Supplemental Aspects of Integrated Marketing Communications* (Fort Worth, TX: Dryden Press, 2000), p. 18.

3. Charles W. Lamb, Jr., Joseph F. Hair, Jr., and Carl McDaniel, *Marketing.* (Cincinnati, OH: South-Western, 2002), p. 13.

4. Lamb, Hair, and McDaniel, p. 301.

5. Tom Duncan, *IMC: Using Advertising and Promotion to Build Brands,* (Burr Ridge, IL: McGraw-Hill/Irwin, 2002), p. 44.

6. Duncan, 47.

7. Adapted from John Burnett and Sandra Moriarty, *Introduction to Marketing Communication* (Upper Saddle River, NJ: Prentice Hall, 2000), p. 79.

8. *The Wall Street Journal,* October 9, 2002, p. A20; and *The Wall Street Journal,* October 10, 2002, p. A9.

9. "Special Report: Leading National Advertisers," *Advertising Age,* June 24, 2002, p. S-32.

10. Warren Berger, "Just Do It. Again," *Business 2.0,* September 2002, pp. 76–84.

11. Lands' End website, www.landsend.com (accessed August 10, 2002).

12. Burnett and Moriarty, p. 411.

13. Shimp, p. 5.

14. Melanie Trottman, "Small Airlines Gain by Cutting Business Fares," *The Wall Street Journal,* July 29, 2002, pp. B1, B4.

16

Integrating Activities and Encouraging Commitment

On a trip to Italy, Howard Schultz was impressed with the relaxed and comfortable espresso bars that he found in Milan. One could sit, converse, and leisurely enjoy an espresso or other coffee treat. Returning to the United States, he convinced his bosses that they ought to try a new concept—a coffee bar. Schultz believed the American public would embrace this new idea. A spot was opened in downtown Seattle, and the rest is history. Today, the business Schultz shaped, Starbucks, is an entrepreneurial success story.

Certainly, Starbucks is known for its phenomenal growth and its sterling record of success. But Starbucks is also known for its commitment to its people, its unique culture, and its reputation for being a great place to work. Starbucks employees, known as partners, are treated with dignity and respect. In fact, the company prides itself on creating a workplace where its partners are engaged, inspired, and rewarded. This philosophy is captured by the inspirational example of Howard Schultz himself.

"Looking back now, I have a lot of respect for my dad. He never finished high school, but he was an honest man who worked hard . . . But he was a beaten man. In a series of blue-collar jobs—truck driver, factory worker, cab driver—he never made as much as $20,000 a year, never could afford to own his own home. I tried to make Starbucks the kind of company I wished my dad had worked for . . . If he had landed a job in one of our stores or roasting plants, he wouldn't have to quit in frustration because the company didn't value him. He would have good health benefits, stock options, and an atmosphere in which his suggestions or complaints would receive a prompt, respectful response."

And that is the kind of company Starbucks has become. Starbucks is legendary for its benefits, which include health, dental, and vision coverage. Breaking from tradition, Starbucks makes these benefits available even to part-timers who work as few as 20 hours per week. There are other special benefits that include health coverage for domestic partners, adoption assistance, and stock purchase plans. But that is just the beginning. The company even has a CUP fund (Caring Unites Partners) that provides financial assistance to partners in times of need. The CUP fund is for special, extraordinary circumstances and is provided in addition to disability coverage and personal leave allowances.

Howard Schultz, chairman and chief executive officer of Starbucks Coffee Co., headquartered in Seattle, WA, waves after cutting the ribbon to inaugurate its store in Tokyo's Ginza shopping district—the first store opened outside North America. Why do you think so many young employees consider Starbucks to be a great place to work?

The company believes in its people and wants them to share their ideas and concerns with management. Through their Open Forums, employees can ask questions and share thoughts with senior management on a regular basis. Awards and recognitions abound, with more than 30 different award programs in place. And the company does not rest on its past success. It's constantly looking for new and creative ways to build a workplace that inspires and rewards its partners. And, of course, this environment builds a stronger bottom line. It's no wonder that Starbucks is ranked as the most admired brand in the food services industry and is perennially listed as one of the best companies to work for in the United States.[1]

As we have noted throughout this text, many interrelated activities must be accomplished if a business is going to be healthy and successful. These activities do not occur in isolation. Rather, as our model of the path to a successful business notes, they must mesh simultaneously if the business is going to achieve its goals in a timely manner. For example, business leaders and managers must know what is going on in the environment. They must know their own current state of internal affairs. They must choose a direction for the business and select appropriate strategies. They must be attuned to customers and provide quality products and services in a timely manner. There are many things to be done and many decisions to be made.

This chapter emphasizes the way the activities of a business fit together. It looks at how businesses are designed and how managers encourage commitment from the workforce. Thanks to these activities, businesses are able to perform in a successful manner.

After studying this chapter, you should be able to:

1. Define *organization design* and *organization structure.*
2. Illustrate the logical way a successful business builds an organization structure.
3. Explain some of the structural concerns encountered in business.
4. Understand some of the ways that businesses are addressing these issues and concerns.
5. Demonstrate the basic dynamics of employee motivation and commitment.
6. Formulate and apply some of the actions managers can take to encourage greater commitment among employees.

The concepts of structure and commitment are key to the model we introduced in Chapter 2. Only with committed workers who are organized logically can the business achieve success. In this chapter, we consider the way the parts of the business fit together and operate to gain the best performance possible.

Two key performance themes are emphasized. First, we talk about the overall design of the business. This issue is important because it affects how work activities are arranged to attain high levels of performance. Second, we talk about encouraging commitment within the workforce. Although this theme has always been important, it is all the more significant in today's streamlined, downsized businesses. Motivated work behavior is critical as managers encourage their workers to do more with less. Importantly, the design and commitment themes fit together. For example, no matter how well jobs are designed, without a committed and motivated workforce, performance will fall short of expectations. Similarly, motivated workers may provide high levels of energy and effort and still fail to meet performance goals if their efforts are frustrated by poorly structured tasks. The good news is that it works both ways. Developing exciting new work arrangements and designs can help build commitment and motivation in the workforce. For example, one popular move of many large companies is to restructure their organizations into smaller units—in essence, to keep an entrepreneurial or small-company feel and entrepreneurial spirit in their operations. Consider General Electric. Instead of having all key decisions made at corporate headquarters, the company is divided into a number of strategic business units. Although all the units are still under the GE umbrella, each unit is really operated as its own business. This approach provides greater speed, more flexibility, and greater sensitivity to customers. Recently, GE went even further when it broke down GE Capital (its financial services business) into four separate businesses.[2]

Building an Integrated Structure and Design

It is the interrelated nature of business that makes the theme of integration so important. The various parts of the business have to be coordinated in some logical manner. **Organization design** deals with how the various parts of the business are coordinated. Organizing and coordinating everything so that the business operates with efficiency and everything that needs to be done gets done is a daunting assignment. This is why businesses develop organization structures.

An **organization structure** is a framework that prescribes the way the business organizes, arranges, and groups the work that needs to be done. It is a pattern of how the business will integrate the various activities. Every organization has a structure. In a very small business, the structure may be informal and unwritten. For example, Jane Long owns and operates Reader's Cove, one of the few remaining independent bookstores in her city. Her husband, Jeb, works at the business on weekends and handles all the bookkeeping. Jane employs three part time salespeople who work in the store at various times throughout the week. Although nothing is formalized, Reader's Cove has a structure. Jane makes all purchase decisions. Jeb takes care of billing and payments and prints the paychecks each week. The salesclerks handle customer matters and provide full service to customers as they shop in the store. Jane and Jeb often meet over lunch to discuss the business, and Jane meets with the salespeople whenever a need arises. As you can see, there is a definition of duties and there is logic to the way the work is arranged.

Certainly, such informality will not work as a business grows larger. At some point, there must be a formal outline of how work will be arranged and integrated. It is this more formal approach to structure and design that we address in this chapter.

Organization structure is developed to integrate the operations of the business in a manner that is as orderly and efficient as possible. Organization structure is really a framework for arranging and coordinating work to use resources when and where they are required and to minimize duplication and redundancy of resources.

Structure should be built logically as the company's leaders consider the jobs that need to be performed and how these jobs must fit together. Suppose that after careful market research, you decide there is a market demand for domestically built high-performance bicycles. You decide to start such a business. You are the president and you call the business Transit Cycles. From your research, you decide to build two models of bicycles—a road bike and a mountain bike. You will design and build the bikes but will outsource many of the component parts.

You decide to assemble a group of people who will design the bicycles. Logically, these people will need to work together in the same area of the business, since much of the information and materials they need for their design work will be shared. These design employees will have engineering backgrounds. They must understand the dynamics of existing competitor bikes and design new ones that will be significant improvements. You decide that initially you will need three designers to work on the road bike and three designers to concentrate on the mountain bike. Logically, these six designers need to report to someone who can oversee their work, provide the resources they need, and coordinate their efforts with other areas of the business. Therefore, you hire an experienced bike designer from a rival firm to manage the design process. This manager will report directly to your plant or facilities manager, who will oversee all production work.

organization design
The way the various parts of a business are coordinated.

organization structure
A framework that prescribes how a business organizes, arranges, and groups the work that needs to be done.

FIGURE 16.1

Partial Organization
Chart

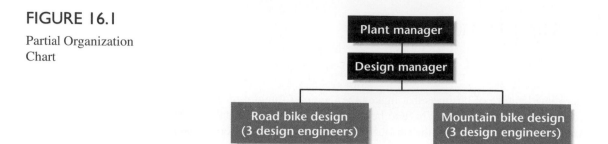

Even at this early stage, an organization structure is beginning to take form. Figure 16.1 portrays the organization structure graphically in an *organization chart.* Although the chart is very basic, there is a logic to it. Positions and jobs are arranged in a way that seems to make sense in helping the business meet its design needs.

Once the design work is done, the bicycles must be built (manufactured) and assembled. The manufacturing process is quite complex. Metal alloys (which you purchase from a supplier) must be molded and formed into frames that meet the specifications provided by the design engineers. This process involves three distinct manufacturing operations. One operation deals exclusively with the frames, another with the handlebars, and another with the wheels. Each of these manufacturing operations employs five workers. These 15 workers are supervised by a manufacturing manager, who makes sure the manufacturing is done properly and manufacturing schedules are met. She also spends a lot of time with the design manager to be sure that the product being built is consistent with what the designers had in mind. Logically, the manufacturing manager also reports to the plant manager. We now have another structural piece, depicted in Figure 16.2.

Finally, once the various component parts are built, the bicycles must be assembled. This operation is done by teams of workers. On most days, there are three assembly teams working. Each assembly team consists of four employees, who perform all the assembly operations. They attach handlebars to frames, add the wheels and tires, assemble all cable linkages and derailleurs (which you purchase from an Italian company), and test the final assembled bike to be sure it operates properly. These teams are led by an assembly team manager who checks their progress, coordinates with the manufacturing area to get parts when needed, and helps the teams from time to time. This manager also reports to the plant manager.

Let's take a look at the structure that has developed in your business and talk about what it means. Figure 16.3 shows the structure used to build the bicycles. What does this structure reveal about the business? First, it clearly portrays the lines of authority and responsibility in the business. For example, a worker who manufactures wheels reports to the manufacturing manager, who in turn reports to the plant manager. This

FIGURE 16.2

Partial Organization
Chart

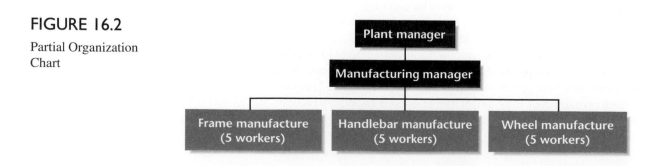

FIGURE 16.3

Partial Organization Chart

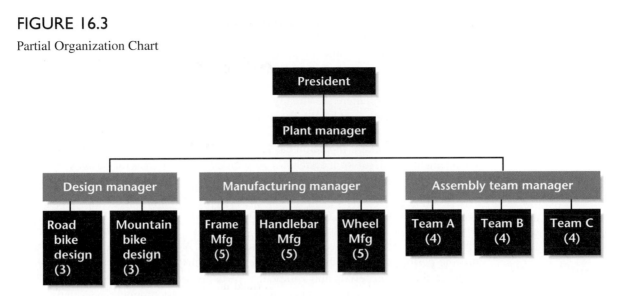

line of authority is known as the **chain of command.** Many managers feel strongly that the chain of command must be followed when communication takes place. The chain of command also leads to another concept, **span of control,** which is the number of employees who report to a given manager. This number will vary depending on the skills of the employees, the skills of the manager, and the complexity of the tasks performed. In Figure 16.3, for example, 12 team members report to the assembly team manager.

Let's look a bit more deeply at the structure. It also shows how your business divides up the overall work to be done. There are some important points to be made here. Obviously, you do not expect all your workers to do everything. Frame manufacturers do not have the background and expertise to perform design work. Further, design engineers should focus on their specific areas and not dabble in unrelated tasks. To accomplish this end, employees are placed in specific jobs and are asked to perform only those jobs. This process is known as **specialization.** You can see by looking at the organization chart the degree of specialization that exists in Transit Cycles.

The chart also shows that specialized jobs are grouped together in a way that seems to make sense. Design jobs are grouped together, manufacturing jobs are grouped together, and assembly jobs are grouped together. This process of grouping similar jobs is known as **departmentalization.** There are a number of ways that a business can group jobs. Our sample business has departmentalized according to *function.*

Some businesses departmentalize on the basis of the *markets* or *customers served.* For example, most banks are organized into commercial divisions and consumer divisions. This grouping assumes the needs of commercial markets are different from the needs of everyday consumers. This customer-based departmentalization allows for more careful attention to the unique demands of both types of customers.

An increasingly popular approach, particularly with global businesses, is to departmentalize into *geographic divisions.* For example, a business with operations in South America, Europe, and Asia may have a separate division for each operation. Again, the assumption is that these unique geographic areas need more discretion in decision making. This grouping should enable the units to be more responsive to customers than could a large business operating from a single headquarters in another country.

chain of command
The line of authority in a business, which identifies who reports to whom.

span of control
The number of employees who report to a given manager.

specialization
The process of placing employees in specific jobs and asking them to perform only those jobs.

departmentalization
The process of grouping similar jobs together in any of several ways (among them, function, markets, or geography).

In most situations, where these divisional approaches are being used, certain activities are still *centralized*. In other words, some activities are done by the firm's headquarters for all divisions rather than duplicated by each division. This is usually the case for expensive services such as computing and financing.

The structure of your bicycle business offers further revelations. Even in this relatively small business, there are already four levels of employees. You are the president at the top level. At the next level is the plant manager. The third level is composed of the various area managers from design, manufacturing, and assembly. The fourth level is made up of the workers in each area. In Transit Cycles, three levels of hierarchy are management. The issue of hierarchy is very important. It is easy for businesses to add more and more levels of hierarchy, but doing so may lead to problems, some of which are discussed in the next section.

It may have occurred to you that the structure in Figure 16.3 is incomplete. Significant areas of the business have been left out. We have included only the activities or jobs that are directly involved in making the bicycles. A number of additional activities must be performed for our business to operate. For instance, people must be hired to purchase the raw materials and component parts needed to build the bicycles. These people will staff the purchasing department, finding the best suppliers, negotiating contracts with them, and seeing that all materials are delivered when needed.

In addition, people must be hired to deal with various retail outlets, encourage retailers to carry your bicycles, and ship the bikes to them. These people are grouped in the marketing department. Some people are needed to track your finances, extend terms of purchase with retailers, be sure payments are received, and handle the payroll. These people are grouped in the accounting area. People in the human resources department will be responsible for hiring and training employees. You also need people in the information systems department to provide information services and support for all areas of the business. Now a more expanded and complete business organization for Transit Cycles (shown in Figure 16.4) has been defined.

The Logic of Structure

As the structure of Transit Cycles unfolded, you began to see the complexity involved. Imagine the complexity of a large business that employs thousands of people and provides a diverse assortment of products or services. Yet the structure of all businesses exists to provide order and efficiency. This point cannot be overemphasized. The struc-

FIGURE 16.4

Organization Chart for Transit Cycles

ture outlines an orderly flow of activities and interactions that keep the business moving toward its goals. The structure is present to avoid the chaos of employees' doing their own thing, without any sense of whether it contributes overall value for the business and its customers. The structure should arrange activities and interactions so that the business is operating in the most efficient manner possible. Unnecessary duplication should be avoided. Clear reporting and communication will ensure that no decision maker is taken by surprise. Businesses realize that structure, control, and order are essential in today's tough and demanding business climate.

Southwest Airlines has a fairly typical organization structure. As you know, Jim Parker is CEO and Colleen Barrett is president and COO. Three executive vice presidents and a senior vice president report to them. A total of 21 vice presidents cover areas such as schedule planning, in-flight service, flight operations, ground operations, fuel management, and government affairs.[3]

Structural Concerns

Companies have long been structured in a hierarchical, pyramidal shape. As we have seen, this type of structure is fine as long as it ensures order and efficiency and helps the business meet its goals of serving customers and meeting performance objectives. But problems can arise when structures become too complex.

Some large companies have numerous levels of management between the president and the lowest-level nonmanagerial workers. In recent years, some critics argue, these traditional structures have become increasingly unworkable. Led by global competitive pressures and the need for efficiency, companies are trying to do three things—reduce costs, make quicker decisions, and get closer to their customers. They found they could do all three by restructuring. The restructuring has gone by many names: downsizing, rightsizing, reengineering, and redesigning to name just a few. While each approach is slightly different in concept, all are designed to restructure the people and positions in businesses and reconsider relationships both within a company and between the company and its customers.

The result of many restructurings has been a much flatter organization. Some of the intermediate levels of management have been eliminated, reducing the number of levels separating top management from customers. At the same time, authority to make decisions has been pushed down in the organization. Now top management must trust lower-level managers and nonmanagerial employees to make decisions that are in the best interest of both the customer and the organization.

Thus far, we have outlined a rather simple organization structure and introduced some fundamental terms and concepts. With this background, we are ready to address some of the structural issues that contemporary businesses are facing.

True, structure must provide order and efficiency to the complex set of activities the business needs to perform. Yet structure must do more. First, it should encourage integration across departments. Information and ideas must flow quickly and smoothly. Second, it should ensure customer sensitivity

THINK ABOUT THIS

1. Some very small businesses pride themselves on having a very informal structure, with few designated links between activities. Do you think such a loose structure is good for a small business? Why or why not?

2. As the business grows, structure becomes more critical. At what point do you think a business needs to begin formalizing its structure?

3. The next time you visit a fast-food restaurant, observe the activities that are occurring. Sketch the structure that seems to exist. What could you change in the structure to help the restaurant improve efficiency and customer service?

and timely response. Third, it should foster employee innovation and creativity. Failing to meet these needs is extremely dangerous in today's competitive environment.

Suboptimization

Unfortunately, some businesses ignore the advice regarding structural concerns. Traditionally, most major businesses in this country have had large, functionally oriented departments that may have had hundreds of people in them. These departments are often minibusinesses in and of themselves. Although there is not necessarily anything wrong with this structure, it can lead to problems. One common problem occurs when the various departments begin to view themselves as the heart and soul of the business rather than as pieces in the larger organizational puzzle. Employees' loyalty becomes tied to their own department. Department success becomes more important than the success of the business as a whole. Employees begin to make decisions that benefit their department but hurt other departments, which can lead to less effective outcomes for the whole business.

For example, the marketing department of a large business wants to sell as many products as it possibly can. In the zeal to make sales, the reps promise faster delivery than any competitor. Unfortunately, they don't check with the manufacturing people to find out whether the products can be made within the promised deadlines. Now the production department is in a bind. Its people work overtime and feel the strain of next-to-impossible deadlines. The accident rate goes up. The number of defects rises. Production runs have to be reworked. Customers become frustrated. In the end, the business may lose an important customer. The situation described here is known as suboptimization. **Suboptimization** occurs when one department, acting in its own self-interest, hurts or inhibits the performance of another department and leads to less effective outcomes for the business overall. When the business becomes too large and extensively departmentalized, the critical holistic focus may be lost and the risk of suboptimization increases.

> **suboptimization**
> A situation in which one department of a business, acting in its own self-interest, hurts or inhibits the performance of another department, leading to less effective outcomes for the business overall.

Bureaucratization

Another problem is that as businesses grow large, they often add levels of hierarchy, most of them in management. Policy and strategy makers become further and further removed from the people who are in direct contact with customers and who are developing and making the products of the business. Control becomes an issue. Upper-level managers frequently develop rules and procedures to tell employees exactly what they are to do in various situations. The organization now has many levels of hierarchy, a formal set of rules and procedures, and considerable distance between the "thinkers" and the "doers." This type of organization is generally labeled a *bureaucracy*.

Numerous problems may be present in a bureaucracy. First, as we noted, large, complex organizations may lose touch with their customers, thus threatening the essential business outcome of customer sensitivity.

Second, bureaucracies are often slow to change and slow to innovate. With so many layers to move through, communication and decision making simply take a great deal of time. Since quick responses are not part of this organizational package, the business outcome of timeliness is often sacrificed.

Third, bureaucracies are rather inflexible. Certain areas perform certain functions and follow specified procedures. While such rigidity helps ensure consistency and control, it also inhibits quick and flexible responses to changing consumer demands. In today's environment, consumers have little patience and often fleeting brand loyalty. The inflexible business often loses in a competitive marketplace.

Fourth, bureaucracies may be frustrating for skilled employees. Rather than fully using their talents, the bureaucratic organization often places these people in specialized jobs with limited variety and autonomy. Instead of encouraging employee commitment, this type of organization leads to job dissatisfaction and frustration, especially for highly talented professional employees.

Solutions to Structural Concerns

Companies that are concerned about reaction time and employee utilization are exploring a number of solutions. Teams, project approaches, matrix approaches, business units, and virtual organizations are being introduced into companies today with varying degrees of success.

Teams

One of the most significant changes in the restructuring era has been the use of teams. Before 1990, teams were not extensively used in businesses except for special projects or task forces designed to solve some specific problem. Increasingly, however, teams are becoming a major way to help make a business more competitive. This enhanced competitiveness occurs for a number of reasons:

1. Teams encourage holistic thinking and minimize the possibilities of suboptimization.
2. Teams' diverse inputs lead to creative decisions.
3. Teams increase members' motivation and commitment.
4. Teams flatten hierarchies, saving time and money and reducing employee frustration.

Teams can break away from some of the limitations and restrictions of the traditional hierarchy. They are much more responsive than the traditional hierarchical structure. Cross-functional teams may be formed around product innovations or new customer needs. As we discussed in Chapters 5 and 14, a cross-functional team may consist of individuals from marketing, production, finance, product development, and human resources, who work collectively to bring about the needed change. Because these teams work on projects and issues by including a range of perspectives, the risks of suboptimization are reduced.

Self-directed work teams are the most progressive and extensive use of the team concept. They have changed the face of production activities at companies such as Ford. Again, as noted in Chapter 5, self-directed work teams are given broad responsibility for carrying out tasks or jobs on their own. The team typically has the freedom to organize its tasks, perform operations, handle problems that arise, and perform quality assurance checks. Often the team is allowed to make decisions that used to be left up to a supervisor. Accordingly, self-directed teams have permitted businesses to streamline decision making. Self-directed work teams are staples at companies such as Kodak, Apple, and Corning.

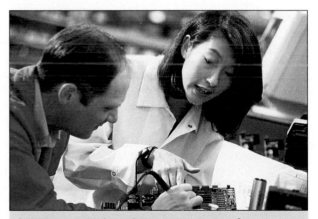

In companies such as this computer repair firm, empowering the employees to make decisions without checking with supervisors allows them to interact closely with the customer to find solutions to problems. This approach may be able to speed service, please customers, and improve employee motivation. Can you think of other businesses where empowering employees may help improve customer service?

Teams of all kinds get input from a variety of people with different skills and different perspectives. This variety often leads to differences of opinion and to conflict. Yet as the team discusses the issues, addresses the conflict, and works toward a consensus, it often finds new ideas and approaches to old problems. If the team works well, it can be a vehicle for making decisions that foster creativity and innovation.

Importantly, teams often allow members more involvement and input, with broader decision-making prerogatives than they have traditionally experienced. This effort to give employees more responsibility and decision-making discretion is known as **empowerment.** Often, empowered team members find their team activities challenging and motivational. They may feel their unique talents and skills are being better utilized. These perceptions may lead to a greater sense of commitment and more interest in their jobs.

> **empowerment**
> The act of giving more decision-making authority and responsibility to workers throughout the organization.

Teams are an excellent way to flatten the hierarchy and to allow for quicker decision making. Consider the team approach of General Motors' Powertrain Division. The division is organized into 22 product development teams. These teams are then grouped into one of four larger teams, called systems teams, on the basis of the frequency of their interaction and their need for coordination. Here is how this approach works: You may be a member of the engine block product development team. You and your team members work together on specific design projects, but you communicate and interact with a number of other teams to be sure that what you are proposing will work and will fit with what those teams are proposing. Your team may meet daily, for example, with the crankshaft team, the pistons team, and the lubrications team. You meet less frequently with the ignition team and the electrical systems team, but those meetings take place to ensure coordination. As a result of the team environment, there are regular meetings, a total divisionwide commitment to innovation, and a sense that everyone is pulling in the same direction. Things get done more quickly and with fewer overlaps.[4]

The team approach at General Electric, known as Work-Out, brings together teams of people from varied ranks and areas—managers, engineers, administrative assistants, line workers, suppliers, and at times, even customers. The Work-Out team focuses on a problem or an opportunity, responding quickly and decisively to present the best ideas and solutions possible. GE assumes that the people closest to the work know best how to do things better. The results are staggering. People feel needed and important. GE wins too. It gets fresh, exciting, and creative ideas.[5]

Some companies have even gone so far as to remove all trappings of a traditional structure. For example, Oticon, the company that pioneered the digital hearing aid, has eliminated all departments, functions, and even titles. Its employees are constantly forming and reforming into self-directed teams to work on projects as they arise.[6]

> **virtual teams**
> Teams that combine the talents and ideas of people worldwide who use technology to communicate in addressing business problems and opportunities.

Some of you may experience a new team approach as you enter the workforce. You may be part of a virtual team. **Virtual teams** combine the talents and ideas of people worldwide who use technology to communicate with one another in addressing business problems and opportunities. With technological advances, these teams may rarely get together physically, yet they still have the advantages of exchanging ideas and challenging one another. Virtual teams create their own unique challenges. People are working in different locations, often in different countries in different time zones, with unique language and cultural differences that must be understood and addressed.[7] Sensitivity to diversity issues, noted in Chapter 7, comes into play here.

Project and Matrix Approaches

> **project organization**
> A structural approach that uses teams drawn from various areas of the business to accomplish high-profile tasks.

When Microsoft developed the Windows 2000 operating system, it used a special approach to structure, known as the project organization. The **project organization** uses teams that bring together a range of talent from various areas of the business to complete a high-profile task or project. In general, here is how the process works: A special project, such as Windows 2000, will be headed by a project manager who is responsible for completing the design. Skilled workers from various areas of the business are pulled together to work as members of the project team. The project team operates as a separate area, and the team's focus is on making sure the project is accomplished. This project organization structure is not new. IBM used the project approach (known as Project Chess) to pioneer the personal computer in the early 1980s.

What prompts this structural approach? The first consideration is speed. When an important, high-visibility project needs to be completed in a limited time, business leaders question whether the existing structure will be able to meet the deadlines. This issue is very important in fast-paced industries in which being first to market a product is critical to competitive success. Second, a business may turn to the project structure when it wants innovation and creativity and fears the existing structure is hostile to these qualities. In a departmental structure, people tend to be concerned about protecting their turf and are reluctant to venture too far from the accepted approaches. Bringing people together as members of special projects teams dispels these fears and encourages innovation.

Today, many businesses are turning toward the matrix approach, which uses the project idea but takes it a bit further. Businesses in rapidly changing fields need to have a number of projects going on at the same time. This situation is what the matrix approach addresses. The **matrix organization** combines the functional structure with the project structure.

In the matrix structure, people are hired and assigned to a functional area of the business and given assignments to work on. They are moved into special projects when their skills are needed. Thus, an employee contributes to both the functional area and the project; employees may contribute their skills and perspectives to several high-profile activities at once. For example, in the research and development arm of Boeing, there will be hundreds of design projects going on all the time.[8]

Through the matrix organization, the business gains the advantages of a project approach, plus an additional benefit: It is using workers in a highly flexible and efficient manner. Employees often feel good about this too. They enjoy being challenged, and the projects are often exciting. Many businesses in high-technology fields use the matrix approach, among them General Electric, Texas Instruments, Boeing, and Dow Chemical.

matrix organization
A structural approach that combines the project structure with the functional structure.

Business Units

There is a growing tendency, particularly among very large businesses, to reorganize their overall operations into business units. For many businesses, this represents a significant change in the way they group their activities. **Business units** are unique product or market groupings that are treated as self-contained businesses. Typically, each business unit has its own performance goals. Accordingly, each business unit can focus careful attention on its products and its customers. This type of arrangement gives the overall business more flexibility and helps ensure sensitivity to customers. Further, as we noted earlier in this chapter, one of the strengths of the business unit approach is that it helps give a very large business more of a small business feel. The financial and other resource advantages of being big are retained. However, each unit can be creative and responsive. General Motors is an example of a very large business that has separate units of the company that focus on its various product lines. These units include the midsize car division, the truck division, the luxury car engineering and manufacturing division, and the Saturn division.

business units
Unique product or market groupings that are treated as self-contained businesses.

virtual organization
A combination of parties (people or organizations) who, although geographically dispersed, are electronically linked so that each can contribute its unique competency in achieving a common goal.

The Virtual Organization[9]

One of the newer structural models is the **virtual organization,** a combination of parties (people or organizations) who, although geographically dispersed, are electronically linked so that each can contribute its unique competency in achieving a common goal. Look at this definition carefully. A virtual organization allows each party to focus on those areas in which it possesses a true distinctive competence. For example, a business may be very good at performing assembly operations in an efficient, low-cost way while adding quality and precision. This competence is where it focuses its internal efforts and resources. All other activities are contracted out to other businesses or individuals through alliances. A remote manufacturer may actually make the product while contract workers take care of the information systems and advertising.

The primary advantage of the virtual organization is that the company capitalizes on efficiency and flexibility. There really is little permanent structure. A business is able to control costs by getting others to perform in areas where it chooses not to specialize. Of course, contracts can be renewed and modified regularly. The business makes limited investment in fixed assets, so its options are open and it can change readily.

Many businesses are using this philosophy. The textbook you are reading is the product of a virtual structural form. The publishing company is responsible for coordinating the book project and for marketing and selling the final product. But the actual writing is contracted to a team of authors. Professors at a number of different universities review the authors' manuscripts. Other remote contractors do copyediting, proofreading, and the selection or development of photographs and illustrations. Still others create the videos. The actual printing of the book is carried out by a separate business. Each party is able to concentrate on its area of expertise and move on to other work once its part of the project is completed.

The Structural Challenge

Managers should always be open to changing existing structures. Indeed, such change may be quite positive. Since business conditions and internal capabilities are always changing, logically, structure must change to meet new business realities. This is a key to successful integration today. Organization structure should be viewed as a tool, not as a limitation. In other words, an existing structure should not stand in the way of what the business needs to do strategically and competitively. A business should first determine its competitive and strategic initiatives and goals. Then it should modify the structure as needed to help meet those initiatives and goals. This focus on structural flexibility will probably be a hallmark of the 21st century.

Encouraging Employee Commitment

As we learned in the previous section, proper design and structure are part of the equation for business success. A creative structure provides a framework that can facilitate desired performance. But it lives up to its potential only when committed and motivated employees are added to the equation.

THINK ABOUT THIS

1. Why is it sometimes difficult for managers and leaders to break from their established organization structures and try some of the structural ideas we have discussed in this section?

2. If you were an employee of a large organization, what would you be thinking if you had just survived a major downsizing by the business?

3. Would you like to work in a project or matrix environment? Why or why not?

To accomplish its objectives as quickly and efficiently as possible, a business needs the right people to work within the structure. These people must be both talented and committed. In Chapter 13, we discussed the acquisition of resources. We noted that businesses must hire people who have the skills and expertise to perform necessary competitive tasks. Further, the business must invest continually in educating and training these workers so that their skills remain fine-tuned and relevant. To fall short in either acquiring skilled people or supporting the development of their talents is a formula for long-run problems.

However, talent alone is not enough. Somehow that talent has to be energized and committed to achieve its full potential. In many ways, this is the most difficult job a manager faces. There is no pat formula. There is no algorithm that always yields a predictable outcome. Each employee is unique. The process of working with people and gaining their commitment to give their all for the business is a perplexing and inexact task.

Understanding Motivation

Gaining commitment is really an issue of **motivation,** an individual's willingness to work hard and expend high levels of effort for the business. Motivation comes from inside. People are usually willing to work hard when they expect to benefit by doing so. In other words, people will expend effort when that effort helps them meet some personal need.

> **motivation**
> A person's willingness to work hard and expend great effort for the business.

In a most basic sense, every action we take is done to meet some need, whether a very short-run need (such as eating when we are hungry) or a longer-term interest (such as performing well in hopes of getting a bonus).

One of the key theories regarding needs satisfaction was developed over 50 years ago by Abraham Maslow. These needs and the ways a business might respond to meet them are summarized in Figure 16.5. Maslow suggested that individuals have five levels of needs. Each level after the first does not become operative until the preceding need has been essentially satisfied. Maslow's five needs are physiological needs, safety and security needs, social needs, esteem needs, and self-actualization needs. Thus, an individual who is out of work and has no money for food and shelter will focus on the two lower needs, physiological and safety and security. That person will not be interested in status or self-fulfillment. A person who is financially secure may be far more interested in making some contribution to society or gaining nonfinancial rewards, such as a plaque that honors him or her as the top salesperson. Managers can motivate workers better if they understand where the workers are on the needs hierarchy.

Another useful theory of motivation is Frederick Herzberg's two-factor theory, outlined in Table 16.1. Herzberg tried to figure out what really motivated people in work situations. He found that one category of factors, known as hygiene factors, will lead to employee dissatisfaction if they are not present in the workplace. However, the increased presence of the hygiene factors will generally not motivate employees to higher levels of satisfaction and performance. Hygiene factors have to do with the context or the environment in which the job is carried out.

Herzberg identified another set of factors, which he called motivators, among them recognition and responsibility. These factors relate to the content of the job. Providing employees with more of these motivators should lead to satisfaction and generate higher levels of performance.

Herzberg's ideas are quite popular. Many experts contend that businesses often spend a lot of money and energy attending to hygiene factors, such as company policies and salary. But they don't pay enough attention to the motivators. They should be creating a work environment that emphasizes the nature of the work itself. When employees receive

FIGURE 16.5

Maslow's Needs Hierarchy

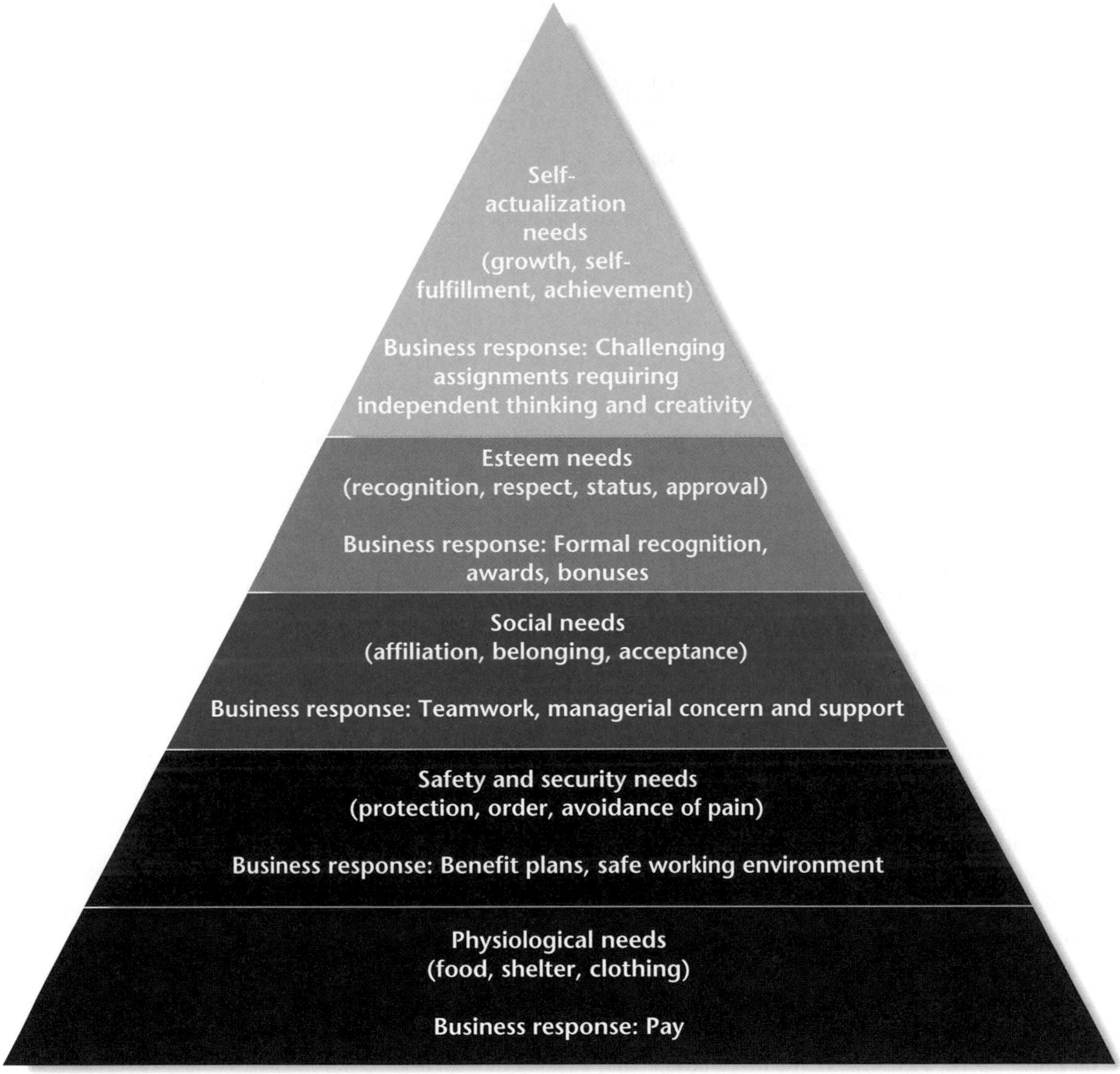

Source: Adapted from Abraham Maslow, "A Theory of Human Motivation," *Psychology Review* 80 (1943), pp. 370–96.

motivators—such as a sense of achievement, responsibility, and recognition—from their work, they feel satisfaction and are motivated to do even better and keep the positive feedback coming. Therefore, managers must be sure that hygiene factors are adequate, but they should concentrate on motivators to attain high commitment from their people.[10]

No manager can command someone to be motivated. All a manager can do is provide conditions that will encourage or lead people to be motivated. Creative leaders can develop a climate and provide rewards so that workers believe that they will be better off by committing themselves to organizational tasks. In other words, managers create conditions in which employees believe they can meet their personal needs by undertaking work activities.

Hygiene Factors (context of the job)	Motivators (content of the job)
• Company policies	• Achievement
• Salary	• Recognition
• Job security	• Responsibility
• Working conditions	• Advancement
• Relations with co-workers	• Opportunities for growth
• Supervisory style	• The work itself

TABLE 16.1

Herzberg's Two-Factor Theory

To understand this process of motivation, let's look at the various decision points that can affect motivation. Susan Moore works in the computing services department of a large manufacturing business. Susan has excellent technical and interpersonal skills. Her job is basically one of troubleshooting. She handles systems problems for users throughout the company. It is a challenging and ever-changing set of assignments. She is on call 24 hours a day. Generally, she likes her job and is quite good at it. Recently, the company installed an advanced computer network for interacting with suppliers and dealers. Clearly, people throughout the business can benefit from the program if they can understand how to access and fully use the program.

Toward this end, the business has plans for Susan. Her boss, Lawanda White, wants her to coordinate and be lead trainer in the software applications. This job will involve a series of two-day meetings with small groups of people within the business, as well as a series of meetings with both suppliers and dealers. Given the number of people involved, Susan will spend the next six months in this coordinating and training job. Susan's boss has just met with Susan to outline the new six-month project. Will Susan be motivated? Will she be willing to exert high levels of effort on this project? Since she is temporarily moving from work that she enjoyed and did well, will she be committed to the new job activities?

The answer is, It depends. Let's assume that Lawanda has clearly outlined the demands of the new project and the specific job that Susan is to do. Therefore, Susan is clear about what is expected of her in this new job. Now she is probably running through some questions in her mind. First, she is probably trying to figure out whether she can meet the expectations of the job. She is assessing whether her efforts can lead to the successful performance of the job requirements. If Susan feels that the job demands are so heavy and resources so thin that the probability of being successful is low (or maybe even zero), she will no doubt have little willingness or commitment. Why should she, if the task expectations are impossible?

However, if Susan assesses the job expectations and is confident that she can complete the job successfully, she will feel that her probability of success is quite high. She now probably considers a second question. What's in it for her? What rewards are likely for performing the job? These rewards may come in many forms. They may be monetary. Or they may be nonfinancially based, such as the chance to work in a new area, be part of a new team approach, take advantage of a telecommuting work arrangement, be given more freedom in making decisions, or receive a promotion. For example, Lawanda may indicate that if the job in training is completed successfully, Susan will be able to do more training, even including training for top executives in the company's international operations. That opportunity would mean travel to a number of countries and the chance to meet and work with some of the top people in the business. Lawanda even suggests that such visibility will probably help Susan advance.

At this point, Susan will mentally evaluate those rewards and decide how much value they hold for her. The potential rewards attached to this job include challenging work, interesting people, the chance to travel, visibility, and activity possibly leading to promotion. Will Susan value these rewards? The answer depends on her unique needs and whether she feels these outcomes will help fulfill the personal needs that are critical to her. For example, it is possible that Susan does not really want to travel, the thought of meeting corporate leaders strikes fear in her heart, and she does not desire a promotion because of the added responsibility and stress. Whereas these rewards may excite some people, they may not be what Susan is looking for. Logically, she may assign a relatively low value to them. On the other hand, Susan may be an ambitious and energetic woman who enjoys travel and meeting new people. She wants to get ahead and rise in the business. So the promotion opportunity is exactly what she has been hoping for. She places high value on these rewards because they are consistent with her needs and wishes.

There is a third concern affecting Susan's motivation: her belief that management will actually deliver the promised rewards. What is the likelihood that successful performance will lead to the desired reward? This decision is critical. Susan may truly want the promotion. It may be of quite high value to her and therefore potentially motivational. However, if Susan thinks management is unlikely to provide the promotion, her motivation will wane. There may be a number of reasons for this outcome. Perhaps the company has frozen all promotions. Perhaps Lawanda has repeatedly made such promises and then failed to deliver. If Susan suspects the promise of rewards is false, the rewards won't motivate her.

You see how three elements interact to affect the presence and level of Susan's motivation. First is her perception of the likelihood that she can successfully accomplish the required tasks. Second is the value she places on the rewards that are being offered. Third is her perception of the likelihood she will actually receive the rewards if she does complete the tasks. This approach is consistent with the expectancy theory of motivation, which is probably the most popular approach to motivation today.[11] A simplified model of expectancy theory is shown in Figure 16.6.

The Manager's Role in Motivation

It is important for Susan's manager to be aware of what Susan is experiencing. While her manager certainly cannot impose motivation, she can facilitate it. For example, if Susan's belief that she cannot succeed in the intended tasks is due to misunderstandings, Lawanda can add clarification. If her belief is due to her fear of being overworked or given inadequate resources, her manager can respond. However, the most powerful way that managers improve motivation is through the actions they take to build a business culture that promotes employee commitment.

FIGURE 16.6

Simplified Model of Expectancy Theory

Organizational task or desired performance	→	Perception of the probability that personal efforts will lead to performance of the task	→	Value placed on rewards that are contingent on desired performance	→	Perception of the probability that rewards will actually follow performance

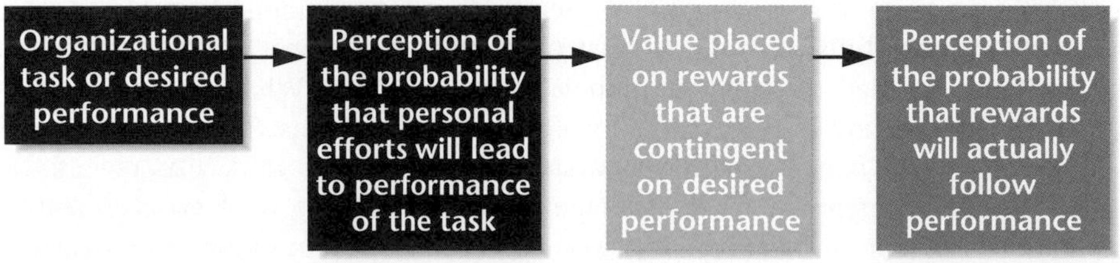

This impact begins with the assumptions managers make about their employees. Early views of managerial assumptions about employees were popularized by Douglas McGregor.[12] These are known as Theory X and Theory Y assumptions.

Managers who make **Theory X** assumptions believe that workers are naturally lazy, dislike work, shirk responsibility, and will do as little as they can in most work situations. It is not hard to understand the actions of managers who think Theory X assumptions portray their employees accurately. These managers offer workers little autonomy or discretion in their jobs. The resulting culture is boss-centered and control-oriented.

On the other hand, managers who make **Theory Y** assumptions believe that workers can enjoy work. They believe workers desire responsibility and want to accept challenges in their work. Not surprisingly, these managers often provide their employees with a chance to exercise their creativity and to be actively involved in decision making. The resulting culture is more open and involvement-oriented.

Which set of assumptions is correct? There is no doubt that some people are indeed lazy and will do as little as possible. Yet good managers realize that Theory Y assumptions may be more relevant. There are two reasons for this conclusion. First, workers often bring important talents and skills to their jobs. To assume that they don't care what happens is probably illogical. Second, astute managers realize that when employees get the opportunity to be involved in meaningful ways, they appreciate it and often rise to the occasion. Making assumptions that are inconsistent with the nature and needs of the workforce can produce frustration, restrict motivation, and threaten a firm's performance potential.

A business culture that helps meet important needs of workers is a key piece in the motivational puzzle. Many factors contribute to a motivational culture, not the least of which is the nature of the managers themselves. So where do we start? How do we figure out how to build a culture of commitment?

Theory X
The belief that workers are naturally lazy, dislike work, shirk responsibility, and will do as little as they can in most work situations.

Theory Y
The belief that workers enjoy their work, desire responsibility, and want challenges.

Building a Culture of Commitment: Becoming an Employer of Choice

Logically, an understanding of workers and what they are looking for from their work seems important to building commitment and motivation. This awareness has led many organizations to focus on becoming an **employer of choice.** Being an employer of choice means that the business displays such a unique culture that it is able to attract, motivate, and retain the high-quality people it needs. If you are an employer of choice (like Stratus Technologies in Profile 16.1), talented people choose to work for you; they choose to stay with you (even when courted by other companies); and they choose to dedicate themselves to your success. Motivation and loyalty prevail, and performance is at its peak.[13] Commitment comes because employees believe that working for your business will somehow meet their needs.

Of course, the trick is putting all the pieces together to build such a special culture. All workers are different. Therefore, it is important for managers to know their people and tailor rewards and approaches to their particular circumstances and personalities. Despite such unique needs, there are certain things today's workers generally look for and expect. These become the foundations that must be in place to become an employer of choice. We will emphasize six foundations: trust and ethics; competitive compensation; interesting, challenging, and meaningful work; employee growth and development; teamwork; and balancing work and family.

employer of choice
A situation in which a business displays such a unique culture that it is able to attract, motivate, and retain the high-quality people it needs.

PROFILE 16.1   STRATUS TECHNOLOGIES LEADS THE WAY

When Stratus Technologies celebrated a new product—the Stratus ft Server system—the maker of business computer servers did it in its usual way. It had a companywide barbecue for employees and friends. Stratus president and CEO Steve Kiely underscores the company's loyalty and commitment to its people. "I have been in this business long enough to understand that the company's best assets go home at night." A commitment to employee growth and development, healthy work–life balance, recruiting friends, and attractive compensation are part of the company's goal of "keeping its most valuable assets happy."

Recognized as an employer of choice, Stratus offers its employees hundreds of growth opportunities. These opportunities include degree programs, state-of-the-art business education from leading universities and private companies, extensive technical training, and a full range of programs supported by its corporate center, Stratus University.

Employees appreciate the friendly work environment and feel the company really cares about them and their well-being. What's not to like? There are kitchenettes in every group, a company fitness center, softball teams, the ATM and StrataStore, and even a concierge service. Judy Reed, vice-president of human resources, puts it all in perspective: "Stratus prides itself on offering our employees the right tools and support to enable them to do the best job possible."

Source: "Stratus Technologies Launches Stratus University," "Stratus Technologies Recognized as Employer of Choice by Leading Experts in Workforce and Workplace Issues," and "Comments from Recent Grads/Co-Ops," www.stratus.com/news (accessed July 31, 2002).

Trust and Ethics

We have already discussed the basics of building strong organizational ethics in Chapter 6. Here, we simply reinforce its importance. It is increasingly clear that workers want to be associated with ethical firms.

A culture of commitment and choice is built on a strong foundation of trust and ethics. People want to work for an organization where trust prevails and where ethical behavior is expected and supported. In fact, one of the primary factors affecting workers' decisions to either stay or leave an organization hinges on whether the employees have developed relationships of trust with their managers.

In today's business world, many people seem cynical about whether their company's top management or even their immediate bosses can really be trusted. In addition, some evidence suggests that younger people are more distrustful of people in general than are older people. In fact, a recent study found that only about 20 percent of today's young people (ages 18 to 24) think that most people are trustworthy.[14]

Therefore, businesses that take steps to build and continually reinforce trust through their communications and actions will more likely gain the commitment of their people. Some businesses build trust not only by what they do, but also by what they do *not* do. For example, chip maker Xilinx does not believe in layoffs. If times are tough, the company offers sabbaticals or early-retirement options to avoid dismissing its people. Bank and credit card processor Synovus Financial has a similar philosophy. With nearly 11,000 employees, the company has had no layoffs in the past 114 years. At W. L. Gore, maker of Gore-Tex, there are no fancy executive perks and no lofty job titles because there are no bosses. Even salaries are determined by a ranking system that is run by the company's employees.[15]

Competitive Compensation

A common reward for encouraging commitment and motivation is compensation, or the money and fringe benefits that are provided for doing work. In general, workers expect compensation to be adequate, competitive with that of other businesses, and distributed fairly.

In today's business environment, the emphasis is on **performance-based pay.** That means the pay received should be carefully and directly tied to performance. In some cases, pay is tied to the individual worker's personal performance. For example, at the end of the year, each employee's performance is evaluated against relevant performance measures. Those who perform best get the biggest raises. In other cases, pay is tied to the performance of an employee's team or project group. If the team saves the company money or completes a special project that brings in thousands of dollars of new business, the employees on the team receive some share of the money saved or made. In some cases, pay is tied to the overall performance of the business unit where an employee works, or even to the overall performance of the entire business.

> **performance-based pay**
> Wages that are tied directly to performance.

Lincoln Electric, in Cleveland, Ohio, the world's lowest-cost producer of induction engines, uses one of the oldest pay-for-performance systems in the country. Nonmanagerial workers are paid on a piece-rate basis; that is, they get paid for how much they produce. There are no limits or quotas on how much they produce as long as quality is not sacrificed. Piece-rate pay rewards people for their personal effort. However, Lincoln Electric also pays a performance bonus based on the overall profitability of the entire business. If the company makes no profit, the workers don't get bonuses. If the business is highly profitable, they receive big bonuses. This profit-sharing bonus plan works, in part, because the company has paid bonuses every year since 1934.[16] Workers receive outstanding wages. What does this pay approach say to the workers? Work hard, work efficiently, cut costs, and profits should flow. When they do, you get more money. Realize the motivational focus of performance-based pay. Better performance, whether at the individual, team, unit, or business level, results in higher pay. The special compensation approaches used at Nucor Corporation are noted in Profile 16.2.

Compensation really consists of two main areas, benefits and pay. You may not ordinarily think of benefits as part of compensation, but they constitute about 27 percent of a worker's total compensation package in the United States.[17] Although benefits can cover a range of

Many companies are making investments that support employee exercise routines. Why do you think businesses are encouraging their employees to take advantage of these exercise opportunities?

PROFILE 16.2   A DIFFERENT LOOK AT NUCOR

With annual sales of over $4.5 billion, Nucor Corporation is one of the largest steel producers in the United States. In a tough, competitive business that has been shaken by foreign competition, Nucor manufactures a broader range of steel products than any other U.S. company and is the most profitable. Nucor openly admits that its success hinges on its employees, more than 7,000 strong. The company seeks to hire and keep the best, most talented people that it can. It wants to hire people who not only have the "right stuff" but also the "right mindset," people who are willing to "treat this like their own business."

Of course, Nucor goes the extra mile to build this desired culture. For example, the organization structure is streamlined, so employees can make decisions and offer needed innovations. Throughout the organization, fairness and respect are pivotal. The company believes in "egalitarian benefits." Thus the lowest-level employee has access to the same benefits as the top-line managers. Company perks for executives, such as special dining rooms, parking privileges, and company cars, simply do not exist.

And then there is the compensation program. People are rewarded for how they perform, not for how long they have been with the company. Performance-based pay extends throughout the business. For example, operating and maintenance employees and their supervisors earn a weekly bonus based on the productivity of their work group. If their productivity is booming, they can make up to 150 percent of their base pay. When the company as a whole is performing at very high levels, the company steps up and pays what it calls an "extraordinary bonus." Everyone in the company gets a share of the bonus, which has run as high as $800 per employee in the past.

Sources: "About Nucor," www.nucor.com (accessed July 8, 2002); and "CEO Describes Nucor's Nearest Competition," www.twst.com/notes/articles/paa619.html (accessed July 8, 2002)

issues, there are three typical categories. First are security and health provisions, such as health insurance coverage and pension plans. Second is payment for time not worked, including benefits such as paid holidays and vacations. Third are employee services, such as child care and counseling. Benefits can be quite important and may affect decisions about whether to join or leave a business. Of course, businesses must always be concerned about the rising costs of the benefits they provide.

Certain benefits are more relevant for some workers than others. Benefits work best when people have a chance to match them to their specific needs. For example, family health insurance is not relevant for an employee who has neither a spouse nor a child.

Some businesses let employees do this matching through a **flexible benefits plan,** under which workers can select from a menu of possible benefits the ones they wish to receive. This approach stands the best chance of assuring the motivational link between the reward (benefits) and the worker's true needs.

> **flexible benefits plan**
> A plan in which workers can select from a menu of benefits the ones they wish to receive.

Many businesses, such as Southwest Airlines, offer flexible benefits to their workers. At Southwest, employees can choose the medical benefits that they want, selecting from a menu those that meet their needs. Employees also have a profit-sharing plan, free travel on Southwest, and discounted travel on routes of selected other carriers. Southwest even offers special benefits options such as an elder care resource and referral program and an adoption assistance program.[18]

Interesting, Challenging, and Meaningful Work

As important as money can be in motivating workers, most people want work that provides some sense of challenge as well. In fact, many consider challenging and meaningful work even more important than high salary and benefits. Thus, another part of the culture of commitment is the nature of the work itself.

Motivation through challenging work occurs when employees are called on to use their skills and talents. Many employees feel frustrated when they are slotted into jobs where they have little chance to use the skills they have. You may have experienced this yourself in a summer or part-time job.

Many employees desire some degree of freedom or discretion in their work. They don't want to be tightly controlled, watched over, and constantly told how to do tasks for which they have background and knowledge. They want a chance to give input on matters they know something about before final decisions are made. They truly want to have some say. Of course, getting input from skilled people not only makes employees feel better, but also helps the business make better decisions and operate more effectively. Increasingly, skilled and talented employees want to know where the business is headed and where they fit in. This knowledge allows them to see that their jobs are important and they make a difference.

In short, workers want interesting, challenging, and meaningful work opportunities. When they get them, they tend to feel better about the work they do. And the work environment tends to energize and motivate them. Companies can do many things to enhance the levels of interest, challenge, and meaning that employees get from their work. Let's explore just a few of these.

Some companies use participation and employee involvement programs to solicit workers' input on matters that affect them. For example, at Dana Corporation, employees are encouraged to post suggestions, complaints, and questions on a company bulletin board. The company encourages its people to post at least two items each month, and all ideas are considered. In fact, the company implements or acts on about 80 percent of the queries it receives. At A. W. Chesterton, an industrial valve and seal manufacturer, CEO Jim Chesterton has quarterly meetings where employees can talk to him about anything.[19]

Employee Growth and Development

Many businesses demonstrate their commitment to employee growth and development through their support of education and training. This approach makes sense. For the organization, training is really an investment in people to help ensure that the business will have the skills and background that it needs. From the employees' point of view, the investment in training helps assure them that they always have cutting-edge skills. It can make them feel needed and important. It also keeps the job interesting and tends to reduce boredom.

Many companies, such as Schwab and FedEx, have their own corporate universities to support continual learning and development. In some cases, the commitment to training is staggering. Financial services company Edward Jones, with over 8,400 offices, spends between $75,000 and $100,000 to train each new investment representative.[20]

Teamwork

teamwork
A situation where employees are treated as key players in the business and where employees want to pull together to help the company succeed.

Teamwork is not simply having people work in teams. Although a lot of work is done in teams, teamwork is really more about a corporate spirit and philosophy. **Teamwork** means that all employees are treated like key players on the larger corporate team, and in turn, these employees want to pull together to help the company succeed. In most cases, companies that emphasize teamwork are strongly focused on satisfying their customers and building a work culture in which people are supported, encouraged, empowered, and appreciated.

Consider the example of Whole Foods Market (WFM), the world's largest organic and natural foods supermarket. At WFM, teamwork is ingrained. Employees, all 23,000 of them, are referred to as team members. Self-directed teams meet to discuss issues and solve problems, team member forums and advisory groups help keep lines of communication open throughout the organization. The company practices gainsharing; if a team comes up with ideas for saving money or making more money, part of the saving or gain goes right back to the team members. Self-responsibility and empowerment are keys. The company's corporate philosophy, known as its Declaration of Interdependence, was crafted by 60 team members who volunteered their time. It's no surprise that the business is growing, and experiencing strong financial returns, and is seen as a great place to work.[21]

Balancing Work and Family

Many workers today are trying to maintain a balance between their work and family (nonwork) lives. Although many companies espouse the value of family friendliness, the bottom-line emphasis on profits can hamper the day-to-day implementation of these values. Management can take a number of actions to help employees reduce the disruptions when work spills over into the family segment of their lives.

One approach is flextime, a work arrangement that gives individual employees some discretion to decide when to start and stop their workday. In a typical flextime system, employees are required to work a set number of hours per day (perhaps eight hours) and must be at work during a core period each day, say between 10 A.M. and 2 P.M. Beyond that, they are free to decide when they start and end each workday. For example, a worker may decide to start at 6 A.M. and leave promptly at 2 P.M., having put in an eight-hour day.

Think of the advantages. Parents can be home early in the afternoon when their children arrive home from school. Other workers, especially those commuting in large urban areas, may choose certain schedules to avoid heavy traffic patterns. Others may simply enjoy the freedom to schedule afternoon activities in the summer.

A second approach is telecommuting. Simply defined, telecommuting is working at a nonbusiness site (usually the home) and using a computer to communicate with the office. Telecommuters work at home several days a week and send their work electronically to their employer. Telecommuters have the freedom to schedule work activities to complement other demands on their time. Also, most telecommuters feel they are more productive at home than on the job, probably because of the reduced number of interruptions.

job sharing
A work arrangement in which two or more employees share one job and split all the duties, responsibilities, and compensation of that job.

The third arrangement that can help achieve a work–family balance is **job sharing,** an arrangement in which two or more people split a job and share all its duties, responsibilities, and compensation (both pay and benefits). Typically job sharers split the workweek. For example, one worker does the job on Monday, Wednesday, and Friday, and the other goes to work on Tuesday and Thursday. Consider the advantages to both the employees and the business. Employees now have more flexibility and free time. They can pursue a career without neglecting their families. Employers often find that job sharing allows them to bring talented people into the business who may be reluctant to commit to a full work schedule. Also, each job sharer probably does a bit more than half as much work as one full-time employee. The downside is that no one person has total responsibility for a given set of responsibilities, and coordination can sometimes be onerous.

A fourth approach is to offer child care provisions. Many companies offer some form of child care support as part of their employee benefits programs. Some businesses go even further. For example, companies such as AFLAC, SAS Institute, Eli Lilly, and Merck are known for their on-site child care centers.

These programs are just the start. Increasingly, companies are looking for creative ways to help workers achieve balance in their lives. Ideas abound. More and more businesses are offering their employees paid sabbaticals. For example, a worker may be eligible for a two-month sabbatical for every six or seven years worked. Other businesses offer months of paid leave or unlimited sick days to care for sick children, spouses, or parents. At American Management Systems, employees who are required to go on extended business trips can have their spouse join them for the weekend, and the company covers the cost.[22]

To motivate and reward its employees, IKEA stores worldwide held a one-time Big Thank You Bonus Day to usher in the new millennium. The company pledged the entire day's sales to its 44,000 employees at 152 stores around the world, and nearly doubled its previous one-day sales record.

Building Employee Commitment: Overall Conclusions

We have presented a number of aspects of a culture of commitment, but it is certainly not an exhaustive list. There are as many employee needs and desires as there are employees. We have highlighted only some of the more critical needs that workers want their jobs to meet. We can expect these themes to be even more important in the future. Managers must understand these needs and offer work cultures that can meet them if they hope to gain motivation and commitment from their employees.

THINK ABOUT THIS

1. Of the various rewards and approaches discussed for building employee commitment, which are most important to you personally? Why?

2. If you were starting your own business, what actions would you take to become an employer of choice?

3. Studies indicate that many managers prefer to have employees on-site rather than as telecommuters. Why do you think this is so? What disadvantages do telecommuters face?

THE BIG PICTURE

As we have noted throughout the text, contemporary businesses must achieve speed, flexibility, and efficiency. They must operate in a logical and orderly manner while encouraging appropriate spontaneity and freedom for new ideas and creative thought. They must have well-reasoned strategies and resources applied to meeting those strategies. This is a tall and at times confusing order in the hustle-bustle maze of the business world. Organizational structure, as emphasized in this chapter, is a tool for helping the business attain its required outcomes. Businesses must recognize, however, that structures and designs have no inherent value in and of themselves. Their value is derived from their capacity to help the business meet its needs for order, efficiency, speed, flexibility, and creative insights. Many businesses are saddled by an existing structure that inhibits the pursuit of these needs. As we have argued in this chapter, business leaders must challenge these structures and modify them when necessary.

In a similar manner, the best business strategy supported by the best available structural design will fall short of success without the day-to-day activities of talented and motivated people. People run the business. They make it work. Strategic plans are daydreams until people make them real. Whereas the structural design establishes a logical pattern of activities and relationships, it's the people who work in the business that make the difference between success and failure. Of all the resources available to a business, which are the most important or valuable—the physical facilities? the giant computer network? the expanding line of credit and secured financial backing? the well-honed system of product distribution? No. People are the most valued resource of any business. Accordingly, building a culture where people feel respected, engaged, and committed may be the most important and most challenging task any manager faces. However, firms must be careful and realistic. Companies that take steps to become employers of choice incur some additional expense. These companies, however, are convinced that their ability to attract, fully utilize, and retain the best talent possible will more than justify the cost.

Summary

1. In virtually every business, important decisions are being made every hour of every working day. The larger the organization, the greater the number of employees making those decisions. The greater the number of decisions, the greater the need for ways to make sure that decisions are coordinated and integrated. Organization design and structure serve that function.

   • What is meant by the terms *organization design* and *organization structure?*

   Organization design deals with how the various parts of the business are coordinated. Organization structure is a framework that prescribes the way the business organizes, arranges, and groups the work that needs to be done.

2. An organization's structure will change as the organization changes. Small businesses have simple structures; large businesses have more complex structures. Nevertheless, every business has a structure that provides a common logic—creating order and efficiency within the business.

- What are some of the basic elements of an organization structure?

An organization chart is the graphic representation of organization structure that shows all employees how work is to be coordinated. Chain of command is the line of authority among levels of employees. Span of control is the number of employees who report to a given manager. Specialization is the placement of employees in specific jobs to which they restrict their work. Departmentalization is the grouping of similar jobs.

3. When a business fails to design a good organization structure, problems will arise. Some problems may be unique to that firm, but others occur frequently in the business world.

- What are some of the common structural concerns a business might expect to confront?

Suboptimization is the result of one department's acting in its own self-interest in a way that hurts or inhibits the performance of another department or the whole business. Bureaucracy is the situation in which many levels of hierarchy result in a formal set of rules and procedures that can inhibit performance. Flattening the hierarchy reduces the number of levels of management.

4. When a company realizes it has problems with its structure, it should begin its search for a solution by looking at what other companies have done in similar situations.

- What approaches have been developed for addressing structural concerns?

(1) Teams. Cross-functional teams consist of people from, say, marketing, production, finance, product development, and human resources who work collectively to bring about the needed change. Self-directed work teams are given broad responsibility for carrying out tasks or jobs on their own. Virtual teams involve electronic teams of members at remote sites.

(2) Project organization. This structural approach uses teams drawn from various areas of the business to accomplish high-profile tasks.

(3) Matrix organization. This approach combines the functional structure with the project structure.

(4) Business units. These unique product or market groupings are treated as self-contained businesses.

(5) The virtual organization. Parties are geographically dispersed and electronically linked so that each can contribute its unique competency in achieving a common goal.

5. The best structure in the world won't perform effectively if employees aren't adequately motivated. It is no wonder that most excellent companies point to committed employees as the key to their success.

- What is meant by commitment and what are its underlying determinants?

Commitment is a matter of motivation. Motivation refers to an individual's willingness to work hard and expend high levels of effort for the business. People are motivated to work hard when doing so meets some of their needs. A number of motivational theories are available to help managers better understand the motivation process, among them Maslow's needs hierarchy, Herzberg's two-factor theory, and expectancy theory.

In addition to understanding motivation theories, managers must make certain assumptions and take actions to create an environment that encourages motivated employees.

- What assumptions do managers make about employees?

At the most general level, managers make Theory X or Theory Y assumptions about their employees. Theory X assumes that workers are naturally lazy and cannot be trusted to assume responsibility. Theory Y assumes that workers desire responsibility and want challenges. Increasingly, companies realize that employees respond to actions that are consistent with Theory Y assumptions.

6. A manager can also improve commitment by building an employer-of-choice culture.

   • What are the foundations of an employer of choice?

   These foundations must be in place: (1) trust and ethics, (2) competitive compensation, (3) interesting, challenging, and meaningful work, (4) employee growth and development, (5) teamwork, and (6) balancing work and family.

Key Terms

business units, p. 415	performance-based pay, p. 423
chain of command, p. 409	project organization, p. 414
departmentalization, p. 409	span of control, p. 409
employer of choice, p. 421	specialization, p. 409
empowerment, p. 414	suboptimization, p. 412
flexible benefits plan, p. 424	teamwork, p. 426
job sharing, p. 426	Theory X, p. 421
matrix organization, p. 415	Theory Y, p. 421
motivation, p. 417	virtual organization, p. 416
organization design, p. 407	virtual teams, p. 414
organization structure, p. 407	

Exercises and Applications

1. Think of a job you have had (perhaps a part-time or a summer job). List the times when you really felt excited and satisfied with your work. Be as specific as possible. What does your experience reveal about motivation and commitment?

2. At that same job, identify someone who seemed to have a low level of motivation and commitment. Given the motivational ideas presented in this chapter, what are some possible reasons for his or her lack of motivation?

3. Survey 10 of your peers, asking them to rank the following job factors in order of importance:

   • Recognition
   • Feeling of accomplishment
   • Job security
   • Intellectually stimulating work
   • Comfortable working conditions
   • Respect from other people
   • Opportunity for learning and growth
   • Opportunity for promotion

- Challenging work
- Good pay and benefits

Write a two-page paper summarizing and explaining your findings.

4. Find information on companies that have recently downsized. (Start your research with the Internet, *BusinessWeek,* or *The Wall Street Journal.*) Explain why the companies believed this form of restructuring was necessary. What are the behavioral impacts on those employees who remain after downsizing has occurred?

5. Look at the organization structure of your college or university. What does it tell you about power and decision making in the organization? Consider chain of command, span of control, and other basic elements of structure.

6. Go to the website for Southwest Airlines (www.southwest.com). Consider the benefits listed for its employees. Which of them appeal most to you? Which do you think would interest someone 20 years older than you?

7. Interview at least one small business owner or manager. How is the task of motivating employees different from that of a manager in a large company?

Too Many Workers? Not for Long

FROM THE PAGES OF

BusinessWeek

Peg Brubaker, vice president for human resources at New York Presbyterian Hospital has a problem, and it's not getting any better. She can't find enough workers, particularly those with special technical skills. She has hiked pay, increased merit pay, and in some jobs, added three extra salary adjustments in just one year. She has even added up to $10,000 in employee tuition assistance. Brubaker puts it succinctly: "All the hospitals and pharmacies were stealing from each other, even in a recession, so I'm hoping this will stimulate the supply."

Experts are arguing that as the economy rebounds, more and more companies will experience labor shortages. The main reason is clear—aging and retiring baby boomers are leaving the workforce and far too few workers are entering to fill the pipeline. The most coveted workers are surely college-educated people with key skills. "Employers could be so strapped for help that they find themselves radically redesigning American work habits to lure people into their ranks."

Older workers become a key. Experts are arguing that companies will probably scrap early retirement options and create incentives to encourage older workers to retire later or return to work. But that is just the beginning. Companies will have to be creative in their approaches to attract the best and the brightest talent. Employers will have to offer working mothers more flexible work schedules. Help with child care and other parental needs will become even more important. On-site day care centers and backup arrangements for sick children will become more common. Training and education programs will be increased. "Diversity efforts . . . could take on new urgency as employers discover they can't rely so heavily on the native white labor pool." Employers will "recruit and train hard-to-place workers," such as those with disabilities and welfare moms. Of course, compensation approaches, such as stock options, will be used. There may even be pressure for governmental involvement to increase the national investment in education and training and subsidize child care.

The message is clear: "If you believe that technological change isn't going to slow down, we're not going to have enough college-educated workers to meet demand."

Decision Questions

1. Which route—more compensation or more training—seems more reasonable in dealing with the issues and problems outlined in the case above?

2. A number of you may participate in an internship program during your college education. What do companies gain through internship programs?

3. What additional creative steps could a business take to ensure that it has an adequate supply of talented workers?

Source: Aaron Bernstein, "Too Many Workers? Not for Long," *BusinessWeek,* May 20, 2002, pp. 126–130.

References

1. "Investing in Our Partners," www.starbucks.com (accessed July 5, 2002); and "Where Companies Rank in Their Industries," *Fortune,* March 4, 2002, p. 78.

2. "GE Capital Is Split into Four Parts," *The Wall Street Journal,* July 29, 2002, pp. A3, A4; and GE website, www.ge.com (accessed August 2, 2002).

3. "Directors and Officers," www.iflyswa.com/about_swa/financials/investor_relations_index.html (accessed October 12, 2002).

4. Steven D. Eppinger, "Innovation at the Speed of Innovation," *Harvard Business Review,* January 2001, pp. 149–158.

5. "Cultural Change Process," www.ge.com/news/podium_papers/culture.htm (accessed July 10, 2002).

6. Richard L. Daft, *Organization Theory and Design,* 7th ed. (Cincinnati, OH: South-Western, 2001), p. 27.

7. For a good overview of virtual teams, see Jon R. Katzenbach and Douglas K. Smith, *The Discipline of Teams* (New York: Wiley, 2001).

8. The Boeing Company 2001 Annual Report.

9. An excellent look at some of the latest research and thinking about virtual organizations is available at the VoNet website, www.virtual-organization.net.

10. For a discussion of the Herzberg theory, see Richard L. Hughes, Robert C. Ginnett, and Gordon J. Curphy, *Leadership: Enhancing the Lessons of Experience* (Boston: McGraw-Hill/Irwin, 2002), pp. 251–253.

11. Victor H. Vroom, *Work and Motivation* (New York: Wiley, 1964).

12. Douglas McGregor, *The Human Side of Enterprise* (New York: McGraw-Hill, 1960).

13. Roger E. Herman and Joyce L. Gioia, *How to Become an Employer of Choice* (Winchester, VA: Oakhill Press, 2000).

14. "Generation Gap Narrowing on Most Attitude Areas, but Young Become More Distrustful of Society in General," The University of Chicago News, October 18, 2000, www.news.uchicago.edu/releases/00/001018.generation.shtml (accessed September 18, 2001).

15. "The 100 Best Companies to Work For," *Fortune,* February 4, 2002, p. 72.

16. Lincoln Electric website, www.lincolnelectric.com/corporate/career (accessed July 30, 2002).

17. Joseph J. Martocchio, *A Primer for Human Resource Professionals* (Boston: McGraw-Hill/Irwin, 2003).

18. "Southwest Airlines Employee Benefits Summary," www.iflyswa.com/careers/benefits.html (accessed October 12, 2002).

19. John B. Izzo and Pam Withers, *Values Shift* (Vancouver, BC: FairWinds Press, 2001), pp. 182, 189.

20. "Career Opportunities," www.edwardjones.com (accessed July 31, 2002).

21. "The Whole Philosophy" and "Our Core Values," www.wholefoods.com/company/philosophy.html (accessed October 12, 2002).

22. Izzo and Withers, p. 52.

17

Using Technology in a Competitive Environment

Look at the following list of companies. You can tell something about them by their names. What do they have in common?

- Allinstruments.com
- Babygift.com
- Collectibletown.com
- Consumercoupons.com
- eCampus.com
- Egghead.com
- Gocowboy.com

- Grantseeker.com
- Handyman Online
- HealthOnLine.com
- Homes.com
- Homeruns.com
- Localmusic.com
- ReptileCenter.com

- Sega.com
- Ticketplanet.com
- Travel-Now.com
- VetAlliance.com
- Vitamins.com
- Webvan
- Zydeco.com

The answer: All were Internet companies that ceased operations during 2001. According to *Fortune*, 519 dot-coms died during 2000 and 2001, with nearly 100,000 people losing their jobs in 2001. What happened? What caused this high number of start-up companies to crash in such a short period of time?[1]

One answer was unreasonable expectations. Many entrepreneurs felt that there was a never-ending demand for any products or services that could be purchased online. That assumption obviously wasn't true. A second reason was that money was too readily available. As we have mentioned repeatedly, the decade of the 1990s was a boom time. As a result, financing could be acquired easily from venture capitalists, from bankers, from initial public offerings, and even from wealthy individuals who were willing to take a risk in hopes of receiving high returns. A third reason was a simple misreading of the market. Webvan, for example, planned to make money by delivering groceries from a central warehouse to the homes of busy shoppers who ordered their groceries online. After burning through millions of dollars, the company closed. Apparently people liked to squeeze the fruit, pick their own brand of green beans, and peruse the ice cream aisle for treats rather than click on a limited selection of items on a screen.

Certainly not all high-tech or Internet-related companies failed. In fact, *Fortune's* 2002 list of the fastest-growing companies in America included Nvidia, a maker of graphic chips; Siebel Systems, a software company; and eBay, the auction business that has been one of the few profitable Internet companies.[2]

Many businesses are rethinking the role of technology and, especially, the value of the Internet. There is, indeed, high value in Internet-based business transactions. But the value comes from careful analysis of situations rather than investment in the latest fad. Companies increasingly use the Internet and technology to make their firms more efficient and, often, more customer responsive.

This chapter discusses the proper role of technology in business. You will note that we don't spend time discussing what computers are or how they work. You know that already. Most of you have been computer literate for years. Our focus is on how companies use technology to become more competitive in their industries.

After studying this chapter, you should be able to:

1. Understand the key role of technology as it affects a company's strategy.
2. Describe how information can be communicated via websites.
3. Explain the concept of e-commerce.
4. Discuss the use of the Web for business-to-consumer marketing.
5. Explain how business-to-business relationships work.
6. Understand how technology can make a company more efficient.

We focused in Chapter 15 on ways that companies communicate with their customers. One way was through the use of information technology, particularly the Internet. In this chapter, we will delve more deeply into the use of technology. We will discuss the role of technology in the strategy of a firm, with particular interest in the use of the Internet. We will discuss how businesses use the Web to sell products or services to other businesses and to consumers. We will then close the chapter by discussing the role of technology in the internal operations of a business.

The Strategic Use of Information Technology

In Chapter 12, we discussed strategies that companies could adopt as they compete with others. Increasingly, information technology plays a role in a firm's strategies. Our three focus companies illustrate three different ways the Internet can become part of a company's strategy. Dell uses an almost total Internet strategy to market its products. Only recently has it moved into anything resembling traditional retailing, and part of this approach—its no-name, generic computer strategy—is somewhat separate from Dell's core strategy. Even the mall kiosks that are popping up are generally connected to the online ordering system. Thus, Dell is very nearly an Internet-only company. Southwest Airlines uses the Internet extensively for online reservations. However, Southwest also has normal telephone reservations, and travel agents sometimes work with the company. Best Buy uses the Internet primarily for marketing products that are found in its traditional retail stores. The purpose of BestBuy.com is to serve those customers who want to purchase online as well as those who want to look at products online before going to the retail store to make a purchase. Thus, the Web serves a relatively limited marketing function for Best Buy when considered as a part of its total operations. As you've just read, each focus company uses the Internet and information technology as part of its overall corporate strategy, even though the relative importance varies by company.

Let's discuss Best Buy further. Many customers have found that home delivery is more of a hassle than a help, as long as other choices are available. Stores such as Best Buy, Circuit City, and Sears have responded to that preference. Customers go online to find a product. They then click to find a store near them that has the product in stock. Once the order is complete, they get in the car and drive to the store to pick up the product, which is waiting for them when they arrive. Best Buy reports that 20 percent of its Web orders are picked up at the store, and the company is even considering installing drive-up windows to serve these customers. This approach, of course, is a variation of the bricks-and-clicks model we discussed in Chapter 15.

As shown in Table 17.1, a survey of Internet customers found that going to the actual store often met their needs better than ordering online for home delivery.[3] Customers

TABLE 17.1

Top Ten Reasons to Buy Consumer Electronics in a Store Rather than on the Internet

1. To eliminate shipping and handling costs.
2. To see a product demonstration before buying.
3. Because returns are less of a hassle.
4. To get the product in a shorter time.
5. To check out the quality of the product.
6. To speak with a salesperson.
7. Because the price is lower in the store.
8. To eliminate using a credit card on the Internet.
9. To pay by cash or check.
10. Because the photo on the Web was not adequate.

Source: Adapted from Jupiter Research/NPD Group Inc., in Nick Wingfield "Click and . . . Drive?" *The Wall Street Journal,* July 15, 2002, p. R11.

were asked why they wanted to buy a consumer electronics product in a store even though they may have ordered it on the Web. It is interesting that customers found that prices were often lower in the store than on the Internet, especially when shipping and handling costs were included. Similar answers were found for customers who were surveyed about buying books in a store rather than on the Web.

Providing Information on the Web

Virtually every public company and thousands of privately held companies now have company websites. These websites provide information ranging from annual reports to company history, to frequently asked questions, to advertisements about product lines. Consider the impact of company websites. If you wanted to read a company's annual report, you used to have to contact the company and request that a copy be mailed to you. Now the annual report can be easily accessed on the Web and read on the computer screen or downloaded or printed for later reading. Because many who want to see the annual report may want only a single piece of information, it makes sense to have the report available on a timely basis on the Web. Having the report online saves time and gives you 24-hour access to company information. Additionally, a number of financial reporting services provide financial performance analyses of companies. The website www.reportgallery.com has over 2,200 annual reports for publicly held companies.

Many company websites contain descriptions of products produced or services provided by the company. In the case of Southwest Airlines, flight schedules are provided

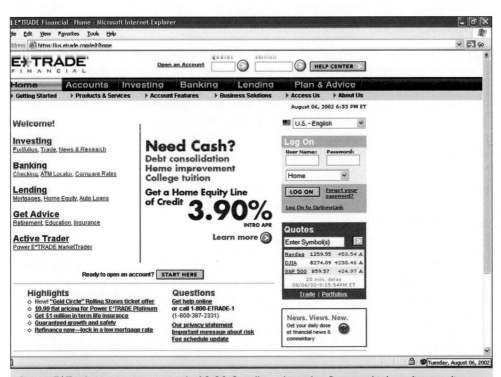

Power E*Trade customers pay only $9.99 for all stock trades. Do you think on-line trading will grow in popularity over the next five years?

on its website. Many businesses, including Southwest, also list career opportunities for potential employees. Thus, people can access websites for diverse reasons.

Keep in mind that the Internet improves communication with customers. It allows companies to select groups of customers to target via e-mail or websites. For example, IBM recently launched a new Web portal aimed specifically at medium-size businesses—those with 100 to 1,000 employees. The site is designed to better serve the product information needs of midsize clients. Rather than getting lost in the maze of pages at www.ibm.com, midsize companies can log onto www.ibm.com/mediumsize. This page then provides them with a number of other links to vendors of software solutions. The site provides information on services that are specific to particular industries, such as financial services or retail. It also allows IBM to highlight its own equipment and services aimed at making midsize companies work more efficiently. This targeted communication would be difficult without the Web portal.[4]

Information-providing websites can be standard, rather routine sites that provide a limited amount of information about a company and serve mainly as a way to contact the business. At the opposite end of the continuum are websites that can be highly interactive, multipage sites featuring a number of products, a fill-in-the-blanks method of registering, and a means to give or retrieve information from the site's originator. For example, General Motors has over 18,000 pages of information that includes 98,000 links to its products, services, and dealers.[5]

Providing in-depth information is the case with some financial websites that allow users to interact with the site. An example is the site developed by The Motley Fool, a financial investment advice service. By logging onto www.fool.com, users can develop a portfolio of stocks to watch. Each successive time they log on and click on "My Portfolio," the site updates the portfolio's stock prices. It will even provide a history of stock prices over a number of different time periods. The website is free, with banner advertisements providing a revenue stream for the providers of the site.

In addition to providing general information about the company and its products, many companies' websites allow users to view their press releases. Going a step further, some even allow users to sign up to receive press releases automatically from the company through e-mail. Some of the press releases announce a technical advancement or new product that the company has developed. Others acknowledge the filing of financial forms with the Securities and Exchange Commission. Still others announce the acquisition of a new subsidiary. Large companies may issue several press releases each day. This service is an efficient and low-cost method of communicating with interested parties.

electronic commerce (e-commerce)
The buying or selling of products or services on the Web.

THINK ABOUT THIS

1. We have stated that most businesses now have websites. Can you think of any businesses that have only a marginal need or no need at all for a website?

2. Many information-providing websites are complex, with frames, animation, videos, and other attention-grabbing aspects. What criteria should guide a manager in determining how glitzy a site should be?

Electronic Commerce

The previous section discussed how companies and their customers can communicate through the World Wide Web. But the focus of that section was on information exchange only. The next logical step is to actually conduct business and make transactions on the Web. **Electronic commerce (e-commerce)** is the buying or selling of products or services on the Web. Electronic commerce is also known as e-business or simply EC. The number of business transactions on the Web is increasing dramatically every day. E-commerce takes one of three forms: consumer-to-consumer, business-to-consumer, and business-to-business.

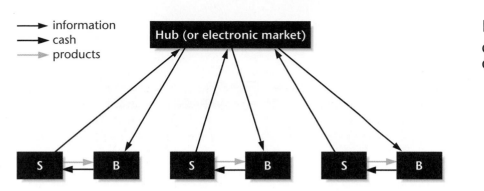

FIGURE 17.1

Consumer-to-
Consumer E-commerce

Consumer to Consumer

Web-based transactions between consumers constitute a relatively small portion of the e-commerce spectrum. In **consumer-to-consumer e-commerce,** one consumer sells a product to another consumer, typically going through an intermediary called a hub or an electronic market (see Figure 17.1). One of the most popular of these is eBay, the Internet auction site. At eBay, sellers list their products with the electronic market. The buyers then look at the hub website and buy or bid on the sellers' products. Once the transaction is made, the seller ships the product directly to the buyer.

Suppose an individual has an accordion she would like to sell. She registers with eBay to list it on its auction, including the minimum bid. After a prescribed length of time, the highest bidder receives the right to the product. Using a credit card, the seller pays eBay a small commission. The buyer arranges to pay the seller, and the seller then ships the accordion directly to the buyer. The growing number of auctions on the Web either sell a wide assortment of products or specialize in one type of product, such as antiques.

consumer-to-consumer e-commerce
The selling of a product by one consumer to another via the Web, typically through an intermediary called a hub.

Business to Consumer

The second type of e-commerce is the business to consumer transaction. **Business-to-consumer e-commerce,** known generally as B2C or BtoC, is electronic retailing. In fact, it is sometimes even called e-retailing or e-tailing. In simplest terms, B2C provides online shopping, 24-hours a day, 7 days a week, 365 days a year. B2C is the use of the Internet to conduct transactions between businesses and consumers. Figure 17.2 illustrates how B2C works. Anytime you have ordered something online, you have used the B2C concept.

All three of our focus companies have a B2C component in their strategies. Dell's primary strategy of selling over the Web is aimed partially at the consumer. Best Buy's www.bestbuy.com is a good example of B2C. Look at Profile 17.1 for another example of an interesting B2C site.

We have previously mentioned retail stores such as the Gap, Eddie Bauer, J.Crew, and Sears. These are predominantly retail stores with add-on business-to-consumer e-commerce. They sell essentially the same products on the Web as they do in their retail stores. Some companies may sell everything their retail stores do plus products not stocked in their retail stores. In the book industry, both Barnes & Noble and Borders have companion websites that sell the same books their retail stores do plus thousands of books that the brick-and-mortar stores do not sell. Other B2C businesses sell exclusively over the Internet. For example, you probably bought this textbook at

business-to-consumer e-commerce
The selling of a product by a business to a consumer on the Internet; also called electronic retailing, e-tailing, or e-retailing.

FIGURE 17.2

Business-to-Consumer
E-commerce

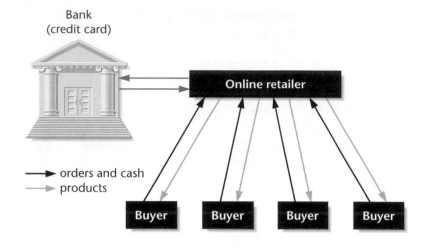

What makes an online retail store effective and successful? A number of factors come into play. First, the website must be interesting. Next, the selection process must be designed so that information and options are readily available and easy to use. Of course, the ordering process must also be clear and straightforward. Finally, there must be on-time delivery with uncanny accuracy. To assure overall satisfaction, what's delivered must match what was selected. If all these steps work, customers generally will report high levels of overall satisfaction with the online shopping experience. There are thousands of e-retailers, but many do not do the job well.

One e-retailer that is consistently rated among the best is the Vermont Teddy Bear Company. The company is known for its special website, its quality offerings, its responsiveness to its customers, and its fun approach. Make no mistake. This is a very successful business operation. In fact, Vermont Teddy Bear Company is the largest maker of handcrafted American-made teddy bears.

Here is the way it works. Assume it's Valentine's Day, the anniversary of your first date, or your significant other's birthday. The key is you want something special and a little different. The Vermont Teddy Bear website is easy to navigate. You get a clear description and a picture of each possible bear option. You can send your own personalized bear-gram or rely on one of the company's standard card messages. Online orders placed Monday through Friday before 4 p.m. EST are shipped the same day. You can even track each step of your bear's trip from the factory in Shelburne, Vermont to its final destination. Or you can receive e-mail detailing the journey. It's a fun and informative site and a nice change-of-pace purchase option. Customer satisfaction with Vermont Teddy Bear's online purchase process runs at an unbelievably high 98% rate! Check out their website at www.vermontteddybear.com. It's about as much fun as you can bear.

Source: Vermont Teddy Bear Company website, www.vermontteddybear.com (accessed, October 14, 2002).

your college bookstore. But you may have purchased it through BarnesandNoble.com or Borders.com. Or you may have bought it from Amazon.com. Amazon.com is a pure B2C company; the other two are mixtures of B2C and retail stores. Still others combine a primary strategy of catalog sales with an Internet component (as you learned in Chapter 15).

Many business-to-consumer companies have also developed affiliate programs. Affiliates work like an extra retail store, except they are online. For example, a small Web-development business may sign up as an affiliate for Amazon.com. A customer visiting the small company's website can link directly to Amazon.com and buy a product. The small business is an affiliate, and Amazon.com is the originating business. The affiliate receives a small commission, and the originating company simply has one more outlet to sell its merchandise.

Many B2C businesses are large operations with many thousands of customers, but creating an online store is relatively simple. Software is now available that allows small companies with a modicum of Internet savvy to develop their own interactive e-commerce sites. Developing an interactive site, along with establishing a credit card processing arrangement with a bank, allows even relatively small companies to have an e-commerce presence on the Web.

Business to Business

Some of the companies discussed above sell to businesses as well as to consumers. Dell certainly falls into this category, as do Southwest Airlines and Best Buy. Other companies, however, are solely in the business-to-business realm. These companies may have begun with the traditional relationship between a supplier and a customer. Over the years, however, the traditional relationship has evolved into one that exists primarily over the Internet.

Business-to-business e-commerce, known popularly as B2B or BtoB, is the use of the Internet to conduct transactions between businesses. This type of interaction is the real growth area in e-commerce. Although business-to-consumer transactions are more visible to the public, business-to-business transactions account for far more dollars of e-commerce because transactions are ongoing between businesses and involve supplies and components that are far more expensive than the typical B2C sale. A number of well-known companies do direct business-to-business selling. Perhaps more notable is that thousands of supplier–manufacturer B2B relationships exist between virtually unknown vendors and their customers—often large manufacturers—to improve cost, efficiency, and delivery times for all businesses involved in the transactions. When working with business customers, vendors or suppliers can adapt their products to the specific needs of their customers far more easily than if human contact were required for each transaction.

> **business-to-business e-commerce**
> The use of the Internet to conduct transactions between businesses.

The statistics for e-commerce and especially B2B e-commerce are dramatic. In 2000, B2B sales totaled $433 billion. But even with a slow growth economy in the years following, B2B transactions are forecasted to reach $6 trillion by 2004 and $8.5 trillion in 2005.[6]

We will consider two kinds of business-to-business e-commerce. The first is direct link transactions between two businesses. Typically, these are supplier–manufacturer links or manufacturer–retail links. The key to these transactions, however, is that the interaction is directly from one firm's computers to the other's. The second type of business-to-business relationship is through the use of a *hub, vortex,* or *electronic market,* three different words for a company that matches suppliers with business customers. The two types are shown in Figures 17.3 and 17.4.

FIGURE 17.3

Direct Business-to-Business E-commerce

FIGURE 17.4

Hub-Based Business-to-Business E-commerce

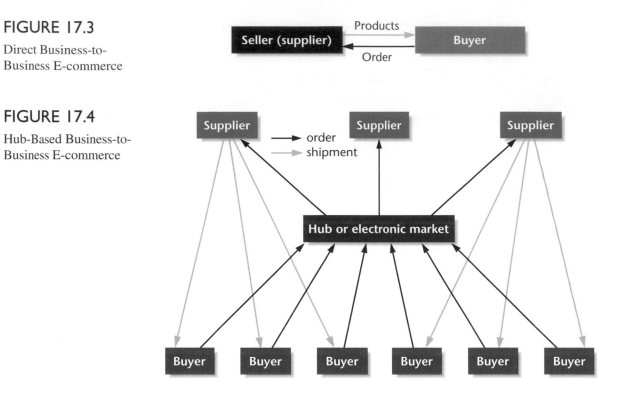

Direct Business-to-Business E-commerce

direct business-to-business e-commerce
The interaction between two companies primarily through computer contact.

In Chapter 12, we discussed the concept of strategic alliances, long-term relationships between two companies who benefit jointly from the relationship. **Direct business-to-business e-commerce** relies on these long-term strategic alliances. The significant aspect of these relationships is that once the agreement is forged and the necessary hardware and software installed at each company's facilities, the interaction becomes primarily computer-to-computer rather than through human contact.

These interactions often involve a supplier and a relatively small number of customers who forge a close working relationship. In Chapter 13, we discussed Lear Corporation. Lear makes interior assemblies for most automobile companies, including GM, Ford, DaimlerChrysler, Honda, Volvo, Volkswagen, and even Hyundai and Rolls-Royce. Lear has 120,000 employees in 300 facilities in 33 countries. Lear's strategic alliance with the Ford Motor Company is a good example of e-commerce. At a specified time when a car is moving down the assembly line, a computer at Ford directs a computer at Lear to build the interior for the car. The computer has all the specifications for the order, allowing Lear to know precisely what to include in the assembly. The seat assembly arrives at the Ford plant approximately 90 minutes later, just in time for installation in the car. Go to the Lear website, www.lear.com, to learn more about this interesting company.

The key to direct business-to-business e-commerce is shared information. This aspect of the relationship requires a high amount of trust between a supplier and its business customer. Many of these direct business-to-business interactions make use of an **extranet,** a private website accessible only by a company and its partners. It works essentially like the Internet except that it is tied only to the parties involved in the interaction. Security is also an issue. It is critical that information is not leaked out of the system. Thus, secure networks must be developed so that information can be transferred over the extranet without fear of loss.

extranet
A private website accessible only by a company and its partners.

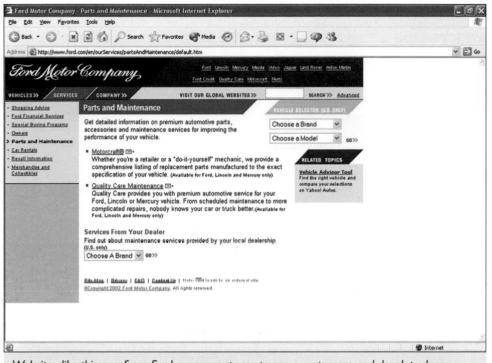

Websites like this one from Ford are a great way to serve customers and develop closer communication between the customer and the business. What other advantages do these websites offer?

Electronic Hub-Based Business-to-Business E-commerce

The second type of business-to-business e-commerce is a transaction that makes use of a hub, electronic market, vortex, or net market maker. In this situation, the hub or net market maker serves as an electronic intermediary. Through its computers, the hub links a number of suppliers to a far larger number of customers (see Figure 17.4).

Electronic hubs or net market makers in e-commerce work much like airline hubs in that buyers and sellers come together and communicate through the hub. The business-to-business hub creates value by reducing the cost of finding customers or sellers. Buyers benefit because they have more choices, and sellers benefit because they have access to more buyers. Interestingly, the hubs become electronic intermediaries that replace and perform much the same functions as wholesalers or distributors in traditional markets. The difference is that products are shipped directly from the manufacturer to the business customer, eliminating the need for a physical distribution center between the two.

Hub-based B2B is expected to grow significantly as companies find ways to reduce their costs of inputs and increase efficiency. Profile 17.2 shows how Best Buy uses a hub-based system to reduce its costs.

In concluding this section, we put e-commerce in perspective with a single question: How many products are transported over the Internet? The answer is, of course, zero. The only thing transported over the Internet is information. Thus, the Internet and e-commerce are nothing but mechanisms to communicate. But they are very efficient means of communication, and they allow companies and individuals to be far more productive than ever before.

> **electronic hubs or net market makers**
> The intermediaries in business-to-business e-commerce.

PROFILE 17.2   SOME OF BEST BUY'S BEST BUYS

Retailers buy products and services far beyond just the merchandise they sell in stores. It is this category of purchases—operational supplies, services, and building materials for new stores—that allows Best Buy to save millions of dollars by using electronic exchanges.

Best Buy's director of supply-chain management says the business can get 100 bids in an hour for materials and services that previously took weeks to obtain. Using Free Markets and WorldWide Retail Exchange, both online exchanges, Best Buy can obtain nearly instant quotes on price-sensitive store construction materials and on services such as rebate fulfillment, which the company outsources.

Best Buy does not use exchanges to purchase retail merchandise. In that case, the primary criterion is to have highly popular products and familiar brands that appeal to customers rather than to have the lowest possible price. For retail merchandise, the traditional negotiation method with suppliers works best.

Source: Dale Buss, "The New Purchasing Department," *Business 2.0,* August 2002, p. 78.

THINK ABOUT THIS

1. Why have websites such as eBay and Amazon.com become so popular? Keep in mind that these companies do not sell anything that was not previously for sale by other methods. Are people buying books that they didn't previously think they needed just because they can now do so on the Web?

2. Business-to-consumer companies and traditional retailers that now have websites are seeing an increasing number of purchases made on the Internet. Do you anticipate that retailers as we know them today will cease to exist? Can you think of some retailers that might switch from a dual method of selling to selling exclusively online?

3. Business-to-business selling is the fastest-growing and least well known type of e-commerce. It often requires a long-term strategic alliance between two companies. What could happen if one of the two companies was sold or merged with a competitor?

Using Technology to Enhance Internal Operations

The discussions in the preceding sections have focused on how a company's strategy can be affected through the use of technology. E-commerce can bring a company's products to its customers with greater efficiency and can increase the size of the market considerably. However, technology helps more than just interbusiness relationships. The operations inside a company can also be enhanced through the effective use of technology. Information technology, in particular, can help a company track its production processes, make processes more efficient, and, at the same time, give the company more flexibility in the way it builds products or provides services.

FedEx is one of the best examples of a company making effective use of information technology. FedEx, the world's largest express transportation company, delivers approximately 5 million items to over 210 countries each business day. It has 138,000 employees worldwide and operates 653 aircraft and more than 44,500 vehicles in its integrated system. It has almost 40,000 drop boxes. FedEx's 2001 revenues were $21 billion. It was ranked seventh in *Fortune*'s list of most admired companies.

FedEx's use of technology both internally and externally is dramatic. It sends over 100 million electronic transactions a day. Its website gives customers a direct window into a shipment tracking database. Thousands of customers a day click their way through the website to locate the status of their shipments.[7] The impact of this communications system may appear to be primarily customer oriented. However, the information system at FedEx is also a key to the operation of the entire company. The system of tracking enables the efficient and timely delivery of shipments.

An **intranet** is essentially the same as the Internet except that it is designed for use entirely within a particular company. Like the extranet that allows a company to communicate with selected partners outside the firm, the intranet allows employees inside the firm to communicate with each other.

Companies are finding that an intranet solves many of their communication problems, not the least of which is the inability of computers in one part of the company to talk to computers in another part. An intranet allows this communication even if different kinds of computers are used. Further, companies are finding that databases can be accessed by users across the company, thereby substantially reducing the need for paper while providing the opportunity for continuous updating of information. Whereas paper-published information is often obsolete almost as soon as it is printed, an internal website can be updated instantaneously and be accessible immediately by large numbers of people. Financial reports, supply catalogs, employee benefits information, corporate phone books, company policies, training manuals, requisition forms, and a host of other information can be stored on Web servers for browsing by employees. The intranets are built in such a way that they are secure from outsiders and insiders who should not have access to confidential information.

FedEx offers clients a number of service features. These features include shipment tracing over the Internet. How does this tracing provide for value for businesses that use it?

> **intranet**
> A computer communications network within a single company.

The Impact of Technology on Internal Operations

The increased use of all kinds of technology and, in particular, information technology, affects all aspects of the production process of a company. For example, we discussed just-in-time (JIT) production in Chapter 13. Information technology plays an important role in JIT, as illustrated in the Lear Corporation example. The amount of investment in inventory is reduced considerably because of the ability to communicate needs better and produce a product just when it is needed.

Flexible Manufacturing

In addition to just-in-time production and inventory policies, another operations issue that is affected by technology is flexible manufacturing. In the past, the traditional approach to manufacturing came from mass-production thinking. Machines were set to produce single operations on a large scale. This approach works well when the business is mass-producing a highly standardized item. The approach yields large quantities of output in a very efficient manner. In short, mass production allows companies to produce large quantities of products at lower costs. Traditionally, this was the approach used by automakers and other large manufacturers on their assembly lines.

Today, however, businesses must be flexible. They must be able to respond to changes in customer preferences and demands, and to do so quickly. Accordingly, mass-production thinking can be out of sync with a needed focus on customer sensitivity and service. Businesses need the efficiency of mass-production thinking, but they cannot afford to alienate customers by being slow and inflexible. One response to this problem is a set of processes known as **flexible manufacturing,** the reliance on highly automated machinery that can be changed quickly to perform multiple tasks. Thus, a given machine may be able to produce a variety of product options. This approach requires machinery that can be controlled through computer-generated commands coming from customer orders.

> **flexible manufacturing**
> Manufacturing with highly automated machinery that can be changed quickly and can perform multiple tasks.

Mass Customization

Mass customization is the design of products and processes with the goal of delivering highly customized products to different customers around the world.[8] The key to mass customization is to build products in modules so that the final assembly is done at the last possible moment before shipment to the customer. Different products can contain different combinations of modules. Companies must integrate their product designs, their suppliers, their processes, and information so that these all fit together. This approach is the essence of Dell's production and marketing. Rather than stocking thousands of computers that are already assembled and in boxes and hoping that people will order them, Dell stocks the components. Employees receive an order and then handpick the components, assemble them into the computer case, and put the final product into a box. So if you order a computer with 10 gigabytes of memory, a DVD player with read/write CD capabilities, a 3.5-inch drive, and two ports, the assembler simply grabs those components from the shelf, inserts them in the case, and puts it all in a box for shipping.

> **mass customization**
> The design of products and processes with the goal of delivering highly customized products to different customers around the world.

Computer-Integrated Manufacturing

Manufacturing industries have evolved into highly technological entities over time. Many technologies have become accepted in large companies. *Numerically controlled machines* have been around for years. They consist of tools, such as drills or grinders, that are controlled by a computer. Industrial robots substitute for humans in doing highly repetitive tasks, many of which are dull, dirty, and boring. A *robot* is a programmable, multifunctional machine that can be equipped with different kinds of arms that allow it to pick up, turn, shake, weld, or paint a part with high levels of accuracy over and over. *Computer-aided design (CAD)* utilizes computers to help design products. High-end computers using three-dimensional graphics can create designs for products that would be extremely time-consuming without the computers. *Computer-integrated manufacturing* integrates all aspects of manufacturing, including design, testing, fabrication, assembly, inspection, and materials handling.[9]

> **enterprise resource planning (ERP)**
> A companywide application software that integrates all departments and functions across a company onto a single computer system.

Enterprise Resource Planning

As we have said over and over, the theme of this book is integration. How do we integrate everything a business does? One way to achieve integration of information and technology within an organization is **enterprise resource planning (ERP),** a companywide application software that integrates all departments and functions across a company onto a single computer system.

ERP allows decisions to be made companywide using a single set of information. For example, financial information from the entire company is centered on a single source rather than being kept on dozens of computers around the company. Thus, everyone in the firm uses the same financial information rather than his or her own particular version of the data, which might differ wildly from department to department or unit to unit. Similarly, integrated customer order information allows companies to keep track of orders more easily and coordinate with manufacturing, inventory control, and shipping. Human resource information can also be standardized, allowing companies a standard way to track information such as wages and benefits across all business units.[10]

Suppose a customer orders a product over a company's interactive website. Immediately, the accounting, production scheduling, and purchasing departments know about it. The accounting area adjusts accounts receivable, records payments, determines costs per unit, and can calculate the impact on the firm's profit or loss. The human resources department is automatically notified so that it can schedule workers for the project. The department can also be alerted to hire workers and to calculate their pay and benefits. The manufacturing module orders material, alerts the quality management area, and sets up production planning and control. When the order is entered, it automatically includes the correct information on pricing, promotions, availability, and shipping options. Thus, the software can integrate the information flow between all sectors of the company.

Consider the case of Possible Dreams, Ltd., a 20-year-old Foxboro, Massachusetts, firm. It has become the biggest creator of Santa Claus collectibles through its Clothtique Santa collection of intricately detailed, handcrafted Santas. Possible Dreams has been delivering Clothtique Santas nationwide and in Europe to more than 15,000 collectors and small specialty stores. Although the firm had been computerized, using ERP allowed it to improve on-time shipments, retain customers, and increase sales. The system allows sales representatives to check inventory levels remotely and provide real-time warehouse management to prevent stock outages and evaluate reorder points. Using B2B communications, the firm can stay in touch with its customers and suppliers, as well as manage its internal operations.[11]

Scheid Vineyards created VitWatch to be a state-of-the-art information system. Through VitWatch, clients have real-time web access to specific vineyard blocks. What advantages does this technology offer for wineries?

THINK ABOUT THIS

1. In the past—and even now, for some companies—mass production was the route to success and profitability. Now mass customization receives much more emphasis as an efficient way to produce products. What accounts for the difference in philosophy and methods?

2. Enterprise resource planning appears to be highly useful as an integrative method of considering virtually all aspects of a company's operations, using a single platform. What kind of training will be necessary to make it work? Are there any downsides to adopting ERP?

THE BIG PICTURE

It is easy to consider technology as a portion of the manufacturing aspect of a business and forget the role it plays in the overall operation of the firm. Yet we need only consider how it affects other aspects of the company to realize how omnipresent technology really is. Information technology affects communication with customers by increasing the ease and speed of communications and reducing the cost of those communications. Financial markets and banks are prime participants in e-commerce. Without the use of credit cards, most of the consumer-to-consumer and business-to-consumer transactions could not be accomplished. Technology influences economics by affecting the supply and demand for products and the opening up of markets in a global arena. Law and ethics are a new challenge because of the differences in the way technology allows people to communicate. Human resources are also affected by information technology since employees can now check their benefits online and make changes in their allocations to retirement and other benefits on the computer.

To illustrate how the big picture is affected by technology, we return to our Federal Express example. We have already stated how information technology allows FedEx and its customers to track packages. But there is more to this story. FedEx has created a business-to-business service called Virtual Order, which integrates the Web catalogs of companies and the ordering from those catalogs on the one hand, with fulfillment and delivery using FedEx's own trucks and planes on the other hand.

Here is how it works: FedEx hosts the Web pages for online catalogs of various companies on FedEx computers. It can even create the Web pages for the selling company if desired. When an order comes in, the buyer is charged, the selling company is notified to ship the product, and the company's database of products is instantaneously adjusted. The order is then routed to the seller's warehouse where FedEx packages the products and loads them on FedEx trucks. FedEx then sends confirmation and invoices to the buyer. If the seller desires, FedEx can even take charge of the entire warehousing operation at its headquarters in Memphis. It also provides 24-hour technical support for the Virtual Order merchants.[12]

From this information, we can see that Federal Express is not only providing transportation of a company's products, but also assisting in marketing those products, storing them, getting them ready to ship, adjusting the client's database, and becoming involved in the payment process. In so doing, however, it also is reducing the human resource needs for the company.

Summary

1. A company's strategy is affected by many factors, including changes in the economy, the company's competitors, and technology.

   • How does technology affect a company's strategy?

   Technology affects how a business competes. Technology provides new ways to communicate with customers and changes the way the company provides services to them. A business that fails to adapt to changes in technology is likely to be at a severe competitive disadvantage.

2. The Internet has opened up tremendous avenues for communicating with customers. Some websites are designed primarily to provide information to customers and other interested individuals.

   • How can companies communicate using the Web?

   The Internet is an efficient way of communicating with large numbers of customers. Some companies put up a simple Web page to provide limited information and invite users to contact the company. Other companies, however, develop massive interactive sites with hundreds of pages or links.

3. Electronic commerce has changed the way businesses operate.

   • What is e-commerce, and how does it work?

   Electronic commerce is the buying or selling of products over the Internet. It can consist of consumer-to-consumer trade, business-to-consumer transactions, or business-to-business activity. The use of computers and the Internet to conduct business is common to all three.

4. Websites for companies such as Amazon.com, J.Crew, and Dell offer ways to buy books, clothes, and computers on the Web.

   • What is business-to-consumer e-commerce?

   Business-to-consumer e-commerce is a way to sell goods or services efficiently to thousands of consumers on the Web. Customers order products from businesses and pay for them with their credit cards. The products are then shipped by way of FedEx, UPS, the U.S. Postal Service, or other means of transportation. Selling on the Web is efficient because it uses computer-to-computer communication. Thus, it can take place 24 hours a day without the need for human interaction.

5. Business-to-consumer e-commerce is perhaps the most well known type of e-commerce. In terms of the dollar amount of transactions, however, business-to-business e-commerce is the leading type of e-commerce.

   • How does business-to-business e-commerce work?

   Business-to-business e-commerce can work either directly between two businesses or through the use of a hub or electronic market. In the direct link version, a supplier and customer form a strategic alliance to exchange information and to order and ship products. In many cases, the companies use an extranet, which is similar to the Internet except that it connects only the two businesses. In the electronic market version, the hub is an electronic intermediary much like a wholesaler in a traditional market. Buyers place orders through the market, and sellers ship directly to buyers.

6. Although information technology is often used between businesses or between businesses and consumers, technology is equally important within the operations of a single company.

   • How can technology make a company more efficient?

   Technology can open up possibilities for efficiency-generating activities such as just-in-time (JIT) management, flexible manufacturing, mass customization, computer-integrated manufacturing, and enterprise resource planning. These approaches allow companies to limit their inventory costs and adjust their manufacturing processes to meet specific customer needs.

Key Terms

business-to-business e-commerce, p. 441

business-to-consumer e-commerce, p. 439

consumer-to-consumer e-commerce, p. 439

direct business-to-business e-commerce, p. 442

electronic commerce (e-commerce), p. 438

electronic hubs or net market makers, p. 443

enterprise resource planning (ERP), p. 446

extranet, p. 442

flexible manufacturing, p. 446

intranet, p. 445

mass customization, p. 446

Exercises and Applications

1. In one minute, write a list of companies that do business-to-consumer e-commerce. Compare your list with the lists of other students.

2. In teams, consider a company that currently does not do e-commerce. How would the company benefit, if at all, by setting up an e-commerce website?

3. Use the company from exercise 2. Describe in no more than two pages what the site should include.

4. Find two business-to-consumer websites. Compare them for ease of use. How do they differ from consumer-to-consumer websites, such as an online auction site?

5. In teams, interview a manager responsible for a business-to-business e-commerce operation. How did moving to e-commerce change how this manager's firm does business?

6. Interview an instructor who teaches operations management (sometimes known as production management). Ask how technology has changed the internal operations of a company in the past 10 years.

FROM THE PAGES OF

BusinessWeek

What's Glowing Online Now

BusinessWeek has created what it calls "BW's Real-World Internet Index." This index is made up of 20 Internet firms that are profitable or nearly so and that stock analysts have rated "buy" or better. These stocks, some of which are widely known and some of which are not, have performed better than traditional companies over the past year—a year not known to be kind to any stocks and certainly not Internet stocks. The stocks include 1-800-flower.com, Amazon.com, eBay, Expedia (an online travel site), Hotels.com, LendingTree, Ticketmaster, and 13 others. Of the 20 firms, 9 are in e-tailing.

BusinessWeek feels that the 20 firms are different from many of the dot-coms that crashed and burned. First, they are fundamentally sound; that is, their concept makes sense. In contrast, the basic premise of many earlier dot-com companies was tenuous at best. Second, the companies are large enough that they have now covered many of their fixed costs. For many Internet firms, the start-up is very expensive, but once the firm grows large enough, the operating costs are relatively small. The key is to reach that threshold of size before running out of money. Unfortunately, many early dot-coms burned through all their venture capital and IPO money before the company became stable. The third aspect that makes these stocks particularly appealing now is that all Internet stocks, like virtually all other stocks, have decreased in value significantly from an overpriced apex a year or so ago. Thus, (as this article was written, in September 2002) the stocks are good investments.

Decision Questions

1. Look back at the introduction to this chapter. What is different about the basic concept of those companies as compared with the stocks on the Real-World Internet Index?

2. What is significant about the title for the group of stocks—BW's Real-World Internet Index?

3. Why are nearly half of the stocks in the index in e-tailing, an apparently risky index?

Source: Timothy A. Mullaney, "What's Glowing Online Now," *BusinessWeek,* September 2, 2002, p. 95.

References

1. Ellen Florian, "Dead and (Mostly) Gone," *Fortune,* December 24, 2001, pp. 46, 47.

2. "Fortune's 100 Fastest-Growing Companies," *Fortune,* September 2, 2002, pp. 161, 166–72.

3. Nick Wingfield, "Click and . . . Drive?" *The Wall Street Journal,* July 15, 2002, p. R11.

4. Kate Maddox, "IBM Launches Portal for Midsize Businesses," *BtoB,* May 6, 2002, p. 3.

5. Efraim Turban, Jae Lee, David King, and H. Michael Chung, *Electronic Commerce: A Managerial Perspective* (Upper Saddle River, NJ: Prentice Hall, 2000), p. 13.

6. Michael Pastore, "Economic Downturn Slows B2B Commerce," Jupiter Research, www.cyberatlas.internet.com/b2b/article, March 21, 2001 (accessed October 18, 2002).

7. Federal Express, website, www.fedex.com (accessed August 30, 2002).

8. This discussion is based on Richard B. Chase, Nicholas J. Aquilano, and R. Robert Jacobs, *Operations Management for Competitive Advantage* (Burr Ridge, IL: McGraw-Hill/Irwin, 2001), chap. 8.

9. Chase et al., Suppl. C.

10. *Medium Business News* (online newsletter), www.ibm.com/mediumbusiness/enewsletter (accessed August 29, 2002).

11. "Possible Dreams, Ltd., Case Study," www.ibm.com/mediumbusiness/casestudy/2402 (accessed August 29, 2002).

12. Turban et al., p. 22.

Model of the Path toward a Successful Business

Vision and Mission

| Indicators of Business Success (Desired Performance) | → | Assessing the Environment and Its Impact | → | Providing Excellence in Products and Services | → | Evaluating Results and Making Changes |

- Achieving financial performance
- Meeting customer needs
- Building quality products and services
- Encouraging innovation and creativity
- Gaining employee commitment

- Diversity trends and issues
- Economic forces
- Financial markets and processes
- Global influences
- Legal and regulatory forces

- Thinking strategically
- Acquiring and using resources
- Providing value through quality products and services
- Enhancing value through communicating with customers
- Integrating activities and encouraging commitment
- Using technology in a competitive environment

- Measuring performance
- Promoting change and renewal

5

Assessment and Change

As we start the last part of this textbook, it is important to pause a moment and consider where we have been. We began this text by introducing the concept of a successful business and how businesses fit together in industries. We then spent time in Part Two discussing the kinds of decisions a manager needs to make and the types of information needed to make those decisions. Part Three looked at various forces outside the business that affect how it operates, including demographic and diversity trends, economic forces, financial markets, global influences, and legal forces. In Part Four, we presented key decisions and actions a firm must take to provide excellence in products and services. These processes include determining the strategic direction of the business, acquiring resources, developing quality products and services, enhancing value through communicating with customers, integrating activities and gaining commitment from workers, and using technology to achieve excellence in products and services.

In this final section of the book, we turn to the assessment of performance and the need for change. A business cannot be truly successful unless it can assess its own performance. As you will learn, measuring performance includes far more than just determining bottom-line financial performance. Further, a business must constantly adapt to changes in its environment and make changes in its strategies and internal operations to maintain its success. We focus on assessment in Chapter 18 and on change and renewal in Chapter 19.

Again, we call your attention to the model on the preceding page. Note that the highlighted element deals with evaluating results and making changes. Note also that an arrow goes from that element back to the indicators of business success, showing that the entire process is a circular one.

18

Measuring Performance

One of the impressive business success stories of 2002 was Procter & Gamble's successful marketing of the SpinBrush electric toothbrush. At a time when most electric toothbrushes were selling for more than $50, four entrepreneurs developed a battery-driven model that they argued could be sold for much less. They offered to sell the rights to Procter & Gamble in 1998. P&G evaluated the production and marketing costs and concluded that the company could make a satisfactory profit by selling the toothbrush for the unbelievably low price of $5. At the same time, P&G measured potential consumer response by assembling a panel of 24 consumers and having them evaluate the product: 23 out of 24 gave strong approval. Then P&G hired the inventors for a year to make sure that the product was introduced quickly. Otherwise, there was a risk that P&G's bureaucracy would be too slow to introduce the product and competitors might get a similar toothbrush on the market.[1]

Notice the role of measurement in the story. On the one hand, measurement of potential profit and potential consumer response was a critical part of the process leading to the introduction of the product. On the other hand, top management's fear of excessive measurement by the P&G bureaucracy caused the company to hire outsiders to help bring the product to market quickly. The managers recognized the all-too-present danger of "paralysis by analysis." In other words, too much analysis can be almost as bad as too little. The best companies constantly struggle to achieve just the right amount of measurement.

Two statements set the tone for this chapter: (1) You can control only what you can measure. (2) You can reward only what you can measure. Managers of businesses must constantly be alert to how the business is doing. They must be able to objectively measure the firm's progress toward its goals. This chapter brings us back to the indicators of business success we discussed in Chapter 2. We now look at ways to actually identify results that help assess how successful the firm is.

After studying this chapter, you should be able to:

1. Describe some major cautions that managers must keep in mind when dealing with measurement.

2. Identify and explain the basic measures of business success in terms of a conceptual model of performance.

3. Explain the primary measures of success from the accounting and financial perspective.

4. Discuss the measures of performance from the customer perspective.

5. Describe the measures of quality and value that can be used in a business.

6. Explain the measures of innovation and creativity.

7. Discuss the most important measures from the employee perspective.

Measurement of performance is essential. Managers spend the bulk of their time planning, making decisions, acquiring resources, developing and implementing strategies, and working with employees to make sure those strategies and decisions are carried out. It is important, however, for managers to also spend time studying performance to check the progress of the business. Performance must be compared with the goals set by the company's managers and the relevant indicators of success. Only when the performance is carefully measured will managers know whether corrective action should be taken. This is the circular aspect of the model in Figure 2.1, which we have repeated at the beginning of each part of the text.

Measurement Caveats

Before addressing the measures individually, we note some important caveats, or cautions, that pervade each of the measures we will present throughout the chapter.

1. Measurements are interrelated and are not performed in a vacuum.

2. Managers must measure both efficiency and effectiveness.

3. Companies must measure processes as well as results.

4. Dynamic measurements are more useful than static ones.

5. Measurement must foster communication.[2]

Interrelatedness of Measurements

Managers do not measure performance in unrelated assessments. It is not as if they have unique containers into which they put different kinds of materials and then measure how full each is. How well a business does in one instance affects how well it does in others. For example, innovation and creativity are important because they result in new products or services for customers. But they are also important because employees may be happier and more challenged, and owners may ultimately be

SOUTHWEST

integrated assessment
The simultaneous measurement of variables in different parts of an organization.

wealthier. **Integrated assessment** is the simultaneous measurement of variables in different parts of an organization. Performance must be measured by an integrated set of assessment variables and techniques so that overall effectiveness of the firm's decision makers can be fully grasped.

Recently, *Fortune* rated Southwest Airlines as one of the 10 most admired companies in the United States. The rankings came from a survey of 10,000 executives who evaluated companies in terms of performance in eight separate categories: quality of management, employee talent, innovation, financial soundness, use of corporate assets, long-term investment value, quality of products or services, and social responsibility. Notice how many of these categories are related or draw upon one another. Quality of management surely is a key to each of the others. Employee talent, quality of products or services, and innovation are related. Most experts feel that social responsibility and long-term investment value are related. Good use of corporate assets leads to financial soundness. Thus, many of these measures draw on others—an indication of the integration of measurement.

Effectiveness and Efficiency

Two overriding issues in measuring business performance are effectiveness and efficiency. These important concepts are easy to confuse. Look carefully at the differences between the two.

effectiveness
A measure of the degree to which a business achieves its goals.

Effectiveness is a measure of the degree to which a business achieves its goals. These may be financial goals, customer goals, employee performance goals, quality goals, innovation goals, or any other outcome that the business deems critical. The key is that a business is effective if it reaches its goals. When a business sets a goal of increasing market share by 10 percent this year and does indeed achieve that, it has been effective in meeting its market share goal. If the business sets a goal of reducing employee turnover by 15 percent and achieves that goal, it has been effective.

efficiency
A measure of the relationship between inputs and outputs.

Efficiency is a measure of the relationship between inputs and outputs. A business may be effective in meeting its sales goals—but only by committing excessive amounts of human and financial resources to its sales effort. In that case, the business is effective (at least in the short run), but it is inefficient. If the business can reach its sales goals while committing fewer human and financial resources, it becomes more efficient. Improved efficiency saves the business money and conserves its resources. As we have noted throughout this text, businesses are increasingly concerned with finding ways to enhance their efficiency.

We measure efficiency by calculating the ratio of outputs to inputs. Businesses may measure efficiency by looking at sales per person, costs per unit, sales per advertising dollar, sales per square foot of retail space, and other output–input measures. It is important to measure efficiency because it gives us a feel for how well the business is using its resources. It tells us if we are being wasteful or investing unnecessarily in plant and equipment or human resources.

Both efficiency and effectiveness are important, and up to a point they are related. For a while, the more efficient a business becomes, the more it eliminates waste, and the more effective it is. After some point—and this point differs for each company—the quest for efficiency may adversely affect the quest for effectiveness. This situation can occur if the business strips resources so much that it reduces its ability to perform. Recently some critics have argued that this condition may have occurred with corporate downsizing. No one would argue that some organizations have some fat in them, but after a point, downsizing may jeopardize effectiveness. Efficiency and effectiveness may begin to move in opposite directions.

Processes and Results

Profit is a result, and a very important one. Defects per million is a result. Employee turnover is a result. These results are important and must be measured. However, it is also important to measure processes. Teamwork is a process. Developing new ways to satisfy customers is a process. Looking for ways to reduce the time it takes to develop new products is a process. We cannot abandon measurement of results, but we must also pay attention to processes.

Dynamic versus Static Measures

The company's balance sheet at the end of the year is a snapshot of the firm's financial health at that moment. It is a static measure. Financial ratios by themselves are static measures. Payroll, benefits paid, the number of days lost to accidents, and the number of customer complaints are all static measures. **Dynamic measurements** are those that include some time element, often comparing results in different time periods. When we compare this week's measures with last week's, or this quarter's measures with last quarter's or the equivalent quarter from last year, the measures become dynamic. We look at historical trends and project them into the future to help predict what will happen. Thus, measurement must be an ongoing, dynamic process. We must continuously collect information for measurement, analysis, and comparison.

> **dynamic measurements** Measures that include some time element, often comparing results in different time periods.

Fostering Communication

Effective measurement requires information from various sources throughout the organization. The results of measurement should also be communicated back throughout the organization. Disseminating results to the lowest ranks will help motivate and focus employees. Thus, the measurement process becomes an integrating device that links units and fosters communication among them. As results are discussed in management forums, they become a central part of the management process. Communication is essential throughout the entire process of measuring performance and making changes.

The Measures of a Successful Business

In Chapter 2, we presented five indicators of a successful business—one that continues to survive and grow and provide value for its various stakeholders. As we turn to analyzing the firm's success in creating value, it is important to compare how we are doing with the goals we have set. Figure 18.1 illustrates the relationships among the five categories, using a model adapted from the *balanced scorecard* developed several years ago by Harvard University professor Robert S. Kaplan and consultant David P. Norton.[3]

As shown in Figure 18.1, evaluation and measurement revolve around the vision and strategy developed for the company. Thus, the goals in each box reflect the vision and

THINK ABOUT THIS

1. Why is measurement important? How does it relate to good management?

2. We suggested five caveats regarding measurement. Add some of your own.

3. Are some of the caveats more important than others? If so, which ones are most important?

FIGURE 18.1

A Model of
Performance Measures

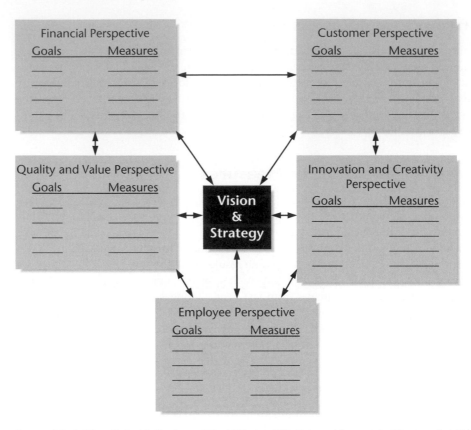

Source: Adapted from Robert S. Kaplan and David Norton, "The Balanced Scorecard—Measures that Drive Performance," *Harvard Business Review,* January–February, 1992, pp. 71–79.

strategies that the firm's owners or managers developed. Note that the boxes are interconnected, indicating that measurement, like strategies, is an integrated activity and must be done with the whole organization in mind. This is the concept behind the balanced scorecard.

There are two other considerations as we begin the measurement process. First, it must include both cost-oriented and noncost measures. Cost-oriented measures are those items on which a dollar value can be placed. Examples are research and development expenditures, supplier costs, design costs, and distribution costs. There are also a number of non-cost-related measures of performance. These items are measurable, but not in terms of dollars. They include market share, complaints, repeat customers, and quality, among others. They may be measured in terms of percentages, numbers of customers, or some technical measure of quality. They are just as important as the cost-oriented measures.

The second consideration is that measurements may be either internal or external. Some measures of performance are clearly in-house. They include number of new products, employee turnover, production costs, and quality measurements. Other measures, however, are outside the organization. External measures include comparison with competitors' performance, market share, image, and customer complaints.

THINK ABOUT THIS

1. How are the five areas of measurement related? How does a change in one area affect another?

2. How does changing the vision or strategy of an organization affect how we measure success? Think of an example.

3. Will internal and external measures usually support each other, or will they sometimes contradict each other?

The following sections will look at each of the broad performance areas shown in Figure 18.1. Little that you will read throughout this chapter is new; we set the stage for these topics in Chapter 2 and addressed each of them in succeeding chapters. But the perspective is different here. In earlier chapters, we looked at how to create performance. Here, we look at how to measure it.

The Financial Perspective

Financial performance is one of the most important areas of measurement. Fortunately, it is also one of the most objective measures of a firm's overall performance. Accounting-related measures have the advantage of being comparable both to industry norms and to historical performance. Financial performance should always be measured using generally accepted accounting practices (GAAP). Accounting-based measures are also more objective than others because they use a common denominator for most measures—dollars. We can measure sales, net cash flow, net profit, and net worth in dollars. Even those measures that are stated in terms of percentages are calculated with dollars. The following paragraphs consider three important measures of financial performance: profit, cash flow, and net worth.

Profit

Perhaps the most common measure of financial performance is profit or net income. In the most basic sense, profit is total revenues minus total expenses, but profit can be measured in several other ways. When we analyze profit, it is important to include dynamic measures. For example, if we looked only at actual profits for the year, then companies such as General Electric and General Motors would appear to be most profitable because they are very large. Therefore, it is more instructive to look at dynamic measures: rate of growth of profits and profits as a percentage of the investment by stockholders (stockholders' equity). Tables 18.1 and 18.2 show the top 10

TABLE 18.1

Top 10 Companies in Profit Growth, 2001

Rank	Company	Percent Increase	Industry Category
1	Sherwin-Williams	1,542	Discount and fashion retailing
2	Wachovia	1,073	Banking
3	Chiron	985	Health care
4	Progressive	792	Nonbank financial services
5	HCA	388	Health care
6	Staples	344	Discount and fashion retailing
7	Baker Hughes	329	Fuel
8	Office Depot	308	Discount and fashion retailing
9	HealthSouth	261	Health care
10	American Electric Power	232	Utilities and energy services

Source: *The Business Week 50,* Spring 2002, p. 34.

TABLE 18.2

Top 10 Companies in
Return on Equity, 2001

Rank	Company	Return on Equity (%)	Industry
1	Maytag	711.5	Consumer products and computers
2	Deluxe	236.5	Office equipment
3	Dow Jones	235.1	Publishing and broadcasting
4	Zimmer Holdings	190.3	Health care
5	Edison International	174.7	Utilities and energy services
6	Colgate-Palmolive	139.2	Consumer products
7	Sara Lee	118.2	Food
8	UST	108.5	Consumer products
9	Wyeth	72.2	Health care
10	Plum Creek Timber	71.3	Housing and real estate

Source: *The Business Week 50,* Spring 2002, p. 38.

> **return on equity (ROE)**
> The amount of profit a firm makes for each dollar of equity invested.

> **earnings per share (EPS)**
> A company's earnings divided by the number of shares of stock outstanding.

Sherwin-Williams reports excellent financial results. Annual sales exceed $5 billion, and dividends to shareholders have increased for 22 consecutive years. Which financial measures would investors be most interested in studying?

firms in two categories in *BusinessWeek's* annual list of the top 50 businesses. As noted in Table 18.1, for one-year growth in profits, Sherwin-Williams was first, Wachovia was second, and Chiron was third. Table 18.2 shows that for one-year return on stockholders' equity, Maytag was first, Deluxe was second, and Dow Jones was third.[4]

In theory, net profit is a simple measure. But in practice, the profit calculation can become rather complex and ambiguous because of the freedom firms have in determining how to classify revenues and expenses. Two similar companies may show significant differences in reported earnings because of differences in their accounting methods. Although there are benefits to having some flexibility in accounting methods, this does put heavy responsibilities on executives to ensure that all record keeping is done in a fair and honest manner. Indeed, companies such as Enron and Global Crossing may have been using technically acceptable accounting measures that lead to erroneous reports of profits.

As noted above, a second meaningful profit-oriented measure of financial performance is profit divided by investment, commonly referred to as **return on equity (ROE),** or the amount of profit a firm makes for each dollar the owners invest. Another of the *Business Week 50* measures is growth in return on equity. As noted, the top 10 companies in ROE are shown in Table 18.2. Other related measures are return on sales and return on assets, which measure the amount of profits compared with the firm's actual sales or total assets.

Another measure of performance for publicly traded businesses that eases comparisons with other firms is **earnings per share (EPS),** earnings (profit) divided by the number of shares of stock outstanding. This measure allows analysts to compare one publicly held firm with another. One business might have more profits than another but have considerably lower earnings per share. *The Wall Street Journal* and other financial reporting services report the EPS of companies in their daily listings.

Cash Flow

Although net income, return on equity, and earnings per share are extremely important measures of success from a financial perspective, cash flow is also a critical measure. Cash flow is especially important when we consider smaller companies over a shorter time period, such as one year or perhaps a single selling season. We discussed cash flow in Chapter 13 under financial resources. Cash flow is important because it involves the actual cash coming into or going out of the business. Many of a typical firm's sales are on credit. Customers may buy products or services from a business but not pay for them for perhaps 60 to 90 days. The sales are counted when they are made, but the actual cash is not received until much later. Therefore, cash is not received or does not flow into the business for a while. Smaller companies with limited financing must be particularly sensitive to cash flow. It is not uncommon for a business to be making a profit but be strapped for cash.

Cash flow is also important because of the seasonal and cyclical nature of business. Consider a toy store. Stores order toys for the Christmas season as early as February. Christmas toys begin arriving in late summer, which is a slack time as far as actual sales go. The firm may have to borrow funds now to pay for products that will be sold months later. This problem is even more complicated if the firm's customers buy on credit. The business may have to pay for goods several months before they are sold and then wait several weeks more before being paid. Thus, the firm's financial health is highly dependent on how well its managers measure and manage cash flow. See Profile 18.1 for another example of the importance of cash flow.

HOW A CASH FLOW FAILURE CAN BANKRUPT A BUSINESS   PROFILE 18.1

Sue Johnson always wanted to own a small business. Her opportunity arrived shortly after her last child graduated from college. A local nursing home owner offered to sell his 15-bed unit to her. He showed her his financial results for the past five years. The home had annual sales of $800,000 and expenses of $700,000, leaving a profit of $100,000 per year. Most of the revenue came from the government which paid much of the monthly costs of the residents of the home. That convinced Sue that the business would be profitable, so she obtained a loan from a local bank, hired one full-time assistant in addition to nursing staff and cooks, and opened for business in January.

Within a few months, Sue discovered a problem that the previous owner had neglected to point out. Most of Sue's expenses were cash payments for employee wages, supplies, and payments on her bank loan. Each month she had to have money to make those payments. But the government did not pay her monthly. Instead she had to send the monthly bill to the government and then wait two or three months, or even longer, for the payment to be made. In January, February, and March, she paid out $10,000 more than she received from all sources. By April, the government owed her $30,000 and she had run out of cash reserves to pay her bills. As May ended, and the government still had not paid Sue what it owed, she went to her local bank for a short-term loan. But the bank turned her down. She then pleaded with the government to pay what it owed her (now $40,000). Sue was told that she would eventually be paid but that she would have to wait another month or two. With nowhere else to turn and unable to pay many of her May bills, Sue declared bankruptcy. In an angry letter to her local paper, she said that her business was profitable, but that the government's failure to pay its bills on time imposed a negative cash flow on her. In her letter, she also warned anyone planning to do business with the government to set aside a large cash reserve with which to pay bills until the government finally paid its bills. And she urged anyone thinking about starting a business to learn about the concept of cash flow. "If you don't," she said, "you can go bankrupt even though your business is profitable."

Net Worth

net worth

The value of a business: for a publicly held firm, its stock price times the number of shares outstanding; for a private firm, its assets minus its liabilities (or its future income in today's dollars).

The final financial measure of performance is the value, or net worth, of the business. The **net worth** of a publicly held firm is simply its stock price times the number of shares outstanding. The net worth of a privately held company is much more difficult to assess. To estimate the net worth of a private firm, analysts subtract its liabilities from its assets to obtain its *book value*. Or they may project future income in today's dollars to get a good estimate of the firm's net worth.

Regardless of whether it is a publicly held corporation, a privately held corporation, a sole proprietorship, an LLC, or a partnership, a healthy firm is one whose net worth continues to increase over time. The amount that the net worth increases from year to year is very much a function of the owner's desire for growth, the environment the business operates in, and the success of management's decisions over time.

Analyzing Financial Reports

Some of you reading this book may land careers in accounting or finance. If so, you will learn how to create and analyze financial reports. Others will learn enough in basic accounting and finance courses to study a few of the major reports and draw some basic conclusions regarding a firm's financial health. Among the concepts you will learn is the need to compare a company's performance with that of the industry and with its own historical performance. And most of you will find it necessary to review the basic financial statements of companies in which you are considering making a personal investment.

income statement

A financial statement that shows a firm's performance over the course of a specific time period, such as a quarter or a year.

Tables 18.3 and 18.4 show two of the basic and important financial statements available for all publicly held companies—the income statement and the balance sheet—using Dell as an example.[5] An **income statement** shows the performance of a company over the course of a specific time period, such as a quarter or a year. It is also known as a profit-and-loss statement, a statement of earnings, or an operating statement. It focuses on sales or revenues and on expenses. Remember that subtracting all expenses from total revenues yields profit (net income or net earnings).

Table 18.3 shows Dell's income statement for the year ending February 1, 2002. Note that Dell calls it a consolidated statement of income, meaning that it is the income statement for the entire company. Each division or profit center of a large company usually has its own financial statements, which are then consolidated into the parent company's statements. Table 18.3 shows that Dell's net income fell from $2,177 million in 2001 to $1,246 million in 2002, or a decline of $931 million. The major factor was a change in revenue. Looking at the table, you can see that net revenue fell by $720 million (from $31,888 million in 2001 to $31,168 in 2002).

TABLE 18.3

Dell Computer Income Statement

DELL COMPUTER CORPORATION

CONSOLIDATED STATEMENT OF INCOME
($ in million, except per share amounts)

	Fiscal Year Ended	
	February 1, 2002	**February 2, 2001**
Net revenue	$31,168	$31,888
Cost of revenue	25,661	25,445
Gross margin	5,507	6,443
Operating expenses:		
Selling, general administrative	2,784	3,193
Research, development and engineering	452	482
Special charges	482	105
Total operating expenses	3,718	3,780
Operating income	1,789	2,663
Investment and other income (loss), net	(58)	531
Income before income taxes and cumulative effect of change in accounting principle	1,731	3,194
Provisions for income taxes	485	958
Income before cumulative effect of change in accounting principle	1,246	2,236
Cumulative effect of change in accounting principle, net	—	59
Net income	$ 1,246	$ 2,177
Earnings per common share:		
Before cumulative effect of change in accounting principle:		
Basic	$ 0.48	$ 0.87
Diluted	$ 0.46	$ 0.81
After cumulative effect of change in accounting principle:		
Basic	$ 0.48	$ 0.84
Diluted	$ 0.46	$ 0.79
Weighted average shares outstanding:		
Basic	2,602	2,582
Diluted	2,726	2,746

Source: Dell Annual Report, www.dell.com/us/en/gen/corporate/investor/investor.htm (accessed October 17, 2002).

TABLE 18.4

Dell Computer Balance Sheet

DELL COMPUTER CORPORATION

CONSOLIDATED STATEMENT OF FINANCIAL POSITION ($ IN MILLIONS)

	February 1, 2002	February 2, 2001
ASSETS		
Current assets:		
Cash and cash equivalents	$ 3,641	$ 4,910
Short-term investments	273	525
Accounts receivable, net	2,269	2,424
Inventories	278	400
Other	1,416	1,467
Total current assets	7,877	9,726
Property, plant and equipment, net	826	996
Investments	4,373	2,418
Other non-current assets	459	530
Total assets	$13,535	$13,670
LIABILITIES AND STOCKHOLDER'S EQUITY		
Current liabilities		
Accounts payable	$ 5,075	$ 4,286
Accrued and other	2,444	2,492
Total current liabilities	7,519	6,778
Long-term debt	520	509
Other	802	761
Commitments and contingent liabilities	—	—
Total liabilities	8,841	8,048
Stockholder's equity:		
Preferred stock and capital in excess of $.01 par value; shares issued and outstanding: none	—	—
Common stock and capital in excess of $.01 par value; shares authorized: 7,000; shares issued 2,654 and 2,601, respectively	5,605	4,795
Treasury stock, at cost; 52 shares and no shares respectively	(2,249)	—
Retained earnings	1,364	839
Other comprehensive income	38	62
Other	(64)	(74)
Total stockholder' equity	4,694	5,622
Total liabilities and stockholders' equity	$13,535	$13,670

Source: Dell Annual Report, www.dell.com/us/en/gen/corporate/investor/investor.htm (accessed October 17, 2002).

Partly offsetting the revenue drop were declines in operating expenses (from $3,780 million to $3,718 million), in provision for income taxes (from $958 million to $485 million), and in the cumulative effect of a change in accounting principles (from $59 million to zero). But adding to the drop in net revenue was a decline in investment and other income (loss). In the year ending February 1, 2001, Dell received revenue of $531 million from that category. The following year, Dell actually lost $58 million on its investment and other income accounts. The 2002 report explains the details of these losses.

Table 18.4 shows Dell's balance sheet, which Dell calls a consolidated statement of financial position. A **balance sheet** lists a company's assets (what it owns), liabilities (what it owes), and net worth (owners' equity) at a specific point in time. Note that Dell's assets fell slightly from $13,670 million in 2001 to $13,535 million in 2002. All but one of the listed components of assets declined. The one exception was the value of investments, which increased significantly. Note also that total liabilities rose from $8,048 million in 2001 to $ 8,841 million in 2002. Finally, note that stockholders' equity declined as a result of a large drop in the value of treasury stock—the stock that Dell, itself, owns.

Large companies typically send press releases to the media when their financial reports are completed. Analysts and other interested individuals can then seek additional information from the companies, including their annual reports and other financial statements. Profile 18.2 is an abbreviated version of such a press release. It reports Southwest Airlines' first quarter earnings for 2002.

Target has been recognized for its financial performance and strength. It has been honored as one of America's most admired companies, one of the best companies for both working mothers and Latinos, one of the best corporate citizens, and as a leader in its commitment to the education and training of its people. To what extent do you think its positive work environment affects its financial success?

balance sheet
A financial statement that shows a company's assets (what it owns), liabilities (what it owes), and net worth (owners' equity) at a specific point in time.

SOUTHWEST AIRLINES REPORTS FIRST QUARTER EARNINGS FOR 2002

PROFILE 18.2

SOUTHWEST

Dallas, Texas, April 18, 2002—Southwest Airlines' net income for first quarter 2002 was $21.4 million, compared to first quarter 2001 net income of $121.0 million, a decrease of 82.3 percent....

Total operating revenues for first quarter 2002 decreased 12.0 percent to $1.26 billion, compared to $1.43 billion for first quarter 2001. Revenue passenger miles decreased 2.5 percent in first quarter 2002 ...

Total first quarter 2002 operating expenses were $1.21 billion, which declined slightly from first quarter 2001. Operating expenses ... decreased ... primarily due to lower jet fuel prices, agency commissions, and profit sharing. These decreases more than offset increases in airport security and aviation insurance costs ...

James F. Parker, Vice Chairman and Chief Executive Officer, stated: "First quarter 2002 was a very difficult quarter for the airline industry, characterized by significant losses . . . We continue to recover from last fall's terrorist attacks. We expect profitability to steadily improve, although earnings for second quarter 2002 probably will fall well below last year's profit of $175.6 million, primarily due to the continued weakness in demand for air travel . . .

"We ended first quarter 2002 with $2.1 billion in cash on hand. In March 2002, the Company issued $385 million of senior unsecured Notes and repaid the $475 million revolving credit facility, which was accessed following the terrorist attacks."

Source: Southwest Airlines Website: www.southwest.com (accessed July 5, 2002).

Other Financial Indicators

debt ratio
The percentage of the company's total assets that are underwritten with debt.

We have listed only three broad financial indicators to measure financial success—profit, cash flow, and net worth. Many other indicators can be used to get a better feel for how a company is doing. Most of these indicators can be calculated from information on the balance sheet and income statement. The following measures are examples of many that you will study in accounting and finance courses. An important indicator that suggests a firm's ability to grow in the future is the **debt ratio,** the percentage of the company's total assets that are underwritten with debt. The more debt a company has, the more restricted it may be in its ability to grow. Of interest in the short run is the **current ratio,** which measure the firm's ability to pay the bills. It compares short-term assets such as cash with short-term liabilities such as loans from a bank. Another ratio that is especially important for retail firms is the **inventory turnover ratio,** which is a measure of how fast a firm is selling its inventory. Other indicators are how well a company collects from creditors, the percent of total revenues that are consumed by administrative expenses, and the amount of total expenses that must be paid each month regardless of the amount of sales.

current ratio
A measure of a firm's ability to pay its bills.

The Need for a Long-Term Outlook

As we evaluate the financial health of a company, we need to look at two comparative pieces of information: (1) How has the business performed over time? (2) How has it performed or is it expected to perform compared with its industry in general?

inventory turnover ratio
A measure of how fast a firm is selling its inventory.

The Business Over Time

Determining the value of a business on a given day is important. But more important is looking at how it has done over time. Thus, one measure might be the average value of the firm's stock over a period of several years. This longer-term outlook would offset the inevitable peaks and valleys in the value of the stock. A significant event in the industry, the economy, or the company can affect the stock price dramatically. It is not uncommon to see a particular stock drop in value by 20 percent over the course of a week. That drop is usually a reaction of the marketplace to some event.

Figure 18.2 uses the example of Best Buy to illustrate the difference between a short-run and a long-run perspective. The figure shows the variation in the price of Best Buy's stock over the three-month period ending November 18, 2002; the variation over the one-year period ending November 18, 2002; and the variation over the five-year period ending November 18, 2002. The three-month chart shows a slight up-and-down movement with the daily averages ranging from 18 to 26. This was a period of some uncertainty in the

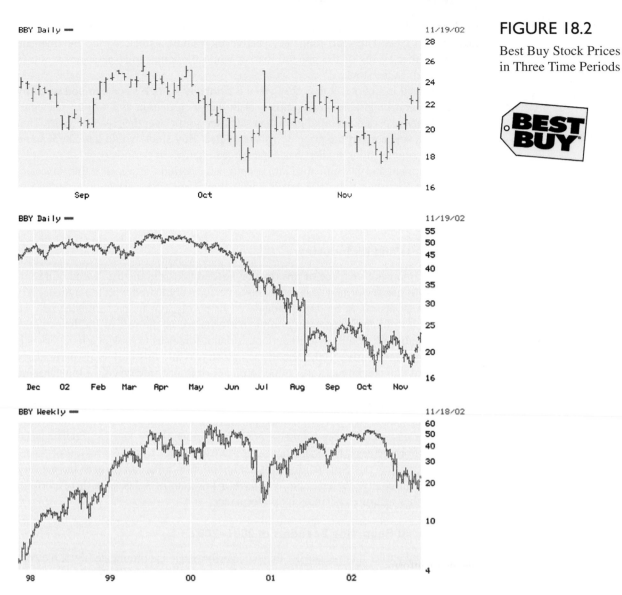

FIGURE 18.2

Best Buy Stock Prices
in Three Time Periods

Source: Best Buy Co., Inc. www.bigcharts.com (accessed November 18, 2002).

stock market indexes. It appears that Best Buy's stock price followed the short-tem variations in the stock indexes.

The one-year pattern shows Best Buy's stock hovering around $50 from December 2001 to May 2002 and then falling into the $25 range for the last part of the year. Thus, Best Buy's stock lost approximately half of its value in less than six months. Does this suggest that Best Buy's stock is not a good stock? To see for sure, go to the Internet and look at the Dow Jones Industrial Averages for the same period. You will see that this major stock market index dropped from 10,500 in May to a low of 7,100 in October. Again, Best Buy's stock followed the overal market closely.

The five-year pattern shows the price of a share of Best Buy stock rising from below $5 in 1998 to nearly $60 in early 2000. It then dropped to a low of around $15 in late 2000—probably reacting to the dot-com crash of 2000—and then climbed back up to over $50 before dropping back to around $25 near the end of 2002. Thus, while Best

Buy's stock clearly fluctuates significantly over time, its stock was still much higher in 2002 than in 1998. The short-range perspective shows how a stock's price can fluctuate based on either events or the general market while the long-range perspective shows overall trends in the stock.

You learned in Chapter 9 that changes in a company's stock price can be caused by something happening inside the company or in the stock market as a whole. The company itself has experienced rapid growth in sales and profit over the past five years. That alone would suggest that the price of a share of Best Buy stock would have kept going up. But the general stock market has experienced significant periods of what might be termed optimism and pessimism. During optimistic periods, it appears that investors pushed Best Buy shares to price levels higher than justified by earnings growth. And during pessimistic periods, it appears that investors pushed the price of Best Buy stock below the level that would be expected based on the company's earnings.

The Business and Its Industry

The second comparative piece of information needed to assess the true value of a company is how it has performed or is projected to perform compared with the industry it is in. A firm may appear to be doing either well or poorly, but its performance may be viewed much differently depending on the performance of the rest of the firms in the industry. The benefit of a long-term outlook is that it forces us to look at a business as it changes over time relative to the rest of the industry. While this outlook is particularly true in regard to financial measures of performance, it is also true when we look at some of the softer measures, such as meeting customer needs, which we discuss next.

Before leaving the financial perspective, consider again the need for integrative measures. In this section, we have discussed profit, return on equity, cash flow, net worth, and stock prices. Many more elements could be included. The key to good financial analysis is thoroughness. Emphasizing one or two variables to the exclusion of others often leads to erroneous conclusions. It is not uncommon for a company to have a very good return on equity, for example, yet have a low rate of sales growth or perform poorly on other measures of financial performance.

The Financial Reporting Scandals of 2001–2002

We mentioned earlier that measuring financial performance is complicated by a plethora of accounting rules that allow a company significant flexibility in assigning and reporting revenues and expenses. Under some circumstances, companies can claim as sales revenue in one year agreements that will not lead to actual cash payments until future years. Firms can overstate profits by not counting certain actions that incur real future costs (such as the granting of stock options) or by failing to write off depreciating assets at a realistic rate. Firms can even cross the line and incorrectly classify items of expense in violation of generally accepted principles of accounting. WorldCom, for example, shocked the investor community in 2002 when it revealed that it had taken what were clearly operating expenses and reclassified them as a capital investment. The result made WorldCom's profit look much larger than it actually was. Similar activities resulted in overstated profits at Enron, Global Crossings, and Qwest Communications.

The potential seriousness of this issue was revealed in a poll of chief financial officers conducted by *BusinessWeek*

THINK ABOUT THIS

1. We have discussed several different measures of financial success. Why is there no single best measure?

2. Why is the cash flow measure so important for small businesses?

3. Why are stock prices on a single day typically not a good measure of the financial success of a company?

at its annual forum for chief financial officers back in 1998, long before the 2001–2002 financial scandals began.[6] Sixty-seven percent of the 160 respondents reported then that they had been asked by other executives in their company to misrepresent the company's financial performance. Thankfully, only 12 percent said they had yielded to the pressures. Nevertheless, the potential for inaccurate financial reports exists and needs to be taken into account not only by investors but also by managers.

Companies today are beginning to take closer looks at their accounting practices. Business leaders are recognizing that part of the measurement of performance must be to ensure that the measurement itself is ethical and meets the most stringent tests. Congress is also getting involved to set more explicit rules regarding what is fair. This stringent attitude among business leaders and rule makers is reasonable because only when the *measurement procedures* are beyond reproach can the measurement of results be totally credible.

The Customer Perspective

The second indicator of success that must be measured is the customer perspective. This aspect of measuring performance includes three areas: meeting customer needs, customer sensitivity and service, and timeliness. You will recall that we discussed these areas in Chapters 14 and 15. We look at them here from an evaluative framework. Here we ask, How well has the company done?

Companies in competitive industries, such as the technology industry in which Dell operates, must constantly monitor both quality and innovation. How does a business know whether or not its approaches to innovation are working?

Meeting Customer Needs

Healthy financial performance can come only if a business successfully meets its customers' needs over time. The difference between a high-quality growth company that perseveres over time and one that struggles continuously is often the degree to which the firm commits to meeting its customers' needs. Assessing performance in meeting customer needs is far more complicated than assessing a firm's financial performance, because there are no easily calculated figures measured in a recognized unit such as dollars. Further, it is nearly impossible to compare one firm's performance with another's because of the lack of a standardized measure. In spite of these problems, some companies are well known as highly customer-oriented firms while others are not held in such high esteem.

The importance of measuring how well a given product or service meets customer needs is that the unmeasured problem will never be corrected until it is too late. Consider a restaurant in your community. The restaurant's food is acceptable, and its ambience is good. But if the service is poor or of erratic quality, customers will not come back. More importantly, they may never tell the owner of the restaurant that they are displeased with the service. They simply do not return. The owner doesn't know what the problem is until it is too late. Word of mouth has done more damage than advertising can correct, and the restaurant slowly dies.

Gap Analysis

gap analysis
The study of customers' satisfaction with a firm's product or service compared with their expectations.

A key to assessing performance in meeting customer needs is a **gap analysis,** the study of customers' satisfaction with a firm's product or service compared with their expectations.[7] This process is shown in Figure 18.3.

Determining the Gap   The first step in gap analysis is to determine whether there is a gap between customer expectations and perceptions. This step entails communicating with customers to determine precisely what their expectations were and how their perceptions of the firm's performance compared. Care must be taken to determine what customers' expectations really are, not what the firm's managers think customers'

FIGURE 18.3

Gap Analysis of Customer Needs

Step 1: Determining gap
• Customer expectations minus customer perceptions equals gap.

Step 2: Identifying sources of gaps
• Incorrect expectations.
• Incorrect product or service design.
• Inadequate actual performance.
• Inadequate follow-up.

Step 3: Taking corrective action
• Commitment to solving problem.
• Communication.
• Reassessment of gap.

Source: Valerie A. Zeithaml and Mary Jo Bitner, *Services Marketing: Integrating Customer Focus Across the Firm* (New York: Irwin/McGraw-Hill, 2000) p. 18.

expectations are. Continuous improvement must aim at closing the real gap rather than what management thinks is the gap.

Gap analysis is often the essence of the plan companies use to enter new markets. Consider Eclipse Aviation Corporation's efforts (discussed earlier in the book) to enter the business jet market. Eclipse was founded by former Microsoft executive Vern Raburn. He was convinced that the corporate jet aircraft currently on the market failed to meet customer expectations in a number of ways. They were too expensive; they needed better flight control and safety equipment; they could not land at and take off from smaller airports; and the operating costs were too high. Eclipse focused on eliminating those gaps. To do so, the company had to find innovative ways of designing and building the jet. In 2002, Eclipse introduced a twin-engine jet that cost $850,000 (one-third the cost of the lowest-priced competitor's product), could land at and take off from any small airport, and had computerized controls and safety features similar to those of the Boeing 777. Eclipse still had to put the aircraft through a year of stiff tests by the federal government before it could be sold to corporate customers. But gap analysis had clearly positioned Eclipse to trump the competition.[8]

Identifying the Sources and Causes of Gaps   The second part of gap analysis requires deeper study to determine the sources and causes of the gap. Gaps between expectations and perceived performance may come from either incorrect expectations, poor design, inadequate performance, or inadequate follow-up. Managers must identify the source because each requires a different kind of corrective action.

Sometimes the gap is caused by nothing more than incorrect expectations. Perhaps the company communicated inappropriate expectations in the first place. The problem may stem from faulty communication in which customers became confused over what to expect. It may stem from a company's management promising more than it can deliver. For example, if a car manufacturer claims that its sports car can go from zero to 60 miles per hour in 7.5 seconds, a buyer may purchase the car and then find that it can achieve that performance only in the most controlled situation. Under normal conditions, the car can be expected to take 9.5 seconds to reach 60 miles per hour. Thus, the company communicated unrealistic expectations for its high-performance car. Interestingly, a buyer of a more traditional car would not have those expectations and therefore would not be displeased by slower acceleration. So the key is to match communicated expectations with the logically expected performance. It is not uncommon today to hear executives telling their employees to "underpromise and overdeliver." This directive means that management wants to avoid an expectation gap.

A second source of gaps is in the design and manufacture of a product or in the development of a service. In this case, customer expectations are assessed correctly, but the product design team develops a product that does not do what it is supposed to do. In service businesses, the equivalent of product design flaws is the failure to develop a system to ensure good service. The equivalent of a defect might be insufficient training of service providers.

A third source of gaps deals with actual performance in producing a product, providing service, or providing after-sale service. This gap may be caused by poorly trained employees, poor internal communications, supplier problems, inappropriate delivery systems, or insufficient coordination between various groups within the organization.

Follow-up service includes warranties and willingness to accept returned merchandise or redo work. Managers should periodically consult with their customers to assess how well the warranties are meeting the customers' needs. Sensitivity to customers who have warranty calls not only builds loyalty, but also encourages customers to communicate even more with the business to let them know how their perceptions match their expectations.

Taking Corrective Action   Taking immediate action will remove gaps between expectations and performance that may have developed accidentally. Most customers accept the fact that companies occasionally make a mistake. Consider the following example: Suppose that you always take your film to a local drugstore chain for processing because it has quality developing and a one-day turnaround. Once, when you returned to pick up your photos, you found the store had lost them. The degree to which you were irate depended partially on how critical the pictures were. Perhaps more important, however, was the store's response to its mistake. Although the pictures might be lost forever, the store manager could give you free film and other goodies to assuage your disappointment. If the manager tried hard enough, the store would not lose you as a customer.

We have mentioned the importance of communication several times in this chapter and, indeed, throughout the book. Communication is perhaps nowhere more important than in removing gaps between performance and expectations. It assures customers that they are important and their concern is a high priority. It helps managers know precisely what the problem is and whether the solution implemented solved the problem. Managers should communicate with their customers, their employees, and their other stakeholders every day. Then when performance gaps do occur, all parties feel comfortable discussing problems and solutions.

Finally, managers must constantly reassess performance and expectations. Continuous improvement truly is a continuous process. It should become a routine task for decision makers to be constantly collecting information, constantly assessing, and constantly improving performance.

Measuring Sensitivity and Service to Customers

The managers of a healthy firm know that meeting customer needs is a key to being financially sound. Managers need to be in touch with customers to assess their needs. The gap analysis is a measurement tool for customer service.

A related but different concept that must also be measured is sensitivity to customers, or how well the business reacts to customer communications. How does the business respond to customer requests and complaints?

Gap analysis is insufficient for this measurement because it assumes a level of customer expectations and company performance. Sensitivity to customers, on the other hand, is often an impromptu action. It involves reacting, on the spot, to accommodate customers. It may even require empowering frontline employees to react immediately to a shifting customer need and then report that shift to higher levels in the organization for further study.

Monitoring customer sensitivity is important because it builds increasing loyalty in customers. It also gives the business powerful feedback from its customers, which can be used for competitive purposes. For example, a computer maker receives a note from a customer saying it would sure be nice if its computer monitors had a little container built in or attached to hold pens and removable memo stickers. The manufacturer's representative responds immediately by sending the customer a container held on by Velcro that she found at a supply store. But the rep also passes the suggestion on to the monitor design department, which redesigns the monitor case with a container that is built into the monitor and doubles as a carrying handle.

A number of manufacturers have telephone hot lines specifically to receive complaints and comments from their customers. Whirlpool dubs its toll-free number its "cool line" because having someone listen to their complaints keeps the customers cool. The cool line is also a ready source of new ideas for the firm's appliances.

Since customer sensitivity is often a one-on-one action, it is difficult to measure how well the company does. Still, indicators such as letters of appreciation provide a clue.

Interestingly, customers will often let the company know when it has done an unusually outstanding job in serving them one way or another. This type of response is above and beyond their response to the normally expected excellent service.

The opposite of the letter of appreciation is, of course, the complaint letter. These must be not only answered but also studied carefully to determine precisely what the problem is and what caused it.

A second measure of customer sensitivity (or lack thereof) is **second-level communications,** those communications that customers make only when their first attempt at gaining satisfaction proves fruitless. Suppose you have a complaint about the answering machine you recently purchased. You take the machine back to the store where you purchased it, and the salesperson tells you the store cannot fix the equipment because it is no longer under warranty. Feeling that you were treated unfairly, you then contact either the store manager or the manufacturer. This contact is second-level communication. The more sensitive a company is to its customers, the fewer second-level communications it should have.

Sometimes companies receiving second-level communications really cannot help the customer. Sometimes the customer's complaint is unjustified, and sometimes it is beyond the company's control. Even when a company cannot do anything to resolve a problem, however, the second-level communication must receive high priority as a way to minimize damage. These communications should be recorded to determine if the problem is unique or common. Both corrective action and preventive action should be taken when possible.

> **second-level communications**
> Communication that customers make only when their first attempt to gain satisfaction proves fruitless.

Measuring Timeliness

There are virtually no areas where timeliness cannot be measured. Measuring timeliness is an important efficiency measure. It is also an important customer service measure.

Manufacturers measure the time it takes to produce a product after the order is received. Suppliers measure how long it takes to make a delivery. Product development departments measure how long it takes to develop and test a new product. Service companies measure how long it takes to provide a service to their customers.

Response time is particularly important when the service is being provided on-site. Arrival at the scheduled time lets customers plan their own activities around the arrival of the service personnel. Measuring timeliness is important, whether the company is a Fortune 500 multinational providing a multimillion-dollar installation or a small clothing store whose owner wants to have the right number of employees on the floor.

Consider the following example: Chili's restaurants measure their timeliness in seating customers. When customers come in, the host records the time they entered, the waiting time promised, and the time they were seated. This procedure does two things. It tells the restaurant managers if the customers were seated in less time than promised—a measure of customer service relating to delivering what you promise. It also gives the managers information about the relative supply and demand for tables in their restaurant. Managers know roughly how long the average customer is willing to wait to be seated before going to a competitor. By recording the waiting times as well as the number of would-be customers who left, the manager can get a feel for how severe the loss of customers is.

Adjusting performance on the basis of the timeliness measure is a judgment call. Having the absolutely fastest service does not necessarily mean that a business will capture market share, but having the slowest service will often cause the business to lose market share when customers have other choices. Managers must determine the trade-offs between timeliness and costs. If response time is at least adequate, the manager may not want to add personnel or change the operating system because the change might be more costly than the benefit of quicker response time. For example, a nice sit-down restaurant might have somewhat slow service. However, if the patrons do not mind and even enjoy the ambience while waiting for their food, the problem may not warrant additional cooking or table service staff. By contrast, if customers at a fast-food restaurant wait more than three minutes, they become upset.

The Quality and Value Perspective

Assessing the third indicator of success, quality and value, is difficult because the measure is something of a moving target. We mentioned that financial performance must be measured in comparison with that of other firms as well as with its own historical performance. The same holds true for quality. Businesses can get a better picture of the quality of their service or products if they benchmark it with that of other businesses.

Quality Indicators

In Chapter 14, we presented eight indicators of quality: overall performance, unique features of the product or service, reliability, durability, serviceability, response time, aesthetics, and overall reputation. You may recall from Table 14.1 that we included examples of measurements of each indicator for both products and services. It is important that specific measurements be developed for each indicator. In most cases, multiple measures can be found. These measures can then be compared with the company's own performance in the past and with the performance of other companies.

Consider measures for a hypothetical bicycle manufacturer, shown in Table 18.5. Performance could be measured by the overall ride or feel of the bike. Features might include the unique quality of the frame or additional accessories that are included as standard on the company's bikes. Reliability is measured by the number of times a bike is returned to the shop for repair. Durability relates to how long the bicycle lasts. Serviceability could be indicated by the ease of changing out parts. Response could be the responsiveness of the dealer in working with customers. Aesthetics relates to how the bike looks. Finally, reputation is the image that the company and the dealer have in the mind of the customer.

TABLE 18.5

Indicators of Quality for a Bicycle Manufacturer and Corresponding Measures

Indicator	Measurement
Performance	Overall feel and ride of the bike.
Features	Frame construction; additional standard accessories.
Reliability	Repair frequency.
Durability	Bike's expected life under various conditions.
Serviceability	Ease of working on the bike.
Response	Responsiveness of dealer to complaints.
Aesthetics	How the bike looks.
Reputation	Image of company and dealer.

Source: Adapted from Richard Chase, Nicholas Aquilano, and Robert Jacobs, *Production and Operations Management,* 9th ed. (New York: Irwin/McGraw-Hill, 2001), p. 267.

Liz Claiborne fashions are known for their style and overall quality. Which of the quality indicators do you think are most important for Liz Claiborne?

Emphasis on Measurement

Dell attributes its success in part to its use of measurements. In 1993, Michael Dell launched an effort to improve performance through better measurement. A consulting firm was hired to develop new and better measurements, which were targeted at Dell's individual business units. Managers of those units were given responsibility for measuring performance and were held accountable for achieving measurable results. Michael Dell recalls that "there were some managers within Dell who resisted the use of facts and data in daily decision making, and as painful as it was for all of us, they eventually left. But for the most part, people were very energized by the change."[9]

Let's consider how to measure quality. First, we must define what we mean by quality in our particular business. Then, we ask customers what they mean by quality. What is important to them? What aspects of the service or product do they like? What do they want to avoid? Blending our definitions and the customers' definitions gives us an idea of what is really important. Next, we set out to find ways of measuring those items. We may measure defects. We may measure the number of phone calls we get from irate customers. Perhaps we measure the number of thank-you notes from happy customers. We could measure the number of repeat customers. We probably should measure the number of lost customers. We measure how long it takes to return a customer's computer. We measure how long restaurant patrons must wait to be seated. We measure the amount of food left on their plates.

We measure anything under our control, but we also collect information on those things that are not currently under our control. Then we see if we can find a way to control them, or at least overcome the problem.

As we discussed in Chapter 14, one of the quality management programs is the Six Sigma approach. A key to Six Sigma is the focus on measurement of results. To measure those results, a company must have a total understanding and acceptance of the Six

TABLE 18.6

Guidelines for Selecting, Setting up, and Getting Results from a Quality Measurement Program

Step 1: Get leaders involved. When upper managers are engaged, you've got the freedom to make real changes—based on what the metrics tell you.

Step 2: Visually represent your metrics. Prominently display them in charts, graphs and diagrams to show your employees what you're trying to do and how they are involved.

Step 3: Metrics must respond quickly. Your measurement system must provide feedback promptly, so you can identify problems and correct them as soon as possible.

Step 4: Metrics must be simple. Avoid setting up complex measurements that are difficult to use.

Step 5: Metrics should drive only important activities. You need to assess the most important factors to measure . . . and then make sure that what you examine will result in information that is relevant.

Step 6: Limit the number of metrics. If you get bogged down in measurements, you can lose time and focus.

Step 7: Take corrective action. Act quickly, then move on to the next project and set new metrics.

Source: From P. Pande, *The Six Sigma Way.* Copyright © 2002 The McGraw-Hill Companies, Inc. Reproduced with permission of The McGraw-Hill Companies.

Sigma principles and their impact. Table 18.6 summarizes some of the principles of the approach. As you read the list of steps in that table, pay attention to the importance of getting commitment and understanding from both workers and management.

Measuring Innovation and Creativity

As we mentioned early in this chapter, it is important to measure processes as well as results. Creativity is a process. Innovations, the new products or services that come from creative efforts, are results. Both are important. Innovation is the fourth area in Figure 18.1 that should be measured. As the figure suggests, we should have goals for and measurements of innovation.

It can be difficult to measure innovation. It is easy to say, "We have a very innovative firm" or "Our people are creative visionaries." It is much harder to prove that. Thus, the measures of innovation and creativity are partially objective and partially subjective.

THINK ABOUT THIS

1. We have emphasized meeting customer needs throughout the text. How would you measure whether or not you are meeting customer needs?

2. Why is it important to distinguish customer sensitivity from meeting customer needs?

3. Step 6 of Table 18.6 suggests that we should limit the number of metrics. Shouldn't we measure everything possible?

Objective Measures

3M is recognized as one of the more creative and innovative firms in the United States. Its culture fosters creativity by giving employees the freedom to take risks and the encouragement to try out new ideas. 3M insists that new products—those developed in the past five years—make up a high percentage of its total product line. Thus, one measure of innovation for 3M is the number of new products introduced each year. 3M's record is impressive, with over 500 new patents awarded in 2001 alone. Growth-oriented firms keep track of additional indicators, such as the length of time to develop a new product, the number of patents held by the company, and the number of new patent applications each year.[10]

Subjective Measures

In addition to the objective measures of innovation and creativity, there are subjective measures. These deal to a large extent with the ambience of the workplace. The number of researchers who receive bonuses for inventions can be a surrogate measure of how creative the workforce is. The number of new product ideas submitted can suggest a climate of creativity.

Many new product ideas never see the light of day. Yet the business must encourage new ideas so that employees continue to be creative. The Post-it Note is a classic example of innovation. This interesting story from 3M includes developing glue that was supposed to be very strong but wouldn't stick, finding ways to trim a microthin slice off the paper to make room for the glue, and even selling the concept in an innovative way. But the product would not exist were it not for 3M's innovative culture. We will discuss more ways a business can foster creativity and innovation in Chapter 19.

More to Come
CHAPTER 19

Firms can also measure innovation subjectively just by assessing the excitement of workers. Often, innovative companies have very low turnover, low absenteeism, and employees who choose to work beyond the hours for which they are paid. But sometimes innovation actually leads to turnover—for example, in high-tech companies. Employees invariably develop ideas or products that the company, because of its limited financial position, cannot pursue. Thus, some employees may leave to start their own business, often with the blessing of their former employer.

The Employee Perspective

The final perspective on measurement deals with employees. A business needs to be able to measure how well it utilizes its workers, how good their performance actually is, and how committed they are.

Workforce Utilization and Productivity

Workforce productivity is relatively easy to measure as long as the workers are producing tangible products for which their individual input is both identifiable and controllable. Unfortunately, this measure leaves out almost all management jobs, most staff positions, and research jobs. It even leaves out most assembly-line jobs, since the rate of efficiency is not individually controllable. It also leaves out maintenance work and other jobs that are not tied directly to production. Thus, it is really quite difficult to assess the utilization of most employees.

Yet analysis of workforce utilization and productivity is important for efficiency reasons. We measure productivity by dividing total sales or total profits by the number of workers in the company. If a firm can eliminate 10 percent

THINK ABOUT THIS

1. How will innovation in an accounting firm differ from that in a manufacturing firm?
2. Why is innovation difficult to measure objectively?
3. If innovation is difficult to measure, how does a business go about rewarding it?

of its workforce and still maintain the same level of sales, it will increase productivity. Similarly, if it maintains the same number of workers but can increase their output, it will experience an increase in productivity.

Workforce productivity involves more than simply dividing numbers. It involves having the right people in the right jobs. It involves having motivated, well-trained employees supervised by effective managers. It involves having sufficient equipment so that employees can do the jobs they are assigned.

A firm can measure underutilization by observing worker behavior, looking at the total output per employee, and benchmarking with other departments or other companies. Sometimes colleagues or even the workers themselves complain that they are not being well used. It is difficult, however, to get an accurate assessment of underutilization because of workers' ability to hide idleness and management's inability to measure output of staff positions.

Overutilized workers can hurt the firm. Overworked employees may seem to be more efficient since they produce more output than others. However, they may eventually become unproductive or burn out if they are continually asked to do too much. One of the problems with downsizing has been that the remaining employees work excessively long hours to make up for the loss of their colleagues. Overutilization is easier to measure because of the visible evidence. Stressed-out employees, defective work, obvious fatigue, absenteeism, and other indicators can give managers a feel for the amount of overutilization.

A third situation facing managers is the inappropriate mix of workers and jobs. In this situation, the company has approximately the right number of employees, but they are misallocated. Thus, one department may have several underutilized workers while other departments are scrambling to keep up with their demands. Sometimes individual workers are simply in the wrong job. They cannot function properly because either they have insufficient training or they somehow got assigned a job that just does not fit their personality. A highly innovative employee stuck in a routine, control-oriented job is an example.

Unfortunately, managers may have little discretion in solving either underutilization, overutilization, or misallocation of workers. For example, budgetary constraints or the inability to reassign work from one person to another may limit a manager's ability to address these issues. Still, measuring the utilization of workers can be useful in assessing the overall health of the company.

Performance Appraisal

performance appraisal

The process a company uses to measure employee effectiveness.

Performance appraisal is the process the business uses to measure employee effectiveness. Performance appraisal may be approached in a number of ways. The intent is to measure how well the employee is doing and communicate that assessment to the employee so that, if necessary, improvements and corrective actions can take place.

Performance appraisal should focus on those activities and outcomes that are critical for performing the job. Both objective and subjective performance outcomes are usually assessed. Subjective assessments such as "works well with team members" or "provides timely information" may be difficult for any one person to assess properly, so some companies use what is known as *360-degree appraisal.* This approach means that employees are assessed or rated by everyone with whom they have key interactions. Co-workers, outside customers, key people in other departments, the boss, and subordinates may all evaluate the employees and offer their sense of whether individuals provide timely information, for example. The range of perspectives should offer a more complete picture of how employees are doing on each performance factor.[11] Most large firms today use some form of 360-degree assessment.

Employee Satisfaction and Commitment

Healthy businesses must have a sense of how employees feel about their work. For these companies, assessing employee satisfaction is fundamental for building the business culture they desire. *Fortune's* 2002 survey of the best companies to work for presents an overview of some of the factors that need to be considered and therefore measured. As you might expect, the list includes good pay, management honesty, good vacation and sick leave policies, treatment of employees with respect and consideration, good retirement and profit sharing benefits, good family policies, and encouragement of involvement in community service.[12] One major form of measurement is to benchmark the company's performance in each of these areas against what is being done by other companies, particularly competitors. In addition, and perhaps more important, management must find ways to measure the satisfaction and commitment of its own employees.

Home Depot provides competitive pay, excellent benefits, teamwork, and a casual work environment. How could Home Depot determine if these policies are having a positive impact on employee satisfaction and commitment?

How do businesses measure employee satisfaction and the level of commitment? A number of approaches are possible. First, managers can infer employee satisfaction and commitment by looking at the levels of absenteeism and turnover in the business. **Absenteeism** occurs when employees do not show up at work when they are scheduled to be there. In general, higher levels of absenteeism suggest higher levels of employee dissatisfaction with the business or their particular jobs. However, a caution should be noted here. Sometimes people are absent from their jobs for uncontrollable reasons, such as personal or family illnesses. These absences have nothing to do with their satisfaction with or attitude toward the job. It is controllable absenteeism, in which employees simply decide not to come to work on a given day, that can be an indicator of employee dissatisfaction.

Turnover occurs when employees voluntarily leave the company. Turnover can be affected by many factors, including the range of other employment opportunities available. In general, high levels of voluntary turnover suggest that employees are dissatisfied with some important aspects of the job. A manager must be careful with assessments in this area. Some turnover is natural in any business. However, if 6 of the 10 employees in information services have left in the past year, some aspect of dissatisfaction is likely to be present. Because of the high cost of replacing skilled employees, the causes of turnover should be identified and addressed.

Some companies conduct *morale* or *opinion surveys* periodically to assess employee satisfaction and overall attitudes toward the business. Some use outside consultants to conduct these surveys to help ensure objectivity and confidentiality. Morale and opinion surveys can be quite detailed and can point out specific areas or practices that employees object to. These surveys may reveal employee views that managers had already suspected—for example, frustration about heavy workloads or disappointment with low pay raises. However, surveys can reveal important employee insights that surprise managers. For example, as a result of downsizings, employees may say that

absenteeism
A situation in which employees do not show up at work when scheduled to be there.

turnover
A situation in which employees voluntarily leave a company.

THINK ABOUT THIS

1. Often the most important indicators of employee performance are difficult to measure. How does the 360-degree appraisal approach provide a better measurement of employee performance than a manager alone could provide?

2. Which is worse, underutilization or overutilization of the workforce? What are the impacts of each?

3. Define *employee satisfaction*. Now apply your definition to an actual company situation. Does your definition work?

they distrust management and feel that communication and respect are poor in the business. While such feedback may be tough to accept, the enlightened manager takes it seriously and searches for ways to improve employee commitment.

Many companies do *exit interviews* of employees who are leaving the company. It is unfortunate that the information is gained after the fact in these cases, but it is still good information. Exit interviews can be extremely accurate and insightful. Since the interviewees are severing ties with the business, they may be willing to share views or concerns they were reluctant to express while they were employees.

Other indicators of employee commitment and satisfaction exist. The number of formal complaints or grievances lodged against management or other employees, attempts to unionize nonunion firms, and strikes or walkouts at unionized firms are all measurable statistics that can give a clue whether employees are satisfied with their workplace.

In addition to these objective measures, a number of more subjective approaches are available. Regular staff meetings to discuss employee problems, recruitment and retention committees, employee focus groups, open door policies, specific opportunities for employees to discuss problems, and even suggestion boxes can all indicate the general level and nature of employee satisfaction.

One subjective measure of employee commitment is how willing employees are to do things above and beyond the call of duty. At Southwest Airlines, it is common for employees to work long hours. It is also common to see them helping co-workers with tasks that are not in their own job description. This loyalty was built, of course, by Herb Kelleher, who served drinks and snacks on a plane when he flew. Or consider this comment from President Colleen Barrett: "I'm a very sentimental person. I like to share good, wholesome thoughts with people. Around here, I'm affectionately thought of as the "Mom of Southwest," and I consider my personal and professional families to be one and intertwined."[13] Loyalty is strengthened when the top people take that kind of interest.

Other companies may have innovative ways of measuring employee satisfaction and commitment. How these employee concerns are measured is not nearly as important as the fact that they are measured and acted on. Companies must constantly be assessing their performance in employee commitment and satisfaction as indicators of business health.

THE BIG PICTURE

Measurement is what distinguishes businesses from other types of organizations. One of the most common questions that has been adopted for general use from the experience of business is, What is the bottom line? Anytime someone uses that term you know that it is time to start considering final results—past, present, or future.

The notion of measuring performance in terms of the bottom line is often misunderstood by the general public. To them, the term is often associated strictly with profits. In this chapter, you learned the error in such thinking. You found out that although financial performance is an important part of measuring performance, there are several other major dimensions. You also learned that successful businesses pay attention to all dimensions of performance rather than myopically stressing one aspect. By now you know that this habit of paying attention to all major aspects of the business is what we mean by the title of this textbook, *Business: An Integrative Approach*. This insight is part of the big picture which you should understand after carefully studying this chapter.

Throughout your career in business, you will probably be faced with situations in which you must explain this point to your employees, your employer, or your fellow managers. Business history is littered with the wrecks of companies that forgot this lesson and focused on one measure of performance to the exclusion of others. The most common mistake is to focus strictly on financial performance. This practice might lead to excellent short-run profits but could be followed by a disastrous loss of competitiveness because of the failure to pay attention to the other aspects of the business.

A second part of the big picture is the recognition that measurement can be carried too far. It is an unfortunate fact of business life that many of the aspects of a business that are most crucial to success are also impossible to measure with a high degree of accuracy. Thus, after all the measurements have been made, there still remains substantial room for judgment by a business leader. To convince yourself of this fact, look back over the earlier chapters and ask whether, in the final analysis, managers have to use subjective judgment. To begin, consider the chapters on the economic, financial, and international environments. All these areas are subject to random disturbances that can cause a company's financial measurements to give false signals. So when managers look at the financial data, they have to make subjective adjustments for such disturbances. Or consider the chapters on quality products, effectively communicating with customers, and encouraging commitment. You can see how a manager's attempt to measure performance in any of these areas must, of necessity, be subjective. But you can also see how the use of performance measures can lead to better subjective judgments.

Summary

1. Daily newspapers make it look easy to measure the performance of a business. They present reports on profits and sales and leave the reader with the impression that everything important has been covered. But measurement is much more complicated. To begin with, a number of important caveats must be kept in mind with any attempt to measure business performance.

   - What are some of the important cautions that should be considered in the measurement process?

   Five caveats are as follows: (1) Measurements are interrelated and not performed in a vacuum, (2) we must measure both efficiency and effectiveness, (3) we must measure processes as well as results, (4) we must measure dynamically, not just statically, and (5) measurement must foster communication.

2. Another aspect of the complexity of measurement is that it involves far more than simply looking at the financial performance of a company.

   - What are the elements of a comprehensive model of performance measurement for a business?

   A comprehensive model of measurement revolves around the company's vision and strategy and consists of measurements in the following five areas of concern: (1) financial perspective, (2) customer perspective, (3) quality perspective, (4) innovation and creativity perspective, and (5) employee perspective.

3. The accounting and financial perspective usually receives the most attention. People not familiar with business probably think of this perspective as a simple matter of reporting sales or profits. But financial performance is more complex than that.

   - What are the major measures of financial performance?

The major measures are the following:

(1) Profit in the most basic sense is total revenue minus total expenses. A second important measure of profit is return on equity investment (defined as profit or net income divided by investment by the owners). A third important measure is earnings per share (determined by dividing net earnings or net profit by the number of shares of stock outstanding).

(2) Cash flow measures actual cash coming into and going out of the business. Cash flow differs from profit because some revenue items do not come in the form of cash and some expense items do not involve cash outlays.

(3) Net worth is the value of a company. For publicly held firms, analysts measure it by multiplying the stock price times the number of shares outstanding. They can also measure it by subtracting liabilities from net assets.

• Where does one find measurement information for a company?

Three primary sources are the following:

(1) The income statement shows the performance of a company over the course of a specific time period, usually a quarter of a year or a year.

(2) The cash flow statement shows the amount of cash that comes into and leaves the company over time.

(3) The balance sheet shows a company's assets, liabilities, and net worth at a specific point in time.

4. Financial measurement is important and basic. Nevertheless, it tells only part of the story. Businesses occasionally show excellent financial performance at a time when trouble is on the horizon because of a failure to adequately meet evolving customer needs, develop new products and services, or cultivate employee relationships.

   • What are the major considerations involved in measuring performance from the customer perspective?

Customer satisfaction involves meeting customer expectations in three areas, each of which needs to be measured:

(1) Meeting customer needs can be measured with a gap analysis, which involves comparing customer expectations with customer satisfaction.

(2) Customer sensitivity and service can be measured by complaints and by communication with higher levels of management.

(3) Timeliness applies to virtually all areas of the business. It can be measured with such indicators as length of time to produce a product and length of time a retail customer has to wait before being served.

5. Another area that requires measurement is the company's progress in meeting its quality goals.

   • How does a company measure quality?

Quality indicators include performance, features, reliability, durability, serviceability, response, aesthetics, and reputation.

6. In today's world, businesses must continually adapt and innovate. Some companies are known for their innovations.

   • What are the major considerations involved in measuring performance from the innovation perspective?

This area involves both objective and subjective indicators:

(1) Objective indicators include average time to market for new products, new-product sales dollars as a percentage of total sales dollars, and R&D expenditures as a percentage of sales.

(2) Subjective measures include the ambience of the workplace and the number of new ideas submitted.

7. Organizations cannot be successful over time without committed employees. Measuring commitment and satisfaction is important for building work environments where employees feel motivated.

- What are the major considerations involved in measuring performance from the employee perspective?

Three themes must be considered:

(1) Workforce utilization can be measured by observing worker behavior and by benchmarking with other departments and companies. Workforce productivity can be measured by dividing total sales or total profits by the number of workers.

(2) Performance appraisals are used to assess the productivity of individual employees.

(3) Employee satisfaction and commitment can be measured by such techniques as employee surveys, employee focus groups, and employee complaint records.

Key Terms

absenteeism, p. 479

balance sheet, p. 465

current ratio, p. 466

debt ratio, p. 466

dynamic measurements, p. 457

earnings per share (EPS), p. 460

effectiveness, p. 456

efficiency, p. 456

gap analysis, p. 470

income statement, p. 462

integrated assessment, p. 456

inventory turnover ratio, p. 466

net worth, p. 462

performance appraisal, p. 478

return on equity (ROE), p. 460

second-level communications, p. 473

turnover, p. 479

Exercises and Applications

1. Most large businesses post their annual reports on their websites. These annual reports contain both balance sheets and income statements. Evaluate the balance sheet and income statement for one of the following businesses: Apple Computer, Southwest Airlines, AT&T, or Kodak. What can you tell about the business, its level of success, and the direction it's likely to move in the future?

2. As a team, identify five important measures of customer satisfaction. Then select a business with which you are familiar. How does it rate on your five measures?

3. Using the measures of service quality discussed in the chapter, evaluate the service quality of your school's food-service provider.

4. In teams, brainstorm measures of employee satisfaction. Then discuss how easy each would be to measure and how accurate the measure might be. Write a two-page summary of your conclusions.

5. As this chapter has noted, measurement must take into account a number of factors. In teams, discuss how this course should be evaluated. Prepare a one-page paper

outlining the measures you would use to determine whether the class has been successful.

6. Interview one manufacturer and one service business in your community. How does each measure quality? In a two-page paper, compare the measures used by the businesses.

FROM THE PAGES OF

BusinessWeek

Steve Ballmer Turns to Metrics

There isn't another company in the world as closely identified with its leader as Microsoft Corp. has been with William H. Gates III . . . But Gates no longer runs Microsoft. He gave up the chief executive role 2 1/2 years ago to his best friend and longtime management sidekick, Steven A. Ballmer . . . The 46-year-old Ballmer is not content to tend the machine Gates designed. His goal: to create a "great, long-lasting company" that will be even more successful.

(T)he new CEO is calling on his colleagues to do nothing less than rethink every aspect of the way they do their jobs. He has put in place a set of management processes aimed at bridging the gap between the sales and product-development sides of the company . . . To make it all stick, Ballmer has concocted a dizzying array of meetings, reviews, and examinations that force people to do their jobs differently. It includes everything from rank-and-file employees grading their supervisors to an accounting system for managers that helps them weigh spending trade-offs . . . Each new process is designed to hook into the next so decisions can be made quickly—and can later be measured. This is light-years away from the ad hoc way Microsoft took action before. The final touch: Ballmer is making adoption of the new corporate values a part of every employee's annual performance review. Ballmer's hope is that his code of conduct will also make Microsoft a better corporate citizen. He says the company's core values of honesty, integrity, and respect must shine through with customers, partners, and the tech industry.

Ballmer's chief challenges . . . are internal. One is the danger that so much attention to management processes and the myriad metrics of evaluating performance could stifle innovation . . . "Policy is an abdication of thought," says former Microsoft chief technologist Nathan Myhrvold. "If you hire process-oriented guys, it's probable that an idea never bubbles up."

Decision Questions

1. What are the benefits of measurement suggested by this article?

2. Ballmer says he wants the company's core values to "shine through" and expects to measure each employee's performance in terms of the company's values. How might a company measure an employee's performance in this regard?

3. Some say that measurement can be overdone. What is the major danger of overdoing measurement according to this article? Can you think of other undesirable results that could come from too much measurement?

4. The article indicates that under Bill Gates, Microsoft was a company that did not closely or systematically measure employee performance. Does this indicate that Gates wasn't as good a manager as he could have been?

Source: Jay Greene, Steve Hamm, and Jim Kerstetter, "Ballmer's Microsoft," *BusinessWeek*, June 17, 2002, pp. 66–75.

References

1. Robert Berner, "Why P&G's Smile Is So Bright," *BusinessWeek,* August 12, 2002, pp. 58–60.

2. Information for this section was adapted from The Price Waterhouse Change Integration Team, *The Paradox Principles* (Burr Ridge, IL: Irwin, 1996), chap.12.

3. Robert S. Kaplan and David P. Norton, "Using the Balanced Scorecard as a Strategic Management System," *Harvard Business Review,* January–February 1992, pp. 71–79.

4. "The Best Performers," *The Business Week 50,* Spring 2002, pp. 27–41.

5. Both statements can be found in Dell's annual report for the fiscal year ended February 1, 2002. www.dell.com/us/en/gen/corporate/investor/investor.htm (accessed October 17, 2002).

6. James Grant, "Lower Stock Prices Will Cure What Ails the Markets," *The Wall Street Journal,* July 9, 2002, p. A18. The original report of the survey appeared in an advertising supplement in the July 13, 1998, issue of *BusinessWeek.*

7. This discussion was drawn from Valerie A. Zeithaml and Mary Jo Bitner, *Services Marketing: Integrating Customer Focus Across the Firm* (New York: Irwin/McGraw-Hill, 2000), chap. 18.

8. J. Lynn Lunsford, "Tech Pioneer's New Business Jet: Seats Six for $850,000," *The Wall Street Journal,* July 12, 2002, p. B1.

9. Michael Dell, *Direct from Dell* (New York: HarperBusiness, 1999), pp. 61–62.

10. "3M Facts," www.3m.com/about3M/facts/3mfacts.jhtml (accessed October 17, 2002).

11. For a review of 360-degree appraisal, see Cynthia D. Fisher, Lyle F. Schoenfeldt, and James B. Shaw, *Human Resource Management,* 5th ed. (Boston: Houghton Mifflin, 2003), pp. 521–523.

12. Daniel Roth, "How to Cut Pay, Lay Off 8,000 People and Still Have Workers Who Love You," *Fortune,* February 4, 2002, pp. 62–90.

13. Nancy Holt, "Workplaces," *The Wall Street Journal,* July 31, 2002, p. B6.

19

Promoting Change and Renewal

It is an amazing story of entrepreneurship, innovation, and the constant drive to improve performance. In the early 1960s, legendary University of Oregon track coach Bill Bowerman and one of his middle-distance runners, Phil Knight, formed a partnership to import Japan's Onitsuka Tiger athletic shoes to the United States. They called their business Blue Ribbon Sports (BLS). But Bowerman was always tinkering with the Tiger designs, looking for ways to improve their performance, and Knight (an accounting major in college) chafed at the idea of improving someone else's products. Soon BLS gave way to a new company that built its own innovatively designed shoes. Today, that company, Nike, is the largest sports and fitness company in the world. And its company symbol, the Swoosh, is one of the best-known corporate symbols on the planet.

Led by CEO Knight, Nike has succeeded through its obsession with creativity. Innovation and change are the corporate watchwords. For example, global creative director John Hoke III has a staff of 75 designers who spend their days making high-performance athletic shoes better and better. From the Nike waffle to air-injected shoes, Nike designers have developed runaway product winners such as Air Jordans, and the company's revenues surged through most of the 1990s.

But even innovation-driven, highly successful organizations are not immune from the sweeping realities of business change. For Nike, the need for change hit in the late 1990s as its domination of the footwear market began to wane. Its advertising superstar, Michael Jordan, had moved out of the spotlight. Worse, many insiders argued that Nike had lost its "cool" image to brands such as Skechers and New Balance. The company's market share dropped 3 percent in just a two-year period.

But Nike, in the spirit of change, responded. Today, annual revenues are close to $10 billion, and Nike has staged a remarkable comeback. Nike has come back by creatively modifying its traditional high-tech performance gear business. New lines, such as Shox, Air Rift, and Air Presto, have led to strong growth in sales.

But the comeback has another unique feature. Many argue that Nike's resurgence is based on "becoming what. . . Phil Knight once swore it would never be: a fashion company." The evidence is convincing. Nike's fashion apparel business reaps some of the highest gross margins in the company. Of course, Nike has long been in the athletic clothes business. But its styles were just that—athletic accessories such as T-shirts, shorts, and sweat suits. Phil Knight saw the need for something more. He hired Mindy Grossman from Polo Jeans to lead the company's new efforts to design, manufacture, and merchandise its apparel line. Now, people are talking about Nike's active wear, which competes with such fashion-focused lines as Ralph Lauren and DKNY. And celebrities still promote Nike. Mia Hamm still has that Nike Swoosh on her shirt, and Tiger Woods has one on his cap. And even CEO Knight now concedes, "We're an apparel company as well as a shoe company."[1]

As Nike knows, the competitive business environment never stands still. A business that experiences glowing profits one year may find itself threatened by a flood of new competitors the next. A unique product that captures a select market niche one year may be cast aside the next if consumer tastes and preferences shift. Expansion opportunities that appear promising may be dashed by a sudden economic downturn and skyrocketing interest rates. Environmental threats and opportunities are always emerging and demanding action. Any change ripples through the business system, causing a series of interrelated challenges. This is the nature of business. This is part of the excitement, challenge, and risk that exist in contemporary business. Indeed, the successful business manager understands that change and renewal are facts of business life.

This final chapter restates the theme of innovation and change that we have explored throughout this book. Further, it offers you a glimpse into the study of change, which is critical for progressive leaders of the future.

After studying this chapter, you should be able to:

1. Describe Kurt Lewin's three stages of change.
2. Understand the nature and meaning of planned change.
3. Discuss the main features of the planned change process.
4. Define *innovation* and *competitive innovation*.
5. Identify some of the common sources or opportunities for innovation.
6. Describe some of the actions that healthy businesses take to promote creativity and innovation.
7. Apply some of the popular approaches to strategic change and renewal.

Throughout this book, starting with the model in Chapter 2, we have emphasized the topics of business change and renewal. Environmental forces and impacts are dynamic and moving. Customer preferences and demands are always shifting. Existing competitors are always fine-tuning their challenges, and formidable new rivals are arriving on the competitive scene at a dizzying rate. Without a doubt, contemporary business faces a turbulent environment that makes change and renewal a necessity of business operations. Indeed, as we have stressed since the first chapter, innovation and change are hallmarks of the successful business.

In the rapid-fire world of business, innovation and change are required for survival. If a business does not change over time, it will slip, lose its competitive edge, and eventually struggle to remain in business. Problems may not be apparent today or tomorrow or even in the next five years. Yet the business that arrogantly assumes it need not change is headed for disaster. To illustrate this awareness, Specialized Bicycle, Inc., has among its assets an old black hearse. Emblazoned across each side of it is this statement "Innovate or Die."

No business, no matter how successful, can isolate itself from the need for change. Consider Dell. Historically, Dell has viewed PC dealers as intermediaries who simply drive up the cost of the machine. Accordingly, Dell's success has been based on bypassing dealers and selling its PCs directly to customers. Yet, that view and approach changed somewhat in the summer of 2002 when Dell announced that it would sell generic, unbranded PCs to U.S. dealers who would in turn sell the PCs to small businesses. Dell even went so far as to offer financing and other support services to its dealers.

What's going on here? Dell recognizes that the best time to consider changes is not when a crisis looms, but when business is strong. Dell sees an opportunity to grow by moving beyond its traditional business. Certainly, this is an aggressive move because it places Dell directly into the territory occupied by giant competitors Hewlett-Packard and IBM. Yet the generic, no-name PCs, known as "white boxes," have about a 30 percent share of the U.S. PC market. According to analyst Bill Shope, the message is clear: "If Dell wants to focus on where it can generate continued growth in PCs, that white-box business is where it needs to be."[2]

Nissan was close to bankruptcy in the late 1990s. Today it is in the throes of a dramatic turnaround. The 350Z is a trendy reminder of the company's new energy and direction. What do you think customers are looking for in the highly competitive automobile industry?

It does not matter who you are. It does not matter how good or how successful you have been. You still must change and innovate. In some ways, change can be more difficult for large and highly successful businesses than for smaller and less successful firms. The successful business can easily become a victim of its own success and the closed thinking that success often spurs: Why should we change when we're the market leaders? This attitude promotes a short-sighted and dangerous stance.

Fifty years ago, the Swiss virtually dominated the world timepiece market. Nearly 90 percent of all watches produced throughout the world came from Swiss companies. Today the Swiss are minor players whose total share of world markets is less than 15 percent.[3] The international watch industry is now dominated by Japan and the United States. Much of this shift is due to new technology, notably the quartz watch. The Swiss were so successful and comfortable with their traditional mechanical watches that they were unwilling to adapt to the advances of the newer quartz technology. In their hesitation, they lost market share, and they are unlikely ever to recover. The odd side to this story is that quartz technology did not come from the United States or Japan. It came from the Swiss themselves. They simply did not accurately assess the impact it would have. Their traditional success paralyzed their movement. They wanted to keep things the way they were.

A small retail department store sold a variety of goods, including toys. Its selection was adequate and its prices were relatively high, so the store prospered—until a new competitor came to the community. Unfortunately, that competitor was Toys "R" Us. The small store's owners knew that Toys "R" Us was coming. Yet they did little to change their merchandise mix or their mode of operations. They finally reoriented their product mix toward craft supplies, but the restructuring came too late and the store failed. The store's managers knew change was critical, but they did not respond.

The Nature and Struggles of Planned Change

There are many ways to think of change. Some change is random and chaotic. It is thrust upon us and forces us to alter our intended course of action. For example, as you and your roommate jump in your car to take off for a spring break skiing trip in Colorado, the car won't start. You have to change your travel plans, unpack the car, and get a rental car instead. Such random change is part of life. Although it can be frustrating, there is little we can do except cope with such annoyances as best we can.

The same randomness occurs in business. One of the things that makes managing a business so difficult is the unexpected and unforeseen events that occur. Some of them are simply minor annoyances; others are major and can have a dramatic impact. For example, as owner of a small manufacturing shop, you employ only 80 people and produce specialized parts that are purchased by a number of larger businesses. This morning your most experienced information systems employee enters your office and declares that she must take an immediate leave of absence. She is visibly upset and barely able to speak. Her 75-year-old mother, who lives 1,000 miles away, has just suffered a stroke. Your employee is the only close family member. There was little prior warning of poor health. There is no way to predict how long your employee will have to be gone. Undoubtedly, her absence will necessitate some significant shuffling of people and will be a major inconvenience for the business. You will probably have to put the morning's planned activities on hold and address this pressing new event. Such unplanned change is part of business life. Through careful planning, you can minimize the unexpected, but you can never eliminate it.

Many organizations have attempted to address the unexpected by having a crisis management program in place. Although crises are generally unexpected and unpredictable, having a plan in place for addressing crises if and when they occur appears to make good business sense, particularly for businesses in which the potential for crisis is high. For example, no chemical company predicts a toxic spill, no manufacturer predicts an industrial accident, and no consumer product firm predicts a public relations gaffe. Yet, a reasonable chance exists that these events will happen at some point. The idea in crisis management is to have a program in place to respond. Some companies even have crisis management units poised to help make decisions and deal with the media when unfortunate events arise. The hope is that the crisis response will help the company bounce back from its setback.[4]

In this chapter, however, we are addressing a different kind of change—planned change. Unlike random and unforeseen events, planned change is intentional. It has been thought through and decisions have been made about how to deal with it. With this perspective in mind, we define **planned change** as the process of intentional movement from the present state toward some future state. This concept is not nearly as confusing as you might think. To explore this notion of change, consider Figure 19.1.

> **planned change**
> The process of intentional movement from the present state toward some future state.

Planned change is systematic, existing in three stages. First is the *present state,* followed by the *actual change,* an alteration of that established present state. The movement or change is toward some new set of activities, events, and outcomes known as the *future state.* This present state–actual change–future state way of looking at change is fairly direct and used often.

You have experienced this process of planned change. You entered this semester's classes with certain knowledge, skills, attitudes, and outlooks. That was your present state. Presumably, you desired a different state or you wouldn't be in college. You desired a future state where your knowledge and skills were fuller and more consistent with the demands of prospective employers. To reach this future state, you engaged in the process of movement. You attended college, studied, reflected on assignments, and perhaps even paid attention in class. Without these movements, the desired future state of increased levels of marketable skills and knowledge would not be possible.

Yet these movements were not always easy. Leaving home and coming to college was difficult for some of you. Disciplining yourself to study was rarely easy. Learning and challenging established views probably took courage. Change implies movement, and that movement, even for exciting and desired changes, is often trying.

This same sense of planned change holds for business. The present state is, of course, the business as it exists today. This present state is made up of existing technology, existing reward systems, existing jobs and activities, and existing structure and design. It also comprises existing views of the market and existing competitive strategies. Planned change occurs when the business takes well-thought-out actions to move from this present state to some desired future state.

Often planned change is prompted by efforts to avoid a crisis. The business realizes that the present state simply is not getting the job done. Without change in that present state, the business will slip competitively. Some businesses are truly innovative. They

FIGURE 19.1

The Stages of
Planned Change

begin the change movements when things are still going well because they realize that change must be ongoing. They also realize that it is easier and ultimately less painful to change before they have to contend with crisis.

Resistance to Change

As basic as this need for change is, we often resist change. **Resistance to change** refers to the strong tendency in businesses (and people) to maintain the present state, to keep things the way they are now. Why is this so? Change implies uncertainty. The status quo represents stability and consistency and, to some extent, security. Change implies the unknown, with all the fears any unknown carries. The status quo builds on foundations and sources of past strengths and past success. Change implies risk, stress, and the burning question of whether things really will be better.

> **resistance to change**
> The strong tendency to maintain the present state, to keep things the way they are now.

Studies indicate that people resist change for very logical and understandable reasons. We emphasize five key reasons many employees resist change.[5]

First, they are not convinced of the need for change. They do not understand why the prevailing system or approaches need to be altered. To them, the change just does not make much sense. In many cases, this lack of awareness occurs because they are not involved in the process of change.

Second, they do not want to lose something of value. This may include their current job status, known work, or even security.

Third, they don't really understand the change and its implications, so they assume they will be much worse off as a result of the change. Generally, this response occurs when people are not given enough relevant information to understand what is really going on. Poor communication and low trust levels increase the likelihood of resistance due to misunderstanding.

Fourth, many people fear failure. They may be afraid they will be unable to develop the new skills and behaviors the change will require. Often they fear they will be less effective with change than they are now.

Fifth, some employees have a low tolerance for change. Their personalities value consistency, order, and structure. They find flexibility and uncertainty quite discomfiting.

One thing should be clear: People who resist change are normal. They are not bad people. They are not malcontents. They are neither slow nor inferior employees. They are people responding naturally to the pressures and difficulties that go with change. And they exist at all levels of the business. It is often against this backdrop of resistance that businesses must struggle with the process of planned change.

The Underlying Philosophy of Change

Businesses today use a number of models of change. Interestingly, most are derived from the work of a single scholar, sociologist Kurt Lewin. Years ago, Lewin noted that successful change involves three stages: unfreezing, moving, and refreezing.[6]

Lewin said that before meaningful change can take place, people have to go through an **unfreezing,** or breaking away from their current thought patterns and behavior. He contended that this step happens only when people become convinced that their present views and approaches are not the best. They must believe that greater success for them and the organization could be achieved with different approaches and behaviors. Remember, one of the key reasons for resistance to change is simply not being convinced of the need for change.

> **unfreezing**
> The first stage in successful change; breaking away from one's current thought patterns and behavior.

moving

The second stage in successful change; the actual change of thought patterns and behavior from the old way to the new.

The second step of the process is **moving,** or the actual change of behavior and thought patterns from the old way to the new. This stage involves adopting new attitudes, values, and approaches. This step is difficult, but if the unfreezing was successful, moving is easier to achieve. It is important to help employees understand the movement that is desired.

Lewin's final step is refreezing—a reinforcement notion. If you have convinced people there are important advantages in changing, then the business must deliver. **Refreezing** means presenting evidence of the promised advantages to ensure that the new behaviors remain. Good results or rewards are critical for solidifying and maintaining the change.

refreezing

The third stage in successful change; reinforcing the new behaviors with evidence of the promised advantages.

The Process of Planned Change

With the basic philosophy of Lewin's model in mind, let's consider its application for the process of *planned change.* Nokia is a Finland-based company that is the world's largest producer of mobile phones and the world leader in mobile communications.[7] Its story is fascinating, and its success has been lauded as an example of business excellence. Losing huge sums of money as a small Finnish conglomerate, Nokia relied on technological talent and keen business and marketing skills to reinvent itself during the 1990s as a high-profile telecommunications company. Today the company employs 54,000 people (nearly 18,000 in the R&D area alone) and pulls in annual net sales of over $28 billion. For Nokia, sitting atop the lucrative cell phone world, the present state looks very good.

Why would a company in Nokia's position consider change? The reason looms on its business horizon, as the wireless world is experiencing some challenging changes. Just look at the numbers: In 1992, there were about 10 million people in the world with mobile phones; today, there are over 1 billion. This increase presents the troubling signal of potential market saturation. In other words, as more and more people who actually want mobile phones already have them, market growth will slow dramatically. Or will it? Industry experts suggest that people upgrade their phones often, looking for more and better features. Customers, now familiar with the basic technology, want new features, services, and functions. Nokia understands that more personal communications will occur over mobile phones. They further realize phones must include multimedia messaging, entertainment, and business applications. The companies that can deliver exactly what these sophisticated customers want are the ones that will grow and succeed.

Though necessary, change is not easy. However, in Nokia's case, change is a top priority. The company recognizes the impact of new technology, and it is always sensitive to the moves of competitors. Success has not blinded the company's management to the need to change.

Nokia's leaders have pushed for change. Yrjo Neuvo, the company's technological guru, notes that "gaining market share is tough work. But you can lose it in a very short time if you do things wrong." That sentiment is shared by everyone from CEO Jorma Ollila on down. President Pekka Ala-Pietila boldly states: "We have to change the whole way we look at the market."

Nokia has a vision and a plan for the future. It believes that the cell phone of the future must be a wireless, portable computer that brings mobility to the Internet. Nokia explains it this way: "Imagine going for a walk and knowing what the weather will be like on the route or buying a movie ticket over your mobile phone and then being shown how to get to the cinema from the point at which you made the call."[8] At the same time, the company sees the need to further develop its role as a leading supplier of mobile, fixed broadband,

and IP (Internet Protocol) networks. Although Nokia Networks currently accounts for about 22 percent of sales, providing network and connectivity solutions is an area whose rate of growth will likely outpace that of the mobile phone market. Of course, Nokia must have the right technologies in place. This approach will allow it to capitalize on one of its other competencies—Nokia's highly recognized and respected brand name. The company's plan is aggressive and logical.

The Nokia story demonstrates the process of planned change, which is depicted in Figure 19.2. The first step in this process is generating an *awareness of the need for change.* This idea is used by today's business consultants as the starting point in the process of change. The awareness is not too difficult when things have turned bad and the business is facing a crisis. This awareness is considerably more challenging to create when the business is achieving good results. As seen in the Nokia example, the successful business tries to build the case for change *before* things get bad. Only after this unfreezing takes place is the organization ready to move or change.

The second step in the process of planned change is the presence of *leaders who will champion the change.* These leaders must step forward and guide the business and its people toward change. Nokia is fortunate to have strong and respected leaders who have been supportive drivers of change. Generally, change is most effective when it comes from the top of the business. Leader behavior shows everyone in the business how important the change really is. Thus, top managers must promote needed changes. They must step forward through their speeches, written pronouncements, and reward policies to provide clear, strong support of change. Particularly during the early stages, the leaders may spend large periods of their time championing change.

The third step is also significant. Leaders must provide a clear *vision of the desired future state* so that everybody knows where the business is headed and what it intends to accomplish. People within the business need this vision if they are to understand and support the change. The vision becomes a rallying point for bringing people into the change process. The Nokia vision of building and marketing a new superportable computer cell phone seems to make sense. It's even part of its culture.

To Nokians (as Nokia employees call themselves), creating a new mobile information society is a central value, and they recognize that voice communication is only the beginning. New multimedia products and services, such as imaging phones, music players, and game consoles are a must, as are strengthened wireless networks. New concepts, such as the Nokia media terminal for home use will give customers the opportunity to watch digital TV, play 3D network games, send and receive e-mail, and tie into interactive services, such as banking and shopping. And the phone innovations continue to stamp out Nokia's special brand of quality and creativity. As an example, there is the new Nokia 7650 camera phone. The handset lets you talk and send messages. But it also takes pictures and lets you send those pictures wirelessly to other phones or to e-mail addresses. The product is sleek and efficient, and even skeptics argue that the quality is surprisingly good.[9] After all, Nokia has always had a sense of vision that's just a bit ahead of its major competitors. The company was the first to launch digital phones, the first to break the cell market into different consumer groups, and the first to launch a combination personal organizer and phone.

FIGURE 19.2

The Process of Planned Change

As you can see from steps two and three, the impact of leadership on change cannot be overemphasized. Although business leaders may use differing approaches to change, good leaders help their people understand the nature and direction of change, recognize the legitimacy of such change, accept risks, and overcome resistance.

The fourth step in the process is to *plan and manage the necessary action steps.* Action steps are the specific things that must be done for the vision to be achieved. Nokia, under the technological leadership of Neuvo, is working on a series of products and technological innovations that will provide the foundation for the kind of ground-breaking cell phone that Nokia believes is needed in the future.

The final step in the process of change is to *monitor and modify* the plan on the basis of feedback. No planned change ever goes completely as planned. The competitive and technological world is simply too dynamic. The implementation of successful change is a process of refining and fine-tuning. Modifying the plan does not mean that the original thinking was poorly conceived; it simply recognizes that adjustments are always needed.

Profile 19.1 describes successful change for the Harlem Globetrotters. Note the action steps that owner and president Mannie Jackson took to turn the business around. These actions changed the business from a stodgy, outdated organization to an innovative, up-to-date, and profitable business. As you look at the changes with the Globetrotters, realize that there is probably no single action that accounts for its remarkable reversal of fortune in a relatively short period of time. Rather, many interrelated actions collectively led to success.

PROFILE 19.1 THE GLOBETROTTERS REBOUND

The Harlem Globetrotters' unique brand of showmanship and athleticism has thrilled audiences for over 75 years. More than just a basketball team, the Globetrotters are thought by some observers to be the most admired, recognized, and publicized sports team in the world. But only a decade ago, the Globetrotter organization teetered on the edge of extinction. With annual attendance as low as 300,000 and revenues a mere $9 million, the organization was losing a million dollars a year. Enter Mannie Jackson. A college basketball star and former Globetrotter, Jackson took over the organization in 1993 after a successful 25-year career as a high-ranking executive at Honeywell. He found an organization that had lost its luster and had become indifferent to its customers. Today, under Jackson's tutelage and guidance, an amazing organizational turnaround has been realized. Annual attendance at games has hit 2 million. Revenues have reached $60 million, and profits have bounced back to $6 million. With a strong fan base and record returns, the Globetrotter brand is hot again.

Jackson's turnaround was based on three key ideas. As Jackson explains: "First, the product had to be reinvented in order to become relevant again; second, customers had to be shown that we really cared about them; and third, an accountable organization had to be created—a real business." The goals and approaches were straightforward. The team would reach customers by once again becoming high-level entertainment. Each game would have three keys: Show the fans these guys can really play the game and play it well; give fans an exhibition of basketball feats they have never seen before (such as unbelievable dunks, amazing shots, and pinpoint execution); and make the fans laugh and feel good. Most important, the entertainment had to be good, clean, family fun. Players were role models, expected to meet and greet their fans and be true "ambassadors of goodwill" throughout the world. The whole package had to be choreographed into a fast-paced 90-minute time frame. Soon the entertainment product was back.

But Jackson added some key business touches. He realized that promotion was central to Globetrotter success. So he brokered sponsorship of his teams (two traveling teams) with major businesses—Burger King, Disney, Kraft, Northwest Airlines, and a host of others. He created Globetrotter Properties, the organization's own merchandising and licensing company. He secured a multimillion-dollar shoe, uniform, and apparel contract. He built strong relationships with the media and the arena owners who would carry the Globetrotter events. Importantly, he began running the organization on the basis of gross profit and break-even analysis, forecasting cost, revenue, and operating profit for every event. He taught his leadership team to pay attention to the numbers and in the process created a culture of accountability. The organization changed and the turnaround was remarkable. But it all came about by following a carefully thought-out and orchestrated plan for change.

Source: Harlem Globetrotters website, www.harlemglobetrotters.com (accessed August 26, 2002); correspondence with Harlem Globetrotter organization (secured March, 2002); and Mannie Jackson, "Bringing a Dying Brand Back to Life," *Harvard Business Review,* May 2001, pp. 53–61.

The Harlem Globetrotters' recent success came from a solid understanding of the customer and a careful application of sound business practices. What kinds of business activities would you suggest for the Globetrotters to extend their pattern of growth and success?

Building Innovative Organizations

Creativity is a pattern of thinking and behaving that emphasizes new and different ideas. Innovation deals with the results, or what is produced through these creative activities. In short, innovation is the successful implementation of creative ideas to create value. As we noted in Chapter 2, creativity is the process; innovation is the outcome. Businesses encourage creativity to achieve innovation.

Despite what many people think, most businesses are potential hotbeds of creativity. People are often very creative if they are given the chance. Unfortunately, all too often that chance is not provided. This is one of the dilemmas of modern business life. Often businesspeople become so concerned with "turf protection," office politics, and

At companies like Merck, research is the foundation of their business and the pathway to success. In 2002, Merck committed nearly $3 billion to its research and development efforts. Why is this kind of commitment so important?

competitive innovation

A change so important that it allows the business to distinguish itself and gain an advantage over its competitors.

formalizing operating procedures and guidelines that true creativity is dampened. This outcome can be deadly. It is also one of the reasons we have focused this book on an integrative view of business.

Businesses must find ways to encourage and even stimulate creativity to gain competitive innovations. A **competitive innovation** is a change so important that it allows the business to distinguish itself and gain an advantage over its competitors. These innovations can be both product- and service-oriented. Consider HBO. Carl Albrecht, president of HBO original programming, is often considered the most original mind in television. His moves have become classic, and they have established HBO as a distinct innovator in the television programming market. It's nearly legend now that four major networks passed on a programming project, called "The Sopranos," before Albrecht gave it a chance. His formula is simply different. Rather than following the crowd with stale, dumbed-down fare, he encourages originality. He also demands top quality all the way—good writing, top-notch direction, and superb acting. Rather than looking for the latest trendy hit, he focuses on creating a brand of excellence. Even the business motto—"It's not TV. It's HBO."—sends the message. And the hits have been plentiful. In addition to "The Sopranos," there's "Six Feet Under," "Sex and the City," "Oz," and a series of award-winning movies, such as *Band of Brothers,* produced by Tom Hanks and Steven Spielberg. As Albrecht notes: "The words we always used to talk about ourselves were, 'different,' 'distinctive,' 'worth paying for,' 'better.' The only way to move forward and win is to take chances and be distinctive." Let's look at some of the ways businesses can generate creativity and gain real competitive innovation.[10]

Sources of Innovative Opportunity

Peter Drucker, an influential business philosopher, identified seven sources of innovation, which are presented in Table 19.1. Some of these sources are outside the business and some are internal. Think of them as changes that present opportunities for innovation.

THINK ABOUT THIS

1. Since business leaders recognize that change is important, why is it so difficult for successful businesses to be proactive in changing before they face problems?

2. Think of a change (perhaps with your family or some organization) that you actively resisted. After reading this section, why do you think you resisted the change?

3. Consider the change that you resisted in question 2. How could the approach to planned change have been used to facilitate the necessary change in your situation?

External Sources

First among the external sources of innovation is *demographics,* or basic changes in the population. For example, the population is aging, educational levels are increasing, and income levels are rising. What will these facts mean for businesses? What will they demand from businesses? What new opportunities for innovation will be possible because of these demographic realities?

Some innovations are fundamental yet significant. Consider the fitness industry. An aging but exercise-conscious population places new demands for innovation on the industry. One innovation that baby boomers appreciate is the focus on personal trainers. Although customized workout programs are more expensive than group or self-directed workouts, it appears that boomers appreciate having their workouts geared to their body styles, needs, and shifting capabilities. They also appreciate the gentle

External Sources	Internal Sources
Demographics.	Unexpected occurrences.
Changes in perception.	Incongruities.
New knowledge.	Process need.
	Changes in industry or market structure.

TABLE 19.1

Sources of Opportunities for Innovation

Source: Peter F. Drucker, "The Disciplines of Innovation," Havard Business Review, August 2002, pp. 95–102.

encouragement of this type of training regimen. At businesses such as Absolute Exercise, customers schedule workouts, and all sessions involve one-on-one interaction between the customer and a professional trainer.

The second external source is *changes in perception.* As Drucker says, "A change in perception does not alter the facts. It changes their meaning, though—and very quickly." The fast-food restaurant business is experiencing such a shift. Some of it is due to a change in customers' perceptions, attitudes, and perhaps even values. Concern about health and fitness has forced many traditional fast-food establishments to focus on healthier menu options.

Health consciousness is not the only shift affecting the restaurant industry. The people at restaurant giant Brinker International recognize another significant change in perception. They believe customers today do not want just the convenience of dining out. Many are looking for unique dining experiences within a reasonable budget. Brinker has responded innovatively with new restaurant concepts. One of these is Cozymel's, which offers authentic Mexican food in a fiesta-like atmosphere that is a different, exciting escape for patrons. The company even suggests that at Cozymel's, the dining is "tropical, not typical." Another is Brinker's Macaroni Grill chain. The restaurant strives to offer fine Italian favorites at affordable prices in an open, warm atmosphere for meeting with family and friends.[11]

The third external source of innovation is *new knowledge,* or new awareness and techniques that allow us to do things we could not do before. New technology is a common example here. Just think of the innovations derived from new technologies in the medical and pharmaceutical industries. Companies battle to be leaders in exploiting emerging technology to bring new life-enhancing and lifesaving products to consumers. Augustine Medical, for example, has been recognized as one of the most innovative small companies in the United States. The company makes surgical warming blankets and other medical devices. It spends large sums of money looking for ways to use the latest technology to produce innovative products. Its Warm-Up products provide heated wound therapy, which improves patient recovery.[12]

Internal Sources

In addition to these three outside sources, at least four sources of innovation lie within the organization. First is what Drucker calls *unexpected occurrences.* These can be unexpected successes that are exploited to build competitive strength. Or they can be unexpected failures that help the business understand its customers more fully.

The second internal source of innovation is *incongruities.* An incongruity occurs when there is a gap between what the business expects or is hoping for and what occurs. As with unexpected occurrences, incongruities are an invitation to innovate.

Let's consider an example of how unexpected occurrences and incongruities can lead to innovation. As the Internet gains in popularity and business use of computer interactions spreads, computer viruses are also spreading at an unbelievable rate. Today there are thousands of known virus strains. This situation has created a unique business opportunity for Trend Micro. Based in Tokyo, Trend Micro is a global leader in antivirus software and services. Its products protect the flow of information on PCs, file servers, and e-mail servers, and the company offers centrally-controlled protection for enterprise networks. In fact, its enterprise solutions have been adopted by Canon, Charles Schwab, ExxonMobil, Hilton Hotels, PepsiCo, and more than one-third of the Fortune 500 businesses. Trend Micro has taken a difficulty, or performance gap, and built a thriving business.[13] Profile 19.2 shows how an industry problem or gap has led to an innovative response in the photo processing industry.

The third internal source of innovation is based on *process need.* As the business operates, people become aware of processes that need to be improved. These needs are the pockets of innovation. Process needs and related innovations are part of the successful company's focus on quality and continuous improvement, as discussed in Chapter 14.

PROFILE 19.2   THE BIRTH OF THE PHOTO KIOSK

The photography industry has seen its share of changes in recent years. One of the most dramatic has been the move toward digital cameras. One of every five cameras sold is digital, and that trend is expected to continue. But there is an unexpected concern and problem—the hassle of printing photos. Printing at home simply takes too long and the quality is often suspect. Even online services are generally slow because they typically send prints through the regular mail system. In an age of instant gratification and one-hour–processing expectations, digital customers are frustrated and disappointed. Herein lies an opportunity to innovate.

That innovation is hitting malls, drugstores, and even amusement parks across the country. Sony, Polaroid, Olympus, Fuji, Konica, and Kodak all have their own versions, but the formula is similar. The industry solution is digital photo kiosks. Here's how they work: You just walk up to the kiosk; insert a chip, disk, or even the camera itself into the kiosk machine; and in about 30 seconds, you have the print. The software is easy to use, and the cost is about 60 cents a photo.

There is even a hidden benefit here. Companies are hoping that the kiosks will help spur future sales of digital cameras. They believe that a number of potential customers have refrained from buying a digital camera because of uncertainty or uneasiness about the printing of photos. The kiosk innovation helps remove that barrier. Of course, the competition is stiff. Polaroid is trying to speed up the process, hoping to be able to process up to 20 photos in two minutes. All companies are looking for ways to drive down the cost. Fuji may have hit on a great advantage. It has landed its kiosks in such plum locations as Wal-Mart stores and Celebrity cruise ships.

Source: James Bandler, "Digital Photos Hit the Mall," *The Wall Street Journal,* May 22, 2002, pp. D1, D3.

Drucker's fourth and final internal source of innovation comes from *changes in industry or market structure*. There have been some dramatic examples of this source. The breakup of the Bell system and the deregulation of the telephone industry created enormous opportunities for innovation. Hundreds of new businesses entered the industry. Most have been searching for new approaches or new niches that will give them a competitive edge.

Drucker's list is certainly not exhaustive, but it does provide a good sense of some key changes and awarenesses that *can* lead to innovation. These sources have that potential, but enlightened managers must act on the potential before innovation can be realized. With that thought in mind, let's examine some of the actions successful businesses take to foster innovation.

Actions for Building Innovation

Creativity and innovation flourish when they are supported through the actions and attitudes of the leaders and managers of the business. These actions provide the foundations that enable the creative and innovative efforts of employees. We will look at seven of the many important actions:

1. Integrating innovation throughout the organization.
2. Encouraging risk and experimentation.
3. Tolerating and learning from mistakes.
4. Embracing diversity and differences.
5. Maintaining close contact with customers.
6. Investing in learning.
7. Using creative personalities.

Integrating Innovation throughout the Organization

Not too long ago, it was popular for organizations to have separate units, often known as creativity centers, whose task was to generate new ideas and innovations. The organizations hoped that the work done in these isolated centers would propel their businesses toward new solutions. Today, the focus has changed. Innovative businesses such as Polaroid, DuPont, and Ford have jettisoned such centers. Even Lucent Technologies' award-winning creativity center—Idea Verse—is now defunct.

These companies have not abandoned their quest for creativity and innovation. Quite the contrary. They are simply approaching it differently. Instead of isolating particular centers to champion innovation, the organization is integrating the process throughout the business so that everyone is involved. Progressive companies such as Kraft and Bristol-Myers Squibb are allotting significant budgets for innovation projects. Each business unit is asked to explore ideas and possibilities, and each unit is provided extensive innovation resources. Within these units, teams have become the center of innovation activity. Innovation champions (people with the knowledge and background to lead innovative efforts) work with project teams to build innovative thinking into their team processes. In turn, teams are recognized and rewarded for their creative contributions. These companies hope that this more integrated focus will breed "cultures of innovation."[14]

That is certainly the case at Procter & Gamble. The company is convinced that the drive for innovation cannot be viewed as something special or unique. Instead, it must be an ordinary part of the way the company does business. Craig Wynett, P&G's general manager of future growth initiatives, comments that "many companies make innovation front-page news, and all that special attention has a paradoxical effect. By serving it up as something exotic, you isolate it from what's normal . . . At P&G, we think of creativity not as a mysterious gift of the talented few but as the everyday task of making nonobvious connections—bringing together thing that don't normally go together."[15]

Encouraging Risk and Experimentation

If organizations are going to innovate and change, they must gain creative new ideas. The organization's leaders must be receptive to these new ideas. They must encourage their people to take risks, experiment with new ideas, and break the established pattern as we see in Profile 19.3. Some organizations gain creative ideas by encouraging their people to think differently. 3M, as noted previously, is a good example of a company where innovation is a way of life. 3M is credited with creating and developing over 50,000 innovative products. Part of its success is derived from its famous "15 percent rule," which encourages and permits employees to spend part of their work time exploring experiments.[16]

Other businesses get a creative edge by paying attention to the novel ideas of their people. Here are two classic examples: Herbert R. Peterson, Sr., a McDonald's franchisee in Santa Barbara, California, introduced a new breakfast item to McDonald's franchise creator Ray Kroc. The unique English muffin with egg, bacon, and cheese became the Egg McMuffin, a mainstay of McDonald's breakfast menu. In a similar manner, Sam Temperato, a St. Louis Dairy Queen franchisee, developed a strange concoction by mixing fruit, nuts, and other ingredients into a vanilla frozen dessert. Temperato knew his product was a winner, but Dairy Queen executives thought it could be too much work for the individual

PROFILE 19.3   EXPERIMENT LIKE CRAZY

Betty Cohen is a corporate strategist at the Turner Broadcasting System (TBS) and the founder of Cartoon Network Worldwide. Her favorite way to encourage innovation is to experiment. She has encouraged her TV and online creative leaders to plot different approaches to the future for Cartoon Network fans. Armed with these approaches, her staff tested all possibilities. Amazing options, everything from "simulcasting Web and TV versions of the same cartoon character premier to a live on-line viewer request weekend to a more interactive on-line action and adventure show," were tried. She wants her people to experiment rather than focus on blowing too much money or placing the wrong bets. Cohen's words are prophetic: "What prevents innovation? The dangerous brew of fear and complacency."

Consider the advice of Nolan Bushnell, an innovation pioneer. Bushnell founded Atari in the early 1970s, then moved in a different direction when he founded Chuck E. Cheese Pizza Time Theater. Today, he is CEO of uWink, an entertainment and game network in Los Angeles. Bushnell's advice: "I think it's essential to build a culture where there's no such thing as a bad idea . . . We have regular compost sessions to come up with new game ideas. We don't debate their value. Our priority is simply to get as many ideas as possible out of individuals' heads and into the group's head."

Source: "Inspiring Innovation," *Harvard Business Review*, August 2002, pp. 39–49.

stores. Temperato brought key executives to his St. Louis store so that they could see how popular the product was with customers. The executives were convinced. Temperato's product, the Blizzard, became the best-selling product throughout the Dairy Queen chain.[17]

Tolerating and Learning from Mistakes

It is one thing to encourage risk and experimentation. It is quite another to accept the downside of that risk and experimentation. That downside is the mistakes and missteps that undoubtedly will occur when people are trying new things. Leaders should realize that the only way to avoid mistakes is to never take a chance. They must view mistakes as a natural part of the creative process and as learning opportunities.

A classic story may illustrate this point. Many years ago, a young manager was called to the office of IBM founder Tom Watson. The young manager had misread a risky venture, costing the company over $10 million. Certain that he was about to be fired, the manager fidgeted nervously. "I guess you want my resignation," he blurted. "You can't be serious," Watson said. "We've just spent $10 million educating you."[18]

This is precisely the attitude toward innovation that successful businesses try to promote. The young manager made a mistake that he could have prevented only by playing it safe. He had to take a risk. He had done his homework. He was prepared. His strategies made sense when they were initiated; they simply did not work out over time in an extremely uncertain and volatile environment. Watson was sure the manager would learn from his mistakes and be better prepared to handle such issues in the future.

Michael Dell openly shares one of Dell's classic mistakes. He even refers to it as a disaster. Some years back, as the industry was transitioning to a new type of memory chip, Dell got stuck with far too many chips of the older kind. Yet that mistake prompted the company to develop an inventory management system that today is one of its strengths. As Michael Dell notes: "At Dell, innovation is about taking risks and learning from failure."[19]

At Pillsbury, "learning histories" are completed for each new project. This is a way of documenting and evaluating projects so that key lessons can be shared, mistakes uncovered, and continual learning is encouraged. There is logic in the adage "If you're not making some mistakes, you're not pushing the envelope far enough."

Mistakes are part of the learning and development that occur in an innovative organization. However, it's important to note that certain types of mistakes should not be tolerated. If a mistake is made because of lack of preparation, faulty analysis, arrogance, or other preventable cause, then negative consequences should follow. Further, making the same mistake over and over is inexcusable. In short, tolerance for mistakes and experimentation does not mean it is all right to be sloppy or unprepared.

Embracing Diversity and Differences

One way to foster a climate of creativity and innovation is to encourage diversity within the business, as we discussed in Chapter 7. Innovative businesses actively build diversity into their activities and operations. Although these efforts can occur in a number of ways, two themes seem particularly important.

First, bringing people of different genders, races, and cultural backgrounds into the business is a foundation of creativity. Indeed, diversity of talent can often provide the information, perspective, and sense that businesses need as they consider changes and innovations.

Of course, as discussed in Chapter 7, people with differing views and outlooks must be accepted and their ideas given a fair hearing when decisions are being made. Such an approach to diversity can lead to tension and uneasiness. But sometimes that is exactly what a business needs to break out of its stagnating comfort zone.

The second diversity theme deals with the use of teams. As you learned in Chapter 16, teams can bring people from different backgrounds and different areas of the business together to solve problems. For example, a small family-owned investment company sees a need for innovation in the wake of the industry's dramatic changes. The firm's president, a 35-year-old who has just accepted the leadership reins from his recently retired father, is concerned that the business may not be setting the pace, given the emerging directions of the industry. He decides that a team of top executives should be organized to identify the strategic moves the business needs to make. This team practice is drastically different from his father's dictatorial approach. A team is assembled that includes the managers from all the key areas of the business. Most of the members of this executive team think in a similar manner. They are logical and analytical, and they carefully assess all risks before committing to action. Their tendency is to follow traditional paths of operation.

One member of the team, though, is different. The financial services manager is always thinking up new ideas, reading about and studying new approaches, and considering different ways of serving clients. As she tosses her ideas into the team mix, others are often bothered. She looks at things differently. She forces the rest of the team to consider a different view. She challenges others' approaches. Although she does not often win the other team members over to her way of thinking, she usually prompts them to extend their thinking. There is no doubt that the team comes up with novel ideas because of her influence. Many of these ideas make good business sense and result in increased revenues.

Once more, we see diversity leading to conflict that can spark creativity and innovation. Again, this result presumes that differences on teams are not only viewed as legitimate but also encouraged. We do need to be cautious here: It will not surprise you to learn that diverse or heterogeneous teams usually take longer to make decisions than do individuals working alone or teams without diversity. Yet most diverse teams, over time, provide better answers to problems and offer more creative solutions.

Maintaining Close Contact with Customers

One key way for a business to stay on the creative cutting edge is to maintain close contact with its customers. Throughout this book, we have heralded customer sensitivity as essential for competitive success. We have said that healthy businesses understand and address the shifting preferences of their customers. Customers themselves are also excellent sources for new areas of innovation. However, this source has no meaning unless business employees listen carefully to what customers have to say.

Sometimes customers point to the need for innovation through their complaints and dissatisfaction with existing products. Ford learned this lesson by listening to both its dealers and eventual car buyers. As the company received comments and explored service records, areas that cried out for change became apparent. Ford addressed those needs through model redesigns. Some of the innovations were quite small (larger trunk space and more headroom in the backseat). Yet collectively, such design changes represented meaningful innovations that better addressed the customers' wishes.

Sometimes staying tuned in to customers suggests new directions. Nordstrom is one of the country's most respected retailers.[20] Its company motto is "Respond to Unreasonable Customer Requests." Living this motto can be demanding, but Nordstrom employees, encouraged to be creative, seem to relish the challenge. Often, all they have to do is provide a little more attention and personal service. At other times, however, they must go further. They have been known to hand-deliver items purchased by busy business customers over the telephone, change a customer's flat tire, or personally pay a customer's parking ticket because in-store service took longer than the time allotted for parking. Nordstrom encourages these creative acts and rewards those who take the extra step for their customers.

Katherine Catlin, of the consulting firm The Catlin Group, contends that one of the characteristics of leading innovators is that they listen to customers. She even argues that "customers and prospective customers are recognized as the single most important source of ideas for product or service development and improvement, market positioning, sales techniques, and industry trends."[21]

Staying close to customers is not always easy. It takes constant attention and diligence. For example, the most popular bicycle during the 1960s and 1970s was Schwinn. The firm's growth was tied to its careful reading of and response to shifting customer demands. For example, when the sales managers noticed young riders modifying their Schwinn bikes with banana seats and longhorn handlebars, the company knew customer needs and expectations were undergoing change. It responded quickly and created the Sting-Ray cycle, which soon became the company's best-seller. Yet this same sensitivity was not repeated years later as the push toward mountain biking began to emerge. Schwinn dismissed the early signs of a new customer mood. In the process, Schwinn missed a key market leadership opportunity as smaller (and more responsive) companies such as Trek and Specialized seized the lead in the lucrative mountain biking market.[22]

Investing in Learning

Jerre Stead has had a stellar business career. He is chairman and CEO of Ingram Micro, Inc., the world's largest wholesale distributor of computer-related products. Stead believes that people are the source of business success because they are the engine of creativity. Ongoing learning is the fuel that people need to generate innovation. Innovative businesses realize that investing in learning is critical to sustaining creativity and innovation.[23]

The idea that businesses should operate as learning organizations is generally accepted today. **Learning organizations** not only adapt to change, but also creatively search for new and better ways of operating and meeting the needs of their customers. Learning organizations are proactive. They are always adapting and transforming themselves in an effort to improve.

The key to a learning organization is that it encourages change and renewal as part of its philosophy, its values, and its very culture. Imagine a business that is progressive enough to say, "The strongest component of our corporate culture is our commitment to continually reshape ourselves and our culture." This outcome is achieved by promoting, on a businesswide basis, many of the actions and approaches we have discussed in this chapter. In learning organizations, leaders are visionaries, sources of innovation are recognized and exploited, and innovative actions are supported as part of the way things are done. The learning organization philosophy prevails among successful businesses.

> **learning organization**
> A business that not only adapts to change but also creatively searches for new and better ways of operating and meeting customers' needs.

Using Creative Personalities

All this talk about the importance of creativity and innovation may be a bit unsettling for some of you. Perhaps you do not think of yourself as creative. Indeed, while some people do seem to be creative thinkers, others—no matter how hard they try—just do not seem to generate much creativity. Maybe some people just have a more creative personality. This idea is both interesting and potentially dangerous. Let's examine it more closely.

THINK ABOUT THIS

1. Look again at Drucker's sources of opportunities for innovation. What do you think the managers of a business need to do to be sensitive to these opportunities?

2. Which of the actions for building innovation do you think is probably the most difficult for a business to put in place? Why?

3. What do you think would happen in a team if all the members were strong innovators? What if all were strong adaptors?

TABLE 19.2

Creativity Style
Assessment

Circle *a.* or *b.*, depending on which is generally more descriptive of your behavior:

1. When I am working on a task, I tend to
   a. Go along with a consistent level of work.
   b. Work with high energy at times, with periods of low energy.
2. If there is a problem, I usually am the one who thinks of
   a. A number of solutions, some of which are unusual.
   b. One or two solutions that are methods other people would generally accept.
3. When keeping records, I tend to
   a. Be very careful about documentation.
   b. Be haphazard about documentation.
4. In meetings, I am often seen as one who
   a. Keeps the group functioning well and maintains order.
   b. Challenges ideas or authority.
5. My thinking style could be most accurately described as
   a. Linear thinker, going from A to B to C.
   b. Thinking like a grasshopper, going from one idea to another.
6. If I have to run a group or project, I
   a. Have the general idea and let people figure out how to do the tasks.
   b. Try to figure out goals, timelines, and expected outcomes.
7. If there are rules to follow, I tend to
   a. Generally follow them.
   b. Question whether those rules are meaningful or not.
8. I like to be around people who are
   a. Stable and solid.
   b. Bright and stimulating, and who change frequently.
9. In my home or office, things are
   a. Here and there in various piles.
   b. Laid out neatly or at least in a reasonable order.
10. I usually feel that the way people have done things in the past
    a. Must have some merit and comes from accumulated wisdom.
    b. Can almost always be improved upon.

Scoring:

Match your answers with those listed below. Give yourself 1 point for each matching answer.

1. b	6. a
2. a	7. b
3. b	8. b
4. b	9. a
5. b	10. b

Add the total number of points. This is your I score (innovator style). Next, subtract your I score from 10. This number is your A score (adaptor style).

Source: From Dorothy Marcic, *Organizational Behavior: Experiences and Cases*, 4th ed. 1995 West Publishing Company. Reprinted with permission of Dorothy Marcic.

Table 19.2 presents a creativity style assessment based on the work of Michael Kirton. Kirton identifies two types of creative people, which he labels adaptors and innovators. Both are creative, but in different ways. **Adaptors** try to figure out how things can be improved. They tend to feel comfortable working within existing boundaries and systems to push for changes that will make those systems better. They change cautiously and in small steps. **Innovators,** on the other hand, are more likely to challenge the existing system and the accepted ways of doing things. They are catalysts for new ideas, often discovering new problems and novel solutions. They are always pushing the envelope of change. Innovators challenge rules, break from customs, and rarely feel constrained by the existing system. Innovators such as Tim Berners-Lee (see Profile 19.4) help reshape our thinking.

Businesses need both types of people. They need innovators to shake things up and break from established approaches. They need adaptors to bring stability and order to the confusion that the innovators can create. Innovators give you the outrageous twists that can be truly groundbreaking. Adaptors have the political sensitivity to take these twists and turn them into acceptable ideas that can actually be implemented.

> **adaptors**
> Creative people who try to figure out how they can improve things by working within existing systems.

> **innovators**
> Creative people who are catalysts for new ideas that challenge the existing system and the accepted ways of doing things.

THE WIZARD OF THE WORLD WIDE WEB   PROFILE 19.4

"Unlike so many inventions that have moved the world, this one truly was the work of one man. He designed it. He loosed it on the world. And he, more than anyone else, fought to keep it open, nonproprietary, and free." He's a low-profile British genius named Tim Berners-Lee—perhaps not a household name—but his invention is. Berners-Lee literally invented the World Wide Web. While working at CERN, a European particle physics laboratory, Berners-Lee wrote the first Web client browser–editor in early 1990. And the World Wide Web was born.

Berners-Lee remains one of the great innovators of our age. Think of the magnitude and impact of his invention. The Web has changed our lives and our ways of thinking about everything from communication to entertainment. *Time* magazine has even recognized Berners-Lee as one of the 100 greatest minds of the 20th century.

His parents, with computer backgrounds themselves, raised Tim in London and encouraged him to think

You could compare him with Thomas Edison, Alexander Graham Bell, or Henry Ford. He is Tim Berners-Lee, and he invented the World Wide Web. Can you imagine what your life would be like without it?

expansively and even unconventionally. They played math games during breakfast. While studying at Oxford University, Tim built his own computer out of an old TV and other spare parts.

Berners-Lee has never sought to make a huge financial gain from his invention. Instead, he has gone the not-for-profit route. Currently, he works as director of the World Wide Web Consortium at MIT. He continues to look for ways the Web can develop into a true force for social change and individual creativity.

Source: Tim Berners-Lee with Mark Fichetti, *Weaving the Web: The Original Design and Ultimate Destiny of the World Wide Web by Its Inventor* (San Francisco: HarperCollins, 1999); "Weaving the Web," www.w3.org/people/berners-lee/weaving/overview (accessed August 29, 2002); and www.pathfinder.com/time/time100/scientist/profile/bernerslee.html (accessed August 29, 2002).

THE BIG PICTURE

Today, the forces for business change are dramatic. Society demands stronger standards of accuracy and disclosure in the wake of troubling business deceptions; assurances of integrity and ethical action; and a commitment to providing value in products and services. At the same time, businesses must maintain their technological edge, continue to innovate, and do all this while focusing on controlling costs. The drivers of change are critical, and they are unrelenting. Yet, this perspective is not new. Although the issues and needs may differ, change has always been a constant for successful businesses.

Increasingly, successful businesses are recognizing that change and renewal are strategic issues. Change must be planned and it must be integrated, covering all areas and phases of the business. In fact, the integrative nature of change and renewal deserves special attention. Thus, it is fitting that we close *Business: An Integrative Approach* with a discussion of the effect of change on the entire organization.

To fully understand the organizational impact of change and renewal, consider the concept of interrelatedness, which proposes that a change in any part of a business system affects all other parts of the system. Throughout this book, we have been discussing the various parts of the business system, and we have been building the case for interrelatedness.

Let's review some of that thinking. In Part Three of the text, we studied the impact of the business environment. We recognized that environmental shifts affect the business and its operations. The presence of a more diverse workforce, a rise in interest rates, the emergence of promising global markets, the possibility of increasing governmental regulation of business, and the threat of a powerful new competitor are all environmental changes that alter the landscape of business operations. To respond to them, healthy and proactive businesses contemplate making some changes in the status quo.

In such an increasingly complex environment, the successful business faces a series of tough decisions. The business must consider whether it needs to change some phase of its actions and operations (discussed in Part Four of the text). The performance measures we examined in Chapter 18 suggest the nature and extent of the necessary changes.

Financial performance and customer needs and values are typically the factors that stimulate change. That emphasis is not hard to understand. If a business feels threatened financially, it must change. If customer value is being threatened (perhaps by new competitors), ultimately, financial performance will decline.

Changes in strategic thinking and customer orientation are often prompted by shifts in the competitive environment in which the business operates. Such changes are not unusual. They are not signs of failure or poor decision making. They are simply the changes a business must make over its history. Some of them can be planned; some cannot. A firm's success depends in large part on how effectively it is able to read the need for change and act in a timely manner. In today's fast-paced, competitive world, business must change, even when things seem fine. The words of Michael Dell are instructive: "You need to encourage innovation when your company's doing well. The last thing you want to do when you're in the lead is become complacent."[24]

All changes must start someplace. There must be some point of entry or initial focus of change. Typically, that change will affect one of the key parts or subsystems of the business. For example, the business may focus change around the people subsystem. We see this approach all the time. When a business announces, in the face of declining profits, that it has decided to scale back its workforce by 10,000 people, the people part of the business is being affected. Perhaps change will focus on the organizational design and structure of the business. The business may reorganize into teams, move to a project structure, look for ways to partner with other businesses, or seek other creative ways to streamline operations and strive for greater overall efficiency. Or perhaps the business will focus change on technology and information. New technology and information sources may be used to help the business be more responsive to customers. The Internet may be used to market items directly to potential customers. Just-in-time inventory practices may be implemented. Outsourcing may be considered to enhance efficiency and reduce costs.

Regardless of the point of entry, change is never isolated in one part of the business. Changes are always interrelated. When a company changes strategy to enhance customer service and improve financial performance, people, design, technology, information, and other processes will change too. If the business downsizes, it will restructure and implement new processes. It will probably have to use information and technology in new ways. If the business decides to reorganize into teams, people will probably be more empowered. Further, information and technology will probably be modified to support the needs of the teams and ensure proper coordination. As a result of their awareness of interrelatedness, successful businesses approach change by looking at all the parts of the business together.

Summary

1. Understanding change is necessary in today's environment. Changes will occur in organizations whether managers plan for them or not. Some changes are forced on a company from external influences. Thus, managers must introduce change into their organizations.

   • What are Kurt Lewin's three stages of change?

   Lewin proposed that achieving change is a three-step process. First, people must unfreeze existing behavior patterns. Second, they must move; that is, the change or movement must be made. Third, there must be refreezing, meaning that positive results will solidify the new behavior.

2. Throughout this textbook you have encountered examples of businesses that have devised highly effective methods of competing. Yet the best of them deliberately changed their successful formulas. Instead of waiting for change to catch them by surprise, these leaders anticipated it and planned for it.

   • What is the nature of planned change in business?

   Planned change is the intentional process of movement from the present state toward some future state. Planned change can be viewed as consisting of three stages: the present state, the actual change, and the future state. Planned change often faces resistance because of the strong tendencies in business to maintain the present state, to keep things the way they are now.

3. Each business approaches planned change in a somewhat unique manner because each business has its own particular strengths and weaknesses. Nevertheless, some common features are usually observed in firms that effectively engage in planned change.

   • What are the main features of the process of planned change?

   The following features constitute a five-part process that is common in planned change: (1) awareness of the need for change, (2) emergence of leaders who champion the change, (3) development and acceptance of a vision of the desired future state that will result from the change, (4) development of an actual plan for change, followed by the management of action steps to implement that plan, and (5) monitoring of the plan's implementation and modification based on feedback.

4. Businesses that are successful in planning change are innovative. In today's business environment, any organization that intends to survive over the long run must learn how to innovate.

   • What is an innovation? What is a competitive innovation?

   Innovation is the successful implementation of creative ideas. A competitive innovation is a change so important that it allows the business to distinguish itself and gain an advantage over its competitors.

5. Many opportunities for innovation are available to businesses.

   • What are the sources of innovative opportunities?

   The three external sources are (1) demographic changes, (2) changes in perception, and (3) new knowledge. The four internal sources are (1) unexpected occurrences, (2) incongruities, (3) process needs, and (4) changes in industry or market structure.

6. Innovation does not simply occur. Concerted attention and action by businesses are necessary to build and support innovation.

   • What are some of the practices that help a business be innovative?

   The following practices provide a foundation that supports creativity and innovation: (1) integrating innovation from throughout the organization, (2) encouraging risk and experimentation, (3) creating a culture that tolerates and learns from mistakes, (4) encouraging diversity and embracing differences, (5) maintaining close contact with customers, (6) investing in learning, and (7) using creative personalities, both innovators and adaptors.

7. Change and renewal must cover all areas and phases of the business. Changes in the various areas are interrelated and must therefore be integrated. Thus business leaders must think strategically about change and renewal.

adaptors, p. 505	planned change, p. 490	**Key Terms**
competitive innovation, p. 496	refreezing, p. 492	
innovators, p. 505	resistance to change, p. 491	
learning organization, p. 503	unfreezing, p. 491	
moving, p. 492		

Exercises and Applications

1. Pick an organization with which you are familiar—perhaps a social group, a fraternity or sorority, or a small business where you have worked. What changes do you think would benefit this organization? Outline the steps you think would be necessary to make these changes happen.

2. Think of businesses you have patronized. Identify one or two you think are the most innovative. What do you see them doing that helps them innovate?

3. This is a team activity. Each team should be provided with a copy of *The Wall Street Journal,* a role of adhesive tape, a ball of string, and 10 paper clips. Using only these materials, each team is to construct a tower, which will be judged on three factors: height, strength, and aesthetic appeal. Teams should be given 5 minutes to meet and plan their tower and 20 minutes to actually construct it. Each team should present a one-page paper on what its members learned about creativity through this exercise.

4. Think of a business where you have worked. Draw from this chapter to determine what that business could do to generate more creativity and innovation.

5. Go to Southwest's home page on the Internet. Southwest prides itself on being an innovative business. What evidence can you find on its website that suggests it really is innovative?

6. Find an example of a business that has recently come up with an innovative product or service. (Look in local newspapers, magazines, and business publications such as *The Wall Street Journal* or *BusinessWeek*). Can you identify actions the business took to support and reinforce creativity and innovation?

A Marvel-ous Recovery

FROM THE PAGES OF

BusinessWeek

Comic book publisher Marvel has suffered through a period that would make even its superheroes Spider-Man, the Hulk, and Wolverine shudder in despair. On the heels of record-setting years in the early 1990's, Marvel was struck by the "bottom-falling-out" decline of the comic book industry. In a few short years, Marvel's readership and sales had declined so deeply that the company was forced to declare Chapter 11 bankruptcy in 1996. But just like its heroic trio, Marvel has fought back. Today, with revenues soaring to nearly $300 million and armed with a new marketing approach, Marvel is flexing its muscle once again.

What's behind this turnaround? Not surprisingly, some needed changes and some novel ideas. Marvel is making a concerted effort to reach a wider audience and is doing so by presenting more sophisticated materials that address serious issues. An example is the release of the new series *The Call of Duty.* This series portrays emergency workers (fire fighters, police, and EMS workers) as action heroes responding to terrorist attacks.

There is also an initiative to "develop new plots using time-tested superheroes and other characters." Marvel hopes to build further interest in and allegiance to such stalwarts as Spider-Man, the Avenger series, and X-Men.

Marvel has also used an innovative theme by tying its comics closely with film releases of the characters. Not surprisingly, the success of the Spider-Man movie helped not only Marvel but also the entire industry. Now, as movie projects based on Daredevil and X-Men (*X-Men 2*) unfold, Marvel will have its comics poised to capitalize on the exposure.

Perhaps just as important, Marvel has emphasized new marketing and distribution approaches. The company has packaged "comics into easier-to-buy bundles for the bargain-conscious reader." And it is creatively using the Web. Marvel provides free comics on its website and reaps income primarily from advertisers. The approach seems to work as the number of visitors to the site has doubled over the past five years.

Marvel's recovery stems from a series of changes for this traditional business. As some observers note, the green that Marvel sees "won't just be the skin of the Incredible Hulk."

Decision Questions

1. It took a crisis before Marvel responded with changes. Unfortunately, this is often the case for many businesses. Why do you think it often takes a crisis to generate action?

2. Why is Marvel's reliance on and ties to the success of films a somewhat risky strategy? How might Marvel hedge to minimize the risks involved?

3. Part of Marvel's new marketing appeal is predicated on the assumption that readers progress through a life cycle. They are fans until high school when they often lose interest to other social activities. Yet Marvel believes that these fans return during their college years. What do you think of the assumptions Marvel is making here? Are they close to their customers with this "market read"?

Source: Billy Cheng, "Comics Clamber Back from the Brink," *BusinessWeek* online, www.businessweek.com (accessed August 29, 2002).

References

1. Richard Rapaport, "Reinventing the Heel," *Forbes,* Summer 2002, pp. 114–119; "How Nike Got Its Swoosh Back," *Fortune,* June 24, 2002, pp. 30, 34; and Nike website, www.nike.com (accessed August 24, 2002).

2. Gary McWilliams, "In About-Face, Dell Will Sell PCs to Dealers," *The Wall Street Journal,* August 20, 2002, pp. B1, B4.

3. Glenn R. Carroll and Michael T. Hannon, *Organizations in Industry: Strategy, Structure, and Selection* (New York: Oxford University Press, 1995), p. 12.

4. Sandra Waddock, *Leading Corporate Citizens* (Burr Ridge, IL: McGraw-Hill/Irwin, 2002), pp. 185–193.

5. This discussion is drawn in part from the classic work of J. P. Kotter and L. A. Schlesinger, "Choosing Strategies for Change," *Harvard Business Review,* March–April 1979, pp. 106–14.

6. Kurt Lewin, *Field Theory in Social Science* (New York: Harper & Row, 1951).

7. This example is drawn from "A Changing and Dynamic World" and other company sites at www.nokia.com, (accessed August 22–August 25, 2002); Andy Reinhardt, "Say Cheese—This Phone Has a Camera," *BusinessWeek,* July 29, 2002, p. 24; and

Janet Guyon, "Next Up for Cell Phones: Weaving a Wireless Web," *Fortune,* October 25, 1999, pp. 224–232.

8. Guyun, p. 232.

9. Reinhardt, p. 24.

10. Polly LaBarre, "Hit Man," *Fast Company,* September 2002, 90–104.

11. Brinker International website, www.brinker.com (accessed August 26, 2002).

12. Leigh Buchanan, "Inside the Idea Mill," *Inc.,* August 2002, pp. 54–61; and Augustine Medical website, www.augustinemedical.com (accessed August 27, 2002).

13. Trend Micro website, www.trendmicro.com/corporate/company_profile (accessed August 27, 2002).

14. Ruth Ann Hattori and Joyce Wycoff, "Innovation DNA," www.thinksmart.com (accessed August 27, 2002).

15. Craig Wynett, "Make It the Norm," *Harvard Business Review,* August 2002, p. 40.

16. 3M website, www.3m.com/about3m/century/experiments.jhtml (accessed August 28, 2002).

17. Jeffrey A. Tannenbaum, "Role Model," *The Wall Street Journal,* May 23, 1996, p. R22.

18. Warren Bennis and Burt Nanus, *Leaders: The Strategies for Taking Charge* (New York: Harper & Row, 1985), p. 76.

19. Michael Dell, "Don't Fear Failure," *Harvard Business Review,* August 2002, p. 41.

20. This example is drawn from Tracy Goss, Richard Pascale, and Anthony Athos, "The Reinvention Rollercoaster: Risking the Present for a Powerful Future," in *Harvard Business Review on Change* (Boston: Harvard Business Review Press, 1998), pp. 93–94.

21. Katherine Catlin, "Practice Makes Perfect," *Entrepreneur,* September 2002, pp. 68–72.

22. Tom Kelley, with Jonathan Littman, *The Art of Innovation* (New York: Currency Books, 2001), pp. 238–239.

23. "Soaring with the Phoenix," www.belasco.com/phoenix/soaring/index.htm (accessed October 16, 2002); "Jerre Stead," www.belasco.com/phoenix/about/stead_bio.html (accessed October 16, 2002); and Jerre Stead, "Values-Based Leadership: The Real People Power," McCord Lecture, Bradley University, Peoria, IL, April 3, 1996.

24. Dell, "Don't Fear Failure."

Glossary

A

absenteeism A situation in which employees do not show up at work when scheduled to be there. (479)

acquisition The purchase of one company by another company. (47)

adaptors Creative people who try to figure out how they can improve things by working within existing systems. (505)

advertising Any paid form of presentation and promotion of ideas, goods, and services by an identified sponsor to a targeted audience. (387)

antitrust laws Laws that prohibit companies from unfairly restricting competition. (276)

assimilation The assumption that women and minorities should blend in and learn how to work within the existing organization and its culture. (170)

B

baby boomers The generation of Americans born between 1946 and 1964. (165)

balance of payments A record of the inflows of money into a country and the outflows of money from that country. (249)

balance of trade The difference between the value of a country's imports and its exports of goods and services. (249)

balance sheet A financial statement that shows a company's assets (what it owns), liabilities (what it owes), and net worth (owners' equity) at a specific point in time. (465)

Baldrige Award The highest quality government recognition that a U.S. business can receive. (368)

bankruptcy A situation in which a firm does not have the money to pay its debts. (272)

bear market A period when prices in the stock market are generally decreasing. (232)

benchmarking Comparing one's practices with those of recognized leaders to determine where and how improvements can be made. (367)

board of directors The individuals elected by the stockholders to oversee the management of the firm. (97)

brand equity The value attached to a brand. (385)

brand A name, term, symbol, design, or image that identifies the products or service of a business. (385)

bricks-and-clicks retailers Companies that have both facilities or stores and a significant online business. (392)

bull market A period when prices in the stock market are generally increasing. (232)

business Any organization that strives for profits by providing goods and services that meet customer needs. (10)

business (integrated definition) An organization that strives for profits for its owners while meeting the needs of its customers and employees and balancing the impacts of its actions on other stakeholders. (126)

business analysis A comparison of projected demand for a product with the firm's ability and cost to produce it. (363)

business culture A set of unwritten values and beliefs about what is proper, right, and appropriate in a business. (143)

business cycle A somewhat regular pattern of ups and downs in aggregate production, as measured by the fluctuations in real GDP. (192)

business ethics The search for and commitment to meet appropriate standards of moral conduct in business situations. (136)

business focus The general direction in which top managers plan to take a business. (300)

business profile An assessment of a firm's strengths and weaknesses. (300)

business units Unique product or market groupings that are treated as self-contained businesses. (415)

business-to-business e-commerce The use of the Internet to conduct transactions between businesses. (441)

business-to-consumer e-commerce The selling of a product by a business to a consumer on the Internet; also called electronic retailing, e-tailing, or e-retailing. (439)

C

capital goods The machinery and equipment used in the production process. (72)

capital intensive Relying heavily on equipment and machinery to produce products. (73)

cash flow The movement of cash into, through, and out of a firm. (340)

cash inflow The money that moves into the business from owners, lenders, or customers. (340)

cash outflow Cash that moves out of the business for any reason. (341)

category killers Large chain stores that specialize in a narrow line of products. (78)

caucus groups Groups of employees who get together to address key concerns relating to members of their particular group. (164)

chain of command The line of authority in a business that determines the movement of official commands down through the hierarchy. (106); The line of authority in a business, which identifies who reports to whom. (409)

chief executive officer The individual responsible for the long-range, strategic direction of the company. (99)

chief financial officer The individual responsible for the overall financial health and strategy of a company. (99)

chief information officer The individual in charge of policy relating to the gathering, use, and storage of company information. (99)

chief operating officer The individual responsible for a company's internal day-to-day operations. (99)

codes of conduct The formal written statements specifying the kinds of things a business believes should be done and those that should be avoided. (143)

collateral Any asset owned by the borrower that is pledged to the lender in case the loan is not repaid. (214)

collective bargaining The process through which company and union representatives work together to negotiate a labor agreement. (282)

commodity markets Financial institutions that offer businesses the opportunity to guarantee the future prices of certain agricultural products and raw materials. (221)

common carriers Trucking companies that transport a wide variety of products for many clients. (81)

competitive advantage An area of competence that consumers value and the business is capable of exploiting. (304)

competitive innovation A change so important that it allows the business to distinguish itself and gain an advantage over its competitors. (496)

competitive pricing Pricing based on competitors' prices for similar products. (398)

competitive strategy The specific approach a business chooses to pursue for addressing its competitive environment. (306)

concept evaluation An analysis to determine if the overall idea fits with the firm's strategy and existing product or service mix. (363)

consumer-to-consumer e-commerce The selling of a product by one consumer to another via the Web, typically through an intermediary called a hub. (439)

continuous improvement The efforts by a business to provide steadily higher quality throughout all phases of its operation. (31); A process in which a firm and all its people continually look for ways to change and improve all facets of the business. (366)

contract carriers Trucking companies that specialize in carrying a particular kind of good for a few customers. (81)

cooperative strategies Situations in which two or more businesses decide to work together for their mutual benefit. (312)

copyright The exclusive right to the use of intellectual property such as books, photographs, music, or cartoons. (272)

core competence An activity or set of activities that a business performs very well or a quality it possesses in abundance. (303)

core values The specific beliefs that a business makes part of its operating philosophy. (142)

corporate bond A loan sold to the public by a business. Buyers may be individuals or financial institutions. (215)

corporation A separate business entity owned by stockholders. (59)

cost-based pricing A method of pricing in which a company figures all of the costs involved in producing and selling a product and sets a price high enough to cover these costs plus a reasonable profit. (396)

creative decision making The process of developing new or different ways to solve problems or capture opportunities. (114)

creativity New and different patterns of thinking and behaving. (31)

crisis decision making Decision making that requires a bold response to a unique, unexpected, and potentially devastating situation. (115)

cross-functional team A group of employees who are selected from various areas of the business and brought together to make collective decisions. (104)

cultural relativism The belief that what is right or wrong depends on the culture of the country where business is taking place. (255)

current ratio A measure of a firm's ability to pay its bills. (466)

customer sensitivity The awareness of customer desires and needs. (29)

customer service The actions a business takes to meet customer needs and preferences. (29)

D

data analysis The study of information to help a manager reach a conclusion about some aspect of the company. (356)

debt financing The money a company borrows from outsiders, such as individuals, banks, or other lending institutions, or raises by selling bonds. (340)

debt ratio The percentage of the company's total assets that are underwritten with debt. (466)

deflation A general decrease in prices or a decrease in the prices of most goods and services. (188)

demand The quantity consumers are willing and able to buy at different prices. (198)

departmentalization The process of grouping similar jobs together in any of several ways (among them, function, markets, or geography). (409)

development team A group of people from various parts of a company who have an interest in the product or service and are selected to develop it into a profitable activity. (363)

differentiation strategy A competitive strategy that is built on providing a product or service that has some unique feature. (307)

direct business-to-business e-commerce The interaction between two companies primarily through computer contact. (442)

direct mail The use of catalogs and other materials sent to the homes or businesses of potential customers. (390)

direct marketing Any attempt to sell a product directly to customers without going through intermediaries such as dealers or other retailers. (390)

discount pricing A strategy of pricing low to increase sales volume. (398)

distinctive competence A skill, activity, or capacity that a business is uniquely good at doing in comparison to rival firms. (303)

distribution sector The wholesale and retail firms that move products from the manufacturer to the ultimate customers or users. (71)

diversification A strategy that entails branching out into an additional area (or areas) of business. (311)

diversified business A business that is involved in more than one type of business activity. (47)

diversity audit A snapshot of how good a job a business is doing in the area of diversity management. (173)

diversity management An approach to management that puts together a well-thought-out strategy for attracting, motivating, developing, retaining, and fully using the talents of competent people regardless of their race, gender, ethnicity, religion, physical ability, or sexual orientation. (170)

downsizing Reducing the number of employees in a business. (327)

dual-career households Families in which both partners are actively pursuing full-time careers. (161)

dumping Selling imports at prices that are below the cost of production and distribution. (258)

dynamic measurements Measures that include some time element, often comparing results in different time periods. (457)

E

earnings per share (EPS) A company's earnings divided by the number of shares of stock outstanding. (460)

economic growth An increase in total spending in the economy. (186)

economies of scale Reductions in a firm's average cost of production that are achieved by increasing the overall volume of production. (309)

effectiveness A measure of the degree to which a business achieves its goals. (456)

efficiency A measure of the relationship between inputs and outputs. (456)

electronic commerce (e-commerce) The buying or selling of products or services on the Web. (438)

electronic hubs or net market makers The intermediaries in business-to-business e-commerce. (443)

employee retraining The practice of regularly providing the education and training workers need to expand their base of skills so that they can meet the needs of business. (166)

employee stock ownership plan (ESOP) An arrangement in which employees buy ownership in the company. (61)

employer of choice A situation in which a business displays such a unique culture that it is able to attract, motivate, and retain the high-quality people it needs. (421)

empowerment The process of giving more decision-making authority and responsibility to workers throughout the organization. (33) (114)

enterprise resource planning (ERP) A companywide application software that integrates all departments and functions across a company onto a single computer system. (446)

entrepreneurship The act of starting, buying, or expanding a business, often with innovative products or processes. (50)

environment of business Those factors or influences that affect the business but over which the firm has little control. (34)

environmentalism Efforts and actions to protect the natural environment. (134)

equilibrium point The point on a graph where the demand curve intersects the supply curve. (198)

equilibrium processes Processes by which the price moves toward its equilibrium point. (198)

equity financing The money invested in a business by the owners. (340)

exchange rate The value of a domestic currency compared with a foreign currency. (247)

exclusive distribution The distribution of a product to only a single outlet in a market area. (75)

expenses The money a business must pay out to make its products and provide its services. (26)

experience curve A concept whereby costs are lowered as a result of a firm's increasing efficiency through experience in making the product; also called the learning curve. (309)

export management firm A firm located in the United States that sells products abroad for another business. (314)

exporting The situation in which a business sells products and services to customers in other countries. (243)

extranet A private website accessible only by a company and its partners. (442)

F

feedback Communications from customers that tell a company how it is doing. (399)

financial markets The places where businesses that need to acquire capital are brought together with financial institutions that help provide the funds. (214)

first-line supervisors The lowest level of management; they are directly responsible for overseeing the work of employees who produce products or provide services. (102)

fiscal policy The raising or lowering of taxes or government spending to influence growth, unemployment, and inflation. (191)

flexible benefits plan A plan in which workers can select from a menu of benefits the ones they wish to receive. (424)

flexible manufacturing Manufacturing with highly automated machinery that can be changed quickly and can perform multiple tasks. (446)

flextime A work arrangement that allows employees to adjust work hours, often to meet other responsibilities. (162)

focus groups Small groups of people who are asked to respond to a researcher's questions. (356)

focus strategy A competitive strategy that is built on positioning a business to serve the needs of some unique or distinct customer segment that is not being fully served by the competition. (308)

foreign exchange markets Financial institutions that offer businesses an opportunity to avoid potential losses when money earned from foreign sales is exchanged for home currency. (221)

foreign sales office A special operation in a foreign country that sells and services products that were made domestically. (315)

form The specific design, size, or model of a product that a customer needs. (373)

franchise A business that grants the exclusive right to another individual or business to use its name and sell its products or services. (53)

franchisee The person or business that purchases a franchise. (53)

franchisor The business that sells the franchise. (53)

free trade A situation in which there are no government-imposed barriers to trade—no tariffs, quotas, or nontariff barriers. (250)

free trade area A geographic area where free trade is permitted among the member countries but imports from nonmember countries are limited. (251)

freedom The power to make one's own decisions or choices without interference from others. (270)

G

gap analysis The study of customers' satisfaction with a firm's product or service compared with their expectations. (470)

Generation X The generation of Americans born between 1965 and 1980. (166)

Generation Y The generation of Americans born between 1981 and 1999. (166)

glass border The tendency for women not to receive international assignments important for their advancement. (161)

glass ceiling Systematic barriers that prevent women from advancing in the organization. (160)

global strategy A strategy in which a business sells a uniform product or service throughout the world. (242)

globalization A way of thinking in which a business regards its operations all over the world as part of one integrated business system. (242)

going public Offering to sell the company's stock to the general public for the first time. (229)

gross domestic product (GDP) The market value of all final goods and services produced in a country in a given year. (184)

H

heterogeneous society A society composed of many dissimilar people with a varied mix of backgrounds, values, needs, and interests. (156)

human resources outsourcing Contracting with temporary help agencies or with consulting firms to provide the people a firm needs. (332)

I

image pricing A situation where a business sets prices very high to indicate the exclusive or high status nature of the product or service. (397)

importing The situation in which customers buy products and services from producers in other countries. (243)

inclusiveness The assumption that it is the business's responsibility to make decisions and take actions so that the talents of all employees can be fully realized. (170)

income statement A financial statement that shows a firm's performance over the course of a specific time period, such as a quarter or a year. (462)

industry concentration The number of firms in an industry and their relative size; often calculated by the C-4 ratio (the percentage of total industry sales by the top four firms). (87)

industry sectors Major groupings of industries with similar characteristics. (70)

industrywide regulation A situation in which a local, state, or federal government controls the entry of firms into an industry, the prices they charge, they way they operate, or even their exit from the industry. (278)

inflation A general increase in prices or an increase in the prices of most goods and services. (187)

initial public offering (IPO) A company's first-time issuance of stock to the public. (216)

innovation New approaches and options that are the result of creative activities. (31)

innovators Creative people who are catalysts for new ideas that challenge the existing system and the accepted ways of doing things. (505)

inside directors Directors who are also company employees. (97)

institutional advertising A communication about the company itself, not its products. (387)

insurance A contract in which one party agrees, for a fee, to reimburse the other for financial damages incurred. (222)

integrated assessment The simultaneous measurement of variables in different parts of an organization. (456)

integrated marketing communications (IMC) The process of developing and implementing various forms of persuasive communications that send a consistent message over time. (383)

intensive distribution The distribution of a product to every possible venue. (76)

interest The price that individuals or businesses pay to borrow money. (190)

international partnerships Arrangements between two or more businesses from different countries that enable those companies to do business more successfully. (262)

Internet marketing The communicating of product information through a company's website, encouraging customers to order online. (390)

intranet A computer communications network within a single company. (445)

inventory turnover ratio A measure of how fast a firm is selling its inventory. (466)

investment banking house A financial institution that works with businesses to get large amounts of financing. (214)

ISO 9000 Quality management and assurance standards published by the International Standards Organization; a common denominator of business quality accepted around the world. (368)

J

job sharing A work arrangement in which two or more employees share one job and split all the duties and responsibilities, as well as the compensation of that job. (162) (426)

joint venture A business owned by two or more companies. (61)

just-in-time (JIT) An integrated set of activities designed to achieve high-volume production using minimal inventories of raw materials, work in process, and finished goods. (339)

L

labor intensive Relying heavily on people as the key to supplying products and services. (84)

learning organizations Organizations that adapt to change and search creatively for new and better ways to operate and meet the needs of their employees and customers. (33) (503)

licensing An arrangement in which a business allows its products to be produced and distributed in other countries by a foreign company. (315)

limited liability Liability of a corporation's owners for the firm's debts only to the extent of their investment in the business. (59)

limited liability company (LLC) A form of ownership that combines the advantages of partnerships and corporations without the limitations imposed by subchapter S. (59)

low-cost leadership strategy A competitive strategy that entails finding ways to reduce the cost of providing a product or service and pass the savings on to customers. (307)

M

macroeconomics The study of the entire economy of a nation. (183)

make-or-buy decision The choice of whether to manufacture a product in-house or buy it from a supplier. (334)

manufacturer's representative A company or person that sells products to wholesalers or retailers on commission. (78)

manufacturing firms Companies that convert raw materials or components into products that may be sold to consumers or to other businesses. (70)

manufacturing sector The broad group of companies and industries that produce tangible objects. (70)

market The place where buyers and sellers meet and bargain over goods and services. (197)

market research The tasks of collecting and analyzing information about the market or potential market for a product or service. (354)

market segment An identifiable group of customers or potential customers that have common characteristics. (357)

mass customization The design of products and processes with the goal of delivering highly customized products to different customers around the world. (446)

matrix organization A structural approach that combines the project structure with the functional structure. (415)

merger The joining of two companies to form a combined company. (47)

microeconomics The study of the behavior of individuals and firms in particular markets. (197)

middle managers Managers below vice presidents down to just above first-line supervisors; they are responsible for translating broad policies into doable tasks. (101)

mission A statement that spells out why a business exists and what the business will do. (23)

monetary policy The changing of the money supply to change interest rates directly, thus influencing inflation, growth, and unemployment. (191)

monopolistic competition A market situation in which there are many firms but each has a slightly different product. (204)

monopolization A situation in which a single firm controls all or most of a market. (277)

monopoly A market situation in which only one firm sells a product or service. (205)

moral dilemma A conflict of interests involving ethical choices. (138)

motivation A person's willingness to work hard and expend great effort for the business. (417)

moving The second stage in successful change; the actual change of thought patterns and behavior from the old way to the new. (492)

multidomestic strategy A strategy in which a business modifies its product or service to address the special needs of local markets. (243)

multinational firms Businesses that have major production and sales operations in more than one country. (261)

N

net worth The value of a business: for a publicly held firm, its stock price times the number of shares outstanding; for a private firm, its assets minus its liabilities (or its future income in today's dollars). (462)

nonbank lender A financial services unit of a large company, which makes loans to other businesses. (215)

nonmanagerial employees Employees in a business who are actually involved in producing or selling products and providing services. (103)

not-for-profit organization An organization that provides benefits to a set of constituents. (54)

O

oligopoly A market situation in which a few firms, with or without differentiated products, dominate the market. (205)

open systems approach The view that any system is comprised of interrelated parts, each influencing and being influenced by the other parts. (15)

operational decisions Decisions that affect the day-to-day actions of the business. (110)

operational information Any information relating to the internal workings of the company that helps it run more efficiently. (344)

opportunity cost The value of the best alternative that is sacrificed to pursue another option. (232) (324)

organization design The way the various parts of a business are coordinated. (407)

organization structure A framework that prescribes how a business organizes, arranges, and groups the work that needs to be done. (407)

original equipment manufacturer (OEM) A company that makes components for another product. (72)

outside directors Directors who are not company employees. (97)

outsourcing Acquiring components or services from outside the firm rather than providing them using company resources. (73)

P

parent company Any company that owns one or more subsidiaries. (61)

partnership A business that is owned by two or more individuals. (57)

partnership agreement A document that prescribes the responsibilities and privileges of each business partner. (58)

patent A government-protected legal monopoly on a product or product design. (272)

penetration pricing Temporarily pricing below competition to gain market share. (397)

per capita economic growth The difference in GDP per person from one year to the next. (186)

performance appraisal The process a company uses to measure employee effectiveness. (478)

performance-based pay Wages that are tied directly to performance. (423)

personal selling The face-to-face communication between a company representative and the customer. (393)

physical resources (1) Fixed assets such as land, buildings, and equipment, (2) raw materials that will be used in creating the firm's products, and (3) general supplies used in the operation of the business. (334)

planned change The process of intentional movement from the present state toward some future state. (490)

price elasticity of demand The percentage change in the quantity of a product or service demanded divided by the percentage change in its price. (201)

price-fixing A situation in which rival firms agree to charge the same price for their competing products. (277)

primary data Data that a business collects directly from customers and potential customers. (355)

primary stakeholders Those stakeholders whom a business affects and interacts with most directly. (124)

prime rate The interest rate that large commercial banks charge their best corporate customers for short-term loans. (223)

private morality Personal moral standards. (138)

privately held corporation A business that has a few stockholders and the stock is not open for public sale. (61)

problem solving Decision making aimed at correcting an adverse situation that has developed. (110)

product advertising Advertising that encourages customers to buy specific products or services. (388)

product or service development The creation of a product or service that provides greater value to customers than previously existed. (360)

product or service differentiation The development of a product or service that differs enough from existing products or services so that customers can distinguish the new product or service from existing ones. (362)

product outsourcing Purchasing a product or component of a product from another company. (334)

productivity The ratio of goods and services provided to resources used. (26)

professional staff Employees who make decisions within their area of specialty that assist others in doing their jobs. (102)

profit The amount of money left over after the business records all its revenues and subtracts all its expenses. (26)

project organization A structural approach that uses teams drawn from various areas of the business to accomplish high-profile tasks. (414)

property rights The freedom to possess and regulate the use of tangible items (such as land and buildings) and intangible items (such as a copyrighted piece of music or a patented invention). (270)

publicity Communication to a mass audience that is not paid for by the company. (396)

publicly held corporation A business with stock that is open for public sale. (61)

pure competition A market situation in which many firms sell nearly identical products and no one firm can raise its price without losing most of its customers. (204)

Q

qualifying the customer Determining whether the customer is likely to purchase the product or service. (394)

qualitative research Research whose results are not subject to quantification or quantitative analysis. (356)

quality The ability of a product or service to consistently meet or exceed customer expectations. (365)

quality management A company's unique approach to ensuring quality. (31)

quantitative research Research that uses mathematical or statistical analysis to reach conclusions. (356)

quota A government's restriction on the amount of a specific foreign product it allows into the country. (250)

R

real rate of interest The rate the borrower actually pays minus the rate of inflation. (225)

refreezing The third stage in successful change; reinforcing the new behaviors with evidence of the promised advantages. (492)

relationship marketing A situation in which the business gets to know its customers, establishes rapport, and develops long-term relationships with them. (385)

research design A plan for determining whom to study and how to collect and analyze information. (354)

resistance to change The strong tendency to maintain the present state, to keep things the way they are now. (491)

resources The people, physical materials, financial assets, and information a firm's managers use to produce a product or service. (323)

responsibility The use of one's property (both tangible and intangible) in a manner that does not unduly infringe on the freedom of others. (271)

retailers Stores that sell directly to consumers. (78)

return on equity (ROE) The amount of profit a firm makes for each dollar of equity invested. (460)

revenue The amount customers pay for the goods and services they purchase. (26) (341)

risk taking The willingness to undertake actions without knowing what the results will be. (271)

S

sales promotions Additional incentives provided to encourage customer response. (395)

secondary data Any data that have already been published. (355)

secondary stakeholders Those stakeholders whom a business affects in an indirect or limited way. (124)

second-level communications Communication that customers make only when their first attempt to gain satisfaction proves fruitless. (473)

selective distribution The distribution of a product to a limited number of dealers or stores. (76)

self-directed work team A group of employees who supervise their own work and are given broad discretion over the direction of their work. (104)

service sector The broad group of companies that provide some sort of service to customers. (71)

silent partners Business partners who typically contribute money instead of being involved in day-to-day operations. (57)

Six Sigma A program that uses proven quality principles and techniques to make business operations as efficient and error free as possible. (367)

small business Any business that is independently owned and operated, is not dominant in its field, and meets size standards that vary depending on the industry. (44)

social overhead capital The purchase of goods and services by government to increase the productive capacity of business. (288)

sole proprietorship A business that is owned by one person. (56)

span of control The number of employees who report to a given manager. (409)

specialization The process of placing employees in specific jobs and asking them to perform only those jobs. (409)

speculation A situation in which a company's stock is bought or sold on the basis of a belief that its price will soon go up or down. (234)

sponsorships Investments in special events or causes for the purpose of building awareness of the company and its products. (395)

stakeholder A person or group that has some claim on or expectation of how a business should operate. (124)

stereotyping Placing people in broad social groups, then generalizing about and labeling them because they are part of a given group. (156)

stockholder Any person who owns at least one share of stock in a corporation. (60)

stocks Shares of ownership in companies that are sold to individuals or financial institutions. (215)

strategic alliances Long-term agreements between firms to work together for the benefit of both. (73)

strategic decisions Decisions that have a major impact on the general direction of the firm. (109)

strategic information Any information about a firm's competitors, customers, and markets that affects its ability to compete. (344)

strategic planning A systematic way of analyzing and responding to a competitive environment. (316)

suboptimization A situation in which one department of a business, acting in its own self-interest, hurts or inhibits the performance of another department, leading to less effective outcomes for the business overall. (412)

subsidiary Any business that is wholly or partially owned by a parent company. (61)

successful business Any business that excels over a long period of time. (10)

supply The quantity businesses are willing to provide at different prices. (198)

supply-chain management Management of the movement of products or components through all the stages involved in the production and delivery of final products to an end user. (370)

sustainable competitive advantage A competitive advantage that competitors cannot duplicate easily. (305)

SWOT analysis An assessment of a firm's key strengths and weaknesses compared with the opportunities and threats it faces. (300)

synergy The combined action of two resources so that their total effect is greater than the sum of the effects taken independently. (47) (324)

T

takeover A situation in which investors (including other companies) purchase enough of a company's stock to control the company. (220)

tariff A tax on an imported product. (250)

teamwork A situation where employees are treated as key players in the business and where employees want to pull together to help the company succeed. (426)

telecommuting A work arrangement in which workers spend part of each week working at home and communicating with the office via computer. (162)

test marketing Selling a product or service in certain select markets to find out what customers think. (363)

theory of justice An approach to decision making that assumes decisions should be guided by equity, fairness, and impartiality. (142)

theory of rights An approach to decision making that assumes there are certain individual rights that must always be protected. (141)

Theory X The belief that workers are naturally lazy, dislike work, shirk responsibility, and will do as little as they can in most work situations. (421)

Theory Y The belief that workers enjoy their work, desire responsibility, and want challenges. (421)

top management The officers of a business who make major decisions for the company and are responsible for the company's performance. (99)

tort A behavior, either intentional or negligent, that harms another person. (285)

total quality management (TQM) A systematic approach to addressing quality issues that involves a total integrated, companywide commitment to quality. (366)

trade deficit A country imports more than it exports. (243)

trade surplus A country exports more than it imports. (243)

trademark The exclusive legal right to the use of a name, symbol, or design. (272)

turnover A situation in which employees voluntarily leave a company. (479)

U

unemployment rate The ratio of the number of people classified as unemployed to the total labor force. (189)

unfreezing The first stage in successful change; breaking away from one's current thought patterns and behavior. (491)

unions Formally recognized organizations that represent a company's or industry's workers. (134)

universalism The belief that there are commonly shared business standards and principles that are accepted throughout the world. (255)

utilitarianism An approach to decision making that assumes decisions producing the greatest good for the greatest number of stakeholders are ethical. (141)

V

value-based pricing A situation where a company determines what customers are willing to pay. (396)

value–price relationship A relationship in which customers get the best possible value from the products they purchase, given the price they pay. (129)

venture capital firms Corporations that invest in risky businesses with high growth potential, usually in exchange for a considerable share of the ownership. (214)

vertical integration The degree to which a firm operates in more than one level of the overall production chain. (73)

vice president A top manager who is responsible for a specific area of the company. (99)

virtual organization A combination of parties (people or organizations) who, although geographically dispersed, are electronically linked so that each can contribute its unique competency in achieving a common goal. (416)

virtual teams Teams that combine the talents and ideas of people worldwide who use technology to communicate in addressing business problems and opportunities. (414)

vision A broad statement of what a business would like to achieve. (23)

W

wholesalers Businesses that serve as intermediaries between manufacturers and retailers. (76)

wholly owned subsidiary A business that is owned as part of a larger business; may be a foreign subsidiary of a domestic firm. (315)

work–family conflict The sense that work and family demands interfere with each other. (161)

workforce diversity The mix of people from differing demographic and ethnic backgrounds and value orientations in an organization. (158)

working capital The money set aside or used for operating a business. (218)

working partners Business partners who play a role in day-to-day operations. (57)

Photo Credits

Chapter 14
p. 361, Photo by Bill Pugliano/Getty Images
p. 364, © Michael Justice/The Image Works
p. 366, Courtesy of Rolex Watch U.S.A., Inc.
p. 368, Courtesy of the United States Department of Commerce, The National Institute of Standards and Technology
p. 372, www.llbean.com

Chapter 15
p. 382, www.coldwatercreek.com
p. 391, www.swavacations.com
p. 397, Courtesy of DeBeers
p. 399, © Robin Weiner/WirePix/The Image Works

Chapter 16
p. 405, © Associated Press, AP
p. 413, © Jim Pickerell/The Image Works
p. 423, © Tony Stone/Getty
p. 427, © Michael Newman/PhotoEdit, Inc.

Chapter 17
p. 437, us.etrade.com
p. 443, www.ford.com

p. 445, www.fedex.com
p. 447, Courtesy of Scheid Vineyards

Chapter 18
p. 460, © Spencer Grant/PhotoEdit, Inc.
p. 465, © Photo by Joe Raedle/Getty Images
p. 469, "Steven's" website, www.dell.com/us/en/dhs/topics/segtopic_steven_home.htm
p. 475, © Monika Graff/The Image Works
p. 479, © Michael Newman/PhotoEdit, Inc.

Chapter 19
p. 488, Photo by Koichi Kamoshida/Getty Images
p. 495, © AP Photo/Aris Saris
p. 496, AP Photo/Mike Derer
p. 505, © AP/Wide World

Logo Credits
Best Buy, Inc., Courtesy of Best Buy Co., Inc.
Dell Computer Corporation, Copyright © 2002 Dell Computer Corporation. All rights reserved.
Southwest Airlines, Courtesy Southwest Airlines.

Index

The *Business: An Integrative Approach*
Online Learning Center

www.mhhe.com/fry3e

Access online study materials, research information, and other internet resources at the Business Online Learning Center.

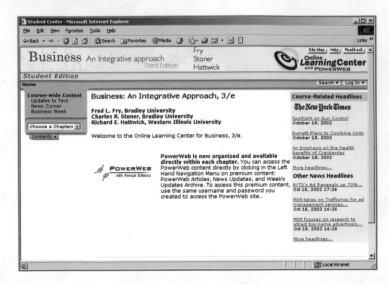

You will find:

- Student Study Map using PowerPoint slides, video clips, and URLs to give you a road map through the information in the chapter.
- Chapter Objectives with summaries to help you review the information in each chapter.
- Direct feeds from PowerWeb — giving you and your instructor up-to-the-minute articles and information about topics in your text.
- Additional chapter quizzes.
- Video Exercises to coincide with the videos your instructor shows in class, and also those on your CD.
- Flashcards to test your vocabulary knowledge.
- And much more!

A password-protected portion of the site is also available to instructors, offering downloadable supplements and other teaching resources.